SUNSET
under the
Poet's
TREE

SUNSET
under the
Poet's
TREE

To Barb

[signature]

GEORGE S. J. ANDERSON

To order additional copies of this book, contact:
Xlibris Corporation
1-888-795-4274
www.Xlibris.com
Orders@Xlibris.com
96997

I dedicate this book to my late wife, Lois Ann Anderson, who took the deadly disease of breast cancer and turned it into a shining moment in the continuum of life.

I would also like to dedicate it to everyone still battling this disease . . .

And for those who lost the battle . . .

They will always live on in our hearts . . .

The Lois Ann Anderson Breast Cancer Support Group Logo

From the year 1993 to 2010, my late wife, Lois A. Anderson, created a quarterly newsletter, which was distributed to almost 350 breast cancer survivors, physicians, nurses, physical therapists, and an array of health care professionals who enjoyed reading the continuing struggles and outcomes in the field of breast cancer. Lois had many personal struggles in her own life but never forgot the front against breast cancer also existed on the local, state, and national levels. As a tribute to her and to the many people who supported and loved her, I felt it was only fitting to include it in this story of her life.

An Extraordinary Life

⚮ *Indicates chapters written exclusively about Lois Ann Anderson*

Preface

Flying Kites (previously released in *Seasons in Cancer* [2000 and 2012])

We measure our lives by the great events that touch us. Every day, our lives continue in their ordinary ways . . . ordinary ways that are comforting in their sameness and their predictability. Then comes a great event, making all our ordinary days seem like a prelude for something that pulls you closer to heaven, or hell, than anything that has happened before. It is an event so enormous, you know you will never experience anything like it again. Two events in my life were like this . . . the birth of my son and my wife's diagnosis with breast cancer. All other events flow away from these like silent circles rippling before and behind them.

One strange surreal day, not long ago, my wife was told she had a serious form of breast cancer. In the surgeon's office, I listened with her for the word "cure"; instead I heard "disease-free survival." I wanted to hear "ten years, five years" or even "she will be okay for a while." But as I watched, her surgeon shuddered the ultimate closing to his epistle. "We will hope for five years. After that, we don't know . . ." Inside me, a wounded cry bore into my animal heart, yet I reined it tightly within me. I wanted to take my solitary voice to the dying embers of the sky and throw this inner rage like a fiery tempest at the forces that sent this disease to her. However, the heavens were silent, and so was I. We both seemed so insignificantly finite as we looked into the infinite sky. We were afraid to close our eyes . . . afraid that when they closed, we would have to say good-bye forever. We wondered when and how and what it would take to be okay again.

Cancer entered my life like a hurricane, knocking down my illusions of what appeared to be valuable, like a house of cards. In the aftermath were the lives around me and a certain will of courage to stand by my wife during her ordeal with breast cancer. At the time, the concepts, predictions, and treatments seemed insurmountable to all of us. Just getting by the enormous hurdle of the word "cancer" was almost more than either of us could bear alone. Despite her poor prognosis, my wife stood against it and survived. In everything she did, in both spirit and demeanor, she wore the mantle of a true warrior fighting this deadly disease. In my eyes and in those who watched with us, she showed us all the stuff of heroes.

Now that the hurricane winds of cancer subsided, the winds of what "could be" still remained, reminding us the fight may never be over and might not yet be won. At the end of this hurricane, the winds of change surrounded us, engulfing us in the same force that nearly swept us away. We took small gasps of air and hoped the massive breathing wind did not drown us in its power. We remembered the strength of the wind when it almost took our breaths away. It made us feel small and powerless. It was unquestionably more powerful than any man . . . Very few could stand against it. In our fear of its potential effect, we could have cowered from it . . . Perhaps we could have hidden from it and never reappeared.

For quite some time, breast cancer made it difficult to consider anything more than what life presented to us each day. As each day faded into the shadows of the past, I realized my wife had been spared for some purpose, some reason that seemed nebulous and out of reach. We eventually realized that living in the past, fearing the predictions of short survival, only allowed our remaining time to slowly disappear. We had to learn that the point of survival was not struggling to hold on to life but that we struggled to live. As the wind passed over us, we had to choose. We could taste the air upon our lips and lose it in a breath upon the moving air, or seize it like a treasure that we locked inside our hearts. This treasure could then become such a part of us that it could change us . . . could make us different souls than what we were or what we could become.

When my son was still a child, I would take him to the top of the hill behind our house on windy days to fly kites. While we were standing there together, I would unfurl the colorful Mylar, loosen the tether line, and allow the vagabond wind to catch the stretched cloth in its unseen grasp. The kite would sail into that unreachable vastness and float high into the sky, challenging the flight of the birds in the air. Caught in the petulant breezes, it seemed to touch the face of heaven in its flight. When the kite held firm in its course and sailed gracefully in the air, I would hand the tether line to him. His eyes sparkled with delight when he realized he held something that could almost touch the distant clouds. Though the turbulent wind at the top of the hill felt as if it could almost burn our skin in its abrasive grip, there was no reason to fear. What existed was the simple delight of sending a child's colorful sail into the sky like a message sent farther than where our mere hands could reach.

Somehow, living with the possibility of cancer returning each day reminded me of the times I flew kites with my son. I thought back upon those days of innocence and realized how we needed to be more like children . . . unafraid of the wind. On those days when I heard the wind outside my window, it still made my heart race. I had to look inside myself to find the heart of a child. There I found that the rage was gone and hope had taken its place. Abandoning our fears of the wind, we were able to launch our kites into the blustery wind, sending them like messages and using it as a force to get closer to heaven than our mortal hands could ever reach without it.

Days no longer seem ordinary when you realize the miracle of having those you love around you. Never take for granted those days that seem ordinary and carefree. Days like these may not be that way again nor as many. Beyond the magic of research, beyond all our mystical science, and beyond all our human potential lies a spirit dreaming of hope. It holds us steadfast in the wind, allowing us to send our prayers upon the wind like children's colorful kites. Our prayers can tell heaven of heroes, warriors, and poets locked in the battle against breast cancer. And if you ever see kites flying against the vastness of the sky, remember to believe in hope. I look forward to what those kites may bring.

I wrote *Flying Kites* between the years 1999 and 2000 for my hospital newsletter. It was written during a tranquil time when Lois's thoughts were disconnected from her own shelved treatments and she could dwell on her role as an advocate for organizations such as the NBCC (National Breast Cancer Coalition), the PBCC (Pennsylvania

Breast Cancer Coalition), the ACS (American Cancer Society), the Linda Creed Foundation in Philadelphia, and numerous agencies founded on principles related to breast cancer advocacy. She believed the only way to combat this disease was to get the words "breast cancer" into the political arena, wherein one is barely able to say the word "breast" in a formal sentence—much less acknowledge this deadly disease as a threat so serious to many women and families that it needed, and deserved, their attention. To illustrate her commitment to this cause, I included a comment taken from her journals.

(From a journal written by Lois A. Anderson)

> *I am a very big advocate when it comes to breast cancer and whatever may be related to it. Lobbying efforts are something that are very important to me. Why? Well, if your legislators don't know about it, they won't know how to vote on it. It is up to all of us to educate these people in Washington, DC, Harrisburg, PA, and our local areas about any and all things that are near and dear to our hearts. That is why I do the advocacy work I do and the public speaking engagements that I make.*

Lois pursued such an astonishing life from the moment she came into the world, overcoming many obstacles in her quest to rise above the ordinary, many conquered even before breast cancer entered her life. I felt her story had to be told. She lived her short life coming from very humble beginnings, rising from all of it, and making changes she hoped would better everyone, when it ended on January 17, 2011. At the time of her death, she was considered a great breast cancer advocate known at the national level.

She was diagnosed with stage III breast cancer at the age of forty in 1992. Signs that could have cautioned her remained muted by an unsuspicious bruise she sustained from an injury several months before her fortieth birthday. In time, she was treated for the initial breast cancer and remained cancer-free for almost ten years, until the cancer returned in 2001. Then when the odds seemed stacked against her, she fought the disease as a stage IV breast cancer survivor (metastatic breast cancer) from the time of that dire discovery until she died in January 2011. She lived eighteen years from the time she was diagnosed, against all prognostications allowing her only five years of survival.

Over the last six months of her life, I began writing a story where I escaped the realities of losing my wife to something I had no control over. In a way, it transitioned into a metaphoric fable, a parallel story of her life. Between the lines, I allowed myself the chance to create an alternate world where the real trials Lois and I experienced on our "last road" together eventually made some sense to me in our unpredictable world. After she died, I began the long process of chronicling her amazing biography and believed I could finish the fictional one. Both stories represent a process of coming to terms with her death and a promise I made to "not let her be forgotten."

I began writing her real life story in late February 2011. After I started, I found stories and journals Lois had written about herself tucked away in boxes and old folders throughout the house. Some of her excerpts are so exceptional that I have included many of them throughout the book. In a way, she will help everyone understand how and why she was able to do what she did in such a short time.

Of all the things I believe the reader should take away from this book is Lois's message of "hope." I believe hope sustained her at times when many of us would have given up. She always believed if you took hope away from a person, it could shorten their life. When I think about her powerful belief that she could overcome anything, I believe it was her "hope" that made it happen.

(From a television interview with Lois A. Anderson, 1997)

If you can give a person "hope," they can go on and fight . . . and they can keep on fighting.

Sunset under the Poet's Tree could only be written using my own perceptions of the events steering Lois's life. The invitation to understand our world as it existed in the late 1960s and early 1970s forced me to begin this story before I ever met my amazing wife. Stories based on my youth and childhood paint this dynamic time of change and turmoil. I felt obligated and responsible to draw the background behind the portrait, showing readers the importance of the times Lois and I lived in. While I didn't know Lois or her family until I met her at the age of nineteen, she came from the same world

George S. J. Anderson

I did and was subjected to its changes, either good or bad. She made my life and the lives of many others better by the way she lived and struggled as a young woman and, eventually, under the shadow of breast cancer. At this point, I invite you to the world I knew before Lois came into my life.

The Newspaper

Tell me about the world . . .

At seventeen, I graduated from high school. The timely subject of most conversations revolved around the lingering war in a place called Vietnam. My friends who are not going to college either quietly enlisted or were unceremoniously drafted into the service. So many of my friends and relatives ended up dead—or if not dead, not really part of the world they remembered, when they returned. Some couldn't get back . . . even with their feet firmly planted on American soil. But I can't begin like this . . .

The world I lived in at seventeen was, in its very essence, the core meaning of the word "irony." In the sounds of the ubiquitous radio and on posters, erratically displayed in the music stores were the sermons of "love" and "peace." Yet with such moralizations, just four years before, I walked into my high school to a gauntlet of tanks and heavily armed National Guardsmen patrolling the grounds around my high school. They were there because of the "racial tensions," which turned our small normally quiet town into an all-out war zone in the streets. We talked of "peace," but there was none to be found. And "love"? That was what we were all looking for.

When summer's sticky fingers, ripe with the lingering vapors of the heat of the passing day, smear themselves on the stagnant canopy of the night, I recall a time that now seems so far away. It was a sweltering summer night I believed I buried deep in the dark memories of my mind. Yet when a hot summer night lingers in breathless heat and the smell of sweat, my thoughts will often go there to remember. It started as an oppressive summer night in early July. The air was heavy and fouled by the smell of garbage, lying full in dented tin cans lining the city street. The night hesitated, malingering with the scorched heat of the day. It seemed unsure of itself, loitering and waiting. It knew something was out of place and pressed its secrets into a silent void.

In the seventeenth summer of my life, I continued to hear this insidious, haunting song . . . Someone named Scott McKenzie was singing . . . "If you're going to San Francisco . . ." The song was so pervasive on the airwaves that summer, it became inescapable. Its message of peace, tacitly woven in its lyrics and reverent allusions, delivered the listener to an almost hypnotic trance.

It was during this same haunting summer that I hoped to find a job through the same private employment agency who provided me with several odd jobs the summer before. I anticipated the agency would find something to keep some money in my pocket for the summer and hoped for a part-time job throughout the fall to help with expenses during my freshman year at college. The agency always managed to come through for me, finding short-term jobs that generally paid little more than minimum wage, but it was always enough for a seventeen-year-old to manage on. The woman running the agency called one day to tell me she had an opening. The job was at the pressroom for a local newspaper. It involved carrying newspapers from their printing presses and then distributing the papers to the workers who would fold the papers together with flyers or advertisements. The only downside was it started at midnight and ended when all the papers were done. So on any given night, I could be there for about four hours or longer.

The idea of working at night intrigued me, and to make it more palatable, the agency was doubling my pay. However, as a warning, the agency explained the newspaper was only trying this method of "stuffing" newspapers until they decided if it was profitable. The employment agency wasn't certain the position would last any longer than the end of summer. Still, they hoped I would take it, since it was the only job available at the time. Perhaps, the agency explained, it would last longer if the newspaper liked what the paper "stuffers" accomplished.

The times were strange and wonderful. They were, perhaps, my last days of innocence. Many of my old friends from high school were either leaving home that summer for college dorms or leaving to go into the service. Because I graduated from high school a year early, I had the option of going to college without worrying about the draft for at least a year. The feared draft was in effect . . . Those called were going to a place called Vietnam. Most of my friends graduated at the age of eighteen or nineteen. Those without a college deferment were either on the roster to be drafted or simply enlisted to avoid the formality. If you had no plans for the future at eighteen or nineteen, the government did. If you had a deferment, it generally meant your parents had enough money to send you to college; if not, your path was chosen for you.

There was a movement rising out of these practices. The young people of the country were up in arms, arguing that they were old enough to die for their country but not old enough to vote (at the time). Protests were breaking out all over the country. I was fortunate. When I turned eighteen, I would already be in college. A deferment would occur without protest provided I was enrolled in a college program should the draft board decide it was ready for me. As fate would have it, I never received the call. Many old friends from high school, I never saw again. A few died of natural causes over the years; too many died in Vietnam. Two of my cousins died there, making the war genuinely touch our families. Our time of innocence was dying too. We would get older. Eventually, we would get wiser, both individually and as a country of men and women looking ahead for better times and healing the wounds of war. But that wouldn't occur for several years.

The music of the times spoke of antiwar protests, free love, hallucinogens, and an emerging drug culture. The drug culture was perhaps the most destructive part of the whole era. Our rock-and-roll heroes seemed to sanctify the use of common street drugs of the times in their songs and by personal use. By the time I would get my first college degree, many of our rock-and-roll heroes died from overdoses of some kind. Many of my friends followed this path as well. "Dropping out," as it was called, was almost the same as dropping over dead. It seemed we were a generation bent on destroying ourselves, either self-inflicted with drugs or in a distant land by a bullet. None of us really felt we had a chance of changing anything. Yet some of us would survive and do that very thing.

I found the newspaper office very easily that first night. The place was a hive of activity with a crowd approximately my own age. Some were young men with long overgrown hair; some were young women with their long hair tied or bound up with colorful bandannas. All of us dressed in the uniform of the times, which demanded bell-bottom jeans and tie-dyed T-shirts. Almost everyone wore a headband of sorts, which for the nights that followed served more to keep the sweat out of our eyes than a statement of "individuality." I found the man I was to report to, who immediately handed me a stack of flyers to distribute to the women stuffing the morning newspapers.

In this job, I found there were runners, like myself, who ran to the pressroom, gathered flyers coming off the press, and then distributed them to the other parts of the team. Those included people who stuffed the newspapers and the men who ran the enormous presses. The paper stuffers were predominately young women about my age . . . a few older women and, even less, older men. Those who weren't as quick as the bosses wanted were stationed at desks and tables in a large office adjoining the pressroom.

First, the main newspaper was printed. As copies rolled off the large presses, I would carry the heavy stacks of paper to the adjoining office, where the "stuffers" would prepare the tall newspaper stacks for the flyers. Once the main newspaper was printed, we started carrying stacks of flyers to the people seated at desks in the office. It was the runners' job to make sure the "stuffers" never ran out of papers or flyers, simply sitting at an empty desk with nothing to do. The job was easy, a real no-brainer. After four or five weeks, I acquainted myself with most of the people working the hours I did.

Mike was a year older and worked various jobs inside the newspaper offices for about a year. This was a job his bosses talked him into. He didn't mind the extra hours. One night, he reluctantly confessed to being a South Street Boy. The South Street Boys were a gang of boys and young men who made it their mission to keep watch over the young white girls of the town so no harm would come to them. The concept seemed benevolent enough, but I knew some of their ideas of "taking care of the white girls" meant vicious, deadly gang fights based on racial differences. Just four summers ago, as I remembered it, the town was besieged by police, artillery, National

Guardsmen, tanks, Black Panthers, South Street Boys, Grenadiers (the other local gang), hatred, and gunfire. Some areas of town still weren't safe for anyone to walk in after dark. Mike said he had connections if I ever had any trouble in any part of town. I just needed to say the word, and he would have an army there in minutes. I believed him.

There was a young African American man called Nate working with us through those early hours before sunrise. Like me, Nate was attending college in the fall with a deferment, lasting until he finished. He was a tall lanky guy and easygoing, with an offbeat sense of humor that made him immediately likable. In spite of the tensions created by Mike's beliefs and Nate's heritage, they got along so well you could have called them friends. Mike liked to pick at Nate's deferment just enough to get him a little defensive, but even Mike was glad Nate could defer going into the service. Nate would pick back at Mike, saying he needed a girl to settle down with and start a family; that way, he too might get deferred. Nate would start pointing out girls he thought would make a nice match for him. Mike would just respond, "Not her, too young. No, too old. Too cranky. Too bossy . . ." To which Nate would respond, "You're just 'too' picky, man. You need to get a life and get on with it." Then the two of them would jab each other in the shoulder and laugh.

About the time I befriended Mike and Nate, I also became friends with two girls working the same shift with us, Melanie and Stephanie. Melanie was a small brown-haired girl of about sixteen, and Stephanie stood as tall as myself with hair as red as fire. Stephanie I estimated to be about seventeen, though to be honest, she never told anyone her true age. She always liked to keep the boys guessing. Both girls tied their long hair back, and because of the sticky summer air, they also wore colorful headbands. I thought they were trying to look like one of our country's rock idols, Janis Joplin. Melanie could have easily passed herself off as Janis Joplin as she appeared on her album cover *Pearl*. Stephanie looked more like the girl on the album cover for *Blind Faith*, only with her clothes on. This was the way of the world at the time, all of us emulating the look of our favorite rock stars. Even Nate had that "Jimi Hendrix" appearance. Mike hadn't caught up with the times quite yet. He still had some of that early "Beach Boys" look and ideology, but he was changing. Mike, only a year or two older than most of us, seemed to be living ten years in the past.

The summer heat was unbearable that night. Mike, Nate, and I had each gone through three cloth headbands trying to keep the sweat from going into our eyes. We took turns going outside, where we pulled off our shirts to wring out the sweat, then came back to let another one of us do the same. The girls, Melanie and Stephanie, looked like scalded rats. Their long hair dripped in spite of using their kerchiefs like a sweatband to keep their sweaty, tangled hair out of their eyes. There was no air-conditioning in either the office or the pressroom, making the stagnant humid air even more oppressive. Because of the heat, some older workers started feeling sick, as the newspapers and flyers grew increasingly higher on their desks. Thankfully, one of the pressroom bosses finally called a halt to the activity.

Everything stood still when the overheated presses started blurring the newsprint . . . like words melted in the swelling heat. Big fans rolled into the pressroom. The large paneled doors, where the enormous rolls of newspaper were taken off tractor trailers by forklifts, were opened to vent the stagnant rooms. The presses were finished . . . at least until the rooms could be cooled enough to start again. The workers were told to get out of the offices until the hot presses cooled down. Workers poured into the streets and alleyways surrounding the building, looking for a place to sit out of the heat. The *Gazette*, as the paper was called in those days, had some of the bosses handing out cups of cold water to everyone, telling everyone to get out of the building until the fans cooled the lower floors of the building.

We didn't know how long the presses would be down, but we knew the longer they were down, the longer we got paid, so we were in no hurry to get back to work. Most of the workers went to the large back doors where the fans were blowing the hot, rancid air out of the building. Mike had a better idea and convinced Nate, me, and the two girls, Melanie and Stephanie, to exit by the entrance door and stand in the front of the building, where it was slightly cooler. Unfortunately, going out the front door meant we could not get back in because, as we all knew, the door would lock behind us. We weren't at all concerned. After all, it was only a short walk to one of the side doors, where everyone from the office and pressroom had congregated, and get back in. Mike was right. It was unquestionably cooler there than where most of the workers had decided to go.

Melanie sidled up about six feet from me, leaning against the brick wall that served as the front of the *Gazette*. Melanie always looked older than sixteen. She could have easily passed for twenty-one at most of the bars in town, and she told me as much herself. She told me stories where she and Stephanie went into several bars and had been successfully served. I was never inside a bar myself, so her exploits intrigued me a little.

"Yes, Stephanie and I once went into the Boars Tavern on Eleventh Street. Did I ever tell you this story?" Melanie asked with a grin on her face.

"No, I don't think so," I said sheepishly as I really looked at Melanie for the first time since I met her.

Stephanie interrupted then started talking about their shared experiences at barhopping. Most of what she told us involved conning some unsuspecting twenty-one-year-olds into buying them drinks. While they talked, I let my eyes wander over the sweat-soaked clothes and form of Melanie. Mike walked in on our disconnected banter, and, without missing a beat, he and Stephanie started a conversation of their own. Eventually, they wandered away, checking in with other people they knew working that night, leaving Melanie alone with me. I didn't mind.

Melanie stood against the painted red brick wall with one foot against it, the other foot firmly on the ground as she looked absently into the night sky. Her body was covered in sweat, and her soaked clothes clung to her like a second skin. She wore a soft light T-shirt, which, against the muted glow of the street lights, accentuated her breasts and feminine form. She wore cut-off jeans, fraying in irregular lines at the middle of her thighs, and a pair of sandals, exposing the delicate features of her feet. She saw me looking and then waved a hand, motioning me to come closer to where she was standing. My heart skipped a beat. I never had a girl invite me to stand next to her. I thought I embarrassed her when she caught me staring. But when I went to join her, she simply wanted to talk.

"I feel like I'm melting out here," she said.

"Yeah, it is pretty hot. I guess the boss realized that when the presses heated up too much."

"How long do you think we'll be out here?"

"I guess however long it takes . . . until the presses are cooled down enough to start running again," I ventured.

"You know, Stephanie and I just live a few blocks from here. We could all go there and cool off if we know how long they will be. My grandmother is up, and she could make us something to eat and some cold drinks."

"Sounds like a great idea. How long do you think it would take to get there?"

"Five minutes . . . we could probably be back here in about half an hour."

"I'm not sure we have that long."

"Do you think we could ask somebody?"

"Yeah, probably . . . but who? And will they really know how long it will be? You know, if we leave and they start the presses while we're gone, we'll all get fired."

"Yeah, that's what I'm afraid of too . . . and I need this job."

"Me too. This is tuition money for school in the fall."

"You're going to college?"

"Yeah . . ." I said, not knowing anything else to say.

"What are you majoring in?"

"Haven't really decided. I'm seventeen now, so I do have a little time to make a decision."

Melanie looked at me for a moment then averted her eyes to the dirty cement sidewalk where we both stood.

"I'd like to go to college when I get done with high school, but I don't think there will be enough money. The money I make doing this job is actually grocery money for us. We all manage."

"How many live at your house?" I asked, wondering what conditions she lived under that forced her to bring money for food into her home.

"Well . . . it's myself," as she held up a finger to count, "my mother, and grandmother, and I have a younger brother." Melanie held up four fingers.

"Where's your dad?" I asked, half expecting her to say he was in the service like everyone else.

"My dad died in a motorcycle accident about five years ago." Melanie turned her eyes from the sidewalk to look me in the face.

"I'm sorry . . . I didn't mean to pry." I tried to act unaffected by her statement, but I really felt sorry for her having to grow up without her father.

"It's okay," she said softly. "It was tough at first, but we all managed to deal with it."

I didn't know how to respond. I just leaned against the wall and looked up into the night sky. Mike slipped in beside me and leaned against the wall, while Stephanie slipped to the other side of Melanie and did the same, putting myself and Melanie between them.

"So what have you two lovebirds been chatting about over here by yourselves?" Mike asked with a certain devilish look in his eyes.

He caught me off guard as I stood straight up and shook my head no. "We were just talking, Mike."

"It looked like more than that," Stephanie chimed in.

George S. J. Anderson

Now it was Melanie's turn to be bewildered. "We were just talking about school, Steph."

"Well, from where we were sitting, it looked like a lot more," Stephanie said, as she winked her eye at Melanie.

"I think you guys are smoking something," Melanie replied as she giggled at me.

"I think she's right, Mike . . . What are you guys on?"

Mike gave me a wink and slapped me on the back. "C'mon, lighten up. Steph and I are just messin' with you."

We were all having a good laugh when Nate showed up and asked what we were all up to. Mike started hassling Nate about girls, and Nate wouldn't bite. Nate knew better than to talk to Mike about girls, especially white girls like Melanie and Stephanie. Instead, Nate turned the conversation to the music of the times. We talked about the Doors, the Beatles, Janis Joplin, the Jefferson Airplane, and, of course, Nate's favorite artist, Jimi Hendrix. Strangely, we all seemed to grow quiet after a while; and from somewhere inside the newspaper office, we could hear the sound of a radio. The words hung in the air, haunting the space around us . . . "If you're going to San Francisco . . . be sure to wear some flowers in your hair . . ."

In spite of the untenable heat, it was a perfect night. We were all at a job that made us some money. We were being ourselves with two lovely girls, and we were at peace with our racial differences. Nate, Mike, Stephanie, Melanie, and I leaned against the warm brick wall intoxicated by the music of Scott McKenzie. "You're going to meet . . . some gentle people there . . ."

"Do you think that's really true?" Nate asked, speaking to no one in particular as he presumed to search the night sky.

"Is what true?" Mike asked calmly as he looked at his feet.

"You know . . . what's happening on the West Coast?"

~28~

"I don't know," Mike said, as he raised his eyes to watch Nate staring at the sky. "All I know is when my time comes to go to Vietnam . . ." Mike trailed off, like he was thinking of something that eluded him, then said, "I don't know."

"You sure you are going?" asked Melanie with some concern in her voice.

"Pretty sure." Mike looked down to his feet again before he went on. Everyone was silent. "My family doesn't have any money. I have a brother in the army now, and it looks like I will be following him . . . over there."

"Does your brother see any fighting?" asked Stephanie.

"Yeah . . . but he doesn't like to talk about it," Mike said in a hushed somber voice.

"It's scary, Mike," Nate spoke up, moving closer to Mike's side. Then as he leaned against the same wall where we all stood, he looked at Mike and said, "We're too young to vote, but not too young to die. We can't drink, but we can bleed. Same coin . . . different sides."

Mike looked up and said, "Pretty deep stuff, Nate." We were all leaning against the brick wall, watching Mike and Nate, and listening to the developing dialogue between them when Mike came off the wall like a shot. He was looking at something over Nate's shoulder as he said, "What the hell?"

Up to now, it was the perfect night. Events were now set in motion to change it. The irony of the times seeped in like the torrid stench of the summer's heat and manifested itself in the thing Mike spotted over Nate's shoulder.

"What's up, Mike?" Nate asked, as he pushed off the wall, straining to see what Mike was looking at.

"What the hell?" Mike said again as he moved toward the street, fixated on something no one else had seen. Nate followed, then me, and then finally the two girls.

"Look at that stupid son of a bitch," Mike said aghast, as we gathered where Mike stood, finally seeing the disturbing vision he spotted in the thick night air.

From a distance, the darkness appeared haloed with scattered streetlights, glowing in dulled washed-out circles by the humid air. As we watched these pools of muted light, we saw what looked like a young white baldheaded man aimlessly lurching back and forth on the dirty sidewalk. He was shirtless and broad shouldered, stumbling down the block on the opposite side of the street like a clumsy giant. Mike knew Melanie and Stephanie were still with us, and there was no quick way to get them into the building. I considered trying to get them inside anyway, but when Mike sensed what I wanted to do, he grabbed my arm and said, "We want to stay still and not draw attention to the girls. Let me handle this." I looked at Mike, but his attention was no longer on me. Mike looked like a wild cat ready to strike. His breathing slowed; he focused his eyes. He was ready to fight. Somehow we knew, or sensed, what was to happen. His vow to protect these girls was going to be tested. He wasn't going to back down if the threat this interloper posed became real. We realized he would fight to the death if needed. We hoped it wouldn't come to that.

"Mike . . . ?" Stephanie sounded upset, even with her most soothing, calming voice. When Mike didn't respond to it, she yelled, "Mike! What do you think you are you doing?"

"I'm going over there," Mike said, believing he would keep the fight on the other side of the street, away from the two girls.

"Mike, I don't think that's a good idea. Just let the bastard walk by us," Nate pleaded.

"Did you see his hands?" Mike asked, giving him a hard, determined look that would have frozen a fire.

We looked into the piebald darkness, finally realizing the dark irony Mike saw below the muted streetlights. The big baldheaded man was wearing handcuffs. He sauntered back and forth, riding some strange tide that pushed him forward, then brazenly pushed him into parked cars along the street. Every time he bumbled into one of them, he reacted to it as an assault, a personal attack. To even the score, he maliciously ripped antennas off the cars he carelessly fell against, smashed random side view mirrors as he staggered forward. We watched Mike's anger growing with the interloper's every step, every broken antenna, and every smashed mirror. We watched, breathing the hot stagnant air, feeling it inside us like a vise, while the bald man blindly made his way toward us. Eventually, he walked directly across the street from us and stopped, swaggering stupidly on the other side of the street, and then rolled his head from side to side like he was looking for something.

"Hey you," Mike yelled at the bald man.

"What do you want?" growled the man, trying to focus on the direction of Mike's voice, just realizing other people witnessed what he did.

"Hey, what's your problem?" Mike continued.

"Fuck you, man, none of your affair!" the bald man yelled, propping his cuffed hands on top of a car roof parked across the street from the *Gazette* building.

"I can make it my fucking affair," Mike yelled back, using some of Baldy's less-illustrious words. Mike was tensing up. His muscles seemed to bulge even more as the bald man insulted him.

"You want to try, pussy?" the bald man chided as he directed his focus on Mike.

"Sure, why don't you come over here, and we can fucking try it right now, asshole." Mike yelled, as a scarlet flush colored his face. We knew when we heard what was said, Mike wasn't thinking. He was just reacting to the insults.

"Mike, don't make him come over here," the two girls pleaded, hoping Mike would stop taunting the guy.

"Don't worry," Mike remarked confidently, "he's not going to do anything."

The bald man plodded across the dirty macadam, oblivious to caution, as a car turned onto the street. When the car tried to drive through, it almost hit him, as he strolled across the street like it was a lazy summer pasture. The driver slowed down, but when Baldy reared up and hit the side of the car with his cuffed hands, the driver sped off, apparently not wanting to get involved in what was turning into an ugly situation. As he stood in the middle of the street, washed by the muted streetlights, we finally saw his face clearly. He was bleeding from the right side of his mouth. Apparently, injuries from a fight transpiring earlier in the night had not slowed him down.

The bald man appeared to be in his midtwenties, older than any of us. He had a tattoo running up his arm, displaying a marine insignia. We watched him swagger over the remaining width of the street, finally stepping onto the curbing near Mike. We saw he wasn't wearing shoes. He was barefoot, manacled, and stank of alcohol. In addition to shaving his head smooth, he shaved his eyebrows, making him appear even more ominous and monstrous. He had chiseled muscular arms and was probably in good shape once, as evidenced by his broad angular shoulders. A small beer belly hung over a pair of khaki shorts, the only clothing he wore. He was covered in sweat. Crusted bloodstains at one corner of his mouth indicated he was struck there, but it hadn't stopped him. Blood covered four inches of each wrist where he tried unsuccessfully to remove the handcuffs. Mike assessed his every move as he walked toward us.

"So, big man," Baldy jeered as he focused on Mike, "whatcha gonna do now?"

"What the hell is going on with you?" Mike asked, looking the guy over from head to foot. "You're handcuffed, no clothes to speak of, no shoes, and you stink . . ." Mike scoffed, standing his ground only inches from the bald guy's face.

"So, like I said, what are you going to do, BIG MAN?" the bald man screamed in Mike's face. He quickly spun around in a circle, showing Mike he was in control of his faculties, and then his words seethed out like deadly venom. "The cops caught me lying on the ground after I got drunk. I smacked the shit out of them after they cuffed me, and then I got away." Baldy hesitated, waiting to see if

Mike thought he was bluffing. "So what do you think you are going to do?" He half spit, half slurred his words as he ranted. Mike tried to circle the man, and Baldy, in turn, countered, not allowing Mike the advantage of getting behind him. Then Baldy spotted Nate standing with me and the two girls.

Baldy had a lecherous grin on his face as he sized up the girls leaning against the brick wall, guarded on either side by Nate and me. He could have picked any of us to address with his foul remarks, but after surveying the four of us, he chose Nate to start on. "Hey, nigger, you fucking one of them girls . . . ? Why don't you send that one over here, and I'll show you how to do it." Baldy said, pointing a finger toward Melanie with his two cuffed and bleeding hands.

Melanie said repugnantly, "You stink, and you're an asshole, I don't think so."

But Baldy wasn't in the mood to be turned down, so he kept at it. "Aw, com'on, honey . . . you want to see what I got for you?"

The bald man proceeded to unzip his fly and stuck his hardened penis out with both his cuffed hands. "See . . . ain't it sweet, darlin'? But you know, right now, I really have to piss."

Mike, meanwhile, was trying to work his way behind the lurching bald guy but backed off when he started urinating behind the bumper of a parked car. "Jeezus, man," Mike said disgustedly. "Did you learn to do that in the marines?"

"Shit, man, I AWOLed the marines about five months ago. That's what the cops found out when they stopped me. They were going to send me back, but I fought them off and got away. Fucking cops are laying on the ground now, wishing they were never born, and I got away." Baldy laughed as he zipped up his fly.

I knew Mike was fed up with this guy, as he persistently watched for weaknesses to subdue him. His allegiance to protect Melanie and Steph was being fundamentally tested. When Baldy directed his crude remark at Nate, we all froze. Even jokingly, making a statement about Nate having sex with a white girl was like throwing gasoline on a fire. Baldy was goading Mike into a confrontation. He knew which hot buttons would ultimately elicit a reaction from Mike. He hoped he would get careless and sloppy. I gave Mike credit; he stayed focused.

The distraction Mike needed was as spontaneous as it was obvious, as he watched Baldy lasciviously inspect Melanie in her clingy wet clothes. Mike looked to Melanie and gave her a wink. Melanie saw the signal then winked back. It was a secret unspoken agreement between the two of them. Melanie understood the insinuation and instinctively knew Mike wanted a diversion. She was it. She watched Baldy observing her breasts through her sweat-soaked shirt with obvious intent. The thought of him touching her chilled her with disgust. She knew Mike would never allow him to ever get that close. She gave Mike a quick glance then spoke up,

"So big man, you from here?" Melanie asked in her sweetest voice.

"Yeah, I'm from here." He continued to run his eyes over Melanie's body. When he looked up, he said, "You look pretty good for a girl in her twenties."

"That's probably because I'm sixteen, asshole," Melanie lashed out.

"Sixteen?" Baldy pondered with a sick twisted smile. "Well, that's old enough to fuck. You up to it, cunt? Think you can you handle all my cock, or should I take it easy on you the first time?"

While Melanie had Baldy's attention, Mike got behind him. Mike moved within two feet of Baldy's back and then crouched down. "Hey, asshole . . ." Mike called from behind him, "you shouldn't be talking dirty to young girls like that." Baldy bolted instinctively, lashing around violently with his cuffed arms, thinking Mike managed to get the advantage behind him, but was curiously surprised as his misfired swing hit the empty air. Mike was ready for Baldy's amateurish counterattack. He lunged with his body weight, becoming a powerful side slash uppercut, slamming Baldy's left jawbone with interlocked fists. An audible crack resounded throughout the empty street in a single echo as Mike connected with him. Baldy went down with a sick thud, landing preposterously on his blubbery white belly. If the scene wasn't so serious and horrible, the landing Baldy made on his stomach would have been comical.

"Nice one, Mike," Nate complimented.

"Yeah, I think I sprained my right wrist when I caught him," Mike said, as he stood, wringing his right arm. Melanie came over and hugged Mike. Stephanie put her arms around him too. I came over, and, with Mike's good hand, we gave each other a high five. All was right with the world again.

"Hey, Nate," Mike ordered, "better go inside and have someone call the cops."

"I'm on it." Nate turned where the bald half-naked body landed, then turned back to Mike. "Mike, you might want to check this out."

Baldy was gone. There was a sparse trail of bloody droplets on the pavement trailing to the curb where two cars were parked close to each other. Mike took charge. "Nate, do what I said and get a phone call out to the police. I'm sure they are looking for this asshole."

Nate nodded he understood and then quickly ran to the open side doors of the newspaper building. We all watched as he pushed through the crowd, still trying to cool themselves outside the doors, then lost sight of him.

"What do you think, Mike? Let him go and let the police handle it, or follow the blood trail and try to hold him until they get here?" I asked, cautiously letting my eyes survey the visible bumpers of all the cars parked along the street.

"Asshole's trying to get away, probably staying low on the street side of these cars. Damn cars run all the way to the corner each way . . . so he could take off, and they'll never catch him." Mike thought for a moment. "Okay, you're going to help. I'm going out to the street side . . . You stay here on the sidewalk. Watch both ways. If you see him, call out. I'll get there, don't worry."

It sounded like a good plan, thrown together as it was in the heat of the moment. I watched Mike walk into the street where visible drops of blood revealed the direction the bald man went. Almost immediately, Mike acted like he caught the blood scent of the bald man fleeing before a pack of bloodhounds. Mike ran three car lengths in less than a second, kicking Baldy out from between the bumpers of two parked cars and onto the sidewalk. Baldy went sprawling onto his elbows. Nate came back and walked up beside me. Baldy might have been drunk, but he was quick. When Mike bolted through the cars, flushing Baldy out onto the sidewalk, Baldy turned over and put a solid kick right into Mike's groin. Mike dropped like a dead animal. If Mike was still conscious, he didn't show it. That left Nate and me to keep him occupied until the police showed up.

"Nate," I whispered, "did you get hold of the cops?"

"No," Nate whispered back.

"Shit, Nate," I said, alarmed at how things were turning out, "we need to get a damned call into the police. Mike is hurt. Baldy doesn't look happy, and he's been threatening the girls."

"No, my brother, it's cool, it's cool. I got someone else to call. I wasn't allowed to make a call, but one of the supervisors said they would do it. So stay tight, my brother, it'll work out."

Baldy moved toward us quickly. With Mike out of the way, his self-confident attitude concerned me as he sauntered up to our little group, directing his attention to Nate, who just returned. "Hey, nigger, where you been? Didn't see you there when I got up. Now you're here . . . What the fuck you been doin'?"

Nate kept his temper. I could see the frustration and anger in his face. What alarmed me further was watching his self-control crumble to dust. "*Just a few more minutes . . . a few minutes . . .*" I thought.

Then Nate did something very clever, with more control than I imagined he could muster under the circumstances. Rather than reacting to Baldy's insults, he engaged his intimidator in a conversation.

Nate began walking back and forth in front of him, keeping the crude intruder's attention, making him work harder to keep Nate in his visual field. Nate started quietly in a very controlled dialogue.

"So you're a marine . . . see any action, Marine?"

"DON'T CALL ME THAT! I've been AWOL for five months, and I'm not going back."

"You afraid?" Nate taunted.

"I'm not afraid of you, nigger," Baldy smirked, moving a few steps toward Nate.

"That's not what I asked, ASSHOLE," Nate screamed back, his residual self-control gone. I don't believe Baldy would have gotten that ugly word out, even once more, before Nate reacted physically to his tormenter. Fortunately, it never had to happen. Mike seemed to come out of nowhere, plowing his momentous weight into Baldy's back full force, slamming his face into the sidewalk with an audible hollow crack. Baldy was out cold. I thought Mike killed him, considering the force he used to take him down. Nate and I rolled him over and saw he was still breathing through bloody bubbles seeping out his nose.

Mike asked Nate, "We get a call into the police?"

"I'm sure they're on their way by now," Nate said.

"Good . . . I'm getting tired of this asshole."

Just then, two police cars came from opposite ends of the street. Baldy was starting to rouse. "What the fuck," Baldy mumbled through his bloody teeth and mangled lips.

It looked like Mike may have broken the guy's nose. Blood was running freely from the corner of his mouth where Mike hit his cheek; the nose was off to one side, also very bloody. The police drove up where we were all standing, jumped out of the car, and then realized we had Baldy on the ground. They asked our group what happened. Melanie and Nate gave an abbreviated version of the events leading up to their arrival. According to one of the officers, Baldy slipped away from them earlier in the night. They acted more than happy to take him back into custody. He was originally picked up for drunk and disorderly. Now, he had a resisting arrest charge as well. Apparently, they were not aware of his claim of being AWOL, but they would be certain to look into it. Baldy was in a lot of trouble no matter how it worked out.

Mike didn't look good and was limping badly. The police offered to take him to the hospital. Mike didn't want to go, but when Melanie explained the events of our ordeal to one of the *Gazette*'s supervisors, he was made to go.

Baldy was still struggling with two police officers as they tried to get him into the backseat of the squad car. One officer told us Baldy fought through four officers earlier in the night. He felt Mike did a pretty good job restraining the guy until they got here. The police were very grateful to us all, especially Mike.

Just before Baldy was forced into the back of the police car, he held his ground, looked Mike in the eye, and screamed through his bloody teeth, "I'll remember you . . . and I will hunt you down. I'LL HUNT YOU DOWN." He screamed, "I WILL REMEMBER YOU." His brutal screams of rage echoed in streets as the officers finally slammed the car door shut on him. Even with the doors locked, Baldy got to his back and tried kicking the windows out with his bare feet. I never saw such animal hatred as I did in those eyes. As they drove away, I hoped they would keep him locked up for a very long time. I was afraid for Mike and, for that matter, everyone else.

Mike was getting ready to get into the other police vehicle.

"You going to be okay?" I asked Mike.

"I think so," he said numbly.

"Baldy made some threats, man. I would watch myself if I were you."

"I heard . . . If he wants to look me up, I'll be waiting for him. I better go."

"Yeah, hope to see you soon."

Nate, Melanie, and Stephanie started calling after Mike, telling him "Thanks," "Be careful," "We'll be watching for you," and "Hurry back," but Mike was preoccupied with his pain. He either didn't hear or didn't care. I never really knew.

The presses were coming back. They said we had about another ten minutes then we were back to work. I heard the radio playing Scott McKenzie's song again. It was the piece that went "You're going to meet . . . some gentle people there." It was the ultimate irony of the moment and the irony of the times. The music played on until the song was over. The night seemed empty, an anticlimax to the scene playing out just minutes ago . . . silent now.

From somewhere inside the *Gazette,* I heard someone say, "The presses are up. Everyone back to work." The intro to Jimi Hendrix's "Purple Haze" was winding up full crescendo on the same radio station when a disenchanted voice hollered angrily, "Shut that DAMN thing off or change the FUCKING station." We were all too preoccupied with the night's events to worry about the radio station. It was just one generation tuning the other one out.

The night continued as it had once the presses started up. Nate and I carried newspapers and flyers out to the office where the women, both young and old, were stuffing them into the morning edition of the newspaper. Melanie and Stephanie were there. Melanie looked as if she had been crying. I tried to get some flyers to her desk, but the other "runners" kept her supply filled; I never had the chance to talk to her. I kept passing Nate in a hallway, running between the pressroom and the office where the women were working; but we were so rushed, we could not pass a word between us.

"Hey, Nate," I tried calling a few times. I could see him, but the best I could get out of him was "Not now, brother, after . . . after . . ." Each time I carried flyers out to the office, I would try to get to Stephanie or Melanie. One time I managed to get flyers to Stephanie.

"Steph, what's wrong with Melanie?"

"I think she's afraid we won't be allowed to come back after what happened tonight. Her grandmother won't be happy."

"It's nobody's fault what happened . . ."

"It's nobody's fault . . . It's just how things are . . ."

"I'm sorry, Stephanie. Tell Melanie we are all sorry."

"It's nice of you to say . . ."

From behind Stephanie, a voice boomed . . . "If you're just going to stand around and talk, then the two of you can get out of here. If you're here to work, then get to it." The interruption was loud enough for everyone to hear. The loud proclamation assured everyone the *Gazette* was only interested in getting a job done, despite feelings, emotional pain, physical pain, or exhaustion.

The dark night turned into early morning sunlight. The sky lighted with soft hues of pink, then yellow, then full sunlight. The night had been sweltering, and the morning sun promised a full measure of the same. It was almost eleven o'clock when the papers were completely finished, and we were "let go" for the night. We all put in about twelve hours that night for a job supposedly needing four hours to do.

I was one of the last to leave. The *Gazette*'s supervisors asked a few of us to help load the vans distributing the paper. I thought Nate would be asked, giving me a chance to talk to him, but it never happened. Melanie and Stephanie left about nine o'clock when the papers were printed and all the flyers were stuffed. I never had a chance to say good-bye to them or talk a few minutes, like our little group did when we finished. All that was left to finish, before I could leave, was collect the folded papers from the office and stack them on the docks or into the waiting vans. Once the supervisors were satisfied with the job, they dismissed the workers who stayed, allowing us to greet the bright oppressive heat as a reward. I walked where I parked my car, covered in sweat and streaked newsprint, rolled all the windows down, and then drove home.

The job lasted another three weeks. Rumor was Mike went to the hospital and was released. Nate returned a few more times but never wanted to talk about that night. The two girls, Melanie and Stephanie, never came back. I supposed the violence of the night spooked the girls' guardian, and they were never allowed to return. And after another three weeks, the *Gazette* figured they could do the job another way, and everyone was let go. The agency found another short-term job, and I moved on. I never saw any of them again.

I guess you could say that night was a turning point for me. Like the times I lived in, full of controversy, full of innocence, violence, and endings. It truly was the end of my youth. High school was over. My life as an adult beginning . . . beginning at the age of seventeen. No regrets, just idealistic promises, hope for the future, and fear.

Whenever I think back on this memory, I always seem to hear the sounds of the old Scott McKenzie song. The song itself seems to speak of all of the most positive ideals of the time, like working together, peace, and trying to attain a better life and make a better place than the one that came before it. Just like my night long ago, it started in peace amid the turmoil, and then it ended in violence. Finally, like the old Scott McKenzie song, the times never generated any peace as it intended, and so its ideals faded . . . It became obsolete and redundant. Yet for me, the idea of a world at peace with itself was enticing. Letting it go was sad. Now I never hear that old song anymore.

It was music I loved too much . . . something I heard almost every day and loved it more each time I listened. It was music I would never hear again. The dream was fading into nothing. It was fading like a memory that served its purpose, then like some enchantment wore off as time progressed on its steady course away from this time, these events. I would never return to this time or this place again. It was a memory fading like a dying rose. The dream fading like a vanished childhood . . . This music I loved too much was over. I could barely stand to let it fall from my fingers. I could scarcely believe it was just a dream, which was over and would never return.

Once upon a Time . . .

Tell me about love . . .

    At the beginning of my sophomore year of college, some friends introduced me to a beautiful girl named Lois. She was a small girl, barely five feet tall, with long black hair worn in loose curls and dark brown eyes. My friends told me in passing she was pursuing a degree in medical technology. When I first met her, I was taking courses in the accounting curriculum; but after taking a few classes, I could not see myself working all my life as an accountant.

    The summer after my freshman year of college, I worked as an orderly in a nursing home near the college. I loved working in the health care system, and my disenchantment with accounting made me think seriously about changing my major. I wanted to take a closer look at health care, and I hoped I could find something financially satisfying where I could apply most of my college credits. Lois, along with our mutual friends, asked me to consider making a course change before the beginning of my next semester. It was on a day I found Lois studying alone in the college pub that she helped me make a decision to look into a nursing career. To be helpful, she assisted me, searching for information on nursing careers in the college library and the muddle of pamphlets, brochures, and manuals existing before the advent of computers. Unfortunately, the college we attended did not offer a curriculum in nursing.

    Lois and I had known each other—or, more accurately, knew about each other—from college classes and mutual college friends over most of my freshman year. She was beautiful and vivacious. I liked her and wanted to ask her out but was deterred when I heard she had a boyfriend. I was certain she had no interest in starting another relationship when she was going out with someone else. She was not a person who cheated on a guy while she was dating him, and I did not want to be "that guy" anyway. Even so, when I turned the situation around, all she really did was help a colleague find some information to make a decision. I did not want to start anything serious with a girl, since my intentions to pursue a nursing program would, by design, take me to another college. Besides, I would probably never see her again after I finished the second semester of my sophomore year. After that, I would be attending a college in a different town anyway.

One day, a close friend of Lois, named Susan, asked me what I thought of her. "She's beautiful, Susan, but she has a boyfriend," I told her.

"She broke up with that guy about six months ago," Susan said with a twinkle in her eye.

"She seems pretty caught up in her work here at college, and I think she has a job. Besides, I don't think she has the time for a boyfriend," I told Susan with a kind of resignation in my voice.

"Well, if you want, I'll say something to her," Susan chided.

I looked at Susan, who had a mischievous grin on her face, then said to her, "Okay, kind of clear the path for me, right?"

Susan didn't say anything but just kept that smile on her face. I just shook my head and told her, "I have a class to catch. See you later?"

It was three months later when Susan came up to me, hit me hard on my arm, and said, "Well, when are you going to ask her?" It wasn't like I hadn't seen Susan in three months. In fact, I saw her almost every day since I had spoken with her about asking Lois out. At the moment, I thought back to Susan's earlier conversation three months before and honestly thought Susan had forgotten to say anything.

"What do you mean 'ask her'? Did you say anything to her?" I asked.

"Yeah, and she has been waiting almost three months for you to make some kind of move."

"I didn't know. I figured if you 'had' said something to her, she wasn't interested."

"Man, you are dense!" Susan snorted. "You haven't noticed she is around the pub a lot more these days. You haven't seen that she has been watching your every move when she is here and you are here."

"It does seem like she is around more often," I said nonchalantly, as I surveyed the pub for any signs that she might be in the pub already.

"So just do it already. Everybody knows you want to ask her out," Susan told me with a bit of anger in her voice.

"Really, then how come I didn't know?" I asked just as peevishly, rolling my eyes at her as I did.

"You men are so dense . . . I expect to hear about a date by the end of the day," Susan instructed with all the charm of a drill sergeant.

"So what do I ask her out to do . . . What does she like?" I asked Susan, honestly wanting her opinion.

Susan feigned frustration, but I could see she was enjoying putting me on the spot. She threw her hands up in the air. "Try a movie, try dinner someplace nice, you want me to do all the work for you?"

"Okay, I'll say something to her when I see her," I said merely to appease her, as I stared down a glass of cola sitting in front of me.

Suddenly, Susan's eyes lit up. "It's your lucky day," she said, as she looked over my shoulder.

"What do you mean?" I asked, startled by her apparent change in temperament.

"Hey, Lois, come sit with us." Susan almost bubbled with excitement.

This felt like a trap. This was typical of the "Susan" Lois and I knew. I was definitely taken "off guard" by Susan's remark and Lois's sudden and unexpected arrival at the college pub. Lois arrived with a group of girls whom she had an early class with. She quickly said something to them, which Susan and I did not hear, and then came over to where Susan and I were sitting. Susan was beaming. I was squirming, and Susan knew it.

"So what are you guys doing?" Lois asked once she put her books on an unoccupied chair and sat down on a chair next to me. Susan had that mischievous look on her face again.

Susan looked at the two of us sitting together. "Well, I thought it was about time I got you two together . . . by yourselves," she said, as she winked at Lois. Lois looked horrified. "By the way, he has something to ask you, Lois." Now it was my turn to look horrified. Susan got up quickly, grabbed her books, and started to walk away, and then, as if she forgot something, turned and said, "And, George, I expect to hear something good later on from you two." Then Susan disappeared into the crowd of students, clamoring to get food or get out of the pub to their next classes.

We both watched Susan make her departure from the college pub, leaving us alone together. I felt more than awkward. I felt disarmed and utterly speechless. Lois looked at me and laughed a nervous laugh. It was a laugh I would know and love for a very long time, but at the moment, it helped to calm the tension. "Well," Lois said, "I didn't see that coming." She looked at me with her clear brown eyes that held me captivated. "Susan told me you wanted to ask me out. You don't have to feel like you have to because of her."

"But I want to," I blurted out.

"So here we are. What do you want to do?"

"What kind of things do you like to do?" I asked, now that the pressure was off.

"Lots of stuff. Movies, eating out. I've been bowling, but not on a first date." She laughed.

We talked for almost an hour then agreed to meet up later in the afternoon after classes to figure out a time for our first date. Susan saw me in the hall going to one of my classes and jabbed me in the side. "So . . . ?"

"We're going to talk about it this afternoon."

"A date?"

"What else . . ."

"About freaking time . . ." Susan said with some very evident relief in her voice.

"Later, Susan."

"I want details. After all, I've been working on this for a while," she said with some propriety in her voice.

"I know . . . I know. I have a class to get to, okay?"

"Sure," Susan said slyly and then added with an almost musical cadence, "but I bet you won't be paying much attention."

"Bye, Susan. I'll talk to you later," I said, emphasizing the word "later."

After my class, I waited in the college pub for about an hour. I knew Lois had a class right after mine, and then she was coming to meet me. The hour came and went, and Lois did not return. After waiting another half hour, I began thinking she had forgotten or, perhaps, she really wasn't interested after all. I was just about ready to get my things and go home when she came running out of the crowd.

"I'm so glad you waited. I was afraid you would leave," Lois said out of breath with a disgusted tone of voice. "They kept us late for a surprise quiz."

I gave her a chance to catch her breath and sit down for a cup of coffee with me. We talked about everything in the world that afternoon. We found we had unknown connections between our two families. It seemed when I mentioned a relative of mine, she knew something about them, and I also knew connections to many of her family members as well. I told her my father was in construction and found her father was an electrician. Apparently, their paths crossed over the years as well. Conversation came so easily with her. It was like we knew each other for our entire lives, not just now. The more we talked, the more we learned about each other. As we both discovered the many inescapable links existing between us, it became almost eerie and, at the same time, wonderful to feel this connected to one person.

When the pub's windows glowed crimson with the last dying rays of sunset, we realized we talked for hours, and we hadn't made arrangements for our date. "How about a movie, then go out for dinner?" I asked.

"Sure. Do you know how to get to my place?" she asked excitedly.

"Not really, but I'm sure it's not hard to get to."

"I live along the river in a little town called Saginaw."

She gave me instructions to get to her home, and eventually, we went on our first date. I remember when we went out, we just talked and talked. We seemed to have such a strong connection to each other. Susan eventually pinned me down for details one day when she found me, and I gave her details. She was excited for both of us.

Lois was so interesting. She came from a poor background financially. She lived in a small house with three bedrooms, a bathroom, kitchen, and living room. She had a sister and two brothers. She shared a bedroom with her sister big enough for a bed, a small vanity, and about enough room to have about a foot-and-a-half walking space around it all. Her brothers' room was smaller, with about a foot of walking space around the room. The family spent most of their time in either the kitchen or the living room. Her sister and her brothers were very friendly and talked to me that first evening while Lois finished getting ready for our first date. Her mother was a small woman, not even five feet tall, who scurried about the kitchen while I was there and asked me about my family between her chores. Her father walked into the kitchen to talk to her mother then disappeared into the house without saying a word to either of us. Even on our first date, I felt some animosity from Lois's father. The only thing he told Lois in my presence was to be back by a certain time. To me, he said nothing but gave me a snarl as I left the house with her. Lois said to him, "Don't worry, old man, I'll be back before midnight."

"Don't worry," I said to her mother, "I'll have her back safe and sound."

"I know you will," her mother told me. Then she added, "Be sure to have a good time."

"We will, Mom," Lois said, and then to me, "We better get going. We have about twenty minutes."

We started seeing each other every time we had a chance. I never met a more-industrious person in my life. She made time for me and continued telling me stories about her family. She spoke of her grandmother and grandfather who helped raise her. Apparently, throughout her early childhood, the situation was not good. Her father was abusive to her mother, and there was never enough money around to do much of anything. She told me on many occasions, when her father was drinking, she went to stay at her grandmother's house to get away from him.

Lois always spoke highly about her grandfather. She told me, when he died, it was the saddest day of her life. I never had the chance to meet her grandfather, but he must have been a good man. When she spoke so lovingly about him, I knew she missed him terribly. He was her hero for so many reasons, but one story stood out over all the others.

One time, she told me a story about her grandfather that summarized how her childhood must have been. On a night after her father was out drinking alone, he returned home and picked a fight with her mother. In the aftermath of foul language and deprecatory remarks, he finished his verbal battery by hitting her. Her mother was very upset and afraid for her children. She left the house when Lois's father was asleep, took the children, and went to her father-in-law's house. When she told him about the incident, Lois's grandfather was very upset. He grew strangely quiet for a moment then said, "Don't worry. I will make sure he never touches you again. You have my word on it." He told Lois's mother to keep the children at his house and stay there until he spoke with his son.

The next day, Lois's grandfather went to her home and sat in the living room after her father had gone to work. According to what Lois told me, her grandfather waited in the house with the lights off, sitting quietly in the dark and waiting for his son's arrival to confront him. Lois told me no one ever discovered what was said between her father and her grandfather, but whatever was said worked. The only thing her grandfather told Lois's mother was this: "If he ever hits you again, I will be up to settle things with my son." No one knew what this meant, but Lois told me when her mother went back home with the children, she could see her father was obviously afraid. He was never physically abusive with her mother again. However, Lois told me her father persisted with verbal abuse. Her grandfather died only a few years after this event. She never forgot him. I was sorry I never had the chance to know or meet Lois's grandfather, but I learned about him from Lois's stories and the stories her grandmother told me over the years. In a way, he still remained standing beside her for as long as she needed him, and that is how love works.

I was fortunate to get the chance to know her grandmother. By our third date, I was called to her grandmother's house, which stood on a high bank overlooking the rolling waters of the river. Her modest home was located down a gently falling hill from Lois's home. At Lois's insistence, we walked the short distance to her house so I could meet her. Apparently, her grandmother heard about me and wanted to meet me face-to-face. I think she just wanted to see if I was up to her standards for her granddaughter. I loved her as soon as I met her. Her grandmother's name was Olive, but the kids called her "Ollie" or "Grandma." Lois preferred the more-conventional term "Grandma" when speaking to her. Olive was Lois's ally in many ways. Even as a teenager, or the young adult woman I knew and loved, she would stay with her grandmother to simply get away from her father. There were times we would sit and talk with her grandmother about how malicious her father was with everyone. Her grandmother once told me she could not believe this was her son. Olive told me of her three sons and one daughter. Lois's father was the only one whose character did not fit in with her other children. I agreed with her grandmother after I had the chance to meet Lois's two uncles and her aunt.

Once invited by her grandmother to a Mother's Day dinner, when she gathered all her children and grandchildren together, I watched in disgust as Lois's father verbally abused his own mother. He walked out with unconstrained rage and did not return to her house for several weeks. Most times, while Lois and I were dating, her father barely spoke to me or simply remained absent until I left. Her father's temper was legendary in the small river town of Saginaw. No one who knew him ever understood his uninhibited wrath, where it came from, or where such a dark frigate harbored. He came from a good family. He was raised in a good home, but it seemed he hated the world. Even when he died many years later, his rage continued to develop, and he magnified any small slights he felt put against him into monstrous memories. I'm sure his anger festered and rotted inside him, becoming something so outrageous; none of us would ever recognize it for what it was. Nothing could ever equal the unchained rage he unleashed on his family.

In spite of Lois's father, I always enjoyed spending the Christmas season with her. Her family traditionally celebrated the holiday on Christmas Eve, and after handing out presents, it was followed by a big Christmas dinner at one of her relative's homes. What made Christmas so special in this small river town was all her relatives lived within walking distance of each other. In whatever weather the season brought upon us, we were able to walk to her uncle's, aunt's, or grandmother's house. It was always quaint and old fashioned; often we were greeted at the door with a cup of eggnog or warm cider. Spirits always remained high, and everyone was happy to get together.

The town of Saginaw still survives with its three main streets running down a slight hill to the river. Intersecting cross streets lace the three main ones together throughout the town. At the end of the main street is a road running parallel beside railroad tracks. Beyond the tracks, the river runs with its constant perceptible rhythm. In the spring, Lois and I would walk along this road after a visit to her grandmother and watch for trains to pass by. The tracks were so wide in places that the river remained the ghost you could only hear. But as we walked, she would show me places where the river not only was visible but also spoke its legacy of the history there. She would tell me stories about the small town and how it came to exist. However, like many small towns, the reasons they flourished were gone. The only reason they persisted in their survival were the families who remained here, and these families were perhaps the only true strength for a town like this to survive.

Six weeks into our dating experience, I knew I wanted to marry her. She laughed at the time, but when I looked into her eyes, I saw the same resolve coming from her. We seemed to be linked almost at once. We found we liked the same things. We had similar experiences weaving the cloth of our childhood. We discovered we were witnesses to our parents' verbal and physical abuse of each other. We promised each other, if we got married, we would never act like this. It made our bond stronger. We often spoke about growing up under these conditions, and it made us sad for both sets of parents.

Through our many conversations, we found not only had our fathers known each other distantly through the construction industry but we also had other family connections. In another conversation, I found Lois's mother worked, at one time, with my aunt, and they had been good friends. The more we discovered about ourselves, the more common ground we discovered. Though we were both nineteen when we met, it seemed we were intertwined in each other's lives long before we found each other. There was a connection between us running deeper than a kiss, deeper than mere physical love. It had roots beyond the time we spent together. To us, it seemed when we were born, we were destined for each other. When we talked about this aspect of our experiences with each other, it always brought chills to both of us. Our connection ran so deep that, on many occasions, I could pick up a phone, and Lois would already be on the line without the phone ringing. We did this so many times during our life together we gave up trying to explain the phenomenon to other people and simply accepted it as our own style of normalcy.

Lois's father eventually realized I was not going to leave his daughter because I had fallen in love with her. He didn't like it. One night, after we had gone to see a movie, he waited up for us. We walked into the living room where he had the entire family assembled, waiting for us to return. When we walked into the room, the situation seemed surreal. It seemed prepared, contrived by some malign design to tear us apart.

He politely invited us to sit on the sofa. Then he started talking to Lois, asking her about the movie we had seen. He seemed almost pleasant, and, at first, I thought he was actually trying to be nice to me for once. When Lois grabbed my hand and gave it a good squeeze, I knew I was in for something else.

"So you're a college boy?" her father asked, sliding forward on the chair, his face red with unrestrained sweat, breath mottled with alcohol.

"Yes, I go to college," I said, trying to give as little information as possible for him to start an argument.

"So, college boy, can you tell me what this is?" he asked surreptitiously, spreading his first two fingers to make the V symbol, his hand only a few inches from my face.

I looked at him puzzled, wondering where this was going, as Lois squeezed my hand even tighter. Finally, not knowing how this was all going to turn out, I answered. "Sure, I know. That's the sign for peace."

"You're pretty smart for a college boy," he said, a red-faced smirk crawled over his face like a poisonous snake. "Now, do you know what this means?" he gloated, preparing me for some kind of confrontation. Knowing he had some sick joke prepared, he stuck his middle finger in front of my nose.

I saw Lois cringe when he did this. I think she would have wrung the blood out of my fingers if she could have at that moment. I saw it as an obvious ploy to start a malicious squabble I could not avoid. I looked to where Lois's mother already hung her head in shame and embarrassment, knowing what was coming next. Her sister and her brothers looked so solemn, I realized, in a moment, they were only there to witness my expulsion from the house. It was a demonstration of power unscrupulously done to solidify his sovereignty of the house, and if he said I was gone, I was gone. I considered how I was going to answer him; I knew I had to be clever. A very unpleasant situation was unfolding. I looked her father straight in the eye and said, "That means 'peace' too . . . just a different kind."

I caught him off guard so badly that even when he tried to be angry, he couldn't. He started laughing so hard he almost fell off his chair. Lois went into hysterical laughter when she realized I had outsmarted her father in what, she knew, was supposed to be a vicious battle between her father and me. Her relieved brothers and her sister told their father, "Serves you right, old man. You asked, and he told you."

Her father, still laughing with tears in his eyes, said to me, "You are one smart son of a bitch." Then before I knew it, he told me, "You know what? You're all right, Anderson. If you want to date my daughter, I'm okay with it."

From that night forward, Lois's father always came out to talk to me, and we actually became good friends over time. He helped us out many times when we needed help, and Lois could not believe I won him over to my side. Lois took it as another sign we were going to be together. Never before, she told me, had her father ever taken an interest in any of her boyfriends. He always embarrassed and degraded them, and she always ended up defending herself in the process. I had won him over myself, and she loved me even more for doing so.

We dated for about three years when I finally felt it was time to ask her to marry me. She agreed immediately, and we prepared for a new life together. As expected, her father was not ready to lose a daughter to this new interloper. He made Lois's preparations as difficult as he could to dissuade her from getting married.

Shadows

Tell me about the darkness . . .

I loved to walk in the dark. In the dark, there were no colors to distract the eyes. On the paths that lay before me, there were no sounds other than my own footfalls. Time had no hold on me here. My progress was unimpeded and led to whatever end there was to gain. In this place, there was peace, but there was also loneliness. Then there are worse things than being alone.

I was never truly alone in my childhood, but many times, I sought my time to be in the darkness. It was a safe place, away from the tumultuous times in my childhood and youth. I went there seeking the peace it offered yet always returned to the lighted places, the places reality washed over in sometimes corruptible colors.

My existence of the time I spent in the light always seemed to be in pain. When I walked in the dark, the real torments of my life always seemed less painful, and I longed for the peace I would find there.

In my early life, I was asthmatic. These times, in the light, in the suffocating reality of not being able to draw one's breath, I tried to find the darkness. Not in the unending night of death but in the darkness where I found peace from the noise and distractions I found in the light.

My parents sought a way to help me, but in the times we lived in, there were often too few remedies to bring me back. So often, in the pain of suffocation, I sought the darkness. Many times I remained there, caught by the desire to stay, yet always pulled back into the pallid light. In the dark, there was no pain, no need to breathe to stay alive. It was a world, albeit a world of dark wonder, where I could survive. In time, I found it would nurture me as well.

I ventured into the darkness to escape those places that caused so much pain. Still, I would go deeper in the dark to find memories, memories of happy times, people who meant something to me, no longer there, and something else . . . something intangible, like wind. There was something there I could feel but could not touch. Whisperings were drawing me deeper . . . deeper than understanding.

The darkness was not an empty place. Yet in its presence, all things seemed intangible. A leaf blowing in the trees and a stone slipping from a ledge were the only sounds, sounds echoing. All the sounds were hauntingly familiar to my senses. Yet they betrayed the depth and margins of my existence here. I sought direction. I listened for any audible proof, telling me which way to go.

This place was not without its barriers. In the darkness, I could feel the bark of a tree, cold and wet from a rainstorm never heard in my ears or felt upon my skin. It was a dynamic paradox. When my mind escaped here, I could be in a different environment every time. Yet it could be the same place, with different seasons, different smells, or another location altogether. I could feel the rise of a hill, a gentle sloping downward that told me I had made it to the other side, or completely flat. The darkness could be filled with vegetation or barren like a desert. Only I seemed to control this.

Usually, when I entered my dark place, it was out of severe physical or emotional stress . . . sometimes both. Depending on my needs, I may have entered by way of a forest, a plateau, a mountain, or perhaps even a grassy plain. Whatever perception existed in reality, an opposite soothing perception laid upon the other side in the darkness. Still I had no sight there, just perceptions, feelings, and for a while, it was enough.

In the Beginning

Tell me about the past . . .

My home was a modest brick house. My mother, never satisfied with it, struggled daily with my father for a bigger kitchen, a bigger room there, another closet, with the conversation ending in bitter arguments with my father. To be fair, our first house was small but adequate for our needs at that time. I never really understood their bitter arguments. Many times I would ask to play outside to avoid hearing their terrible confrontations with each other.

If you asked my father what kind of work he did, he would tell you that he was a farmer. In reality, he was a contractor who built houses. He knew everything a person needed to build a house from the ground up. I found out, in my later years, that my father was not only a mason who could lay blocks and bricks but also a highly prized stone mason as well. My father came from a long line of masons. Laying bricks was second nature to him, and he could make money doing it, but his real love was working with rough-cut stone. He always told me that the uglier the stone or brick was to hold in your hand, the more beautiful the wall would be made from it. True to his nature, he indeed seemed to construct incredibly beautiful walls from the most rugged stones and sometimes irregular handmade bricks.

His talents did not lie strictly with stones and bricks. His knowledge of building houses enabled him to do all the carpentry and masonry needed to get a house standing. He employed others to do the plumbing and electrical work, but by then, he had the house standing by himself.

As for his self-proclaimed occupation as a farmer, he was not wrong. By the time he was in his early thirties, he had accumulated more land than any one person or corporation in the county. His dream, he once told me, was to keep the land as a farm and give it to my brother and me when we were older. His plans were to develop some of the land into communities with himself and his sons building the houses on these properties. His hope was to teach us everything he knew and then assist us in his own way. His dream, visionary, would go on for several generations, considering the amount of land he had accumulated to this point in his life.

But dreams die. In reality, both my brother and I were terrible asthmatics, and his attempts at teaching us the farmwork almost cost us our lives. When I ended up in the hospital at the age of seven with double pneumonia and asthma, my mother brought a swift and terrible end to his dream. My father was able to fight for his dream until I was about twelve years old. When my illness showed no signs of relenting, and my mother had demoralized and defeated the dream at every turn, my father relented and sold the farm land at a pittance of what it was worth. Once the dream died, my father was never the same. He still built houses, but his intentions to teach my brother and myself died when the farms were put up for sale and lost forever.

The home my maternal grandmother occupied in the city was a lovely brick row home that had a great backyard with flowers, a cherry tree, and an overspreading grapevine. My grandmother was very proud of her home and kept it meticulously clean. Inside, the furnishings were modest, and a few of her things were actually very valuable. She had a mahogany table with lion's claw feet in her dining room where we all took our Thanksgiving and Christmas meals. There was a less-expensive, well-worn table in the kitchen, which served as the place for the regular meals she served the rest of the year. My maternal grandfather was alive during that time, but he did not live with my grandmother. From what I could tell at that young age, he had abandoned his family long before I was born.

Once in a while, I would overhear whisperings he had spoken to one of my aunts or uncles. As I grew older, the whisperings stopped, and I was certain he must have died. It was always a strange story as to why he left them. My grandmother would never speak of him but left a black-and-white photograph of a young soldier hanging on the wall above her telephone in the living room. When I asked my grandmother who he was, she would, at least, tell me he was my grandfather when he was younger. When I asked where he was, she would sigh and tell me, "I don't know." If I pressed for anything more about him, she simply stopped talking or would change the subject.

I learned two things from these conversations with my grandmother. First, when you don't like how the conversation is going, change the subject. Second, and probably more important, sometimes not knowing everything is how some people want it to be. Sometimes, even memories are far too painful to be brought up in the light of a conversation. Some memories need to stay in the darkness, not to be seen, not to be heard.

On a farm nestled in the curling hills of the country lived my paternal grandparents. The land was clothed in green meadows, and dark woods nestled in the lowlands. A stream ran through the farm where my brother and I ran and played on many hot summer days. Yet everything we did was not play on the farm. Many times we went to the fields to carry water out to the men working there. At times, when our asthma was in check, we would ride out on the empty wagons with my grandfather and then ride back to the barn with fully loaded hay wagons. There was joy and a sense of accomplishment when my grandfather told us we did a good job, even though I never felt that I was doing much to help.

At the farmhouse, my grandmother would take care of my younger brother and me when our asthma surfaced. Still we were never left in our misery alone. Our grandmother would have us set the table for the men working or, if the asthma wasn't raging, we would bring in wood for the woodstove. It was a beautiful but simple life.

One of the great lessons of my early childhood occurred on this farm. It wasn't one of those events that stayed with you at the time. It was more like the sense of what it was like being in that moment that made the impression. Every summer, when the crops were to be brought in from the fields, all my grandfather's neighbors came from the surrounding farms to help. No one had to ask; there were no formal invitations; they just knew it was time. The work laid out before them in the ripe summer fields was simply and methodically completed. When my grandfather's farm was done, everyone moved on to the next farm with tractors, wagons, and other farm equipment and did the same for them. Everyone kept working until all the crops were brought in, stored, or sold to outside vendors for every farm. There was a sense of camaraderie and good feelings that I never experienced anywhere else or ever again.

My grandfather died when I was fifteen years old in 1969. It seemed the farm died with him. All those wonderful years of helping out on the farm passed into the darkness of the past. It seemed everyone who had been part of the farm's history faded away with him. My grandmother seemed lost after he died. The farmhouse where they lived, still filled with my memories of joy and pain, stayed abandoned for many years. Eventually, one of my cousins married and needed a home to raise a family. He finally took it over and revamped it.

After my grandfather passed away, my grandmother could not bear to stay alone in the house where he died. He died in a bedroom in the farmhouse the day before Thanksgiving. He had been ill for only three days, driving him to his bed. My father and my uncles never saw their father bedridden in all the times they were alive. They knew something was very wrong when my grandmother informed them he was bedridden. My grandfather must have known something was wrong for some time. He started building my grandmother a new house to live in just three months before he died.

It took another three months to finish the house after he died. She stayed with one of my uncles until it was completed. My grandmother lived there until she died at the age of ninety-six. She continued to run the farm, with the help of her sons, until she was ninety-three. After she died, the farm was never the same. It was another memory fading into the shadows of the past.

The old woman was hustling pots over the hot stove. She did so with the experience of someone who had raised a large family. Every burner was occupied with something, and she knew just how much heat and how long each kettle needed for the food to be just right. The kitchen smelled of fresh apples, herbs, and the best of freshly cooked foods. She hardly noticed the young boy who sauntered in and found a seat at the kitchen table.

"Grandma." The boy had a serious look about him as he tried to get the old woman's attention.

"I'm busy right now," she said, as she moved a boiling pot from a burner and replaced it with another of uncooked potatoes.

"But, Grandma," he insisted, "I have a question."

"Can't it wait until after dinner?" she asked somewhat petulantly. She was busy. What could the boy want that was so very important?

The boy sitting at the kitchen table was her seven-year-old grandson. He was sick more times than he was well. It was 1960, and the world was changing, not always for the better. This child was definitely one of her favorites. She knew he almost died from an asthmatic attack earlier this year, and the whole experience had almost devastated her. You had to be careful with his diet and keep him away from dust and animals. The diet was difficult enough to control when all the other grandchildren could eat whatever they wanted. The biggest problem was the boy's love of animals. The old woman loved cats. She had two housecats. One was a red tabby named Sandy. The other cat was black and white with white patches on the throat and a white tipped tail named Patch. The boy loved to play with both of them, and every time he did, his asthma started up. So to remedy this, the cats had to spend the whole day, while he was here, in her cellar.

To her, it just didn't seem right that her grandson had to miss out on so much of his childhood because of asthma. She felt badly, since her household chores of keeping the house running, making meals, and taking care of her grandson made for a very full day. Still, when she had the food at the table, she would find time to answer the boy's questions. For now, the boy simply put his head down on the table into folded arms and waited patiently for his grandmother to finish.

Eventually, the old woman caught up most of her cooking, and whatever pots she left on the stove were put on simmer. She looked over to where the boy was sitting patiently.

"Now, what did you want to ask me?"

The boy still had a very serious look on his face as he pulled his head from his folded arms and sat up in the chair. "Where do we go when we dieGrandma?"

The question was not what she was expecting. It was even more unnerving knowing that this boy almost died six months earlier. "Why do you want to know that?" she remarked with some concern in her voice. "Are you feeling sick?" she asked, realizing how tired he looked to her now that she was really looking at him.

"No, I feel all right. But where do we go when we are not here?"

She sat down at a chair next to him and took his hand. "I believe we go to heaven when we die."

"Is it nice there? Will I see you from there and my mom and dad?"

"I believe it is supposed to be that way." The old woman was getting concerned. None of her grandchildren ever posed a question like this to her before. This seemed very serious to her. She could tell by the look on her grandson's face that it was very serious to him as well. It seemed he still had something to ask her, and she prodded him along. "What brought all this up?" still with concern in her voice.

The boy turned to look her straight in the eyes and said, "Grandma, I think I died for a little while a few months ago."

The old woman looked horrified. She couldn't speak. She couldn't move for a few minutes while her grandson delivered the rest of his story.

"Grandma, don't be afraid of me. I just want to tell you something, and I don't know what it was. I remember not being able to breathe at home. I remember telling my mom that she needed to let me go if I stopped breathing. It is the last thing I remember until I woke up three days later in my bedroom with my dad. Did I stop breathing? What happened to me for those three days?" he finished and then seemed to be hesitating, waiting for a response from the old woman.

"Is that what this is all about? You don't remember those three days at all?" she said somewhat emphatically, not realizing how she sounded to her grandson. She looked for a response and, not getting any, continued saying, "What I know is this. You stopped breathing that night, and your parents took you to the hospital where they worked on you. They did not think you would survive, and your parents took you home. Your mother and father took turns watching you while we all prayed that you would get better and return to us. After three days, you woke up, and you got better. Does that answer your question?" She looked at him, almost relieved herself that this was what he was after the whole time.

"Sort of, Grandma," he answered somewhat hesitantly like she left something out of her story that he still needed to know.

"Is there something else you wanted to know about that time?" not really thinking there would be any more details to be discussed.

"I remember a dream I had during those three days," the boy said, as he tucked his head into his chest as if he was embarrassed to go on.

"What was your dream?" she asked, now firmly convinced the boy had something very deep to talk about with her.

"I dreamed I was in a place where there was no light. I looked all around and finally saw a small white dot below me. It was the only thing I could see in all the darkness. I found out that I could move just by thinking about it, so I went to the dot. As I was moving, I realized I had no pain, I had no problem breathing. It was nice. As I got to the dot of light, it got bigger and bigger. When the dot of light got to the size of a large room, I saw five people in white coats working on something at a table. They didn't seem to know I was there, so I floated above them and took a look at what they were working on." He looked up at his grandmother to see how she was taking this. She looked frozen in her chair, almost as if his words were magical, casting a spell of immobility over her. Seeing this as his only chance to tell his story to her, he continued, "I was on that table, Grandma. They were working on me. I suddenly got afraid and didn't know what to do. Then as I was confused as to what to do, a brilliant light opened behind me, and a voice came out of it. I could hear it in my mind more so than an actual voice. It asked me if I wanted to stay or go back. The voice told me I had to choose quickly, but it also said I still had a little time to think about it. I told the voice I better go back because my parents didn't know where I was. The voice was nice and told me that it was okay to go back, so I lay down in my body and went to sleep again in my dream." The old woman no longer looked frozen, but the boy could see that she was crying. While he still had the courage to ask, he continued, "Grandma, was I in heaven? Did I die?"

The Orange

Tell me about childhood . . .

Sometime before my father sold his farmlands, the world was a different place. One summer, when I was about nine years old, my mother allowed me to stay with my grandparents on the farm. She made it a well-established fact that my brother and I were very bad asthmatics before she left for work that day. After she was gone, my grandfather tried to find ways to keep our day interesting. He tried to show us things we wouldn't see anywhere else but on a farm. He showed us the chicken coop, which was essentially a small room attached to the barn, where we actually helped him gather eggs. My grandfather knew we could not spend much time in the coop because of the straw, but he gave my brother and me just enough time to see what it was like to gather eggs for breakfast. He wanted to show us where things, which we took for granted, really came from. He taught us many things over the few years we had with him, especially me.

On a day like any other summer day, the men came from the neighboring farms to help harvest the rolling fields of hay. My grandmother set the long wooden table in the kitchen with bowls of steaming scrambled eggs, fried potatoes, stacks of fresh bread and toast, an array of homemade jams and jellies, and homemade butter she put out in bowls. She had several old bowls topped with apples and other bowls brimmed with cut fruits readily available on the farm that time of year. The men working the farm that morning filed into the house, but only after Grandma's enforced urging for all the men to wash their hands in the washroom before coming into her house. The washroom was a room just outside her kitchen door, supplied with two old ceramic basins and a bar of soap. It was my grandma's intention that no man would come to her table with dirty hands . . . This was how she did it . . . no arguments.

Washing your hands before a meal was no small thing. First, each man had to walk to the back of the house, basin in hand, and draw a modicum of water from the hand pump they found there. When the basin was filled to satisfaction, it was brought to the washroom where a bar of soap was provided to wash with. When finished washing, the man would throw the water out into the yard, and the basin was handed to the next in line. Each man took his turn at this obligatory ritual. Grandma actually watched from the screen door adjacent to her kitchen, assuring everyone sitting at her table had clean hands.

When everyone was seated along the sides of the long table, my grandfather would call for a prayer. My grandmother, although always busy, never failed to come to the opposite end of the table from my grandfather. It was only when both my grandmother and grandfather were seated that the prayer was actually said, and breakfast was started. All through the summer, these kinds of gatherings took place on the farm. When one farm was harvested, my grandfather, my father, and my uncles would take their tractors, wagons, and other equipment to another neighbor's farm and do the same for them. And at any of the neighbor's farmhouses, the same sense of family dinners and breakfasts continued until all the farmlands were done.

One day, when the kitchen was cleared, there was bowl of fresh oranges left over. My brother and I always helped Grandma clear the table, while the men left to get started with the balers and wagons. I asked my grandmother if I could have one orange. She told me I could if it didn't bring on an asthmatic attack. About the time I asked her for the orange, my grandfather was lacing up his boots outside the screen door leading to the kitchen. He heard the entire conversation I had with my grandmother. He looked in, but since he was pressed for time, he quickly told my grandmother where the men were working and to have the boys bring water out to the men in a few hours. By the time he was gone, I already peeled the orange and devoured it in gulps. I really enjoyed the orange, but known only to myself and my parents, it was one of those foods I was forbidden to eat. My reaction to citrus fruit was moderate to severe, depending on how sensitive my system was at the time.

Of course, my asthmatic reaction was never an immediate response; and sometimes any response was very minor, and I could tolerate the slight shortness of breath it caused. It seemed, at first, the reaction would not happen at all; but when my brother and I started carrying water to the men at midmorning, I felt a very strong allergic response from eating the orange. By the time I carried water out to the last crew of men piling hay bales on a wagon, my asthmatic response was as bad as it could be. The men stopped collecting the bales of hay and drove me back to the house on a half-filled wagon of hay. My one uncle carried me into the house. I was wheezing and sweating. My grandmother got a cold washcloth and washed my face and mouth with the hopes it may have been the field dust setting me off. Still, none of these measures helped. My father and grandfather just brought in a full wagon of hay and arrived at the house to find I had fallen sick again.

My father was upset over how I was gasping for breath. My wheezing was so bad he considered taking me into the hospital. Back then, there were very few medications for asthmatics. I remembered one of my classmates dying from asthma when I was in second grade. My doctor prescribed some kind of red liquid medicine that helped me, but it wasn't always successful. My father got a teaspoon of it and made me swallow it. I spent the rest of the late morning and the early evening sleeping off the medication. When I finally awoke about an hour before sunset, I was able to breathe much easier. I was hoarse from the drying effects of the medication, but I could breathe and cough up some of the clear phlegm obstructing my airway. The men were still out in the fields, but my grandfather was there with me. He stayed behind to keep watch over me, while my father, who was younger and could get more done, went back to the summer fields of hay.

"What happened to you, boy? You gave your father a pretty bad scare this morning," my grandfather said. He was sitting in his favorite chair next to the TV, positioned near the back of the kitchen where I slept on the daybed. Normally, he would sit here after supper, have a cigar, and tell the grandchildren stories. He looked very serious this time, which made me unsure of the reason he was really here.

"I don't know, Grandpa . . . maybe there was more dust in the fields than I thought."

"Do you think it was something you ate?" His eyes seemed benevolent, but he still had his eyes fixed on me as I answered.

"I don't think so," I said but then realized maybe he heard me ask Grandma for the orange.

"Your grandmother said she gave you an orange. You can have oranges, can't you?" he asked calmly and quietly.

What came out of my mouth next was a lie. I knew it was a lie as soon as I devised it but went with it anyway. "I'm okay with oranges. I can't eat other things like nuts or chocolate, but oranges are okay."

"I'm not so sure. Your father tells me you are very allergic to oranges."

I was terribly ashamed. I just lied to my grandfather, and the worst of it was, he knew it. "I'm sorry, Grandpa. I thought I would be able to eat it without any problems . . . but then I got sick."

My grandfather never got angry with me. He remained calm and even toned the whole time he spoke with me. "I'm sorry you got sick, but think about what all this did to people. Your grandmother is upset because she thought she almost killed you by giving you the orange. Your father is upset with you and your grandmother because he feels she should have known you are allergic to oranges, and you, for telling her different. Your mother is upset with all of us because she didn't want you here on the farm to begin with. Your mother sees this as your father's failure to protect you, and your grandmother's small gift of an orange almost killed you. Do you see what a small lie can do now?"

My illness did not preclude me from the lie I had told my grandfather. I understood a little of what my grandfather was telling me. I tried not to cry, but the whole situation weighed heavily on me. I wanted to answer my grandfather somehow, but there were no words adequate for a nine-year-old boy to explain himself. My grandfather moved from his chair and put his hand on my head and said, "I think you know now to tell the truth when you are asked something . . .

especially something that can hurt you and other people. I'll tell everyone they can come to supper now." My grandfather turned, walked out the kitchen's screen door, and called from the porch that supper was about to start.

I hadn't realized how late in the day it was. The last hay wagon arrived from the fields, and the men were unloading the last of the hay into the barn at this very moment. I was disoriented because my grandmother should have had the table set for supper and there were no plates, silverware, or cups on the table. While I slept that afternoon, my grandfather helped my grandmother make a makeshift table outside the kitchen for the men to eat from. My grandfather wanted me to have a place to myself for a while to think and to get better. He didn't want the men coming into the house with the hay dust on their clothes to set off the asthma again. He also wanted me to think about what I had done. I fell asleep again before the supper cleanup was finished. I woke up long enough to realize I was going home with my parents after dark. It was a beautiful summer night with the sky filled with stars and a full moon's light. I knew I would dream of my dark place.

Stones

Tell me about the dream . . .

In the quiet solitude of the darkness, I chose to question those events of life that, from time to time, summoned me here. My illness always plagued me, sometimes for no other reason than "fate." Still, I believed everything had a purpose. Everything had a reason that would be revealed in time. Yet no answers were forthcoming from the darkness. Though sometimes I believed there were answers either from my inner self or from the world that existed, somehow suffering had to have a reason. In the darkness, I found there were no reasons for suffering or pain or man's inhumanity. But I did find something . . . something I never expected. I found the story about the Village of Stones as I was sitting beneath the unearthly spires of a spreading tree.

Once there was a place, a village, where when you are born, you are given a stone to carry for your entire life. Timothy lived there in the village of Stock, one of many villages that lay near the Great Wall where their stones were placed at the end of their lives. His story is chronicled here . . .

"Hello, Timothy, it's a fine morning to be alive, is it not?" spoke the voice of Benjamin the shopkeeper. Benjamin, never just "Ben" or "Benny," was a tall swarthy man whose business was not just selling cloth and garments to the women of the villages but also one who knew the business of the entire village of Stock.

Timothy was a pensive young man. He barely spoke more than a few words, like "Yes, it is a nice day" or just "Hello, how are you?" But today, this pensiveness seemed to melt away to curiosity, and he asked Benjamin a question.

"Benjamin . . ." Timothy said, as he addressed the older man.

"Yes, Timothy . . ." Benjamin responded as he held Timothy at eye level.

"What have you heard about some of the villagers wanting to breach the wall?" Timothy knew this was a sacrilegious question to ask Benjamin in the open street, but he had heard rumors and whisperings that were ominous.

"What have you heard?" Benjamin recoiled, looking about for anyone who might be listening. The idea of being confronted publicly on this topic would give him an unwanted notoriety that he did not wish to have.

"Well," Timothy hesitated, as he looked up and down the streets, checking for anyone who might overhear them. At this hour, the streets were abysmally vacant. The early morning travelers and villagers were not yet out this morning. The night's fog, dampening their skin, was only starting its departure as the morning sun, just barely above the distant hills, started to evaporate the mist lingering in the lowlands and along the curbing of the streets.

"There's no one here, Timothy. We can talk," Benjamin told him. *"So what have you heard?"*

"I heard some of the villagers wanted to open a passage through the wall and explore what is on the other side."

"I've heard some of that talk too . . . Thing is, the wall has been here forever. Legend has it the wall was put there by our ancestors for a reason."

"That's just it . . . what reason?"

"Well, the legend never really comes out and tells us what the reason is . . . just that a reason, a very powerful and devout reason, existed for them and for us. It was so important, all our ancestors

implored those who exist now and those who existed before us to continue to maintain the wall and to continue to build it."

Timothy stared into the empty cobbled streets. When he finally spoke, it was in a whisper. "Could it be we are ready?"

Benjamin turned his head away from Timothy for a second then, as he turned back, spoke quietly, "Ready for . . ."

"What's waiting on the other side of the wall?" Timothy said impatiently.

"Listen, Timothy, the teachings of the elders are clear. No one is ever to cross over the wall, much less breach it, and let whatever is on the other side enter the villages. From the wall, which lies to our east and stretches north to south to the frozen lands, we have fertile and expansive lands. The villages extend from the wall to the western sea, and no one has ever needed or wanted to cross the wall for any reason. Everything we will ever need or want is here."

Timothy looked at Benjamin, personally hoping to have the chance to say something, but realized Benjamin was definitely into one of his speeches, and Timothy did not dare interrupt. Benjamin continued, "Our ancestors, or the elders, gave us very clear instructions. We are all given a stone when we are born. Our stone is placed into the wall when we die. The stone is reverently given to us to symbolize, in a very real way, our link to the lands we live in. The stone is a very real reminder we exist and we are a part of the villages. In fact, this idea represented in the stone is so very powerful that each of us must take our stone with us if we are to be away for more than three days. So strong is our collective belief, we know we can be no further than three parcels from our stone or else we die within three days. And . . . are you listening, Timothy?"

"Yes, you're reciting the Three Rules. Everybody knows them from the time we are in the 'waking phase' of our childhood."

"Then you know how necessary the wall is, and how revered. It would be heretical and sacrilegious to remove any stone from the wall. Every stone in the wall represents a person's life. Removing any

stone would be like stealing a person's life, his or her legacy to the villages . . . and that, in and of itself, would be a reason not to touch the wall."

Benjamin, in his waistcoat and parson's hat, pondered the young man called Timothy as they both stood outside his shop this foggy morning. Timothy was soon to be married to the financier's daughter, Catherine. Catherine's father, Michael, cleverly chose an enormous rock for his daughter's birth many years ago to ensure she would never be too far away from him. The rock was so huge, it would take four sturdy men to lift it. If it were, theoretically, to be moved, it would take a strong cart and four strong horses to move it to a new location. Benjamin thought Timothy felt hindered by his betrothed's obvious determents. Was this what Timothy was concerned about? Benjamin was certain Timothy knew the third rule of the villages, though neither one brought it up in the conversation. Still Benjamin wondered what was on the young man's mind.

"So, Timothy, not to change the subject, but how are you and Catherine getting along?"

The shift in conversation brightened the young man's mood considerably. Timothy's face, though just moments before was quite dour, now changed to a far more characteristic countenance. "She's fine, sir. The wedding plans are going along quite well. Her father says she is driving him mad with her excitement."

"Well," Benjamin covered his mouth to prevent Timothy from seeing a smile creep over his face, "that should keep our banker friend in his office a lot longer these days."

"Sir . . . .?" Timothy looked perplexed at Benjamin's reaction.

"You know what I mean, Timothy. Catherine and her mother will drive your future father-in-law to distraction. Michael will want to be out of that house to keep his sanity." Benjamin could stand it no longer and finally had to laugh out loud.

Timothy could not help himself. When Benjamin started to laugh, he just had to join in. Before long, the two of them had bantered so many scenarios of Michael's household, with an excited bride-to-be, an extremely nervous and overprotective mother, and, of course, a very conservative father who felt left out of the damage, that the two of them laughed so hard a deaf man could have heard them.

"Well, Timothy," Benjamin intoned as he pulled a set of keys from one of his many pockets, "I need to open up. I'm surprised we haven't seen anyone yet, though they're sure to be along presently."

"I'm sure they will be. It is the end of the solen, and everybody will want to stock up on supplies . . . myself included," Timothy said, as he started to turn away.

"So you'll be getting along then . . ." Benjamin said, almost saddened Timothy had to be away. He was a very nice young man, and Benjamin liked him.

"That I will, sir. I am on my way to the village of Glade to pick up some solvents for my father's business. I hope to be back by the middle of the afternoon. Have a wonderful season if I don't get to see you."

"You too, Timothy."

And the two parted company that morning. Benjamin watched as Timothy made his way out of sight, walking quickly over the cobbled streets of Stock. He put the keys into the door, opening the shop for what promised to be a very busy day. Still . . . thinking back on Timothy's conversation, he again realized he never brought up the third rule. The third rule stated when you die, your stone is placed into the wall by your loved ones, unless you place it there yourself in which case, you have only three days to live.

"Never mind," Benjamin said out loud. Timothy has enough on his mind. Besides, he knows the Rules of Three, and it simply didn't apply to their conversation anyway, so he let it go.

Benjamin entered the shop, pulled up the window shades, and started pulling beautifully colored cloths from their shelves to place on sale for this morning's activities.

✺

The mists melted off the cobbled streets of Stock as Timothy made his way north, out of the village. Mists still lingered in the small alleyways in cool shadows where the sun still hid from them. In the fields, the fog was trapped beneath the rays of yellow sunlight, where it evaporated like a ghosts caught off guard in its penetrating light.

Timothy moved through the village streets, meeting little else than the sunlight and the shadowed alleyways. When he emerged on the other side of the village, he stopped and let his eyes wander over the expansive stone wall that separated the villages from something unknown to him, something forbidding yet intriguing.

The lifestone Timothy's father had chosen to give him at his birth hung from a leather pouch nestled on his chest. Unlike his beloved Catherine, his stone allowed him to travel at will anywhere in the villages. Most of his friends contained their lifestones in a similar manner, keeping them in small but discreet locations, which was common for the young men. Some kept them in small pouches or pockets lining a coat or shirt. Some may have had a pocket secured in a leather belt, keeping their lifestones close and safe as they traveled about the other villages. The young men of the villages were encouraged to travel and promote trade of goods and services to and from the neighboring villages. Many of the villages had unique goods indigenous to each, and getting such trade was not only wise but profitable as well.

As it was this day, Timothy made his way from Stock to the neighboring village of Glade on foot, since his father could not spare him a horse. The horses were needed by his brothers for working the fields at his father's farm. However, the farm was not the only business his family managed. His father ran a successful leather business, and part of the goods he needed were found only in the village of Glade. The other part of his family's success was created by his father, which he kept as a "family secret." It was this "secret" that made Timothy's family business unique. People from every village would come to buy his father's leather goods. The leather had a remarkable durable quality, proving to be almost legendary throughout the villages.

The villagers who knew about his family's business always stopped by when they visited Stock. Jakob, Timothy's father, was more than willing to produce his leather products provided his friend, Leon from the village of Glade, could keep up with his needs for solvents.

In the village of Stock, Benjamin finished placing his colorful wares for the upcoming sale. He put needles and bobbins and multicolored threads on round and cone-shaped spools, along with yards and yards of colored yarn wound in neat tight bundles, into carefully manicured displays. Skeins of fabric were displayed with an arm's length of fabric splayed over wooden trestles designed to appear like waves washing the tables in shades of vivid color. Shoppers were already starting to observe and sort through some of the items he had on display just outside his doors . . . items placed with the intent of drawing customers inside his doors for larger purchases. Excited babbles drifted through the doors as he prepared his books, anticipating all the upcoming transactions. All in all, it seemed like a wondrous day for selling his wares. Still, trepidation lingered like a dark stranger stepping into the shadows as some of the villagers wandered into his store.

"Hello, Benjamin," called Sarah. "How are you this morning?"

"Quite well, Sarah. How are things out on your farm?"

"Well, Seth is out harvesting the wheat fields this morning. It will probably take all day and into tomorrow before he gets it all in. He should have a good day for it once these mists dry up."

"I should say so," Benjamin nodded.

"Well, I must get some fabric and threads for my new dress. There's a wedding in the works, you know?" Sarah said, giving Benjamin "the look" from the corner of her eye.

Benjamin smiled back. "Why, yes, I just spoke with Timothy this morning as I was opening up. He seemed to be in a hurry to get somewhere."

All-knowing Sarah spoke up as if Benjamin knew nothing. "His father sent him up to Glade to get some materials for his business. I'm sure he wanted to get finished so he can see Catherine later today."

Benjamin gave Sarah a big smile, letting her know her secret was not such a surprise. "Yes, at the hour I saw him, I would say he was getting an early start. If he pushes himself, he should be back from Glade by early afternoon."

Sarah gave Benjamin a wry little smile, telling him their conversation needed to close. "Benjamin, it is very nice talking with you, but I have a million things to do yet today. I must get to them. By the way, do you have any pink or rose-colored threads I could look at?" Sarah said, as she brushed off her wide brimmed straw bonnet. The bonnet, tied loosely at her neck, glided gently to her back without falling off.

"If you follow me, I believe I have several shades of pinks and rose-colored thread I can show you." Benjamin put his hand on Sarah's shoulder and led her to the bin containing the colors she was looking for. Once Benjamin had Sarah settled where she contentedly examined the threads, he began thinking of the strange conversation he had with Timothy this morning. Was Timothy aware of some dark plan to breach the wall, or was it just idle talk among the young men these days? Either way, Benjamin was concerned. The Old Teachings were clear about "not" breaking through the wall. Still, the other argument was, there were no clear teachings about what happened if someone did breach the wall or what would be found on the other side. Benjamin's thoughts weren't so much what was on the other side of the wall but what was the wall preventing from getting through to the villages. He merely pushed his thoughts to the back of his mind, knowing full well no one would be so brazen or heretical to make any attempt to force a way through the wall. He turned his thoughts back to the business at hand as he watched his store filling up with customers. "It is going to be a wonderful day," Benjamin whispered to himself as a big smile grew on his face.

Foundations

Tell me about her past . . .

Lois was the first, and only one in her immediate family, to ever go to college. She had good grades, which rewarded her with a few small scholarships and a student loan. The rest of the money she made working at a five-and-dime snack counter in a mall, located halfway between her home and the college. She told me she made most of her money in tips from her customers. Still, it was barely enough to manage paying her college courses and have anything left to live on.

I came from a different background where my parents could afford to send me to college, and they simply paid my tuition if I didn't have it myself. I worked evenings at a steel plant welding parts, earning three times what Lois did. Many times when she was working, I would stop by, grab something to eat, and leave a huge tip. She protested, but I told her I really wanted her to have it. When we went out, I would take her to places she had never been. When she started getting used to my interventions, she found interesting places that neither one of us experienced, which created a special unique history with each other.

At the end of my sophomore year of college, I earned my first associates degree at the age of nineteen. I was to start at a major university in the fall, matriculating into their nursing program. Matriculating meant I would not be in the nursing program officially until I had a few of the university's credits under my belt. However, after completing a full-course load for one semester, I was told I would not have a problem entering the nursing program as an existing student. Entering their nursing program as a new student was impossible, since the program was severely limited by its stringent admissions policy. Their plan for me was to leave the college I was attending with an associate's degree in biology, start as an incoming student in an undeclared major in the fall, and by spring of the following year, start a degree program in nursing at the university.

Lois and I agreed earlier in the year I had a better disposition for science and the arts than numbers and mathematics. I loved the short-lived experience of working at a local nursing home earlier in the year and felt a nursing degree would be a good fit. Besides, at nineteen, the draft would be checking up on my progress in college very soon. A medical career would mean a deferment until I finished college at the very least. If I were to be forced out of college at this time, it would mean an almost immediate draft pick for me. Lois was very happy I had made the choice to go into a medically related field. I was to start my fall semester at a satellite of the university located in our town. So while we would be in different colleges, we would at least be in the same town. Lois was going to stay where she was to finish her BS in medical technology.

In July, I received an ominous call from the incoming university saying they would not allow me to matriculate into their system. I was very angry, but no argument I gave would change their mind. They were "sorry," but it did little to help me. Not only did this move on their part leave me without a school to attend in the fall, but it also made me a prime target for the military draft. It wasn't just disappointing. . . it was terrifying.

When I told my parents what happened, they were upset. My father, a veteran of World War II, came from a family of military veterans. My own grandfather had been a sergeant of engineers in the army in World War I, with all of his sons doing their military duties thereafter. Had my grandfather been alive at the time, I would have gone to him for advice, but he died about four years before. Even with all this military background in my family, we had two casualities in the family from this war, and my father did not want one of his sons to be another. He told me if I did not find a way back into school before the draft came for me, he would send me to Canada himself. He was not a man who said things lightly. I took him at his word. Still, I didn't want anyone doing anything illegal for me.

Later that day, when I managed to see Lois, I told her the problem I had because of the university's decision. She was really upset, and when I saw tears come into her eyes, I knew she realized the implications of what happened. She told me she had some connections at the local hospital, and she wanted me to wait until I heard from her to do anything. The next day, Lois had a phone number for me to call at the hospital's school of nursing. They were still accepting students at that late date, and it was still possible to start with their current class. The beauty of this nursing program was their whole first year was still at the college where Lois was finishing her third year.

The next day, I called the phone number Lois had given me. They told me they still had a few openings in their program, so I immediately cancelled everything for the day and concentrated on filling out the paperwork to attend the school in the fall. I told Lois later in the day that not only had she saved me from sitting out for a year waiting, but she also made me less of a target for the impending draft rolls. I was grateful to her and loved her even more for really helping me as no one else seemed to be able to do. By September, I was in a nursing program, still attending the same college with Lois. It was another change in events that brought Lois and I closer together.

After my first year of nursing school, I really began to see the proverbial "handwriting on the wall." There were two types of programs for nurses at the time . . . a diploma program and a degree program. While it was possible to continue your education in nursing with a diploma program, it seemed, at the time, few colleges would accept the nursing credits from the diploma schools. Most, if not all, programs at the colleges would accept college credits for nursing from another college program without having to repeat the courses. In my last few months at the diploma school, I looked into several college programs and finally found one I could do and afford. I talked to Lois about my decision, and though she would not be seeing me every day at college, she also believed it would be the right decision over the long run.

Eventually, I ended up going to college about forty miles away, full-time, while Lois continued her final year in clinicals at the hospital. We were both horribly busy, but we always found time for each other, even with our crazy schedules. Lois graduated a year ahead of me because I switched into a college degree program after my first year of the diploma school. Even then, we still found time for each other, though I had clinical twice a week and worked full-time in the evenings as a welder. Some nights when I finished work, I'd find her waiting in the parking lot for me. Sometimes we would just talk, and other times we would go to an all-night restaurant and get something to eat or have coffee. It never seemed to matter to either of us where we met. We just wanted to be together, and it was enough.

When I graduated with my second associate's degree in 1975, I could not get a nursing position in all of Pennsylvania. Many of the diploma schools that still existed had overproduced registered nurses. Even nurses who had graduated from these hospitals could not find work in the very institutions that manufactured them. Most of the nursing graduates that year either had to travel far away or find work in other fields until a nursing position opened up for them. I was lucky enough to find an extern program for graduate nurses about an hour and a half from my home. It was not a realistic commute, and I generally stayed in a rented apartment near the hospital and came home every chance I had to see Lois. What college had been unable to do, my job finally did. The distance and the remote area where I worked made it more and more difficult for Lois and me to get together. I asked Lois to watch for nursing jobs around the area where she worked, and finally, after seven months, Lois found a job in the same hospital where she worked. I was finally able to get back home and to her.

With my job near her, I was able to get into a more-predictable schedule. We both worked together to get compatible schedules so we could be off together. I asked her to marry me in late 1975, and what I knew six weeks after I met her became true in 1976.

The Swing

Tell me about magic . . .

Summer at the farm in 1964 was magical, especially when my two cousins Dave and Scott arrived with their father. When it was time for my grandfather to harvest the fields of hay and wheat, he would call for his four sons, my father, my three uncles and their families, and whatever neighbors he could rely on to come to the farm to help with the harvesting. The farmhouse was always bustling with activity around this time each year. Of myself and my cousins, David was the oldest, with myself next, then my brother, and then Scott, who was the youngest. We were all within a year or two apart in age, which made for wonderful playmates during the summer months.

My brother and I were standing under my grandmother's old pear tree when David and Scott jumped out of my uncle's car and bounded toward us. We could hardly contain our excitement as we planned all the things we would do with our day. The men were gathering outside the main farmhouse, deciding who was going to be baling hay, who would be driving the tractors out to collect the bales after they fell off the baler, and who would be driving the filled wagons back to the barn for stacking in the nearly empty barn.

Grandma made a simple breakfast consisting of cut pears, oranges, and cherries picked from cherry trees growing near the farmhouse. She also had some raspberries freshly picked from the thorny brush, which served as a backdrop for the woodpile next to the house. There were bowls of steaming scrambled eggs, a plate piled with bacon, and a plate stacked with toast. The butter was served in a bowl, not sticks, and there was a plate of cut assorted cheeses as well. The colorful meal was displayed on the long wooden dining table for the men working the fields that day. Grandma always insisted that everybody had a full stomach so they would be able to work until lunch.

Of course, to us four boys, what we saw was a beautiful summer day, the cool breezes lightly moving through the tall grasses in the meadows, and shaded glens of trees that bordered the sides of the fields. A tractor path, which was actually a well-worn dirt road, curved gently around the bottom of the hill, where the farmhouse stood at the top. The road started at the barn and traveled in a meandering course through the fields of wheat and hay to the main road, where it met the next farmhouse. This was no accident. The road gave access to the neighboring farmers, allowing them to get on the farm easily with their equipment to help harvest the burgeoning golden fields.

As rituals continued in their ordinary ways, it was determined that we four boys would be responsible for carrying water out to the men working the fields. But since there were so many men, my grandmother brought out big enclosed tins of water to be carried out on the wagons for the men to use as drinking water. This meant the men wouldn't need water until they came back at lunchtime, and we could fill them up at the house. Besides, David, Scott, Thomas, and I were all asthmatics. And though we wanted to help in the hayfields, our asthmatic problems could flare up if we were exposed to the hay dust. Scott was perhaps the most prone to attacks, as was I. My brother and David seemed to have much less of a problem. As a result, my grandmother tried to keep us away from the hayfields and the storage of the hay as was possible. It was a task that proved to be difficult, since we were boys trying hard to be like our fathers.

David was the first to consider our situation. "Well, it doesn't look like they'll be needing much help from us. What do you guys want to do?"

It took us a moment or two to consider what our day was going to be like when we all decided on exploring the farm. My cousin Scott came up with the first suggestion. "Why don't we go into the barn and jump off the rafters like we did last summer?"

I spoke up first, "Because the men have cleaned the floor of all the loose hay so they can bring in the new stuff. I saw Grandpa forking the stuff out the back door of the barn this morning. He shoved it into the corral behind the barn."

Then my brother Tom said, "Yeah, remember we almost got killed last year on the pitchforks the men left lying in the hay. If I hadn't landed next to one, one of us may have gotten speared."

"I remember that"—as David rolled his eyes—"We were all lucky on that one."

"You know what we could do?" I said, as I set my mind running over things that I saw in the barn just this morning. Everyone was looking at me. "I saw a long thick rope, which I know Grandpa never used, coiled up in the chicken coop."

"So what do you want to do with a long rope?" David asked.

"First, let's see if it's still there, and then I'll show you," I told him.

"Okay, everybody to the chicken coop. Last one there is a loser," David taunted. David loved to torment his little brother Scott, but since Scott was standing closest to the chicken coop, he had a really good head start.

The chicken coop was actually a tack room built into the side of the barn. In order to get inside, we had to push open the big sliding barn door, squeeze inside, and open the door to the coop. The door to the coop was latched with a wooden bar, which had to be lifted to get in. Since Grandma kept a good stock of chickens, we had to be careful not to let any out or she would put an end to our lovely day. We had to be careful.

Scott ran like a hunted man. He made it to the barn door first but was too small to push the enormous door back. I made it next, with David close behind. My brother closed the gap and was soon on us as well. All four of us collided at the barn door and started pushing. The door moved enough to allow one person at a time to get through. David slipped through first, then me, followed by my brother, and finally Scott. We all stood in front of the chicken coop door immersed by the total darkness of the closed barn. The only light coming in was sliding through the opening the barn door made as we had entered. Cautiously, we allowed our eyes to adjust to the darkness. We had to make sure the chickens stayed away from the door before we entered.

"Can you guys see anything near the door?" David asked, squinting to see through the door to the chicken coop.

"I'm still blind from the sun. Give me a second," I said.

"I think we need more light," my brother said, as he tried to push the heavy barn door open a little further. He couldn't get it to move. Scott joined in, but even with the two of them, they could not move it.

David told them, "Just let it go. If anyone comes looking, they probably won't notice that the door's barely open. If you open it any further, they might see it and check it out. So give it up."

"Okay already," Scott said sullenly.

My eyes were getting used to the darkness. I saw the chickens were mostly on the other side of the room from the door. With the others still arguing about how wide they needed to open the barn door, I slipped inside the coop. There was enough light to check around. I knew roughly where Grandpa kept the rope. I felt around the dark entryway, and finally, there it was, the long coarse rope I came for. I was surprised how heavy it was. I called for David to lend a hand . . .

David came into the coop and gathered about half the rope on his shoulders, and I took the other half. We slipped out of the coop without disturbing any of Grandma's chickens. We had to take the rope off our shoulders and then sent our two younger brothers through the narrow opening at the barn door. Once my brother Thomas and my cousin Scott were outside, David and I pushed the heavy coil of rope out to them. It was all they could handle. When the rope was out of the barn, David and I left the barn and pushed the barn door shut together. The rope was free, and I had a wonderful plan for it.

"So now what?" my brother asked.

"Now we carry the rope to the black walnut tree that sits at the top of the hill near the house."

"Are we going to tie the rope up and climb the tree?" David asked.

Scott caught on before anyone else. "No, we're going to make a swing. Right?"

"Exactly." I laughed.

"That is a really cool idea, but where are we going to set this up, and how are we going to get the rope over the limbs?" David the pragmatic asked us.

"I don't know yet, but I think we will figure it out," I said unceremoniously.

David and I gathered up the heavy rope and carried it to the black walnut tree. When we arrived, we searched for a branch that would support a swing. We knew the limb had to be fairly level yet strong enough to carry one of us. It had to be high enough, but not too high, that we could reach it. Our eyes surveyed the possibilities. Finally, we all decided on a relatively level branch that appeared to be perfect for our swing. The problem with the limb was it was in a place where we could not climb.

"So I guess we better take the rope back to the barn," David said sarcastically.

"Not yet. Let me think about this," I said, ignoring David's negativity.

"This is really getting boring," Thomas pouted.

"Yeah, I thought we were going to make a swing," Scott said impetuously.

"Come on, guys, help me think of a way to get that rope up there," I pleaded.

"So if we come up with a way to do that, how are we going to fasten it to the limb so it doesn't come down?" David the spoilsport asked.

"Simple . . ." I said exasperated, "Once we get the rope over the limb, we will pull it so the two strands of rope hang down. Once that is done, one of us can climb the rope to the limb and wind the rope around the limb like a coil until we use enough rope to tie to a board to it to make the swing. We just need to get the rope over the limb."

"How about a rock?" Tom asked.

"What?" we all asked together.

"You know, throw a rock over the limb with the rope attached," Thomas said.

"That's a good idea, but the rope is too heavy to tie a rock to it," I said.

"Yeah, but if we get a thinner rope, then tie a rock to it and throw it over the limb, we could take the thinner rope and pull the thicker rope up with it," Thomas explained.

I had to admit, it was a great idea. I looked around at the rest of them to see if anyone else had a better plan. I should have known my older cousin would be the first to ask a deterring question.

"Where are we going to find a thinner rope?" David asked.

"Well, Grandpa keeps a box of baling twine up in his tool shed," Thomas explained. "We can borrow it long enough to get a rock tied to it and then go from there."

"So do you know where this box of twine is?" I asked.

"Yeah," Thomas said, "Scott and I can get it and bring it back."

"Okay, you two go for the twine, and Dave and I will look for a board to use as our swing."

The two younger boys took off like a shot. David and I left the rope beneath the old black walnut tree and went to the woodpile to look for a board that would work. It didn't take long for our younger brothers to locate the twine. David and I sorted through the wood pile and finally found a nice board suitable for a swing. We finally had everything we would need to make it.

"Okay, everybody, look for a rock that will carry the twine over the limb," David ordered.

We went into the field, and three of us came back with rocks. One rock was barely a stone not heavy enough to carry much of anything. The other two were pretty good. David tied one of the stones to the end of the twine then said, "Are we ready?"

"Yeah," I said excitedly, "go ahead."

David threw the rock, but it missed, going under the limb by at least three feet . . . "Let me try again," David said confidently, as if he knew he would get it over the limb this time. His next throw went just below the limb. The rock sailed through the air as the twine trailed behind it like the tail of a kite. "Well, this is working out well," David said, disgusted by the way things were going.

"Maybe the rock is too heavy," I said.

"So try the other one," Scott said.

We unfastened the heavier rock and then quickly tied the twine to the other one.

"Okay, this feels better," David boasted. "I know this one is going to make it." But when he threw the rock, it hit the limb, knocking the twine off the rock altogether. The rock sailed out into the thick grass in the field, as the twine fell softly in coils beneath the limb. We wound up the twine so we could try again. David looked for the rock but couldn't find it.

"Well, I guess that's that," David said exasperated.

"What do you mean?" I asked.

"We're not getting anywhere with this. Every time I try to send the rock over the limb, I miss," David told me angrily.

"Let me try then," I said coolly.

"Like you're going to get a rock over that limb. It must be twenty feet at least!" David exclaimed.

The two younger ones were frustrated. They were too small to throw a big-enough rock over the limb, and David was already angry.

"Just let me try," I implored.

"I think we should just give up and do something else," my brother said.

"Okay . . . tell you what . . . let's tie the rock on the twine once more and let me take a shot at it. If it doesn't work, we'll go down to the creek and look for crayfish or something." I looked at everyone to see if my plea for another try was getting anywhere. The two younger ones lay down in the grass and wouldn't answer. I looked toward David.

David threw up his hands. "Okay, one shot then we're done."

Our younger brothers refused to help us. They were angry because they felt they had no real part in this adventure. They couldn't throw a rock over the formidable tree limb.

"Okay, the rock is tied on," David told me. "You ready to try it?"

"Yes," I said, not really sure if I could really throw the rock that far in the air myself. I looked over at David, and he looked at me.

"Good luck," he told me. He spoke the words like he really meant it.

"All right, here goes." I watched David throw the rock overhanded to get it across the limb. My idea was to throw it underhanded from just below the tree limb. I walked to a spot below the limb and, using both hands, threw the rock into the air. It was one of those magical moments when the air goes out of your lungs and everything goes into slow motion. I knew when the rock left my hands, there was something special happening, like a moment that is supposed to occur in the continuum of time. The rock seemed to rise like it was caught on a pillar of air, rising up and over the limb. The twine followed like a trail of smoke from a jetliner. Then as it passed over the limb, the rock trailed the twine in its downward wake. A reverent hush fell over us as the impact of what happened penetrated our gloom.

"You did it," David gasped, as our two younger brothers sprang from their grassy resting places.

"Wow," Scott and Tom exclaimed, as I stood dumbfounded over the rock that passed across the limb.

"Come on guys, let's get the rope and pull it over," David shouted, trying to get me to move.

"I really did it. I got it over," I said under my breath, as the rest of them worked on tying the twine and the rope together.

David looked over at me and smiled since he overheard my remark, "Yeah, so let's get the rope over the limb now."

David and Scott finished tying the rope and the twine together, while Thomas and I untied the magical rock. Once the rope was tested against our knot, we started pulling the rope over the appointed limb. We all thought something else would happen to deter our rope from going over, but the rope slid easily over the limb.

"Well, the hard part is done," I said.

"So how do we get the rope so the two ends are fairly equal when they touch the ground? We can't cut the rope. It's too thick to do that," David exclaimed.

"If we let one end run to the ground and then wrap the excess rope around the limb, we could get the other side just as long as we want it," I said.

"Yeah, that would work, but we can't keep throwing a rock over a limb. We were lucky it worked once. Getting that rock over twenty or more times would be impossible." David the antagonist was back again.

"I listened to what David said, and he was right. We weren't going to get a rock over that limb nearly enough times to get the rope the right length or secure it to the limb properly to have a safe swing. The only way I knew to make this work was climb up to the limb, using the rope, and wrap it myself.

"I need you guys to hold one end of the rope," I told David.

"You're going to climb up there?" David asked me as a shocked look molded his face.

"You want to do it?" I challenged.

"No way. You can do it. What do you want us to do?"

"I figure with the three of you holding the rope, I should be able to climb it. When I'm there, I'll straddle the limb and wrap the rope around it until we have about two equal lengths."

"Okay, this I got to see." David laughed, though, to be honest, I wasn't really sure I would really make it.

The three boys, David, Scott, and Thomas, stayed on the ground and held one end of the rope. When they had it secured, I started pulling myself up the coarse prickly rope. I was about ten feet off the ground when I tired out and stopped. David asked, "Are you okay?"

"Yeah," I answered, "just taking a rest. How are you guys doing?"

"We can hold it," my brother Thomas said.

"As a matter of fact," David interjected, "I think we can help."

"What do you have in mind?" I asked, as I felt my hands slip a bit on the abrasive rope.

"Hold on!" David told me, using his most serious voice. "Okay, guys," David said, as he turned to address the two younger boys, "pull."

I held on to the rope even tighter. David and our younger brothers started pulling. At first, the rope seemed to hang up on the rough tree bark, and then with the three of them working together, the rope started to move. The rope only moved an inch or two at first, as my hands burned raw on the rope, then they were moving me upward a foot at a time. "I don't think I can hold on, David," I called out as I approached the limb, almost fifteen feet off the ground, with the objective getting closer each time they pulled. Then I heard David tell the younger boys, "Okay, we need one good last pull to get him up there fast. You ready?"

"Yeah, we're ready," Scott proclaimed loudly and determinedly.

""Let me know when . . ." Thomas told David.

"You ready up there?" David asked me from his spot on the ground where I wished I stayed at that moment.

"What choice do I have?" I asked disgustedly as I started getting nauseated in the summer heat. I began to realize how futile this whole project actually was. My hands were in agony from holding the rope. The cramping would not stop, and I wasn't sure I could move from the rope to the limb when the time came. Of course, the alternative of falling almost twenty feet from this point did not appeal to me either, so I held on for whatever came next. I felt like I was in limbo, caught between heaven and earth. Both concepts didn't look very positive from the perspective where I lingered at the moment. As these thoughts ran through my mind, I felt myself rising, not in one-foot jerks but as one steady movement. I looked down and realized what the three of them had done. Each of them had taken the rope and secured it to themselves like a harness, and they were walking away from the tree, pulling me up. It was a very good idea, since the strength was leaving my hands.

"Come on, you guys, pull . . ." David tormented the two younger ones.

"We are pulling . . ." Scott replied breathlessly.

I held on. Cold sweat popped out and poured off my skin. It was probably ninety degrees up here, but my skin was cold and sweaty. Then my hand touched the limb . . .

"Hold it," I hollered with as much strength as I had left.

"Wait . . . hold up, guys," David bellowed at the two boys

The rope stopped. I looked up at the limb that had been so much trouble. I felt like passing out, yet looking at the limb up close made me angry. I could get up to the limb or I could slide down the rope and let this idea go. "No," I said, "you don't beat me that easy."

I took one hand off the rope and wrapped it around the limb. When I was sure my arm was secure, I left the security of the rope behind me and put my other arm around the limb. Now I was in the most dangerous position of the entire climb, hanging by my arms off a limb twenty feet off the ground. I was surprised by the silence up here. Again, another magical sensation went through me, telling me I was following a predestined path. I could not see the other three on the ground, and none of them made a sound. Something struck them too, and I knew by their silence that something was happening.

I swung on my arms until I had one leg over the limb. Once that was accomplished, I got the other leg up. Now I was hanging off the bottom of the limb like an orangutan. I thought I must look funny to the guys on the ground, but no one laughed . . . no one made a sound. I couldn't see the boys on the ground and wondered if they had run off. I called out, "Hey, are you guys still there?"

"Yeah, be careful," David said. I could hear the caution in his voice.

It was encouraging to know I hadn't been abandoned. Now I had to right myself and get to the top of the limb. I looked around and saw a small but sturdy branch growing out of the top of the limb. I grabbed it and started shifting my weight over the limb. I was in shorts and a T-shirt, and my bare legs were getting scraped open by the tree bark's rough surface. I finally got my chest over the limb and then pulled my legs up and over. I sat on the limb and felt the cold sweat and nausea pass as I took a few minutes to regain my strength.

David called to me from below, "How are you doing up there?"

"A few scrapes and out of breath. Give me a second."

"That was amazing," one of the boys said.

"What's it look like from up there?" my brother asked.

I hadn't checked the view, but the question intrigued me. I looked around and saw the expansive fields, the forest, and the top of the farmhouse. It was an amazing scene seeing everything from this level. Looking over the fields, I began to realize I would probably be the only one to ever see the farm from this tree limb. No one would ever venture this far up the black walnut tree again. It was a strange feeling to know I was the first one to do this, and I would probably be the last.

"So are you ready to start?" David asked.

"Yeah, I think so."

I straddled the limb and hoisted the long end of the rope over the limb for the first time. It was fairly easy. I pulled it up and wrapped the rope over the limb again and again and kept asking the guys on the ground if we had used up enough rope to balance the two ends. David was supervising, and before long, we had made about ten or twelve wraps around the limb.

"Dave, test the rope before I come down and make sure it doesn't slip."

First, David hung on the side of the rope they pulled on, and it didn't move. Then he tried the other side. He felt it give a little, but nothing slipped. Wrapping the rope, as we did around the sturdy limb, made a nice width between the two ends of the rope. When we finished, we had the two ends far enough apart to fit a good wooden seat.

"I think that will do it," David said proudly.

"We couldn't have done it without everybody," I said.

"How about you slide down awhile, and then we'll look for a way to tie the board on."

"I think I'm ready to come down," I said with obvious relief in my voice.

Going down the rope was far easier than going up. I put my feet in the rope and held on with my hands. When I touched the ground again, it seemed the magic I sensed in the tree was fading.

"You look bad," David said, trying to determine if I was strong enough to keep going. "How do you feel?"

I looked at him and, with a breathless laugh, said, "A little scuffed up but actually pretty good."

The job of fastening the board to the heavy rope was our next challenge. Tom and Scott looked at the thick coarse rope, shaking their heads.

"I guess we didn't think of that," my brother Tom said.

"The rope is so thick we can't even put a knot in it," Scott agreed.

David looked at the rope and saw it was made by three smaller ropes bound together with a thin wire. "Here, watch this," he said.

David picked up an end from one of the ropes and slid the thin wire off the end with his fingers. Then he started untwisting the thick braided rope. When he was done, he unwound about a foot of the stranded rope on each of the rope lengths hanging from the tree. The result thinned the rope from one thick cord to three smaller ones. Smaller ropes that could be cut, tied, positioned in any way we wanted.

"That will work," I said. "But how do we attach the board?"

"Let's use Grandpa's tools to make some notches and a hole." David said. Then he looked over at my scraped legs and soaked T-shirt and said, "You stay here and rest. We're going to look for a saw or something to notch out that piece of wood we found." The three of them started off. I thought I was alone when David turned around and yelled, "We'll be back." David and the two boys hurried off to see what they could find. It wasn't too long until all three came back with something.

I was exhausted by my climb into the black walnut tree. David had been right to let me stay in the shade, while they ran off on their project. My arms and hands cramped into knots that curled my fingers while I waited for them to return. I flattened my hands into the cool green grass beneath me and waited for the uncomfortable feelings in my arms to pass. In a while, I started to feel like myself again. I was still sitting beneath the black walnut tree when they brought back the finished piece of wood.

David wasted no time in setting up the swing seat. He fished one of the three strands of rope through a hole they drilled into the wood, then took the other two strands and tied them around two carved notches on either side of the short wooden plank. When he was done, David sat in the finished swing to test his weight against the knots he made and then let each of our younger brothers try it out. We were proud of what we accomplished. When it was my turn to try the swing, I found, in some mysterious way, part of the magic I sensed on that unreachable branch in the black walnut tree passed into the swing as well. Eventually, we all took our turn sitting in the swing and experienced the magical sense of flying over the fields of corn that grew near the farmhouse. It made me happy to see the joy the swing brought to the faces of my brother and two cousins when they sailed into the idyllic summer sky.

The rest of the day we spent building a small tree fort that was just a platform we placed up in an old mulberry tree growing near one of Grandpa's corncribs. Then we went down to the creek in the afternoon and built a small dam across the water and swam in the backed-up water when the afternoon sun was too hot to do much of anything else. All the while, the men were bringing in the hay from the fields and filling up the barn. When supper was ready, we all sat down, exhausted by our endeavors. The men told stories about how their day went and the various problems they had with the equipment. They were talking about the different ways they fixed problems with the balers and tractors when Grandpa brought up seeing the swing. All eyes turned to the four of us as we explained our long tale about making the swing.

When we finished telling our stories, my father and my uncle were upset. They couldn't understand why we wanted to be so foolhardy as to attempt such a thing. "Besides, where did you find the rope?" they all wanted to know. After I told them where and how we came by the rope, my father and all my uncles were angry at us. My father told us the rope was used to lift and lower bales of hay into the loft. Then my uncles backed him up, saying we should not have taken it out of the barn without asking. From listening to the conversation, I realized David and I were going to take the brunt of the trouble when we got home. It was then my grandfather, who had been listening to all of them, said, "Boys, I didn't use the rope anymore. It was okay to use it. Besides, I have other ropes that are much easier to use than that old rope. You probably did me a favor by using it." He gave me a wink, which meant he was all right with what we had done. "Besides, you boys have something you can do when you come to the farm that will keep you out of trouble." With that said, he continued to eat his supper. My father and my uncles looked thunderstruck. If it was okay with my grandfather, it was okay with all of them, and no one was to get into trouble over any of it. I knew my grandfather, and I knew he would check back with both David's father and mine to see if either of them had punished us. If they had, he would deal with his sons in his own way, and they knew not to go up against their father. David and I were off the hook.

So this was the story of the swing and how it came to be. All the things the four of us did that magical summer day passed away over time. The dam we built lasted about a week when a thunderstorm came along and, with a rush of rainwater, washed most of our dam away. Whatever remained, time wore away with such deliberation; no one would ever know that once on a summer day, four boys had played there. The same was true of the tree house. When Grandpa removed some corn from the corn bin about two years later, the weight shifted, and it fell against the mulberry tree, crushing the tree with our little platform. The corn bin had to be taken away afterward, and the mulberry tree was burned where it stood. Like the dam, no one would ever know it was there.

However, the swing was magical. The swing was still there many years later. Whenever any of us went to the farm, we used the swing. No matter what the season, or if it was one of us, or all of us, the swing was there. Many of my younger cousins were not even born when we made the swing. Even so, they would tell us how much they enjoyed having it through their childhoods. It was always up to David, myself, Thomas, or Scott to tell the story of the swing and how Grandpa took up for us. We were grown men with families of our own when we heard the swing had to be destroyed because the tree was dying from a disease that affected black walnut trees. Some of the limbs were rotting and falling down. The swing still was there, but it wasn't safe to use anymore.

It was sad to know the swing was finally gone. Yet it was like that single summer's day locked in a piece of our childhood for almost thirty years. My grandfather died a few years after we made the swing, and my grandmother, twelve years younger than he, lived to be ninety-six. The swing outlived them both. My grandmother even saw some of her great-grandchildren play on it before she died. When I think back on the swing, I remember a long-ago perfect summer's day, which was magical.

Steps

Tell me about her dreams . . .

When it came to our wedding, I had the opportunity to watch Lois's version of organization firsthand. She found a beautiful wedding gown at a price that was phenomenal and rented a hall for the reception for about seventy-five people. With meticulous care, we managed to keep rosters of who wanted to come to the wedding to that amount. Then we discussed the wedding party. We decided to have two bridesmaids, the maid of honor, two groomsmen, and the best man. The maid of honor would be her sister, and the best man would be my brother, our most logical choices.

One night, as we looked over stationery for the wedding invitations, I said, "I'm glad your father is helping you out with all the wedding expenses." I made the remark, thinking how far her father had come to accept me. Since it was traditional for parents to help when it came to a marriage, I thought her father was happy for her. I was wrong.

Lois didn't look up from the stationery when she said, "My old man isn't doing anything for me. I am paying for everything myself."

I pulled back from the portfolio of wedding invitations and looked at her in disbelief. I thought she misinterpreted her father's intentions as I asked, "But he is helping you out with some of the wedding arrangements, isn't he?"

"No . . . he isn't doing a thing to help me. My mom is helping with the dress and helping me decide what needs to be done, but he controls all the money. My mom can only help me with the things that don't cost anything." Lois looked at me for a response. I looked back with horrific surprise. She still had something else to say and wanted to know how I would take it. "My father tells me that he won't be there to walk me down the aisle."

"You're not serious," I said, shocked that her father would be this dismissive of his oldest daughter. "Why is he acting like this? Doesn't he know it is a great honor to walk his daughter down the aisle to her wedding? Besides, isn't getting the wedding together stressful enough without having to worry whether he will show up or not?"

Lois looked at me with a clever smile, which puzzled me. "Don't worry," Lois said with confidence, "I already asked my uncle to walk me down the aisle if my father persists in being ignorant. That puts my father on the spot, not me. I will not let him ruin my wedding day . . . I just won't."

So it was—we planned for the wedding without the help of her father. I heard from her sister and brothers that Lois and her mother had many heated arguments with her father in the days leading up to the wedding, but he would not relent.

Then something unexpected happened. My brother was placed into intensive care just six weeks before the wedding after a work-related accident. It was three weeks of waiting to discover whether my brother would live or die from his extensive injuries. Somehow, he managed to get out of intensive care and recuperated on the general floor for another three weeks. I realized he would not be out of the hospital before the wedding, much less be in any condition to walk. As the eleventh hour approached, I made the decision to have my cousin step in as best man.

My brother was markedly upset he could not be there for the wedding but gave his best wishes and told me he would do anything to help within his power. Something eventually clicked with Lois's father, and just a few days before the wedding, he finally agreed to walk her down the aisle. Lois was ecstatic but skeptical. She told me she would believe it when she saw it, keeping her uncle on standby just in case he pulled something in the minutes before the wedding.

Our wedding day finally came on September 18, 1976. The church was filled with family members and friends. Lois's father did indeed walk her down the aisle as he promised. We had a beautiful wedding and a beautiful reception afterward. I had my car packed and ready at my parents' house to leave on our honeymoon as soon as we left the reception.

When we arrived at my parents' house, I unsuccessfully tried to start my overburdened car and discovered the battery was dead. I called my brother at the hospital and asked to borrow his car. He was delighted he had something he could do to help us and agreed to lend his car to us. We unpacked my car and loaded his with our luggage. We were finally off on our new life together in a borrowed car with most of what we owned in the trunk. We were happy, and we were together.

Before we were married, I traveled extensively up and down the East Coast with my parents. I traveled to every state between Connecticut and Florida by the time I was fourteen. My parents always investigated the historic sites in the states we visited. My father, a real Civil War buff, always pointed out sites where battles occurred and the significance it had on history. He had a library of books dedicated to the Civil War and became so fluent he once took the lead away from a guide trying to explain the significance of the battlefield we were touring. His discourse was so interesting, the people on the tour applauded him when he was done. To say I had an enchanted childhood was putting it mildly, but Lois was not as fortunate as I.

I sadly discovered she never had the chance to travel any farther than the New Jersey shore in her entire life. Her parents went there year after year. Other than a few areas around where she lived, she had not traveled any farther than her own backyard. When we discussed where to go on our honeymoon, I told her about Williamsburg, Virginia, a beautiful and historic place where I visited many times as a child. Before we decided to go there, she investigated and studied everything she could find about it. She thought going to Williamsburg was a wonderful decision and was very excited she would finally travel to a different place . . . discover new things . . . learn something new about the world she lived in. She was, at long last, going to Virginia, a place she never dreamed of.

After we arrived, Lois wanted to see and do everything. The beauty of the many gardens, the ambiance of the old buildings, the quiet walks after dark, the brick walkways, and taverns set the stage to fall in love with the place. The year we married, Williamsburg was going through a centennial year, and the bustling activity in the town was enormous. Lois enjoyed that destination more than any other, and over the years that followed, we succeeded to go back many times.

In later years, we traveled to the western side of Virginia, the states of North Carolina, South Carolina, New York, Canada, Florida, and so many destinations I could not begin to list them all. We traveled as far north as Massachusetts. We went as far west as Seattle, Washington. Eventually, Lois became more traveled than I. As her job proficiency increased, she was sent to conference after conference in different states by her employer. She saw the Sears Tower in Chicago, ate a steak in Texas, and saw the "brickyard" (a colloquial term for the raceway at the Indianapolis 500 where the original paving was made of bricks not asphalt) in Indianapolis. She saw destinations I only heard about. Lois became a young woman who never had a chance to explore the world she lived in as a child, but it opened up to her as an adult. She absorbed what she learned and found places to visit I would never see. She became a constant learner and a constant doer.

Our first three years together, we did not have a lot of money. We worked long hours, and Lois introduced me to many interesting foods like spaghetti and Spam. Spam, I thought, was a product of my imagination; but when Lois served it, it was pretty good. Lois seemed to know how to stretch money, and incredibly we were actually able to save some money for a new house.

One of the advantages my family had was my father's ties to the construction business. As forethought in his younger years, my father bought three acres of land to build houses for my brother and me. He felt that once we were married and had sufficient money to start a house, he would build one for each of us on these lots. However, my father insisted we have ten thousand dollars to begin construction of a new home. While this does not seem like a lot of money now, it was a small fortune for a young couple back at that time.

My job as a nurse, while stable in 1976, paid less than what people made flipping hamburgers. Lois and I agreed that I needed to find a trade or profession paying more money to start a family and build a house. The following years, I spent in school to learn a new trade. After a year of school, I was hired at a local manufacturing plant at twice the pay I was making as a nurse. The irony was, I made more money to move steel than save a life or improve someone's health. It made us question the sanity of the world.

Making more money in my new job, and with what we had managed to save, we finally had enough to start building our new house. In the spring of 1979, Lois discovered she was pregnant. So as we were building our home, we were also building our family. We moved into our home in November 1979, and our son was born in January 1980. Though she was only five feet tall and very pregnant at the time, Lois came out to the building site every day and helped sweep the floors, paint, and do whatever she could do to help. My father, who was not an easy man to impress, was very impressed Lois would get out and get her hands dirty like the rest of us. Lois's father and brothers helped put in the electrical work for the house. Building our house was a family project, and with everyone's help and support, we were done with it in six months.

Like me, Lois was under the scrutiny of my parents as well. My father told me, before I married Lois, I could marry a rich girl as easily as a poor one. He meant he did not think Lois was bringing anything into the family. Both my parents felt I married a girl of a lower station in life than myself. I believe Lois felt that way herself, which made her try to be the best person she could be. No one ever dreamed how far this need to exceed would take her.

My father's innate ability to work mathematics in his head made his world one of logic and a good argument. Lois often times disagreed with him, which led to many interesting discussions between them. I remember once when Lois won him over in an argument, he was so impressed with her intelligent dialogue that he told me, "She's pretty smart. I like talking to her." Once my father was convinced, my mother started to look closer at the potential in her daughter-in-law. Every time Lois and I visited, my father would try to catch her in an argument. They were always good-natured about it, and I swore my father purposely studied something in the news just to keep up with her. I watched my parents fall in love with her even before our son was born.

We were barely in our new house and settled when our son was born. I didn't know a thing about babies, and Lois had to teach me everything. All the grandparents just hovered over our son, and we never had a problem with babysitters when we needed a night out. And, of course, when holidays came, we were invited to too many places to ever imagine getting to see everyone. I remember having some minor disagreements with Lois as to who we were going to see and which relatives were going to be disappointed. Lois, I, and our son became the center of attention for both grandparents' worlds for many years. After some time, some new granddaughters and grandsons finally came along, and our son was not so much the center of the universe for which Lois and I were both grateful.

The world went on, and we all moved on with it. Our ordinary days were both peaceful and loving as they passed and we grew. We planned vacations, had adventures, and generally lived an ordinary life in a world of changes and turmoil. We planned our life as though we would be together for a very long time, hoping those hopes everyone has and dreaming dreams that gave us solace in the darkness.

Secret

Tell me more of the dream . . .

As I grew older, the sojourns into the darkness grew less frequent. And on those occasions, when I did venture there, there seemed to be more-ambient light present than ever before. The light was phosphorescent. The vegetation in the haze glowed and outlined itself in hues of what existed in the darkness, like it had something to reveal to me . . . a secret. Something I was to understand but not really know. It was there I dreamed of the wall again . . .

Leena washed last night's dishes by the window, which framed the ambient light of the early morning sunrise. Her hands, covered in suds, picked up another pot, another dish, and washed them squeaky clean, then placed them in a homemade dish rack by the sink.

The light seeping through the window was muffled orange, streaked with hazy yellow, as it reflected off the morning fog. It looked like, when the foggy mists burned away, it would become a beautiful day. It would be perfect for her and her daughter Catherine to go shopping in the village. Leena actually felt more excited about the upcoming wedding plans than her daughter Catherine. Her husband, Michael, criticized Leena's leniency for allowing Catherine to make all her own decisions regarding the wedding plans and draining his pockets. However, Leena seemed not to abide his advice, knowing full well she wanted Catherine to have the best wedding the village of Stock ever saw.

Leena's husband was the chief officer of the villages' banks, and in the capacity of finances and money lending, he was financially sound, perhaps even rich by the standards of the villages. Michael was a fair man, and it was never said of him he took advantage of anyone.

As Leena looked from her kitchen window, she watched the fog rising in the distance; eventually, she saw the mists part. The small break in the haze allowed the morning light to paint golden colors on the ancient stone wall, which seemed to stretch out into forever, running like a stone serpent beside the many villages of the east. Whatever idyllic thoughts she rendered now sobered as she pondered its existence, its reality. The wall stood before her time. It stood throughout her time as it would after her.

She knew as every family bore a child, a stone was given to the infant, where it remained a guarded possession until that life ended. It was then that the stone would be taken by the family or a close friend and placed into the wall as it had been for centuries. Some infants were given possession of stones no bigger than their hands; others were smaller. However, in Catherine's case, her father chose an enormous stone for her. Leena was, at first, amused by the gift of such a large stone for their daughter, but the implications were obvious. Michael, her father, never wanted Catherine to stray too far from her home.

But now, as Catherine got older and was considering starting her own family, the idea of the large stone only served as a symbol of confinement. It made Catherine resentful of her father and the home where she was raised. Her older brother Stephan was given a small pocket-sized stone at his birth, which he carried in his coat pocket or the small leather pouch his wife made for him. This allowed Stephan to travel to many villages without restrictions anytime he decided. There were limitations on Catherine because of it, making her feel trapped and isolated. At least, things were that way until Timothy took notice of her. Timothy changed Catherine's world, and that hope of change lessened the weight of her stone.

Leena watched as the sunlight revealed more of the stone wall. While she watched through the clear rippled glass window, she imagined she heard the whisperings of the villagers who spoke of what lay on the other side. We all wondered about it throughout our lives, but no one ever ventured there. No one needs to, *Leena thought.* Everything we need is here. Plenty of land, food, shelter, family, and friends . . . it was all here. Everyone was happy to live here. *Yet the mystery of what lay beyond the wall remained for her and all the people of the villages.*

Transitions

Tell me about the child . . .

In 1982, the job paying a decent wage for our little family was terminated. The layoff, I feared, was just the first of many, leading to a complete shutdown of the plant two years later. When the layoff came, Lois and I were seriously thinking of having a second child. However, the loss of a good-paying job and our change in resources put our dream out of reach. I was on unemployment for six months, looking for a job to cover the existing bills. I still possessed my nursing license and attempted to find work with the nursing facilities around our area. I was told I would make much less than 75 percent of what I made moving steel around. With my prospects of finding work close to home becoming poor to nonexistent, Lois suggested I look into work outside our area. Her idea proved successful two weeks later when I found several available nursing jobs in the Baltimore area. It was a forty- to fifty-mile commute, but it was one of the best decisions we ever made together.

The position I found was in a major hospital and started as a forty-hour work week, which was to last three months. During those three months, I had to travel to Baltimore every day and be oriented to the hospital. They were eight-hour days that, many times, ended up to be ten hours or more, starting and ending with the one-hour drive back home. The drive from work helped me decompress from all the events happening throughout the day. When I drove to work over the days that followed, the drive helped me reinforce the courage I needed to get through the rugged orientation process.

After three months orientation, I was allowed to work on the floor independently. The hospital was using a new concept known as weekend option for which I had originally been hired. This meant I would only have to work two twelve-hour nights on Saturday and Sunday and get paid for forty hours. The idea came about because a nursing shortage occurred in Baltimore and many metropolitan areas throughout the country. The hospitals in the area needed to get nurses. Hospitals, like this one, were willing to do this because, like most other positions in the country, nurses also liked being off their weekends. It was a good way to have the weekends covered and allow the forty-hour nurses off the weekend. For those of us that worked the weekend, we had the entire week off until Saturday night when we returned. It was a good selling point for both situations.

As a result, my job made it possible for Lois to work through the workweek while I watched of our then two-year-old son. Lois was home almost all of her weekends, allowing her to work through the week when I was off. As far as the money went, it was actually more than I made at the steel plant in our hometown. It would take several years for the nursing shortage to affect our local area like it did in Baltimore.

Lois and I were able to see each other every night except the two weekend nights I worked. The world was in such turmoil with so many people laid off and looking for work, we did not trust the possibility of having a second child. We feared our fortunes would change again, and we would end up impoverished with two small children to support. I knew from Lois's history she would not bring children into the world that were not loved and cared for, so we decided to wait.

After our son was old enough to go to preschool for an entire day, I returned to school for computer electronics for a year. I heard computers were going to be in great demand, and having skills in this emerging field appeared lucrative. I managed to graduate with a perfect 4.0 average. We hoped this training would land a position closer to home. I found a position, but the field of electronic controls eventually pulled me farther away from home with longer hours than I wanted. The changing world was not cooperating with us. In 1987, I was resigned to return to nursing in our area. I was happy to find wages had improved. A local hospital offered me a weekend option plan, which I immediately accepted.

Throughout this turmoil, Lois stood by and supported me regardless of what I was dealing with. However, by this time, she also needed a change in her career path. I gave her the same advice she had once given me. So in February 1988, Lois looked into a position at Mercy Medical Center in Baltimore. After some preliminary orientation, she took the position for a chemistry medical technologist for the night shift. Her hours were a little more exacting than mine had been, so her forty-hour week was "really" a forty-hour week plus the one hour commute to and from work. She also found the drive helped relax her. We found we were both happy with the arrangements. I was home during the week for both Lois and my son. I had to work the weekends, so if she had a weekend to work, we would have one of the grandparents babysit our eight-year-old son while we both worked. We had time together, we could be home with our son, and if we couldn't, his grandparents loved to stay with him. It was the best situation we ever had for our household since we were married.

At Mercy Medical Center, Lois thrived. Her superiors noted her drive to exceed, and because of her commitment to succeed, she was scheduled for many outside conferences. The conferences she attended were offered all over the country. Her attendance brought new techniques, procedures, and potential new equipment into the hospital's laboratory. She became well versed in almost all the equipment at Mercy Medical Center, becoming their lead technologist in only two years. But like me, she longed to get a job closer to home.

So after working three years at Mercy Medical Center, she found a position at Metpath Laboratories in Timonium, Maryland, in 1991. Again, she excelled in her work and was sent to additional courses and training in other states for one to two weeks at a time. The move to Timonium meant Lois had a thirty-minute drive, as opposed to the one-hour drive she made into downtown Baltimore. It was finally the perfect blend of our talents and time.

Things were going so well, we thought again about a second child even though Lois was nearing the age of thirty-nine. We discussed the options and the timing very seriously, then decided to wait a little while longer. We never had the chance to make it happen.

(A depiction of the "Poet's Tree" by Brooks Anderson, 2012).

The Poet's Tree

Tell me more about the dream . . .

Once I entered the dark realm, I found myself beneath an impossibly large spiraling tree. I knew the form suggested a tree as the phosphorescence illuminated the network of interlacing branches in a bath of eerie light. A kind of negative impression of its mass and size imprinted itself in the darkness. Somehow I knew I needed to sit, then rest, sleep, then dream beneath it. I can't remember moving. I transcended there. Within those moments between heartbeats, it happened. It became clear a vision, perhaps I could describe it as an enlightenment . . . or an epiphany. I didn't know what this place was, but I knew it was a place of reverence.

"Jonathan," Nathan called out, his form hidden behind an old tree leaning heavily against the enigmatic stone wall that stretched out forever.

"Yes, this looks like a good place to start," Jonathan said, surveying the long imposing wall. "The height of the wall is shorter here, and these huge fallen trees should hide our work. We should be able to work safely without any uninvited interruptions."

"I've been thinking about this," said Amelia, rounding the broken tree trunk obviously felled long ago by storms and strong winds.

The three friends were joined by two others. Victoria, a tall fair-haired woman about fifteen solens old, walked near a thick swarthy-looking young man they called Fog. Fog inherited his name when his friends noted that his deep voice sounded like the horns sounding over the hills on foggy nights. His real name, Fogerby, was purposely mispronounced by his tormenters for so long, he simply accepted the name Fog.

Amelia was not to be dismissed so easily by Jonathan in the presence of their friends. She looked at each of their arrivals, then continued her intense questioning: "What are we looking for on the other side of this wall, Jonathan?"

"Destiny . . . ," Jonathan said flatly, trying to locate a foothold in the stone wall.

"Destiny?" Amelia exclaimed as her small face, outlined by her long brown hair, twisted into a scowl. "How can you call this blasphemous act 'destiny' when we have been taught this wall is sacred? Sacred in the memories of the ones we loved, sacred in our thoughts of our ancestors, and sacred in the price of our own lives placed as stones in this wall. Why are we doing this, Jonathan?"

Victoria lagged behind Fog, walking lazily on the old unattended path running to a steep incline at the base of the wall. The path they walked on, they all knew, was called the "Last Road."

The name was not prescribed because it was the last road ever built by the villagers. The intention of the name meant it was the last walk any soul of the villages would ever take when they died. This was the road family and friends traveled to carry the lifestone of a fallen loved one and place it into the wall forever. Victoria saw a widening in the road and passed the slow-paced Fog, walking quickly to a place beside Amelia.

"You call this 'destiny, Jonathan? This is just an act of rebellion in my eyes," Victoria chided, now standing with her childhood friend Amelia.

"But it is destiny," Jonathan said calmly, not ever looking over his shoulder at the two young women obviously upset with him. Instead, he continued inspecting a large stone lying just beyond his reach. "Destiny, in my eyes," he continued, "is just another way of saying, 'This is our future. This is what we, as a people, need to find and put to rest for all time. We need to erase our fears and

misconceptions of our past.' If there is something to fear on the other side of this wall, then we will find it. As a team, we will go forward and discover, either for good or bad, what is on the other side of this wall. No more second-guesses, no more fear of the dark foreboding of our ancestors, no more bogeymen, no more childish fears . . . We will have facts. And facts are much better than frightening fairy tales our fathers and mothers told us in the dark. I don't want to live my life in a fairy tale anymore. I want to know what it is we are afraid of, if anything."

"I agree with Jonathan." The massive hulk named Fog boomed from the base of the wall where several ruined trees leaned tenaciously against the stone pilings. "We owe it to ourselves and our families to know what we are afraid of. We will find it on the other side of this wall."

"So if we find horrors on the other side, then do we say, 'Sorry, everybody, we found out that you were right after all . . .' then what? Do we return and tell everyone we desecrated the wall just to validate their fears? I'm not sure I can do that. I'm not sure any of you can do that," Amelia said, walking in deliberate circles around Fog and Victoria.

Jonathan finally stopped and looked at them, standing below his perch on the wall. He raised his hands like an offering to the gods and said, "What if there are no horrors? What if everything we ever heard was just some story to keep everything in tow . . . to control us . . . to keep us all from being something more than what we are? What if, instead of horrors, we find treasures . . . or secrets to make our lives better? What truths lie hidden behind this cursed wall?"

Jonathan looked sanely calm and more confident than any of their small group could ever remember. Amelia always saw Jonathan as a good friend, almost like a brother she never had. His strange attraction to investigate the other side of the wall after his mother died tried Amelia's patience and strained their friendship. The only reason she was even here was to talk Jonathan out of opening the wall. He seemed to have none of it. It was as if breaking through the wall would bring his mother back. Yet, Amelia realized, Jonathan really understood nothing would bring her back. Still, she could not reason what dark motives drove him to breach it. While they faced each other, Amelia at the base of the wall and Jonathan halfway up, he continued speaking. This time he looked directly at Amelia.

"Imagine," Jonathan said, "our ancestors realized they created something so advanced, so wondrous, but also so dangerous, they created the wall to keep it away from all of us. Then they created the myth about the wall so no one would ever try to find the secrets lying on the other side. Realize too it has been a century of centuries since the wall was created, and all we really do is add our 'lifestone'... the measure of a life. Is that really all we are in the wide scheme of things? Are we just a small stone, a rock at best, to be placed into the wall when we die? I, for one, would like to counter that. No, I want to reject that myth. Because I think we are more . . . more than just a stone . . . more than a tiny piece in this massive wall."

Jonathan turned away from his friends, picked a small stone from the wall, and threw it into the weeds growing near the Last Road. "For you, my forefathers, my mother, my ancestors." With that said, Jonathan began gathering larger stones, throwing them irreverently to the base of the wall. Nathan and Fog started clearing the loose stones from the bottom of the wall, moving them to one side, then to the other, forming a rudimentary path.

Nathan, lean but rugged looking, considered Victoria's and Amelia's parts in all this. After he moved a stone as big as his hand, he looked at the two girls and said, "Well, Victoria . . . Amelia"—he handed a basket to each of them—"you both ready to start?"

Victoria took both baskets from the skinny tangled-haired man, knowing Amelia wanted no parts of this desecration. She knew Nathan was rebellious. If there was some antiauthority activity going to happen, there you would find him. If there was some outrageous activity or feud, Nathan would be there. Now here he was, handing out baskets to collect and move stones from a wall older than time itself. It was the ultimate sacrilege . . . the ultimate, perhaps final, act of rebellion, and Jonathan was calling it "destiny."

"Well, Victoria," Amelia said, as she took one of the baskets from her, "what should we do?"

"I partly believe in what Jonathan is saying, but I understand what you are saying too. I think we should help, but when the time to cross over to the other side of the wall comes, I'm not going. I'm afraid of what we'll find there."

"Me too," Amelia said, fumbling with the handle of the basket. "Yet I'm not so sure once the wall is breached that we will be able to get through."

"What do you mean?" Victoria asked, wrinkling her forehead in a perplexed manner.

"What if whatever is on the other side comes pouring through it the second the wall is finally opened? What if we are all killed by something the wall is keeping out?"

"I don't think it will be like that," Victoria grimaced; she turned away, looking to collect some of the smaller stones the young men dislodged.

"Neither do I, but I would get ready to run the second that wall is breached," Amelia said, fear knotting her entire being.

Jonathan's cavalier yell came from a point near the top of the wall, "Hey, watch out, everybody. I'm throwing a big one down this time."

Amelia, concerned by Jonathan's arrogant defense of what he was doing, leaned against one of the fallen trees. She was not convinced what they were doing was right. She was amazed when they all began picking up the fallen stones, piling them in neat mounds next to the failing wall. These were not merely pieces of stone . . . these represented people's lives.

A chill convulsed her, becoming a violent shudder, almost knocking her to the ground. For a moment, her vision went dark and then blurred . . . She felt nauseated . . . She was going to be sick. Somehow, she still had the will and strength to stand. When the chill passed, she started to feel faint. Leaning heavily against the fallen tree, her perceptions of what she saw in front of her changed. Instead of watching Victoria, Fog, Nathan, and Jonathan breaking into the wall, quartering the fallen stones to either side of the pathway, she saw red tendrils and thick mists rushing forth from the aperture. She watched Jonathan running, screaming as some sort of indistinguishable orb attached itself to his back with silky red threads. She could not see her other companions but heard sounds of impossible animal screams . . . She knew they were human cries . . . but who or what could generate such agony? Then as quickly as these visions began, they stopped, leaving Amelia dripping in cold sweat.

Victoria collected some small stones in her basket and then turned back when she realized she never saw Amelia start gathering. From her position, she watched the color drain from Amelia's face as she struggled to keep her balance. She looked like a ghost tenuously holding on to a reality that no longer existed for her.

"Amelia, are you all right?" she called out.

Amelia leaned heavily against the fallen tree to support herself. "I'm not sure . . . I think I just saw something."

Victoria was alarmed. They were so careful not to let anyone see what they were doing. "Where?" she asked, thinking they had been discovered.

"Right there . . ." Amelia pointed a finger at the unopened passage Jonathan started into the wall, as some color returned to her face.

Victoria looked around. She saw nothing but the three young men furthering their ingress into the wall. Looking back at Amelia, seeing how pale she had become, made her realize something was very wrong. "What did you see, Amelia?"

Amelia stood straight up, supporting herself against the fallen tree. She looked down where one of the stones Jonathan had carelessly thrown landed near her feet. She leaned down, picked up the small stone, and then handed it to Victoria. She vacantly spoke a single word, "Destiny."

1-17-2012 A Life Ended Too Soon by Brooks Anderson

Small Signs

Tell me about that summer . . .

It was the early summer months of 1992. Lois was in our downstairs recreation room roughhousing with our twelve-year-old son. I was in the kitchen upstairs preparing food and sauces to start supper on the grill. I could hear the two of them laughing and yelling at each other playfully as I worked. I laughed to myself, knowing the sounds meant they were enjoying the afternoon. It made me happy to know all were at peace. It seemed so idyllic at the time; I never saw what was coming next.

As I sliced peppers and zucchini, I was distracted by the sound of a muffled thud followed by Lois's scream. I dropped everything and rushed downstairs, not knowing what I would walk into. When I made it to the bottom of the steps, I found Lois sitting on the sofa half crying, half laughing, holding a hand on a spot just above her right breast.

"What happened?" I asked calmly as I could, realizing she was injured.

"It was my fault. I stepped in front of Jim when he was showing me his karate kicks," she said calmly, still keeping pressure on the site.

"Jim, you have to be more careful," I told our son. "You can really hurt someone doing that."

"I know, Dad," he said rather sheepishly, knowing he was probably in trouble later on.

I looked over to where Lois was sitting and noticed she was starting to feel the sting of the injury and asked, "Do you need some ice?"

Still not looking up from the sofa, she said, "No, I think it will be okay. Just let me sit here awhile. Go ahead and get supper started."

Seeing she was still in pain, I said, "Ice would help."

Lois gave me a smile then said, "Stop fussing about me. I said I would be okay. Besides, Jim and I are hungry. Right, Jim?"

Our son nodded in agreement with his mother.

"Okay then. I'm just about ready to take the food outside and get started."

At the time, it seemed such a small event. Our lives were spoken about in the words of ordinary and peaceful. For the first time in our lives, nothing blocked our way. We had our home, our family, everyone was doing well, and we were finally working in stable jobs with a steady income. We were secure enough that we planned a trip to Disney World in Florida at the end of the summer. The day was beautiful to be outside. Later, when I had the food prepared and Lois settled down, we went outside and had a wonderful meal on the deck behind our house. For someone looking down on this, they would have seen a happy, contented family enjoying a lovely summer day. No one, not even us, would have thought the accidental injury would end up saving Lois's life and changing all of ours in the process.

Almost a week after the kick occurred, Lois showed me the small one-inch bruise at the top of the right breast. I asked if it hurt, and she told me, "Well, it feels bruised, but that's what it should feel like."

I had to agree, but the following month after her menses, she showed me the bruise again. Instead of shrinking, the bruise grew into a thin crescent over the top of the right breast. Once her cycle ended, the bruise seemed to stabilize and grew smaller. However, the bruise was never smaller than the one I saw the first week after the initial injury.

Three months later, we went to Disney World as we promised our son. When we had a quiet moment, I asked how the bruise was acting. What she showed me concerned and frightened me. The bruise, which started as a one-inch mark above her breast, now circled the entire right breast. Lois had two menstrual cycles since the initial bruise, and each cycle exacerbated the growth of the bruise to the point it was now.

"What do you think is happening?" she asked me, knowing my background as a nurse.

"I don't know what is going on, but the hormone fluctuation is definitely causing more bleeding under the skin. It looks painful," I said, trying not to be alarmed.

"I made an appointment with my ob-gyn when we get back," she told me. "As far as pain . . . it's not really pain . . . It feels more tender than anything else. I know this is not good. I will probably need surgery at some point."

"I'm hoping it is just some weird deep-tissue tear that needs to be drained or repaired," I said, thinking this was an injury-related bruise, nothing else.

We enjoyed our time at Disney World with our son that summer. We got back home, went to work, and resumed the life we loved until Lois saw her gynecologist in September 1992. Lois would be turning forty on October 6, so when her gynecologist could not find anything on an exam, he sent her for her first mammogram. He also suggested he would recommend a surgeon to check out the area where the bruising started. According to Lois, we were all working on the premise the bruise was injury related.

We never suspected anything. We never believed anything could enter our lives that could change our values or test our beliefs. Fate would not be on our side this time, but "destiny" still had many life chapters for Lois to write. She would write them well with courage and conviction. She had, to this point in her life, survived many battles, fought for the things she believed in, and protected those she loved. Her world was changing, and no one saw it coming, for if we had, it would have been like hearing the rampaging thunder before a storm. The rain would still fall; the best we could have done was watch the rain. We did . . .

The Fence

Tell me about a kiss . . .

Most of the time I spent with my maternal grandmother in the city existed looking through barriers. There were the windows, dusty from the street, smooth, flat, without edges, whisper clean on the inside and smeared by rain and probing fingers on the outside. Outside, it was the close-knit walls like a maze, dark and twisted, that seemed to barricade us all. The other barriers, which may seem strange to mention, were the fences that ran between the properties behind the houses. Of course the fence that ran behind my grandmother's house to the garage at the end of her property is the one this story is about.

The sidewalk became my play area while I stayed in town. I used it as a highway for cars, a plateau for my army, and a road to Dodge if I played cowboys and Indians. It was whatever my imagination decided I would play that day. Alongside the sidewalk ran a wire fence made of interwoven arches running from the top of the fence to the ground. Its construction gave the appearance of miniature arches running between the backyards to the garage at the far end of the property. The fence was sturdy and unbreakable. A small child might be able to put their hands through the fence with little problem, but even a small animal like a cat or dog could not pass through the tightly interlaced wires. The fence was supported on steel poles set in concrete with one exception. In the middle of the neighbor's property, an old walnut tree stood. The laborers, who built the fence long before I stayed with my grandmother, were forced to incorporate the huge tree into the fence. By doing so, the walnut tree became the focal midpoint of the fence.

From the back of my grandmother's house to its most distant point, where the modestly built garage stood, was perhaps fifty feet. While small to an adult, the distance was huge to a child of eight or nine. It was a wonderful play area for a child. It was enclosed, safe, and easily observed by my grandmother's many stares out her kitchen window. On the other side of the sidewalk was a rope tied from one post to the next running the entire perimeter of the yard. We were told never to cross the rope or we would be punished. It meant we would be confined to the house for a week or so. Being confined to the house was not something either I or my brother preferred to do. To stay out of trouble with Grandma, we stayed between the rope and the wire fence.

The utter confinement bred the seeds of imagination. It was the polar opposite of my adventures on the farm, different, not better, not worse. Besides, my brother and I loved it here. It was here that imagination formed, starting from the great wide world of the farm and ending in the smallest world on a dusty sidewalk. A new world grew from inside us. It was here, on an imaginary road to nowhere, that I could be anything and everything. It honed the skills of my imagination.

Next door, where the walnut tree grew, lived a girl and a boy about the same age as my brother and I. In spite of the fence that acted as an obvious deterrent, we all played together during the summer. Bobby and Joy were a diversion when my younger brother had to take his afternoon nap, something my grandmother insisted on. I being the older brother meant I had some privileges my younger brother did not. Many times when I played alone, Bobby would come out, and we would play race cars on our parallel sidewalks. Sometimes we would get all our cars out and play traffic jam. We would line up twenty toy cars and pretend there was an accident on the road, and we would have to get people to the hospital. Other times we pretended to be cowboys hunting the bad guys. Bobby was perhaps a year or two older than my brother, but it still made him younger than me. His sister, Joy, was about a year older than me. Though Bobby was a lot of fun to play with, I always liked when Joy came out to play with us.

Joy would not play with cars or toy guns, though. She was a typical girl and loved dolls and playhouses. When she came out, she forced Bobby into tea parties and playing house. The exceptional part of Joy was her fiery-red hair and blue eyes. I never really got close to a girl before, and Joy made it known she didn't like boys as a rule, but Bobby and I were okay to play with.

Since I stayed with my maternal grandmother for many years over the summer, I got to watch my friends Bobby and Joy grow up with me. My brother was eventually old enough to join us in our backyard playground, and he and Bobby had many adventures as well. Since Bobby was younger than Joy and me, the natural tendency for Bobby to play cars and army men fell to my younger brother. When Joy came outside and wanted to play house, we needed the other players to join in on our house play. Joy would enlist my brother and Bobby, who were none too happy to be pulled away from their toys.

As we all grew up in our tiny world, Joy would ask me real-life questions.

"What are you going to do when you grow up?" was one of her favorites. Of course, the conversation eventually got back to marriage, children, and where are you going to live? We decided when we both grew up, we would get married to someone. She wasn't sure whom she would marry but said she couldn't marry me because I was a year younger than she was.

Most times when we played in the yard, both my grandmother and their mother kept watch over all of us. It was a fact the four of us suspected but didn't really know until later. Both my grandmother and their mother would call each other on the phone to keep watch on all of us. The adult women would do this so if one of them ever needed to go out for something, someone could keep an eye on us. As children, we suspected we were being watched, but none of us knew of the pact that existed between my grandmother and their mother. Even so, it was child's play for us. It was innocent. Nothing would happen or could happen in our little enclosed playground. Besides, there was a fence that kept both Bobby and Joy on their side of the fence, and me and my brother on the other.

On our last summer together with Bobby and Joy, there was a different feel in the air. I knew it when my brother and I started playing in the yard. We got out the box of toy cars and army men, but neither of us seemed to be too interested. So we just got the toys out, lined them up, and looked at them. Eventually, we just walked to the end of the sidewalk where the garage stood at the end of the yard. We were listless, yet we were boiling with energy. We both hoped Joy and Bobby would come out to play. My grandmother saw the two of us moping about and asked what we were doing. We said we were waiting for Bobby and Joy to come out.

My grandmother, who had been leaning out the kitchen window, said, "Well, I'll call them and see if they are home." My brother and I looked at each other in surprise. Our grandmother had a secret way to contact the neighbor next door. It was the first time my brother and I realized she probably had been doing this for quite some time. Joy once told me their phone number was unlisted, which meant Joy's mother must have given Grandma their phone number at some time. This also meant they probably had spoken together more than once over the years. We felt betrayed—"betrayed" because the adults did not let us know we were under constant watch. But in a way, it was comforting to know we were important enough to merit observation by both women. Still, it was a revelation to us that we were never away from someone's surveillance.

After a few minutes, my grandmother called out the window that Bobby and Joy were on their way back from the movies and would come out to play when they were back. Her answer satisfied my brother and me. We returned to playing with the cars and army men we set up earlier. Even as we played, my brother and I sensed something different about that summer. The toys were not as entertaining or as interesting as before. It was more difficult to focus on creating imaginary worlds where we always won the battles or rescued the day. We were growing up. Toys were almost a thing of the past, though we still thought of them as a way to pass the time. When Bobby and Joy returned, we understood why we felt like we did.

Joy and Bobby came out to play like they normally did on those long summer afternoons. We all gathered by the fence with Joy and Bobby on one side, myself and my brother on the other and talked. We caught up on the things we did together the previous summer, and then we talked about the things we did in school. None of the things we usually did on a day like this ever entered our minds. We simply stood there talking for hours. Joy and I talked about music we liked on the radio, while Bobby and my brother talked about school and the teachers they liked. While the conversation was interesting, we hardly realized no one was playing with anything. The toys we left stayed where they were, and neither Joy nor Bobby brought anything out to do. It was about time for my mother to pick up my brother and I, before we realized all we had done was talk.

The next day, when my brother and I went out to play with Bobby and Joy, they were all dressed up like they were going out somewhere. Bobby solved the mystery of his Sunday clothes when he told us they were moving away. Joy seemed upset but explained she was not upset with either my brother or me. She held back saying anything more for a moment then asked me to meet her down by the tree. She said she wanted to tell me something and give me something. Bobby looked at the two of us then said, "We have to say good-bye, but we will write to you. Right, Joy?"

"Yes, we will try to write." But Joy's tone of voice did not really convince me they would.

"Maybe we could write to you," I said. "Do you have an address, a phone number to reach you and Bobby?"

"We don't know yet," Joy said to me, somewhat irritated.

"You don't know?" I asked, puzzled that someone wouldn't know where they were going to be living.

"My dad didn't come home a few weeks ago, and my mom said we can't stay here anymore," Joy said, as tears welled up in the corners of her eyes.

"Did he get hurt? Was he in an accident?" I asked, concerned that Joy and Bobby had lost their father.

Joy turned away from me because she did not want me to see her cry. Bobby looked away from my brother and then told me, "My father moved in with someone else. That's all she knows. That's why she can't tell you anything . . . We don't know." Bobby, in his childlike innocence, went to his sister and held her hand. Joy brushed him away then turned to me. With her cheeks still wet with tears, she said, "Come on, let's go to the tree. There's not much time."

I followed her to the tree, Joy on her side of the fence, and I on mine. She leaned against the fence and told me she liked me a lot. She told me if we would have had the time, she could have been in love with me. I knew I liked Joy, even though she was a girl, but love? I remembered all those summers when she and I would play together, and she would send our younger brothers to play by themselves. I had wondered what she did with the rest of her year. Did she think of me, because so many times I thought about her? Was I just a playmate or more than that? I was almost twelve, and Joy was going on thirteen that summer. So could love exist in children so young? My heart was pounding, and I still hadn't said anything to Joy. I stuttered, "But you're leaving . . ."

"I know, but I wanted to tell you before we left." Joy was still leaning against the fence like she wanted to get as close to me as she possibly could. "It just doesn't seem like there's anything else to say," Joy muttered as if she was going to start crying again.

Then I asked, "Are you going right now? Don't we have any more time than right now?"

"No, this is all the time we have. We are leaving as soon as we say good-bye to you both. You have been good friends over our summers together. My mom thought it was only right to say something."

"Could we write to each other?" I tried again as a last resort.

"Sure, but I'll have to write first. I don't have an address where you could write to me yet. Your grandmother's address is the same as mine, except the house number, so I could write first."

"I will miss you," I said with my head bowed.

"I'll miss you both, but especially you."

I raised my head until I was looking into Joy's face. Her cheeks were wet with tears. I leaned against the fence and put my fingers through the wire fence. She put her fingers through and intertwined them with mine. The fence wires became smaller over time, never allowing our once smaller hands that ability to put our hands completely through. Still, we had the bodies of children and the tree trunk blocked the view from my grandmother's window and her mother's window. We leaned our faces against the wire fence as Joy said, "This is to remember me by . . ." It was an awkward but simple kiss, lasting just the briefest of seconds. It was given without time or a place to be by ourselves and a strong wire fence to separate us. Apparently, our being out of sight made both my grandmother and Joy's mother nervous. Almost simultaneously, they started yelling for us to come into the house.

"Good-bye," Joy said to me as we walked slowly to our separate houses.

"Good-bye. I won't forget you. Write to me soon." I felt my heart breaking. Somehow, watching Bobby and Joy slowly walking into their house for the last time made me think it was the last time I would ever hear or see them again.

Bobby and Joy left their home in the early part of June that summer. I waited for some kind of word from them all summer long, but no letters came to my grandmother's house. After school started, I asked my grandmother if she had heard anything from their mother over the summer. She told me Joy's mother had called her sometime about July to say she wasn't coming back again. Apparently, Joy's mother had moved to somewhere in Ohio but did not give an address. I told my grandmother Joy promised to write. According to my grandmother, Joy's mother had not settled into a permanent place.

By Christmas, I was concerned something happened to them. When I saw my grandmother for Christmas dinner, I asked if she heard anything more from any of them. Grandma told me she had a brief conversation with Joy's mother just after Thanksgiving. She told Grandma everyone was doing okay. She was staying with relatives with Joy and Bobby. She didn't want to give out an address or phone number of the family member she was staying with.

Eventually, both my grandmother and I lost touch with them. I never saw or heard from them again. An older couple moved in next door to my grandmother. She was delighted, since they shared more in common than Joy's mother. They also shared a love of gardening as did my grandmother. Soon, the naked mud yard, which served as Bobby and Joy's playground, grew into a lush garden of flowers, fruit trees, and grass. The walnut tree continued to stand where it was.

My times of coming to the city to stay with my maternal grandmother were drawing to a close. I was growing up most of those last summers I spent on the farm. In time, I stopped thinking and worrying about Bobby and Joy. In my mind, I saw them both grow up and be happy . . . but I never really knew. I never forgot them. I never forgot Joy and my first kiss. A kiss given behind a tree, in front of my grandmother and Joy's mother, and a fence meant to keep us apart, a feeling strong enough to break barriers and make it happen anyway.

It seemed so small at the time, but the kiss was given against all odds and restraints I somehow realized in time how courageous love can be. It takes a lot of courage to love, and that perhaps, more than anything, is what Joy left with me. Perhaps the courage to love is the most powerful lesson any of us can ever learn . . . and I learned it from the heart and hands of a child . . . one I used to know.

Transformation

Tell me about change . . .

    With the results of the mammogram in her gynecologist's hands, he called Lois into his office to discuss the results. Lois was told her results did not show anything to be concerned about. The mammogram results revealed the tissues were too dense to be read, a common finding in a young woman, as Lois was. However, because the bruising continued to spread, he felt Lois needed a surgeon to check out the site. We knew something was wrong. We just didn't know how wrong until later.

(From a journal written by Lois A. Anderson):

*   I had been to my gynecologist for my annual exam in June of 1992 and everything was normal. He gave me a request to have a baseline mammogram done before I turned forty in the fall. However, before that could happen, and just about one month later, I was accidentally hit by my son as he demonstrated his karate moves. I got in the way and got caught by a move that hit me across my right breast. I had a bruise but I didn't think anything of it. But the bruise recurred about the time I was ovulating in August.*

*   This scared me and I set up the appointment for the mammogram as soon as I could get it. The mammogram was reported as "tissue too dense to read," and the radiologist referred me back to my gynecologist. I called the gynecologist but was unable to get an appointment until almost mid-September. I did a self breast exam the night before this appointment and found a lump. This was the first time I had anything that was palpable and I was scared. Needless to say, I slept very little that night.*

*   During the exam the next day I called the gynecologist's attention to the lump I found. He could very easily feel it as he said to me, "You want to know what this is, don't you?" "Of course I do" was my answer and I*

was referred to a surgeon for biopsy. I saw the surgeon the very next week and the biopsy was scheduled for October 12, 1992. The surgeon performed the open biopsy with the thought in his head that this would only be fatty necrosis because of the injury I had suffered. However, that was not to be the case.

(End of journal entry . . .)

On Monday. October 12, 1992, Lois's surgeon did a biopsy of the right breast. We were told, considering the injury, he felt it could be endometriosis of the breast. This condition, under these circumstances, was very rare to find in the breast, but also very possible.

Ten days after the biopsy, the surgeon wanted to see Lois in his office to report the findings of the biopsy. He scheduled her to be the last patient to be seen, and at the time, I thought nothing of it. Lois still worked during the day, so his office staff would have tried to accommodate her schedule. I knew Lois was very nervous, as she was entirely too quiet, saying very little on the way to the office. When we arrived, we found the waiting room completely empty. I thought it was strange, but since Lois was the last patient to be seen, it did not seem terribly out of place. Usually, the nurse would take Lois back to the exam room; but this time, the surgeon himself opened the door and asked Lois to come back. A chill went down my spine. Lois's surgeon, a normally gregarious person, seemed grave and serious. Something was very wrong. I could tell by the robotic way Lois walked back with him she also knew something was wrong.

No more than five minutes later, the surgeon came back and asked me to go back to the exam room with Lois. In the exam room, I found two prearranged chairs sitting together, with Lois seated in one of them. Another chair sat farther back in the room where the surgeon sat with a folder in his lap. Upon entering, I realized the room was prepared for both of us. The surgeon had me sit down next to Lois, and from behind, his nurse stood by the open door. Lois slid her hand into mine. She was cold as ice. She was shaking uncontrollably and seemed like she was going into shock.

"I have some bad news for you both," he started, as Lois and I sat stunned by what was yet to unfold. Lois went from just being cold to almost completely stiff and frigid; she started to lean heavily against me. Somehow I thought he was going to tell us she needed a mastectomy to stop the progression of the bleeding around the breast. That much I had been prepared for. I was not prepared for what he said next.

(From a journal written by Lois A. Anderson)

I remember returning to my surgeon's office for a follow-up exam about ten days after the biopsy had been done. My husband came along and he was in the waiting room while the surgeon took care of me. There was something very strange about this appointment, but I couldn't quite figure out what it was.

As the surgeon did his thing, we conversed. For some strange reason my mind must have picked up on something he said or maybe it was how he said it, I don't know, but a bright white neon flashing light went off in my head that read, "This is Cancer." It kept flashing its very white bright light until the surgeon said he had some news to tell me. He asked me if I wanted my husband present. Of course I did, and he went to the waiting room and my husband returned following the surgeon back into the exam room.

(End of journal entry)

"You have breast cancer . . ." the surgeon informed us with barely a second to recover ourselves.

I did not know how to respond. Lois could not speak and simply went from her frozen state into a mountain of tears. The nurse said something, but I tuned out everything but my wife's tears. The surgeon continued talking, but I couldn't follow anything of what he was saying. It took me a moment to realize I was crying, and Lois was almost hysterical with tears. The best we could do was to make another appointment in a week to discuss options. The one thing I did remember was the cancer had been there a long time. One of the lymph nodes the surgeon removed was completely riddled with cancer.

Somehow, Lois regained her composure long enough to ask, "How are we going to tell Jimmy (our then twelve-year-old son)? He will think he is the cause of this."

The surgeon's actions and words had been well thought out. He told us this: "I've known about your diagnosis for a few days. I spent the whole weekend trying to find the words to tell you about the cancer. I knew there would be a problem telling your son, and I think you need to tell him he is the hero in all this. In fact, if he had not hit you at that exact spot, at this time, this cancer would have been too far along to do anything to help you. Right now, the laboratory results tell us this is a stage III breast cancer. It's not good, but treatable. We'll know more after surgery."

We both acknowledged the surgeon's advice on how to tell our son about his role in finding her cancer. We both felt this approach was a good one. In fact, it was true. We made an appointment for a week later. We went home to tell our son and everyone else that cancer had invaded our home. Everything had changed. The world we had lived in ended abruptly. The quiet realm where we existed, made decisions, and went on family outings and vacations died on that day. Camelot was burning. A terrible enemy had breached the walls. The essence of what we believed to be valuable changed as we grasped for that which our enemy, cancer, was trying to steal. Our lives of planning for next year and the years after it were gone. That certainty of waking up alive and in good health the next day was no longer a distinct or probable possibility. Everything we believed as our future of possibilities disappeared, because cancer would not allow us any certainty of what tomorrow held. Sometimes it was difficult to consider "tomorrow" in terms of living through it, much less a span of time we could take for granted. After a cancer diagnosis crosses the threshold of one of the lives you care about, you savor the special moments of your life, and the lives around you, in an entirely different way.

(From a journal written by Lois A. Anderson)

As my husband stood beside me, the surgeon in his best and most empathetic way softly broke the news to us. I remember holding on long enough to say, "Oh my God, what are we going to do about Jimmy?" The surgeon replied, "You know I've been thinking about this all weekend long. Why don't you try to make Jimmy the hero in all of this? Present it to him in a way that if this accident had not happened, he probably would not even have his mother in another year or two." I was so glad that I was guided to this surgeon by my referring doctor because I don't think any other surgeon would have been able to handle the situation the way he did. I lost it after this because I had my answer on how to handle my son. At that point my twelve-year old son was the sole important person in my world. My husband, who was and still is a registered nurse, could take care of himself, but my son still had a lot of growing up to do. Without a mother I didn't think he could grow into the man he now is. Because of the extent of the cancer in my breast and because we knew a lymph node had already exploded with tumor cells, a mastectomy was recommended. The surgery was scheduled for November 23, 1992, a few days before Thanksgiving.

(End of journal entry)

At her next appointment with the surgeon, Lois discussed her upcoming mastectomy and lymph node dissection. We discussed the need to see an oncologist after the surgery. Lois decided on a new oncologist just starting in the local practice near our home. The right-sided mastectomy and right axillary node dissection took place on November 23, 1992.

(From a journal by Lois A. Anderson)

My emotions were on a rollercoaster at this time, and a dream kept taking place over and over again for about two weeks. I would go to sleep and, after several hours, a scene of an old wooden ship like the ones used by the Pilgrims, moored beside an old wooden dock would begin. I was standing by the gangplank of the ship checking off names on a list. I could see some of the faces as clear as could be, but others were shadowy. However, I could tell there were both men and women here going into this ship. My amateur psychological interpretation of this dream is that I was loading people onto a ship who were helping me and who would be helping me in the future to battle this breast cancer. I also knew there would be rough seas and calm seas ahead for all of us in this ship.

Another step I took during these first weeks after my biopsy that helped me get through all of this was I made a vow to myself that I remain true to even today. I vowed that

I would do whatever it took so that any woman did not have to walk in my shoes as a breast cancer patient. This took a lot of introspection and I know my husband thought I was headed for a major depression, but it was something I had to do in order to heal myself from inside out. Little did I know that this vow would lead me into volunteering for local, statewide, and national organizations and that it would change my career.

Dream inside a Dream

Tell me about the dream . . .

As I grew, the banishing darkness parted with thin gauzy light. Luminosity dressed in deep mists danced like rivers through the familiar wooded ravines where I traveled before. Confused and undecided by their spectacle and complexity, I aimlessly choose direction, chasing rivers of light to the end of consequence, stopped by barriers of outcropping rock or an open field spanning forever . . . with nothing in sight. When I stirred from the dreams of seeking, I awoke rested, not enlightened. It was the shadows' intention to map the course I would follow there.

It was only in the dream within a dream where I would stumble upon the great tree. From there, I returned to the waking world to write poems from recollected time when I stayed, dreaming beneath its dark branches. There was the destiny I longed to find again. In this conscious dream, I would lie near a river of light to sleep. Dreaming as a sleeper in a dream, I dreamed I woke again beside the great tree. Whispers, vague and unintelligible, assaulted my mind . . . then abruptly went silent. It was in silence where I heard the birth of words, crying at their inception. The inarticulate words were slaved in despondent discord, yet in their wholeness, great truths were revealed. I knew their memories and sought to write their beautiful sadness. If only I could remember . . . sometimes I could. Yet in the waking world, only fragments of this broken vase of dreams remained. With mere fragments I tried to piece together memories, eventually truth would reveal its epiphany in a line of words.

Leena finished with her morning household rituals then started wondering what her daughter Catherine was doing.

"Catherine . . . Catherine!" she called loudly from the bottom of the stairway leading to the upper bedrooms. "When are you coming down? It's about midmorning, and I have yet to see or hear anything from you." Leena made a few steps up the stairs and stopped. "Catherine . . ."

Catherine sat on her bed with a thick leather-bound ledger Timothy gave her after their engagement. She was writing in it when she heard her mother calling. The ledger was to use at her discretion. Timothy hoped it would act as a kind of guide, or list, in which she could write things down to help with the wedding plans. Catherine thought she would keep lists of who to invite to the wedding, what she would wear, what Timothy and his groomsmen would wear, flowers, food, the whole thing. The ledger was special because the tooled covering was made from the valued leather from his father's shop.

Timothy made the ledger for Catherine. He carefully inscribed the leather cover with the words "To My Love." It made the book so personal she did not want to use it as a wedding planner. After thinking what she wanted to do, she decided the beautiful ledger would become her personal diary, a book to put her dreams into. In the leather-bound ledger, she kept her thoughts, her daily routines, her time with Timothy, and her time with her family. She thought of the ledger as a "scribe-keeper," a written journey of her days for as long as she existed. She was writing some of her thoughts when she heard her mother calling.

"Catherine . . . Catherine, what are you doing?"

"Just jotting some notes, Mother. Did you need me for something?" Catherine answered petulantly.

Leena appeared at the doorway of Catherine's room, hands on her hips, her flowered skirt almost brushing the floor. "Do you know what time it is? We have at least a dozen places to be today."

"I thought my day was pretty clear. In fact, Timothy will be here in the afternoon when he gets back from Glade."

"Well, I think I can get you back a little while to visit Timothy, but I need you along to get fitted for your wedding clothes. Also, there are places we need to be where I need your decisions. So hurry up and get dressed. We need to make the most of the morning, okay?"

Catherine turned to her mother with a smile. "Yes, it sounds like fun. Let me put my book away. I'm sure Timothy will understand." Then as an afterthought, Catherine said excitedly, "Maybe he could come along and help."

Leena rolled her eyes. She was trying to get Catherine moving. "That may depend on Timothy's father, Catherine. It's the end of the solen, and his family is very busy."

Catherine, not to be dissuaded, continued her insistence to bring Timothy along. "Well, I'm sure he would let Timothy go along if you said something to Jakob."

"I'm not about to come between Timothy's father and Timothy, so let's get moving," Leena told her daughter.

"Oh, Mother, how hard would it be? I'm certain Jakob would be okay with letting Timothy off a few hours, especially if you asked him."

"Let's see what Timothy has to say when he gets here. He may know if his father needs him badly this afternoon or not."

"Yes, okay," Catherine smiled. She knew she could talk Timothy into anything.

Catherine closed the leather book that had become her diary, tying the leather straps to hold it closed. She placed it under her bed for safekeeping. Her quiet day suddenly became very busy. She went to her closet, removed a beautiful blue dress, and placed it on the unmade bed. She looked out her bedroom window and took a few seconds to watch the road leading out of Stock, where it wandered through the many hills and glens to the neighboring village of Glade. The road known as Wall Road ran parallel to the stone wall, set just a parcel away from it. Catherine smiled, as she thought Timothy passed by her house not but a few hours before she was awake. She was sure he was thinking of her when he passed by. She was looking forward to their afternoon when he arrived.

"Catherine," Leena called from the kitchen, "I don't hear you getting ready."

"Oh, Mother, be patient. I have my clothes out, and I won't be that long."

"Well, hurry up. The day won't wait forever."

"Yes, I know," Catherine sighed, as she pulled her brush through tangles of her golden hair. The leather book stayed hidden beneath Catherine's bed. Little did she know it would be the last time she would see the ledger again.

The village of Glade was six or seven parcels north of the village of Stock. To the south of Stock, the nearest village was the village of Lexington, where livestock was bought and sold; and beyond were the villages of Roe, Tansumas, Landell, Worthingdon, and Rossland. There were many villages beyond these, but Timothy did not know all their names. To the north, it was much the same. The village of Glade stocked many tools, ointments, and solvents, which were bought, sold, and traded with the other villages. Wendow, located just north of Glade, was known for its fine glassware and tableware for the village homes. North of Wendow was Bridgedom, known for its famous bridge, which spanned a deep ravine where a visitor could not see the bottom. The Great Bridge, as it was called, created a way to the more-northerly villages of Vigil and Emansupass. Beyond, the mountains sprang up, and the roadways became scarce and difficult to determine by ordinary means. There were oxen roads for travelers, but travel was very difficult and treacherous for horses and wagons. Travel beyond Emansupass was generally taken using footpaths and an experienced guide if you were traveling to the Northlands. Truth be told, very few passed beyond this most northern village. Still, some ventured there into snow-covered mountain passes for hunting and for knowledge.

It was said somewhere in the mountain passes was another village lost by time and disuse. The legends surrounding this particular village were haunting and ominous. This particular village was to have been a center for learning at one time. If it ever existed, it would be a great find, since it was reputed to have held a spectacular library, which held secrets about the origins of the villages and the wall.

The name of this legendary village was Winterland. If the old stories about the village were true, then why did no one ever find it and return to the villages to share the knowledge or its location to others? Almost everyone believed the village of Winterland was a myth, and most people did not have any great need to quest for "library books." The people of the lower villages used their time working the fields and following the simple lives their ancestors followed for centuries. The need to find the mythical village of Winterland was not enticing enough for anyone to risk their life trying to find it. As a result, it stayed the myth . . . a tragic legend.

𑿗

Catherine hurried Leena to and from the crowded shops of Stock. Catherine flew from shop to shop like a bee, lighting from one flower to another, briefly examining each shop's wares. Leena hopelessly requested Catherine to stop long enough to examine and price some of the goods they were seeing.

"Catherine, please slow down," Leena pleaded, almost out of breath.

"But, Mother, these cloths are beautiful. I don't know which one I would pick," Catherine said, rushing her mother toward a sheaf of richly colored materials.

"Well, we need to decide some things today, some next week, and some can wait awhile. But if you are to have a wedding dress, I need materials yesterday," Leena scolded.

"Benjamin's store had some pretty cloths . . . ," Catherine stated sheepishly, "that I've had my eye on for weeks." Knowing her

mother's thriftiness may not coincide with Benjamin's price for the items she had seen made her reluctant to bring up the subject.

"Anything Benjamin might be able to sell or trade us today would make me happy to negotiate with him," Leena said, intrigued by her daughter's ability to have actually made some decisions on her own.

"Well," Catherine said, putting a finger to the side of her pursed lips like she was thinking, "yes, I believe the cloth we need might be there."

"If we are to get done in time for you to see Timothy when he gets back, we better hurry to the other side of the village as soon as we can, right?" Leena asked, looking directly into Catherine's face to get her attention.

"To be honest, Mother, I haven't seen anything in these shops to interest me. But I have been watching Benjamin's shop this past week and saw something that would be beautiful material for a wedding dress."

"It's settled then . . . to Benjamin's store . . . in a hurry," Leena proposed.

In the very busy streets of Stock, Catherine and Leena set out for Benjamin's shop. Their way was impeded by the multitude of customers out for bargains and stocking supplies for late solen. Catherine watched the time closely, since Timothy promised to be back from Glade in the early afternoon. Still, something was giving her a deep chill as goose flesh fell on her arms and neck. The day was very uncommon for late solstice. Instead of the normally cold air, the morning was humid and warm like a summer's day, making this feeling of coldness most peculiar.

Leena was having a hard time keeping up to her daughter on the rough cobbled streets. She was about to tell Catherine to slow down when Catherine stopped in the middle of the street. Her daughter seemed to stare off into the distance while passersby walked around her from all directions.

"Catherine, whatever are you doing?" Leena asked, concerned by her abrupt change of pace.

"I just felt strange for a moment, like a deep chill just passed over me," Catherine said, trying to shake off the feeling.

"I hope you're not getting sick. That's the last thing I need right now with all these errands to run today."

"It seems to be passing now," Catherine said, as she started feeling a little better.

Leena reached out and touched her daughter's forehead, "Well, you feel fine, not too warm there." Then Leena brushed up against Catherine's forearm as she tried to move away. Her forearm felt as cold as a corpse, yet the color was still good. "Perhaps we should get you into the shade and rest a little . . . I think you just had too much sun," Leena said, concern coloring her voice.

"All right, Mother. I am feeling a little better, but a short rest would be good for both of us, I think."

Leena looked around and saw an unoccupied bench near a dress shop. She led Catherine to it and had her sit down. Leena sat with her, pulling Catherine's hands into her own. "What's wrong, sweetheart? Are you getting the 'jitters' about getting married?"

"No . . . Timothy is a wonderful man, and I love him very much. This is something different. This is like what people tell me happens when you are too far away from your lifestone."

"But, Catherine, we're not even one parcel away from your stone right now. I'm sure it isn't that."

"I know, but I felt something you and I know cannot happen this close to the stone Father picked for me." Catherine thought for a moment then said very seriously, "Mother, no one would try to move my stone away, would they?"

Though Leena thought the idea was preposterous, it was something she hadn't considered. It was a grave accusation. If such a thing were to occur, the person or persons involved in moving or taking another person's lifestone would be considered very serious. The powers that controlled the lives of the various villages would exact severe justice. A person who moved a stone beyond three parcels of the owner would be required to place their own lifestone into the wall. Afterward, the person would be stricken with a terrible illness. The illness would last three days. That person would be given one chance, and only one chance, to return the person's lifestone to them before their stone became a permanent part of the wall. If this wasn't accomplished, the thief or thieves would die at the end of three days. There were no exceptions. There wasn't anyone born in the villages unaware of the consequences of stealing someone's "lifestone." Still, Leena was concerned about her daughter's feeling something was wrong.

"Catherine, how are you feeling now?" Leena asked, unsuccessfully keeping concern out of her voice.

Catherine, after resting a short time, felt the coldness pass as if it never happened. Yet for her, the incident was disquieting. She rubbed over her arms then ran a hand over her brow. They felt normal to her again. She looked at her mother and said, "I feel fine now. You may have been right about being out in the sun too long."

"Well, if you feel like that again, stop me, and I'll get you home."

"I do feel good again. Should we continue on to Benjamin's store?"

"You're really feeling okay?" Leena asked, not convinced Catherine was being honest with her.

"Of course, don't be silly," Catherine said, laughing, "We have to get some of our things done today, or it will be worse to get done later on. Isn't that what you've been telling me all day?"

"You're right, of course. Let's go."

Leena and Catherine abandoned the bench residing before the shop then walked through the crowds clustered on the cobbled streets.

They passed Arch Street and Glydow Avenue, where the most unique treasures were displayed in picturesque windowpanes. Transient onlookers pointed here and there, looking through the elegant shop windows. Leena and Catherine moved through the crowded streets, talking about the wedding, the nice weather, and other things, as they made their way. Never once did they bring up the incident Catherine felt in front of the dress shop. Eventually, after walking a parcel in excited conversations, they found themselves in front of Benjamin's shop.

"Look, Mother, in the front window . . ." Catherine's excitement was as obvious to her mother as it was to anyone standing within earshot.

Leena crossed in front of her daughter and saw the most exquisite white cloth, with just the faintest trace of pink, produced by gossamer pink threads woven in lines through the material. Leena watched the sunlight reflect brightly on the pink threads, giving the illusion it had a pinkish glow, though it still appeared white. "I'll bet Benjamin will want a pretty price for this!" Leena stated, shaking her head.

"We can look around for something else," Catherine said, disappointed by the tone in her mother's voice.

"Before he disappoints us with a price, let's go inside and see what else he may have to offer. It will be difficult to outdo this material, but we'll look anyway. Is that all right with you?" Leena asked, hoping Catherine hadn't set her mind on the material in the window.

Before Leena could catch her next breath, Catherine grabbed her mother's arm and pulled her toward the open door of Benjamin's shop. "Sure, let's go in."

Catherine led Leena into Benjamin's shop. The shop was crowded with noisy customers looking for heavy materials to make clothes for the upcoming winter solstice. Most customers were just looking at the bales of cloth Benjamin offered. Yet quite a few were buying heavy wools and tassel cloth to make shirts and heavy pants.

Benjamin also had a hundred small bins of buttons to choose from. There were large ones, metal ones, bejeweled ones, and very simple ones of coined bone for everyday use. There were laces for tying up or bunching materials in a cinch. Ribbons of all colors lay on the tables he prepared after Timothy had spoken to him. There were sewing needles, knitting needles, and all kinds of sewing and darning equipment. Benjamin had skeins of yarns of all colors set on wooden spools. It was a fascinating spectacle for the eyes to see, drawing many customers into his store, which pleased Benjamin very much.

"I'll bet I know what you ladies are looking for." Benjamin smiled, seeing Leena and Catherine approach him.

"And you would be right . . ." Leena playfully chided.

"Yes, your busy day is coming up, and I have a lot of cloth on sale that may interest you, if you don't mind an old man showing you around," Benjamin said, extending an arm toward Catherine.

"Not at all," Catherine said, as she took the arm leading her toward the front of the store.

"It just so happens I got this cloth in a few days ago," Benjamin said excitedly. "Not too many people are in the market for it, and my vendor, though realizing its value, also understands very few people would have a use for it. So he decided to sell it at cost," Benjamin said, looking in Leena's direction before continuing, "which makes it very cheap." He pulled Catherine to the front window where the beautiful white material with the glowing pink threads waited for her. "This is it. What do you think?"

Catherine could not believe Benjamin led her to the very window where the beautiful wedding dress material was displayed. Leena, close behind them, heard every word Benjamin spoke. Catherine could barely contain herself. "Oh, Benjamin, I love it. We saw this outside the store and were going to ask you about it, but you figured it out before I could get in a word." Catherine turned and hugged Benjamin as her mother stood back and left out a sigh. "How much?" asked Catherine, barely able to breathe.

"Why don't you stay here and get acquainted with the cloth . . . Don't be afraid to touch it. I hear it is nearly perfect cloth," Benjamin told her.

"Are you sure?" Catherine asked, sliding into the display window to touch the fine material.

"Of course . . . and while you examine the material, I will discuss a price with your mother. Is that all right with you, Leena?"

"Well, if it's a fair price," Leena said dubiously.

"I think you will find it a very fair price," smiled Benjamin, leading Leena off to the side. Catherine continued to admire the fine pink threads and beautiful craftsmanship of the cloth. She could hear her mother and Benjamin nearby, haggling over the price. The sunlight profusely illuminated Benjamin's display window as shoppers looked in to see Catherine's mesmeric stare and gentle touching of the beautiful cloth. Some simply passed by with hardly a notice, while others looked in, giving Catherine a wink and a smile.

Leena and Benjamin finally returned to give Catherine news that he and Leena had bartered for the price on the whole skein of material. Catherine looked at her mother in disbelief. *"The whole skein, Mother?"*

"Benjamin gave me such a good price I've decided to buy the whole thing."

Catherine was ecstatic. *"What kind of gown are you thinking of?"* Catherine asked, thinking her mother was using the whole thing on just her gown.

"Quite a beautiful one, my dear daughter. And with what's left, I will make sashes, belts, and inlays for your bridesmaids' dresses. What do you think of that?" Leena asked gleefully.

"I think it is a wonderful idea," Catherine said, jumping up and down in the display window. *"I'll have to tell Molly, Andrea, and Leona as soon as I can so they don't go get something else."*

Benjamin stood nearby, a big smile on his face, and said, "So what do you think, Catherine? Do you like it?"

Catherine leaped down from the display window and gave Benjamin a big hug. "How did you know? How did you know I would love the material you had on display?"

"Somehow, when the vendor brought the cloth to me that day, I was thinking of you and how nice you would look in a wedding dress made of such fine threads. When the vendor gave me such a good buy on it, I just had to tempt your mother and you. I was fairly certain no one else in the village would need or want such fine materials. Even now, watch as they admire the finer goods. However, when it comes down to buying, they simply purchase the things they need. I don't judge them. We are, as you know, simple tradesmen and farmers. Fancy clothing made of such fine cloth as this is a rarity. But I knew Stock was up for a wedding . . . and here you are. I guess you could just call it 'destiny.'"

That was when the world changed for Catherine, Leena, Benjamin, and the whole village of Stock.

Inner Storms

Tell me about the storm . . .

Those first months, after the right-sided mastectomy, were difficult for Lois. She wanted to fit back into the world. She told me many times she did not feel part of the world anymore. She felt alien and out of place in a world where everyone had two breasts, where most advertisements and TV shows exemplified women who were whole and unblemished by the scars she now wore. So many times I told her she was the same person on the inside. It was the outside that changed. But something had changed. She was angry at the disease. She knew it would take her life prematurely, and she did not want to leave this world without making some kind of mark upon it. She wanted to do something that mattered. She told me during her treatments, "I do not want to be forgotten." It was a vow I made to myself to never allow that to happen. When I told her I would not forget her, she would smile and tell me it was really up to her to make this happen. Yet to see her at the time, she was barely able to get to her job and back without needing twelve hours sleep or more. At the time, it did not appear she would be able to make her part of the dream a reality. We all underestimated her, even herself. No one, not even Lois, realized what impact her life's story would make upon the world.

After Lois returned home from the hospital, a crescent-shaped incision marked the place where a breast once existed. Metal staples and two Jackson Pratt drains completed the intrusion. One drain, located at the lower part of the incision, drained fluids from the chest area. The second drain, located at the extreme top end of the incision, extending just under the right arm, drained an area where the axillary node dissection was done. Lois needed these drains for almost a week. She couldn't get a proper bath in the hospital and desperately wanted to get cleaned up. However, warnings foretold, she would not be able to get water on the incision or the drain sites without risking infection. We found by installing a hand sprayer in the showerhead, we could direct the water spray anywhere we wanted it to go and, more importantly, where we didn't want it to go. To do this, we wrapped plastic wrap around her entire right shoulder and taped it into place. This way, Lois was able to take her shower unassisted, with the right shoulder covered, and with the hand sprayer, she could get a good shower on her own. The only help she needed was someone to hold the sprayer when she washed her hair, allowing her to use both hands.

Once her surgeon removed the drains, he sent her to physical therapy and, more importantly, her first visit with the oncologist. While she progressed with physical therapy, she started a chemotherapy protocol based on the results of something called a ProdEX panel. I recently looked for the ProdEX panel on the Internet but could not find anything on it. Apparently, it is not used anymore; but in 1992, the results indicated whether or not the tumor sample would respond to the known chemotherapy protocols of the time. When the oncologist evaluated this panel of test results, he decided a regimen of Cytoxan, Adriamycin, and 5-fluorouracil as the treatment of choice for Lois's type of breast cancer.

With the mastectomy out of the way, Lois needed three months of physical therapy. The worst part of the mastectomy was regaining strength and mobility. The right arm was very weak, and moving it above her chest area was, at first, impossible. First, she had to get the strength back into her right hand using a soft rubber ball she squeezed throughout the day. Lois did two exercises to regain her mobility. One called "wall walking," which involved taking her right hand and using the fingers to move the arm up the wall, pulling her arm higher every time she did it. Every day, she had me watch her progress. The other exercise involved a short piece of rope. By using a short rope we slung over a door, she would take her left arm and use it to pull the right arm to an upright position. This was difficult, but it was the best exercise she performed to get the right arm above her shoulder.

What wasn't expected on her profile was the presence of osteoclast-like giant cells. As the name presents, it was a large cell normally found in bone tissues, not breast tissues. It meant Lois was one of those rare people who fell into a class of breast cancer statistics where less than one-tenth of 1 percent of known breast cancers existed. With further research, Lois found most of these recognized cases existed in Norwegian women. Its presence in breast cancer tissues was never determined to be good or bad prognostically. However, Lois's mother was of Norwegian decent, which conclusively followed the results of her profile.

Lois started chemotherapy in mid-December 1992. She was to continue chemotherapy for six months, then start an estrogen receptor antagonist. An estrogen receptor antagonist is a medication used to block the effects of estrogen on estrogen receptive breast cancers, which was the situation for Lois. When she completed her chemotherapy, the oncologist would consult with a radiation oncologist and then continue with radiation treatments for six weeks.

To further improve her recovery, Lois continued her scheduled physical therapy sessions where they taught her activities she could eventually do at home. However, they had therapies and exercises they wanted to supervise. Of course, as with any exercise, cramping and discomfort associated with pushing muscles beyond their endurance started. At night, when Lois was at rest, the shoulder and chest spasms became so unbearable she would end up crying out in pain. We tried muscle relaxants and pain meds, but she didn't like trying to overcome the "groggy" feeling occurring the next morning. Frustrated by the pain and the aftereffects of the medications, we asked the physical therapy department if they had any remedies not involving medications. One therapist had an idea and recommended my attendance at a physical therapy session with Lois. She wanted me to learn a technique called "myofascial release." The therapist explained by gently putting my hands on either side of the healing scar, I could release the muscle tightness with firm, but gentle, pressure. After I learned the technique and used it at home, Lois had no need for pain medication and recovered more quickly without them. I appreciated the invitation to learn the technique. It was something I used with Lois for the next eighteen years, and it worked every time. By the end of three months, Lois regained 75 percent of her original strength and mobility of her right shoulder.

Lois's first chemotherapy treatment started the second week of December 1992. On Christmas Eve, her hair fell out in clumps. She knew she would lose her hair, but she wanted to get it shortened after Christmas. When she lost her hair, the effect was as dramatic as the timing. She went from a full head of hair on Christmas Eve morning to a head of fine short hairs by Christmas night. The alopecia (as the technical name for baldness is called) could not have been more untimely. I think Lois hoped it would happen after Christmas, but as fate would have it, it came at a time when Lois wanted her close family to see her as something other than a cancer patient. For her, it was very disheartening.

Lois later told me she did not feel she had cancer until she lost her hair. With her hair gone, she really knew, perhaps for the first time since her diagnosis, she had cancer. "It never became real for me until I looked in a mirror and saw I looked like a hostage from a POW camp," she told me bitterly. I felt badly for her this Christmas. She finally started feeling more like herself since the surgery and first tumultuous chemotherapy treatment, when this happened. Now, losing her hair became one more loss in the many battles she had to overcome on her long road back to find herself.

Between chemotherapy visits and physical therapy visits, Lois became accustomed to her rigorous schedule. She recovered in slow meticulous steps. We didn't know how her tumor markers were doing until all the chemotherapy and radiation treatments were completed. It was a time of upheaval and changes. Some days she had victories, and on others were defeats and disappointments.

(From a journal by Lois A. Anderson)

After the mastectomy was completed we found that I already had a locally advanced case of breast cancer, Stage III to be exact. Because of that I began chemotherapy treatments with the recommended drugs, Adriamycin, Cytoxan, and 5-Fluorouracil exactly one month later. I had a horrible time with nausea and vomiting, but you have to remember these were the days when Zofran was only available as an intravenous infusion. There was no Kytril, Emend, or Aloxi. I would always get through the first several hours after the infusion, but about five PM every Friday evening after the treatment, the nausea would begin. After several rounds of trying Compazine and some other older anti-emetics, the only drug that seemed to work was Decadron. My husband, the registered nurse, gave me an injection and I was okay for the rest of the evening, but again on Sunday afternoon and into Monday morning I would again suffer with the nausea. After several tries we got it down to a schedule of taking the Decadron pills on a regular basis throughout the weekend after my once a month treatment.

My chemotherapy treatments went on for six months ending with the last one in April. In May of 1993 I began Tamoxifen for five years to reduce my chances for recurrence."

(End of journal entry)

Three months after the surgery, in January 1993, Lois had enough of her diet of recuperation. On her next visit, she asked her surgeon to allow her to return to work. He did so reluctantly, seeing her strength had not returned. When he found she traveled thirty miles away to get to her job, he was even more skeptical. I spoke up and told him I was in a position to drive her to work every day if this was what she wanted. The surgeon relented, very pessimistically, and told us he did not want her driving herself until he gave permission to do so, and not before. Lois was excited he offered her this much. When we were home, Lois went to the telephone and started calling her friends at work. She told them she would be at work the following Monday.

Chemotherapy was particularly exhausting for her. So many times, treatments forced her to sleep for almost six hours after getting one. When the surgeon gave his blessing for her return to work, I wondered how she would manage it. She was still weak and seemed to require all the sleep she could get.

By this time in my life, I was fortunate to be working five miles from my home. I was easily available if anything went wrong while I was working. I worked night shift, allowing me to be available during the day or evening, provided I had six hours sleep before I returned to work by 11:00 p.m. By my calculations, I could be back home by 7:45 a.m., get Lois to work by 9:00 a.m., and then return by 10:00 a.m. I could sleep a few hours and then drive back to Timonium by 5:00 p.m. I knew it would be difficult, but not impossible.

As it turned out, I only had to take Lois to work for one week. After the first week, she insisted on driving herself. On those first days, when she drove to work, I worried about her making the thirty-mile trip to Timonium. It took time for everyone to realize Lois was not going to let this disease interfere with her life. She always accepted help when she needed it, but when she didn't . . . well, you back off.

I well remember taking her to work her first day. Lois barely had the strength to get into the car. I brought a pillow for her to keep the right arm elevated and a warm blanket to keep over her for the long January journey to her position at the laboratory. When she was in the car, she fell asleep immediately and stayed asleep, until I arrived at the parking lot on the laboratory grounds where she worked.

I parked the car near the entrance. I watched her sleeping next to me, unaware we had arrived. I could not foresee how this small five-foot woman, as weak as she was, would ever get through an eight-hour day. I woke her up and told her we arrived. She looked at me and smiled.

"I'll wait if you want me to," I said, thinking she would tire out in an hour or two. I thought I would stay where she knew she could go to rest if she needed.

Then as if she knew what I was thinking, she told me, "No, I'll be able to do it."

"I'll just sleep in the car," I protested.

"No, you need to sleep and then come back here to get me. So let me do this," she told me emphatically.

There never was any way to argue with Lois once she made her mind up to do something, and this was one of those times.

Lois got out of the car, picked up her belongings, and slowly walked up the sidewalk to the door. She slid her badge in the door and then walked inside. In spite of her protests, I remained in the parking lot for about thirty minutes, thinking she would be back. When she did not return, I hoped her coworkers would take care of her until I returned in eight hours.

When I was home, I went to bed. I did not sleep well, thinking the phone would ring at any minute. When my alarm went off, I jumped into my clothes and drove the thirty minutes back to Timonium. I barely arrived, waiting just a few minutes before the scheduled time in the parking lot, when Lois and many of her coworkers walked out the door.

The woman I left that morning was not the same person I collected at the end of the day. Instead of being slow and tired, she was limber and strong. She was smiling and laughing as she jumped into the passenger side of the car. She was excited and enthusiastic to make it through her first day.

"So I'm guessing things went well," I said, assuming her transformation determined she had a lot to tell me.

"Everyone just had to come over and hug me. They were so glad to have me back. They even made this huge banner that stretched over the whole lab. Look"—she showed me her still-filled lunchbox— "I didn't even eat my lunch. They ordered out."

Lois was so excited and relieved to know everyone wanted her back. She felt valuable. She felt alive. She felt she belonged in the world again, and accepting her back was an enormous gift. It was a gift only her coworkers could give to her. It was such a huge welcome back for her. It was not only her job but also her self-esteem, her sense of being human again, and her "welcome back" to the world she lived in. It was a role they gave her, and it was a role she wore with pride. She was no longer just a body broken by cancer. All through the years, she never forgot that day. Of all the things it taught me, I learned this: acceptance and love are stronger medicines than the best drug on the market. I saw what these two entities did for her at the beginning of her breast cancer ordeal, and I believe it is what kept Lois alive every day she had with all of us.

Within a few days of my driving her to work, she decided her surgeon needed to give her the permission to drive herself. She made the call and set up an appointment so he could see she was strong enough to drive again. What the surgeon saw, between the previous visit and this one, was a remarkable improvement of her functioning. Neither I nor the surgeon knew what to make of it other than Lois's sheer determination to get on with her life. Returning to work was the best therapy she could have received. I don't believe another month of any type of therapy could have been any more effective, though she continued physical therapy and chemo during the time she returned to work full-time.

Lois continued to drive herself to and from work, getting stronger and more confident every day. She scheduled her chemo sessions late on a Friday, allowing her the weekend to overcome the fatigue and nausea that occurred afterward. For the remainder of her chemo sessions, ending in late April 1993, she missed only one day of work, which was a Monday after a particularly difficult session. Once chemotherapy was completed, Lois thought the radiation treatments would be easy by comparison. She started tamoxifen in May 1993, while her oncologist made the consultation for radiation therapy. Radiation treatments would take her into the first weeks of August.

Lois was finally her happy self again. The surgeon's prognosis of five years of disease-free survival did not dissuade her from doing everything of which she was capable. During her first three months of recuperation at home, we both attended I Can Cope classes together. It was there where we made contact with several other couples going through breast cancer treatments as well. It was nice to watch these women get together and talk about their experiences. I remember about five or six of them talking, comparing notes, and then hoping to talk to each other again at their next meeting.

One night, Lois approached one of the nurses teaching the course and asked about starting a support group for breast cancer patients. Apparently, the thought was on the instructor's mind as well, noting how the breast cancer patients gathered together on the nights they held classes. By the end of 1993, with the support of the facility and other breast cancer survivors, Lois cofounded the support group known as Surviving Breast Cancer.

(From a journal entry dated August 28, 2007, by Lois A. Anderson)

Along with another breast cancer survivor and the oncology coordinator at our local cancer center I helped establish a breast cancer support group, the first such group for the York area. Our first meeting took place in September of 1993 with a huge turnout . . . so large that the room overflowed with women who recovered from breast cancer and women who were still being treated for the disease. Today this group still remains in operation. I also write, edit and publish a newsletter for this group that is distributed to over three hundred breast cancer patients, survivors, and health care professionals in this area. This group also put together several breast cancer awareness walks in the mid 1990's with me as the co-chair of those events.

(End of journal entry)

In June 1993, the radiation oncologist saw Lois and recommended six weeks of radiation therapy. It was no surprise her surgeon and her oncologist both felt the same way. Lois was to get a treatment every day except weekends for six consecutive weeks. The radiation oncology center set up an appointment to do the mapping and tattooing for the radiation treatments for early July 1993. On the very day the green markings were completed, she returned to work to find an impossible barrier to cross . . . another problem beyond her control. To tell the story accurately, I included an excerpt from Lois's writings.

(From a journal entry by Lois A. Anderson)

At the same time I began the Tamoxifen, I was referred to a radiation oncologist to see what radiation could do to reduce this recurrence rate even further. I saw the radiation oncologist in June and by July I had no job and was being tattooed for my radiation treatments. It's funny because I saw the radiation therapist for the radiation simulation and tattooing in the morning and in the afternoon a group of us were called into the conference room at work. That afternoon we found out that the small lab where we worked had been bought out by Corning Labs and we were all going to be out of work unless we wanted to work in one of their larger labs near Rockville, Maryland. Because Rockville was a two hour drive from my home, there was no way I would be able to move with Corning to Rockville and I was out on layoff. However, before that was done I sat down with the Human Resources Manager to explain my situation. Because I advocated for myself, Corning covered all my radiation treatments, all the blood work I had to go through over the next six months, and all the follow-up testing, such as a bone scan and other x-rays over that same time without charging me a thing. Not even one cent. For all of that I am eternally grateful to them because they could have put me on COBRA and then I would have had to pay the monthly insurance rate for the coverage.

I really hit bottom emotionally at this point too, because I had no job and when first notified of the buyout, and the worry of having to pay for all my treatments was overwhelming. It was then that my husband went to work. Unbeknownst to me he called everyone he could think of to help pull me out of the depression pit I was in. I was invited to a meeting of a group of women in Lancaster, Pennsylvania that would later become the Pennsylvania Breast Cancer Coalition. This was only the beginning of my volunteer work.

(End of journal entry)

Lois had not quite finished her radiation treatments but felt she needed to start looking for another job. She was very self-conscious. The radiated chest wall was very tender, and wearing a weighted prosthesis against it was nearly impossible. In addition, she had green markings running up the right side of her neck, not covered with the medium-length red wig she wore to cover her baldness. Both problems were a deterrent, but Lois, with her wisdom and creative instincts, solved both problems herself. First, she spoke with the radiation oncologist about something to put on her skin for pain, which would not interfere with the radiation treatments. Once an appropriate ointment was ordered, Lois had a seamstress make a formed pocketed bra with a soft inner material she could wear against her irritated skin. She filled the pocket with a lightweight batting material she purchased at a fabric store. Covering the radiation markings was more difficult.

Lois was trying to look for a job while undergoing the last of her radiation treatments in the hottest month of the summer, August. Being able to cover her body without showing scars, radiation erythema, and the telltale tattooing up the right side of her neck, while looking like the clothing you wore as a woman during the summer months, was a challenge. She decided to go shopping.

I remember shopping at store after store, never finding the kind of top she needed. She was frustrated by the search. The summer tops for women were just too revealing at most of the stores we normally shopped in. I told her perhaps looking at a discount store might give us something different than what she normally bought. She was willing to try anything. So during the last two hours of shopping time, we finally found some tops with very short sleeves (but sleeves) and a high mock turtleneck neckline. It was perfect. She bought six of them. She liked them so much, she went back the next day and bought six more.

With her most betraying problems solved, Lois began her job search. Her first day of interviews went well as far as her great work history and qualifications, but when the interviewer asked if she ever had a long-term illness, the interview was over. Day after day, her interviews went like this. She grew quiet, and I saw the fight leaving her. She wasn't able to do anything about the inequity where people with long-term illnesses were being passed over for jobs (at the time), but she certainly remembered it later in her life. Her political career, which to this point had not been considered, would bring up this concept of "genetic discrimination" again. When the time came to speak up, she would be ready.

She came home the first day of her job search frustrated, angry, and troubled. She felt the only thing left in her life was to be an unemployed breast cancer survivor. The only thing defining her was a breast that no longer existed and cancer, which was, at the moment, in remission. She could not understand how a highly educated, experienced woman, like herself, could be erased by a society that valued the very traits she possessed. How did breast cancer take that all away from her?

Radiation treatments were taking their toll on her. Her job search was so frustrating, she cried every time she remembered what happened when she dropped off a resume. She told me she felt worthless, and I would not be able to maintain the household bills, house payments, and bills for treatments if she didn't get into a job fairly soon. Some of what she said had some truth to it, but with our savings, and with some overtime, we would be all right. But even I realized it wasn't just the financial issues that were bothering her. She lost the essential thing that defined her—being a viable productive woman, which was what she was. She felt society had forgotten her . . . It was making her less than what she was or could be. I hated what this disease had done to her, but I despised the fact the world would not even give her a chance.

Seeing Lois headed for a major depression, I called the oncology center asking for suggestions. One oncology nurse told me to get Lois in touch with a group of women starting a "grassroots" movement to bring breast cancer to the forefront of the political arena. This was perfect, considering what happened on her job search. I thought, if Lois could tell these women what happened, they might be able to help her. I asked the nurse to have them call her.

The other thing I did to help Lois was calling the hospital where she worked just three years before to see if they would be interested in hiring her back. Though she resigned, Lois maintained many of her friendships she made working there. I knew some of her friends, so it seemed like a logical place to start. Through a series of phone calls, I eventually made contact with one of her old friends who had been promoted into a position where she could make a decision to hire her. She told me she needed to make some inquiries, but she wanted Lois back, breast cancer or not. I told her I would have Lois call her in two weeks. She said this would work out for both Lois and herself. Two weeks later, Lois had her old position back as a medical technologist with Mercy Medical Center in Baltimore.

When Lois made the call to Mercy Medical Center in Baltimore, she was ecstatic. She discovered I made the initial calls to her old friend and was grateful she would be able to go back to work once her radiation treatments were completed. Seeing a future as a productive human being did more for her than being treated for breast cancer. It was "hope," and her hope to do something more with her life than she did with the first forty years of her life, that drove her to excel.

By the end of August 1993, Lois completed her radiation treatments and finally returned to work. After a long-fought battle lasting from October 1992 to August 1993, Lois was able to resume an almost-normal life again. Her hair returned, and as it did, her lovely upbeat disposition started to grow back as well.

In September 1993, some of Lois's initial work, while undergoing breast cancer treatment, began to take shape. The oncology nurse, along with another breast cancer survivor, worked with Lois to start their breast cancer support group. They had their first meeting in September with about thirty women coming to the first meeting. Lois wanted the concepts of education, advocacy, information, and emotional support to be the guidelines steering the group during its existence.

Just a week or two before the first meeting of the Surviving Breast Cancer support group, Lois met with a few women who began the Pennsylvania Breast Cancer Coalition or the PBCC. The PBCC had been active, at the urging of another national group known as the National Breast Cancer Coalition (NBCC), to petition then president Bill Clinton to increase funding of breast cancer research. In 1993, one in eight women chanced getting breast cancer within their lifetimes. Both groups, the NBCC and the newly formed PBCC, sent their members to Washington DC to deliver thousands of petitions collected across the country to President Clinton. Being part of that history-making march on Washington had a definite impact on Lois. I think getting caught up in the spirit of political change showed her she could do something to help other women from having to walk the same path as she did. As Lois once said, "I vowed that I would do whatever it took so that any woman did not have to walk in my shoes as a breast cancer patient." In time, she would make changes, both as part of a group and as an individual, that would change the course of breast cancer history.

(From a journal by Lois A. Anderson)

In September of 1993, I participated in the march held on the streets of Washington, DC while our NBCC (National Breast Cancer Coalition) leaders presented petitions to President and Mrs. Clinton and Donna Shalala after helping to get many of these signatures myself in York

County. Because of my efforts and others, Pennsylvania ended up with almost 300,000 signatures from our state residents. And again, from September 1996 through April 1997, I distributed and collected signatures on Petitions for NBCC's 2.6 campaign.

(End of journal entry)

(From a letter by Donna Duncan of the Linda Creed Breast Cancer Foundation [LCBCF] to George S. J. Anderson, dated Monday, April 25, 2011)

Lois got involved with National Breast Cancer just after she was diagnosed and went to DC the following spring or fall. NBCC introduced her to Linda Creed Breast Cancer Foundation as we were the coordinator for PA. We are one of the founding members of NBCC and the President, Fran Visco, was LCBCF's representative to the planning meetings. LCBCF helped fund some of the initial activities of NBCC. Lois worked with us as part of her work with NBCC. Lois became a "Field Coordinator" and was responsible for Central PA for Linda Creed/NBCC.

Sunrise Morning

Tell me what you heard . . .

   With determination, I found the dream within a dream each time I tried. Maturing, discovering the facets and dimensions of my soul, made my requisite return wax and wane like cycles of the moon. I found solace in my own direction and, yet there were times I was involuntarily swept back to find familiar specters lingering in this world. Within my burgeoning awareness beneath the great tree, I discovered a thin horizon glowing in a muffled line pushing light through the layered branches. As I watched the thin light unfolding, I was startled by the figure of an old man leaning against the tree, his face hidden by the shadows, his form outlined in a penumbra of hazy blue-pink light. I did not approach, not knowing if I had stumbled upon a friend or a foe. The old man spoke with the voice of my grandfather and then walked to the other side of the great tree and vanished.

   I stood immobilized by the dream of the sunrise morning undecided. The choice to journey deeper into the dream or to awaken resided in silent ripples flowing behind and before, washing to unseen shores. What was he was trying to say? What did he want me to do? What did he mean by saying, "We don't leave our loved ones behind"? So I decided to dream . . .

   A sound cracked like an impossibly large tree losing a massive limb. The sky, violated by purple hues, birthed ominous black clouds swirling like madness, dominating the sky above the village of Stock. The ground tremors rose slightly and then shook violently, bursting every glass windowpane on Stock's streets, lanes, and alleyways. People outside buildings were knocked across the cobblestoned streets, as waves of splintered glass became lethal projectiles. The tortured street dust rose from an unquiet sleep, filled with lethal glass shards and splinters, and shrouded the devastation lying beneath its mocked veil. As survivors of the open streets collected themselves, they found their exposed skin bleeding or hanging in shreds. Many were not as fortunate, as dead lay in glass-riddled sanguine pools, victims of mortal wounds. Throughout the village, wails of pain broke free even before the glass fell completely to the ground. Catherine and Leena remained untouched, as was Benjamin and everyone in his shop. The glass burst outward, and those in the street were slashed and cut by the exploding glass. Everyone inside a building appeared unharmed.

"What happened?" Catherine screamed, throwing herself at Leena, sobbing hysterically.

Leena cautiously looked around, trying to find a place to get Catherine out of Benjamin's shop window where pitiful horrors, once their friends and neighbors, lunged and grasped with bloodied hands and torn bodies for something stable. Leena looked at Benjamin who could only stand and stare, giving the impression he was paralyzed. His color drained, making him look like a pale stone. He started wavering, and if not for a steady hand spared from Catherine's grasp, he would have fallen into a table of colored ribbons.

"Come on, Benjamin," Leena screamed, "we need your help."

Benjamin was disoriented and in shock. He looked toward Leena and Catherine and, for a few moments, tried to remember who they were. He couldn't determine whether he was at his shop or at home, dreaming this nightmare in his sleep. The shop looked ruined, a timber beam broken free from its ceiling mounts hovered a few arm's lengths from the floor. Leena finally worked her way loose from Catherine's grasp and walked a step toward Benjamin. She put her hands on either side of his face and screamed,

"Benjamin . . . Benjamin . . . we need your help." Leena couldn't stand it any longer. The stress of the day, Catherine almost fainting in the street, and now this were too much to bear. Leena started to cry. "Oh please, Benjamin . . . please help us . . . please. Don't fall apart on us . . . just don't."

Benjamin leaned heavily against the tousled table of ribbons. His shallow breathing slowed as he tried to take a few deep breaths. His eyes stayed unfocused, and a moment passed where he was seeing double. Echoes, which were once voices, faded in his ears. They were replaced by piercing screams, muffled and distorted. Then a voice sounded closer to him. It was somewhat clearer. He heard someone crying out his name. "Benjamin, please, please help us!"

"Whaa . . . tt . . . What do you say?" *stammered Benjamin vaguely, trying to awaken from this dream.*

"Benjamin." *Leena had calmed her tears slightly, but Catherine was clinging to her waist like a small terrified child. She fought to get a response from Benjamin, speaking loudly and with force.* "Benjamin, wake up, wake up please . . ." *she implored.*

Benjamin regained enough of his vision to see Leena and her daughter Catherine against a background of bloody faces running past the blown-out windows once gracing the face of his shop. Against a din of screams, cries, and desperate shouts, he heard Leena speaking. He strained his ears to sounds of a stray whisper that finally formed coherent words. From a distance, he thought he heard Leena asking for help. This couldn't be a dream, *he thought. When he spoke, he could not believe the thin, stretched voice he heard to be his own.* "Leena," *Benjamin sputtered.* "Leena, is that you?"

"Benjamin, thank the Winds you are all right."

"I'm not so sure that I am, but . . ." *Benjamin took a closer look outside his broken windows. What he saw gathering in the distance concerned him greatly. His resolve strengthened. He began to feel some strength returning. He took a deep breath, trying to clear his head.* "Leena, we all have to get out of here. Come with me. I have a cart and horse ready behind the store, provided nothing happened to them."

"I just want to get home and make sure everything is all right," *Leena said with some urgency.* "I also want to make sure Michael is all right as well. Could we do that?"

"If there's time. I want to check on my wife and family too. But there isn't much time, I'm afraid," Benjamin said, trying to keep the fear out of his voice.

"Why?" Leena looked perplexed. *"Why don't we have much time, Benjamin?"*

"I'm not sure," Benjamin said, still recovering from the formidable quake. *"But I might know what has happened."*

"What was it?" Leena asked, concerned for herself and her family.

"There just isn't time," Benjamin urged a little more forcefully. *"We have to get our families and get out of here."* Benjamin looked at Leena and saw a sense of alarm register on her face. *"Really, Leena, we have to check on those closest to us, gather them, and then we have to move . . . and quickly."*

"What are we waiting on, Mother?" Catherine sobbed. *"We need to see Father. I hope Timothy and his family are all right. Maybe he didn't go to Glade after all. Maybe he made it back . . . maybe . . ."* Catherine started to cry in big heaving sobs.

Leena grabbed Catherine and Benjamin by their hands. *"Come on, Benjamin, lead us to your cart. We have work to do."*

Benjamin, still not in control of his faculties, weakly followed Leena and Catherine to the back of his shop. All the while, he urged his struggling customers to get home quickly. He found the door under some fallen skeins of green fabric and pushed them aside to reveal the handle. He pushed the handle down and led Leena and Catherine down the short narrow hall to the outside door where vendors once bargained over goods for him to sell and display. Benjamin's thoughts were not on his wares as he hurried down the wooden staircase to the alleyway. He was hoping his cart and horse were where he left them, tethered in the small barn behind his shop. He led Leena and Catherine there now.

The barn door was closed, just as he left it before he spoke with Timothy earlier this morning. Glass shards and dust littered the scattered straw just outside the door. Large glass shards were forcibly embedded in the wooden door like crystal talons. Benjamin broke through them as he lifted the long wooden bar trussed across it. Inside, the barn was dusty and smelled of sweet hay. "Millie," Benjamin called. The horse whinnied in the darkened barn. Benjamin went to the tethered horse. Remarkably, she was unharmed. "Come on, Millie, time to pull the cart," Benjamin said, walking the horse to a two-wheeled cart and then working the harness on her. As Benjamin finished preparations, Leena and Catherine pushed the barn door open to its widest point, allowing Benjamin access into the narrow alleyway.

"Come on, ladies," Benjamin shouted once the horse drawn cart cleared the threshold. He stopped horse and cart in the back alley where Catherine and Leena waited. "We have to get moving," Benjamin urged.

Catherine jumped into the cart with Leena behind her. Once seated, Benjamin hurried the cart through the narrow corridor as fast as his horse would take them.

"Leena," Benjamin shouted behind him, "Michael's place of business is on the way to my house. We'll check there first."

"Thank you, thank you," Leena shouted back. Leena was back in her seat when she remembered her unanswered question. She moved closer to Benjamin's ear and shouted over the sound of hooves and wagon wheels clattering against the cobbled street. "Benjamin . . ."

"Yes, Leena?" Benjamin shouted back.

"What has happened here this morning?"

"I don't know, maybe it's a natural disaster like an earthquake, though I've never heard of one in these parts."

"Yes," Leena shook her head, "but you suspect something else, don't you?"

Benjamin neared the end of the long alley, slowing to make the turn onto the main street. From their vantage point, Leena, Benjamin, and Catherine watched people running past the cart, blood running from their eyes, faces covered in blood and dust. There the return of screams and cries rifled against the walls that once drowned out their plight. In the aftermath, shops and homes caught fire as overturned candles and spilled hearths caught combustibles, feeding the growing flames. Benjamin ushered Millie into the street of bleeding souls and novice fires flourishing out of control. Benjamin was justified in not answering anything as her eyes surveyed a scene that defined the purgatory of the Four Winds. Without blinking, taking in the horrific view before her, she addressed Benjamin. "What are we waiting for . . . Move, on Benjamin," Leena said.

"I must agree . . . and move swiftly as we can," concurred Benjamin.

Catherine, awestruck by the events unfolding before her, spoke, "What happened?"

Benjamin shook his head, ushering commands to the horse for her utmost speed. Under his breath, so no one could hear, he spoke a single word, "Destiny."

⁂

Jakob finished his preparations to start tanning after sending Timothy to Glade in early morning. The leather business was very lucrative with bridles, saddles, bags, and boots requiring his fine leathers. Jakob was working on a technique to bond inferior leather scraps with good leather and other materials to make ropes stronger than the ones currently used by the villagers. His idea was sound. Leather scraps, normally thrown away, would become a new and better product. Resources often limited many villages to a handful of practical commodities. However, if this idea worked, he could eliminate waste and offer better ropes to the villagers of Stock. As a consequence, people could barter for rope in Stock without traveling ten parcels south to Lexington. However, he needed supplies from Glade to make a first attempt at his project.

On that quest, he sent Timothy, the oldest of his sons, to Glade where his friend Leon ran a solvent shop. Timothy was familiar with the journey to Leon's shop. He wanted to offer his son a horse but couldn't spare it with the crops coming in, so Timothy left this morning on foot. If the load was light, he could carry it back in the leather sacks Leon provided. If not, Leon would undoubtedly lend Timothy a horse to bring the supplies back to his shop.

Jakob bade Timothy farewell long before the sun awoke in the sky. He expected his oldest son back by midafternoon but hoped he would return earlier. Jakob was excited and eager to begin this new project.

Alexis, Jakob's only daughter, entered his shop about midmorning, while Jakob detailed leather handbags . . . something women of the villages heatedly bartered over.

"Father, have you eaten anything this morning? You and Timothy were up terribly early . . . Why didn't you call me?" Alexis asked.

Jakob, startled by her quiet intrusion, looked up from his detailing. He watched his beautiful daughter glide to his side. "I'm sorry, but no . . . neither one of us had anything to eat."

"Well, I brought you some bread, cheese, and fruit along with a skin of water. Poor Timothy will have to fend for himself," Alexis chided. A mischievous look stole the innocence from her face.

"Don't worry. Leon and Penny will force-feed him before they let him return." Jakob laughed, seeing the joy he lost when Linda died reborn in his daughter's face.

"Oh, so that's where he's off to so early today?" Alexis pondered a moment, and then asked, "So what are you two trying to do out here?"

"Trying to fashion a rope made of leather. But the tensile strength has to be better than either normal leather or rope. I sent Timothy to Glade this morning for solutions Leon and I discussed a

few weeks ago. Leon is preparing them specifically for me so Timothy will know he has the proper solvents."

"So this is all really theoretical then?" Alexis mocked *lightheartedly.*

"Come on, Alexis," Jakob played back, *"can't you let a couple of men be about their work in peace?"*

"Of course . . ." She smiled. *"That's what I'm here for."*

"Off with you then. Don't you have some chores to do?" Jakob asked a little more sternly.

"Sure." Alexis was on her way out of the backroom shop then thought about Timothy. She turned back to her father and asked, *"Father, when did you say Timothy would be back?"*

"About midafternoon, I should think. Why?"

"I don't know . . . a funny thought just flew through my head. Probably nothing." Alexis hesitated in the doorway a moment. When her father cast a puzzled look in her direction, she turned around and said over her shoulder, *"I have things to do, and so do you, so I'll see you at supper."*

"Thanks, Alexis, and tell your brothers Andrew and Lamin to come down here. I have some tables I need moved to set up this project."

"Sure, Father," she replied from the doorway. She just stepped out the door when she remembered her other brother. She turned back again and asked, *"What about Eric?"*

Jakob shook his head and said, *"I almost forgot Eric. Tell Eric to get the lower hayfields cut so it can dry a day or so. Then I'll have your four brothers down there in a few days and bring it to the barn when it's ready."*

"I'll tell them." Alexis turned back to the main house, walking the stone footpath her father built after she complained

about getting muddy feet walking to his shop. Traveling up the slight rise, she reflected on her missing brother, Timothy. In her mind, where thoughts and dreams coexisted, she dreamed she saw Timothy leave under a barely rising sun. But when the sun set again, he had not returned. "Probably just being silly," Alexis whispered to herself. Still, it felt real enough. Alexis loved Timothy and knew how dedicated he was to their father and the business. She also knew how he felt about Catherine. He wouldn't leave that way unless he was forced to.

As Alexis neared the house, she saw the sky turning a strange purple color. Alexis hurried to the back door of the stone farmhouse. Eric was still inside, looking out a window at the strange sky.

"Eric," Alexis called out as she entered the doorway. "Father wants you to cut the hay in the lower fields today."

"Alexis, do you see this?" Eric exclaimed.

"Yes, I saw it on my way back from the shop. What do you think it is?" Alexis asked, her thoughts twisting from the list of tasks to what was happening in front of her.

"I've never seen anything like it . . . It looks like the sky is on fire now," Eric said, his eyes widening at the bizarre spectacle before him.

Alexis put some things she brought from the shop on the table then turned back to the window Eric was watching from. "Let me see, Eric," she said, pushing Eric to the side of the small window facing north of the farmhouse. "The sky has gone from some kind of purple to a strange red color."

"That's what I mean," Eric told her, upset she blocked his view of the phenomenon. "First, the sky was dark purple, then black, and now it turned red. Do you think it's a fire somewhere in the village?"

"I don't know. We should have heard alarms going off. But so far, I haven't heard anything."

The two of them watched until the farmhouse started shaking violently. After that, all the windows of the farmhouse exploded outward.

༔

The village of Glade was under sunny skies when Timothy made his way to Leon's shop. The aromatic smells in the streets were mixed with sweet and caustic odors. Leon's shop was one where both pungent and caustic aromas escaped into the meandering streets of divergent odors. Timothy walked to the hewn wooden door and pulled the heavy iron knocker. Leon must have been on the other side waiting, as Timothy's next attempt almost pulled him into the house when the door opened quickly with his hand still on it.

"Sorry, Timothy, I hate that knocker. I don't like hearing it more than once . . . gets on my nerves, and I'm edgy enough as it is, people tell me," Leon spoke quickly with clipped words, like there wasn't time to get them all out. Timothy stood with his hand still extended, as Leon grabbed him and pulled him inside.

"Leon, my father—" Timothy started, but Leon interjected, finishing his sentence.

"Sent you here to pick up four special solvents for tanning leather he doesn't have. Am I right?" Leon smiled gregariously.

"Well . . . yes," Timothy stammered to get a few words out.

"Come on then. I have them ready in my office all wrapped up and ready to go. You should be able to carry them, but trying to get four packages back over the seven parcels to Stock will be quite an undertaking. So I bridled a horse to take them back. Is that all right?" Leon chuckled. "Just tell your father to bring the horse back when he comes to Glade early next week. I know he'll take good care of Sebastian . . . that's the horse's name, you know?"

"Well, I didn't, but it's a good thing to know," Timothy said.

"Oh yes, the packages . . . Let me get them for you." Leon left Timothy waiting in the brick foyer while he hurried off for Jakob's packages of solvents. While Timothy waited, another voice, much calmer than Leon's, called out, "Timothy, is that you?" It was Penny, Leon's wife.

"Yes, Penny, it's Timothy."

"I'm sure Jakob sent you off without anything to eat this morning. Am I right?" Penny asked.

"Yes, that's about right." Timothy laughed.

"Well, come to the kitchen. I have lunch all prepared for you. And you're not talking me out of it, so don't try," Penny chided. "Leon, let the packages where they are awhile. Timothy is going to eat something before he goes. So get out here." Penny led Timothy into her large brick kitchen. There were two hearth ovens built next to one another in one wall and a large metal woodstove on another wall. The remaining two walls were covered with cabinets from the floor to the ceiling. She had large kettles stocked into the corner and other pans, skillets, and cooking utensils hung from rafters above their heads. In the center of the kitchen, Leon built a stone table with a polished top and several wooden chairs. The entire kitchen was a wonder of sturdiness and utility.

"Come on, Timothy," Penny ushered him into a corner chair, "let's get something into you." Leon hadn't arrived, but Penny and Timothy heard him jabbering away long before he entered the room.

"Penny, I was just wondering what wonderful food you have for us . . . Is it meats, cheese, fruits, a lovely pudding, possibly a fruit pie, or something even more special than that?" "Leon was many things," *Timothy thought as he smiled at the old man,* "but above all, he loved Penny's cooking . . . and he loved Penny more than anything else in his life."

"Well, if you sit down, I'll bring the food out." Penny laughed as she watched Leon pantomime her traditional way of delivering food to the table. Leon finally sat down and poured three goblets of

cold water, one for each of them. Penny served homemade breads and fresh fruits picked that very morning. Next, she brought cut melons and went to the woodstove to bring steaming hot meats and eggs. When everything was on the table, she sat before a plate of food and ate with them. Leon led the conversation, as Penny interjected questions about Linda, Timothy's mother, Penny's childhood friend. Talking about his mother often made him sad, but Penny's stories about his mother when they were younger always made him feel she was still with him.

"Linda was a beautiful dark-haired girl," Penny recounted. "She loved life. She and I would run through the meadow grass just outside Stock where some old trees fell against the wall. It was a beautiful spot, and still is, I'm told. We played around those old trees for hours then came back home all muddy and dirty. Our mothers would scold us for being so careless. It wasn't that we were looking to get dirty, you know, we just forgot what we were wearing and ended up looking like dirty street urchins by the time we got there. Your mother, Linda, always had the best excuses. She would tell her mother she heard voices coming from the other side of the wall. We told our mothers we were scared, so we both scurried under the heavy fallen trees to hide. Other times, she blamed our appearances on our roughhousing brothers who shoved us down in the dirt. There were always times when she could manage an equally convincing story to keep us out of terrible trouble."

"Did my mother really hear voices from the other side of the wall?" Timothy asked Penny, suddenly attentive to her story.

"I don't remember. It was a long time ago, you know. All I can say is, I never heard anything. I think it was just an excuse Linda used to stay out of trouble."

"So what did my grandmother say to her when she told her she heard voices?" Timothy was curious, because hearing voices near the wall was a foretelling of the Four Winds, and he wanted to hear more about his mother.

"Why so interested, Timothy?" Leon asked, squinting his eyes in concern.

"*I just wanted to know what my mother was like when she was alive . . . when she was younger,*" *Timothy corrected himself.* "*Most times I remember my mother, she was sick. It's nice to hear of a time when she wasn't.*"

Leon felt terrible questioning Timothy this way. Of course, Timothy wanted to hear about his mother. And why not, memories from a friend as good as Penny were probably a lot like a visit from Linda. Leon put a hand over Timothy's apologetically. "*Sorry, Timothy, I didn't mean anything. Penny, go on with your story . . . We were talking about Linda's mother, Timothy's grandmother.*"

"*Well,*" *Penny said, rubbing her chin with the fingers of her right hand, searching the air for words to say. She finally dropped her hand and said,* "*It was a very long time ago, but if I remember right, Linda never got into trouble using 'voices behind the wall' as an excuse, which I thought, at the time, was odd. Because when I got home and tried to use that excuse, it never worked. I always got into trouble.*" *Penny laughed, turning her attention toward Timothy who had a smile on his face again.*

Leon rolled his eyes at Penny when Timothy wasn't looking. It was an unspoken sign between them, which meant, "*Get things moving along.*" *Besides, Timothy needed to pack up and return home with Jakob's solvents.*

"*Well, Timothy, I better get you on your way before Jakob sends out a search party for you. Or worse, your fiancée, Catherine, might show up, none too happy I've kept you,*" *Leon said lightly as they all got up from the table.*

"*I don't think you need to worry on either one's behalf. My father knows I will be back later this afternoon, and Catherine is not expecting me until midafternoon.*"

"*Until we get you packed and riding back to Stock on Sebastian, I wouldn't be so surefire certain you will be on time,*" *laughed Leon.*

"*Yes, Timothy, you and Leon make your preparations, and I will make quick work of tidying up. Move along, you two . . . and,*

Timothy, say hello to Catherine and your father from us when you see them today."

"I certainly will . . . and thanks for feeding me." Timothy smiled back, as Penny went into the kitchen to get their dishes off the table.

They walked through the rear brick foyer to Leon's office. There on Leon's desk was a large wooden box and a leather-strapped burlap bag. "Give me a hand with this, Timothy." With Leon on one side and Timothy on the other, they lifted the box, placing it on the leather-strapped burlap bag. The leather straps were part of a harness, Timothy discovered, used to secure a box like this to a riding horse.

"Now all we need is Sebastian," Leon said, opening a door to a brick-lined staircase leading off the back of the house. Beyond the curved staircase was a small brick courtyard. On the opposite side was a modest-looking stable with five horses waiting to be walked. Leon and Timothy hurried down the steps where Leon introduced Sebastian to Timothy.

"Here he is, all saddled up, and ready to go," Leon announced.

"He looks fast," Timothy noted, seeing the sleek lines and smooth brown coat of the horse.

"He is. He should be able to carry you and your packages in short order back to Stock," Leon said with pride. "He is one of my best horses. I'll miss him until he gets back. I know Jakob will take good care of him until I see him next week. Well, let's get him loaded up, shall we, and then you can be on your way."

"Sure thing," Timothy added. But before they had the package off the ground, the earth trembled beneath their feet. "What was that?" Timothy stammered.

"I don't know." His words were barely spoken when the ground beneath their feet rebelled in violent shaking. The wrenched earth

threw them to the ground. The windows of Leon's house exploded, and if not for Leon's decision to keep glass windows out of the stable and courtyard construction, they would have been cut to shreds. When the tremors stopped, the frightened horses displayed their terror by kicking and neighing inside the stable's confining stalls, threatening to break out of the protective structure.

"Easy, Sebastian, easy," Leon shouted, pushing off the brick-covered courtyard to a standing position.

"What's going on?" Timothy screamed from his position on the ground. "What's happening, Leon? I never saw anything like this." Timothy was shouting, waiting for something to follow. Then screaming started in the streets of Glade. The sounds of wailing rushing down the alley from the streets beyond them was so pervasive, Timothy and Leon heard it in the courtyard.

Leon, recovering his senses, thought of Penny still inside the house. "Wait here . . ." Leon said quickly to Timothy. "I have to check Penny. Don't go anywhere," he commanded.

Over his shoulder, Leon hurriedly asked Timothy to calm the horses and then bravely ran into the house. Timothy heard Leon's voice drifting though the shattered windows. "Penny, Penny, where are you? Are you all right?" He heard fear in Leon's voice and, at times, Leon's sobbing. Timothy was afraid to follow, guessing what might have happened to Penny. The wailing he heard from the streets beyond the house supported his nauseating fear something was terribly wrong. Then he heard Penny's voice.

"Leon, I'm over here." She didn't sound injured. He heard Leon weeping when he found her.

Timothy examined the surroundings. It was a safe confined space, surrounded by the house, the walled perimeters of the courtyard, and the stable. The only way out was the alley leading to the streets of Glade. The buildings surrounding Leon's house and shop gave little clearance to view the sky boiling to a hideous purple. Timothy looked between the structures, seeing the darkness materialize over the visible rooftops of the village. "What is happening?" Timothy unknowingly whispered.

Leon hurried out of the house with Penny on his arm, leading her to the bottom of the staircase. "Steady now, my dear, careful going down the stairs," Leon said with a gentle, but frightened, voice.

"You're the one who should try to be steady," Penny said, trying very hard to be brave, but failing, as tears ran from her eyes. Penny wiped her face with the apron she still wore. As her eyes became accustomed to the outside light, she realized how the sky had darkened.

Leon watched Timothy as he made his way out of the house with Penny. He saw his gaze fixed on something. Leon looked into the sky above the rooftops and saw the violet sky boiling over them. Penny stopped, fiercely squeezing Leon's hand, and gazed with them. None saw a sky like the one before them in their lifetimes.

"Do you think it is a bad storm, Leon?" Penny asked timidly.

"If it is, I've never seen anything like it," Leon replied, not taking his eyes off the ominous purple sky.

Timothy remained silent, never acknowledging Leon and Penny's presence beside him. He looked pensive and worried. Penny jabbed Leon in his side, getting him to notice, then pointed at Timothy's mortifying stare. Leon understood Penny's concern as soon as he saw him and called out to the boy. "Timothy . . . Timothy . . ." Leon called, trying to break his concentration on the threatening sky.

Timothy heard his name. Finally, breaking free of his gaze, he realized Leon and Penny were standing together, watching him. It was like an enchantment, which mesmerized him. He worried about the dark forces, which changed the sky so dramatically. He remembered rumors he heard whispered in the streets of Stock. Concern must have shown on his face like a broken mask as he faced Leon and Penny.

"Leon, I heard rumors about some young men and women planning to breach the wall. You don't think this is what happened,

do you?" Timothy asked, his troubled eyes averting to the disquieted ground.

"Damned fool kids . . . It certainly would explain things," Leon chafed. "I certainly hope no one would be that foolish. Why, if the village council hears of this, there will be a heavy price to pay . . . a very heavy price. And if you ask me what I'd do . . ."

"What happens if this is true?" Timothy interrupted, his gaze returning to the portentous purple sky swirling above them.

"I don't know. Nobody knows. But I do know that whatever was removed from the wall must be put back to set things right again," Leon said with disgust in his voice.

"So they just have to put the stones back into the wall, and this will all stop?" Timothy asked Leon, looking for some hope to hold on to.

"I know. It sounds too easy, so it probably doesn't work that way. But I think someone should find out if this really happened, and it is not just some weird storm. Maybe it's not what we think it is," Leon pondered hopefully.

"What should I do, Leon?" Timothy asked, confusion muddling his decisions. "If it is a break in the wall, I don't know where it is. It may not be safe to cross there."

"I'm going to saddle another horse and go with you. We will investigate this together and see if what we suspect is true. I'll take you to Stock and then travel farther if it is necessary. If no one has seen or heard of a breach, then this is something else, like a storm or an earthquake perhaps." Leon turned to Penny. "Pull the shutters closed on the house until I get back. If the house is not safe to stay in, take a horse and travel north to your sister's house in Wendow and wait for me there. There are three good horses left in the stable. One of them should be able to get you there. I'm going to get Timothy back to his father. Then if I find anything or any news about this, I'll return here and look for you. If you're not here, I'll come to your sister's house. Do you understand?"

George S. J. Anderson

Penny looked at Leon in shock, "But, Leon, what if something happens to you?"

"Nothing is going to happen. If I should run into any trouble, I have Timothy to help me. When I get to Stock, Jakob will help me. You have nothing to worry about. If things look bad, both Timothy and myself will come right back."

Penny thought about the options, and though she was content in staying where she was until this mystery was sorted out, she also saw the logic in finding what they were up against. Instead of protesting, Penny said, "I'll get the house cleared and closed up. When I'm done, I'll come to the stable and get one of the horses ready to go. If you're not back by sundown, I'll make my way to my sister's house. Is that what you want me to do, Leon?"

"For preparations under fire, it sounds like a very good plan, my dear," Leon said, as Penny put her hand into his. Leon kissed Penny then sent her to the house to begin preparations. He went to the stable and saddled a horse. When all was ready, he motioned for Timothy to follow him. "Okay, Timothy, let's take it easy until we find something to worry about."

"I agree, Leon. Take the lead. I'll follow."

Leon and Timothy rode south, hoping they would pass the outer borders of Glade by midafternoon. With any luck, they would reach the village of Stock before the sun went down. They rode over a mayhem of blood and scattered glass covering the main streets. They heard people crying behind closed doors where random screams of pain pierced the silence. The sounds lingered in collected echoes abandoned in faraway places. The journey south of Glade was littered in darkness and flourishing smoky fires. As they progressed, they found discarded bodies of villagers, fatalities of glass projectiles, and hysteria. Many lay in scattered piles by Samaritan villagers with no choice than to leave them behind. Some bodies were so callously mutilated; it froze Leon's heart to what might lay beyond the southern borders of Glade. Leon, once full of ideas, began to doubt his plan to get Timothy back to Stock.

At the outskirts of Glade, they saw a ragged-looking man traveling the road from Stock. He limped painfully along the road, moving quickly as he could, calling out to Leon and Timothy as they approached.

"Thank the Winds I found you. Don't go any further," the ragged man warned, trying to catch his breath.

"Who are you?" Timothy asked, perturbed this disheveled man interrupted his way back to Stock.

"A merchant from the village of Lexington who came up to barter for goods at Glade," he offered as a way to gain their confidence.

"What happened to you?" Leon asked skeptically. "For a merchant, your clothes look like rags, and it doesn't look like you have anything to trade or use for currency."

"I had to leave it all behind when the quaking started. I was a few parcels north of Stock, on my way here, when it began. It spooked my horses, and I was thrown off. I lost everything." The ragged man sobbed.

Leon observed the expansive injuries covering the man's body. Though his clothes were torn and stained with blood and caked dirt, they were once fine clothes, something a merchant would wear. Leon dismounted his horse and approached. "Look, I want you to get on my horse, and I'll lead you into Glade." Leon looked to Timothy. Timothy was indignant, glaring between Leon and the direction of Stock. Leon turned his attention again to the ragged man, "So what's your name?"

"Rand . . . my name is Rand," the man said reluctantly, or perhaps, it was unheeded exhaustion seasoning his voice.

"Rand," Leon mused, rolling the name over on his tongue. "What are the chances of getting into Stock by this road?" He pointed toward Stock and then assessed the dark look on Timothy's face.

Rand looked horrified. *"You don't mean to go there . . . The road is gone, everything is gone between here and Stock!"*

"What do you mean the road is gone?" Timothy interjected, *finding something of interest in Rand's epistle.*

"I mean, when you heard the big quake, it caused a big crevasse that swallowed the road between here and Stock. Stock is cut off from the northern villages." Rand could not console Leon and Timothy with his news.

Timothy, still sitting on his horse, turned and looked down at Leon. "How do I get back, Leon? Everyone I know and care about is in Stock. Could there be another way into my village?"

Leon wanted to be empathetic but knew he had to get Rand to a healer. Besides, Penny was, no doubt, still at the house. If they delayed their return any longer, Penny would be on her way to Wendow. They needed to make a decision quickly. He could take Rand to Penny for healing if they hurried.

"Rand, were there any safe ways around the opening you saw?"

"I didn't stay long enough to get a good look . . . but I would say probably not."

"What did you see?" Leon urged, *trying to decide whether it was safe to allow Timothy to go on or not.*

Rand, exhausted from his injuries and their questioning, was barely able to stand, much less walk, any farther. Numerous deep cuts and scrapes peppered his torn arms and battered legs, though nothing looked fatal, but the pain was bright and drained what energy he had. Rand spotted an old log and limped sluggishly toward it. Once there, he sat, motioning Timothy and Leon to join him. They brought the horses, dismounted, and then tied the horses to a strong sapling nearby.

Leon was getting impatient. Penny could be ready to leave the house at any time. He wanted to get back, and this fool, Rand, wanted to sit and have a conversation. Timothy was ready to run off into who knows what, and Rand's only opinion on Timothy's return to Stock had to be waited on.

"Come on, Rand, what's going on?" Leon snapped. "Tell me, or I leave you here to rot or until the next rider comes along, which, at this rate, could be days from now. I need to know right now."

"You can't send the boy back that way." Rand's exhaustion hunched him over, but fear lifted his dirty blood-streaked face, as he looked directly into Leon's eyes. "There's more wrong than the road, Leon." Tears welled at the corners of his eyes as he spoke to him. "I saw things . . ."

Blood and Paper

Tell me about struggle . . .

The brief interlude of peace slipped behind us as the calendar pointed its map of days at 1994. It was a concept of Lois's making during this year to begin writing a newsletter for the support group. Her first newsletters were simple typewritten pages, photocopied and stapled together to distribute at support group meetings. However, as years progressed, with the advent of new computer systems and the Internet, the newsletter became more sophisticated. The complexion of the newsletter changed over the subsequent years, but the concepts Lois founded it upon remained constant during the years she wrote it.

The newsletter was called *Surviving Breast Cancer;* the title was proudly faced in bold print at the top of the page followed by the mission statement that said, *"Our mission is the support of breast cancer survivors and their loved ones through Education, Advocacy, Information, and Emotional Support."* Every newsletter contained information from the national level, the local area, which incorporated highlights and events pertaining to breast cancer; group news, which informed members who was speaking to the group and the topics to be discussed; and finally, the editor's corner where Lois wrote about issues affecting her personal life and what she was doing to improve herself and others.

As the newsletter matured, the local oncology physicians began to question where their breast cancer patients were getting such detailed information. The breast cancer patients started coming to visits with more-relevant and up-to-date information than ever before. They came with questions, which, in some cases, the physicians were not prepared for. Physicians eventually discovered Lois's newsletter, which provided their patients with information and tools to be more involved in their care. They needed to catch up.

The oncology physicians and nurses began requesting copies of her newsletter for their offices so the information Lois wrote would be available to them as well. From my perspective, the newsletter put both the patient and their physicians on a more-level field of discussion. By doing this, patients were more informed, and physicians were more prepared to have meaningful visits with their patients. The information Lois provided brought many of these same oncology physicians, nurses, and specialists to the support group where they visited and discussed many topics of interest with the breast cancer survivors. The support group branched out into the community, in turn, making it the largest breast cancer support group the area had seen to date. At its peak, there were close to 350 members in the group's mailing list with about thirty to fifty members coming to the meetings once a month.

In 1994, Lois listened to many breast cancer survivors express concern for their husbands and significant others about the effect their illness had on them. The concern seemed universal and had deep impact on the emotional "well-being" of the breast cancer survivors attending the group. What Lois discovered was many of their husbands, boyfriends, and significant others were unable to talk with the breast cancer survivor, and in some extreme cases, they could not bear to look at them. Some situations were so bad, divorces, breakups, and abandonments loomed on the horizon for many of these women. Many nights, Lois came home and cried when she told me the stories these women shared. She wanted to help, but nothing was available to give anyone immediate intervention. The problem, as she saw it, came from a lack of a support system for the men who were the actual caregivers for these breast cancer survivors. Lois, being the woman she was, set out to find a solution.

One night, after a particularly heart-wrenching session, Lois asked if I would consider heading a support group for the men. She told me stories she heard coming from the support group and explained she needed someone who had been through the breast cancer process to head it. "Besides," she told me, "you're a nurse, and you are the husband of a breast cancer survivor. You are in a unique position to help these men."

I knew she had not asked without thinking about the consequences, either good or bad, of taking on a support group like the one she proposed. I told her I would have to think very hard about doing it. At the time, I was looking for stories of people in a similar situation to my own. There were a few books out there, but nothing like an organized support group for men. I realized a freestanding support group, like Lois proposed, was not only innovative but ground breaking as well. The concept was monumental both in scope and in the potential good it could achieve.

If I was going to do this, I wanted to be prepared. I set out to find any and all resources I could for men supporting a breast cancer survivor. Most of what I found was information written by women telling men how they should feel, what they should do, and what they should say to their loved one struggling through breast cancer. I was extremely frustrated to find there was little to no information written on this by men. I wanted to find one honest book written by a man who had been through the breast cancer experience and who could share that emotional roller coaster on the topic with other men. I think it was the sheer paucity of materials for men (at the time) that eventually helped me decide to create the support group for them. After sharing my findings with Lois, I told her there was a definite need to make this group a reality. I didn't know how it would work out, but I told her I would try.

So by the next meeting, Lois announced the beginning of a men's support group starting at their next meeting. Lois was very excited to have the men come to a meeting of their own, as were the members of her group. Lois set the meetings up to be inclusive for both, so the information, advocacy, and educational segments of the meetings had both the men and the women together in the same room. For the emotional support part of the meeting, the men were given a space apart to "open up" and share what problems and thoughts they had with the rest of the men.

By the end of 1994, the men's support group was initiated. Unlike the women's support group, consisting of a core group of women who attended religiously, the men's group was more tentative and transient. Most men came to the group to hear what was being said, then returned to their lives generally after three or four meetings, either changed by the experience or made to "give up," with future consequences lying on their horizons. I enjoyed being involved with the men's group over the years, but in 2001, I had to leave because of scheduling difficulties at my job.

With no one to lead the men's group, it eventually faded into the past. In hindsight, it was an opportunity I was grateful to have taken. It was something Lois taught me about the power of a shared experience. That experience opened my eyes and the eyes of many. Some stories the men told me were so powerful, I eventually shared one of them with the world. I called the story "A Brief Shining Moment," which was published in *Chicken Soup for the Volunteer's Soul* in 2003. The men's support group was a great idea for its time, and perhaps there are, or will be, others like it again when the need arises.

Lois continued to work on projects outside the confines of the breast cancer support group with the Pennsylvania Breast Cancer Coalition (PBCC) and the American Cancer Society (ACS). In 1994, Lois felt the need to volunteer for the *Reach to Recovery* program sponsored by the American Cancer Society. The basis of the Reach to Recovery program is to match women who have been through breast cancer treatment and have been cancer-free for at least a year with newly diagnosed women. The context of meeting a woman who has been through the same experiences you are facing is a powerful step toward recovery.

At one time in Lois's recovery process, she was visited by a Reach to Recovery volunteer, and the experience was never forgotten. Lois felt this was a way for her to personally give back to the organization that gave her hope when she most needed it. She was cancer-free for a little over a year, which qualified her to make visits. Lois had some initial training she needed before she could go out on her own. However, once her training was over, she gave the program her all. She was so informed when she made her visits to fellow survivors that physicians who heard about her from their patients requested her to speak with subsequent breast cancer patients they referred.

Another project Lois became involved with was the Look Good, Feel Better program also sponsored by the American Cancer Society. The program was centered on volunteer beauticians and cosmetologists helping breast cancer patients in treatment with applying makeup and other beauty aids to help diminish the outward effects of chemotherapy and radiation therapy on their appearance. Lois was such a good spokesperson, the American Cancer Society asked her to appear on a cable television show to speak about their program. The public's reception of the program was so positive, the TV studio asked her to come back to speak in front of the cameras about the formation of the breast cancer support group.

By the end of 1994, the breast cancer support group had over one hundred members, from only thirty at their first meeting, in just a little over a year. Throughout these activities, Lois continued to work full-time at a job located one hour from our home. When I asked how she was getting everything accomplished, she would simply tell me she had a full-time "work" job and a full-time "volunteer" job, and both were important to her. Yet even with all she was accomplishing on those fronts, Lois never forgot she was a mother, a wife, and a member of a family. She never forgot a birthday, anniversary, or holiday for her brothers, sister, nieces, nephews, brothers and sisters-in-law, and other family members. All of it was important to her. Life was important. Every day was important, and it was celebrated as best it could. However, by the end of 1994, Lois was again in a battle to save her own life.

By December 1994, Lois had another scare. Had she not been vigilant of her health and the signs in her body, she may have lost her life. She just saw her gynecologist for a yearly endometrial biopsy of the uterus in early December. This was done yearly to evaluate the effects of tamoxifen on the lining. After a biopsy, it was not unusual for some spotting to occur. However, this time, Lois noticed the bleeding was not stopping as it usually did. This went from very slight to heavy bleeding, lasting from December 13, 1994, until the first week of January. The bleeding should have slowed to a stop the week following the biopsy, but it continued and became increasingly worse. One night, I suggested she get a hemoglobin and hematocrit drawn while she was at work. I knew this test would evaluate how much blood loss occurred and if she could recuperate from it. Lois had her blood drawn and tested that very night at the lab where she worked. She called me back with the results, which shocked her. This same test was completed a week before her biopsy when the hemoglobin was 14.1. The hemoglobin she quoted me over the phone was down to 8.6. So in about three weeks, she dropped her blood supply by about 40 percent. If the blood loss continued at these levels, she would need to be hospitalized for transfusions before they would even consider an operation to stop the bleeding. If the bleeding didn't stop and nothing was done, she could bleed to death.

When she called me with her results, she was in Baltimore, an hour's drive from our home. I happened to be off work that night, and the results she discovered concerned us both. She asked me to call her gynecologist with the results of her blood work and ask what they would want her to do. In early 1995, there were no cell phones, and we relied on phone books to find phone numbers. So all the calls I had to make were looked up and made from our home phone, which took some time. Fortunately, the HIPAA laws were not even thought of at this point in time, which would have deterred timely treatment and consensual information exchanges. So when I called the on-call gynecologist, I was able to relate the information to her without having to fill out forms in triplicate. The gynecologist's suggestion was, we needed to get the bleeding slowed or hopefully stopped. The gynecologist told me if the hemoglobin dropped below 8.0, any surgery would be delayed until the counts were above 8.0. If the hemoglobin dropped below 8.0 and the bleeding wasn't stopped, Lois would be in danger of bleeding out to the point of unresponsiveness and death. The gynecologist's plan was to start Lois on hormonal treatment to slow the bleeding so Lois's hemoglobin would stabilize above the 8.0 level. I agreed with her. She called a prescription to the hospital's twenty-four-hour pharmacy where I picked up the prescription overnight and had it ready for Lois when she returned from work the next morning.

After the call with the gynecologist, I called Lois back with the news. I could hear the fear in her voice when she answered the phone. It would still be six hours until she would begin the hour's drive back home. Overall, it would still be seven hours until she could take the first dose of hormones. Lois asked me the name of the hormone the gynecologist prescribed. After I gave her the name, she told me she was going to research it then call back. I remember waiting nervously by the phone until three o'clock in the morning, waiting for her call. I was almost asleep with the phone by my side when it rang. Lois regained her composure but said she wasn't convinced the hormone the gynecologist ordered was the right thing. Her research found it was contraindicated in breast cancer patients and she could not take it. I asked if she wanted me to call the doctor back, but she insisted she would take up the discussion with her own gynecologist when she returned. I asked how she was feeling with her low hemoglobin. She said she felt pretty good other than the tiredness that now had a demonstrated rationale. She promised me she would have no trouble driving home in the morning, though I did not feel terribly reassured. She told me to get some sleep, and she would see me when she was back.

When she returned at nine o'clock the next morning, she looked exhausted. I think her normal workload at the hospital and the blood loss was starting to affect her. In spite of her exhaustion, she went right to the telephone, armed with a folder filled with information on the prescribed hormone, and made her case. Apparently, she was told by her physician, there was no other way to stop the bleeding than the hormone prescribed by the on-call gynecologist. I did not envy Lois's physician, knowing Lois had her end of the conversation well researched before making the call. However, she felt, as did her gynecologist, the breast cancer risks were worth accepting in order to arrest the bleeding long enough to perform a transvaginal hysterectomy. Finally, on January 12, 1995, the surgery was performed. The surgeon told Lois, the uterus, which looked relatively normal on the inside, was actually covered with large benign tumors over the outer surface. The tumors enlarged the uterus, a structure normally the size of a small pear taken out in one piece, to a size that required it to be removed in four pieces.

Lois spent about twenty-four hours in the hospital. The surgeon wanted her to stay a second day if she wanted, but she said she felt so good she wanted to go home. So on the morning of January 14, 1995, Lois came home to start her recovery. Her surgeon cautioned her not to do too much on her first few days back, but Lois talked me into taking her out shopping. I was delighted to do so, but I reminded her of the warning her surgeon had given. Apparently, her need to shop outweighed her need to rest; and at her insistence, we went to the local mall. She lasted about two hours when exhaustion got the better of her. I took her home and put her to bed. She finally accepted she had a major surgery, and it would take about three weeks to recover.

Lois returned to work as a medical technologist sometime in early February 1995. She always seemed to heal incredibly fast, and soon she was back to her support group and her newsletters. It seemed the group, the newsletter, and Lois burgeoned in all directions. She continued to get informed physicians to come and speak at the support group. The men's group continued to flourish. It was the year Lois would be nominated to a first-ever peer review panel for the Department of Defense. It was also the year Lois met a woman by the name of Diane Sackett Nannery, and it would be history in the making.

Blind Vision

Tell me about seeing . . .

One thing was constant: the tree was a perpetual presence in my lucid dreams. Like me, it was dynamic, growing stronger, and burgeoning in the passage of time. In the embryonic glow, I watched it expand its appearance above me in multicolored leaves and blossoms, and below, in magnificent root structures working through the rocks and soil, unseen but existing. It was a being with two natures . . . the visible, obvious to all, and the invisible, seen only by those who dream. Yet both exist and are dependent on each other to survive. It was like the body you could feel and the soul paired with it. In this sense, this world within a world existed and paralleled my waking world. I would come here for a lifetime.

"I believe I saw what is to happen when the wall is broken," Amelia told Victoria, as Victoria laid her half-filled basket of stones on the ground.

"But you said 'destiny,' the same word Jonathan used. But . . . it didn't sound the same as when Jonathan used it," Victoria said, pulling a kerchief from her pockets and wiping Amelia's cold, sweat-covered forehead.

"I didn't mean it the same way he did," Amelia responded, leaning heavily against a fallen tree.

"You look ill, Amelia. Should I take you back home?" Victoria asked, her concern for her friend mounted. She knew the boys would get through the wall on their own without their help. She worried if Amelia didn't start back soon, she may not make it back at all.

Amelia looked at Victoria dubiously. "Did she think I would let the boys down when they expected my help? Did Victoria hope to gain their approval with me gone? Or was she really trying to help me?" *Amelia admitted to herself, the longer she stayed, the weaker she felt. She was Victoria's friend, but Victoria was at a point in her life where scoring points with the boys was more important than friendship. She wanted to stay, hoping she could talk Jonathan out of opening the wall. Yet this sudden weakness concerned her. She wasn't sure she could stand, much less carry stones in a basket.* "Victoria might be right," *she thought,* "though I feel I should try to keep going." *Eventually, Amelia looked at Victoria and said,* "I'll try to keep working, though I have to tell you, I don't feel well . . . at all."

Victoria watched her friend wavering against the fallen tree. She didn't like what she saw happening to her. "What's wrong, Amelia? What are you feeling?"

"Just dizzy . . . like I'm too weak to stand anymore."

As Amelia started to explain, Fog walked from behind a cluster of fallen trees. Jonathan ordered him to check up on the two girls. After jumping from the wall, he stepped cautiously on the loose stone path they started as a passage. He watched from behind the trees as Victoria hovered over Amelia then shook his head. His massive presence known, he traveled the remaining distance between them and addressed Victoria, "What's up with her?"

Victoria snarled, noting his condescending attitude for Amelia never changed. "Fog . . . I don't know. I looked over . . . and she looked bad. I just came over to help her."

"So is she going to be okay or what?" *Fog asked, his obvious disdain for the two young women seething from his voice. He could see they were trying to get out of the hard work. It was so apparent: one pretends to be sick, the other one wants to take care of her so they can both sit back and do nothing.*

"I'm right here, Fog," *Amelia moaned, disgusted that Fog dismissed her presence.* "I'm not deaf or mute. I think I'm getting sick. That's all."

"Such a waste of time," Fog muttered, loud enough for Amelia and Victoria to hear the contempt in his voice . . .

"What's a waste of time, Fog?" Victoria snapped back.

Fog turned his nose up at them. He decided he didn't want to get into anything with Victoria. Fog turned and started walking back the path leading to the wall. Victoria had other ideas. She wasn't one to let things go. Fog wasn't surprised when she left her sick friend to come after him.

"Okay, so what's your problem, Fog?" Victoria said, flush with anger. Teeth clenched, fists together . . . she had the whole *"angry female"* body language all down . . . ready to take him on.

"My problem is, we seem to be the one's moving the stones while the two of you sit back and talk to each other. I thought we were all in this together," the relentless Fog insisted.

"So being a woman is a problem for you boys?" Victoria asked, just a finger length from his face.

"Not so much that you're women . . . more like you both are more concerned about yourselves than really helping us," Fog shouted back. Fog was angry. He wanted Amelia and Victoria up and moving so they could open the wall before they were discovered. If they were caught, the consequences could be dire. This thought brought another idea to Fog. *"You know, we could all be brought up to the Council of Villages and have our own lifestones put into the wall prematurely, right?"* Fog put his question before her as a point of law.

Victoria held her anger for a moment then said, *"We all know it is risky to be here. I know if we get caught, we are doomed. We both want to help, but Amelia is too sick to do anything, and . . . and if none of you want to stop what you're doing, I am willing to get Amelia back home."* Victoria looked at Fog for some kind of reaction and, seeing none, continued, *"Otherwise, Fog, maybe I'll stay here, and one of you can take her back."*

"*I'll talk to Jonathan . . . see what he has to say,*" *Fog sneered, turning toward the opening in the wall, leaving them behind.*

"*Don't bother . . . I'm getting Amelia out of there. She's sick, and I don't know why I bothered to come here, considering how you think you have all the work to do anyway. I'm going, and Amelia is coming with me. You can tell Jonathan that.*"

Fog stopped and then turned back to Victoria. "*You two are worthless anyway . . . just go. Jonathan will be angry and disappointed, but I know you two don't care . . . so just leave. Remember this as you crawl back to Stock: when we discover all the wonderful things on the other side of this wall and claim it as our own, you get none of it . . . nothing . . . like you were never here . . . like you never existed. So go . . . GET OUT . . . and KEEP YOUR MOUTHS SHUT, LITTLE GIRLS!*" *Fog screamed at them.*

"*WE'RE LEAVING!*" *Victoria screamed back, tears welling up in her eyes as Fog walked out of sight. Victoria turned toward Amelia and found her vomiting in the tall lush grasses between the fallen tree trunks.* "*Amelia,*" *Victoria yelled at her,* "*can you walk?*"

"*I'll have to take it slow, but I think so,*" *she said, wiping her mouth on some dried leaves pulled from a fallen tree.* "*I feel terrible, and Fog was so mean to us. I wish I could stay and show them we are just as good as they are.*"

"*Well, I think that day will come soon enough. They don't know what they are up against when they break through the wall.*" *Victoria hesitated then pulled Amelia against her, forcing her arm around Victoria's neck.* "*Okay, you ready?*" *Victoria asked.*

"*Yeah, let's get out of here. My father will know how to fix this,*" *Amelia said weakly, though she wasn't certain anybody could make her feel better. With Victoria guiding her toward "Wall Road," Amelia started to improve. It felt possible she might make it to her father's house with Victoria's help. They were almost out of the tall grass when Amelia went cold again.*

"*Amelia . . . Amelia,*" *Victoria gasped when Amelia went limp. "I'm not able to hold you up." Victoria stopped, gently sliding Amelia's sagging body into the tall grass. ":Come on, Amelia, don't pass out on me now."*

Amelia lay on the grass, her eyes darting back and forth, up and down, her flaccid body devoid of movement. Victoria thought she might stop breathing or begin seizures, but neither happened. Instead, Amelia continued the strange eye motions a few moments, then sat straight up and started sobbing uncontrollably. She looked directly at Victoria and said, "We have to leave this place now or we are going to die."

The strangeness of Amelia's appearance as she spoke placed an icy knife of fear through Victoria's heart. She not only heard Amelia's words but somehow also felt them . . . and they were sincere. "All right, Amelia, we're going. Can you get to your feet?" Amelia surprised her as she bolted from the ground as if suddenly cured. Yet looking into Amelia's eyes, she saw emptiness. It was like looking at a ghost.

Victoria grabbed Amelia's hand and pulled her to the road leading south into Stock. Amelia plodded forward with jerky steps, somehow keeping pace with Victoria's lead.

"Are you able to go any faster?" Victoria pleaded. Amelia stared ahead vacantly and said nothing. Victoria finally pulled Amelia off the dusty dirt road to a copse of dry grass beside them. She sat down and looked at Amelia staring absently at the road before them. "I can't make it back pulling you along like this," Victoria cried.

Amelia managed to understand her friend was upset with her. She broke her reverie long enough to speak. Her voice sounded like her but had a strange edge to it. "We need to hurry now. Jonathan is almost ready to break through."

Sitting in the grass and hearing the change in Amelia's voice was disconcerting. Amelia was disconnected and distant. Victoria looked at her friend and questioned her. "You say we have to hurry, but you have done nothing to get us out of here any faster than I can manage by myself. It's up to you to get moving. Do you think you can walk any faster on your own? Are you still so sick you can't walk on your own?" Victoria got up from the grass, walked to the road, and surveyed both directions. She saw no one. "If only someone would come along with a cart or wagon, we could get back faster." Then she turned back to Amelia, staring south toward Stock. "Do you have anything else to say?" Victoria screamed at the empty person she knew as her friend. "Any more enigmatic warnings, Amelia?" Victoria angrily shuddered as she threw herself in the dry grass and started crying.

Amelia broke her mesmeric staring toward Stock and walked where Victoria sat with her head against her knees, hands grasping her legs like a circle. "I don't mean to frighten you." Amelia spoke in monotones, steady and without hesitation. Victoria automatically glared at her. Then after a cursory observation, Amelia appeared to have recovered from her strange behavior. Still, Victoria was not completely satisfied her friend was in her right mind once again.

"Well, you have frightened me. I thought you were dying. Then I thought you lost your mind. And now . . . I don't know what you are doing." Victoria got to her feet. "You say we have to leave . . . so let's move and get out of here."

"I need you to do something right now," Amelia said as empathetically as she could.

Victoria looked at her friend, stupefied by her impertinence, "What could you possibly want me to do other than run all the way to Stock and hide?"

"I need you to travel to Glade and warn them the wall has been breached."

"But that hasn't happened yet," Victoria yelled, throwing her hands in the air, disgusted with Amelia for being so unreasonable. "For all we know, the guys may have given up, since we weren't there to help them. And you really don't know there is anything bad on the other side of the wall. For all we know, it could be a paradise on

*the other side. If you hadn't been so sick, we would be there too,"
Victoria argued.*

*Amelia stepped up to Victoria and stared into her eyes. "It
wasn't just an illness, Victoria," Amelia rasped as though her throat
was very dry. "I saw things . . . things that are to happen when
Jonathan opens our world into the world beyond the wall. What I
saw was our destruction."*

*Victoria, shaken by Amelia's comments, still maintained her
good judgment. She tried to think things through before commenting.
"Yes, but you were sick. And from what I can tell, you're still sick.
All this stuff you supposedly saw happened when you were sick . . ."
Victoria continued, barely taking time to catch her breath, "and you
are sick. These are just delusions caused by a fever or dehydration.
They aren't visions or prophecies."*

*"You can believe or you can doubt. I've seen what will happen
when the wall is opened, Victoria. You must go to Glade, and I must
continue to Stock. There are certain people who need to know what
has happened and what needs to be done to stop the destruction of
our world. Whatever this illness is . . . still affects me. I am still seeing
things—things that are coming. Things that have no part in our lives.
We need to decide now. We need to get the warnings out. I need your
help," Amelia pleaded.*

*Victoria looked at her friend doubtfully. She wasn't convinced
Amelia was having some kind of foresight. She wasn't sure Amelia
hadn't simply pretended to be sick so she wouldn't be involved if
things went wrong when the wall was opened. Victoria was ready to
argue with her when Amelia took her hand and put something into it.
Victoria gasped when she saw what it was.*

"Take it," Amelia said, as a single cold tear ran from her eye.

"I can't . . . won't," Victoria stuttered.

*"Yes." Amelia paused, then turned away again, staring down
the road toward Stock. "I'm dead already anyway. You may still have*

a chance. I know you don't believe me, but it is my hope you will. At least respect what I am asking you to do."

"Amelia, what will this accomplish other than convince me you're serious?" Victoria gasped, knowing what Amelia was asking of her. "You know once your lifestone is three parcels away, you only have three days to live."

"I know, Victoria. But I also know if you manage to return my stone within three days, I may survive."

"Take it back then. I don't need it. I'll do what you want. Just keep your lifestone, Amelia. I'll go . . . Take it," Victoria pleaded, trying to keep tears from clouding her eyes.

"Keep it . . ." Amelia commanded loudly.

"But why? Do you want to die so badly?" Victoria implored.

Amelia turned to her friend and said calmly, "Dying badly is what I don't want to do. Knowing when death is coming and preparing for it seems more humane and dignified than what the things on the other side of the wall have planned for me." Amelia smiled weakly at her friend, then seeing no reaction from her, she turned and faced the road back to Stock.

Victoria was speechless. If Amelia was so certain she was at the end of her days that she wanted to die on her own terms, then she would do what Amelia wanted.

"Take my stone, Victoria. It can protect you a little while," she said, as she stared into the distance, unheeded by her thoughts, the fleeting passage of time, or Victoria's constant pleadings.

"But I have my own lifestone with me. Can't it be enough to see me through?" Victoria asked, seeing a possible argument to save her friend.

Amelia did not turn to face her but spoke calmly, self-assured of her response. "Yes, your stone may help you, but to stop the things on the other side of the wall, you must give it up. At least, using my *stone, you will have a chance to live. If you need to use your own, you will suffer my fate as well."*

"I don't know what you mean, Amelia . . . keep what away?" she protested.

Amelia did not acknowledge her. "You need to go soon. Let me tell you quickly what I need you to do. Then you must leave," Amelia said, turning to face her friend. "You must travel as quickly as you can to Glade. There you will find a young man that goes by the name of Timothy . . ."

𝕏𝕏𝕏

Nathan was working alongside Jonathan as Fog rumbled into the narrow shaft they cleared. "How are the girls doing?" Nathan laughed.

"That's what I came to tell you. Amelia was sick and almost passed out," Fog said, resentment seething from his voice.

"So what's wrong with her, Fog?" Jonathan asked, looking up from the pile of stones he was moving.

"Let me finish . . ." Fog interrupted. "So Victoria decided . . . no, let me put it this way, she demanded that SHE take Amelia back to Stock."

Jonathan's face soured. "So you're telling me they are both gone?"

"Yeah, but Victoria put up such a fuss and decided on her own that she and Amelia were leaving. I yelled they were cowards. But Victoria just yelled back. Then they just picked up and left."

"I'm sure your attempts at gentle persuasion no doubt hastened their decision to leave," Nathan mocked as he pulled more stones from the center of the shaft.

"Hey, I tried to stop them, but when I turned around to come back here, they were already walking off the site," Fog protested, thinking he did all he could to stop the two girls from leaving.

"Did you warn them against saying anything, Fog?" Jonathan asked ominously.

"Yeah. They know if they say anything, they will have the same responsibility in it that we all do."

"Or"—and Jonathan emphasized his point—"they will miss out on a major discovery. A discovery, I may add, to put an end to all things, like fear and hypocrisy represented by this wall. It will open a new Age of Enlightenment and discovery . . . and we will be revered as heroes."

"Let us not forget what we are here for," Nathan intoned. "How about less discussion and more clearing the path?"

"I'm for that," Jonathan said.

"Me too . . . ," Fog said, as he pushed by Nathan and Jonathan, taking the lead in clearing stones.

Fog led the way before them. When Victoria left with Amelia, the three hollowed a cavity in the wall like a small ravine. When the ravine was deeper than the top of their heads, they began a tunnel. Once the tunnel started, each took a turn at digging, while the other two transported the loose stones away from the entrance. Progress was slow, but their efforts would realize what they came for. Fog, who had the lead, called back to Jonathan, "Hey, you might want to get by me and take a look at this."

Jonathan, moving the stones just behind Fog, called back to him, "We're going to back out so I can get in front of you. Can you just tell me what you're seeing?"

"I think we're almost through. I see light from the other side. I think you should have the honor of breaking through, unless you want me to do it." Fog laughed with excitement.

"Okay, Fog, let's back out, and I'll finish the job." Jonathan chuckled. The three men, giddy with their imminent discovery, exited the small tunnel. Once outside, Fog relinquished the lead to Jonathan, whom he felt should break through first, since it was his discovery to unfold.

"Onward to paradise," Jonathan stated with egregious intonation. Then without a pause, he walked into the tunnel. "Come on, let's all get there together," he said, motioning Nathan and Fog to him.

The end of the self-made tunnel glared with a strange blue light. On the side where Nathan, Fog, and Jonathan came from, the midafternoon sunlight was bright and golden. Looking at the light from the other side of the wall, the light was conclusively different. The few stones remaining before them comprised a stone mesh, which spilled a bizarre blue light into the tunnel. Although the light was strange, it did not betray any danger to the three ambitious interlopers.

"I say it's time we broke through and put an end to these old superstitions," Jonathan said, as he cleared some stones. Soon a small hole opened, and Jonathan looked through. "Other than this side is darker than our side of the wall, I'd say we have nothing to worry about."

"What do you see?" Fog asked, watching Jonathan push enough stones out of his way to force an opening.

"What's he saying, Fog?" Nathan asked.

"Don't know, but Jonathan's out on the other side of the wall now. There's an opening, but I'm too big to get through it. I'm going to clear more stones, then follow me."

Fog put his head through the opening and looked around. "Hey, Jonathan, where are you?" The blue light was dazzling and sparkled with bright purple spots. Fog realized the opening was a few arm's lengths off the ground on this side, but he couldn't see Jonathan. He called out again, "Jonathan, stop fooling around, where are you?" Fog was frustrated by Jonathan's obvious need to discover something interesting but felt trepidation as he moved through the opening. He heard Nathan calling behind him.

"Come on, Fog, if you're not going through, let me by," *Nathan complained.*

"Probably nothing to worry about, Nathan. I just can't see where he went. To be honest, I don't see anything but these sparkly purple lights shining in blue mists. Jonathan must have moved away from the wall. I don't see him."

Fog finished removing the stones blocking his way and pushed through. He crawled down the slight incline of dislodged stones and called back to Nathan, "I made it, Nathan. You can come through. You should see this place."

Nathan lingered in the tunnel above Fog, looking out the opening they created. "Fog, don't move. I barely see you. This blue stuff is hard to see through."

"Yeah, I know. I also noticed we barely hear each other. This place seems to affect our hearing too," Fog yelled his words, though Nathan was only a few arm's lengths from him.

Nathan pulled himself from the opening and slid on his belly to where Fog stood. The muffled silence distorted his senses as he took a position next to Fog. When Fog yelled "I'm glad you finally got through," it sounded like a whisper.

"So what do we do?" Nathan yelled, standing next to him.

"We should try to find Jonathan."

Nathan looked around at the miasma of blue-flecked air besotted with purple sparks. He looked for identifying features in the landscape, but the lack of distance vision made it impossible to get any bearings. "Fog," Nathan yelled, "we need to figure out how we are going to move around here without getting lost. I barely see the opening in the wall where we came through. We need a plan to get back here."

"You're right," Fog yelled. "Too bad we never thought about bringing some rope or something to mark our way with us."

"We didn't know what we were up against until we saw this place." Nathan thought a moment then yelled, "You know, we could tear strips of cloth off our shirts to use as markers, dropping them close enough together to spot our way back here."

Fog looked at Nathan skeptically but agreed; it was a better idea than he could think of. "Okay, let's do it."

"I'm going to strip off my shirt and tear a piece off to put up there at the hole where we came from. Then we are going to mark the way with no greater than two arm's lengths till the next one." Nathan looked around at their surroundings and was astonished by the intense nothingness he saw around him. "This blue stuff is really hard to see through."

"I've noticed," Fog replied in his loudest voice.

Nathan pulled his shirt over his head, while Fog yelled at the top of his lungs to Jonathan. He shrieked several rounds of "Jonathan . . . Jonathan . . . answer me!" into the thick blue air. When he turned around to face Nathan, he gasped, "What is that?"

Nathan looked down at his chest where his lifestone was hanging from a burlap pouch. The pouch was glowing red and emanated fine tendrils of light, which successfully stabbed the blue mists, parting them. There was a clarity surrounding the pouch that could only be seen on the other side of the wall . . . the side they left behind.

"Wow!" Nathan shouted. "Why is it doing that?"

"I don't know, but if you take it out of the pouch, it might actually work like a torch to light this place up," Fog suggested.

Nathan pulled the lifestone from his pouch. As he did, the stone glared with a brilliant red light; and in its light, the blue haze moved almost five arm's lengths away from them. When Fog saw what Nathan did, he pulled his lifestone from a pouch hanging around his neck as well. The two lifestones worked as torches in the blue murkiness.

Fog was astonished. "I can't believe this. I always thought these lifestones had no purpose other than to mark our lives after we were dead."

Nathan rolled his lifestone in his hand, watching the way the red streamers of light cut into the blue cloud. "Apparently, they have another purpose on this side of the wall that we were not aware of."

"It's angry," Fog said, as he looked at his lifestone, glowing red and sending long wispy fingers into the blue air.

Nathan shook his head at Fog's remark, as he perceived something had changed. He turned to Fog and said, "Have you noticed, we can also speak in our normal voices without having to yell at each other?"

Fog looked to Nathan and remarked, "You're right! What is happening?"

"I don't know, but I do know this will make it easier to search for Jonathan," Nathan stated as he looked about the strange empty landscape with wary eyes.

"Look, Nathan, footsteps." Fog pointed as Nathan looked at the rippled ground and saw places where the ground was disturbed near Fog's feet. The footsteps were like their own with no other signs of disturbed ground around them.

"These must be Jonathan's prints. They lead away from the wall and head to the east," Nathan said, as he shook his head. "Why didn't he wait? He must have known how dangerous it would be if we got separated."

"Dangerous?" Fog exclaimed. "What's dangerous about this place other than its blue and you can't hear in it?"

"Come on, Fog," Nathan said seriously, "this place isn't natural. So far, in a nonthreatening way, this place is defending itself.

This intense blue stuff that we can't see through, the muting of sounds, even this lack of landmarks . . . it's all put together to deceive our senses. Like it wants to get us lost . . . make it so we can't find our way back to the wall." Nathan paused and looked around in every direction. Fog did the same.

"You know, Nathan, you're right about this place. But I'm not so sure it's 'nonthreatening.' Jonathan is no dummy. After a few steps away from the wall, he would have stopped until one of us got through to be with him."

"So you're saying you didn't see the fantastically huge head he developed, thinking he was going to find treasure here? You didn't suspect for a moment he wanted to get through first so he would be the first to claim it?"

"He's not like that, Nathan. He would have waited," Fog protested Nathan's assessment of Jonathan's behavior. Fog surveyed the area around them and said, "Something either lured him away or dragged him off. Either way, it's out of character for Jonathan to just wander off like this."

Nathan looked at Fog by the reddish light cast by their lifestones. He sat down on the ground near a mark in the rippled sandy floor . . . a mark they both felt may have been a footprint made by Jonathan. Nathan seemed despondent as he started drawing circles in the rippled sand with a fingertip then looked up at Fog. "I know how you feel, Fog. I feel the same, but this"—Nathan swept an arm about him, motioning at the blue fog—"this is much more than we bargained for. Even if there is something of value here, how will we find it? How will we even get it back?" Nathan looked at Fog then rose to a standing position. "If we're going to do this, then we better mark our way. Let's tear pieces of cloth out of this shirt and drop them from time to time to find our way back."

Fog looked at Nathan suspiciously like he lost his mind. "I thought we already decided to do that anyway," Fog stated, looking into the maddeningly silent blue mists.

"Let's do it then. When we run out of cloth, we are going to turn around and get back here. Agreed?" Nathan stated as logically as he could, trying to make Fog understand they may be in danger.

"Agreed," the lurching hulk that was Fog said, as he started moving further into the blue as Nathan followed him.

Within a few steps, Fog saw more disturbed earth. He pointed it out to Nathan quietly, as if they were on a hunt, not letting the hunted hear or see them. Nathan nodded silently, as he pulled a strip of cloth off his shirt and dropped it on the ground. They kept on a straight path, dropping strips of cloth as they went. In another few arm's lengths, something laid on the ground that put Fog to screaming.

"Nathan! We have to turn back. Turn back . . . turn back now!" Fog's retreat was unexpected. He knocked Nathan to the ground as he ran away blindly. Nathan, now at eye level, saw the thing that ripped the courage from Fog's heart instantly.

"By the Winds," Nathan gasped. "What have we let loose?"

Jonathan's head was ripped from his body. Parts of his spine, still dripping with fluids, were attached to a glowing purple sphere. The sphere was ripe with pulsing red tendrils that grasped and flowed like vessels across its surface. Jonathan was dead from Nathan's perspective. What happened to the rest of his body, he could not tell. As he watched in abject terror, Jonathan's head tried to speak. It was grotesque, and the sounds made were unintelligible. The sphere somehow enervated Jonathan's vocal cords, his eyes, and his facial muscles. The sphere supporting Jonathan's head seemed to keep it alive. Though Nathan clearly knew this abomination wasn't Jonathan, he still called out to him, "Jonathan, what has happened?"

Nathan tried to get to his feet but found his legs would not move. It wasn't fear that paralyzed him. He realized too late another purple orb descended over his legs. He looked down only to see this horror consume him. He tried kicking, but nothing below his waist responded. The red glow from his lifestone grew dim as he started screaming.

 Fog ran blindly, hoping the opening in the wall was in front of him. He searched the barren ground for scrapes on the rippled earth or dropped strips of cloth marking the way back. His fear mounted as he realized he missed the first markers. When the horror of Jonathan's head mounted atop a purple sphere precluded any logic, the event sent him on an unguided course into these impenetrable blue mists. Now he was lost. He tried searching in wider and wider circles, hoping to find just one torn strip. There was nothing to use as a landmark. Several times, Fog found his own footsteps and realized he traveled a path leading back to a place where he started. To see his footsteps comforted him, in some way, but he realized staying in one place endangered his life. He continued moving until his arm brushed against something. He turned quickly, prepared to run. It was the wall. He made it to the wall . . . but which way was the tunnel? Was he north or south of it? Rubbing his fingers over the rough stones, Fog felt along the wall, hoping to find the marker they left by the entrance . . . but which way? Nathan would know. Nathan would follow the cloth strips back to the opening. Despite knowing the blue mists muffled his voice, Fog screamed out, "Nathan, Nathan, can you hear me?" Fog looked in all directions, careful not to lose contact with the wall. His lifestone continued to glow five arm's lengths away, allowing him limited vision of the barrenness surrounding him. Other than the stone wall, he had nothing to gauge his direction. He had to move forward. Yelling was futile. With no answers to guide him, he moved north. Every step along the wall was soundless and unnerving. He sensed danger here. His mind played back the scene of what remained of Jonathan. He hoped Nathan ran away and was waiting at the entrance. "We should never have come here," Fog mumbled to himself.

 Fog moved stealthily along the wall, cautiously staying within an arm's length distance away. He kept watching the uniformly rippled ground, illuminated a short distance by his lifestone, looking for any signs. Anxious, unsettled to the point where he was ready to turn and move south, he saw the first signs of disturbed ground. The mark looked like a shoe print turned on its side. It was definitely a mark made by one of them. Fog felt relieved he was moving the right direction. "I might get out!" he thought. Tension mounted in beads of perspiration, running into his eyes, blurring and burning them as he walked. "Just a little farther . . . there must be more tracks." *Still, as he advanced, there was nothing but the rippled ground. Fog was frustrated, abandoned, and feared for his life. Doubt rose inside him like an acid gruel.* "Could the footprint be Jonathan's? He could have been thrown by one of those purple things and landed on the side of his foot. That would explain the one footstep . . . then nothing. Or did the one footstep mean he walked into the barren terrain to nothingness?" *Either way, he was still lost. Whatever clue the footprint revealed eluded him as the barren lands cloaked themselves beneath the cerulean mists. When Fog's doubts resurrected, overshadowing his decision, the leading edge of the lifestone's red light crossed something. Fog moved where the red light passed. It was a piece of torn cloth lying against the wall. It was fate. This very piece had to be within several arm's lengths of the opening. Fog moved closer to the wall and looked at it closely. The opening had to be there. The maddening blue haze was unrelenting, making it impossible to see through.*

Fog decided to climb the wall where he was and chance he could find the opening. "It must be nighttime on the other side of the wall now. That's why I can't see any light through the wall." *Fog continued moving until his hand knocked against some loose stones. Something moved beyond the red glow of his lifestone. Fog moved up the wall, clumsily dislodging and disturbing the stones as he moved sideways. He could not risk missing the opening. He saw it . . . the place where Nathan placed the first torn strip. Between the cold sweat boring into his eyes and the tears, Fog caught a furtive glimpse of a shadow slip inside the opening.*

Fog called out to Nathan, but muted silence answered him. He ran his hands along the loosened stones that fell when he and Nathan broke through the wall. Fog followed his senses and found the next torn strip Nathan placed at the tunnel's entrance. Fog's world seemed so close, but yet he felt so very far away from home.

Fog touched the stones around the opening in the wall. Light from the other side should have come through, but even time was distorted here. He wasn't sure of time anymore. Fog moved his lifestone into the opening and climbed inside. Even here, the blue air continued to distort his vision. "What if the blue mists invaded and removed his world? What would happen then?" *Fog asked himself. Fog never saw his world again. The purple orb pulled Fog's head into itself, while a second orb settled on his legs. There were no screams as the orbs ripped his body in two, while numerous smaller orbs pulled the remaining two halves to pieces. The red light of Fog's lifestone went out as the blue air moved beyond the wall, into the world of the villages, with thunderous consequences.*

This picture was created with the slides Lois had made of her breast
cancer cells as they appeared under the microscope. Brooks Anderson took
the slides, found a section he felt was interesting and had the computer
generate an alternate composite of the cells. He then used the composite to
create a stencil. The stencil was then put over a piece of wood
and the wood was cut to create a kind of type face. He used about three
overlays to create the three dimensional effect. He called the piece
"1-17-2011 A Life Ended Too Soon".

The Stamp

Tell me about destiny . . .

Locally, Lois's name came up in the news many times when breast cancer issues arose. At the advent of her support group, she was interviewed by our local newspaper with an article titled *"Breast Cancer . . . A New Activism."* Others noted her forward and formal speaking ability and utilized her on television shows from 1993 until 1995. And still other newspapers beyond the local level started following her success with articles such as the American Cancer Society's *Look Good, Feel Better* program.

As Lois's name continued in the spotlight of the media, her influence over how breast cancer topics were treated became topics of conversation. One of her goals was to get breast cancer literally "out of the closet" and into the open. She wanted people to discuss it openly, and she hoped that open, honest discussion would bring up new ideas or, at the very least, take some of the stigma associated with breast cancer away forever. In 1992, when Lois was diagnosed, if the words "breast cancer" were spoken at all, they were spoken in private or not at all. Women who had breast cancer did not speak about it and seemed to be either ashamed or afraid to discuss it with anyone. By not speaking, many women who had experiences with prosthetics, reconstructive surgery, back pain, shoulder pain, and other problems associated with the removal or partial removal of a breast were isolated from other women with similar problems. There was a huge untapped resource of information held by women who had gone through the experience and survived that was underutilized by silence. Lois broke the silence of the times.

By 1995, she was allowing women with breast cancer to speak about the disease by bringing it into the media and by speaking about it herself. Opening this door to breast cancer survivors put the topic of "breast cancer" on the front burner. No longer did items like wigs, breast prosthesis, specially made bras, lymphedema sleeves, and devices stay in the footlockers of the medical community. Open discussion brought open competition with better prosthetics, better wigs and hair products, better supportive wear, and improvements in overall care. I believe, with Lois acting as their spokesperson, that women with breast cancer finally had tools available to them to make them whole again.

Lois continued her struggles to get information about breast cancer into the forefront in 1995. But once that struggle started being picked up by others, she wanted to know "why" breast cancer affected some people and not others. In her own experience, she knew there was a genetic component involved when the biopsy showed osteoclast-like giant cells, a finding only found in Norwegian women as was her mother's family. However, she wondered if anyone had ever determined whether work environments, diet, exercise, where you lived, and what stressors you had in your life may have been elements of a breast cancer diagnosis. This was a journey started in 1995 and lasted until Lois died in 2011. Lois started many such journeys over her short life. However, the journey Lois made going to a conference on "pesticides" in Philadelphia in 1995 would have to go to something called "destiny."

Sometime during the spring of 1995, Lois found information regarding a conference to be held in Philadelphia on the topic of pesticides. She told me she read an advertisement on the proposed talks. Some of the presenters made vague inferences to a cancer link to common pesticides and fertilizers used in the production of our food. Lois knew the references to cancer were, at best, ambiguous, but she told me she intended to question the presenter regarding a link to pesticides on food and its relationship to cancer. Some of her interest was generated by the location of our home. Before we built our home, the ground had been used a farmland for decades. Surrounding our home were acres and acres of farmland still used, still fertilized, and still protected by the common pesticides used by farmers throughout the country. Contracting a stage III breast cancer at age thirty-nine going on forty certainly made Lois question what else, other than her genetics, contributed to her diagnosis. Lois felt attending the conference might be a study in futility, but it would satisfy her curiosity. Her hope was the chance to make some good contacts, which might help her in the future, either for information or for references to other professionals.

Lois left for Philadelphia that spring morning with only small expectations for the conference. However, when she returned from Philadelphia in the early evening, she was very excited by what happened there. Apparently, the conference went as she expected. Though she did get to ask questions of the presenters, it seemed the audience was dominantly comprised of people interested in cleaning up the environment. There were a few questions raised regarding a link to cancer and the use of modern-day fertilizers and pesticides, but the answers were not forthcoming or remained vague or unclear. She told me she was sitting near a woman asking some of the same kinds of questions she posed to the presenters. They sought each other out and decided to have lunch together.

From what Lois told me, neither one of them was aware that the other was a breast cancer survivor when they sat down together for lunch. After they talked awhile, Lois discovered her new friend was a breast cancer survivor like herself. Her name was Diane Sackett Nannery. According to what Lois told me about Diane, she was part of a large group of young women living in the same area who were all diagnosed with breast cancer within a short period of time. According to Diane, these young women lived in the same housing development and were diagnosed with breast cancer within a few months of each other, making her suspect an environmental agent of some kind. Diane lived in New York and worked for the United States Postal Services. She was attending the conference on pesticides, looking for a link to her breast cancer, as was Lois. Diane was working on a project, which caught Lois's interest and mutually could have great implications for both of them.

Diane had petitioned the post office twenty-eight times over the years since she was diagnosed. She felt the breast cancer movement needed something else. She suggested the creation of the first-ever breast cancer postage stamp. Diane believed since she worked for the U.S. Postal Services, they would have been receptive to the idea of a breast cancer postage stamp. She found, instead of being receptive, the postal service was quite the opposite. She told Lois of her many attempts to bring the stamp into existence and the many difficulties she encountered along the way. Diane felt she was up against the wall with the concept of a breast cancer awareness stamp and was running out of ideas on how to pursue it. The one difficulty Diane encountered was one she had not expected since she worked for the postal service. The postal service did not want to start producing stamps that supported social issues or health issues like domestic violence, heart disease, or breast cancer. The postmaster general felt if one organization for health or social issues was addressed with a postage stamp, it would only lead the way for all others to follow thereafter. They told Diane the postal service was not interested.

Lois was outraged and suggested to Diane they exchange phone numbers and e-mail addresses to keep in contact with each other. Lois believed Diane was onto something that had potential to bring the breast cancer movement to light. If this stamp could be produced, then breast cancer would be brought to national attention, and this was something Lois felt was important for the times. In 1995, breast cancer was just starting to be spoken about openly. Like Diane, Lois felt the breast cancer movement needed something else . . . something else to bring it to the attention of the nation and have it present every day in the form of a postage stamp. This would keep the momentum going in the right direction and in a good direction. In 1995, the chances of getting breast cancer in a woman's lifetime were one in eight. Out of one thousand people (of both sexes), that would affect 125 people, or 12.5 percent of the entire population. No matter how you look at it, that is a lot of people. Now, considering most of those people were women, that's a lot of women affected by breast cancer. Now imagine you put that formula against the entire population of the country, and the numbers get staggering. Getting the warning out about breast cancer to the women of this country or, at least, making them aware of the problem was terribly important to both Lois and Diane. They went to work trying to decide what the next course of action was.

Lois and Diane contacted each other within days of the pesticide conference and came up with a plan. Lois suggested she would begin another campaign to petition the post office with signatures from all over Pennsylvania and then move the petition drive into Maryland where she worked. Diane was already into a petition drive in New

York, and together they felt the impact of that many signatures might change the mind of the postmaster general.

Within days, Lois spoke with the PBCC (Pennsylvania Breast Cancer Coalition) after she created a petition form for distribution. Meanwhile, Diane sent Lois a drawing of what she felt would be a good example of what the stamp should look like. The elements of Diane's postage stamp were simple. There was a pink ribbon displayed over the whole surface of the stamp with the words "Breast Cancer Awareness" printed up the side of the stamp. Lois had me copy the image onto larger sheets of paper, which she used at stations where the petition was to be signed. Concurrently, the PBCC issued a newswire letting people know where people could sign the petition. Most of the stations were located in Central Pennsylvania, especially around the larger towns of York, Harrisburg, and Lancaster (where the PBCC is located). Within three months of the petition's exposure, Lois and the PBCC received 11,800 signatures requesting the first breast cancer awareness stamp. Lois sent the first wave of the petition drive to the post office with word she had not yet penetrated the eastern and western points of Pennsylvania . . . meaning Pittsburg and Philadelphia had not had the chance to collect signatures.

From what I was told, the postmaster general was so impressed by the petition drive launched by Diane and Lois that they surrendered and told Diane and Lois to please stop. They would create the stamp, but they would be the ones to design it. Lois and Diane were happy the stamp would finally be created after twenty-nine attempts, but they were also skeptical as to what the stamp would look like.

In June 1996, the stamp was issued. I believe Lois and Diane were relieved by its appearance when they finally saw it. Actually, the post office did a beautiful job with the creation of the first breast cancer awareness stamp. They used Diane's idea of the pink ribbon symbolizing breast cancer but made it smaller. They also used the words "Breast Cancer Awareness" along the side of the stamp, as she had done with her version. What changed, and what was both provocative and beautiful, was the image of a nude woman with her back toward the viewer with a smaller version of the pink ribbon resting on her shoulder. I remember some controversy occurred over the appearance of the stamp, but controversy fueled discussion, and that was a good thing. Breast cancer survivors made it to the national level because of Lois's and Diane's efforts.

Opening this door for breast cancer awareness also opened the door for other social issues to be brought to the forefront. Over the years that followed, movements like domestic violence and heart disease also had the chance to voice their concerns in the image of a postage stamp. Eventually, a better idea for a breast cancer awareness stamp emerged, where the stamp issued was more expensive than the going postal rate. The proceeds from the sale of this stamp went to breast cancer research. Still, if the first battle for a breast cancer awareness stamp had not been won by Lois and Diane, nothing would have followed. It was a great victory on many fronts.

Back in York, Pennsylvania, Lois was honored with a breast cancer awareness plaque, which highlighted the stamp and the year it was approved for distribution. Lois oversaw the operations of three simultaneous stamp celebrations on the day the stamp was issued. I did the driving that day because Lois was exhausted from setting up displays at the three post offices the morning of its issue. She was interviewed by the network television stations from our area and spoke briefly at all three locations. By the end of the day, she was exhausted but happy the stamp had been issued. Lois became part of breast cancer history that day, though to her, she did not see her impact or what it did to bring breast cancer to the forefront of discussion.

(From a journal entry by Lois A. Anderson)

In 1995, I conducted a petition drive to support a breast cancer awareness stamp proposed by Diane Sackett Nannery after having met Ms. Nannery at a conference on pesticides held in Philadelphia. With the help of the Pennsylvania Breast Cancer Coalition, I received 11,800 signatures within three months time. When the stamp was issued in June 1996, I organized and conducted "celebrations" for this stamp at three local postal facilities where breast cancer information was distributed to the public.

(End of journal entry)

In 1995, another opportunity presented itself when Lois was nominated to the Department of Defense Breast Cancer Research

Program. Lois was the first of many breast cancer survivors to be part of a peer review program that combined breast cancer survivors (known as consumer advocates) with physicians and scientists dedicated to breast cancer programs. Proposals were sent by scientists and physicians throughout the country to the Department of Defense Breast Cancer Research Program with the intentions of receiving grants to continue their work. After these proposals were evaluated, a vote would be taken to either accept or reject any given proposal. Each proposal had to be voted on by a panel of three. Every panel of three consisted of two professionals and a "consumer advocate" who contributed a full vote. Lois had the privilege of being one of the first such consumer advocates to cast votes on grants that helped scientists and physicians bring leading edge work on breast cancer treatments to the forefront, allowing treatments out to the public as quickly as possible. She made contacts with physicians, scientists, nurses, social workers, breast cancer survivors, and many other breast cancer advocates from all over the country. Her contacts with well-known scientists and breast cancer survivors helped fuel discussions in her newsletters to her support group. As she learned new things from her discussions with some of the leading minds of the country, she would bring their concepts and suggestions back and offer their new ideas to her support group and, quite often, to her own physicians. Lois often said she was trying to find answers not only for herself but also for any woman diagnosed with breast cancer. She never wanted another woman to have to walk in her shoes as a breast cancer survivor.

(From a journal entry by Lois A. Anderson)

I feel that our learning process should be lifelong. I take each day as it comes and try to learn something new every day and the area of breast cancer is my priority. I think that to be an effective advocate, one must keep up with the ongoing research and scientific discoveries taking place on a daily basis. I am constantly reading articles and have an innate hunger for learning all I can about breast cancer. For this reason, many women in my area will seek out my advice on breast cancer issues and treatment decisions.

I am already a part of the breast cancer research/ policy process through my consumer advocacy efforts with the Department of Defense. However, I feel it is necessary to expand this influence and be able to use it in a more effective way on both a state and national level. I am constantly searching for ways to become more involved as an advocate within our local hospital systems, on a state level, and on a national level.

On the local hospital level, I plan to find any committees that would enable me to use my breast cancer advocacy skills and seek out opportunities to serve here, even if it takes going to the CEO of the hospital system.

On the state level, I have several connections within the Pennsylvania Department of Health that I intend to ask about any opportunities in which I can serve on committees, etc., within their department to use my advocacy skills for breast cancer patients.

And on the national level I intend to keep applying for any and all positions wherein a breast cancer advocate could be used to serve within the Department of Human Health Services, the National Institutes of Health (NIH), the National Cancer Institute (NCI), or any other national agency.

(End of journal entry)

The above journal entry may seem like an impossible, idealistic commitment, but by the end of 1996, most of the elements she wrote about, she actually got to do. All the while, her breast cancer remained in remission. To have seen her, then you would have seen a picture of health. She was strong and persevered in what she believed in, which was making the world a better place for breast cancer patients and survivors. On a more-local level, she was invited to speak to her first class of LPN students at one of our adult education programs in 1995. The teacher of the LPN program was so impressed with Lois's dissertation that she was invited back twice a year from 1995 until 2010. There were other events beginning in 1995 that would become the seeds of discovery as the year unfolded.

Eluding Change

Tell me about the changes . . .

I entered the dark place calmly, awed by the growing phosphorescent light. I was evolving, changing, and aware of the scent of inspiration. The great tree graced a peaceful river, glowing translucent blue, which drifted beside it. Approaching the shallow shoreline, I saw within the sand's detritus the harbored crop of smooth, worn stones. "The sand comes from the stones, dissolved by the water's unending currents." The voice of my father said like a hollow echo. I searched to find him, only to realize his voice was the only expression the great tree allowed. My father's revelation was the answer to a question I asked long ago when we hunted in the woods. In that time of wonder and innocence, the question was more relevant than his answer. Now the answer was the seed of truth. The truth was in the stones . . . a wall of stones . . .

She traveled almost two parcels from where she and Amelia parted. Moving quickly, she watched people walking, riding carriages, or leading their horses south into Stock. She hurried past merchants and travelers pressing north toward the village of Glade to sell or bargain for goods and wares. Now, the road to Glade was mysteriously empty. Victoria needed to find Timothy and relay Amelia's message before she lost her chance. The first tremor knocked Victoria to her knees. It should have frightened her, but she knew something would happen as soon as the wall was broken. The tremor, though unwelcome, was a minor condition to be endured. Amelia's warning concerned her more. Remembering her promise, Victoria rose to her feet, brushed the dust from her clothing, and moved on. As the promise quivered in her thoughts, the next terrible wave of quaking began, disrupting her resolve like nothing she experienced before.

It was a rumble in the distance, rising in a most terrible sound and shaking the brittle ground with quaking thunder. Victoria, knocked to her side, grasped a patch of long grass and held on. She felt the earth beneath her vibrate with such intensity, her hands felt like fire. When she looked at the ground, she realized what was happening. The ground blurred with shattering vibrations. Then as quickly as it started, it stopped. Victoria, faced with her knowledge of the terrible power Jonathan released through the wall, felt empty and subdued. But there was no time for empty tears; what Amelia predicted came to pass. When the earth shook again, it was not a violent shaking but quivering, like the death throes of a dying animal. Then a horrible ripping sound came from the south, terrifying Victoria and forcing her to stand and witness what was coming.

Victoria looked south and watched a tree line collapse into a deep ravine. As the dust cleared, she watched the formation of another crevasse several armlengths away. She watched it fill with something like blue smoke. It seemed like a living entity, moving and searching for something beyond its grasp. She moved closer to the blue miasma filling the deep fissure and dipped a finger into it. It didn't feel like anything, yet it was strange. Behind her, someone whispered her name . . . "Victoria . . . Victoria . . ."

Victoria turned quickly, shocked that anyone who knew her could have found her in the middle of nowhere. There was nothing but a deep, wide ravine filled with the peculiar blue fog. "Victoria . . . Victoria . . ." the voice called. It was strange and familiar. Yet on some primordial level, it terrified her, keeping her frozen where she stood.

"Victoria . . . turn around," the voice commanded.

Victoria stammered with fear, "Who are you? How do you know my name?"

"You know me . . ." the voice said with a pitiless laugh. "Turn around and see me."

Victoria was not prepared for what met her when she turned. There, floating on the blue mists before her, was a purple orb. Growing red tendrils writhed across its surface like crimson snakes. It floated in the blue mists . . . mists saturating the crevasse like a low moving river. Its confines were demanded by the split edges of broken stones, hampering its advance. Victoria estimated the orb to be almost five arm's lengths across. It floated on blue mists contained inside a ravine approximately the same size. Its most grotesque feature was Jonathan's head and torn spine immersed in some bizarre way inside the purple-skinned surface. It spoke again using Jonathan's mouth, seeing with his eyes.

"I've found paradise, Victoria. What do you think?" the hideous Jonathan-thing asked with an unpleasant laugh.

"You're not Jonathan . . ." Victoria gasped, not believing she was truly seeing the unnatural thing before her.

"You're right, my dear," the thing hissed. "But I would have you join me," it taunted, attempting to lure her closer. Victoria remained frozen by the horror before her. The orb developed a long crimson tendril and steered it with deadly aim toward her. The tentacle-like protuberance was fast, quick as an arrowshot. But in its haste to take her, it misjudged the distance, falling short by an arm's length.

Victoria, betrayed by her frozen fear, was finally shocked to her senses and took cover on ground behind her. The tethered red projectile retracted, scorching the ground where it landed. She stayed in the tall grass, hiding behind a small rock wall she found abandoned there. She needed to escape from this thing and get to the village of Glade like Amelia wanted. Now her way was blocked. The Jonathan-thing stayed to torment her.

"Come out, Victoria. This is your destiny," its queer sinister voice commanded her. "Nowhere to go, Victoria . . . nowhere to go." Another imprecise projection spun from the orb and launched its attack, touching the rock wall where Victoria lingered. Stones atop the old wall burst, cutting Victoria's arm with stony shrapnel. "I smell your scent, Victoria. I smell the stink of your fear. I know where you are, and I will fulfill your destiny," the Jonathan-thing stated soullessly. "You can't go forward, and you can't go back. Let go of

this world and come with me," the thing hissed with the ruined voice that was once Jonathan's.

Victoria drew her body close to the ruined remains of the wall then screamed, "I'm not coming with you. I would rather die."

"If dying is what you want . . ." the Jonathan-thing mocked, "I will happily relieve you of your life. Just come out and see me."

Victoria knew she was trapped. She was terrified, but in her fear, her anger breathed in courage. It was in that moment she decided to fight past the horror before her. She glanced around for a weapon but found only the broken splintered stones destroyed by the living red projectiles that still confined her. She looked through the scattered stones and found one big enough to damage it. She measured the weight of the stone in her hands and imagined she could throw it forcibly to damage the sphere that taunted her. She pressed the rock into her right hand, hiding it from the monstrosity's sight, as she stood and peered over the ruined wall. The seething purple sphere with Jonathan's head was still there . . . waiting.

Mocking her, using the most deprecatory tones, the Jonathan voice said calmly, "So there you are, Victoria. Come closer and meet your destiny. I will favor you with my attentions. You stink of fear, of sweat, of blood . . . of human violation. Let me cleanse the world of your stench and fear. I will make it a better place where you stand. Let your agonizing gods receive you into their arms."

"May the Winds knock you down and send you back into the icy depths of redemption, you putrid piece of garbage," Victoria screamed as she pulled herself from behind the broken rock wall. Without a moment's hesitation, she defiantly threw the rock squarely into its mocking face. The force smashed the forehead with a sick crushing sound, leaving a scored dent in the ruined skull. The impact stunned the odious purple orb momentarily, and then Victoria watched as multiple pseudopodia blistered to life on one of its sides. Victoria dove like a shot behind the failing wall as an unformed tendril shot out in her direction. It landed beside some rocks near her feet then vainly slithered toward her still out of reach. Again the thing missed its mark, angering it further. Seeing how close this strike came made her *realize it would only be moments before the thing closed its distance, and she would be taken. Victoria started to cry though not from fear. This time she wept tears of anger, and she was going to fight.*

From beyond the small rock wall, the Jonathan-thing mocked and tormented her, "Oh, Victoria, look what you have done." Victoria stayed hidden behind the remains of the wall. "You've been a very, very bad girl . . . I have been patient with you, and I'm giving you another chance to come out and meet me. After that, I may have to come to you and deal with you there," the Jonathan-thing said nonchalantly as if nothing happened.

Victoria was burning with anger. She stayed below the wall's edge and screamed, "So what does that mean, you bastard . . . You're going to kill me, or are you just going to change me into one of your purple friends?"

"You'll see . . ." was all the Jonathan-thing said. Then the air went silent like a closed empty room.

"What's he up to?" Victoria whispered as she looked for another good rock. Not finding one large enough to do damage, she sifted through her pockets, hoping to find a small knife she kept for cutting ropes when she helped her father. There she felt the stone Amelia gave her. "Oh, Amelia, I've killed us. I can't get out. When he comes to kill me, he kills you too. I won't be able to get your stone back to you."

Victoria thought to when Amelia gave her lifestone to her. She thought Amelia just wanted to make a point of telling the truth, but she said something else, "Remember, Victoria, my stone may protect you, but only for a little while." What did she mean? *Victoria pulled Amelia's lifestone from her pocket. She was amazed when she saw the reddish glow suddenly push back her feelings of dread and hopelessness.*

"What are you doing back there, Victoria?" the Jonathan-thing spoke up suddenly. The thing sounded fearful, not as sure of itself as it had before.

Victoria watched Amelia's lifestone glowing in her hands. "What will this do?" she whispered in amazement. "If I use this to escape, will it only work once? If it stops glowing, will Amelia stop living?" Victoria was torn by indecision. Either choice, to use Amelia's lifestone to save herself or chance losing her life by trying to escape, involved loss. "It isn't fair . . ." Victoria whispered through tears and clenched teeth. Mustering what courage she had within her, Victoria spoke to Amelia as if she stood beside her. "I can't stay here, Amelia." She lifted her head from the splintered rocks. Victoria, her tear-streaked face covered with dust, her arms cut and bleeding, spoke out as reciting a prayer to the Four Winds, "I have to use your lifestone to survive . . . if I survive. And I promise to bring your stone back. If something happens to me, we are both doomed. So, Amelia, if you can hear me . . . wish me luck." She broke down and cried like she had never cried in her life.

In her tears, the Jonathan-thing taunted her, mocking her tears and her misery. "Victoria," it hissed with contemptible solace in its voice, "praying for your life to end so quickly? Why don't you come out, and I'll provide you with the answers to all your prayers? I'll help you with your decision . . ." Then the Jonathan-thing laughed while another pseudopod formed on its surface. "It is time, Victoria . . . time to meet me . . ."

Victoria rose slowly from the refuge of the aged wall. She wore the steadfast resolve of a warrior. She spoke with confidence and strength. "You want to meet me . . . Is that right, you big purple jackass? You're not, Jonathan . . . Jonathan would never treat a friend like this." Now it was Victoria who taunted the thing that terrified her for so long. She was no longer afraid . . . she was furious. She moved away from the purple sphere, keeping Amelia's lifestone out of sight.

The purple orb acted shocked by Victoria's sudden brazen behavior. It couldn't decide its next move. Victoria saw its indecision and used it to her advantage, putting as much distance as she could between the orb and herself. When the Jonathan-thing realized what she was doing, it set an underdeveloped tendril flying at Victoria. Again it fell short, and the ground trembled slightly with uncontrolled anger.

"What's wrong, purple boy? Can't get it up?" Victoria laughed hysterically. Instead of escape, Victoria turned to taunt her tormenter. "You wanted to meet me . . . well, here I am. What do you have in mind?"

The Jonathan-thing pulsed with an inner light and renewed vigor. Multiple red tendrils grew over the orb's surface. The changed face of Jonathan grimaced at Victoria with bulging wild eyes. With a feral scream, it attempted to free itself from the blue mists that bathed it.

Victoria realized her indulgent mistake for retaliation. She was terrified by the renewed industry of the monster before her.

It attempted to close the distance between them, trying to climb out of the misty ravine on numerous new-formed red cilia. She watched in horror, realizing its frustrated efforts would not allow it beyond the mist-filled crevasse where it sat. Frustrated by its confines, the orb developed a new way to move, extending its environment. She watched the orb's cilia move pieces of earth, tearing through the ground and allowing the blue vapors unrestrained egress into another ravine. The blue mists poured into the opened depressions, and the purple orb followed. If the orb continued, she would be trapped inside a circle of moats. She had to make her move and make it quickly.

To delay her escape, the Jonathan-thing defiantly tormented her, shooting half-developed pseudopodia in her direction. The tethered projectiles fell short, burning and scorching the ground in their retreat. Victoria had to move. The thing was breaking through stones and earth to another low spot in the surrounding ground. The trap would be complete in moments. She was torn by the possible loss of Amelia's lifestone and the possible loss of her life. Her indecision gave this malign destroyer the opportunity to take her. Victoria wanted to live. She needed to deliver a message to someone named Timothy. "Let Timothy live with the weight of Amelia's sacrifice," Victoria said under her breath. Then Victoria raised Amelia's lifestone above her head, and an immediate red glow bathed the area around her almost twenty arm's lengths across. The space was certainly enough to get by her tormenter, provided it actually worked against it.

To Victoria's amazement, the red glow froze the despicable orb where it floated on the blue mists. It was paralyzed by the red light. Its time forced to a standstill. Victoria moved quickly across a chasm not yet been broken by the purple sphere. She moved rapidly past blue mists, dammed against a thin wall of earth and stone. She looked up to see the frozen face of Jonathan, his spine and neck embedded in the strange metamorphic sphere. She didn't have time to ponder the fate of the three young men, who were her friends, who obviously breached the wall. There were no signs of Nathan or Fog. She hoped they did not suffer Jonathan's traumatic end. She cried for them as she made her way toward the road to Glade . . . back where she promised Amelia she would go.

As Victoria left the site of her entrapment, the reddish glow of Amelia's lifestone faded. It returned to the simple stone it once was. Victoria realized the lifestone only worked in the presence of the purple orb. "This might be useful in the future," she thought.

As she moved away from the ruined site, she heard terrible screaming and thrashing coming from the Jonathan-thing. She won this battle, but for how long and at what cost? Would Amelia's lifestone work again when she needed to call upon it? Or was Amelia's life already spent on Victoria's safety? Victoria's only thought as she ran forward, unimpeded on the road to Glade, was to fulfill her promise to Amelia and take her message to Timothy.

Patchworks, Roses, and Weeping Cherry Trees

Tell me about hope . . .

What do we really leave behind? Are they footprints in the snow, some vague indecipherable etchings in the sand? Will anything stand the apoptosis of time, or will it be erased by the winds of science and technology, blown like insignificant dust into unknown frontiers? What answers lie within the effigy of our lives? What kind of world did we leave behind? Did we point the way? Will our accomplishments be realized in ashes . . . or stones? Did we find truth in places where blind visionaries left it undiscovered, leaving behind a valuable piece of the puzzle of life? Was it arrogance that drove us, or faith? Did we believe, or did we hope? From the moment of our birth to the moment of our death, we are given a space of time to show the worth of our being here.

In 1995, the American Cancer Society had an idea to create a patchwork based on what breast cancer survivors and their family members experienced during their struggles with breast cancer. The idea evolved into an undertaking that came to be known as the Skin Deep Project: Stories in the Fight against Breast Cancer.

The requirement to create a patch designated each square to be ten inches by ten inches and should be created by a survivor or someone affected by a breast cancer survivor, such as a husband, child, sister, brother, and so forth. The patch could be created from anything, paper, cloth, cardboard, plastics, or whatever the person felt comfortable working with. They could be quilted, as some were, or be drawings, words, combinations of many concepts, ornate, or as simple as a survivor simply writing her name on a square. With this elaborate medley of creativity, a "patchwork" would be fashioned by fixing each ten-inch square onto a larger twelve-inch square and lacing them together with pink ribbons. Pink ribbon was used as it denoted "breast cancer awareness."

It wasn't until the summer of 1996 when someone from the American Cancer Society called my home and asked if Lois or I would contribute a square to their display. I spoke with Lois later that day, explaining the requirements of the American Cancer Society's Skin Deep Project entries. She thought it was a good idea and asked what she should put on her square. I told her, "Whatever you think would explain how you feel about getting breast cancer." At the time, she said she would think about what she would like to do. Jokingly, she added she wasn't too artistic, and I would have to help her. I agreed, knowing it would mean a lot to have her own square. Later that evening, Lois asked if I could draw an old-style ship sitting at a dock. I told her I could and then asked what she wanted to do with such a drawing. She said, "Do you remember the dream I had with all my doctors, nurses, and unnamed people coming to the ship to help me?"

I remembered the night she told me about her strange dream then told her, "Yes, I remember. Is that what you want me to draw?"

She gave me a smile and said, "Do you think you can do it?"

I laughed and then said. "Just tell me what you want me to draw, and I will make it happen."

Later, Lois and I sat at the kitchen table where she told me what she wanted me to draw. We tried three versions of a ship tied to a dock. When I had the version she wanted me to do, I went to the study and used pastels to draw it in color. I used parchment to create the drawing of the ship at dock, leaving a spacious cloud over the ship to write the words she wanted. By the next day, I had her square completed. Since the drawing was on parchment, the pastels tended to smear. I asked her to get the square laminated so it wouldn't be ruined in transit. She took the completed artwork to a place where she had it laminated the next day, and the result was absolutely beautiful.

The following day, I called the American Cancer Society. I told them Lois had her square finished, but I still had to do one myself.

They were happy we made the pieces because they only had a little time left to get them into the office and bound together. I told them I was happy to do this and wondered how they were making out. They told me they had a total of four squares, including mine and Lois's.

"How long do you have to accept entries?" I asked, thinking I must have missed something.

"A little over two weeks still remain," the volunteer said.

"Are any more squares coming that you know of?" I asked, with the hopes York County would not show up on the capitol steps of Harrisburg with a display of only four squares.

"That's all we know about right now," she told me.

I asked the volunteer, "Would you like me to make some phone calls?"

"We don't have much time. But if you think you can help us, it would be appreciated."

"I'll do what I can," I told her.

After I got off the phone with the American Cancer Society, I called Lois at work. I told her the "patchwork" from York County for the American Cancer Society had the potential to be a futile effort due to inadequate support of survivors and families. I could tell she was upset. I told her I would make some phone calls the following day to get people interested in the project. She agreed to help, but she was on a long work schedule at the time, and she would make calls over the weekend. That night, fueled by the desperation of having only four squares for York County's "patchwork," I found my inspiration to make a square.

When Lois was diagnosed in 1992 with a stage III breast cancer, it seemed she lost contact with those of us not affected by cancer. She felt alone and alien. Chemo and radiation only solidified these feelings, making her feel and look the part of something not part of this world anymore. Cancer possessed some innate power that sought a way to remove each person's identity and their sense of belonging to the human race. When Lois realized her staging of breast cancer meant a premature death, a shortened life, she was afraid her life had gone by without contributing anything by which she could be remembered. She told me once, "I don't want to be forgotten." It may have been her fear of dying that caused her to tell me this, but I remain haunted by her words, even to this day. Somehow, I wanted to let her know, let her feel, she would be remembered, especially if the cancer treatments were ineffective.

When the first anniversary of her diagnosis with breast cancer arrived that first year, I wanted to do something special for her. I came up with the idea to give her twelve roses, white ones, all except one. The twelfth rose had to be pink . . . symbolizing her first anniversary as a survivor of breast cancer. Then each year and every year thereafter, on the twelfth day of October, I would give her another pink rose to replace a white one. The first year I did this for her, she wondered what the significance of the one pink rose was. She told me she liked the white roses but preferred pink ones. When I explained what I had done, she cried. It was a good cry, and then I continued to make this an annual affair every year. It was a good story, and it had to do with breast cancer, so I wrote it down so it would fit on a ten-inch-by-ten-inch square.

Over the week, I contacted about thirty breast cancer survivors on Lois's list from the breast cancer support group. On the weekend, I handed the list to her, and she contacted even more. By the end of the two-week period, the American Cancer Society in York had about sixty squares to carry to the capitol rotunda in Harrisburg, Pennsylvania. By October 1996, the York County patchwork and all other participating counties gathered at the Capitol building in Harrisburg, Pennsylvania. Patchworks from all over the state were put on display at the rotunda for a period of three weeks. A large reception and legislative lobbying day took place the first day of the display. It was orchestrated to make our state legislators more aware of the implications and consequences of breast cancer on the patient and her family. Because Pennsylvania had the fourth-highest rate of breast cancer in the nation, the American Cancer Society felt their responsibility lay in educating our legislators about the disease.

It was something to be proud of. The effect of seeing all those stories, as they related to breast cancer, in one place was sobering and emotional. The patchwork was comprised of survivors, friends, and families who had something to say or just stood as witnesses to the devastating reaches of breast cancer. The feelings one felt standing before the six-foot-by-six-foot structures (almost two of them for York County), reading the stories, and letting the beauty of the artistry and courage sink in were so powerful. It was a feeling that, over the following years, people wanted to experience again and again. A decision was made to leave the invitation open to anyone who would want to submit a patch to the existing patchwork. Unfortunately, no further patches arrived for the rest of 1996.

When the Skin Deep Project (the patchwork) returned to York, it was displayed for a time at the Apple Hill Medical Center. It also had a short-lived display at York College. Afterward, it was put into storage at the American Cancer Society. The patchwork went unnoticed until late 1997.

In late September through early October 1997, the Skin Deep Project was displayed at the York Cancer Center during the Pennsylvania Breast Cancer Coalition's photo exhibit known as *67 Counties/67 Women: Facing Breast Cancer in Pennsylvania.* The Skin Deep Project was there to acknowledge those who had presented a square to the patchwork in 1996. A second function was the hope that other breast cancer survivors, their friends, and their relatives might contribute a square to the existing work. Unfortunately, none did; yet through this display, it was learned a real interest and need to see the patchwork existed. After the display at Apple Hill, the patchwork went on tour in York County through the rest of 1997 and 1998.

Finally, in March 1998, the York Unit of the American Cancer Society had an opportunity to extend an open invitation to anyone who wanted to place a square on the patchwork. The American Cancer Society was approached by the Strand Capitol complex in the city of York to become involved in their production of the musical *Carousel.* With the advance sales indicating a very successful turnout, an effort to spearhead interest in creating another full patchwork was attempted. From this attempt, another thirty squares arrived at the American Cancer Society before the night of the musical. The night

Carousel played at the Strand Capitol Complex, the entire patchwork was erected in the lobby. Several hundred people saw both the original and the new patchworks that night for the first time. The entire patchwork contained a total of ninety squares and, if placed side by side, ran the length of eighteen feet by six feet high.

After the night of the musical, the patchwork went on display at the Galleria Mall. The West Manchester Mall, Apple Hill, Memorial Hospital, the Jewish Community Center, Glatfelter Insurance Company, HealthSouth Rehabilitation Center, and many other places around the York community. It was displayed by the American Cancer Society at events like Relay for Life and at the World's Greatest Yard Sale. As the patchwork moved from one place to another, the comments of the profound impact it made were a common occurrence. It made its mark on the community by promoting breast cancer awareness and helped people understand what impact breast cancer has on the woman and her family. Survivors who contributed a patch were proud they took a stand and spoke up. The stories from the patchwork, no doubt, moved someone to act to get a mammogram, see a doctor, get help, and get information before it was too late. Lois made sure the patchwork was seen and information was passed out with every viewing.

Eventually, the patchwork started showing signs of wear and deterioration. I eventually asked permission of the American Cancer Society to take pictures of every square on the patchwork with the hopes of at least preserving the idea and some of the legacy it represented. I took the pictures, which remain in a small photo book with some of the stories intact. Even though it exists in this small way, it is nothing to compare with the original concept. Seeing something that enormous made an impact like no other. The patchwork is now in storage, and until a way to keep it permanently displayed and preserved is found, it will stay where it is. Yet in its heyday, it was something to be seen.

Lois's love of the weeping cherry tree influenced many members of her breast cancer support group to adopt it as the symbolic tree of breast cancer awareness for their group. The weeping cherry tree Lois and I planted in our front yard the year before her diagnosis with breast cancer must have inspired her. We were always delighted by the long cascades of pink flowers showering our lawn with a carpet of pink petals every spring. Lois's perspective of the pink-colored flowers supporting the beauty of the weeping cherry tree in our yard seemed to make it her logical choice for the breast cancer support group.

In 1995, the breast cancer support group members asked the cancer center, where their meetings were held, if there was a piece of ground where they could start a garden. The group wanted to start something they called the Garden of Hope where they would place various plantings that would bloom pink flowers through the spring and summer months. The center was happy to allow this project for the breast cancer support group, and the weeping cherry tree was the first planting to be placed in the garden. The promise of spring flowers symbolized, to the survivors, a promise of life and hope both in this world and in the one after. Before this first planting occurred, some of their members died from breast cancer. Planting this first tree was a way to remember and honor them. The surviving members found hope for life after breast cancer in the symbol of the flowering pink tree.

At the time of the planting, Lois told one reporter who came to interview her, "It's about the day-to-day continuing of our lives." The event was so important to Lois and her support group members, she wanted me to write a poem to read at the tree's christening. I included the entire poem here, but only the first stanza was read at the planting of the weeping cherry tree in June 1995.

Litany of Hope

Watch as the Wind whispers
Through these willowy stems . . .
They are Survivors,
With softly bending branches,

Kneeling in silent prayer . . .
Leaves like clasped hands
Unfold Spring-pink blossoms
Held like a rosary of hearts

That sing out
> *With their Litany*
>> *Of Hope . . .*

Daughters of Eve.
> *The challenge of the Wind*
>> *Has called you*
>>> *To this urgent Cause . . .*

With your hopes
> *And yearning hearts*
>> *Upon the wild Wind's roar*
Send your prayers
> *Blowing like pink petals*
>> *Over Eden's Door . . .*

Each time I wander past the front window of my home, I look outside to see the weeping cherry tree Lois and I planted the year before her diagnosis. I still reflect about the day we planted it, knowing she chose that particular tree to become the focal point of our front yard. It was still that innocent time when she was blissfully unaware of how soon she would leave this ordinary life behind. But like many things she accomplished during her short lifetime, and the many events and opportunities that emerged before her, I had to believe in what I call "destiny." Over time, I consciously decided not to question "fate" whenever it arrived on my doorstep dressed in work clothes or in finery.

The year 1995 was filled with surprises and many new beginnings for Lois. The year was dynamic and productive. Within its harbors were the beginnings of the Skin Deep Project, the planting of the support group's weeping cherry tree, a newsletter with wonderful reviews by physicians and patients, a burgeoning breast cancer support group, and Lois's induction into the Department of Defense scientific peer review panel for the first time. It was also the year she met Diane Sackett Nannery at a chance meeting in Philadelphia, a city they shared between them on a day where "fate" brought them together. She didn't realize it then, but the legacy of her life began to write itself. It was what she hoped for. She didn't want to be forgotten, and, in some small way, she never would . . .

Thunderous Light

Tell me about promises . . .

What my father told me about the stones beneath the mountain streams became a clear memory beneath the massive tree. "Different stones wear away to nothing at the bottom of the streams," he would tell the boy walking beside him in the mountain woodlands. When the autumn-colored trees surrounded the perpetual sounds of water splashing over the rocks littering the bottom of a streambed, he would say, "A piece of quartz becomes smooth and beautiful like a gemstone, while sandstone washes away to nothing. Eventually, what remains lines the streambed with a sandy layer all through the mountain ravines." As I realized his underlying parable, the lesson found a seat in my memory. I was unaware of the rays of red and purple diffusing through the branches of the great tree with the first morning light, almost screaming its birth in a weightless glow.

"Which rock are you?" whispered the voice of my grandfather through the muffled silence I wore like a cloak.

"I don't know, Grandfather . . . I don't know . . . ," I whispered, without strength of conviction or substance in my voice.

"Are you the sandstone?" my grandmother asked, standing as violet silhouette of what she was, outlined in a penumbra of scarlet.

"No . . . not sandstone . . . something else . . ." I tried to answer . . . but I could only speak the words in colors of light . . . silence strangled me, but in my consciousness, I heard my answer nonetheless.

"He is the stone that doesn't break . . . ," my father replied, his voice booming like a god standing above me on an unseen cloud. Then all went silent . . . blurred transparent light colored the visible horizon. I could hear my breathing. I listened as a stone fell someplace out of time and knew I was alone again.

Amelia knew Victoria was past the breach. She felt some of her life's energy leave the second she passed her lifestone to Victoria. She knew the sudden weakness in her shoulders, legs, and arms meant Victoria traveled more than three parcels away. "Good for you, Victoria," Amelia whispered through her thinning breath. To make her situation worse, she distanced herself from Victoria with every step she made toward Stock. Amelia knew any hope of seeing Victoria again was futile. The only hope for the world, as she knew it, lay in the self-sacrifice of a girl named Catherine . . . a girl she desperately needed to contact.

The visions and tellings she heard outside the site of the open wall explained how to mend it. "Find a girl whose name is Catherine," the voices told her. "By her own free will, she can mend the wall with a single stone." It was all the telling voices said.

"Enigmatic, but concise," Amelia told herself.

Amelia heard rumors of others with visions and tellings of future events, but even she was a disbeliever. People who claimed to see visions or hear voices near the wall were banished to a mythical place called Winterland. Banishment to a place that doesn't exist sounded benign at first, but the way to Winterland was through jeers, degradations, and stoning by the villagers. People banished to Winterland usually died while hiding in caves, forests, and places abandoned by the people of the villages. Showing your face to a villager when banished was certain torture and degradation. No one killed a prophesier. They were left to die on their own. Being banished to Winterland meant you were considered less than a human being, less than an animal, a dead person not fit to fill the space they existed in.

According to the story her mother told her, to keep her from misbehaving, Winterland was a pariah among the villages destroyed *a century of centuries ago by people who grew to despise what it stood for. According to legends, it was once a thriving village located in the mountain passes north of Emansupass. It was a place of learning. Teachers used their knowledge to help the youngest of the villagers understand the trades, finances, philosophy, history, art, and, foremost, science and mathematics. From the legends Amelia heard as a young child, Winterland destroyed itself by the nature of the competition it fostered among its students.*

Whisperings of this far, other village told a fatal story of a group of corrupt young men who used twisted truths and physical confrontation to hurt or destroy others in order to subjugate those they would defeat. They felt superior and created ways to hinder anyone showing signs of surpassing them. Their brutal offerings consisted of sessions of physical and psychological torture, which ripened their depravity to other atrocities. In time, they believed their superiority entitled them to do anything they wanted. They subdued young women and raped them, letting them know their cruelties were above the justice they would find in Winterland. Any young woman who protested their defilement was admonished for lying and sent back to her family in shame. This detestable group destroyed many young men and women who came to Winterland to prove themselves. However, the vicious physical attacks, the creative well-placed lies, the faultless alibis proving innocence to their superiors, and their outstanding eminence in the eyes of the Council of Winterland put them beyond reproach. With the blindness of their teachers and administrators to protect them, these thugs designed atrocities to discourage and damage anyone they targeted. The educators encouraged their competition, and when they secretly began killing students, retaining their superiority over their competition, they were never stopped. Their depravity went unchecked and grew rampant. Teachers aware of this group either looked the other way or encouraged their methods of eliminating their competition. It was the epitome of depravity and immorality.

The destruction of Winterland arrived when a girl named Heather was raped and killed by the boldest, most brutal competitor Winterland ever produced. His name was Christian Losse.

On the day Christian demanded the brutal initiation of a new student, named Jeremy, the fate of Winterland was sealed. Christian chose Jeremy, thinking he would make a good addition to the collection of thugs he utilized to rule the hallowed halls of Winterland. It was his physical stature that impressed Christian. Jeremy was a big man, broad shouldered, muscular, and stood a head taller than any student Christian ever met. When Christian confronted him and demanded his subservience, Jeremy laughed him off. The outraged Christian engaged three of his thugs to subdue him. Then according to Christian's orders, they were to beat him senseless. However, Jeremy fought back, knocking them to the ground almost effortlessly. The incident made Christian Losse the laughing stock of the school.

Christian never tasted failure. To him, failure was a bitter meal he would never swallow. He never failed, and this fool Jeremy would pay the price of failure, not he. He told his thugs to follow Jeremy secretly, watching for any weaknesses. They found one. Her name was Heather, and Jeremy was head over heels in love with her. Christian knew another confrontation to humiliate Jeremy would be hopeless. So as a lesson, he cowardly plotted to ruin him by destroying his beloved Heather.

Christian clandestinely set a trap to separate Heather from her friends, but her friend Rebecca saw his two thugs walking beside her just before she disappeared. His group of vicious animals covertly abducted her, using a rehearsed distraction to hide her presence. When restrained, they shoved her into an open toolshed where he and his thugs repeatedly raped and eventually killed her. When Heather's friends, Justin, Christine, and Rebecca, realized she was missing, they told Jeremy. They started searching but could not find her. A howling snowstorm, unlike any storm seen in a century, struck the school grounds, making their search impossible. With the blustery snowstorm raging, Justin and Jeremy struggled through blinding snow, fighting their way through freezing temperatures and frozen doorways, and tried vainly to get the attention of the school authorities. They begged for help, but everyone either refused or resisted doing anything, telling them Heather was probably drunk, passed out in somebody's room.

It wasn't until morning, when the snowstorm passed, that Justin and Jeremy opened the doors to an arm's length of snow covering everything in a sepulchral white veil. Jeremy alone, overwrought by Heather's mysterious disappearance and eager to find the girl he loved, dashed headlong into the deep snow in the muted light before sunrise. He went to a shed he tried to check before the storm encompassed the grounds. The shed door was half open when Jeremy arrived. Hoping Heather took refuge there during the storm, he shouted her name as he struggled through waist-high snow. The floor inside revealed a trail of blood leading out, disappearing under the snow. Inside, blood-soaked clothes were torn to shreds. The clothing was what Heather wore when she disappeared. The trail of blood was impossible to follow beyond the door.

Justin, concerned for his friend, followed his tracks in the snow. He found Jeremy hunched by the toolshed door. Jeremy pointed to the ominous signs of a brutal attack and the shredded bloodstained clothing. When Justin calmed Jeremy to where they could both think, they decided to keep the torn clothing as proof of the attack. Still, if there was a chance Heather was alive, they needed to find her. They found two brooms inside the shed and then dusted the snow off the trail of frozen blood. They worked together, following the serpentine path to the outer wall encircling the perimeter of the school grounds. The blood stopped at the wall. The wall was too tall to climb, especially for someone injured. Sweeping the snow away a short distance in both directions, finding nothing, they decided each would follow the wall in opposite directions, calling out if they found anything.

It was Jeremy who found the icy blue hand, outstretched, frozen in midair, reaching from the snow. Apparently, Heather didn't die as quickly as Christian hoped. She must have crawled from the shed after they abandoned her. Injured and disoriented, Heather crawled in enormous pain, looking for help, and finding none, struggled to the outer wall and died. Jeremy, recognizing Heather's hand, screamed with inconsolable tears. Justin, hearing his friend's anguish, ran where Jeremy held the frozen hand of his beloved Heather. Justin pulled the snow off her naked body and placed his cloak over her. He tried to pull Jeremy away, explaining they needed to report what they found. But it was a hopeless gesture. Jeremy would not abandon her. Justin had to leave him. He struggled through the deep snow and found Rebecca and Christine waiting for his news. The young women were devastated by what he had to tell them. Justin told them he needed their help, explaining where he left Jeremy. He sent them, with instructions to bring him back, while he found a way to report Heather's suspicious death.

It took a very long time for Rebecca and Christine to comfort Jeremy. They found him holding Heather's frozen body where Justin left him. Rebecca found an officer of the school to take Heather's body away before Christine could convince him to come back to report her death to the headmasters. An irate Justin supported Jeremy when they revealed their allegations about Christian Losse to Winterland's officials. After hearing their story, they were reprimanded for their slanderous insinuations that Christian Losse was responsible. The authorities lauded Christian with the highest honors for his dispassionate nature in competitions. He, with his fellow classmates, defeated every team in every sport. They were in the top honor rolls in every class . . . every subject. Christian was the epitome of Winterland's vision of their ultimate success. Christian's lackeys provided him with a credible alibi, which the Council would not contest. When Jeremy insisted on reporting the events leading to Heather's death to an outside tribunal, they expelled him instantly with dishonor. The Winterland Council put Justin on dishonorable probation for interfering with a school investigation. Jeremy left Winterland's grounds unassisted but swore revenge on those who killed Heather.

When word of Jeremy's vow of revenge reached Christian, he invented a strategy to placate Justin. Confronted by Christian's thugs, Justin was helpless. Christian watched Justin writhe as his thugs beat his legs to splinters. He laughed at this impotent protector of Heather's remaining friends . . . Christine and Rebecca. With Justin out of the way, the two girls had to protect themselves. The girls knew they were the next targets of Christian's sick revenge. They had no intentions to be raped or killed, possibly both under the circumstances. With Justin gone, the only person left to help them was the ostracized Jeremy.

According to the legend, when Christine and Rebecca told Jeremy what Christian had done, he went insane. However, it wasn't the kind of insane where he screamed and ranted. This kind of insanity was silence, introspection, and a plan so cunning that not only would Jeremy get revenge for Heather's death but he would also bring down the gates and souls of Winterland forever.

Amelia remembered this part of the legend well. According to the old stories, Jeremy went to Justin. Together, they devised a plan to trap Christian and his followers in the heart of the school . . . the library of Winterland. Patiently, they waited . . . they waited, keeping Rebecca and Christine cloaked and invisible . . . They waited for the tempo of Heather's death to calm a bit. Then the night finally came to put their plan to work.

Christine and Rebecca came out of hiding and made themselves innocently visible to Christian and his followers. On the appointed night, the girls went into the library when it was about to close. On plan, Christian and his deviants followed them. Christine evaded Christian's clumsily devised ambushes as long as she could but was overtaken by Christian's animals, which wasn't part of Jeremy's plan. Christine's sacrifice gave Rebecca time to hide. When Christian's gang of sadistic animals cornered Christine, they forced her onto a hard wooden table. Two thugs wrestled her arms, while two others tore the clothes from her body. They had the advantage, gloating about their debased intentions of raping her first to humiliate her and then beating her to death afterward. Before anything happened, Jeremy appeared from nowhere with a blazing torch in his hand.

No one really knows what was said, but the sight of Jeremy in the room startled Christian. He responded by sending most of his thugs to attack him. Christine battled two attackers, while Jeremy fought the others alone. In the desperate fight, Jeremy's head was struck from behind with a heavy book. Jeremy staggered, blood running from his ears, but he still managed to stand. Christian saw his chance to deliver a fatal blow, striking him squarely in the chest with the large bloodstained dictionary he still held in his hands. The heavy blow took Jeremy to his knees. Rebecca remained hidden in the shadows; unable to help her friends . . . she knew it wasn't supposed to happen like this.

The evening before they realized their plans, Jeremy prepared the stage. Behind the veil of a moonless night, he pumped thousands of gallons of flammable fuel from Winterland's stores onto the library's flat roof. The walls surrounding the roof were nearly two arm's lengths high, keeping his industry hidden from inquisitive eyes. He plugged the storm drains and then filled the enormous rooftop pool to capacity.

On the night they lured Christian into the library, Jeremy pierced numerous small holes through the roof with an elongated drill bit he fashioned earlier. This allowed fuel to seep slowly into underlying structures, finding avenues to thousands of books nestled securely on library shelves. Once accomplished, he decended on a ladder to the library below to rescue the two girls. By the time he met them, provided they could be elusive enough to confuse Christian and his thugs away from them, they would have Christian so deep inside the library he would have no way to escape. According to Jeremy's plan, when the fire caught the initial tinder, it would undermine the roof and bathe everything below it in an inferno, the likes of which would never be seen again. They would make their escape through a trapdoor set into an elevated roof near an outer wall. The way to the ground was a rope Jeremy tied there the night before. Their escape was to be used before the fires caught well enough to bring down the roof and oil over Christian and his followers. It never worked that way.

Once Christian caught Christine and subdued her with several blows to the face, the plan for their escape was over. They beat Jeremy senseless, they thought, and then turned their attentions to Christine lying naked and helpless, screaming hopelessly for this horror to stop. But Jeremy wasn't finished. Confronted by Christian and his gang of animals savagely raping Christine, he came off the floor with renewed fury. Jeremy fought like a lion, severely injuring many of Christian's accomplices, but in the end, the sheer number of assailants overpowered him. The fight left him as Christian smashed the blood-soaked dictionary into his chest again and again until he barely breathed. Rebecca remained hidden until the smell of dripping oil became unbearable. The acrid smell drew Christian's attention away from the ongoing rape and savage beating. It was in their moment of absolute surrender to the fates of Christian and his followers that Rebecca made herself known with a burning torch.

As the story went, Amelia remembered, people think Rebecca believed the original plan could still work. Some believe she provoked Christian to release Christine and Jeremy since the people found their poorly survived bones clustered next to each other in the charred debris. However, some people feel Christine's and Jeremy's injuries must have been too severe for Rebecca to get them to the roof. And here is where the story of the fire becomes blurry. Did Christian try to stop them from escaping and Rebecca threw the torch as a means of preventing the attack? Or was it the more popular theory that once confronted with no possible means to escape, Rebecca decided to sacrifice herself and her friends for the greater good? Perhaps she perceived her final act a design to destroy the decadence, fashioned and nurtured by competition, thriving inside a wall of impenetrable rules created by its distinguished authorities, to end Winterland. Whatever her reason, Rebecca threw her torch into the dripping oil, causing a ball of flames to explode like a blistering fountain that rose so far into the air, the villages of Emansupass and Bridgedom saw the flash in the night sky . . . or so they say. The roar of fire released a sudden blast of thunder, and the world that was Winterland shook at its insistence. Unable to contain the fire at the site of the library, several buildings surrendered to its insatiable hunger and became engulfed in flames. Physically, Winterland was over . . . yet it was Justin that finished it.

Justin was the only one left to tell the story. He knew the plans made by his friends should have worked. It was a simple matter of piecing together what he knew, with the way their bodies were found, to realize what transpired. He knew the outcome of the fire would be twisted into something else by anyone left in Winterland's service. Justin wrote the truth behind the fire, sending copies to friends in nearby villages . . . and within days, the story went to the ones beyond. When the villagers heard Justin's account of Winterland's atrocities, families came and extricated their children in droves. Between the extensive destruction of Jeremy's fire and failing support of the villages, Winterland fell to abandonment.

The teachers condoning Winterland's detestable history were, at first, hunted down by horsemen who ran the hated teachers to death before their horses. Most willingly went into isolation, never to return to the villages again. To assure their isolation, the letter W was branded into their forehead. Any known teachers of Winterland who tried to hide were brought to trial. Those refusing the brand were allowed to be hanged or run to death before the horsemen. Most chose to be branded, though it only delayed death a little while. Those with the brand were exiled to the frozen northern wastelands, where they were most certainly doomed to a frozen death.

After the fall of Winterland, no one dared use the word "teacher" for fear of the severe punishment dealt by the villagers. From that time forward, trades, history, finances, and whatever passed for sciences and mathematics were passed down through families. Somehow the system worked. No one called it "teaching." No one was ever known as a "teacher," as the knowledge of the treachery that occurred at Winterland tainted the word. People who were good at something were known as "knowledgeable." Or as they were more commonly called in Amelia's day, "seekers."

Of Winterland, only the terrifying legend survived. If there ever was such a place, it was gone centuries ago. Whatever knowledge it possessed was gone with it. It was, to Amelia, a fairy story designed to teach and frighten people from falling into the deviancy of "competition." In Amelia's world, everyone had a place. It was only by a marriage or by apprenticeship, where you worked with a skilled tradesman, that anyone changed their position or standing in life.

It was a slow painful death to admit being a carrier of a prophecy, of a telling or vision. Being a prophet or a person with a telling was to accept the same fate as a "teacher"; both were avoided and despised . . . both ended in exile. Still, she feared the implications of exile to the place called Winterland. Of her own visions and instructions, from voices no one could hear, she assumed people might find her mad. Yet the breach caused considerable physical damage and danger to her world. Surely someone, like herself, might be believed in these grave times. Someone might listen . . . might believe what she said to be true. Yet in the gravity of the situation, Amelia felt it was her duty to the villages . . . her last dying act, to warn them. And if by warning them, they could save themselves, perhaps her life would count for something, either despised or revered.

In spite of every footstep becoming a small agony, Amelia pushed on. The first day away from her lifestone would be painful but tolerable. The second day, she might still get around, but the pain and the weakness were sure to set in by the end of it. By the third day, she would need someone to look after her. It would be her day of dying. Amelia did not have much time. Today was a certainty, and perhaps as much as half a day after that. But then, she would need to find someone, someone who would allow her to die in peace and gratefully bury her body in the accepted traditions of the villages. She knew Victoria would not make it back in time. Amelia knew this from the beginning. All they ever had was hope.

As Amelia drew close to Stock, she noticed thick gray tendrils of smoke rolling from the eastern side of the village. Though filled with fear and foreboding, she kept moving until she passed some scattered buildings on the outskirts of Stock. There were people dying in the street. Fire, smoke, and broken glass covered the worn cobblestones. People were running about, fearful of the events happening around their village. Amelia stopped a passerby. "Sir, do you know a young woman named Catherine?"

"I'm sorry, girl," the man replied. "I need to get my wife to the healer. She was hit by glass, and she is bleeding badly. I'm sorry." Then the man ran quickly as he could through the smoke-filled street, leaving Amelia alone.

Amelia moved on, trying to find someone to talk to when she spied an old woman crying. "I'm sorry to disturb you, ma'am, but have you heard of a young woman named Catherine who lives here?"

The old woman was so besieged by her tears and her sorrow, she could only shake her head no.

Amelia wanted to cry herself. The whole world was in shambles. She looked up and down the cobbled streets, trying to find someone for help. Just then, something told her to check Benjamin's shop, just across the street from her. She hurried across, past piles of bodies lying to the side, broken glass everywhere, people crying, smoke and fires . . . all caused by Jonathan's quest to break through the wall. She was ashamed of her inability to stop him, but if she could get to Catherine, she might still redeem herself in the eyes of the villages. When she entered Benjamin's shop, she was aghast by the destruction she saw there. She heard something hit the floor and then saw a woman struggling to find the front door. The woman was blinded by blood-soaked hair and billowing smoke pouring through the broken windows of the shop.

Amelia found the woman's hand and guided her through the smoke and broken glass. When their feet met the solid ground of the street, the woman turned to Amelia and said, "Thank you, my dear. I could not see anything after the windows broke and smoke filled the shop."

"Please, ma'am," Amelia pleaded, "do you know where I might find a young woman named Catherine?"

The woman's disheveled black hair covered a deep cut across her forehead and some minor cuts, but otherwise, she braved the consequences of the destruction well. She looked at Amelia and said, "Catherine was just here with her mother, Leena. I saw them leaving with Benjamin out the back of his shop. If you hurry around this side of the store, you may still catch them."

"Thank you . . . thank you," Amelia squealed. "I'm going right now. I think I know where they are."

In spite of the growing pain in her limbs and shoulders, Amelia ran like the wind to the alleyway leading to the back of Benjamin's shop. There she heard echoing hoof beats of a horse at full gallop. She ran to the center of the passage, hoping Benjamin would see her in time to stop. She looked into the smoky, shaded alley, unable to see anything through the thick smoke. Within moments, Amelia saw a horse and cart hurtle toward her around a blind curve. Almost upon her, she waved and screamed for the driver to stop. However, the cart's momentum was too fast to stop in the distance left between them. Amelia jumped away just as the cart was almost on top of her. She hit the cobbled street with her shoulder as she screamed, "Catherine . . . Catherine, please stop. I must tell you something . . . something important. Please stop, Catherine . . . please." Amelia cried out from her pain, but more so from the realization of her final failure. As she managed to a sitting position, her eyes blurred with tears. She could never get to Catherine now.

And It Was the Beginning . . .

Tell me about questions . . .

It was a year of conclusions, a year of beginnings, and a year of continuations. I think back in 1996, and I remember Lois's ability to gather the resources around her. Her chance meeting with Diane Sackett Nannery in Philadelphia caused the first breast cancer awareness stamp to be created. A phone call from the American Cancer Society, pleading for Lois to contribute her patch to the Skin Deep Project, not only caused their efforts to be successful but also spearheaded a novel approach to inform the public about breast cancer. She spent a second year as a consumer advocate to the Department of Defense scientific peer review program. Then in 1996, she was invited to sit as a consumer reviewer for these same panels later in the year.

Lois continued to write her quarterly newsletter to over two hundred breast cancer survivors, physicians, nurses, and other health-related personnel. She continued to get speakers for her group and brought any national news into the local media. She continued biannual testing of her tumor markers and her yearly mammogram on the remaining breast. From the results of her exams, it was decided she was healthy and cancer-free for the time being. Though her health was stable, she was troubled by disturbing breast cancer news she started hearing in the media during the summer of 1996. By the end of the year, Lois began to hear rumblings of dire changes being discussed by one of our nation's most prestigious cancer affiliations, the National Cancer Institute (NCI). By the end of 1996 into 1997, Lois and other breast cancer advocates took on a battle that would not be soon forgotten.

By November and December 1996, there was definite news that the National Cancer Institute was raising their recommendations for women to start screening mammograms at the age of fifty. This was a marked change in the traditional standard of care for women. It was a dramatic departure from the standards already in place by other established and respected cancer agencies such as the American Cancer Society, Sloan Kettering Cancer Center, and others across the United States. The original standard recommended screening mammograms to start at age forty. This was the standard for many years and was recognized and understood by women across the country. Recommending this change to fifty undermined those agencies still recommending the old standard and clouded women's perception as to when they should really begin screening themselves. According to many old records I have been able to resurrect, the atmosphere surrounding the NCI's recommendation became so heated, many outraged women across the country spoke out with defiant belligerence against the NCI's decision on mammograms. Discussions broke out in the newspapers, magazines, television, and, in particular, the Internet.

Lois was markedly upset by the NCI's decision not to recommend mammograms to women at age forty. To her, this appeared to be a decision with dangerous consequences, which drove confusion into the minds of American women approaching their forties. It was also a personal affront to Lois who found her breast cancer at age thirty-nine and was officially diagnosed at the age of forty. The controversy struck home with her. I wasn't surprised when she made it her personal crusade to fight the decision of the National Cancer Institute.

Throughout the years, to this very day, the controversy continues to be discussed as new technology comes to the forefront. The controversy came up again in 2008 and 2009, but by this time, Lois's health was fragile, and she was not able to return to the battle the way she did in 1997. However, in late 1996, Lois was ready to do battle with the large, well-established, and respected NCI. It was now a very tiny David and a mammoth Goliath that would enter this arena of controversy in early 1997.

Lois participated in several online breast cancer support groups at the time. On almost any night, she was in discussions with other breast cancer survivors and, at times, the family members of the survivors. They would discuss the news of the day as it related to the

NCI's recommendations about mammograms. Many nights I sat with Lois when she would show me the e-mails she sent and her return e-mails. Every time I read one, I found a story of fear and outrage over a decision affecting every woman across the United States. What was evident in her early e-mails was, not only were the women of this country watching this decision closely but women all over the world were also doing the same.

At first, Lois received e-mails from New York, California, Florida, and almost every state in the Union. They were asking the same thing, "Why would the NCI make such a horrendous recommendation?" Later that year, closer to Christmas 1996, Lois started receiving e-mails from women and female physicians all over the world. Lois chatted with a physician in Australia and another breast cancer survivor in Norway. She received several e-mails from Great Britain and a few from France. Sometimes the person sending e-mails was not fluent in the English language but had taken the time to get an interpreter just to e-mail Lois. I tell you this to illustrate how important this decision was to the women of the world and how much faith they had in Lois to do something about it. By the end of 1996, there was no longer any doubt; women of the world were focused on the decision made by the NCI. They were also concerned about an anticipated response by women in the United States. Never before had any medical decision ever made, by any authority, cause such a heated debate.

From January 21 through January 23, 1997, the National Cancer Institute (NCI) director, Richard Klausner, MD, convened a panel of scientists, which concluded regular mammograms were not necessary until a woman reached the age of fifty. Dr. Klausner disagreed with his own panel, as did the American Cancer Society and many health care agencies. This decision created confusion for women approaching the age of forty as to when to get their first mammograms. The NCI's recommendation, "It is up to the individual and her physician as to when to do the first mammogram," was at odds with the recommendations of other agencies. When all the literature spoke of prevention, when all the insurance companies believed prevention was cheaper than treating an illness, how did the NCI come up with such a statement? A Swedish delegation had been invited to the consensus panel to share new information on this age group. Their evidence showed a 16 to 25 percent mortality reduction using screening mammography in the forty- to forty-nine-year old women. Their evidence in 1997 was the latest available evidence on this age group. They were completely ignored. Some members of the panel were outraged. Jennie Petrek, MD, of Memorial Sloan Kettering Cancer Center in New York City, resigned from the consensus panel because of the decision.

By January 1997, the NCI's decision to recommend women to begin screening mammograms at the age of fifty became so contested, the media carried the story every day. At the urging of Lois's many Internet friends, she made a decision to make contact with the National Cancer Institute. Lois, after making several calls, eventually spoke with Dr. Alan Rabson, acting deputy director of the National Cancer Institute (in 1997). After some discussion, he had Lois call Dr. Richard Klausner, then director of the National Cancer Institute (1997).

In Lois's conversation with Dr. Klausner, she discovered he did not agree with his own panel regarding the mammogram decision. Lois wanted to know what he needed to persuade the panel to overturn their decision so the NCI's recommendations would align with other existing cancer organizations. Dr. Klausner suggested Lois needed to get anecdotal evidence to be used as proof of diagnostic validation of women's lives saved by the use of mammograms under the age of fifty. He told her he felt the more cases he could present, the more convincing his argument would be to change the minds of his own panel.

Lois made contact with Dr. Klausner during the last week of January 1997. The National Cancer Institute was to reconvene their meeting on the mammogram recommendations on February 25 and 26, 1997. Dr. Klausner needed whatever anecdotal information Lois could obtain and verify with documentation a week before this conference took place. This gave Lois just a little over two weeks to get the information, verify it, and then send it to Dr. Klausner before the conference. The enormity of Dr. Klausner's request was staggering. How could something with such enormous consequences be accomplished in two weeks?

Lois went to work immediately. She sent out a mass mailing to her friends on the Internet asking for their help and their stories. She explained anything they could gather needed documentation to be sent to Dr. Klausner. After setting up her Internet contacts, she called the Pennsylvania Breast Cancer Coalition (PBCC) and asked their permission to send a newswire across the county asking for anecdotal evidence to submit to Dr. Klausner for the conference on February 25 and 26. She explained everything had to be in place by February 20, the last day Dr. Klausner would be able to accept anything.

According to the conversation with Dr. Klausner, all the anecdotal experiences needed to have the person's name, address, and age of their first mammogram, age of diagnosis, type of breast cancer, and a brief overview of how the person felt about screening mammography before the age of fifty. The newswire was sent out to the public on January 31, 1997, and said:

CALL TO ACTION

PBCC SEEKS MAMMOGRAM EVIDENCE FOR NATIONAL CANCER INSTITUTE CONFERENCE

In response to the inability of the National Institutes of Health to resolve the mammogram age controversy, the Pennsylvania Breast Cancer Coalition is issuing an immediate CALL TO ACTION! This effort is spearheaded by Lois Anderson, York County Captain for the Pennsylvania Breast Cancer Coalition, who is collecting anecdotal evidence from any woman in the Commonwealth whose breast cancer was detected by a mammogram under the age of 49.

"The controversy surrounding the age women should begin getting mammograms is causing DEADLY CONFUSION," said Pat Halpin-Murphy, President and Founder of the Pennsylvania Breast Cancer Coalition. "This callous disregard for women's lives means that women in their 40s will die from breast cancer!"

Ms. Anderson, a breast cancer survivor and advocate, immediately activated her support group. She said, "We must end this furious debate. We know women in their 40s are dying of breast cancer and that early diagnosis with a mammogram can spare them and their families from needless tragedy. We do not accept the National Institutes of Health's decision and we demand a resolution."

We are compiling this data at the request of Dr. Alan Rabson, Deputy Director of the National Cancer Institute (NCI). It will be presented at a conference February 25 and 26 by Dr. Richard Klausner, Director of the NCI.

Women should fax their data to the PBCC at ********. Each report should include: diagnosis date, type of breast cancer (if known), age at diagnosis, names, address and phone number.

This gave the entire country of women twenty days to get the information to Lois, compile it, and send it to Dr. Klausner in time for him to evaluate the evidence and present it at the conference.

There was no time for discussions anymore. Women had to stand up and be counted in an effort to reverse the decision of the National Cancer Institute. Still not everyone agreed that the NCI's decision to start screening mammography at age fifty was wrong. From the scientific standpoint, it was agreed mammography was not a perfect tool; too many false readings made it unreliable. There were others that contested "self-breast exams" were not necessary, saying a woman needed a professional exam to be sure something was truly wrong. Even Frances Visco, president of the National Breast Cancer Coalition and a breast cancer survivor, spoke at a Senate Appropriations Subcommittee and said, "I am appalled at the resources we continue to devote to this question. We have to save the outrage for the fact that we don't know how to prevent this disease, how to cure it, how to detect it truly early, or what to do for an individual once we do find it" (*American Health Consultants*, "Breast Cancer: The Disease State Management Resource," 1997, 37).

Visco's statement in 1997 was absolutely true. No one in 1997 knew what to do about breast cancer. Fighting for screening mammography, an imperfect tool at best, seemed to be using an enormous amount of resources for something that didn't work all the time for everyone. So I had to ask myself, "Why was the mammogram decision so important? Why would anyone want to continue such an imperfect tool? Why not save the outrage for better, more-sophisticated tools to find and treat breast cancer?" The answer was simply this: this fight was never really about mammograms. The fight was really about when a woman was to begin screening themselves for breast cancer. Mammograms were the vanguard, the "golden mile" a woman achieved when she turned forty . . . the time you started screening yourself in earnest for breast health. When you look at it this way, it is much easier to understand the meaning between the lines.

By the time most women reach forty, they have had all or most of their children. Hormonal changes, lifestyles, and generally midlife changes affecting the bodies of women start occurring around the age of forty. Does it happen for all women? No, of course not . . . but recommendations for other diseases existfor prostate cancer, colon cancer, and other cancers. So based on a general overview of when we know breast cancer emerges in the lifetime of women, why not keep the initial screening age of forty intact? Why change it to ten years later when we already know a substantial number of fatal breast cancer occurrences happen before the age of fifty? It is while the hormonal presences are in the breasts, enabling fertility, which the more-fatal breast cancers seem to survive and burgeon throughout the body. It is only after the body disables this hormonal system in women that any occurring breast cancers appear more easily controlled and better able to be survived. So knowing this, why deny women under the age of fifty the signpost that says, "Start screening at age forty!"?

I can't begin to fathom the scientific and technological advances of our current times or even the times as they existed in 1997. Every day, even by the hour of every day, new advances occur to help women screen themselves for breast cancer. The object of discussions in 1997 was when to begin screening. Using mammograms as the vehicle on which to base the discussions was just a point of form. If we used the term "xenograms" (a fictitious test that could catch all types of breast cancer) in place of the word "mammogram," I don't believe the contentiousness would have persisted for as long as it did. So getting your "xenograms" at age forty would have been okay for most of the women of our country, but getting a mammogram at age forty . . . now that was a problem.

However, the fictitious and elusive "xenogram" did not exist in 1997, and it does not exist at the time of this writing either. We still search for it and hope for it. So until the perfect "xenogram" exists, what do women do to protect themselves, and, more importantly, when do they start to do it? And there is the real question: "When do women start to screen themselves and with what crude (but existing) tools?"

On February 4, 1997, I wrote a letter to the editor about an article written by Larry Hicks on January 29, 1997. My letter exemplifies a little of what was happening over the entire country.

Mammogram needed earlier than 50

I'd like to thank Larry Hicks for his article on the National Cancer Institute's negative decision on mammograms for women under 50 years of age. I facilitate a men's support group involved in helping men deal with their wives' diagnosis of breast cancer. More times than not, the men tell me the cancer was spotted on a mammogram. Many of the men indicate that their wives were less than 50 years of age when the cancer was found. Therefore a real benefit to early detection through the use of mammograms at ages less than 50 exists.

I believe Larry hit the "nail on the head" when he wrote about the kind of message the NCI sent women. The NCI's decision to not recommend mammography for women between the ages of 40 and 49 places too much of the decision-making process on the average woman. Many times these women do not have the time or the inclination to investigate this decision in their lives. This is a complex issue! American women are being told to make their own decision to have mammograms. I hate to tell the NCI this, but the women of this country have always had the right to decide to have a mammogram or not. The NCI's decision makes it unclear to women as to when to have a mammogram, not whether women think it is a good idea. This ambiguity might prove deadly for the women below 50 thinking about when to have their first mammogram.

And Larry, you're right about self breast exams. Done properly they are the first line of defense in the fight against breast cancer. I am very fortunate that my wife is still alive four years after her diagnosis of breast cancer because of self-exam. Self breast exams and mammograms . . . good things to tell the woman in your life. Thanks Larry.

George S. J. Anderson

Co-facilitator of the Men's Group of

Surviving Breast Cancer Support Group

I'm sure when conversations about the impact of breast cancer on society occur; the conversations only look at the front end of the story. There are people behind the math, behind the statistics, behind the sciences and technology, and the media. Breast cancer predominately affects women. To lose a woman before the age of fifty, be it your wife, sister, daughter, aunt, mother, or friend, to this disease is devastating when their life ends. The impact on society is not simply the loss of the breast cancer patient; the impact is a profound and expensive loss. So not giving women recommendations to begin screening until age fifty would have had serious consequences. So this is something to consider as I tell the rest of Lois's story . . . amazing, as it is true.

Twenty days were given to Lois to accomplish a feat almost desperate in comparison to the years of research and knowledge base standing before her. The best minds in the country and the world, backed, no doubt, by lobbyists and interested parties hoping to cut health care costs, gathered before her. An unknown band of fellow breast cancer survivors, yet to make contact, would be her army if such a militant force still existed in a world where conformity and silence became the new norm . . . where complacency was a virtue to be admired. Lois was their tiny David pitted against the wills and knowledge of the NCI. In spite of the enormity of this task, Lois still believed she was doing the right thing. She felt getting the NCI to align its recommendations with other breast cancer agencies throughout the country would solve the confusion as to when to begin screening women.

After the newswire went out on January 31, 1997, Lois and I waited for the women of this country to respond. Every day, we continued to read stories regarding the mammogram decision as the newspapers, magazines, and television stories carried the latest developments. The Internet was a hive of heated discussions. But now, Lois offered the women of this country a way to actively participate in changing this decision. We spent the last night of January 1997 listening and waiting.

The woman who once told me, "I don't want to be forgotten," was about to put her mark upon the world. In my experiences with cancer, I have seen how it marks itself in a cruel irony but leaves a legacy of heroes, warriors, and poets. Sometimes change comes into our lives and makes us different people than the way we were before, and sometimes we get the chance to change things. Breast cancer came into my wife's life and changed her. Now her chance to do something about it came to be. Neither Lois nor I was prepared for what happened after the newswire went out.

At first, it seemed nothing would happen as our phone sat quietly, waiting for calls that never came. On the second day, the phone started ringing. The first calls came from women across the state of Pennsylvania. At first, calls came sporadically then multiplied so quickly, Lois could not finish one before another came in. For hours, the phone was filled with callers all over the state trying to realize the conditions Lois needed to present documentation of their case before Dr. Klausner. Many callers voiced their protest against the decision made by the NCI, and others wanted to help, promising Lois faxes or mailings of their information before the NCI meeting at the end of February.

On Tuesday, February 4, 1997, senators Specter and Hutchinson were instrumental in passing a nonbinding U.S. resolution recommending mammograms to forty- to forty-nine-year-old women across the country. It passed, 98-0. It did not change the NCI's decision. More needed to be done.

On February 5, Dr. Richard Klausner spoke before the subcommittee on labor, health, human services, education, and related agencies about the "mammogram decision." During the same week, Lois appeared on three local television stations calling for stories from women helped by the use of a mammogram before the age of fifty.

By the end of the first week, calls continued both day and night. Calls started coming from all points in the country with promises to fax or mail Lois the information she needed. I fielded hundreds of these calls during the day when Lois worked, and she handled the calls at night when I worked the night shift. The stories these brave women told were, at times, heart wrenching. Others just called to say they appreciated what Lois was doing for the women of this country but did not want to give out their information. There were young women under the age of forty that told us their stories and were willing to send information on how a mammogram helped to save their lives, but since Dr. Klausner and Dr. Rabson only wanted anecdotal stories from women ages forty to forty-nine, we would not be allowed to use them. We sadly told them they could not be counted, which was a devastating loss. We heard stories from affluent women, poor women, and members of families where their wife or mother found their breast cancer too late to be helped, all calling us to protest the decision or offer their information to Lois. The response from the women all across the country was staggering. Yet Lois would only be allowed to present those stories with documented proof of survival after a mammogram detected breast cancer. We were confronted with the real face of a country of breast cancer survivors wanting to speak but found the confines of Dr. Klausner's restrictions unacceptable or unattainable in the time constraints offered . . . so many faces remained in the shadows . . . too many remained uncounted.

Lois was delighted by the responses she was getting. Every day, we received documentation she needed to present to the NCI. However, in some documentation were flaws that made the information she received useless to Dr. Klausner and Dr. Rabson. She started evaluating what she could use and what she could not. Though disappointed by some responses, she was still getting reasonable amounts of good documentation from the women sending their stories, their anecdotal evidence. Then something unexpected started happening in the second week.

Calls from women across the United States continued to come in, and Lois and I continued requesting the appropriate information from them. Then calls started coming from Canada. After I received five or six calls from there, I told Lois what was happening. She felt somehow the newswire crossed our northern borders, and the women from Canada were calling with the hope they could participate in some way. I told Lois I hated to turn them down, but Dr. Klausner and Dr. Rabson were very clear on what they wanted for the conference. Lois told me it was unfortunate they could not participate, but the rules about what types of anecdotal evidence Dr. Klausner would accept were clear . . . American women between the ages of forty and forty-nine saved by the use of a mammogram; no others were to be included. That same evening, Lois continued with calls, and again some calls came from Canadian women asking how they could help. Lois asked why they were calling, since only American women could participate in the collection of anecdotal evidence. Their answer was simple: this fight, this struggle, was about the screening age women were to begin. Mammograms were only part of the screening process, but the age they were to begin screening was their real issue. They found the American concept held by the NCI contemptuous of the women of the world and found Lois's crusade to change it both important and courageous.

This helped Lois feel better about what she was doing since it came when she had about sixty or seventy anecdotal records with very few days left before they had to be sent to the conference with the NCI. It was after the calls from Canada started that calls from Great Britain, Norway, Ireland, and other countries across the Atlantic Ocean began to call. I remember a call I received one night when I was off work. I received a call from a woman who stated she was from France. She called using an interpreter to tell me her story of how a mammogram saved her life in her early forties. I had to tell her through her interpreter that I wished her well, but I could not use her story because I could only use stories received from American women. After the call was over, I felt deflated. This woman had used her own money to make a transatlantic phone call, called at a time that was a different time zone than ours, and found an interpreter who spoke English so she could communicate with us. I began to realize the implications of the NCI's decision, and the women of the world were siding with Lois, my wife. It was a chilling experience to be sitting in the same house with someone who was making history.

When Lois woke up the next morning, I looked at her and said, "This is not about mammograms anymore, is it?"

She nodded and said, "I think this is a bigger fight than what I first thought."

After telling her about the call I received in the early hours from France, I said, "It took a lot of courage for that French woman to make that call. She had to plan, get people in place, and then tell us her story, a story we cannot use because of the restrictions."

"I know." Then she said, "The world is watching us now. The decision the NCI makes will affect the world, even though they think they are just doing it for the women in the United States."

"We have to do our best for them."

"We will," Lois said with emphasis, then as an afterthought, she continued, "I sometimes wondered if I was doing the right thing. But hearing from people all over the world lets me know this is the right thing to do."

"Even if the NCI will never hear any of these stories from other countries?" I asked.

"I know how you feel about it, but the NCI will never know about these calls. The NCI has jurisdiction in the United States only. The money that affects the women who have breast cancer is only spent on American women. That is why the restrictions to American women in the United States was placed on the anecdotal stories I can bring to the NCI."

"No one will ever know how brave these women across the world have been to offer their stories to us," I said.

"Perhaps someday I will get to tell the whole story. For now, I have to concentrate on what I can do, and not on what I can't."

"I know . . . and you weren't given much time to start with," I said. I could see the weight of what she was trying to accomplish sink into her. It made her resolve to do her best for all the women who had called even stronger.

I don't believe Lois ever told anyone about the calls we received from foreign countries. I tell you now, to let everyone know how important the NCI's decision was to the world. My call from the woman in France was not the only foreign call I received. I received calls from England, France, Italy, Australia, Norway, Denmark, and countries all over the world, all wanting to help Lois deliver anecdotal evidence of breast cancer survival after a mammogram between the ages of forty and forty-nine. In spite of the efforts from these countries, Lois and I were unable to use any of their stories. However, their efforts reenergized her and made her realize the eyes of women across the world were on the United States, and Lois would not let them down as she prepared anecdotal stories for the upcoming conference of the NCI. How the NCI handled the mammogram decision was now a world matter, whether they were aware of it or not.

On February 14, 1997, Lois appeared with Dr. Wanda Filer (then Pennsylvania's state surgeon general) in a radio broadcast at the *Pennsylvania Round Table* program. The topic was "Mammograms and the National Cancer Institute's Decision." The program was about thirty minutes long, and though it was a radio program, many women and interested parties tuned in and listened. They were interested in what Dr. Filer and the woman going up against the NCI's decision had to say. It was one of those remarkable historic radio shows in the history of the radio station.

Lois, foreseeing she would not have enough anecdotal evidence to persuade the NCI, sent out the following letter to Senator Arlen Specter on February 19, 1997.

February 19, 1997

Senator Arlen Specter
*** Hart Senate Office Building
Washington, DC, 20510

Dear Senator Specter:

This letter is a follow-up to a phone call conversation I had with Allison Dekosky, an aide in your office, on February 14, 1997 regarding the mammogram controversy now taking place.

I am a breast cancer survivor, advocate, and York County Co-Captain of the Pennsylvania breast Cancer Coalition, and as such was very angered and dismayed over the NIH Consensus Conference decision to NOT routinely recommend women between 40 and 49 years of age be screened by mammography. My anger and dismay prompted me to mount a campaign to collect stories from women less than 50 years of age whose breast cancer was diagnosed by a mammogram. These stories will be sent to both Dr. Richard Klausner and Dr. Alan Rabson, Director and Deputy Director respectively of the National Cancer Institute, prior to the meeting of the Advocacy Board to the NCI on February 25th and 26th.

A copy of the PBCC press release and copy of a notice placed in physician offices follow this letter.

My breast cancer was not initially found on my mammogram, but a benign lesion was. However because I was having bruising symptoms in my breast, my radiologist and gynecologist both recommended I see a surgeon. Because of my education and training as a Medical Technologist and my husband's work as a Registered Nurse, we agreed to see a surgeon. On exam, a lump was found, biopsied, and turned out to be Infiltrating Ductal Carcinoma with Osteoclastlike Giant Cells. A full 0.1% of all breast cancers are of this type. This rarity makes things scary for me, as no one knows why these giant cells are in the tumor nor what they do there. In a way a mammogram did save my life—the mammogram forced me to seek additional help to find out what was wrong. Many women without enough medical knowledge when confronted with a situation such as this would choose to watch and wait. For me waiting would have caused my death within two years according to my surgeon. I was 39 years old at the time of my diagnosis.

I was very happy to see that the Senate Subcommittee on Health and Human Services passed a nonbinding resolution recommending screening mammograms for women between 40 and 49 years of age. Many tumors are being found in this age group as the use of mammography grows and because, in general, more breast cancer is being found in younger women. According to the CDC the incidence of breast cancer increased 34% from 1973 to 1992.

I would be very happy to testify at any hearings to be held on the mammography issue. I feel that mammograms are an essential screening method that SHOULD be used to detect breast cancer in women ages 40 to 49 and even younger if there is a family history of the disease. At the present time, MAMMOGRAPHY is our ONLY TOOL we have to detect breast cancer early. In addition, the earlier breast cancer is detected, the higher the survival rate will be. Early detection without mammography is an illogical concept to me. How can we take mammograms away from these women and tell them to decide for themselves when many physicians do not recommend mammograms and when many women do not have enough medical knowledge to aggressively ask for these tests.

As you can see my frustrations, dismay, and anger run deep and I would be willing to testify or do anything to stand up and be counted regarding this issue.

Sincerely,

Lois A. Anderson
Co-facilitator and founder of Surviving Breast Cancer Support Group at the York Cancer Center and York County Co-captain of the Pennsylvania Breast Cancer Coalition

Sometime after Lois sent the letter to Senator Specter, the NCI decided to postpone the "mammogram decision" until the highly emotional, highly charged atmosphere surrounding it cooled. Lois had collected a little over two hundred anecdotal stories with the appropriate documentation to be used as evidence to be presented before the scheduled NCI meeting on February 25 and 26. Now the meeting was not going to take place.

It was a remarkable journey to hear so many breast cancer stories from survivors all over the country and all over the world. It was an incredible effort, on Lois's part, to compile over two hundred stories and put them into a usable form for Dr. Klausner to present in the now-postponed conference. Copies of the evidence were sent to Dr. Klausner by Lois in the allotted time. She had hoped for many more, but to get over two hundred documented stories organized and mailed to Dr. Klausner in a little over two weeks was, in itself, phenomenal. Lois was certain, when the conference finally reconvened, Dr. Klausner would use them to help change the minds of his colleagues regarding the "mammogram decision."

On February 23, 1997, I received a phone call from someone asking for Lois. The caller asked if Lois would like to appear on a Senate subcommittee hearing regarding the use of mammography for women ages forty to forty-nine. I asked the caller for a phone number for Lois to call back, and the caller obliged. I then asked the caller if he was ever told how much he sounded like our state's Senator

Specter. The caller laughed and said, "That's probably because I am Senator Specter."

I told the caller I didn't believe him, but I would give Lois the message and the number when she returned home from work. The caller told me it would be okay but to have her call as soon as she got in.

About an hour later, Lois came through the door and asked me, "Did you get any calls over the last few hours?"

"Yes," I told her, "someone called and asked if you would sit on a Senate subcommittee."

"What did you tell them?" she asked, concerned I may have been less than cordial with the caller.

"I just asked if they could leave a phone number for you to call them back . . . and I did," I said nonchalantly, not really believing any of this was happening.

Lois furrowed her brow and asked, "Did the caller tell you who they were?"

"Well, yes. The guy sounded a lot like Senator Specter, so I told him he sounded like the senator."

"You didn't?" she gasped. Then she laughed at me and said, "You goof . . ."

"Yes . . . I did," not understanding I just told Senator Specter I didn't believe he was who he actually claimed to be.

"Oh my god, I better call him back. Where is the phone number?" she asked, as she furiously scrambled to the phone, still shaking her head at my naiveté.

"Over there by the phone," I told her, starting to believe she was contacted earlier in the day about this.

Lois made the call. After she finished, I could see she was very excited about something. "I just spoke with Senator Specter's secretary. They want me to testify about the mammogram decision, and they want all the anecdotal evidence I have so far to be presented at this meeting."

"You aren't kidding, are you?" I asked, only half believing what I was hearing. I sat there dumbfounded for a moment, trying to take in what just happened.

"No . . . and I have to pull everything together as quickly as possible," Lois told me as she headed downstairs to the office. "Come on," she said, "I need your help, or this is not going to happen."

I followed Lois downstairs to the office and the computer we both shared. The stories Lois collected were in a small cardboard box waiting on the desk. Lois asked me to take the box to the post office and make six copies of all the anecdotal records she had collected. She wanted enough copies on hand to give to Senator Specter and whoever else needed them at the subcommittee hearing. Lois always believed in being prepared and organized, especially for an event such as this.

On February 25, 1997, the day the NCI was to have held its panel to discuss the mammogram decision again, a letter came for Lois. It was a letter from Senator Arlen Specter of Pennsylvania formally inviting her to testify before a special hearing of the Subcommittee on Labor, Health and Human Services, and Education.

United States Senate
COMMITTEE ON APPROPRIATIONS
Washington, DC, 20510

MEMORANDUM

DATE: February 25, 1997

To: Ms. Anderson

SUBJECT: Hearing on NIH Consensus Development
Conference on Breast Cancer Screening
In Women Ages 40-49

TIME/DATE: 10:00 AM., March 3, 1997

PLACE: Milton S. Hershey Medical Center, University Drive Hershey, Pennsylvania, Hospital Auditorium located on the ground floor

Thank you for agreeing to participate in this special hearing of the Subcommittee on Labor, Health and Human Services and Education Appropriations. I have called this special hearing to discuss the findings of the NIH Consensus Development Conference on Breast Cancer Screening in Women Ages 40-49.

BIOGRAPHY

Please FAX one copy of your biography <u>no later than 10:00 A.M. WEDNESDAY, FEBRUARY 26, 1997</u> to the Subcommittee Office.

TESTIMONY

In order to help organize the hearing, I am asking that you submit your written testimony <u>no later than 12:00 NOON, FRIDAY, February 28, 1997.</u> Please FAX one copy of your testimony to the Subcommittee office. Please bring 50 copies of your testimony to the hearing for distribution to members of the public and the press.

All statement and accompanying material that you wish to have printed in the hearing record should be typed single spaced on one side of the paper with a one inch margin on all four sides. A floppy disk MUST be submitted for ALL statements and additional material along with an original copy. Please indicate on the label of the disk the type of word processing software used to prepare the documents. NO FAXED statements or inserts will be inserted in the record—they must be ORIGINAL COPY.

If you have any questions regarding this hearing, please contact ******** at *********.

I look forward to your participation in this hearing.

My Best.

Sincerely,

Arlen Specter

Chairman

Subcommittee on Labor, Health and Human Services and Education

As she had from the beginning of February, Lois continued to receive and compile anecdotal stories from all over the United States. By March 3, 1997, Lois walked into the field hearings held at Hershey Medical Center with 226 anecdotal stories from women under the age of fifty whose lives were saved by the use of mammograms. All of the stories were collected in the first twenty days of February . . . a remarkable feat by anyone's standards. I often reflect on the magnitude of their stories and the number of phone calls we received. How many voices, crying to be heard, were left out of this already extensive list of breast cancer survivors? Only Lois and I really heard them . . . The list she carried was but a frail piece of what we knew was the true story of the nation's women . . . the world's women.

As I've said . . . Lois believed she was doing the right thing for the women of this country. But more so, I believed Lois was doing the right thing for the women of the world. On the day she went to testify, she told me she was nervous as the day we were married. I had to tell her she was going to do well, which she did. I would include her testimony here, but it would be redundant, in that her comments were well covered in her original letter to Senator Specter. Her drive and passionate concern, exemplified in her desire to help everyone have the chance to find breast cancer before it reached the levels where she had found her own, was the compelling force she used to gather her courage. She never wanted another woman to walk in her shoes as a breast cancer survivor. It was a true heroic effort any woman ever saved by mammograms and for those yet to be saved by them in the future. Senator Specter carried all 226 stories, along with Lois's testimony, and made them part of the Congressional Record.

On March 4, 1997, Senator Specter met with Donna Shalala and put pressure on her to have the NCI change its decision. By March 11, 1997, another letter from Senator Specter arrived in the mail for Lois.

March 11, 1997

Ms. Lois A. Anderson
York, Pennsylvania *****

Dear Ms. Anderson:

I want to take this opportunity to thank you for taking time out of your busy schedule to participate in the March 3, 1997 Subcommittee on Labor, Health and Human Services and Education hearing at the Hershey Medical Center.

As I stated at the hearing, the absence of a clear consensus on mammogram screening for women in their 40's may discourage many women not to consider mammography screening.

Your testimony has proven to be very useful in my talks with the National Cancer Institute and members of the National Cancer Advisory Board as we work to quickly resolve this important health issue.

I look forward to work with you in the future on this and other matters.

My Best.

Sincerely,

Arlen Specter
Chairman

Subcommittee on Labor, Health, and Human Services and Education

The mammogram decision of 1997 was finally over. Women across the country could again count on getting a mammogram at age forty without any repercussions. Can we say, Lois was one of the deciding factors in overturning the NCI's decision? Perhaps history will have to be the ultimate judge of that. There are times I think back on all this and still conclude this controversy was never really about mammograms. I believe the whole debate was really about the age women were to begin screening. If we had been talking about a fictitious but perfect screening test, would we have asked women to wait to screen until the age of fifty? I don't believe we would have left a decade's worth of women without something to screen themselves for breast cancer . . . neither did Lois.

Even while Lois was testifying before a Senate subcommittee, holding a full-time job, and gathering anecdotal stories to present to the NCI, she received a letter at the end of February 1997, congratulating her on winning a Jefferson Award.

On February 27, 1997, Lois received her letter from our local NBC affiliate, channel 8. The letter was sent to inform her she was going to be awarded the Jefferson Award. Every year, five local individuals are chosen to receive this award. In 1997, Lois was one of those five individuals chosen from a pool of 276 nominations. According to the letter she received, the Jefferson Award was given for outstanding public service benefitting local communities. The award was designed to recognize the countless individuals across the country who are performing extraordinary public services in their local communities.

From what we could tell, it was from the number of letters our NBC affiliate received that convinced them to choose Lois for this award. Since the mammogram decision had not been decided at the time the letter was sent, we concluded her actions regarding it had no bearing on the award. However, excluding the mammogram decision of 1997, Lois certainly had many achievements to be proud of. She started her work with breast cancer survivors back in 1992 even before she finished treatment. In the years after, she cofounded an amazing breast cancer support group, produced a very informative and, at times, controversial quarterly newsletter for over two hundred breast cancer survivors and health care professionals, was a voting member on the Department of Defense peer review panels for Breast Cancer Research Program for two years, helped many cancer organization with the passage of bills and agendas that affected breast cancer patients and their families (such as House Bill 2082, which allowed a contribution of the Pennsylvania tax bill to be allocated to breast cancer research), and she helped to get the nation's first breast cancer awareness postage stamp. I told her, as we read the award's letter, that this wasn't too bad for a breast cancer survivor who hasn't quite made the five-year mark for survival. Lois just laughed and told me she hadn't realized she had done all this. I told her she was too busy to keep tabs on herself to which she just shook her head and gave me a hug.

After the "mammogram decision" was finalized, Lois made preparations to receive the Jefferson Award. The ceremony was to be held on April 28, 1997, giving her a little time to get prepared. Still she had other commitments to complete before that important night. Shortly after her testimony on March 3, 1997, Lois was chosen by the American Cancer Society to participate in a program they called Models of Hope. The Models of Hope program allowed breast cancer survivors to voluntarily work as actual models to display lines of clothing to be on sale at the major stores in our area. It was a huge morale boost for those women who felt devastated by the ravages of what breast cancer and its treatments took away from them. Lois was very proud to have been chosen to participate in this program. On April 12, 1997, Lois spoke to a convention of the Reach to

Recovery Certification Program concerning her role in the National Cancer Institute's "mammogram decision." Finally, Lois had cleared her calendar and prepared herself for the upcoming reception for the Jefferson Award.

(From an editorial by Lois A. Anderson dated March 3, 1997)

On Monday February 24, two phone calls placed to me that evening brought with them some very exciting news. The first call came from senator Specter's office in Washington DC asking me to testify at a Senate Subcommittee Field hearing to be held March 3rd in Hershey. A faxed letter arrived the next morning telling me exactly what I had to do in order to participate in this hearing. A copy of my resume had to be faxed to his office by noon on Wednesday February 26. I also had to fax a copy of my testimony to his office by noon on Friday the 28th. There were many frenzied phone calls and faxes coming and going that entire week as I was still receiving stories from women diagnosed with breast cancer before the age of 50 by the use of a mammogram. I got the testimony together and George typed it up for me so I could send it out before noon on Friday. At 9AM on Friday the fax was sent through and several hours later I called the Senator's office to make sure his aides received it. Because of all the phone calls and faxes our phone bill for the month doubled itself overnight. At the hearing on March 3rd I was never so nervous, not even when I was married. Two panels gave testimony—Dr. Mary Simmonds, a Medical Oncologist, Dr. James Evans, a breast surgeon, and Dr. David Van Hook, Chief of Mammography at Hershey Medical Center. All of these physicians agreed that mammograms should be done annually from 40 on up. The second panel of which I was a member also had Lorene Knight, an African American breast cancer survivor, and Representative Katie True from Lancaster County. My testimony took an emotional tack. Lorene Knight approached the issue with the American Cancer Society data and from the African American higher breast cancer rates. Katie True approached the issue from the monetary side saying that we probably would not even be testifying if it weren't for the fact that the health care costs are being cut as much as possible and mammograms in this age group are one place to start. The senator asked for our comments in summation and then made a promise that if necessary he would push for legislation on this issue. That made me very happy, but now all I need to do is hold him to it.

> *The second phone call that evening came from WGAL-TV 8 telling me I had won one of the Jefferson awards and that my nomination would be sent to the national committee. I will be presented with the medallion at a banquet at the Valencia Ballroom on April 28th. I have to thank all the people who nominated me and you know who you are. The spokesperson from Channel 8 said there were 6 in all and that was out of 276 nominations! And if anyone wishes to attend the banquet just let George or me know. Take care all.*
>
> *With warmer days spring is on the way,*
>
> *Lois*

I believe Lois's participation in the Jefferson Award production was one of her greatest joys. A week or so before the ceremony, Lois was interviewed by one of our NBC news anchors, Dick Hoxworth. They met at the York Cancer Center with a complete news crew and videotaped the interview. It was Lois's time to shine as her broadcast reached out across the area with her story. Once the taping was completed, Lois needed to sit for still photographs, which would be published in the local newspapers and for use as still frames for commercials to be shown on television before the ceremony. On the night of the award, Lois had friends and family sitting at three of the large tables, which held about twenty people per table. She was introduced by the NBC news anchorman, and Lois began her short speech.

As was Lois's style, she never took any of the credit for what she did herself. Instead, she thanked her friends, colleagues, and family for helping her accomplish the things she had done. I think it was her sense of humility and graciousness that won the hearts of the audience. When she was done, the audience gave her a standing ovation that lasted several minutes. I looked across the audience and saw every table was standing, even those in the audience who were there for the other award winners. Her story was so incredible, so inspiring, that no one was untouched by the words she spoke with humility and grace. Even I wept when she spoke of my assistance and the support given to her by her son. She told us all she would never have achieved so much so fast without everyone's help. At the time, both Dick Hoxworth and Lois glanced over her work on the mammogram decision and the NCI. No one in the audience actually knew what the woman before them did for the women across the nation. Eventually, the ceremony concluded, and everyone went home. Lois left with the Jefferson Award displayed on a carved oak display, which she placed in our living room. They gave her a case to keep it in, but she preferred to keep it out for anyone to see when they came to visit. It stays there to this day.

About a week later, Lois was back in Washington DC.

(From an editorial by Lois A. Anderson, June 4, 1997)

On May 5th and 6th, I attended the National Breast Cancer Coalition's Advocacy Conference. The Conference was very informative and sparked many women into action to lobby their congressmen on LOBBY DAY, May 6th. A rally was held in the morning on the steps of the Capitol building with many politicians, breast cancer advocates, and survivors participating. Lobby Day was the culmination of the NBCC's Campaign 2.6 to get 2.6 million signatures on petitions to increase breast cancer research funding. We surpassed this number by a huge margin. Those petitions were presented to Congress by groups of women who visited or lobbied their congressional representatives for the funding and special legislative initiatives. My deepest thanks go out to all of you who participated in this petition campaign. I was able to present the signatures you collected to Senators Santorum, Specter, and Congressman Goodling. These men and their legislative aides were impressed by the fact that they were able to personally see the signatures of their constituents on the petitions. They were also impressed by the fact that you took the time to collect these signatures. You have made a difference and will continue to do so.

Besides funding issues, we discussed other legislative initiatives now before Congress. One of these was genetic discrimination legislation, which would protect anyone found to have a genetic predisposition for a disease from losing their health insurance and above all, their jobs. It is time for this country to pass legislation like this! We did not ask for bad genes and really cannot be held responsible for predisposition to a genetic disease. Please notify your Congressman that you support this legislation. It would not only apply to those with inherited breast cancer but anyone with a genetic disease.

During his commencement address at Morgan State University in Maryland, President Clinton called on Congress to enact legislation that would prohibit health insurers from using genetic information to determine eligibility for insurance. I agree with him, but even this does not go far enough. Those with genetic problems need complete protection from having their lives ruined by financial hardships that could result from an inability to obtain insurance. We all need to write to our legislators about this issue. Please do so now!!

Will summer ever get here?

Lois

Lois went back to her ordinary life, though nothing she ever did was ordinary anymore. She went to Northern High School on May 9, 1997, and spoke to a group of young female high-school students about the importance of doing breast self-exams. On May 11, 1997, she was asked to go to York College to do an interview for the alumni news. On May 27, she appeared in Harrisburg, Pennsylvania, with then-governor Tom Ridge for a ceremonial signing of the Breast and Cervical Cancer Bill. This bill allowed Pennsylvania residents to allow a donation of their tax dollars to go to breast and cervical cancer research by placing an additional line at the bottom of the income tax form for donations. In June 1997, she was presented with a resolution by the York County commissioners; and on July 1, 1997, she was presented with the Golden Eagle Award for her public service in regard to breast cancer. She spoke again before a Longaberger convention on July 19, 1997, where she spoke about the affairs of breast cancer and was again requested to speak on another radio talk show on July 23, 1997.

By September 8, 1997, Lois was again sitting on the Department of Defense peer review program for breast cancer research and concluded those meetings on September 11, 1997.

(Editorial by Lois A. Anderson, August 4, 1997)

As I sit here writing this newsletter, I have 32 scientific proposals staring at me from across my living room. So, I guess you're wondering what scientific proposals are doing in my living room. Well . . . I have, again, been selected to serve as a breast cancer consumer advocate on the Department of Defense's Scientific Peer Review Panels for Breast Cancer research. For those of you who do not know what this is, please let me explain.

In April, the Department of Defense (DOD) sends out a Broad Agency Announcement asking for scientific proposals for breast cancer research. The proposals are submitted and divided up by topics and then split further into several manageable groups for each panel to study and comment on after reading. I now need to wade through 30 more of these proposals and write comments on 18 of them. I will be in McLean, Virginia from September 8th through the 10th wrangling with twelve other scientists to decide which proposals will be funded. The panel I am attending this year has to do with behavioral sciences and deals with psychosocial issues in breast cancer. I am looking forward to these panels and how what I do affects the direction of research.

On another front, I want to be sure that you do not confuse the Breast Cancer Awareness stamp with the stamp that was approved by the President and Congress for Breast Cancer Research. It seems that our local press has confused these two stamps and has linked the two in the public's mind. The Breast Cancer Research Stamp, which can be sold for up to 8 cents above the cost of a first class stamp, has NOT been printed yet. Please continue to use and purchase the Breast Cancer Awareness stamp. It does make a statement on all your mail.

School days are here again,

Lois

By September 17, 1997, Lois was again before the York County commissioners being presented with a proclamation declaring October as "Breast Cancer Awareness Month" in the city and York County area. By October 23, 1997, Lois again spoke before the television cameras for Fox News on breast cancer and had a second interview for our local CBS station on November 5, 1997. Between the dates of October 8, 1997, and December 2, 1997, Lois held five or six presentations on breast cancer for then core states banks.

During that time, Lois continued to watch over her own health, which now required an EGD to evaluate a growing problem with esophageal reflux, a condition where chronic heartburn and gastric pain are unrelieved by conventional methods. Lois did all these things and continued to work full-time at night at her position as a medical technologist in Baltimore, Maryland, which is a one-hour drive from our home. The stress of such a full agenda was starting to take a toll on her, which I pointed out. She told me that she felt obligated to help the women of the nation and our local area. I understood her commitment, but I also knew that no one could continue the unrelenting schedule she had before her. She assured me she would try to let the momentum of her life calm down. I thought about what she was telling me and realized that she had the chance to do a lot of good with the rest of her life, however short it might be. I accepted that she was one of those exceptional individuals who really could change things for the better. It had to be enough for me to sit on the sidelines and hope.

Before 1997 concluded, Lois told me she was considering returning to college for a master's degree in social work. She told me she looked into Temple University, which had a satellite facility at our state capitol in Harrisburg, Pennsylvania. To attend classes, Lois had to travel about an hour from our home to the north to arrive at the university's doors. At the time, she was the picture of health, and she had found her employer had a tuition reimbursement program, which would allow most of her costs to be covered. I again told her I was concerned that adding the additional stress of her return to college would be detrimental to her health in the long run. After many discussions with her, we decided that it may be a good idea, particularly if her health failed in her later years. It was a prediction that haunted me for many years. She started taking some elementary courses she needed to enter the program during the fall of 1997. By the time 1998 arrived, Lois was enrolled in graduate classes at Temple University, Harrisburg campus. As she told me many times, "Sometimes we get the chance to change things."

Lessons from the Poet's Tree

Tell me about commitments . . .

"What would you do for love?" the disembodied voice asked inside me. I watched as the new light washed the branches and multicolored leaves over my head. "What was that?" I asked, aware of a presence speaking to me. Brutally tired from many sleepless nights, I found the dreams that placed me beneath the tree again. Was it a question about love? I thought to myself. "What would you do for love?" the voice asked again. "Who wants to know?" I asked, searching for my questioner. No one answered. No one presented themselves as I s explored the grounds around the great tree. "What do you want?" I asked, perplexed by the nature of the question.

Again, no answers were forthcoming . . . just the question. "How do you want me to answer? The greatest poets of the world could not do it with all the poems and songs written since time began." I sat with my back against the poet's tree and tried to dream. I seriously pondered the disembodied question again and then said, "I would give my life for love . . ." No response came as branches rustled with the wind's song blowing through them on a variant breeze. "Is that what you wanted to hear? Is that the answer you were waiting for?" I asked, not expecting a response. I was not disappointed by the silence.

I leaned against the tree, waiting for answers that never came. The silence was fertile ground for dreams to take root as I started sleeping . . . "Would you sacrifice her love to make her immortal?" it asked as I closed the door and entered the dream about a wall of stones.

Catherine heard someone call her name. She turned quickly and spied a young girl sitting in the street behind them. She vainly tried to hear what the girl was shouting. "Benjamin, that girl knows my name. How can that be?"

"I don't know, nor do I care. We need to get away from here," Benjamin stated loudly over the clack of the horse's hooves and carriage wheels rumbling on the cobbled street.

"Stop," cried Catherine, "I need to find out what she has to say. Everything we need to know is in her message."

Leena looked at her daughter skeptically. "What do you mean, Catherine?"

"I saw the girl before, Mother. It was in the marketplace when I felt sick. I thought I was seeing things, but that girl was looking for me." Catherine pointed back where the girl's profile was shrinking as Benjamin distanced them away. "There is something she needs to tell me."

Leena was concerned by Catherine's reaction to everything happening around her. Still, her daughter rarely asked for anything. They weren't far from where they spotted the girl. What harm would it be to turn back and take the girl where she wanted to go, other than upsetting Benjamin? Which was, to Leena, superficial at this point. Besides, the girl was fighting for her life under the same conditions as themselves. Perhaps they could help her.

"Benjamin, turn around," Leena ordered, an inherent authority weathered her voice.

"You're kidding, right?" Benjamin said incredulously, looking up to see Leena staring at him fiercely.

"No . . . I want you to turn around and find that girl. She could use our help, even if she was just making an attempt to get our attention. I'm sure she has a family somewhere that is worried about her . . . so turn around now!"

Benjamin begrudgingly slowed the carriage and then turned back toward his shop. After a short distance, they found the dirt-

smeared girl crying on the corner. "Okay, girl . . . we're back for you," Benjamin said with abject disgust.

"Benjamin!" Leena scolded. "You don't have to be that way with her."

"In case you haven't noticed," Benjamin added with an angry mocking voice, "this place is falling down around us. We don't know why . . . and we 'were' trying to get to safety and check our loved ones before you had me turn around to pick up this waif."

Leena gave Benjamin a stern look, then said with very controlled cadence, "This will only take a moment . . . then we'll be off." Leena looked down where the girl remained, sobbing softly at the street corner. With a voice only a mother could bring to bear, she ordered her, "Come on, girl . . . get in the cart now."

Amelia was in physical pain. Moving started small agonies, rising in unsolicited pain, which was freezing her joints. She was afraid and upset. She found Catherine at least . . . she barely believed they turned back to get her.

"What's your name, girl?" Benjamin asked brusquely.

"Amelia," she said, brushing tears from her eyes.

"Well, Amelia, you can get into the cart or sit here. Either way, I'm putting the whip to the horse in a blink," Benjamin taunted, wanting desperately to be away from this place.

"I'm sorry . . . just give me a second," Amelia told Benjamin, as she pulled herself from the curb and slowly rose to her feet. Leena, thinking the girl looked ill, got out of the cart not only to help but also to prevent Benjamin from rushing off, abandoning the poor girl on the street. Amelia was grateful for Leena's help as she settled into the cart and met Catherine for the first time.

"What's your name?" Catherine asked, as she could not hear the conversation she and Benjamin had for all the noise on the streets of Stock.

"Amelia," she said softly.

"How do you know me?" Catherine asked.

Tears came into Amelia's eyes once again as she realized she would probably alienate Catherine as soon as she presented Catherine with her story. "I know we never met, but I was told to ask you for a great sacrifice," Amelia said, as she lowered her head as to not look at Catherine's face.

Leena, listening to their conversation, asked, "Who told you about Catherine, Amelia?"

Amelia looked at her feet, wondering how she would explain the peculiar request she was asked to carry. Even to her, no matter how she approached it, her story sounded unbelievable. Amelia decided to tell her story from the beginning. Perhaps the truth was the only way to explain it. She hoped to be convincing, but if she failed, her own sacrifice would be in vain.

"Catherine," she said, raising her head to look at her, "I was at the wall helping some friends break through to the other side . . ."

Leena, Catherine, and Benjamin gasped at Amelia's words. Leena finally overcame the shock and asked, "You mean you are responsible for all this destruction happening around us?"

"What in the name of the Winds were you all thinking about?" Benjamin shouted, as the clatter of wheels on the rough stone streets was almost too loud to shout over. "You have doomed us."

"I know what you think," Amelia sputtered through a freshet of tears, "but I tried to stop them." Sobs racked her to the core of her body.

Benjamin stopped the cart, with intentions of throwing her off. Leena was too shocked to respond as she looked at this small girl, barely fourteen or fifteen seasons into her lifetime. It was Catherine who finally spoke. "Amelia," she said softly to the young girl, "tell us what happened at the wall."

Amelia started her story, telling Catherine, Leena, and Benjamin how she and her friends, Jonathan, Nathan, Victoria, and Fog, came to the wall, intending to get to the other side. She told how Jonathan sought to break the superstitions surrounding the wall's history for centuries and how he hoped to find some kind of treasure on the other side. Benjamin, of course, asserted just how preposterous the idea was but had to admit he too was curious about what lay on the other side of the wall over his lifetime. Leena was appalled anyone would disrespect the old beliefs but agreed with Benjamin she was curious as well. Now curiosity turned to fear as the streets of Stock lay littered with broken glass, smoke, and blood. Now with the wall breached, no one knew what was safe. Amelia explained that before the wall was opened, she became ill. It was Victoria, her friend, who pulled her away and sent her back on the road toward Stock.

"So is Victoria in Stock with you?" Catherine inquired.

"No," she said, laying her head in her hands, "I had to send her to Glade."

"But why?" Leena asked. "Surely you would have been better off together than alone?"

"Because she had to find someone named Timothy and give him a message," Amelia said, raising her face from her hands.

"Timothy!" Catherine gasped, sitting up abruptly. While Catherine's interest resided in her new friend's story, her revelation hit her like a bolt of lightning.

"Who told you these things?" Benjamin insisted. "Before today, Catherine never met you. Now you say a friend of yours, named Victoria, is off looking for Catherine's fiancé, Timothy, to deliver a message?"

Amelia was shaken. "You mean you know someone named Timothy?"

"Yes . . . yes . . ." Catherine cried. "Timothy is the man I am to marry, and I love him very much. What is going to happen to him? What message is Victoria carrying to him?"

"Where did you get these messages?" Leena broke in, concerned Amelia's strange revelation was nothing more than a fabricated story.

Amelia hesitated. If she told them the truth, she risked exile, but the bigger risk was not being believed. She looked into their faces, not knowing how to reveal the events that brought her here. Slowly, almost in a whisper, she began, *"I . . . heard. I was near the wall . . . at the fallen trees."*

"You're speaking of the old trees that fell in a storm about three or four parcels north of Stock?" Benjamin asked.

"Yes," Amelia stammered, not certain she could continue.

Benjamin looked back at Leena who already had him fixed in her gaze. They gave each other a brief glance of concern, and then Leena turned her head to Amelia, *"You are telling us you heard the 'voices'?"*

Again, Amelia was unsure of herself. Leena could be setting a trap to cause her exile. She only wanted to give her message and then find her father. Exile would keep her from ever seeing her father again. Her name would be defiled, never to be spoken again. At best, she had two days to be with him before the end of her life. Not telling Catherine what she had to do would mean the end for everyone. She needed to tell her, no matter what the consequences. Amelia looked to Leena then said, as meekly as she could, *"Yes . . . the voices."*

Catherine, mesmerized by the conversation, asked, *"Amelia . . . you said you had a message to give me. What is it?"*

Finally, Amelia could deliver her message to Catherine. Whatever happened from this point forward didn't matter. She would give her message; then with or without their help, she would make her way to her father's home, where he would care for her until she died.

"The voices told me you were the only one who can stop what is happening to the villages."

"But how?" Catherine asked.

"The voices said, 'Find a girl named Catherine. By her own free will, she can block the wall with a single stone.' Amelia finally passed the message. Her job was done. All she had left was to find a place to die.

Catherine was astonished. What did this girl Amelia sacrifice to deliver her message?

"We have to think this through, Leena," Benjamin protested. "What this girl is asking Catherine to do is lay down her life to make up for the treachery of those young hoodlums she calls her friends! It's not Catherine's problem. She did not cause the problem, so why should she be the one to pay so dearly to undo it?" Benjamin understood the problem now. He also understood what consequences existed if Catherine did what Amelia suggested.

Leena was beyond any response she could make to Amelia. Amelia looked to Leena and said, "I gave my lifestone to Victoria to protect her from the things coming through the wall. It is my first day away from it, but I'm feeling the pain it makes when it is too far away. If I could make one request of you, could you take me to my father? He will care for me through my passing. It was the only way I could get her to carry a message to Timothy."

Hearing Amelia's request, Catherine's eyes welled up in tears. "Mother, we must take her to her father. But before we do . . . Amelia, what message is Victoria carrying to Timothy?"

Amelia was tired and in pain. Catherine's message was bad enough, though she didn't understand how one person's small stone would stop the invasion coming through the wall. Sifting her thoughts, she remembered the message Victoria carried for Timothy. She turned to Catherine. "The voices said, 'Tell Timothy not to return to Stock, since nothing he could do would change the events that happened there.' The voices continued to say, he was to continue northward into the mountains and find a mythical place that will make Catherine immortal."

"Immortal?" Catherine exclaimed. "No one is immortal. No one would ever dream they could be immortal."

"Maybe what the voices meant is you could manage the supreme sacrifice, and Timothy will find a way to keep the curse of the lifestones away from you if he finds this place," Benjamin stated.

"That doesn't sound quite right, Benjamin," Leena said, exasperated by his superficial analysis.

"So what do you think it means?" Benjamin directed at Leena.

Catherine looked as perplexed as Leena and then turned to Benjamin and said, "Benjamin, Mother, I think we all know what Amelia means."

Leena looked to Benjamin. Benjamin lowered his head, "Leena, I think I understand what Amelia and Catherine are saying."

"Yes, but I don't need to hear this right now," Leena replied.

"People are dying, Mother," Catherine stated in a monotone voice.

"I know . . . I know, my dear daughter, but I can't accept this. There is another way . . . not this." Leena's frozen finality punctuated the matters of the message. She understood the implications of Amelia's message but wanted no part of it.

Amelia was puzzled. It seemed her strange message had some real meaning to them. Even Catherine understood something. How can one person's lifestone stop a threat as large as this? *Amelia thought, then asked, "Does Catherine's stone possess more power than other stones? Why did the voices send me to torment your beautiful daughter like this?"*

"You do not know my daughter. Do you, Amelia?" Leena asked coldly.

"No, until this day, I have not met her or heard anything about her."

"Then you are not aware that her father bestowed her with one of the largest lifestones ever given to a child. The stone sits in front of our home. My husband did this to assure she would never stray too far from her family, even in marriage. The stone is too large for Catherine to carry. In fact, it would take at least four strong men to move it at all. To carry it any distance would require a strong flat cart with two or three strong oxen to even move it. You see, Amelia, your message from the voices is exactly what is needed, but I cannot sacrifice my daughter to do this."

Amelia was horrified. The voices knew what was needed. People who loved Catherine were not going to make it easy. Amelia no longer possessed the strength to protest. She just wanted to go to her father's house. Feeling the weakness and pain take siege of her bones, she told Benjamin, "I need to get to my father. My time is short. I would, at least, like to tell him good-bye and that I love him."

"She's right, Leena," Benjamin spoke softly. "We need to get Amelia to her father. We'll use our travel time to decide what to do . . . agreed?"

"Very well then," Leena said soberly. "Let's be off."

Catherine was silent . . . and thinking.

Amelia directed Benjamin to her father's house. As they traveled, they discovered ravenous fires devouring neighboring fields and buildings uncontrolled. When they arrived at the lane leading to her father's house, Amelia saw their gutted home burning, fire crawling over charred blackened timbers piercing the rubble. The smoke was impenetrable beyond the devastated structure, making further inspection or exploration impossible. Amelia cried out, "What will become of me, there's no one . . . no one."

At Leena's persistence, Benjamin was persuaded to invite Amelia to stay with his family if no one from hers could be found. Amelia accepted and told the reluctant Benjamin she was grateful for his help. With this settled, the little group continued their search for Leena's husband.

Michael's office was a small wooden structure with a coverd porch built beside the road to their home. As they approached, Leena was grateful to see the structure unscathed, apart from the exploded glass She thought Michael might be outside inspecting the damaged windows, but no one was there. She jumped off Benjamin's cart even before it stopped, then ran up the three porch steps to the door of her husband's office. She shouted through the broken door, "Michael . . . Michael . . . are you here? Please answer." When she pulled the door open, she found him fighting through scattered ledgers, papers, and overturned furniture. She ran and wrapped her arms around him.

"Leena, why are you here?" Michael asked, surprised by her sudden appearance in his overturned office.

"We came for you," Leena said, leading him from out of the broken office through the front door to the waiting cart.

From the porch of his ruined office Michael saw his daughter sitting with two people. He couldn't see them clearly through the effluent smoke and dust. "Catherine came too?"

"We were shopping for materials to make a dress. We just found something I thought would work at Benjamin's store when this happened," Leena explained, sweeping her arm across the burning landscape as a demonstration of the destruction that lay around them.

Michael looked at his wife curiously, then asked, "What was it—a storm . . . a quake?"

Leena looked into Michael's eyes and said, "We believe someone broke through the wall, Michael."

"That's just not possible," Michael replied incredulously.

"We found a young woman who says it is true. She's called Amelia, and she is very ill. She passed her lifestone to save her friend's life. Amelia is dying. I have much to tell you. But I will tell you when we are safely on the road home."

"We should go then," Michael said, his mind still reeling from his wife's revelations of the events unfolding around him.

"That's why we are here. We came for you, and then we want us as far away from Stock as we can get. We need to get away from here," Leena said, urgency drifting into her voice.

Michael could not take it all in. He was afraid and confused, and for once in his life, he did not have a workable plan to get them out of this danger. Leena led Michael to the waiting cart. He got in, said something to Benjamin to thank him, and then they were off again. As they traveled toward their home, Leena tried to explain the events of the day to Michael.

Benjamin's house was first on the way to Michael's home. Benjamin left his passengers off long enough to check that his wife and children were safely out of danger. As he gathered some belongings, Benjamin's wife came out to speak with Leena. Michael saw the girl Amelia was suffering and in a lot of pain. When Benjamin returned, Michael told him, "When we get Leena and Catherine to my house, I'll stay with you. You're going to need help with Amelia. I overheard your wife when she spoke with Leena. She cannot take anyone in at this time."

"Yes, the neighboring families came to her when their homes fell in the quake. She is a kindly woman, and I don't blame her for doing this, but the house is overcrowded! We just don't have the room."

"So you couldn't convince her to leave Stock?" Michael asked.

"No, but she wants me to take you and your family as far away as you want and then return. She doesn't believe the wall was opened . . . to herthis was just a bad quake."

"Is that what you believe after hearing Amelia's story, Benjamin? A quake?"

"Until I see it differently . . . I have no reason to leave. The quake was devastating, to be sure, but we can rebuild the village."

Benjamin continued, *"I think you may find Timothy's father better help in this situation. He lost his wife a few years ago. Alexis, his daughter, picked up most of the household duties, but with Timothy in Glade, there will be an empty room for her there."*

Michael considered this option, knowing he could not care for Amelia when he moved his family away from Stock. Michael turned to Benjamin standing beside him at the side of the cart. "The girl doesn't look too good. It would be best to find one of her relatives to care for her even if we can't find her father. Do you really think Jakob will want this responsibility?".

"I hope they will help her. I will continue sending out word to anyone knowing the whereabouts of Amelia's father, but I wouldn't hold my breath. You should have seen her home, Michael. I don't believe anyone survived that fire."

"We can hope, Benjamin," Michael said.

"It seems to be the only thing we can count on, isn't it?" Benjamin said, crestfallen by the events surrounding them.

Leena finished her conversation with Benjamin's wife and then returned with Catherine at her side. "Your wife thinks Jakob could help Amelia until we find her father."

Michael looked to Benjamin for a response, but he said nothing. After an uncomfortable pause, Michael told Leena, "That's what we discussed, but first, we are going to drop you two off at our house. I'm going on with Benjamin to help with Amelia. She's too sick for Benjamin to watch while he's trying to get to Jakob's farm."

"I think that's a good idea. Catherine and I will get things together in case we have to move quickly."

"I'll be back with Benjamin as soon as Amelia is settled at Jakob's farm . . . if they'll have her," Michael said, with sadness tainting his voice.

"They'll take her in, sweetheart. No one can be so cruel to not take in a child," Leena said sweetly to Michael.

"Yes, but this child had something to do with what is happening around us. People have died today. She won't be easy to have around when they find out she heard voices. They'll say she's mad and exile her to Winterland. It would be her death sentence," Michael said, listening to Amelia's moaning just a few arm's lengths from them.

"I think she chose her death sentence already, Michael. We just need to keep her comfortable until she passes." Leena walked to the side of the cart and laid her hand on the side.

"I know," Michael told his wife. "I just don't like it."

Benjamin came from behind Michael and clapped him on the shoulder. "Are you all ready?"

Leena motioned Catherine back into the cart. Soon they were aboard, and Benjamin pulled away from his home, taking Leena and Catherine to theirs.

When they arrived, Catherine and Leena disembarked, leaving Michael, Benjamin, and Amelia to continue to Jakob's farm. The world they lived in changed. Many lives were lost, yet many more would die before the night ended.

※

Leon looked at Rand suspiciously, as did Timothy, pulling the horses where Rand was sitting. "Things?" Leon asked, as he approached. Rand looked at Leon and Timothy from where he sat. His bloodshot eyes glared from the dirt-streaked face and aged lines. He looked through dust-covered eyelids and said, "I don't know what I saw, but whatever it was filled not only the split earth but every low spot as well."

"Explain it to me, Rand . . ." Leon said, the frustration of being delayed coming through.

Rand looked from the stump and started his story. "Once the quaking was over, a deep crevasse ran from a place near the wall and split the road going to Stock. I was knocked to the ground during the quake and, not sure of my bearings, took a few moments to collect myself. My horses were scared off, and except for the clothes on my back and a little money bag I keep on me, everything was gone. I saw the large crevasse running across the road and wondered how deep the trench went. I walked to the crevasse and looked in. While I saw how deep it was, a blue fog started pouring into it like water from the direction of the wall." Rand hesitated and then looked at Leon to see if he believed anything of what he was saying.

"Go on . . ." Leon prompted, wanting to get to the bottom of this bizarre story as quickly as possible.

Rand looked down at his hands and continued, "I kept watching this blue stuff pour in, like I said. Then I noticed these odd purple orbs floating in on the stuff. I was about to reach in and grab one when, all of a sudden, one of them started growing some kind of big red spike. It really didn't do anything, but I thought it was better to leave well enough alone, which I did." Rand looked to Timothy then to Leon, almost hovering over him.

"Then what happened?" Leon asked, intrigued by Rand's story a trifle more than he anticipated.

"Well, it had been awhile since the quaking stopped, and I was sure someone else must be around, so I started looking. Eventually, I saw a man standing on the other side of the crevasse. He hollered across the river of blue mists and asked me what was going on. I was about to yell back when a red spike, like the ones I noticed growing on the orbs floating in the mists, shot a long red tendril toward him. I watched it wrap around the man's waist and cut him in two. After that, I wasted no time getting out of there."

Timothy, silent until now, asked, "Did you see anything else on the way here?"

"When I started running here, I didn't look back," Rand responded, slowly realizing how skeptical they were of his story.

"Nothing followed you?" Leon asked, knowing how upset Timothy was, cut off from his home village of Stock.

"I never looked back!" Rand repeated, frustrated by Leon's imposing questions.

Leon was frustrated as well. He raised his eyebrows and asked the question a different way. "I mean . . . was there anyone else on the road to Glade with you?"

Rand said with disgust, "Of course there was! But everybody was in a hurry, just like me."

"So where did everybody get to Rand?" Leon asked, thinking he finally got inside this old fool's impropriety. Just like he thought . . . the old boy's lying for free room and board for the night. The story is just too ridiculous. Leon looked back at the road where Rand supposedly came and saw no one traveling there. At this hour, travelers should be coming in droves for lodging and meals, settling in for the night before traveling to the other villages at daybreak. Where were they? Could there be something to Rand's strange story?

Rand looked at Leon, trying to judge whether he believed him or not. He couldn't read Leon's stare, so he continued, "Some stayed on the road, like me. Others abandoned the road and went off into the woods. I heard others say they were going to higher ground to set up camp for the night. Some travelers I met decided to find lodgings in the western villages closer to the great ocean and trade. Very few were comfortable traveling the road along the wall. They were afraid . . . I think." When Rand finished, he lowered his head and clasped his hands in his lap.

Timothy listened intently to Rand's story. Like Leon, he was convinced the old man embellished his story. Timothy asked Leon, "Do you want me to ride a few parcels south and look for these 'things'?"

"No, Timothy. I will get Rand back to the house. If Penny is still there, she can tend to his injuries. You stay here and watch the road for anyone. If you see someone, try to bring them back to the

house. Once Rand is settled and I keep Penny from leaving, I'll come back for you. Unless you return before I get a chance to come get you. Do you understand?" Leon asked, as quickly as he could get the words out of his mouth.

"Yes, Leon. I'll bring anyone I find wandering around out here back to the house. If not, you'll be back for me. Is that about it?" Timothy would have laughed at his friend if the situation was not as serious as it seemed to be.

"You got it, boy." Leon smiled back at Timothy, then turned to Rand. "Okay, old man, hop up on the horse. We got stuff to do, and we have to do it fast."

"All right . . . All right," Rand declared. "Can't you see I'm tired and in pain?"

"Yeah, so let's get on with it," Leon chided. When Rand finally crawled up on Leon's horse, Leon hollered to Timothy, "Find the highest hill you can and watch this road. If anyone comes, I want to talk to them. I want to verify this old fool's story with someone else. Understand?"

"Yes, Leon, I understand. I will keep watch." Timothy resigned his feelings; he wanted to be back in Stock with his beloved Catherine. Yet if Rand was right, and the wall was breached as he suspected, he was isolated from his family and Catherine. He would wait and hope for the arrival of a stranger to verify Rand's story.

Leon knew how Timothy felt; he turned to the boy before he left and said, "I know you think you have better things to do, but if this Rand fellow is correct, then you would be in danger if I let you return."

"I know. I'll be careful, Leon. I promise."

Timothy watched Leon lead his horse away, with Rand slumped over in the saddle. When they were out of sight, Timothy got on his horse and rode to a hill where he could survey the road into Glade. Within a few moments, he watched a distant figure stumble slowly toward the village. He led his horse down to the road to meet the oncoming stranger. When he was close enough to see, he realized it was a girl of about seventeen seasons. She wore a tattered brown dress, common for the girls of the villages. In spite of her young age, she looked exhausted.

"Hello there," Timothy called.

"Hello," the girl in the brown dress replied. Then she asked, "Is the village of Glade much farther?"

"It's less than half a parcel," Timothy replied.

"My name is Victoria. Do you know a young man named Timothy?" she asked, breathing heavily from exertion.

"I am Timothy," he replied, questioning the coincidence of meeting someone who was looking for him.

"I can't believe my luck. It has to be fate that brought you here," Victoria panted. "Are you from Glade?"

"No, I was here on business when the quake hit. I am from Stock originally," Timothy explained. "Where are you from, and why were you trying to find me?"

"I am also from Stock," Victoria said, then hesitated before answering the rest of Timothy's question. "I was on my way back to Stock when I was cut off. I had to turn around and come here."

Timothy, intrigued by the girl's story, asked, "You asked if I knew someone named Timothy, and I am he. Were you looking for me for some reason . . . a message from Stock from my father or my fiancée?"

Victoria was still catching her breath. She looked where Timothy sat on the horse and told him, "Yes, I have a message for you, for certain. First, I was told to tell you not to return to Stock. There is nothing you can do to change the events happening there."

"Well, Victoria, I got that message loud and clear from my father's friend, Leon, who has been helping me since this whole thing started. But who gave you this message?" Timothy asked.

"That part is not as easy to explain," Victoria said under her breath.

Timothy shook his head at her. "Somehow, Victoria, I think this may take a while to sort out, won't it?"

"There is a lot to tell, and there isn't much time. The wall was breached, and there are monsters coming through it," Victoria blurted out.

Timothy recalled the conversation between Leon and Rand before they left for his house. He looked to Victoria and said, "Victoria, I believe you. My friend Leon discovered a man traveling from Stock just a short time ago. His story, in many ways, reflects your own. For now, you need to travel with me to Leon's house for food and shelter. We need to find Leon and tell him your story."

Victoria closed the distance between them then climbed up behind Timothy for the ride to Leon's home in Glade. When they arrived, Leon was waiting. Fortunately Penny did not leave the house before Leon arrived with their first guest. Penny just finished packing and was cleaning up, when Leon arrived with Rand. Now, Timothy returned with another guest. He called out to Leon, standing at the front door, looking like he was guarding his home. "I've brought a friend, Leon. Now you don't have to come after me . . . I made it back myself."

"Who do you have, Timothy?" Leon shouted, as Timothy led his horse in front of him. Timothy stopped the horse and had Victoria dismount where Leon was waiting.

Victoria wasted no time in introducing herself as her feet touched the ground. "My name's Victoria. I came from Stock. I couldn't get back, so I came here hoping to get help."

"She saw monsters, Leon," Timothy added to her introduction from his position atop his horse.

"What kind of monsters, young lady?" Leon inquired.

Victoria proceeded to tell them about her encounter with the bizarre purple orb. She explained the orb's attempt to encircle her with trenches to trap her inside a circle of blue mists. She purposely left out the part about Jonathan's head and spine being attached to it, allowing it to speak and threaten her life. She felt it wiser not to tell the dialogue occurring between her and the Jonathan-thing. She could tell Timothy and Leon were not quite ready to hear about all that.

After telling her selective story to the two men, they were joined by Leon's wife, Penny, and the merchant, Rand, rescued by Leon earlier in the day.

"Good of you to join us on the front stoop, Rand. Penny, I want to introduce you to our young friend. Her name is Victoria. She could not return to her home in Stock after the quake. She had quite a story to tell, sweetheart," Leon said, speaking to Penny nonchalantly as if he had not a care in the world. Leon seemed to be taking this news like he was entertaining on a pleasant summer evening, with glasses of lemonade, ice tea, cold sandwiches, and stories told on the porch. He looked over his shoulder to his older guest and said calmly, "Rand . . . her stories were a lot like yours."

"It's like I told you. These purple spheres are killing people!" Rand exclaimed, excited to hear someone verified his story.

Victoria spoke up, explaining, "Yes, and one tried to trap me. The thing I saw was digging trenches around me. It means they are capable of creating passages to allow them to move one place to another." She sat down on a porch step, leaning her head like she was thinking, then said to no one in particular, "That means they will be able to come here . . . in time."

"That is a problem," Leon said, his detached attitude disappearing as he looked at Victoria.

"It also means, in time, all the villages will be in danger from these things," Rand said, preoccupied by the growing darkness he saw in the distant horizon over the skies of Stock.

Rand looked to his feet and then back at Leon. "I think these purple spheres, orbs, or whatever they are, are at war with us."

"That would explain why the wall exists . . . to keep them there and not here!" Timothy piped up.

"It sure does explain a few things," Leon said, as he got up and then walked back and forth on the front porch. He stopped, like he had an epiphany, and then said, "But the mystery of the wall is still not entirely clear."

"What do you mean?" Penny asked, wiping her hands on her apron.

"Well, first, why did anybody want to open the wall to start with, and who? Next thing, why do these purple things want to kill us . . . Are we food or something they need?" Leon stopped, watching their reaction, then continued, "And last, how do we stop them?"

"All good questions . . ." Rand spoke to the thin air, where no one listened, though everyone shared his thoughts.

Penny interrupted, "Leon, it's getting late in the day. Sunset is bearing down and will be upon us very soon. I think it best to stay here tonight and, if we need to, be ready to move north in the morning."

"I think that is a wise thought," Rand said over his shoulder, then slowly turned toward the horizon over Stock. "I also believe we would serve ourselves to station a guard in case these things get closer than we want during the night."

Timothy was restless and needed something to take his mind off Catherine. Not able to return home made him feel useless and guilty for not being there with her. The tension was getting to him. He looked whereLeon hunched over a railing on the porch, looking like he was thinking about something. Timothy asked nervously, "Leon, *should I take a horse and look for others that might join us? It could be the villagers have gone indoors or left for other parts, but it may do well to look for others who haven't found a safe place for the night."*

Timothy's suggestion was actually good. "Go ahead, take a horse, and check the streets around my house until sunset. If you find anyone who needs a place to stay tonight, direct them here. When you're back, we will have dinner and then decide what we are going to do next." Leon gave Timothy a nod that meant "Get going." Then Leon turned to the others on the porch and said heavily, "Go inside . . . light the candles. This may be the last good night any of us have for a very long time."

Everyone was too tired to protest Leon's commands. Leon turned his eyes to the street where Timothy mounted his horse. He watched as Timothy gracefully trotted his horse to the end of the street then disappeared from sight. "The Winds be with you, boy," Leon said as a little prayer. He turned to watch Penny usher their two guests into the house before she turned back.

Penny walked where Leon was standing. "What do you think Timothy will find there on our streets?"

"I think everyone has gone to cover or they moved on to other places. If Timothy finds anyone, I will be surprised. Besides, he only has a short time to find anything."

Penny looked at her husband suspiciously. "If you knew this, why did you send him off by himself?"

Leon turned to look into his wife's eyes and said, "Because I want to talk to Victoria myself. There is something wrong with her story, and I want to get to the bottom of it before Timothy returns."

For the first time since Penny met Rand and Victoria, she agreed with Leon's observation. "Yes, I've noticed it too. Something about her doesn't add up. Besides she is much too quiet for a girl her age, even if she is well behaved."

"Yes, but it's stranger than that. She told us she was attacked by purple orbs. Rand saw one and ran the other way, which is what most of us would do. Victoria tells her story like the orb was toying with her, like it could communicate. I'd like to know how that happened."

"That is strange," Penny said, as her brow furrowed as it did when she was thinking about something. "Do you think I could help draw her out?"

Leon looked into Penny's eyes and smiled, "I was hoping you would."

Penny slapped him on the arm. "You don't have to make such a game of it . . . just ask me straight out." Penny laughed at Leon, since it was his way to get her to agree to something he wanted her to do.

"I will need all the help I can get, and I'm not sure how much help Rand is going to be," he said, playfully rubbing his arm where she hit him.

"Don't underestimate him, dear. At least he told the truth. Victoria's story seems shaky. Rand may be a great help yet." As she was leading Leon toward the front door, Penny's thoughts went to Timothy. How was he doing out in the streets? Did he find anyone? How soon would he be back? Would she and Leon have enough time to convince Victoria to tell her real story? *Leon opened the door for her. She stepped inside, watching her husband glance back at the darkening shadows growing on the streets of Glade.*

Timothy led the horse through the empty streets. He saw few signs of anyone other than an occasional chimney puffing smoke where people decided to stay. Throughout the village of Glade, he saw the destruction of glass windows but little else. Then he heard distant echoes of hammers falling on wooden planks coming from one of the streets. Following the sounds, he came upon a shopkeeper and a group of four men nailing wooden boards over windows and doors. The shopkeeper yelled, "Boy, do you know what happened?"

Timothy stayed on his horse while he told the men what he knew of the quake, the break in the wall, and the purple orbs Victoria and Rand spoke of. His story frightened the men. Before he could invite them to Leon's house, they decided to gather their tools and return to their families. The shopkeeper told Timothy they would travel from Glade in the morning with their families. They would travel west or north to escape the danger from the south.

The shopkeeper thanked Timothy for his news and urged him to find safer ground himself. Afterward, the shopkeeper and his workers departed. The sunset was dying in gasps of pinks and purples. Soon the long nocturnal colors would begin painting the streets of Glade in grays and blacks. Timothy knew it was time to start back to Leon's house. He left the darkening silence to return to his friends.

"Victoria, would you mind helping me in the kitchen?" Penny whispered, putting a hand on her shoulder.

"Of course, what do you want me to do?" Victoria replied, surprised by Penny's somewhat secretive tone of voice.

After Penny secured Victoria in her kitchen, she instructed her on what needed to be done. "Well, let's get some dishes on the table for starters, then we can cut up some bread, then cheese, and some cold meat. I still have some apples and pears in the cold cellar if you wouldn't mind getting them. I'm afraid I can't get the fire going, since I don't know how long we are going to be here."

"That's okay. I'm sure everyone will understand. Where is the cold cellar?" Victoria asked, unaware Penny was laying a clever trap by making her comfortable in the kitchen.

Penny showed Victoria the way to the cellar. When she returned with apples and pears, she showed her how to cut the bread she made earlier. Then she showed her the cupboards where she could find the dishes to set the table. While Penny kept Victoria's attention on dinner preparations, she started digging into her story.

"Leon tells me you were attacked by one of these purple orbs . . ." Penny led off.

"Yes, it started to surround me by digging trenches to let in the blue mists. They seem to need them to move around," Victoria said in a carefree way, knowing she was over this part of the story before.

"How did you get in such a predicament? You must have been very close to the breach . . ." She tried to lead Victoria, but the girl remained silent this time. "Victoria . . . you came with a message for Timothy. He told me about it before he left on Leon's errand." Again, Penny waited for Victoria to respond. When she remained as silent as before, Penny continued, "You told him not to return to Stock. You told him he could not undo the events happening there . . . am I right?" This time, Penny turned away from cutting apples and looked at Victoria.

"Well . . . yes . . ." Victoria stammered.

"Although that message makes good sense under the circumstances, it really isn't much of a message . . . especially coming all the way from Stock, am I right?"

Victoria nodded in affirmation.

"What concerns me," Penny continued, "is who sent this message, and why send it to Timothy? Anyone thinking about going to Stock right now could have received that message. Why not send it to the whole village? Certainly, we will all stay well away from Stock until it is safe to travel there again. So the message to keep away is pretty evident." Penny stopped awhile, leaving Victoria mulling in her thoughts. After a few moments passed in silence, Penny said, "Victoria . . . if there is something else . . . something to help us or Timothy, please be out with it."

"Penny, please don't be mad at me. I've been trying to tell you something important." Victoria sat down on a stool and wrung her hands in her lap.

"Be out with it then, girl. What else could you possibly want to tell us? The world, as we know it, is in danger of becoming no

more. There is a threat to our south that we haven't been able to see. Though I will say, what happened so far seems very ominous."

"My friend Amelia sent me with two messages for Timothy," Victoria began, looking at her pale hands as she spoke.

"We know about the first message . . . ," Penny said, as she repeated it to Victoria, hoping to make it easier to tell the second one, *"stay away from Stock."* Penny watched Victoria hesitate. *"You know we would have done this whether you came to warn us or not."*

"I know, but that was the easy part to tell you . . . ," Victoria said, as she raised her head to talk to Penny. *"The rest is not so easy."* Victoria lowered her head in shame. She started, *"My friends, Amelia, Fog, Nathan, and Jonathan, went to the wall this morning with the intentions of breaking through . . ."*

Penny gasped, *"So it was you and your friends that did this!"*

"It was a stupid idea. Amelia got sick before the boys really got started. I tried to take her home before they broke through the wall."

Penny was shaking. She tried to sound calm, as she asked, *"So what happened?"*

"Amelia started to behave strangely. She started telling me she heard voices near the wall, and we had to get a message to someone named Catherine and someone named Timothy. My message was for Timothy, and I found him. I don't know if Amelia found Catherine or not."

"Victoria," Penny hissed, *"you said Amelia had a message for Catherine as well? Do you know who Catherine is?"*

"No," Victoria replied, recoiling from Penny's question.

"Catherine is Timothy's betrothed. His fiancée . . . the love of his life," Penny shrieked at her.

Victoria would not go any closer to Penny but tried to draw her off. "Now it all makes sense . . ."

Penny's anger diffused after she realized the girl's ignorance of the significance of finding these two distinct people connected by each other's hearts. She turned to Victoria and asked, "What makes sense?"

"The messages . . . for both of them," Victoria said, as she watched Penny lean close to her face.

Penny spoke slowly, meaning to make Victoria understand every word she said to her. She started close to her face, as a whisper, to get her attention, then started getting louder with every word, "I'll tell you what I want you to do. First, you and I are going to stop these 'cat and mouse' games with my questions. Second, I want to hear whatever the message or messages were for Timothy, then what you know of the message for Catherine. And last, I want an explanation for why the wall has been breached." Penny was screaming at her in her frustration. "Am . . . I . . . clear?"

Victoria backed away from Penny, never taking her eyes off her. "Yes, ma'am . . . we are clear."

Penny continued, "Because if you and I are not clear, I'm putting you outside to fend for yourself tonight. And . . . if we are to leave here tomorrow morning, which I daresay is a very good possibility, I will insist you are left behind."

Victoria looked tearful. She believed Penny's intention to be true to her word. Now was the time for truth, no matter what the cost might be. She tried looking for the kitchen door as a last resort, but Penny moved and blocked the way. She looked through tear-filled eyes and told Penny how she came to be at the wall. She explained how Amelia became sick and then gave the two instructions for Timothy. Amelia had a message for Catherine, which she was to deliver to her in Stock. "It's why we split up . . ." Victoria interjected into her story.

"Go on . . ." Penny said, "you're doing fine."

Victoria continued, "When we got to the road, Amelia was starting to feel better, but the strangeness hadn't gone out of her voice. She told me we had to split up. I didn't want to leave her that way, and I wasn't sure I believed she really heard the voices. I just thought she was sick and that was how she was, you know, when she was sick. We argued about that. It was when Amelia gave me her lifestone that I knew she believed what she heard, and it made me believe her as well."

"You mean that poor girl is going to die just to prove what she was saying is true?" Penny asked, trying to keep the horror of what she heard from entering her voice.

"You must understand the wall was not breached at the time. We were safe at that point. The thing is, Amelia told me our lifestones can act as protection. I didn't know what she meant until I was caught by one of the purple orbs."

Penny, intrigued by Victoria's story, urged her to continue. She listened as Victoria told her about the moments before the breach.

"Amelia and I spoke of two sets of messages. One message for Catherine and two messages for Timothy. The message for Catherine was she could block the wall with a single stone by her own free will. The messages for Timothy were to not to return to Stock because he could not undo the events happening there, and the other one, which I found to be very strange . . ." Victoria hesitated, looking into Penny's face for some empathy there.

Penny just looked at her stoically, then said, "Please go on. I have to admit, what you have told me so far is peculiar in its own telling. So if you don't mind, finish telling it. I will decide if it is enough when I've heard it."

"The last part of Timothy's message says he is to find a mythical place that will make Catherine immortal. It's someplace north in the mountains," Victoria continued the story of how the purple orb she encountered was constructed from Jonathan's severed spine and attached head. She said it looked as if the head and spine were ripped out of his body. She told Penny how she had been repulsed and *horrified by its appearance as it tried to act like her friend Jonathan. The orb absorbed some of Jonathan's attributes but didn't behave as Jonathan. She explained her escape and how using Amelia's lifestone protected her as she slipped by the orb.*

Penny listened patiently to her story then asked, "You said Amelia gave her lifestone to you?"

"Yes . . . I still have it with me."

"And from what you tell me, the lifestone glows red in the presence of these orbs, and when the glow is present, the orbs are not able to move?"

"That's what I noticed when I got away from the one that looked like Jonathan. Amelia said it would protect me, but she will die if I can't get it back in two days," Victoria explained to Penny, rifling through her dress pockets to show Amelia's lifestone to her. "That is Amelia's lifestone!" Penny gasped when she saw it. It was not the nature of the villagers to show another's lifestone like this. To prove the stone she displayed was not her own, she pulled out the small leather pouch holding hers to show Penny as well.

When Victoria showed Penny the two lifestones sitting side by side, she realized the supreme sacrifice Amelia made for her friend Victoria. The action, driven by the purest intentions, put tears in Penny's eyes. There was nothing that would outweigh one person laying down their life for the survival of another. Certainly, what Victoria was saying had to be true.

Penny heard Leon opening the front door. He was speaking to Timothy, who just returned. The news Victoria told Penny would make good dinner conversation if they didn't choke on the shock of hearing it. However, this news needed to be told. Victoria's message to Timothy needed to be heard so he could make a decision. Leon needed to understand Victoria's presence was not accidental. If there was any possibility of returning Victoria to Stock, allowing her to return Amelia's lifestone before it was too late, then it had to be done. A lot of decisions hung in the confines of her household. Penny needed everyone to understand Victoria was a messenger . . . a messenger with upsetting stories. She did not want time wasted blaming the girl for the information she carried. She would smooth them over. Now was the time for action, not words. Words would be useless against the orbs.

"Timothy, did you find anyone?" Leon asked as he guided Timothy through the front door. "Did you tie your horse up out back?" he added, concerned the horse wouldn't be ready to use the following day if it wasn't cared for.

"I put the horse in the barn before I came around the house. I wasn't sure anyone would have heard me if I had used the back door." Then to Leon, "As far as I could tell, I traveled most of the streets around here. I found four men a few streets over boarding up a building before they moved their families out of Glade. When I told them the story Rand told us about the orbs, it confirmed they were doing the right thing by leaving. Not one wanted to stay here tonight. Otherwise, the streets were deserted. I didn't knock on any doors, but there were no lights burning in any I passed. The whole village looked abandoned. I think we need to move on in the morning as soon as we can. It feels like there is danger here. I can't see it, but I feel it."

Penny looked at Timothy wearily pulling off his dusty short coat. Penny walked to him and put her hand on his shoulder. "I know what it is you are feeling, son." Timothy said nothing as he turned to look at Penny. "Victoria and I had a long talk while you were gone." Penny turned to face everyone in the room. "I believe all of you need to hear what she had to tell me. If we are safe tonight, then good, we get out in the morning. After you hear her story, we may want to consider moving out right after dinner." She looked to Leon squirming to get to the barn to feed the horses. "Do you hear me, Leon?"

Leon was unconvinced anything Victoria said could be that bad. "What possible danger are you speaking of, Penny?"

"Let's sit down, and we'll all talk," Penny said, as she spread her arms over the dinner table, indicating everyone was to take a seat. Leon pulled a chair at the end of the table for himself, while Timothy took a seat to the right, and Rand found a chair to his left. Penny sat *at the opposite end of the short sturdy table, while Victoria found a seat beside Rand. The food on the table was cold but abundant. It would be the last good meal any of them would have for a very long time. The conversation started with a question from Leon directed at Victoria. There were shouts, tears, reconciliations, and a willful need to develop a plan after hearing the news she told them.*

"Does anyone have any suggestions as to what this means?" Rand asked.

Timothy looked upset, but he was the first to speak up. "I believe the voices asked Catherine to seal the wall by sacrificing herself. Placing the lifestone her father gave her when she was born in the wall might actually work. As for the rest of the message Victoria had for me . . . I'm not sure."

Then Leon, who had asked very few questions, looked to Timothy. "Why Catherine? Why is her lifestone so important?"

Timothy looked wearily at Leon. "Because the wall is breached, and it is very likely her stone is large enough to seal the breach. It would mean only one person would have to make that ultimate sacrifice. It might also mean there is only one chance to seal the wall. Others may be willing to sacrifice themselves, but even collectively, it will not be enough. To be honest, I'm not sure." Then Timothy looked to where Victoria sat next to Rand. "If these things are here to kill us or take us captive, it must mean sealing the breach won't be easy. Multiple tries at stopping them will mean more lives lost just to seal it off."

Both Leon and Rand nodded in agreement as a small quake hit the area near Glade. The tremor silenced the conversation for a short time, while their own thoughts of surviving this horror troubled their minds. In their hearts, they knew their way of life was threatened by the things behind the ever-present wall. Everything they believed was valuable now seemed insignificant against the possibility they would die so ingloriously, without reason, without any significance. The quake didn't last, but its essence was enough to make them realize how they came to this table, at this time, and they were grateful for the time and the camaraderie.

Leon broke the silence. *"We need a plan. One to do the most good in the shortest time."*

"Yes, Leon, I agree," Rand spoke up. *"Does anyone have any thoughts to what we should do?"*

"I think we have to consider what Victoria has to say about all this. Her experiences with the orb that attacked her may help us," Leon said, as all eyes fixed on Victoria.

Penny looked at Victoria, twitching nervously while the entire table waited for her to say something. *"Don't be afraid, dear. We just need to know what happened so we can put together some kind of plan. Go ahead,"* Penny said, trying to encourage the young girl. *"Tell us about the orb you encountered."*

Victoria looked up from her place at the table and recounted the events that led her to Glade. When she said all she could, the table shook with another minor quake. It seemed to the small table of friends that the orbs knew of their betrayal.

Leon sat silently at the head of the table. He folded his arms before him and made a quick glance at all of them. He raised his hand in a fist and slammed it onto the table. *"I think we need to work our way into Stock."*

Rand was shocked. *"Why would we want to do that? How could we do it even if we wanted to?"* He waited to hear Leon's defense but then added. *"Besides, these things are blocking the road to Stock. Haven't you been listening to what Victoria and I have been telling you since we got here?"*

"A lot of the villagers were heading west," Timothy added, hoping to diffuse an argument between Rand and Leon.

"And that's what we're going to do," Leon said, as confused looks came from everyone at the table. *"We must get to Stock to make sure the message Amelia carried made it to Catherine."* Leon looked at Timothy and said, *"Son, Catherine may have to make the ultimate sacrifice to save all of us. I know your heart must be heavy knowing*

it is a choice between her and everyone else. But that chance doesn't even exist yet because it is possible she is not aware that she can help."

Timothy bowed his head in resignation. Leon was going to ask the love of his life to ransom her lifestone to save them all. Timothy thought, What does Leon want me to do? Does he think I can or will convince Catherine to put her stone in the wall? It is a debt she pays too dearly for. I can't do that. I cannot ask her to do this for us all. Timothy wiped his tears on his sleeve then told Leon, "Catherine will do it . . . She will do it if she knows what is at stake. But don't ask me to tell her this . . . don't ask."

Leon put a hand on Timothy's shoulder. "I'm sorry, but we have to make sure Amelia delivered the message, or no one may ever know we had a chance to put a stop to all this." Leon turned to the rest of the table. "If what you said is accurate, Victoria, your friend Amelia has about two days left. Her first day, which is over, would have been her best day. After that, she would be very sick, not likely to travel around and find Catherine. Her third day would be in agony. It would be out of the question to expect her to be coherent enough to deliver a message to anyone by that time. If Amelia could not get the message to Catherine on her first day, then it hasn't happened, and we are all doomed." Everyone at the table looked at Leon but could not come up with a good argument against his summation.

Leon saw the pain on Timothy's face. He looked to Victoria. "Victoria, there were two parts to Timothy's message, am I correct?"

"Yes, sir," Victoria replied quietly.

"How did the second part go? It was strange as I remember and vague. But since everything else the voices told us has a ring of truth in it, then perhaps this does too," Leon asked, trying to give Timothy some hope for Catherine.

Victoria thought for a moment then said, "Timothy is to travel northward to a mythical place in the mountains. He can make Catherine immortal if he does this."

"So there is a chance for Timothy to keep Catherine alive?" Leon asked, hoping Victoria knew more of the message's intent.

"I don't know what that means . . ." Victoria stated, "Amelia said that is what the voices told her." Then she looked toward Leon and said, "I think it sounds like a horrible curse to be immortal because you would watch everyone you ever loved die before you. I would feel terribly alone if I were immortal." She suddenly remembered Timothy was still upset over Catherine then said, "But the message was not clear either. It might just mean that Catherine may be able to live a normal life without her lifestone. Like I said, I don't know what the message means."

"I think if there is a chance to save Catherine, someone should make the attempt," Leon spoke to everyone. He looked to Timothy. "Son, I guess that responsibility is yours. The voices designated it would be you who would find this place and save her. It is my thoughts and intentions that you need to try."

"But I feel a journey to a place that may not even exist is pointless!" Timothy protested bitterly. He fully wanted to get back into Stock to see Catherine and his family. He would fight beside Leon to get there if he would have him. "There is no guarantee I will find this place. Even if I do, will it really save Catherine?"

Leon was sympathetic but firm in his resolve. "I think you need to take the chance, my boy. The only way to stop these things is to block the wall with a single stone. I daresay getting a stone that large to the site will be an enormous feat in itself. And I know it is not a comfort to you, but Catherine's lifestone may be large enough to stop what is happening. I believe Catherine herself will be willing to make the sacrifice. It will be the people around her who love her who will be the hardest to overcome. It makes me sick of heart to ask you to do this, but I must. From what the voices say, it has to be of her own free will that she does this." Leon turned Timothy by his shoulders to face him. "It will be up to you to save her. You have to believe this."

Timothy looked into Leon's face. "But how, Leon? I don't even know what it is that I am looking for. Even if I do find it, will I make it back in time for it to do any good?"

"Perhaps we can help you there." Leon turned to those at the table, then back to Timothy. "If we can get to Catherine, fighting our way into Stock if we need to, we will delay her from placing her stone for as long as we can. We'll buy you time. I'd like to say I could give you four or five days at least, but it will all depend on how aggressive the purple spheres really are. If I can give you more time, I will. You just have to do your best to get into the mountains and find whatever it is you need to find."

"Thanks, Leon . . . I think," Timothy offered, resigned to the task before him.

"Rand . . ." Leon shouted.

"Yes, I'm right here," Rand spoke with some hostility.

"Will you help Timothy get a fresh horse from my stables in the back of the house then help him with the harness?"

"Of course!" Rand replied, then turned to Timothy and said, "Come on then, you probably know the stables better than I do. We'll find you a good horse, and then you must be off."

"Will all of you make ready to get out of here as well?" Timothy asked, concerned they were getting him off to safety but not themselves.

Leon answered him, "Yes, I sent Penny and Victoria to get satchels of food prepared for our journey into Stock. You are to drop by the back door to the kitchen before you leave. Penny's orders . . ." Leon said, as he winked an eye at him.

As Timothy and Rand hurried back to the stables to find a horse, they heard crunching sounds coming from the south. "I think our purple orbs are working their way here," Rand remarked with concern.

"I think it's a good idea to be getting away from Glade, though it's only a few hours until the sun is up, and we'll be able to see everything around us," Timothy said, throwing the saddle on his horse, while Rand fitted the harness. They finished fitting his gear, and then Timothy hoisted himself into the saddle.

Rand still held the stirrup as he looked at Timothy. "Young man, I don't know what goes through your heart since this horror came to light, but I think you have a lot of courage. May it see you through to wherever you may be going. May the Four Winds be blowing in your direction to make your passage easier and lighten your heart."

Timothy was moved by this man he once thought of as a stranger. In such a short time, Rand showed them he was a friend. "Thank you, Rand. Take care of everyone, especially Leon. He may try to take chances he shouldn't if he gets forced into it."

"Ah yes, I suspected as much! I will look after him most of all." Then as an afterthought, he said, "Don't forget to stop by the back door before you leave. Penny will be furious if I left you leave before saying good-bye to her."

"I will." Then he added, "And thanks for helping everyone."

"Believe me, you've helped me far more than I've helped you. Now get going. I need to stay here and get some horses hitched up to a wagon. Be careful, Timothy!" Rand said, as Timothy trotted his horse to the back door of Leon's home.

Penny was waiting as Timothy guided his horse toward her kitchen door. He dismounted then went where Penny had waiting satchels filled with food and water. "For your journey . . ." Penny said.

"Thank you . . ." Timothy continued to look at Penny like he had something else to say. He turned around to get back on his horse then turned back to Penny and said, "If Leon finds Catherine, can you tell her from me that I love her and I will do anything I can to save her?"

"Yes, of course, Timothy. And I'm sure she already knows you do love her. As for the rest . . . well, that will really be up to the path of the Winds, will it not?"

Timothy looked distant. He was torn between riding off to a destination that might not exist and traveling with Leon, where he might at least have the chance to say good-bye to Catherine. He would have to live with this moment forever. Finally, to Penny he said, "The choices are hard."

"I know, but to not make choices would be the end of everything."

Timothy nodded in affirmation and then said, "When will you all be leaving for Stock?"

"Just after we get you along. Leon thinks we can head west to the village of Notting, and if the way is not blocked by these things, we'll try to move south to the village of Adonnas. If there is a way from Adonnas to Stock, we will find it. I am only hoping we can be quick enough."

Timothy mounted the horse then looked down at Penny and said, "Good luck to you all. I will try to find this place, wherever it is. Tell Leon I will spread the word of this tragedy to each of the northern villages I pass through."

"I'll tell him. And, Timothy . . . don't give up hope." Then Penny added, "Hope is all any of us really have."

"So I'm going to say good-bye to you now . . . I must get going," Timothy said, as he pushed his horse toward the northern borders of Glade.

"We will all pray to the Winds for you, Timothy. May the speed of the Winds be at your back," Penny yelled as Timothy rode off and out of sight. Penny turned back to go inside her house, perhaps for the last time, for all she knew. She gathered up the satchels of food and water she had prepared in her kitchen and carried them out the door where Rand was finishing the harnesses for the horses to be hitched to the wagon. She carried the armload of satchels and placed them on the wooden bed of the wagon. She looked to Rand and said, "Timothy's gone now . . . I wished him well from all of us."

Rand could feel the deep emotions Penny had for the young man. He was almost like a son to her, and it hurt to see him off to such a strange destination . . . such a strange end. "I wished him well too," Rand said.

After Rand and Penny said their good-byes to Timothy, they secured what supplies they had on the wagon. Meanwhile, Leon and Victoria ran through the house looking for knives, swords, crossbows, flintlocks, and powder. Leon carried two cases of his solvents, in case he could never return to his home, to the front porch. They brought everything the wagon could carry and then waited for Rand and Penny to pull up with the wagon.

After a few moments of silence, Rand hitched the horses to the wagon. He escorted Penny into the wooden seat. "Up you go, missus. Leon and Victoria should be waiting on the front porch with housewares, dried goods, solvents, other paraphernalia I don't know about, and any weapons they could collect on short notice."

Penny rolled her eyes at Rand when he spoke about the weapons they would be carrying but said nothing. Rand knew, after Leon heard Victoria's story of her encounter with the orb, he felt better having some weapons with them. Victoria also said her shots at the orb with ordinary stones seemed to have no effect. However, she did say she could damage parts that were still human. True, ordinary weapons may not have any effect on the orbs, but having weapons along was a better plan than no weapons at all. Leon also considered the possibility of finding desperate people who would steal their food or take their wagon. Having weapons would deter anyone from trying to take anything.

By the time Penny and Rand drove around the house, Leon and Victoria had a fairly large cache of boxes and equipment on the porch. "In the name of the Winds, Leon," Rand exclaimed when he saw the enormous stash on the porch, "how will the horses pull all this stuff with us on the wagon besides?"

Leon looked to Penny with an imploring look in his eyes, but Penny would have none of his nonsense. "Rand's right. Either some of these things have to stay or we need to hitch up two more horses to haul all this."

Leon looked to Victoria to evaluate the situation. Victoria thought Leon must be joking to ask a girl her age for advice. Unfortunately, she was wrong. "What do you want me to say?" Victoria asked, puzzled by Leon's obvious attempt to use her to gauge the extent of the danger lying before them.

"You've seen these things, and you have the only experience of dealing with them. What weapons would you choose to bring?" Leon asked her, sincerely wanting her advice.

"The only weapons I had were Amelia's lifestone and a few plain rocks. Both had some effect on the orb, but neither one really stopped it. It's possible some of your weapons may do something against them. As for how many or what types of weapons . . . I don't know. I do know one orb was more than enough to fight off. By now, there must be more of them, and having enough weapons to fight them seems to be a good strategy."

"Then we're going to hitch up two more horses," Leon proclaimed. "Rand . . . Penny, go back to the stable and hitch up two more horses to this wagon. Victoria, go with them and help. I will stay here and sort out what we will take and what stays here. Go ahead . . . We need to hurry. I don't know how much time we have anymore."

While the three rode the wagon back to the stable, Leon went through the things Victoria and he piled on the porch. He took a step back and gazed at the house where he made his home with Penny. "I hope to see you again, old friend." He looked at the road leading to the stable and heard Rand moving the wagon toward the front porch. Rand arrived with the additional two horses. They got off the wagon and helped Leon load the remaining supplies. By the time they were done, the faded crimsons and ascending yellows of the morning light were born on the new horizon. But in the south, the sky glared back with an eerie blue. No one spoke of it as they gathered on the wagon and made their way west to the village of Notting.

The Undiscovered Trail

Tell me about discoveries . . .

By 1998, Lois and I looked back at the history and progress of the breast cancer support group. In hindsight, we realized some survivors and friends from the group were gone, snatched from the world by the specter of breast cancer. It was a sobering thought to comprehend a disease, which almost seemed possible to conquer with the available tools (chemotherapy, radiation therapy, physical therapy, available tests and monitoring), could still take a life at any time. From the onset of the disease, every breast cancer survivor needed to remain vigilant while she watched and waited for any signs of reoccurrence. It was a fine line to walk. It was a fine line to live on, much less one to grow and blossom on. Yet Lois seemed to manage both with the time she had.

Lois always had a plan and a list to make those plans work. As 1998 began, Lois pulled a new calendar and placed her work schedule on it, then her school schedule, as she knew it at the time, and every event she knew she would be involved in for the year. By the end of the first week of January, she had the entire year planned out, with family vacations, birthdays, holidays, and anything she could predict that would happen throughout the year. As she started college, it seemed she had it all worked out. Then inevitably, calls came asking her to lecture or appear at events she had not planned on. It was more stress on an already stressful schedule.

Lois started some preliminary courses at Temple University over the summer of 1997. In late 1998, she was accepted into the graduate program for social administration. Though I registered my concern she was spreading herself too thin, she assured me she would slow down on other breast cancer-related activities if she felt she needed to. As the year began, Lois was involved with many activities involving her breast cancer support group, including the quarterly newsletter, the NBCC and their activities, the PBCC, the Linda Creed Breast Cancer Foundation in Philadelphia, the American Cancer Society, and the Reach to Recovery Program, among others, a full-time job in Baltimore, and finally, a nearly full-time schedule at Temple University by year's end. Fortunately, no signs of breast cancer recurrence existed during that time. Her tumor markers from March 1997 (CA 27-29 test) registered as below 20, which, as tumor markers go, were very good. Overall, she said she felt good and wanted to be a part of helping women survive, so I did not protest her decision to be this incredibly active. Although, looking back on her decisions at the time, her additional burdens continued to worry me that she had taken on too much.

Somehow, Lois managed to juggle all the elements she accepted with such grace; she accomplished a great deal with very little time wasted between projects. She enjoyed all the activities she was involved with and continued to make every effort to keep a steady and persistent watch over her health. She had her tumor markers drawn in March 1998 with the CA 27-29 registering at 20; later during the summer, her CA 27-29 registered just 13.8. If there were going to be problems with breast cancer returning, the tumor markers were certainly not showing anything. Just for anyone reading this, so as not to draw an incorrect conclusion, Lois's tumor markers worked for her. This is not true for everyone.

This was Lois's first full year off tamoxifen, a drug that limits estrogen and prevents estrogen seeking tumors from occurring. Lois was on the tamoxifen protocol since finishing her chemotherapy cycles and radiation therapy for about five years. Now she was facing any residual breast cancer on her own . . . no more treatments . . . no tamoxifen to keep the cancer away. And now, a grueling schedule to complete by anyone's standards. The idea that she was on her own made her more vigilant to be watching herself for evidence of reoccurrence. Many times she would ask my advice as to whether I could feel any lumps in the remaining breast. Most times I would only verify what she found herself. She religiously received her yearly mammogram, which, in 1998, was negative for any significant changes, though in December 1998 she had two fibroids removed from the left breast. For the year, Lois remained healthy.

In early February, Lois was asked to speak at a local bookstore on breast cancer issues from an advocacy level and from a survivor's viewpoint. The store had been haunting her from the previous year to speak. Women wanted to hear about her political activities and her life story. Then in mid-March, Lois was asked to participate in the American Cancer Society's Models of Hope program. With her regular work schedule, an hour's driving time, one way, a college schedule also an hour's drive away in the opposite direction, and her other obligations, the added activities began to take a toll. By the end of March, Lois ended up needing a scan to evaluate increasing joint and bone pain.

Of course, everyone, including Lois, thought the cancer returned as metastasis to her bones. However, the scan did not reveal metastasis but rather arthritic changes that were part of her aging process. However, the pain was bad enough to make an appointment with a specialist who started her on medications for arthritis. These were medications she took regularly with increasing prescription changes for the rest of her short life. The meds were effective without any lethargy, enabling her to continue her commitments to the many activities she was involved with. However, I felt this event was a precursor to something else. I voiced my concern, but she was not willing to hear it at the time. It seemed the world needed Lois, and I was willing to help her as much as I could. She continued with work, school, and the ever-increasing demands for her time and presence.

(Excerpt from an editorial by Lois A. Anderson, March 1, 1998)

It's that busy time of year when spring rolls around and everything starts coming to life. Change is inevitable, so everyone says, and my life is no different. I am, at the ripe age of 45, considering a major career change—not just something that may add to my Medical Technologist background, but a possible shift in a completely different direction. I'll let you all in on the secret when the plans are finalized.

Waiting on those daffodils,

Lois

On March 26, 1998, Lois received a letter stating she had been chosen for the JCPenney Golden Rule Award. This again was a coveted award given to those people who offered extraordinary community service as a volunteer. The award had a grant of $1,000 attached, which could be designated by the awardees to an organization that they worked with. Lois chose to give this donation to the PBCC (Pennsylvania Breast Cancer Coalition) for assisting her with the "mammogram decision of 1997."

Throughout the year 1998, Lois, myself, and several other volunteers set up and displayed the American Cancer Society's Skin Deep Project. This was no easy task, considering the "quilt," as it came to be known, was two panels measuring six feet across and six feet high, which needed to be folded without damaging the delicate structure. There was also a framework, which needed torn down and rebuilt every time the "quilt" moved to a new location. It was never a one-man, or woman, operation.

Since the Skin Deep Project was a very successful teaching tool across York County, Lois felt the American Cancer Society needed to extend an invitation, again in 1998, for additional squares to be added to the original work. The activities of displaying the "quilt," and the deep impact it made on anyone who saw it, started drawing media attention. On Friday, April 14, 1998, our NBC affiliate chose to do a story on Lois and her work with the "quilt." The TV station was so impressed, not only by her work with the "quilt," but also by her work on the national level, they decided to do a second interview just outside the station at a picnic table. The second interview was broadcast a few days after the original interview for the "quilt." The media attention again put Lois in the spotlight, and more people wanted to meet her or have her speak at their groups. Instead of being able to slow down, Lois's efforts intensified.

By April 19, Lois was given the honor of cochairing an event in Lancaster County known as the Race to Research. The race was held by Hadassah, the Women's Zionist Organization of America Inc. The head of the Race to Research sent Lois a letter on May 6, 1998, thanking her for her assistance. Yes, it was a thank-you letter, but it said so much more than that. It was indicative of the impact Lois was having on everyone. I include the body of the letter here.

Dear Lois,

The rain has stopped, skies are clear again and I am ever thankful of meeting you and having you as our honorary chairperson for the Race to Research. I thank you and George for coming to Lancaster on the two occasions for media coverage and on race day.

Learning of all your strengths has taught me a valuable lesson that I will never forget. I applaud all your hard work and talents in founding the Surviving Breast Cancer Support Group and the many other projects and initiatives that have come before you.

There's a sign that I pass on a local road here in Lancaster that says, "You can give without loving, but you can't love without giving." I thought of you at the time, and how you Lois, have that quality as a woman.

M****** U****

On April 22, 1998, Lois walked into the ceremony for the JCPenney Golden Rule Awards. It was held at the White Rose Room at the York Fairgrounds. That night, the room was beautifully decorated with tables of white linens topped by candlelight. The tables were set with shining plates and dinnerware. Everyone was dressed in their finest clothing, awaiting the unforgettable stories to be expressed by the area's most incredible volunteers. The ceremony was flawless and beautiful that night. Almost all of Lois's immediate family and my family were there to support her, along with close friends and associates. When her name was called, she accepted the award with the grace and humility, which was always her way of accepting praise and recognition. One of the excerpts I wrote about Lois for that special night follows and was published by the PBCC in their newsletter.

"I do not want to be forgotten," she told me a few days after her diagnosis. Before the diagnosis, she was simply a thirty-nine-year-old woman going through the daily rituals of running a household, getting to work on time, and making sure our twelve-year-old son got to school. Breast cancer took the familiar life she knew. It transformed her into a different person. Not just in the obvious physical sense but in a totally different way. She became better, stronger, and potentially more alive than any of us had ever seen. She truly sees the beauty in the moment and goes about living like it could be the last moment of her life.

George S. J. Anderson

It seemed Lois could not get out of the spotlight. Her schedule was rigorous, and thankfully, her health remained good. She continued her part-time college schedule and full-time job while she was pulled by one organization or another trying to have her speak or appear for them. In spite of her growing exhaustion, she still made time to follow her volunteer work. She continued to find speakers for her own support group, wrote an eight- to ten-page newsletter every three months, and followed any activities where people called and needed her help and expertise. Not quite catching her breath from the Golden Rule Award, Lois appeared at Northern High School on May 1, 1998, to speak to the young woman at the school on the importance of self-breast exam and breast health. Finally, she had a few weeks to recover until she went to Philadelphia for the NBCC's first Project LEAD conference.

When the NBCC created Project LEAD, their intentions were to educate their advocates so they would understand the science they would review. Lois was one of the first advocates to attend these conferences. As additional LEAD courses were added to their program, Lois would attend them. Each LEAD course would take three to five days to complete. Lois writes about her first attendance of the Project LEAD courses in her editorial.

(From editorial by Lois A. Anderson, June 9, 1998)

It's nice to be back home after having attended Project LEAD in Philadelphia from May 27th through the 31st. Project LEAD is an intensive course for the breast cancer advocate presented by the National Breast Cancer Coalition. This course trains one in the science, Epidemiology, and leadership skills necessary to being a public breast cancer advocate. Project LEAD was a wonderful experience for me and for those of you interested I have articles and other information from the women I met. Any of you are welcome to attend Project LEAD and I would encourage you to do so. For more information just ask me at our next meeting or call me at my home. My son's last week of school is beginning with all the activities surrounding his graduation from high school so please forgive me if it takes awhile to get back to you. After June 6th things will be normal at our house again.

Now for letting all of you in on my secret mentioned in the last newsletter. I have been accepted to graduate school in the area of social administration—that's social work—and will start classes later this summer. I am looking forward to this move with great anticipation and hope it will lead me to even greater endeavors.

Looking forward to life's changes,

Lois

We exist in this time, this place, only once in a lifetime. We wander this undiscovered trail finding the world on wings, the moon lost in nocturnal treetops, and the ruins of thunder collapsing in the rain. It is a source for untapped energies, untapped endurance, and strength. Lois believed in the moment where inspirations become the reality of life. I believe she never really lost her way here but thrived in the discovery of new ways, new directions, and new and exciting discoveries that might potentially end breast cancer forever.

After attending Project LEAD in May 1998, Lois finally had a quiet time to live her normal life again. It only lasted until September 1998 when she was again called to sit on the Department of Defense peer review panels. I don't believe many people realized how deep her impact was on the national level. One publication I found that may explain how powerful her influence was on the scientific community may be explained by this short blurb found in our local newspaper.

(From the *York Dispatch*, Wednesday, August 19, 1999: People You Know)

Lois Anderson of York has been selected by the Department of Defense U.S. Army Medical Research and Material Command to participate as a consumer reviewer on its Breast Cancer Research Scientific Peer Review Panels, which will be meeting next month. This is the third year in a row that she has been selected to participate as a consumer reviewer. She is one of only 31 women in the United States selected to serve as a mentor consumer reviewer on these panels.

Her anticipation and excitement of again being a consumer advocate is reflected in her editorial.

(Editorial by Lois A. Anderson dated, August 28, 1998)

These are exciting times we live in—from new treatments for breast cancer to research discoveries to my own life and the changes breast cancer has wrought.

New treatments, including Herceptin and some of the newer drugs, are some of the less toxic therapies to come along in years and represent a manifestation of the work started by the National Breast Cancer Coalition.

New research, backed by the Department of Defense, the National Breast Cancer Coalition, and the National Cancer Institute, is some of the best medical research and most directed research to have been done in years. Breast cancer survivors' presence throughout the process made scientists consider what they were doing and how it would affect those stricken with breast cancer. Our voices and our faces must continue to work to make our presence known as something that is real to these researchers and not some obscure end point in the process.

And on to the excitement in my life—I am eagerly anticipating meeting other breast cancer survivors/ advocates, breast cancer researchers and scientists at the peer review meetings to be held in September at Norfolk, Virginia. This will be my third year to attend these meetings to help decide funding for research proposals submitted to the Department of Defense. The Pennsylvania

Breast Cancer Coalition's annual conference represents another excitement with its ability to provide a large educational meeting for anyone with an interest in breast cancer. Again this year I have been selected to help present a workshop on advocacy. An upcoming television appearance about my favorite subject—breast cancer—will be another exciting challenge and last, but not least, is the official start of classes for my Master's Degree in Social Work.

Exciting times for me and I hope for you too. Take care and hopefully each one of you will attend the 5th birthday celebration of our group at our September meeting.

Anticipating a wonderful Fall season,

Lois

Just after the peer review panels were over, Lois headed to Washington DC to participate in "The March" held by the National Breast Cancer Coalition on September 26, 1998. After she returned home, she was scheduled to appear on a television program, called *Medically Speaking,* with one of our local surgeons. The program was a thirty-minute interview highlighting the medical and surgical advances to thwart breast cancer, but it also emphasized Lois's personal struggles with breast cancer and her important role as an advocate who utilized funding for research in the breast cancer forum. After the program aired, it again put Lois in front of the media, and breast cancer survivors from everywhere responded.

However, the effects of breast cancer surgery and its concomitant side effects continued to affect her. Muscle shortening and overuse of her right dominant arm, where the breast was removed just six years before, required her to return to physical therapy. On her forty-sixth birthday, October 6, 1998, Lois was suffering with severe pain and limited movement of her right arm and shoulder. Now, in addition to an almost impossible schedule, Lois had to find time to add two sessions of physical therapy per week to her agenda. Though she was not happy about this new wrinkle in her schedule, she had no choice but to accept it. Eventually, once the therapists got the arm moving again, I was called in by the therapists to learn the treatment techniques they used to keep her arm flexible. One technique was called "myofascial release." It was a technique I used time and time again to loosen her shoulder and give her flexibility over the rest of her life. Lois used to kid me, saying she liked having her own personal nurse around the house, especially when her shoulder started giving her trouble, which was quite often.

Even with her frozen shoulder, Lois continued to teach others about breast cancer. By October 9, 1998, only three days after her first physical therapy treatment, she taught self-breast exam at the Susquehanna Valley's Women's Fair. On October 13, she spoke to women before the Pennsylvania Breast Cancer Coalition on the topic of "political advocacy." On October 14, she spoke to the group known as the Women of Today about her breast cancer experiences. This group was so impressed by her accomplishments and her ability to speak intelligently about the breast cancer forum as it existed in 1998, they nominated her to receive an award from their group.

Sometime before the last days of October 1998, and the end of the year, Lois found two lumps on the left (remaining) breast. Tumor markers taken in September were unremarkable and did not indicate any evidence breast cancer had returned. One night, after her bath, she asked me to check and feel the same lumps she felt. Lois was concerned about her findings, and it was always enough to convince me. She showed me places where she felt something. When I checked, I also found them. She looked up at me and asked, "What do you think it is?" It wasn't a situation where she didn't understand the implications; I believe she just wanted validation she was doing the right thing, for the right reasons.

Knowing my wife was never one to simply accept anything on face value, I evaluated what she experienced over the past few months. She had a frozen shoulder. This was something she had not experienced since her mastectomy. She had joint pain in her knees, shoulders, her hips, and lower spine. Though tumor markers were not showing anything, my concern mounted as I considered the overall picture. I knew her thinking had to run along the same paths. I looked at her and told her, "I don't know what these are. But I can tell you are worried, and honestly, if you are to be sure about what they are, they need to be biopsied."

"Those were my thoughts too," she told me. She proceeded to speak to her surgeon whom she asked to biopsy the two sites. One site was to the upper part of the left breast, and the other was on the outer side. Lois was very anxious to have the biopsies done as was I. If these sites turned out to be a return of the cancer, it could explain the numerous painful sites as something other than arthritic changes. Lois was very anxious to have the biopsies done. There were days she waited when she would be on the verge of tears. Having the weight of a possible reoccurrence on your mind, while trying to lead your daily life, isn't easy. Nothing I could do or say seemed to make her feel any better. The only thing I could do was be there for her if she needed me.

Finally, on December 10, 1998, Lois had the two biopsies done. She could go home after the biopsies with instructions to keep the breast supported. This meant Lois had to wear a bra twenty-four hours a day, since the incision on the top of the breast could gap if the weight of the breast pulled it open. This had to be done until the incisions healed. However, with time, the top incision gapped. She continued to keep it supported, but now the incision care included daily cleaning, topical antibiotics, and, eventually, oral antibiotics. The gapping caused Lois a significant amount of pain, and she constantly observed for any signs of infection. Eventually, the biopsy reports revealed the lumps were fibroids with calcifications; neither was cancerous for which we were both grateful. The incisions finally healed in the early months of 1999.

In spite of doing continued physical therapy for her right shoulder at home with me, and a very painful, slow-healing incision on the top of the left breast, Lois wrote a six-page newsletter for her support group. Her editorial was full of hope and good news. There was not one mention of the personal problems she was enduring at the time. To all who read it, the newsletter was just another great effort by Lois to educate the members of her support group, physicians, and related health agencies that received her newsletters.

(From editorial by Lois A. Anderson, December 30, 1998)

By the time this newsletter reaches you 1999 will be upon us. I hope that all of you have had a good Christmas and a Happy New Year. The holidays have come and gone and we are faced with the boring time of year and little to do. Might I suggest that we all take time for ourselves and relax? Curl up with a good book—perhaps one in this newsletter or one you received for Christmas.

This time of year, too, makes me want to reminisce about the happenings of 1998. Perhaps the best thing to come our way is the advent of Herceptin for breast cancer treatment, one of the biggest advances in years. New protocols for using drugs already available are another example of the "bests" to be realized this past year. Moreover, don't forget the surgical advances that include the use of sentinel node procedure for axillary dissections.

My life has slowed down a little. However, classes will begin January 18th, and I must prepare a lecture for the LPN students on January 28th. Then I'm off to try to get speakers lined up for the next quarter's meetings. February and March will bring some excitement with them since I have been selected to review proposals for the Healthy Woman 50+ program administered by the Pennsylvania Department of Health. Well, so much for my "calm and boring" time of year!

Here's to 1999, may it be our best year ever,

Lois

Looking back on 1998, I would say it was probably one of Lois's last good years as far as her physical condition. The two incisions healed, as I've said, but the insurance company she dealt with at the time did not want to pay for two biopsy sites on the same breast. The insurer could not understand why the surgeon chose to do two incisions over doing just one. Considering the top wound barely healed due to the weight of the breast pulling the one-and-a-half inch incision open, leaving the other one-inch incision on the outer side of the breast, which healed normally. It was conservative for the surgeon to do the surgery in this manner. The insurer did not see it this way. They felt one incision from top to side would have given both biopsy sites. Their idea, though appearing logical, was enormously impersonal and would have created a disfiguring scar that probably would not have healed. Lois had to submit pictures of her left breast incisions to her insurance company with documentation from her surgeon in order to protest the claim. The battle with the insurer took time out of her overbooked schedule, exhausting her further. It took almost the entire year of 1999 to resolve this. By having this battle on a personal level created a precedent for other women with similar surgeries from having to go through this kind of impersonal treatment.

The year 1999 loomed before her with opportunities in the area of breast cancer treatments and information. She did not disappoint anyone.

Voices from the Past

Tell me about the voices . . .

In a place I knew well from my nocturnal journeys, the tree appeared within a dreamlike swirl of morning mists and fragrant smells of a new day. It was pleasant here, and I felt my dreams more clearly than I ever did. The lines governing the world of the dreamer and the experience that was the world blurred. The lines of the tree grew like a haunted gray silhouette emerging against a peaceful river. The slow waters stirred lazily, spilling across smooth rocks placed indiscriminately between the river's shores. Waves lapped peacefully against the dreamlike shoreline just beyond my shoulder. I knew I was not alone, yet no one appeared to disturb my reverie.

"Forget your way?" the voice of my grandfather asked me as he rounded the tree to face me. A penumbra of light surrounded him, making his face all but invisible yet outlined his body in bright outline.

Though amazed he would be able to appear, I responded, "I always find a way back, Grandpa." My heart was yearning to talk to him once more . . . tell him all my secrets . . . tell him about my life since I saw him.

"Remember . . . I am with you. All good things never die . . . They stay with you because they are a part of you." Though I couldn't see his face, I knew he smiled at me. He turned away, walking behind the great tree.

"Don't go. Please don't go," I called, hoping to hear just one more word.

Then he turned for just a glimpse and asked, "Did you dream?" His last word slipped away like grains of sand through an hourglass. His lighted outline became a shadow, and I knew he was gone. I wasn't sure I would see him again. The lines between the dream and the world blurred and then dimmed. Within the peaceful stirrings near the river's edge, I found my way to dream again.

Timothy was on the northern outskirts of Glade by the time Leon started toward the village of Notting. His immediate destination, the village of Wendow, was conservatively ten parcels north of Glade. From Wendow, he might push his horse the additional twelve parcels to the village of Bridgedom the day after. It was there, at Bridgedom, where a magnificent bridge spanned the Great Ravine of Tondell. It was said the North Wind became angry at his brother, the East Wind, and in his rage blew rocks and stones at the small mountain of Tondell where he was hiding. When the East Wind continued his torments behind the mountain, the North Wind blew the mountain down, causing a deep fissure in the earth as deep as two parcels. The folklore said their sisters the South Wind and the West Wind came between them to stop their bickering. As a result, the Four Winds found that if they worked together, they would keep a balance in the lands of the villages with no further destruction. As a result, the Great Ravine of Tondell was explained by the folklore surrounding it. Of course, great respect was generated for the North Wind when villagers saw the deep chasm cut into the earth. However, the real wonder of Bridgedom was the bridge that spanned it.

First and foremost, Timothy had to reach the village of Wendow before midday or his chances of going farther would be out of the question. To complicate matters, Leon sternly instructed him to pass the information of the broken wall and the great danger it caused in the villages of Stock and Glade.

Timothy left Leon's house before the sun rose. The day he left Stock on his father's errands, he had food and a few hours' rest, but no sleep. He felt weariness in the core of his body. He would be careless if he took chances. Timothy set his horse at a slow trot for Wendow. The horse kept pace, but Timothy fell asleep while the horse continued on the road. It was nearly nightfall when he arrived at the border of the village. It was a wasted day . . . He needed sleep. Going into Wendow after sunset was hopeless if he were to pass his message along. The village lodgings were closed when he arrived. He decided to wait until morning . . . He needed sleep.

He saw a copse of trees bounded by rock formations to either side a short distance from the road. It was a safe place, off the road, where he could sleep. He rode behind the rocks and then stopped behind some trees, keeping them secluded. He disembarked and then tied his horse to a tree. He unpacked a little of the food Penny sent with him, then pulled a blanket from behind his saddle and laid it on the ground. After a few bites of bread, exhaustion demanded its payment and drove him into a dark sleep.

Sleep opened the gates of troubled dreams. He dreamed a white-gowned figure was standing off at a distance on a misty ridge. He tried to reach the apparition, but it turned and started walking away. He called out, "Catherine . . . Catherine, it's me, Timothy." But when the figure turned toward him, it had no face. The shock almost stirred Timothy awake, but exhaustion drove him to another place . . . another dream.

He was wandering through massive sharp rocks and snow. The air was wretchedly cold, and the winds were fierce. Trying to keep his face out of the cold wind, he turned toward a flat face of solid black stone. The stone face had strange etchings on it. It seemed to be a kind of ancient writing, indiscernible to Timothy, but it meant he was on the right path. He did not know how he understood, but in this dream, he realized he was searching for something. He felt a sense of urgency but didn't know how to proceed. He stood, looking at the flat face of rock, trying to decipher something to tell him what direction to go. He was freezing, hungry, and bone tired, but he knew he had to go on. But which way . . . which way? He cried in the sea of hopelessness, knowing he was lost. Sliding against the snow-covered rocks, overcome by exhaustion, he fell into a blinding sleep as snowflakes filled his eyes and clothes, covering him in a melancholy white. While he slept in the snow, he dreamed a dream within a dream.

He was in a bright green meadow. It was an unformed dream, not quite ready, as only a small space was created around him. He watched the meadow reveal itself, eventually expanding a world and extending in all directions. The meadow was unlike anything he encountered in Glade, Stock, or any villages he knew. He felt he was standing in the center of the world. To his side, a stream materialized and then swelled to a parcel across like a river. Timothy put his foot in the water where it came to his knee. The water was knee deep the whole way across! A huge spreading tree, its long leafy tendrils dragging in the lazy current, stood on the other side. Not understanding the dream's intentions, he crossed the river to the great tree. Here, the dream was powerful, forcing him to lie on a grassy swell near the tree. The sound the water made, moving lazily against the banks, acted like a powerful sedative. Entering this peaceful sleep, there were no dreams, only a void of darkness.

"Timothy . . ." a hollow voice called. "Timothy . . . you must wake up . . ."

Timothy woke beneath the great tree. He looked about and saw no one. "Who called me?" Timothy asked, looking for the source of the voice. He stood and walked to the other side of the gigantic tree. "Is anyone here?" No answers were forthcoming. Timothy was tired but saw the way the sun neared the horizon; it was late afternoon here. Or was it? He was dreaming. He stepped away from the tree and suddenly went cold, bumping his head into a solid snowy mass. He looked at his arms and saw his coat covered in snow. The moon was in the sky, and the etchings on the stone face before him formed words in its luminescence. He traced the words with a finger, but when he rubbed the snow from his eyes, everything disappeared.

The woman in the white gown stood on a dusty road a great distance from Timothy. Timothy did not want to see her empty face again. He did not understand the meaning of it, and really didn't want to. Instead of turning, the figure simply pointed. "What do you want of me?" Timothy asked the haunting figure. The specter simply continued pointing to the north. "I am heading north . . . Is that what you want?" The woman in the white gown walked into a cloud of dust, disappearing into nothingness. This time, the dream did wake Timothy.

Timothy awoke inside the grove of trees bordering Wendow. Somehow, his excessive exhaustion allowed him time to sleep, but the dream within a dream woke him by early afternoon. The timing was good. He could get news of the danger from the south to the villagers of Wendow and then continue to Bridgedom before nightfall. He picked up the satchel, pulled a skein of water, and drank half of it before rummaging through the bag for an apple. He ate it quickly, tied the satchel to the saddle, and rode off quickly.

He arrived in the busy streets of Wendow, where afternoon merchants and shoppers looking for bargains filled shops and open-air traders. He stopped at a booth and asked the merchant if he knew anyone who could circulate news quickly. The merchant directed Timothy to a tall stone building adorned with sculpted stone falcons, their mirrored wings overspreading the doorway. It was the office of the village crier. Timothy pushed through the crowd and went inside. The village crier was skeptical and appalled by the news Timothy carried. He said he wanted a messenger to verify his story before he would cry it on the streets. He wanted to know who sent him. Timothy explained how he was isolated from his village and how Leon had taken him in. When the man heard Leon's name, he took Timothy at this word. He did business with Leon in the past and knew he was a reputable man . . . not someone who spread rumors. The crier knew Leon would not send such devastating news without reason.

Timothy explained he could not stay. He needed to travel to Bridgedom as soon as his business was done. The crier said, "Be assured, I will tell them. I will still send a rider to assess the situation. Then if need be, we will send militia or whatever help Stock and Glade may need. Does that sound reasonable to you, young man?"

"Of course . . . of course. It sounds fine. But why do you suddenly believe me?" Timothy asked, perplexed by the man's willingness to believe his story.

"Because Leon is a good man. He would only ask for help under the most dire circumstances . . . and this sounds like one. The other reason I believe you is your description of the quakes and tremors. We felt them, but not as strong as the ones you describe at Glade."

"Thank you, sir." Timothy added, "But I must hurry and deliver this same news to Bridgedom."

"Call me Thomas," the crier said.

"Thank you, Thomas," Timothy called over his shoulder, as he turned toward the door.

Thomas called him back, "Before you go, I must give you the name of someone in Bridgedom who can help you get the news of this disaster to the villagers quickly." Thomas took a piece of paper from a polished wooden writing desk and wrote a name. "He lives at a house built against the bridge entrance . . . name is Amos."

"Thanks again," Timothy said, taking the paper from Thomas. He turned toward the door, then turned back and said, "I hope to see you again."

"Myself as well, Timothy," Thomas added sadly. "May the Winds help you on your journey and keep you well."

When Timothy was at the door, he turned to wave good-bye to Thomas. He left the building behind and mounted his horse. He had fifteen parcels to ride before he made it to Bridgedom. He only had a little time before dark fall. It would be night before he would get there. He had no time to waste.

Benjamin pulled the cart up to the darkened house. Night robbed the light from the sky as Leena, Michael, and Catherine left the safety of the cart and moved cautiously toward their house. There, embedded in the front yard, was the massive stone Michael gave Catherine the first day of her life. Amelia, too weak to move, saw Catherine's stone and gasped, "Benjamin, that's Catherine's lifestone?"

"Yes, it is an enormous one, I must say. But I've seen it, and I know how big it is."

"Catherine can never move it far enough away to escape the things coming through the wall, can she?"

"I'm afraid not," Benjamin said somberly.

"That poor girl is trapped . . . just like I am," Amelia whimpered as a tear ran from her eye.

"Don't say that," Benjamin blurted out, not wanting to hear any more of her suffering voice than he had to. "Between Michael, Leena, and myself, we will find a way to save you both," Benjamin said, though he was not convinced he could help either of the girls. He hoped Leena or Michael would think of something, but it was probably a long shot at best.

Michael came to Benjamin. "We'll need to move Catherine's stone to a safer location."

Benjamin understood his concern for his daughter but knew they were not equipped to move it. "We can't . . . We need help, Michael."

Michael understood. "Timothy's family is just a little ways from here. I could ask them for help."

"Then what are we waiting for?" Benjamin asked impatiently, wanting to get started.

"Be ready to go when I get back." Michael left Benjamin a few moments then returned. "Let's go . . . and hurry. Leena saw blue mists traveling in a meadow only half a parcel from our back window. I don't think we have much time."

Benjamin pulled Michael into the cart before he could take a breath. They were finally traveling the rutted dirt road toward Jakob's farm. Amelia sat on the backseat of the cart, watching the distant trees outlined in stars. She spoke to Michael, "Don't forget me. I'll help where I can."

Michael felt sorry the young girl lost her youthful strength trying to get her message to his daughter. He knew she was dying and could do nothing about it. Michael turned to Benjamin and said, "Amelia doesn't look good. When we get help from Jakob, we need to find her father . . . if he is still alive."

"I saw the house burning . . ." Benjamin told him, replaying the sight of smoldering timbers piercing the ashes where a house once rested beneath fragrant flowering trees . . . gone now.

"Her house is less than half a parcel from Jakob's house. Could we try another run and see if anyone might know where he is?" Michael said like an impatient father caring for a sick child. "I think we owe her that much."

Benjamin only had to glance at Michael's grave face to realize how serious he was. "I'll try, but if we get stopped by these things, I will have to bring her back."

"That's all I am asking," Michael said, relieved Benjamin realized the seriousness of their predicament. Michael looked at Amelia and saw her pain grimace brightly as they rode over the darkened roads. Michael turned to Benjamin and whispered just loud enough for him to hear, "I think she is dying, Benjamin."

This time Benjamin did not take the time to look at Michael's face. He knew what he had to do. Benjamin shouted to the horses, and they picked up pace. They were off to Jakob's farm as quickly as the horses could take them.

🛆🛆🛆

Apparently, Thomas didn't wait until his rider returned. Leon's word was good, and it must have been enough to convince Thomas. As Timothy made his way through the puzzle of streets, he listened to the echoing bells of town criers delivering the terrible news he brought from Glade. He turned his attention away from his viral news and rode his horse quickly through the winding streets of Wendow. He never slowed long enough to hear their proclamations but knew he kept his promise to Leon. He felt good but wished his news had a happier message.

He had much to do. Bridgedom was fifteen parcels to the north after reaching the northern borders of Wendow. Finally, the streets broke away to the open road, a place where Timothy could see farther than the next cross street. He left the horse run, kicking the dust and stones behind him.

He pushed his horse over the first three parcels toward Bridgedom. The mare's hide started lathering with white foam, its breathing became heavy and labored. Timothy had to give the animal a well-deserved rest. He dismounted and then walked the horse off the road. He saw a flat place where the grass grew abundantly greener and the rush of water flowed unseen behind it. Thirty arm's lengths from the road, he found the stream. Leading the horse into the water, he pulled the saddle from its back and then used his hat to pour water over the overheated animal.

Timothy looked at the horse and realized the futility of what he doing. Timothy and his horse were exhausted. He had one night's sleep over the past three days. His horse was doing about as well. To accomplish what he needed required him to skip resting and keep moving. He leaned against a tree, while his horse walked into the cool stream and drank water from its calm surface. Timothy's heart was beating fast from whatever remaining energy he had. He had to rest.

"How will I do this?" Timothy shouted, frustrated by his limitations. "If I am injured or killed by exhaustion, I will do no service to Leon or Catherine. I must be careful." Timothy looked where the horse lay down in the water to cool itself. It was an unnatural thing for a horse to do and revealed how tired the animal was. "I hope the Winds will forgive the borders of my abilities. Fate may kill me, but I will not kill myself. I will rest." Timothy looked at the horse and said, "We need to rest now. We did what we could today." Timothy walked to where his horse lay its head against a bank of grass growing near the water's edge then said, "When I awake . . . we will be off," he said, sweeping his hands over the horse's mane. "We will do this . . . we will." Timothy walked to a nearby tree, sliding his back down its smooth trunk to the ground. It was there he fell into a deep and dreamless sleep. He did not awaken until early rays of sunlight caught the corners of his eyes.

✗✗✗

With Rand's help, they hitched the last two horses to the wagon. They left Glade with their belongings well after sunrise became an old memory. The village of Notting rested eight parcels to the west of Glade. Leon pushed the horses as fast as he could, considering the pulling weight of the wagon. Penny leaned toward Leon and admonished him, "You're going to tire the horses running them like this."

Leon looked at Penny's frown, then in resignation said, "Yes, you're probably right. I better back off them." Leon, not slowing down, looked cautiously at every horizon. "I don't see any danger, but I wanted to get away from Glade as fast as I could. I think the orbs may already be invading the edges of our village."

"It's possible," Penny said, "but I hope they stay away . . . Overall, I'd say most of the villagers already abandoned the village."

Rand spoke up, "Penny may be right. What the girl, Victoria, was saying, the orbs seem drawn to where people are. Empty buildings may not entice them."

"Hope you're right," Leon said over the clatter of hooves tearing up dust on the road.

Leon pushed the horses a little harder, seeing where the road cut up a small hill rising before them. Even the increased momentum didn't help as the horses slowed to a trot by the time they crested the hill. At the top, Leon stopped the wagon.

"Why are we stopping?" Victoria asked, trying to focus through the light blinding her eyes.

"By the Winds . . ." Rand exclaimed in horror.

"Oh, Leon," Penny gasped, looking beyond the road before them.

From the hilltop, they looked upon a maze of channels excavated by the purple orbs. Leon and Penny, who only heard stories about them, watched in amazement. Rand and Victoria watched in horror at the sheer numbers of hideous spheres working diligently at stopping their progress.

Rand clasped a hand on Leon's shoulder to break his attention. "We have to get past these things."

Leon turned away from Rand and marveled at their amazing industry. They were meticulous, controlled, and very effective at what they were accomplishing. The ravines they cut into the earth using the red pseudopodia as cutting tools were just deep enough to channel the blue mists from one low spot to the next. There were three main ravines placed about a half parcel apart. Then there were smaller, shallower ravines surrounding and running through the three main trenches. The illusion appeared to make all the branches passable by the orbs. It was a deception, and Leon realized their intent. Leon believed most of the ravines were made too quickly and remained too shallow for the orbs to navigate. Both Victoria and Leon's stories verified they needed a very deep ravine to move through. The majority of these shallow depressions appeared to be tracks in the soil the orbs created, allowing the blue mists to fill them. The appearance of the blue mists filling an area much larger than what really existed was clever and visually deceptive.

The scene looked impossible to overcome. In fact, if not for the information Rand and Victoria supplied, Leon might have decided not to move on. It was Victoria who finally led Leon through the incredible maze.

"I know how to beat them," Victoria said. She pulled Amelia's lifestone from beneath her shirt. To everyone's amazement, the stone glowed red and emanated fifteen arm's lengths in all directions from the rear bench of the wagon. She climbed down and walked in front of the horses.

"What do you mean to do?" Leon shouted at her, too far from her to pull her back. "You'll be killed if one of those orbs decides to attack us."

"They won't attack," Victoria said confidently. "Just follow me." Watching her walk into the mists, Leon sat helplessly as the woman-child, Victoria, moved through the blue misty river, streaming defiantly before them. To Leon's amazement, the blue mists parted and allowed Victoria to walk right through. Still standing in the middle of the churning mists, she motioned Leon to move the wagon and follow her. Leon wasted no time as he commanded the horses to follow. The girl led them, walking untouched by the blue mists and purple orbs. Leon and his astonished wagon of passengers passed through unimpeded.

Leon finally drove the wagon out of the mists to the safety on the opposite side. Perspiration lay beaded on his brow. He could barely open his hands from the reins, so tightly he held them. Victoria walked through a quagmire of dangerous orbs and a minefield of rugged terrain like it was child's work. Leon looked at Victoria, staring up at him. "By what magic have you done this?"

Victoria almost laughed at the terror written on Leon's face, but thought better of it and maintained her solemn expression. "Remember, I told everyone at your house. It is what Amelia told me to do before we parted. She told me her lifestone would protect me as long as I had it in my possession." Victoria looked at Penny and Rand, listening intently to her. She continued, seeing her new friends thought she was something working outside the forces they believed in. "But Amelia also said in three days it would not work anymore. Three days from when I left her, Amelia will be dead. When she dies, the lifestone dies . . . that is why I must get it back to her."

"How did you know this?" Leon asked, while Penny and Rand looked behind them, watching the continued industry of the purple orbs as they cut and channeled paths into the lowlands.

"The voices Amelia heard near the wall . . . they told her these things," Victoria told Leon with a pleading look in her eyes.

"Anything else they told her?" Rand asked sarcastically while he turned forward to face Victoria.

"No . . . a lot I figured out myself when I was attacked by the orb that killed Jonathan." Victoria's amusement, short lived as it was, dissolved completely with this last confession.

"Do you know how to destroy them?" Leon asked, thinking Victoria was still keeping something back that could help them.

"Not really . . . but Amelia's stone gets weaker each time I use it." Victoria looked to Penny and Rand, hoping they would say something to get her off the witness block with Leon.

"Well, from what I just saw . . . ," Penny remarked from the front wagon's bench, "if one stone can slow them down this much, then collectively, what would several stones do? For that matter what could a whole village do?"

Victoria considered Penny's idea but questioned the strength of Amelia's lifestone. The first time she used it, the glow extended twenty arm's lengths; this time it was less. It meant the lifestone was getting weaker as Amelia did. Soon her lifestone would be useless. Amelia said Victoria's lifestone would help her as well, but until now, Victoria never thought to use it. Amelia knew her lifestone would work. Now Victoria considered the possibility her own might work, perhaps better than Amelia's. She reached inside her shirt to the small leather pouch lying at her chest and pulled out her lifestone. In the presence of the orbs, her lifestone glowed with a crimson penumbra, emanating almost thirty arm's lengths away from her. She looked to Leon and said, "I think you might be onto something. Can everyone take their lifestones out with me?"

Leon rummaged through his coat and brought out with a stone as big as his hand. Together the two stones emanated a reddish light almost sixty arm's lengths across.

"By the winds," Leon exclaimed, watching the red glow extend to its greatest distance away from them. "Together they are more powerful than by themselves!"

"Let me try too," Penny exclaimed. Penny held her lifestone up with the two others. The force of the red glow carried all the way

to the mire of blue mists behind them, striking one of the purple orbs, which stopped and fell into the swirling blue mists.

"We have a way to stop them," Rand proclaimed.

"I think so," Leon returned. "But this is useless until we get to the villages and tell them."

"Yes . . . yes, I agree," Rand said. "Let's be off. We have to tell as many people as we can and quickly."

Leon snapped at the horses; the wagon again jumped forward toward the village of Notting. Everyone put their lifestones in places where they would rest until they were needed. Everyone remained silent while the morning sun rose, revealing the western edge of the village of Notting.

♦♦♦

Jakob, with his sons Andrew, Lamin, and Eric, heard the thunderous hoof beats hammering against the cobbled lane running in front of their home. Alexis, Jakob's only daughter, stayed inside the house until she knew who came to call.

"Jakob," Benjamin called fiercely from his two-wheeled carriage, "please come over here."

"What's this all about, Benjamin?" Jakob asked, as he walked to the wooden cart, looking where Michael held a pale sickly-looking girl.

"There's not a lot of time to explain," Benjamin said. "The wall was breached, and the whole village is in danger."

"That was the quake we felt father," Alexis said, leaving the safety of the house to stand next to her father.

"Who is the girl, Michael? She's not someone I've seen or met in Stock before . . ." He looked at Benjamin, suddenly too quiet for his liking. "A friend of Catherine's?" Jakob asked looking at Michael holding the girl close to him.

~341~

"A lot of questions . . . not much time for answers," Benjamin stated almost apologetically.

"Yes, but we owe Jakob some kind of explanation before we can ask for help, Benjamin," Michael proclaimed as Benjamin shook his head at them.

"What kind of explanation?" Jakob asked suspiciously, seeing the peculiar behavior Benjamin and Michael were exhibiting.

"The wall was breached!" Benjamin bellowed. He continued, now that he had everyone's attention, *"And now, we are at the mercy of the things coming from the other side of the wall."*

"What things, Benjamin?" Alexis asked suddenly, afraid of what Benjamin was trying to explain.

Though Amelia was too weak to move, she still had her voice. She watched as Michael and Benjamin hopelessly attempted to convince Jakob anything was wrong. She looked to Alexis and spoke to her. *"Things, Alexis, which have no right to be here."* Amelia struggled weakly against Michael's hold. *"You felt the quakes . . . The things coming through the other side need the low grounds to move about."*

Suddenly, everyone's attention focused on Amelia and Alexis. *"So why quakes?"* Alexis asked

"Because it opens seams in the earth . . . They make fissures deep enough to gain access to another area."

"What are these 'things' you speak of? Have you seen them yourselves?" Jakob asked, skeptical his visitors were panicking over stories they heard passed around the village.

"I've seen them," Michael finally confessed. *"I was going to Adonnas on business when the first quake hit. I was at the western borders of Stock when the shaking knocked me to the ground. A ravine opened between me and my horse. A strange blue mist poured into it, filling the rift in the ground. When I stood up, something moved in*

the mists. *A purple-colored sphere floated there on top of the mists. I thought I'd be cautious and stay out of sight. I ran behind a tree then watched as the thing grew a stringy red tentacle that it shot like an arrow toward my horse. It wrapped itself around the middle . . ."* Michael trailed off. He shuddered before he went on. *"It tore the horse in two . . . I never heard a horse make such an anguished sound. Then it took the pieces and tore them up over and over again until nothing was left except undistinguishable parts of a bloody carcass. I stayed hidden behind the tree until the orb disappeared into the mists. I made my way to my office and stayed there until Benjamin showed up with Catherine and Leena. I think the orbs hate life, and they are doing whatever they can to erase us from the surface of the grounds we keep. They are here to destroy us."*

Benjamin never heard Michael's story, and it made him think. He didn't respond for a moment, then asked, "You mean the orb did not take any part of your horse for food or keep any parts of it?"

Michael looked at Benjamin, obviously frustrated his story was questioned. Jakob listened intently, trying to understand Michael's implications. "Benjamin," Michael finally said, "the orb just picked up my horse and utterly and completely destroyed him. It took nothing . . . then it moved away like nothing happened."

"Then the orbs are just here to destroy," Jakob stated, staring at Michael holding the girl Amelia.

When Amelia sighed loudly and slumped against him, Michael became alarmed by her sudden weakness. "Amelia, are you all right?"

"I think Victoria just used my lifestone. I get weaker each time she uses it. I feel it."

"You mean you do not possess your lifestone?" Jakob asked, shocked that someone would give their stone to another for safekeeping.

"I needed Victoria to get a message to Timothy, and she needed more protection than what her lifestone could give her. Besides, she

had a hard time believing me, and I needed her to go before the wall was breached."

"So you were there . . . ," Lamin, the third oldest son of Jakob, asked, "at the place where the wall was breached?"

Amelia could feel what little energy she had fading with every breath she managed to take. She felt feint, and a graying mist seemed to be growing over her eyes. She looked to Michael then to Benjamin. "Tell them, Benjamin. I no longer can." Though she wanted to stay aware long enough to see her father again, Amelia finally went into the graying mists of sleep . . . a place where she would not return.

Michael pulled Amelia against him, keeping her from falling against the floorboards. Benjamin tied the reins to the bar at the front of the cart then stepped off where Jakob waited. "Jakob, we do not have the time to do this, but I have to explain what I know so you and your sons can help."

"So the quakes were more than just the earth shaking?" Jakob asked.

"Yes, when the wall was breached, something came through, something violent. Apparently, Amelia and her friend Victoria were near the wall where this happened. Amelia had some kind of encounter and sent Victoria to Glade with a message for Timothy. I don't know if she ever got there. Amelia came here with a message for Catherine. Miraculously, she was able to find Catherine in all the confusion. When she finally had Catherine's attention, she told her she alone could stop the orbs by placing her stone in the wall."

Jakob looked at Benjamin with some concern. "But won't that make Catherine part of the causalities?"

Michael spoke from the bench where he was holding the unresponsive girl. "That's why we're here. We wanted to bring Amelia here to be looked after, but she wants to be with her father, and we will try again. But we also have to transfer Catherine's stone to a safer place . . . Catherine too for that matter. Leena and I wanted to get out of Stock, but we can't leave Catherine behind. Her stone must follow wherever she goes. If the orbs possess some awareness of what we are doing, they may be cognizant of the potential threat her lifestone represents to them. The orbs may try to annihilate Catherine or her lifestone before she decides what she will do."

"We plan to fight them," Benjamin stated with authority. "I, for one, do not relish the thought that we sacrifice such a young vibrant girl to stop these things just to save ourselves."

"But what if we find she is our only weapon against them?" Andrew, Timothy's oldest brother, asked, knowing full well Timothy would fight anyone who forced his Catherine into doing this foolhardy deed.

"Then that will be Catherine's decision. Not mine . . . not anyone else's," Michael said, as the cold knife of reality cut through his heart.

"So you want to move her lifestone to some other place?" Jakob asked Michael.

"I haven't considered where a safe place would be, but I know leaving her lifestone lying half buried in my yard in full view is not the safest place," Michael replied.

"I believe getting her lifestone on a wagon and, at least, making it mobile will give us a better chance at keeping both it and Catherine safe for a while. At least until some decisions can be made," Benjamin told the small group.

"Eric, Lamin, Andrew . . ." Jakob shouted to his sons. "Go to the stable and hitch up some horses to the biggest wagon we have and get back here as soon as you have it ready. Bring shovels and pry bars. We're going to need them." The young men did not protest and hurried off to the stable as their father told them. Jakob addressed Michael and Benjamin again, "What will you do with the girl?"

Amelia moaned softly in deep sleep as Michael looked to Jakob and said, "We need to get her to her father. It was the last thing she asked us to do for her before she stopped talking."

Though Jakob felt Benjamin's sudden arrival was an intrusion, he also had a daughter, and his heart went out to the father of this one. He looked at Benjamin and said, "Then be off and get her there. My boys and I will head out and meet you later at Michael's house. If all goes well, we may have Catherine's lifestone on the wagon by the time you get back. For now, we will bring Catherine and her lifestone back here. We'll leave it on the wagon in the closed barn where it will be out of sight." Jakob paused; he realized he had taken the planning away from Benjamin, who was looking at him defiantly. "It's a plan, Benjamin. We can all decide what to do after we meet at Michael's house, okay?"

"I will be off to find Amelia's father then, I suppose. I'll see you all when we get back," Benjamin said, as he summoned the horses and rode off, with Michael holding Amelia tightly against him.

Jakob sent his sons to his shop where they went to work preparing and collecting the tools he had asked them to gather. He had Alexis close the shutters on the house and had her lock them as if a storm would be coming. A storm was coming, and it was already on their doorsteps.

Andrew came up to tell his father that Lamin and Eric were bringing up the wagon. Jakob turned to his sons as they stopped the wagon in front of him. "Let's get this done. This is Timothy's fiancée we are trying to protect. If Timothy were here, I believe he would want us to do this. If what Benjamin and Michael say is true, Stock is probably cut off from the other villages already. I think we should prepare for the worst. Timothy may not be able to come back unless we stop these things and patch up the wall somehow." Jakob turned back toward the house, thinking Alexis returned there. Instead, she was standing right there with them, waiting for her father to issue orders to her just as he had for his sons. "You never fail to amaze me, my daughter. I need someone to keep an eye on the place while we are gone. Can you do this for me?"

"Of course, Father. If you want, I will get a meal together for everyone. I'm sure no one has had time to eat anything with all that has happened."

"Just wait until we get back. It could be quite a while until we get Catherine's lifestone on the wagon," Jakob told his daughter as he turned back to his sons waiting for him to climb on. Jakob climbed to the front bench of the wagon then waved good-bye to his daughter. Lamin took the reins, moving the horses toward Michael's house.

They were greeted by Leena and Catherine when they arrived. Leena seemed upset Michael was not with them as promised. Jakob explained, *"Leena, that girl wasn't even able to talk when she left my place. I've never seen the 'stone sickness' before, but from what I could tell, the girl was in a bad way. Benjamin needed Michael to watch the girl while he drove the horses. I understood they tried to find her father once before."*

It upset Leena to think that the small girl she had once thought of as a nuisance could now be dying in her husband's arms. She looked to Jakob and said, *"Yes, Benjamin tried to take her back to her home, which is just a little ways from your place. What they found was burning ruins . . . No one was there. That poor girl gave so much to get her message to Catherine . . . Now she has no one to care for her . . . no one to cry for her."*

"And no stone for the wall when she's gone. She has stone sickness because she gave her lifestone away." Jakob tried to reassure Leena.

"Is there anything you want Catherine or me to do?" Leena asked, trying to take the attention off Amelia's last days on this earth.

"Michael and Benjamin feel this house is no longer safe for you or Catherine. While we move Catherine's lifestone onto the wagon, it would be best to pack any belongings you want to take."

"Where do they think a safe place would be?" Leena asked with some impetuousness.

"Certainly not here, where her lifestone is out in the open. We all felt it best to come out to my farm and stay until we can sit and decide what to do."

"And what does come next?" Leena asked angrily.

Jakob didn't have time to deal with Leena's anger. He simply turned away and said, "I don't know."

Jakob's sons had unloaded the tools and backed the wagon up to the site where Catherine's stone lay half buried in the soil. Lamin looked to his father and asked, "Ready?"

"Anytime you boys are ready . . ." Jakob responded. Lamin and Andrew swung the picks into the ground around the perimeter of the large stone, while Jakob and Eric lifted the loosened soil and moved it away.

"This is a really big stone," Eric said to his brother Andrew.

"This is going to take all night to move. Alexis might just as well make breakfast," Andrew replied.

"You boys need to concentrate on what you're doing," Jakob interjected. "We want to get this stone on the wagon and out of here as quickly as possible. Chattering won't get it done, so keep at it, boys."

Eric and Lamin looked at each other, giving each other a silent nod, which meant they better do as their father asked. Lamin raised the pick and drove it hard into the packed earth around the stone. Andrew moved the loosened soil, and neither of them said a word to each other.

"She looks pretty bad, Benjamin," Michael said, pulling the unresponsive girl against his side.

"We've been this way before, Michael. If we're lucky, we might find someone this time. It looks like the fires burned out," Benjamin said, as he drove the cart closer to the site that was once Amelia's home. He continued on the road until he came to the charred ruins. Benjamin looked around but saw no one. "Hello," Benjamin called

loudly. "Hello, is anyone about?" Before long, a figure moved from behind an old elm tree, one untouched by the fire.

"Hello," the distant figure called out, "what do you want here?"

The figure continued moving toward Benjamin. It was a man's voice who called back. "Do you know a girl by the name of Amelia?"

"She's my daughter. I have been here these past two nights waiting for her to come home. Has something happened to her?"

The man walked next to Benjamin. "Your daughter has the stone sickness. She's already well into her second day."

This man lost his home, and now he was most aware he would lose his daughter. "What happened?" he asked, looking at Amelia lying against Michael's side. She looked like she was sleeping, but the color of her skin told him otherwise. Tears welled in the man's eyes as he reached to take his daughter from Michael's arms. Amelia's limp body finally lay in the arms of her father. He looked to Michael and asked, "Do you know what happened? What did she do with her lifestone?"

Michael looked into his grieving face. He knew Benjamin wanted to get this business over with as soon as possible, but Amelia's father deserved an explanation. This girl was not just a problem to unload on her father. She made the ultimate sacrifice to warn Stock. Michael would not allow Benjamin to dismiss her so easily. "She wanted to get back to you. We made her a promise we would do so. Do you have a place to stay? A place where we can talk? I have a lot to tell you and very little time to tell it."

"I'll take Amelia to my sister's house on the next hillside. We can talk there. Follow me." The man carried his daughter in his arms as he walked before Benjamin's cart, leading the way to his sister's home. It was a slow solemn procession where the creaking of the wooden cart wheels and horse hooves cladding on the hardened dirt road seemed like prestigious litanies for their fallen messenger.

The door to the modest cottage on the hill opened as the small entourage arrived, spilling bleak candlelight like a specter crawling on the ground to meet the new arrivals. A woman appeared from the light and asked, "Who is calling at this hour?"

"It's Amelia. She has the stone sickness. With the rising of the sun, she will soon be in her third day," her father said to the woman standing at the threshold.

The news was not taken lightly as the woman softened her voice and said, "Bring her in. I'll get a bed ready for her." She disappeared inside the house, while Amelia's father carried his daughter's almost lifeless body inside.

Michael jumped down from the cart and tried to convince Benjamin to do the same, but he wouldn't budge. "I'll keep an eye on the cart and water the horses while you make explanations. We did what we set out to do. Now we need to get back just as soon as you are done," Benjamin stubbornly replied.

"But Amelia is his daughter. Some reverence for her, Benjamin . . . It's all I'm asking," Michael implored.

Benjamin said nothing. He turned the cart around and prepared to go back the way he came. He found a trough of water and led his horses to it. Michael saw Benjamin did not want to be part of this, so he turned and followed Amelia's father inside.

Benjamin sat impatiently, waiting for Michael's return. From the top of the hill, he could see the southern borders of Stock and a fair distance to the north. "It can't be sunrise yet!" Benjamin spoke loudly to himself. As he watched the horizon to the north, he saw a growing reddish glow as if sunrise came from that direction. Benjamin smelled the burned air, then realized the reddish glow he saw coming from the north were fires set by the villagers. They were setting fires to keep the orbs out of the village! He watched the glow form a great circle across every horizon he could see. "The orbs have us under siege! The villagers are surrounding the village within an enclosure of fire!" Benjamin exclaimed as he watched incredulously.

He was ready to knock on the cottage door when Michael appeared and walked slowly to the cart.

"How did he take the news?" Benjamin asked with modest concern.

"Much better than I would have," Michael replied.

"We need to get back."

Michael had nothing more to say, simply nodded agreement, then caught the acrid scent floating in the surrounding air. He looked at Benjamin and asked, "Do you smell that?"

Benjamin aimed a finger at the red glow rising in the horizon to the north. "I've been watching it since you took Amelia in with her father. I think the villagers set fires to keep the orbs away."

"We better hurry. I hope Jakob and his sons have Catherine's lifestone on the wagon. They'll be wondering what took so long."

"I think they'll just be happy we returned Amelia to her father before she died," Benjamin said, not realizing how cold he sounded.

Michael looked at Benjamin sternly but said nothing. He was emotionally exhausted telling Amelia's story to her father and aunt. He didn't want or need another confrontation. He shook his head sadly, while Benjamin drove the cart over the rough dirt road.

Sunrise began its steady drift forward when Benjamin started toward Michael's home. Yet for a short time before the sun rose in the east, Michael watched a glowing red mist rising from the northern borders of Stock, pitting itself against the growing pinks and reds of the new day. An army had arisen during the night, built moats, filled them with tar and oil, and set them ablaze. Michael hoped it was enough to keep the orbs out of the village. Little did he know hope was failing in the village of Stock.

A Chance to Change Things

Tell me about her time . . .

Until 1999, I worked as a registered nurse within an extended care facility located fifteen minutes from our home. With the changes being made to our facility by insurers and new government regulations, the unit I helped create was coming to a close. I still loved what I did and started searching for facilities that might be starting a unit similar to the one I was leaving. I found one . . . fifty miles away.

Having a position locally was convenient and allowed my participation with our monthly meeting of the breast cancer support group even the nights I worked. My new position was an hour's drive away, with twelve-hour night shifts, starting at 7:00 p.m. The breast cancer support group started at 6:30 p.m., lasting sometimes until 9:30 or 10:00 p.m. I explained my commitment to my new employers, and for two years, they accommodated my request to be scheduled so I could run the men's support group with my wife, Lois. The problem was, after two years, they would no longer guarantee I could schedule this night off once a month. It was an unforeseeable change of events that I hoped I could remedy. When I look back at the year 1999, I would say it was a year of transitions. Some changes were heartbreaking, and others were wonderful.

Lois understood my need to move into the new position. Staying where I was implied a possible layoff or, at least, a pay cut. Neither option was realistic, as we were financing our son's tuition for his first year of college. Stresses came from every side, and Lois did her best to keep everything from slipping away. Though it was not what we wanted, Lois suggested I continue the men's support group every other month for as long as possible. This worked for a while, but in 2001, the men's group had to dissolve. Trying to get time scheduled off for the men's support group was growing impossible and caused a lot of tension at work. But everything that eventually transpired with the men's group happened in 2001 . . . I would be getting ahead of myself.

At the beginning of 1999, Lois received the report that the lumps she had removed from her left breast in December 1998 were calcifications, not cancer, which reduced some of her anxiety. The open wound at the top of the breast continued to concern her because if it didn't close, it wouldn't heal. Lois started having arthritic pain and coupled with the open wound on top of her left breast just made her miserable. I felt helpless to do anything for her. With her pain, and what we saw was occurring with the men's support group, I knew she felt depressed. Still, she continued the activities she could do.

On January 12, 1999, Lois received the following letter from the American Cancer Society.

Dear Lois,

Thank you for agreeing to speak at the American Cancer Society public issues forum "Let Your Voice Be Heard: Legislation Affecting Cancer Issues" at the Capitol. The program will take place January 21, 1999, from 1:00 PM to 5:00 PM in the East Wing of the Capitol. A Networking Reception will follow the program from 5:00 PM to 6:30 PM in the East Wing Rotunda.

We are asking you to speak on what you personally have done to advocate for cancer issues, such as your work on the Breast Cancer Check Off, Etc.; and what those concerned with advocating for cancer issues can do to follow your example and make a difference. This is what we are trying to get across with this program, that we can make a difference regarding legislative issues, so you may want to discuss the advocating you do for breast cancer, your fight against the disease, etc. You should plan on making your speech last 15-20 minutes.

The agenda will also include local legislators who will share strategies on health related issues and legislation. Topics to be discussed will include: health related legislation issues, building relationships with public officials, how to lobby your legislators, and how cancer related issues can "compete" with other special interests.

We are very excited to have you speaking at our program, and are looking forward to seeing you there. If you have any questions please don't hesitate to call me . . .

Sincerely,

****

Educational Representative

On January 18, 1999, Lois began graduate studies at Temple University. Starting studies in earnest was one of the best things she could have ever done for herself. Once she started, I again voiced my concern she might have taken too much on, but she showed me on her calendar, how she had her time regimented to accomplish what she needed and have time for herself. The tumor markers from September 14, 1998, confirmed her CA 27-29 to be only 13.8, a decrease from the previous 20 reading. This finding fortified her argument, which was enough for me.

On January 21, 1999, Lois was well enough to deliver a speech on "advocacy" to the American Cancer Society's Capitol Region public issues forum named "Let Your Voice Be Heard." The woman I knew and loved was back in control again. She rose above the surgery and the arthritic changes in her knees and back and, at least, looked and acted like the person who would shake the world by its roots.

On the last day of December 1998, Lois was contacted by the northeastern branch of the Women of Today, asking Lois to be nominated as their 1999 Outstanding Woman of the Year. Lois accepted their invitation to be nominated and later received confirmation she would receive the award in the early months of 1999. Lois was very excited and wrote the story in her quarterly newsletter.

(Editorial by Lois A. Anderson, March 4, 1999)

Well, it looks like the groundhog might have been right after all, but I won't say that too loudly. My tulips and daffodils are almost two inches above the ground and going strong. And, speaking of going strong, I hope you took a good look at all the spring events over the next several months. Looks like there's something for everyone and that's probably not all, so stay tuned to the updates at our next several meetings.

As for me, I have been chosen to receive the Outstanding Woman Award from the Pennsylvania Women of Today. I feel quite honored by this group. The award will be presented at a luncheon on March 6th in the Yorktowne Hotel when this group holds its statewide conference for 1999.

Don't forget the Breast Cancer Check off on your state income tax as you file all those forms. The money goes toward research and was a hard earned reward for the Pennsylvania Breast Cancer Coalition. Last year $285,000 was raised. We hope 1999 brings at least double that amount.

Watch for the flowers and have a happy Spring,

Lois

On March 6, 1999, the Pennsylvania Chapter of the Women of Today honored Lois as the Outstanding Woman of 1999 for the State of Pennsylvania. Then on March 24, 1999, the northeastern division honored Lois with the Northeastern Outstanding Woman of the Year for 1999 with their celebration. After Lois received these awards, I asked lightheartedly, "Is this a new trend for you . . . getting a major award every year?" Lois fired back with her own brand of laughter and said, "Well, that's what people do when I get out and get things accomplished." I had to agree; people appreciated Lois taking time out of her life to keep breast cancer issues and treatments in the forefront. I was very proud of her, and she knew it.

By the time March 1999 closed, the wound at the top of her left breast finally healed. It had taken daily cleansing, antibiotic ointments, Steri-strips, gauze dressings, and wearing a supportive bra to bed every night. The medications from her physician tempered the arthritic pain in her back and knees. Lois was now on daily medications, which had to be taken the rest of her life. She also needed to be on clorazepate, a benzodiazepine, at intervals, to help with indiscriminate periods of vertigo triggered when she was overtired.

After the awards ceremonies passed, Lois concentrated on her studies. She focused on her schoolwork but continued searching for new information on breast cancer. On days not at school or work, she would investigate the Internet for stories. If either my son or I found a newsworthy article related to breast cancer, she would verify the story with Internet sources, find others who had written about the same subject, and then she would use it in her newsletter. Over time, Lois kept a stack of newspapers, journals, and magazines piled at the end of our dining room table to use for her newsletter. Between newsletters, the pile would get enormous. She was driven to keep people interested in the advances scientists, physicians, and legislators made to eradicate breast cancer every day. The irony, as I perceived it, were many of these advances were the direct or indirect consequence of Lois's activities with the Department of Defense, the National Breast Cancer Coalition, the American Cancer Society, and other agencies she worked with to eradicate breast cancer from the roster of deadly diseases.

Until late spring of 1999, Lois continued her studies, worked a full-time job, and ran the household. Her hands were full, to say the least. If she wasn't writing something for classes, she was researching information on the latest breast cancer advances. Even on days not at work or school, she would work well into the early hours of the morning, getting only four or five hours sleep a day. Our adult son, who was still home to attend college, pointed out his mother's lack of sleep and her exhausting lifestyle. I took a second look at her activities and realized how tired she was beginning to look. Together, our son and I told her to get more sleep, or she might push herself into a recurrence of cancer. Of course, it was only superstition on our part. We had no basis for believing our foolish assumptions. We had no analysis to justify our concerns. There was, however, a real concern stemming from driving exhausted on the interstate, but such arguments landed on deaf ears. Still, we wanted Lois around for a while, and pushing herself to this "extreme" to exceed seemed foolhardy. Lois dismissed our concerns and told us we were worrywarts. She agreed that she was obviously "tired" but felt "fine" otherwise. We were told there was no reason to be upset with her schedule. She was doing what she wanted to do. We asked her to, at least, slow down a bit, but this only irritated her, and she seemed determined to do even more.

In early 1999, Lois was invited to the television studio at York Cable Access Television to record a show about the Skin Deep Project. She brought several people who contributed a square to the "quilt" to record their stories. She had me prepare slides and some written narration, but the gist of the program were the women's stories about their experiences with breast cancer, or a lost loved one, to this treacherous disease. After the show aired, YCAT received a tremendous positive feedback from the community. It was, perhaps, the most significant TV program Lois ever recorded; and between 1999 and 2000, it aired several times. It was Lois's last TV recording with them. Lois displayed the thirty-minute video to her support group in June 1999 to honor the women who helped with the program. Lois placed a short blurb into her newsletter for upcoming events for this showing of the video.

Our June 16th meeting will feature *Lois Anderson* with a *legislative update* and explanation of some terminology used in the newsletter. We will also view a tape done for York Cable Access Television (YCAT) on the *Skin Deep Exhibit: Stories in the Fight against Breast Cancer,* which features several of our group members.

As it was for Lois's career with television programs, it also ended the era for the Skin Deep Project. Showings of the "quilt" continued a few more years, but eventually, requests to see the work faded to nothing. The "quilt" was eventually retired and put in storage.

Lois attended the NBCC conference in Washington DC from May 23 to May 26, 1999. During her time there, she lobbied her state senators and congressmen to either initiate financial aid or continue financing breast cancer research. Her continued efforts with the NBCC produced allies and friends and, more times than not, additional commitments and resources. Her newsletter released on June 1, 1999, tells about her many activities related to breast cancer.

(Editorial by Lois A. Anderson dated June 1, 1999)

Welcome to those of you who are new to this newsletter. I think you'll enjoy it. With this newsletter, we are beginning our 6ᵗʰ year of publication, and in September our Support Group will be 7 years old. What a record! Also in this newsletter, we are announcing the beginning of a new section on websites that may be of interest to all of you. These sites will focus on women's health and cancer.

By mid-June, my classes for this year will be finished and I am looking forward to a two-month vacation from studying, seminars, and paper writing. As I write this newsletter, I am two-thirds of the way through a Loss and Grief course in Temple University's graduate school. It's been an exciting and fulfilling school year for me.

I have just returned from the National Breast Cancer Coalition's Advocacy Conference and annual lobbying day. I had a chance to catch up with old friends and make some new ones. My roommate was a 21-year old woman who won the Miss Albany, Georgia pageant, a stepping stone to the Miss America Pageant in September. Her platform is breast cancer and she is very involved in the issues surrounding breast cancer. She was a member of the lobbying team from Georgia, and we, both, were able to share much information and feelings with one another.

A small group of our members has formed a committee to put together a resource pamphlet for breast cancer patients in the York County area. If anyone is interested in helping on this committee, please call me. Any help you can give is welcome.

The ceremony, in which I received the Outstanding Woman for 1999 from the Pennsylvania Women of today, was beautiful. I was very moved by it. A slide show was put together by this organization about this award and me. One of these times we will present it for the rest of you because I'd like to have all of you share in it.

Take a look at the article on the STAR trial at the end of this newsletter. You'll be hearing more in the weeks to come about this clinical trial.

I guess that's all for now. Don't forget the picnic in July.

Have a good summer and be careful not to burn.

Lois

On June 17, 1999, Lois participated in the Pennsylvania Department of Health's technical review. Lois's college courses were finished for the summer, but people seemed to find her, asking for her help and expertise, which were becoming renowned.

(From a thank-you letter from the Pennsylvania Department of Health to Lois A. Anderson dated July 19, 1999)

Dear Ms. Anderson:

Thank you for assisting the Cancer Prevention and Control Program with the review of applications submitted in response to the Healthy Woman Project's Request for Applications (RFA) 98-07-11. All members of the technical review committee worked so well with Department staff in conducting an effective review.

It was a pleasure to work with you on this initiative. We look forward to working with you on future cancer control initiatives.

Sincerely,

Director: Bureau of Chronic Diseases and Injury Prevention

Manager: Cancer Prevention and Control Program: Bureau of Chronic Diseases and Injury Prevention

New advances were being made that addressed breast cancer and the treatments of the times. In 1999, the STAR program was initiated, which weighed the values of tamoxifen (which was the appropriate treatment for breast cancer after chemotherapy and radiation therapy were completed) against a drug called raloxifene, which was used (at the time) to treat the effects of osteoporosis. The news (of the day) hyped the study with hopes that raloxifene would become the new tamoxifen. The hype escalated to such extremes, Lois had to write to the newspaper, asking them to clear up the discussion. The news hype started to have women believe raloxifene "was" the new tamoxifen. However, at the time, the study between the two drugs just started, and there was no data to support a correlation between the two drugs. Lois eventually took it upon herself to write a story to clear up the controversy.

(From the *York Daily Record*, Sunday, June 13, 1999: An article written by Lois A. Anderson)

Drug not proven to prevent cancer

On page 3C of the May 26 edition of your newspaper, in the article entitled, "Breast cancer tests begin," reporter Tom Joyce states: "Raloxifene, commonly used to treat the brittle bone disease osteoporosis, has proven to be effective in preventing breast cancer."

This statement is completely and utterly wrong and presents information to the public, and especially women, that is not correct about this drug manufactured for Eli Lilly. Unproved statements such as this are a disservice to women.

Nowhere in the package insert for "Raloxifene" (trade name Evista) does the manufacturer state that this drug prevents breast cancer. Obviously, your reporter did not understand what was being presented at the press conference about the Study of Tamoxifen and Raloxifene (STAR) clinical trial held at the Apple Hill Medical Center on May 25.

Raloxifene cannot be prescribed by physicians for the prevention of breast cancer because it was only noted anecdotally in previous clinical trials for the efficacy of Raloxifene in preventing osteoporosis that the rate of breast cancer was somewhat decreased in the women receiving this drug.

The STAR trial was designed to try to answer the question of whether Raloxifene does prevent breast cancer with fewer or lesser side effects than Tamoxifen (trade name Nolvadex) does.

Tamoxifen is the only drug currently approved by the Food and Drug Administration for the prevention of breast cancer, and it is the only drug that can be prescribed to prevent breast cancer, a disease many women fear.

A breast cancer survivor, breast cancer advocate, and breast cancer activist, I just returned from the National Breast Cancer Coalition's Conference held in Washington, DC, where Dr. Norman Wolmark, one of the investigators of the Breast Cancer Prevention Trial (BCPT) was attacked there by various advocacy groups for the design of the STAR trial. I feel I must point out the errors in your report. I would be remiss if I did not take this opportunity to educate the public in the errors contained in your article.

I would also be remiss if I did not point out the fact that a Letter to the Editor on page 7 of the same edition lacks complete information about Tamoxifen's (Nolvadex) side effects. I am referring to the letter from Jerry Lewis, MD, senior medical director of Zeneca Pharmaceuticals.

Dr. Lewis states that "the risks of therapy, while serious, occur in less than 1 percent of women on Nolvadex" (referring to the healthy women in the BCPT trial using Tamoxifen to prevent breast cancer). This statement is true.

However, one must look beyond this statement to the actual data generated by the BCPT and see that when dividing the women into those under the age of 50 and those over the age of 50, the serious side effects of endometrial cancer, stroke, and blood clots in the legs and lungs occurred predominately in the women over the age of 50 and not in the women under age 50.

In my opinion, the risks and benefits of taking Tamoxifen to prevent breast cancer must be clearly understood by women prior to taking this medication for prevention, and only a woman and her physician can make that decision after careful evaluation of the risks and benefits as they apply to each individual case.

As you can see from the article, Lois did not mince words when it came to correct information. As it was in her newsletters, all information was clearly checked and verified. Any story or information she found was verified with other sources and had to say the same thing, or it wasn't used. It was unfortunate our local newspaper reporter crossed swords with my wife. She was clearly not putting up with misinformation. She was so concerned her support group was getting the wrong information; she had a clinical trial coordinator explain the entire STAR program in an article to her June 1, 1999, newsletter. This way, she felt assured that no members of her support group misunderstood the information, and if need be, they could share the proper information with others.

The summer moved on with heat, humidity, and slower-paced activities. Our outdoor cookouts, vacations, and annual summer picnic with the breast cancer support group passed into simple pleasant memories. Having Lois home over the summer was almost like having a normal family life once again, something we hadn't experienced since her diagnosis with breast cancer. We made the most of the summer months, taking short trips on weekends when we were both off. Sometimes we visited the homes of our friends or family for cookouts and get-togethers. It was a simple summer, with easy expectations and no real surprises, but one.

Over the summer, at a family gathering, we discovered her father lost a tremendous amount of weight. Her father, an electrician his entire life, was working as a driver for a supply house to make ends meet in his retirement. Her mother was bussing tables and taking orders at a local pizza shop to help with their household finances. It seemed, in their retirement, her parents were struggling. Her father, who controlled the finances, could not see the sense of spending his money on doctor visits and simply refused to go.

Lois and her siblings were concerned by his sudden weight loss over the winter and early spring. They thought the worst and suspected his drinking problem had the consequences of liver or pancreatic cancer. They convinced their father to make an appointment with the doctor for a checkup. Afterward, they understood the reason for the sudden weight loss.

Unknown to his children, the physician diagnosed her father with diabetes several years earlier. However, he went unchecked, refusing doctor visits. During the scheduled visit, the physician found his blood sugar to be over 400. There, he admitted to drinking beer and water to settle an unquenchable thirst, frequently a sign of an elevated blood sugar. His physician prescribed an oral hypoglycemic, with instructions on doing blood sugars at home. The physician wanted daily blood sugars to verify this new medication effectively brought his sugars into normal limits.

Lois knew her father would not be compliant with the daily blood sugars or his medications. To protect him from his own ignorance, she set up a network, which included herself, her sister, and two brothers to check in on their parents weekly, particularly her father, if not more often. Since the four siblings could share the responsibility, they divided it up on a weekly basis. Of course, Lois coordinated their efforts. When she got word her father was not checking his blood sugars, he either got a nasty phone call or Lois showed up on his doorstep.

Their father's diagnosis of uncontrolled diabetes actually came as a relief to Lois and the rest of the family. It answered a lot of questions about his past and present behavior.

Still, it was a long-term commitment. Every four weeks, Lois would take her turn driving the twenty-mile journey to her parent's home. Once there, she prepared her father's medications for the upcoming week. Other than a relatively good control of her father's diabetes with oral medications, both parents were physically healthy and active. Time would move on, and this would change. Eventually, her father was compliant with his blood sugars, and Lois was able to check in periodically once the sugars were under control again.

Having elderly parents with chronic and deteriorating medical conditions is an inevitable part of life. Her parents needed her, and in spite of her own problems, she stood by them and did her best. In later years, the repercussions of their medical conditions would herald definite mediation on Lois's part.

Our son finished his first year of college but seemed disenchanted with what he was learning. His grades were adequate but not outstanding, so Lois and I had a serious talk with him. Over the previous summer, our son landed a job with a local television studio and was mastering the very things the communications degree would do for him. After talking with him, we believed he needed to continue another semester to be sure. If it didn't work out, then we were willing to look at another school more conducive to what he wanted to learn.

It was disappointing for both of us, since we graduated from the same college years before. Still, we understood it was his decision to determine what he wanted to do, and we would be there to help him. Eventually, by the end of 1999, our son decided to change schools and follow a course of study he wanted to pursue. The new college was almost five times more expensive, and we put a second mortgage on the house to send him. In the end, it was well worth the cost, and he finally graduated in 2001 with a degree in electronics and computers.

Our son was not the only one attending college that year. Lois also made preparations to return to classes as you can read in her September newsletter.

(Editorial by Lois A. Anderson dated September 1, 1999)

Well, it's back to school time and that includes me. This year my courses include one on research and another on grant writing and fund raising. Guess my real life experiences will help as I've been involved in both subjects at some point in my career and volunteer work.

The past several weeks have brought an explosion of conferences, conventions, seminars, and meeting notices to my mailbox, many of which I do not have space to list in this newsletter. It seems as if everyone wants to hold an event during October, but it is impossible to attend them all or you'd die of conference-itis and overload of the brain. A few not listed will be mentioned at out next meeting.

Don't forget to come out and support the Pink Ribbon Walk.

That's all for now. I have a few politicians to write to about some breast cancer issues. If you'd like to help with letters and postcards to your senator or House of Representatives member, please contact me. The National Breast Cancer Coalition needs your help.

Working for breast cancer issues with the politicians,

Lois

The year 1999 was the last year of the century. Many looked at the end of the century as the end of the world. Some saw signs of our portentous end, while moviemakers and doomsday prophets used the end of the century to confirm their beliefs. Some worried about our digital clocks and computers setting properly to the new century. We called this phenomenon the Y2K problem. Businesses, hospitals, and people in general ran to stores for devices, computer programs, and new clocks to help overcome the Y2K "crisis." While there was some concern about overcoming the Y2K problem with computerized documents and timepieces, the new century was not something to fear. Change is inevitable, and it was coming with or without preparations.

Some more-courageous forward-looking people saw the dawning of the new century as a new beginning. Lois believed this would be the century where breast cancer could become a thing of the past. She certainly foresaw the new developments and treatments happening over the upcoming months and years. Her understanding was based on her perspective of having served on many of the country's leading breast cancer panels such as the American Cancer Society's ACT Lead for Congressional District #19 in 1999 and her previous contacts with the Department of Defense peer review for breast cancer research. Instead of seeing the end, she saw the beginning. At the end of everything, there is always a new beginning.

(Editorial by Lois A. Anderson dated December 1, 1999)

> Everywhere you look everyone is talking about Y2K —
> so much that, frankly I'm tired of hearing about it. The
> year 2000 is the beginning of a new century—a century in
> which I hope we can conquer cancer once and for all. We
> are making slow but steady progress, which will continue
> with help from all of us.

> For me, the year 2000 means I am about one-third
> of the way through my graduate studies. Studies, which
> I hope, will change my life and the lives of those around
> me. It's a scary thought to be making such a change at
> this stage in my life, but I'm sure this change will be worth
> the effort.

> Have a Happy Y2K,

> Lois

The new century eventually came, and all the negativity surrounding the advent of this new beginning faded into obscurity. Our son started his new college, and Lois prepared for the next grueling part of her studies. I was in the process of publishing a book within the next few months. We entered the new century with our eyes open to new beginnings, new experiences, and hearts filled with hopes, dreams, and aspirations.

The Dimensions of Shadows

Tell me about their lessons . . .

The light filtering through the obscenely beautiful branches could not but inspire a dream of places unseen by those who never did. There were voices, madly shuffled together, blending with the rustling flowers and leaves. The voices faded in and out like light, shadowed by objects passing over and away. My thoughts remained confused by the cacophony of sound, rendered with perceptions of shadowed beings shimmering in the melee. I wanted a single thought to be its vanguard and drove a manifest word into the surrounding madness. "Stop."

Silence dropped like a shroud. "What do you want of me?" I asked, looking for some sign that whatever I entered might still be present. "You called me to the Poet's Tree. Why?" I asked, not knowing which direction an answer might come. "Who are you? What are you?" I asked, frustrated by the wall of silence imposed by my questions.

One whisper surfaced in the air, followed by three shadows. "We are what went before. You know what we are, and who we were," one shadow said in a familiar feminine voice.

"Grandma?" I asked, knowing she was gone from the world almost ten years.

"Yes, and your grandfather and other grandmother are here . . ."

I looked to the three shadows, thinking I would find physical attributes, but their forms remained dark and insubstantial. My grandfather, gone from the world . . . almost twenty years, spoke next.

"You will be tested. You will know if you are the sandstone or the rock that doesn't break."

"But, Grandpa, the river of time wears us down until there is nothing left," I protested.

"We will be with you through it all," my other grandmother said. Her voice softened to a trailing whisper as the shadows faded. "When we come to take you from the river of Life, will we find a smooth beautiful stone or a handful of sand on the streambed?"

The rock that doesn't break . . . It did not sound like an easy journey. I lay my head against the Poet's Tree and slipped into a troubled dream.

The melancholy sun hovered low in the sky during the time the villagers called "early light" when Leon fought through the minefield of orbs outside the village of Notting. Now, it was "mid light" as he drove his wagon through the streets of Notting. Notting was busy, bustling with activity, when the wagon rumbled through the cobbled streets, laden with passengers and weapons. Onlookers, seeing Leon's tired face and wagon equipped for a hostile encounter, pulled back in silent fear.

"Leon," Rand called, "these people have no idea of what we went through. They are going about their business as if nothing happened."

"Perhaps nothing has happened here," Leon replied without resolve. Exhausted from the events they survived, Leon observed the unnatural normal pace and the unblemished peacefulness existing in the village of Notting. Rand was right. They didn't know the existence of the horrible dangers a few parcels east of their village. He faced Rand and said, "This may be a place to rest and make preparations to fight our way into Stock tomorrow."

"These people need to know they are in danger," Rand insisted.

Leon was not in the mood to fight. He packed his belongings, closed his home, and fought across a treacherous field of orbs without sleep. He was exhausted by the events of the past days. They all needed a good meal and a long rest before they continued. He looked at the passersby making a wide berth around his wagon. "They don't seem very receptive to bad news," Leon said sarcastically.

"What do you think we should do?" Penny asked, wiping the few hours of restless sleep from her eyes. Victoria slept soundly on the pile of blankets lying behind Penny's bench.

Leon thought a moment, wondering how he would convince these people they were in danger. Once done, how would they convey the news from this village to the villages beyond? Ruminating on how he would accomplish these things, he remembered how he sent Timothy on this same mission alone. He wondered how Timothy managed the responsibility he dealt to him. While he sat here, not knowing the next step, he turned to Rand and asked, "Rand, do you ever do business with Notting?"

Rand thought a moment and then said, "Move forward a few streets to a place called Banyon Street. Stop in front of a store called Omar's and let me out. I know a man who may help us."

Leon pushed the horses and wagon three streets forward where Rand told them to turn. Thirty arm's lengths from where they turned was a sign that clearly stated Omar's. Rand jumped from the wagon and then motioned Leon to wait. It was only moments when Rand returned and said, "Go to the end of this street then turn behind the buildings. Omar has buildings behind his store, a lot like your place. There's a stable behind his business . . . food and water by the back kitchen door . . . and Omar is a good host. He wants to hear everything we have been through. Let us rest, eat, and then decide what to do next. He especially wants to meet Victoria, since she was the one to see these things."

"Were they even aware of the quakes here?" Penny asked.

"We didn't take much time, but I did ask if they were affected by them. He told me everyone thought they were rumbles of thunder, nothing more," Rand said quickly.

"I need to rest the horses." Leon was weary, bone tired from the ordeals preceding his arrival. "Wake Victoria. Her stories should impress Omar with the nature of this threat. When I have the horses settled, I'll join you for food and much needed sleep. We need to be ready to move into Stock before the sun comes up. Take advantage of the time we have to rest. Does that sound reasonable?" Leon asked them.

Rand nodded agreement then climbed aboard to awaken Victoria. She was in such deep sleep, she was unaware they made it to Notting. When she woke enough to stand, Penny and Rand led her into Omar's shop. Leon watched the three tired travelers stumble through Omar's doors and then pulled the wagon and horses inside the barn behind the shop.

Shackled by fatigue, Leon's mechanical care of the horses and belongings pushed him to where he could barely move. When he finished, he struggled to the back door of the shop and knocked. The door was opened by a young woman who introduced herself as Omar's servant. She led him to a table set with simple but abundant food. To Leon, the table looked like a fine feast. While he made his way to Penny, he watched as Rand and Omar staged a heated discussion with Victoria. Penny was eating when the young woman led Leon to the chair beside her. The servant girl asked what she could get for him. Leon said, "Whatever Penny is having . . ." The girl smiled then went into the adjoining kitchen. Leon leaned toward Penny and asked, "So how is everything going?"

Penny turned and whispered, "Omar's having a time understanding how all this happened."

"He's not the only one! We were chased out of Glade by those things," Leon said, unimpressed by Omar's ambivalent nonchalance. When Penny rolled her eyes at him, he knew everything was not as it should be. "Something wrong, dear?" Leon asked, a little more seriously, picking up Penny's signal.

"Omar is not convinced the orbs exist," Penny said, as Omar overheard her conversation with Leon.

Omar, picking up the conversation between Leon and Penny, said, "If these things exist, why aren't they here where we can see them?"

Leon looked where Omar sat smugly in a huge armchair. "If you don't believe them, Omar, believe me. I just left my business and home in Glade to come and tell you, you are all in danger. If you choose to ignore us . . . so be it. But if you are as wise as I hope you are, you will ride five parcels east of Notting and see for yourself."

Omar thought a moment, then said, "Okay, I'll send an envoy there, and if what you say is true, a warning will go out." Omar looked to Rand, then Victoria, then where Leon and Penny sat together. "Eat, then sleep. When you are awake, I will have answers and then make a decision. Until then," he continued, "I will check your story."

"Fair enough," Rand stated.

"I agree." Leon said. "I've had enough to eat. Just point me to a place where I can sleep."

Omar had the servant girl escort them to clean comfortable rooms where they could sleep. Meanwhile, Omar called for a rider to investigate Victoria's story. After hearing Omar's stories, the rider was terrified. Omar would not be disappointed.

※※

Jakob, Lamin, Eric, and Andrew dug around the large rock residing in Michael's front yard. "Do you think we have enough ropes and pulleys to lift this thing out of the ground father?" Andrew asked impetuously, sore from the extensive digging he did to release it from the ground. Jakob took the shovel from him and handed him a pry bar.

Jakob said, "We should get enough leverage using the horses and ropes. At least, I hope we do."

Eric stopped digging and sniffed the air around him. "Do you smell burning oil in the air?"

"Yeah, I've smelled it for the last quantum," Lamin said. "It seems to be coming from the northern end of Stock."

"So what do you think it is?" Andrew joined in.

"Boys!" Jakob stated loudly. "Concentrate on what you are doing. We will figure what the smell is later. Could be someone lit a patch of field on fire and used too much oil to get it started. Right now, we need to get this rock on the wagon and be out of here."

Lamin, Eric, and Andrew knew better than fight with their father. They put their shoulders into the shovels and pry bars, and within a short time, they were able to move the large stone onto the wagon. They were loading their tools when Benjamin and Michael returned.

"I see you managed to get Catherine's stone on the wagon," Michael said.

"It's more of a big rock . . . ," Benjamin said, irritated by wasting their time talking, "than a stone. Don't you think, Jakob?"

Jakob looked at the two men and said, "I think it would be best to be out of here before we are discovered."

"Have you been up to the house?" Michael asked Jakob.

"Yes, we told Catherine and Leena to wait until you returned. They are inside."

"I'll get them," Benjamin insisted.

Michael remained in Benjamin's cart, all the while observing Jakob's sons securing Catherine's lifestone to the large wagon. He looked where Jakob stood giving orders to his sons, then furtively back to the door where Benjamin went to retrieve his wife and daughter.

Jakob watched Michael restlessly observing everything. A father himself, he imagined Michael wrestled some inner demons; but before he could say anything, Benjamin came back with Catherine and Leena.

Catherine watched her father squirming on the front bench of the cart. "Father, you made it back. We were afraid you were stopped along the way by someone looking for Amelia."

"We were careful not to let anyone near us until we knew she was back with her father."

"Amelia is with her father then?" Leena asked, as she and Catherine took their seats on the bench behind Michael.

"Yes, he was happy to find his daughter." Michael hesitated, then went on, his head lowered, "When I told him she gave her lifestone to her friend Victoria, he went pale . . . then he wept over her. I tried to explain why she did this, but his grief was too great to have understood any of it. I told him anyway. It didn't seem to make any difference to him . . . His daughter had come home to die in his arms. What could I tell him? What could I say that would make any difference? I felt helpless. Her father's house burned in this catastrophe so he has gone to live with his sister. That's where we took Amelia. He carried her inside, and then Benjamin and I returned. I don't think Amelia's father will have long with his daughter until she draws her last breath. This will be with him the rest of his life."

"I'm glad she found her way home," Catherine said with tears in her eyes.

The little caravan started back to Jakob's farm. Jakob's sons rode along the sides of the wagon. Standing on makeshift runner boards, they kept watch on the tension lines holding Catherine's lifestone on the wagon. The horses strained against the weight of the stone, while the wheels groaned in protest. Still, their expertise in moving the big rock was successful; and eventually, the wagon gained stronger footing on the tightly packed earthen roadway to Jakob's farm.

Seeing the difficulty Jakob had with the wagon's weight, Benjamin suggested he move ahead, taking Leena, Michael, and Catherine to the farmhouse, where a very worried Alexis would be waiting. Jakob agreed with him and told Benjamin to tell his daughter that he would be along as soon as he could.

The roadway was certainly better than Michael's front yard, where the weight of the wagon cut deep into the soft earth. Still, as the hardened road moved behind him, Jakob practiced caution with the heavy load. Several times he shouted for Andrew, Lamin, and Eric to jump off to patch a rut or fill in a hole where the horses might have difficulty pulling the wagon through. If they weren't careful, the weight could split a wheel or break an axel as they returned. The road home distorted itself into a tiring and tedious ordeal. They anticipated an uncomplicated journey, but it twisted into a day of exasperating work. The late evening sun spread eerie red beams through the trees growing beside their barn, when they wearily pulled their cargo inside, hiding the stone from onlookers.

None expected their return to be so late. Yet by the end of the day, the stone was hidden, and all the exhausted souls rested well that night. The next day would prove trying. The orbs were circling the village of Stock, while everyone slept peacefully inside the farmhouse, in the heart of pleasant fields around them. All through the night, Stock's villagers were digging trenches around the perimeters of the village. All available tar, oil, and combustible materials urgently thrown into the trenches created dangerously large fires the orbs could not cross. People died trying to stop the orbs; some villagers were ripped apart by more than one at a time . . . Sometimes it was only one to end a life. The orbs were winning, and the discovery of stopping them stayed sealed in smoke, fire, and silence.

𝖷𝖷𝖷

At dusk, Omar woke Leon. "What you told me is true. I've sent messengers all over Notting and riders to the villages beyond to relay the news to be ready, if need be. You may have saved us with your story." Omar stopped, pondering a thought that crossed his mind. "But how do we defeat them?"

Leon, still waking from his deep sleep, did not understand what Omar said. When he regained his bearings and realized his surroundings, Omar told his story again, making sure Leon understood. Leon looked at Omar, focusing on his question before he spoke. "Victoria told us only one person is capable of saving us. Her name is Catherine."

"But by what manner of magic will she accomplish this?" Omar asked, intrigued yet puzzled by this news.

Leon understood Omar's reluctance to accept his answer. His throat was dry with sleep, and he needed a drink. *"Have you some water?"* Leon asked. Omar turned and poured some water into a glass sitting on a table near him and handed it to Leon. Leon emptied the water with a single swallow. He felt the water hit the bottom of his empty stomach, and the cramping helped to further waken him. *"That's better. Now we can talk."* Leon looked to his host, who seemed the epitome of skepticism.

"I'm not sure you will believe or understand what I am to say," Leon started. Leon looked to Omar for a reaction. Not seeing any change in his expression, he continued, *"I'm not entirely sure I do either. I can only tell you what was told to me."*

"And what was that?" Omar asked with some interest.

"As I understand it, Catherine's lifestone is the only stone large enough to place in the wall to seal it off again. However, she must do this by her own free will, or it may not work."

Omar started pacing the room and stroking the side of his face. This news had an effect on him, and the concern on his face was authentic. He stopped and turned to Leon. *"Does Catherine know about these things?"*

Leon sat on the side of the bed and ran his fingers through his thick white hair in an attempt to clear his head. *"She may already know, but as you can imagine, she will forfeit her life in the process. It will not be an easy choice for her or her family."*

"Sacrifice one for the good of all, it sounds like a bargain," Omar said like there was no discussion needed.

"Could you do it?" Leon asked with obvious disgust in his voice. *"If it was you instead of Catherine, a girl you do not know nor will you ever be likely to know, would you do it?"*

"That's not really the point here, is it, Leon?"

"My point is, if Catherine decides to do this, her sacrifice should be held in supreme reverence, not just a story about some unknown girl who contributed a stone to block off a hole in the wall."

"You know this girl, don't you, Leon?"

"I met her once on a trip into Stock. I know her fiancé, Timothy, quite well, and he loves her with all his being. He would never allow anything to happen to her."

"Then he has the weight of the world on his shoulders. Saving her destroys everything. What will be left to love?"

"This is not Timothy's choice . . . it's Catherine's!" Leon exclaimed with some anger in his voice.

Omar paced the room, thinking about the information Leon provided. "Please, my apologies for upsetting you, but I see no other way to stop these things from invading our villages. Catherine must do this, or we will all perish."

"But doing this of her own free will?" Leon stopped him from continuing. "How difficult will that be?"

The discussion between Leon and Omar was loud enough to wake Rand and Victoria. They hurried into Leon's room to join the conversation. Rand was listening for some time and entered first. "I really don't see any alternative but to sacrifice hundreds. Hundreds of people might close the breach by placing their lifestones into the hole where these things are coming through," Rand added, thinking the consequences of this possibility would decimate the populations of the villages.

"But there was the message for Timothy . . ." Victoria started, as she walked through the door to Leon's room.

Omar looked in Victoria's direction. "What message . . . I did not know of this, Leon. What does Timothy have to do with all this?"

"Go ahead, Victoria, tell him the rest," Leon said remorsefully, knowing he had held this information from Omar.

"Catherine is Timothy's fiancée. Leon sent him to the north to find a way to make Catherine immortal."

"That is impossible!" Omar said. "There are only a few villages to the north, and after that, there is only the desolation of the icy wastelands." Omar turned to Leon. "You have sent him to his death, Leon. There is nothing there but scary children's stories to keep them in line and legends of places no one ever found."

"There were two messages, Omar," Rand interjected. "If the one is true, which we all believe will save us, then why shouldn't the other one be considered true as well?"

"But even if it is possible, will that mean she won't die three days after her stone is placed into the breach?" Omar asked, skepticism pooling in his eyes.

"We really don't know what it means," Rand replied. "It was the message Victoria's friend Amelia told her to pass along to Timothy. We felt it was a chance for Catherine to survive, allowing her stone to block the path of these things."

Omar looked dejected. "It seems Catherine is doomed either way, doesn't it? She could die in three days or survive so long that all of us here, including her great love, will pass away, leaving her alone with nothing but an eternity of time before her and an eternity of memories behind her."

"If that is indeed the meaning of the message . . ." Leon spoke up. "It might also mean she could survive without her lifestone, lead a good life with Timothy, and die of old age like the rest of us."

"That's not what 'eternity' means, Leon," Omar argued.

"I know that," Leon replied with abrupt contempt. He looked to the others for support, but his companions had no answers. "You have to realize the message Victoria brought was somewhat cryptic. I *don't think we can take it at face value." Everyone was watching Leon now. He had their attention, though it was the last thing he wanted. Leon shook his head at them and said, "It was the best plan we could come up with after we heard Victoria's message. I don't know if it was the right thing to do, but Timothy is on that journey now. We can't call him back. Our decision to send him may serve us well, in time."*

"We all hope so," Rand added.

Unknown to the group in Leon's room, Penny stood outside the door listening. "Hope is really all we have now," Penny said, as she entered, looking at Leon compassionately. "Hope is all any of us have."

Everyone looked at one another, knowing Penny was right. Then Rand spoke up, "Omar, we have to be going. As always, thank you for your help and your hospitality."

"Think nothing of it," Omar replied.

Leon gathered his belongings then walked to the back door of Omar's shop. There, Rand, Penny, and Victoria gathered, busy securing their belongings on the wagon. Omar provided enough food and water for two day's journey, though they hoped their trek would not outlast the provisions. Leon hesitated near the front step of the wagon, as his three passengers moved into their seats.

Omar watched Leon hand his parcel of belongings to Penny and then asked, "Do you have everything you need to get into Stock?"

"I think so," Leon said, as he surveyed the contents of the wagon. Omar had taken the liberty of hitching Leon's six horses to the wagon for which Leon was very grateful. He gave Omar a nod of his head, which was his way to say thank-you, then climbed into the front bench. Omar understood and nodded back.

"I guess we'll be going then," Penny said. "My best wishes to you all. Remember to use your lifestones wisely. Victoria thinks the

lifestones lose some power every time you use them. From what I've seen, it's probably true."

"We'll be careful," Omar said, waving them off. "Get started. Notting knows how to protect itself because of your help. Go now . . . help Catherine, help save the village of Stock." They were the last words Leon heard from Omar as he pushed his horses toward the village of Stock.

⚶

"They're burning oil and tar in hand dug trenches around the northern borders of Stock. The fires are keeping the orbs from entering the village," Benjamin told Jakob after Catherine's lifestone was securely hidden in the barn.

Michael held the kitchen door for Jakob as he entered the farmhouse. "From the top of the hill where we left Amelia with her father, the trenches seem to be working. They can't keep the trenches burning forever. This is just buying time."

Jakob was exhausted from the laborious day but understood Michael's concerns. He may have to sacrifice his daughter. He didn't want to be the one to tell him. Michael had to come to this conclusion himself, but they had to be careful in how they handled it. He looked to Michael and said, "The problem will be, how long the oil, tar, and combustibles last? When these run out, we will be at the mercy of these purple orbs, or spheres, or whatever this threat looks like. Amelia thought these things had no concern for us. Their only motivation is to kill us and take the lands we inhabit . . . if that is truly the only reason they want to murder us." Jakob searched the room, watching how the news of Stock's battlefront against this threat influenced the mood of his family and friends. "We may have to think of alternatives before long," Jakob said, turning his eyes toward Catherine.

"We can't seriously consider Catherine should do what Amelia suggested?" Leena spoke up. "That's a death sentence for her . . . I won't let her . . . We will have to think of something else."

Benjamin, silent until now, put forth his thoughts, "Leena . . . Catherine . . . I know how difficult it must be to consider what Jakob is saying. If he is right, it may come down to sacrificing Catherine's lifestone in order to save us all. Amelia said, however, it has to be Catherine's choice. We can't decide for her."

"But Amelia also said Timothy could save Catherine if he finds a way to do it," Leena stated contemptuously, disturbed by Benjamin's abject unconcern of her daughter's feelings.

"From what I have heard," Jakob interjected, "we don't know if Victoria made it to Glade. We don't know if she was able to get word to Timothy for that matter. It may be we have to defend ourselves. We may run out of options."

Catherine, silent until now, finally spoke, "I have listened to everyone talking about what to do. No one even considered what I want to do." Everyone went silent; they knew Catherine had a good heart. They knew if Catherine had the choice to make herself . . . she would do what would be considered the ultimate sacrifice. Catherine looked to her mother and father. "Mother, I know you love me, and I love you too, but to save me and allow everyone to die would be intolerable. How could we both live with ourselves in the aftermath of this . . . if there is an aftermath? Without my sacrifice, our world may not survive. The orbs will overrun us eventually and destroy us completely." Then Catherine turned to her father. "Father, you know I was never fond of that enormous stone you picked for me." She laughed as Michael shamefully put his head into his hands. Catherine thought she upset him and continued, "But now, it may be the very thing that saves us. Besides, if Timothy has the message, he is already on his way to do whatever he can to save me from this fate."

"But there is no way of knowing my son ever got the message," Jakob said with suppressed alarm. "What you're asking us and your parents to do is allow you to kill yourself. I, for one, do not want my son returning to find we sacrificed you to save all of us, especially if there is another way to stop these things."

"I agree with my father," Andrew interrupted. "Timothy can figure out a lot of things, but he may turn against us if we allow you

to do this." Eric and Lamin quickly agreed with their brother with a nod of their heads.

Catherine looked into each of their eyes and said, "I know how much you all love Timothy and me. We mean the world to each other, and you all mean so much to both of us. Nothing that happens will change that. But if you don't allow me to sacrifice my lifestone to the wall soon, all we loved and cherished will be for nothing. If all we hold dear is destroyed by these hideous orbs, then they have already won. If I lay down my life for all of you, for Timothy, and all the people in the villages, then I leave this life with a full heart . . . and a full life, no matter how short it may be. I want to do this for everyone . . . for us all."

"And Timothy . . . ?" Alexis spoke up, trying to support her brother's prior argument with Catherine.

Catherine looked to where Alexis stood in the kitchen doorway. "Timothy may yet find a way to stop me from dying. Like Benjamin said, the messages were not clear. 'Immortal' may mean I can live somehow even though my lifestone will already be embedded in the wall. We need to believe in hope. Hope will die with us if we are destroyed by the orbs."

Alexis wasn't finished. "Timothy loves you. He is not going to understand why we would all help you destroy yourself. We need to try other ideas, some other plans, until we know for sure he got the message from Victoria. Let's give Timothy some time to fulfill his mission before we set out on ours. That's all I'm asking for . . . some time."

Catherine took a moment to ponder Alexis's words, then replied, "I agree to waiting . . . for a while. But if Stock begins to lose the battle, then I must do this."

By dusk of the third day, Leon sat on the outermost borders of Stock. Throughout the day, Rand walked beside the struggling wagon using his lifestone against the orbs for as long as he was able. The little band of travelers found that the continued use of the lifestones not only weakened the person using it but also lessened the effects against the orbs. So many times the orbs threatened their progress, and every time, each used their lifestone against them. Rand was on the verge of total exhaustion. He managed to stay on his feet by leaning against the moving wagon. Leon feared he would stumble and the wagon wheels would run over him. He finally stopped and made him get into the wagon, while Penny took over. He resisted, but Leon was adamant, not willing to risk the life of any of them just to prove their courage or stamina. Finally, Rand submitted and lay on a pile of blankets spread over the floor of the wagon. He was asleep within seconds.

Penny was next to use the power of her lifestone against the orbs. As she felt her strength failing, she asked Leon to take over before she was too exhausted. She took the reins from Leon and rested while she drove the wagon. Before long, Leon had to stop, leaving Victoria to take his place on the road beside the wagon. When Victoria could no longer manage, they drove to high ground and made camp for the night.

From a wooded knoll, they surveyed a field of blue haze four parcels across, teeming with purple orbs nodding above its surface time to time as if taunting them. Beyond the safety of this knoll lay Stock, encircled by distant trenches of fire they watched burning from their vantage point. At times, the mild wind blew the smells of burning wood and oil, mixed with sounds of men shouting to each other, to their woodland knoll. The mixture of smells, sounds, and ominous vista portrayed before them took any sense of strength they had and crushed it.

"We have to get in there," Penny said, leaning her head against Leon's shoulder.

"We are exhausted. We will stay here and rest until morning." Leon took a second glance at the blue mists where the orbs continued roiling in and out of the haze just a half parcel from their camp. He turned to Penny and said, "We will post a guard and allow the others to rest peacefully. By morning, we may recover enough to use our lifestones again. By then, we might stand a chance of making it into

Stock alive. If we choose to go tonight, I'm not certain any of us will make it."

Victoria listened to the discussion between Penny and Leon then sat up petulantly and argued, "But Amelia's lifestone . . . I still have it. We may be able to save her if I can get it to her."

"Too risky," Rand sighed, waking from his light sleep. "We aren't strong enough to punch through that field of orbs . . . ," he said wearily, pointing to the expanse of blue mists just a short distance beyond them, "at least not at this point." He looked to Leon and said, "In the light, we may find another place where we can get closer to Stock without having to fight our way through such a great distance." Then Rand turned to Victoria. "I know you feel responsible for your friend, but I feel she realized her fate the day she gave you her lifestone." Rand saw tears welling up in Victoria's eyes. He sat up and extended his open hand toward her. "May I see Amelia's stone?"

"Why?" Victoria cringed.

Rand hung his head but continued, "Because I believe her time is almost gone. It will be up to us to place it into the wall someday."

Victoria pulled Amelia's lifestone from her pocket, unable to look at it. She was afraid Rand was speaking the truth. She held the stone tightly in her hand, thinking if she didn't look, she would not need to see it. Amelia couldn't be dead. They only spoke three days ago . . . three days.

Rand sat there, hand extended toward her, waiting. Seeing Victoria stymied by her own fear, he said, "Victoria, you can hold it. Just let us see it in the presence of the orbs."

Victoria turned her head as she extended her arm and opened her hand. She could not look, but Rand and the others saw what they suspected. As Rand predicted, the red glow that proved to be such a powerful weapon at one time merely lit with the faintest glimmer of red in Victoria's hand. Rand was right. Amelia sacrificed herself to save her friend. Victoria finally looked at her hand and watched the glow fade to almost nothing. She was crying. They felt her loss; watching her grieve was almost unbearable.

"Put it away, Victoria," Leon commanded gently. "You have honored her by warning the villages as she wanted. We won't let her sacrifice go unnoticed."

A New Century

Tell me about the next century . . .

The dawning of 2000 marked the beginning of the most exciting times. It was the year I published my first book. I think Lois was more excited than I. For me, it was just another step in many small steps to put the book in the marketplace. For her, it was a shining achievement, and she was very proud of me. Of course, she wanted to do everything she could to make the book successful. She took on the responsibilities of media involvement and her connections with various agencies to make this possible. Her first newsletter tells of her excitement with the new book.

(Newsletter by Lois A. Anderson dated March 1, 2000)

Well, it is said that "breast cancer stuff" slows down over the winter, but not this year for me or for my husband, George. Things have kept going full speed for some time.

First of all, George completed his book and has signed a contract to publish it. The publisher has been working on the layout of the book for about two weeks and we're hoping to hear more from them very soon. My little crystal ball tells me that book signings and promotions are in our future. The book covers the time during which I was diagnosed and treated for breast cancer and what was going on in his life during this same time. The book is built around the theme of the seasons of the year and thus the title . . . Seasons in Cancer. The male view, professionally, as a registered nurse, and personally, as a caregiver to his wife, and father to his son, are represented. The emotional tugs and pulls on him are all in the book.

Second of all, I have been appointed to the Consumer Advisory Panel of the Oncology Nursing Society. This is a group of oncology health care consumers, which includes patients, survivors, family caregivers, and consumer advocates. These panel members will advise the Oncology Nursing Society on matters related to cancer care. I am very honored and proud to be selected as one of the 15 members of this international panel.

School is coming along very well. Some of you will be receiving a survey in the mail about our newsletter as part of a research project I am doing for one of my courses. Don't fret because it will be a quick one page survey to find out what you do/do not like about this newsletter. In advance, thanks for your help. Results of the survey will be available soon after my class is finished in May. Call me for a copy if you'd like the full report. That's all from my corner.

Warm days and bright flowers

Are on their way,

Keep that in mind as the last

Of the snow melts away.

Lois

PS. The following story written by my husband was published in his hospital's newsletter. Copies of the newsletter are extremely difficult to come by because people have taken the story home to their loved ones or just to have themselves. The newsletter is almost extinct within the hospital since most have been absconded from the bulletin boards throughout the hospital by people who loved the story.

It was clear to everyone that she had a very full schedule. Fortunately, her personal struggle with breast cancer was not a prevailing thought, but she was past the five-year mark of her initial prognosis and not actively treated for the dormant breast cancer during this time.

Lois was nominated to sit on the consumer peer review panel for the Oncology Nursing Society this year. She was no stranger to panels like these, having experience with both the Department of Defense's program and the American Cancer Society's peer review programs. Lois felt she was chosen to be a lead person to help initiate their program in 2000. She expended many hours at home, creating a working model for their program to follow. She would spend the next three years in this position before the ONS dissolved the program in 2003.

Lois continued her studies pursuing her master's degree and continued her full-time job throughout the year. Any time she had for herself, she spent researching the next newsletter. Adding my book to her list of activities with the additional responsibilities of being an ONS consumer advocate did not appear to affect her. I was very proud of what she was achieving, not only for herself but also for the greater good of all breast cancer patients and survivors. On the other hand, I was increasingly concerned by her long hours, sleeping only four or five hours a day and then pushing at 100 percent. To fully understand what she could accomplish with her time, you need to realize she commuted fifty miles to and from work almost every night of the week; and the two days in school, she traveled an additional fifty miles to and from school (in the opposite direction). There were days I would not see her except the time she spent sleeping. I was increasingly concerned her exhaustion would trigger a serious illness.

Lois left for Washington DC on March 10, 2000, after returning from her classes, for the NBCC's team leader training program to be held March 11 and 12, 2000. I remember pulling her luggage from the attic, while she quickly assembled what she needed to wear in Washington. She scheduled her CA 27-29 for the day after she returned. She left that evening for Washington DC tired, but in good spirits. I was working with the publisher, finalizing the details of my book. I told her I would be getting the final version done while she was at team leader training.

"Then I know you won't get into trouble while I'm gone," Lois told me with a grin on her face, as I explained how my weekend was going.

"I'm too busy to get into trouble." I laughed as she packed her suitcase.

"Me too." Lois laughed. "I don't have the time to breathe, much less get into anything else. I have my plate full."

I knew I was probably going to come off the wrong way when I told her a little more seriously. "I hope you haven't bitten off more than you can chew."

"I'll be all right," she said just as seriously. "I'm driving down a day ahead of time. When I get in, I'll have dinner, then I'm going up to bed." I know I had a pained look on my face because she turned back and said, "I'll call you when I get there, okay?"

"Just to let me know you got there safely, right?" I asked.

"Don't worry," she told me with some emphasis in her voice. She pulled the bags off the bed to the floor and said, "Could you put these bags in the car for me while I wash up a bit? Then I have to go. I need to check in by nine, and it's five thirty already!" She looked around, like she forgot about something, then said, "It's a three-hour drive. I got to get moving." She hurried off to the bathroom to get ready.

I grabbed the luggage and called back. "I know. I'll put the bags in the trunk so you can get them out easily when you get to the hotel."

Lois took a few minutes to clean up and change out of her school clothes. I hurried to the car and placed her luggage in the trunk with the handles out so she could move them easily when she arrived. She was walking from the kitchen door when I finished. "Wow that was fast," I told her.

She jumped into the car and rolled down the window and said, "Call you later." She gave me a quick kiss. Then she was on her way to Washington. I went back inside, turned on the computer, and started reworking the changes for the book. It was going to be a long weekend for both of us.

She arrived at her hotel in Washington DC about eight thirty that evening, when she called.

"How was the drive?" I asked, remembering how DC traffic could be.

"I got into the traffic about seven thirty. By that time, the bad traffic was pretty much out of the way," she told me, as I recognized the weariness in her voice.

"Can you still get something to eat? I'm sure the dining room won't be open that much longer," I said, knowing she hadn't eaten anything but some breakfast I had made for her earlier that morning.

"I'm going to check in, and then I'm ordering room service," she told me with a small giggle.

"Did you run into anyone you know yet?" I asked, thinking others may have arrived early like her.

"No, I think I'm here by myself tonight. Tomorrow is when the big group starts coming in."

"I better let you go. You need to get moving or you won't get any sleep." Then as an afterthought, I said, "If you want to call me back after you get settled, I'll probably still be up. I hope to get this manuscript done by Monday, so I plan to be awake for a while."

"Okay, but I'm going to eat first," Lois told me with some emphasis in her voice. Then she giggled again and said, "So you miss me already."

"Get going," I told her, laughing back.

"Call you later," she told me before she finally hung up.

I went back to the manuscript, but my heart was not in it. I stopped and waited by the phone after sitting absently at the computer screen for about a half hour. About an hour went by before the phone rang.

"Well, I'm all checked in and waiting for room service," Lois said, as she left out a sigh.

I was so glad to hear from her. We had so very little time to just sit and talk. since she was pulled from one place to the next one almost every day. "I'm glad you got settled," I told her. Then thinking she just wanted some sleep, I said, "Well, I'll let you go. I know you just want to eat then get to bed. I just wanted to know you were all right."

"I'm good," she said with a little laugh. "You know I had to make this a collect call, and it will go on my bill when I leave. How about I give you the phone number of the room and call me back in fifteen minutes? My food should be here by then, and you can talk to me while I eat."

"Okay, fifteen minutes then," I said. I looked at the clock on my desk, which read nine forty five. At ten o'clock, I called Lois in Washington DC and we talked while she ate a tuna fish sandwich, some soup, and a bag of potato chips. Our conversation drifted from what she would be doing the next day and who she would be meeting, to how I was doing on the manuscript, and then when she would be coming home and what needed to be done at home. Then I asked her if she just wanted someone to talk to because there wasn't anyone there that she knew. "Yeah, I knew about all the stuff we talked about, but it is just nice to hear you talk to me."

"I like talking to you too, but we don't get much of a chance these days. I'm off in the office on the computer, and you always seem to be going someplace," I said with some sadness in my voice.

"I know," Lois said with resignation. "But things will slow down eventually."

We talked and talked. The conversation reminded me of the times I spent on the phone with her when I first met her in college. She wanted to be home with me, but there were so many commitments she had made pursuing ways to improve the lives and health of breast cancer patients and survivors that, it seemed, she was beginning to lose herself. But this night, she wanted to make that connection with me again. We talked about an hour and a half on a collect call from Washington DC to York, Pennsylvania. I remember the call cost almost thirty dollars, but it was worth every penny. We talked until she finished eating and was starting to get drowsy. She told me good night and that she loved me, and I told her the same. I was able to go back to my manuscript and finished it by three o'clock in the morning.

On March 13, 2000, Lois had her tumor markers drawn. On March 14, 2000, the CA 27-29 came back with a result of 22. This, though not alarming, was the first time her tumor markers rose above 20 since the middle of her chemotherapy sessions in 1992. The number concerned me, knowing her markers were relatively accurate for the presence of tumor activity.

I remember Lois discussed this increase with her oncologist, and they agreed the findings were not that remarkable, considering the stress and exhaustion Lois endured at the time. The oncologist recommended she "slow down" a little, and hopefully, the number would stabilize or decrease by her next testing. Together, they felt her markers would be adequately evaluated in twelve months. Even Lois dismissed the tumor marker as a stress-related finding and continued to work even harder, doing the things she loved, doing things that would eventually make a mark on the world.

Lois was again asked to sit on the peer review panel for breast cancer research for the Department of Defense in the spring of 2000. This was the fifth, and last year, she could be asked to participate on this panel. She also sat on the Consumer Review Board for the Department of Defense later in the summer. This was her fourth year working with this panel.

Lois continued her studies and excelled in her position in Baltimore. Other than seeing my wife a few hours in the afternoon, when she slept four to five hours, I did not have a chance to see her. When she was home weekends, or an occasional day off work, she would be studying or writing papers. I too was busy with a publisher who needed additional projects completed so the book could be published. By the time Lois wrote the June newsletter, the book was in its final stages. The newsletter was only six pages long, but she was very proud of the book and made sure to mention it in the newsletter.

(From newsletter by Lois A. Anderson dated June 1, 2000)

At this point I have completed one-half of my graduate studies toward a Masters in Social Work and I feel the little light at the end of the tunnel is beginning to shine. Right now that light is only a pinpoint but it is getting larger and brighter, slowly, but surely.

I, also, just returned from a Peer Review Session for the Department of Defense Breast Cancer Research Program. Concept awards, totaling $3.5 million dollars, were selected and ranked by six panels of scientists and consumer advocates. Our results were sent along to the Integration Panel to determine which awards from all the panels would be selected and funded. I saw some very amazing and novel ideas in breast cancer research presented in these proposals, and I was able to discuss other research with the scientists during our breaks. I found out that for women whose tumor becomes resistant to Herceptin, a new approach using the ERBB3 signaling pathway is being studied intently to determine if a monoclonal antibody, like Herceptin, can be developed. The ERBB3 gene, it seems, may be involved in this resistance to Herceptin. I met the researcher who has been dubbed the "Father of Angiogenesis," Dr. Judah Folkman. He participated in one of these panels. I came away from the panels knowing that the money the NBCC lobbies Congress for each year is being spent very wisely. Breast cancer is a very complex disease and there are no easy, simple answers.

George's book is coming along. The final corrected copy should be at the printers. If anyone wants to see his biography and the cover of his book go to ************* on the web. I'm getting anxious to see a final copy of "Seasons in Cancer."

Wishing you a good summer

Lois

By the end of summer, my book was published, and I received ten copies. My publisher had problems getting enough books printed to supply the waiting audience. The inadequate supply of books created many episodes of frustration among me, my publisher, and Lois. During the summer months when both of us should have been relaxing, Lois worked diligently getting word out to the newspapers and local magazines about the publication of my book. She even managed to get a short paragraph inserted into *Baltimore* magazine. We had a reporter lined up for an article in the *Washington Post*, but we never got to utilize it. My publisher just could not keep up with the demand, and books were sold before they ever saw the inside of a bookstore. Somehow, in late summer, I obtained fifty copies for my hospital to sell. I signed the books rather unceremoniously and took them to the gift shop where all fifty copies disappeared within two weeks. I wanted to do a book signing at our local bookstore but could never get a shipment large enough to sell to everyone who wanted copies. My year with the book was both exhilarating and frustrating. Lois worked very hard over the summer trying to get promotions set up for the book and was equally frustrated when we were unable to get a supply. Frustration led to exasperation, and eventually we both had to let the book ride the course the publisher was taking it.

By September 2000, Lois was beginning her new school year. This was the first year she had to do an internship. She chose Johns Hopkins Oncology Center in Baltimore, Maryland, as her field placement. It was a good choice because when she finished her shift at Mercy Medical Center, she only had to drive a few blocks to Johns Hopkins. It was certainly better than driving from Baltimore to Harrisburg, a one-way trip of over one hundred miles, which had to be done once every week. However, having a field placement meant when she was done with her eight-hour night shift in the morning, she would turn around and work another eight-hour shift at her field placement. Add all that to an hour's drive to work and an hour's drive back to home from the field placement, and you can easily see an eighteen-hour day in the making. All too frequently, the eight-hour day at Johns Hopkins would turn into nine- and ten-hour days, making Lois's time to stay awake even longer, making her more exhausted. Fortunately, she only had to do this twice a week, with a trip straight from Baltimore to Harrisburg once a week. There were times when two or three days could go by without me ever seeing her. On the days I did, she looked tired and very irritable. It was difficult to get her to eat anything at home because of her extreme schedule, so she generally grabbed something on the run. Even with this impossible schedule, she insisted on doing the publicity for my book, working with the ONS, and writing the newsletter. Lois writes about all this in her editorial.

(Editorial by Lois A. Anderson dated September 1, 2000)

The new school year is fast upon us and I'm slowly getting used to the idea of being back in school again.

However this year will be a little different for me because I must do an internship, which in social work terminology, is called field placement. My field placement will take place at the Johns Hopkins Hospital's Oncology Center in Baltimore, Maryland. I feel very honored to be able to do my first year fieldwork at Hopkins because normally, they only take second year students. (Yes, I have to do this for two school years to complete my requirements.)

Along with school, another thing to keep me busy is working as a publicist for George's just published book. "Seasons in Cancer" is a very touching chronicle of what my husband went through while caring for me during my treatments for breast cancer, keeping our family life going, assuming household duties, and caring for our son all while still holding down his job as a registered nurse and caring for other breast cancer patients. I look back now and see just how rough it was for him, but the good news is we've made it through all of that and have come out the other side a changed, but closer couple and family. This book is a wonderful book, not only for breast cancer patients, survivors and loved ones, but a good one to give to those families facing any life threatening diagnosis. The men will especially enjoy many parts of the book. Ladies, get your hankies out because you'll need them!

Working as a publicist, though, does have its ups and downs. I've learned a lot about marketing and advertising and what to do to get people to look at this book. Eventually, we will have a book signing at one of our meetings. I know all of you are excited about this book and have asked about getting copies. For now, the book is available on the website and at the gift shop at GBMC in Towson, Maryland. Yes, George signed all of GBMC's copies. Locally, an autographed supply in York Hospital's gift shop and the Cancer Center might be nice too, but that remains to be seen. It would be especially fitting since both institutions are involved in the book. After all, that's what makes a book real too, being able to see the places where parts of the book took place.

Ah well, time for me to stop rambling and get on with the pre-school studying that I need to do. Hope you have a beautiful autumn.

Don't let the acorns hit you on the head,

Lois

Before starting her internship at Johns Hopkins, Lois found that her time there may not be considered a part of her social work training. Though Johns Hopkins is a world-renowned institution, and it would appear any work there would be valid in any school system, the fact was Temple University did not possess a contract to send a student there. Lois accepted the field placement at Johns Hopkins because of the incredible experiences she would get, and as she said in her newsletter, Hopkins never accepted first-year social work students. To be accepted under these circumstances indicated Lois was an exceptional student, and the Johns Hopkins instructors recognized this. Lois discussed her situation and this extraordinary opportunity at Johns Hopkins with several advisors who felt they shouldn't have a problem getting a contract drawn up between the two schools. However, about four weeks into the field placement, there were problems. In addition to the incredulous school and work schedule she maintained, she now had to shoulder the responsibility of getting a contract initiated between the two schools.

As Lois continued her grueling schedule and intense experiences at Hopkins, she was making daily phone calls to both the Harrisburg and Philadelphia campuses of Temple University, trying to get the contract between the two schools completed. On days I was home from work, I saw her get two hours sleep, get up to make phone calls, and then get back in bed for another two or three hours before she had to get ready for work. If the phone rang, she was up to answer it, hoping for news the contract was completed.

Never before had a student of Temple asked for a field placement at Johns Hopkins. Roadblocks, red tape, and contacting people who would not return phone calls or paperwork became daily occurrences. Lois's frustration level was so high that many times I would find her in tears when I got home from work. She asked me many times for help when she physically couldn't manage the calls herself. However, the complexity of what she was trying to overcome were things I could barely fathom, much less do anything to help. The few times I made contacts for her quickly became dead ends because the person on the other side of the phone would not speak to anyone but the student. Telling Lois I was truly unable to help her, since Temple University would not accept anything I had to say about her just made her angry. She had nowhere to direct her anger, so many times it was directed at me. Eventually, I had to walk away and allow her to work through this herself. This frustrated her even further but solidified her resolve to make the contract between Hopkins and Temple happen.

Samuel Clemens (Mark Twain) once wrote something that said the moment he learned something was also the moment he lost something. I felt this same sentiment watching Lois struggle through her first field placement. It seems when you accept something you learn, you have to let part of your innocence go. Losing innocence feels like a "little death" of your soul. Truth and facts are the cement meant to fill those places where our innocence dies and falls away, but it only serves to make us colder, more ambivalent, and more diagnostic than what we were. Joy is harder to find. A kind of detachment from the world seems to happen, and the only people you find to communicate with are the ones who have gone through the same processing as you. They are unable to share their innocence about some of the magic that is life. I saw what was happening to Lois, and I did not like what I was seeing. Innocence was dying, and I was afraid the magical connection we had with each other was dying as well.

The week after Thanksgiving, Lois told me she had resigned herself to the fact that her time at Johns Hopkins would not be considered as credits toward her master's degree. She said she still had a commitment with Hopkins until the end of the school year in May but wasn't sure she would be able to do it if Temple University didn't come through with the contract. It was during this same time, while she was off for Thanksgiving vacation, that she vented her frustration with the whole situation between the two colleges. Nothing I could say could make her feel better, and many times what I said simply made her break down into tears. She stayed to herself for quite a while after this. No one could break through the shell she had gone into. Somehow she still managed to get a newsletter out in early November before she became overwhelmed with finals in December.

(Editorial by Lois A. Anderson dated November 1, 2000)

With October's Breast Cancer Awareness month and November's National Caregiver month over, life becomes a bit slower for about two weeks in my household. However, to fill in the gaps, there are always papers and process recordings to write for school. I am truly longing for a bit of a vacation, but that won't happen until January of 2001. So now it's grin and bear it, because eventually all this will pass.

George's book is now available on the internet and now an audiobook is available too! The publisher will soon be doing a second printing of the book. For those of you who want to order the book please go through the websites. A book signing will take place in 2001, and eventually George will sign books for our group.

I have been working to get a small group of women together to work on a resource booklet for breast cancer patients. Several of the original committee had to resign due to other commitments. We still need more help. If you are interested call me at my home phone. The work would involve contacting agencies to list in our booklet. It is very simple to do. All you need is a telephone, pen, and paper. Please consider helping your fellow women with breast cancer by joining our group.

Well, I've got to starting writing a speech for the Forge Hill Women's Organization so it's time for me to close.

Keep yourself snuggly warm in this cold weather,

Lois

It was sometime in early December when the contract between Hopkins and Temple finally came through. I thought it would improve Lois's disposition, but it seemed more anticlimactic to the damage the whole affair had on Lois's outlook. Problems with getting books from my publisher, frustration with newspapers and magazines that couldn't do interviews since we could not guarantee book availability in the time frames they wanted, an unending barrage of schoolwork, and people requesting more and more of Lois's time simply wore her down. By the time Christmas arrived, Lois and I could barely speak to each other. She finished her work for the semester in the week before Christmas. She was frustrated by my publisher and wanted to know why I couldn't be more proactive in promoting my own book. I told her I had no control over the supply of books. When I asked her to stop promoting my book until a reasonable supply could be set up, she told me to do the work myself from now on. It was not the answer I wanted to hear from her, but I felt she had, at least, removed one burden from her shoulders. She did not take it that way. By mid-2001, we became very distant with each other. There were weeks on end where we barely spoke to each other. In time, we only communicated enough to keep the household running.

The century year was one that remains bittersweet in my memory. It was a year that began with so much promise and ended with heartbreak and resignation on so many levels that it would be impossible to tell it all. I still looked forward to the next year with thoughts of compromise and new hopes. In some ways, it worked out that way, but in others, the tragedies were just beginning.

The Rock That Doesn't Break

Tell me about the stone . . .

Turbid colors washed the horizons beyond the shadowy branches of the noble tree. Troubled dreams kept me from my time here. I longed for some voice to materialize in the silence, but memories jumped inside me like repetitious platitudes with no wisdom attached to them. They were only sounds from the outside world, clattering for me to return. For now, I tried vainly to grasp for something to take back to the waking world, but silence would be my wages at a time I desperately wanted a voice to speak.

I sat down next to the tree where my inspiration grew and touched a rock smoother than any stones strewn about the base of the great tree. It was a curious-looking stone, almost glassy but complex in its many opaque colorations. I picked it up, turning it side to side at first and wondering at its smooth hard surface. I finally turned it over, and a single word had been engraved into it. The word was "me." I angrily threw the rock into the other stones. Many stones broke from the force of my throw, and I refused to retrieve it.

"What do you want of me?" I asked. The answer hung in the silence surrounding me. "Let me dream . . . let me dream . . ." I begged. I lay my head against the base of the great tree and prayed for a dream. In time, the dream came, and I was swallowed up by it.

Timothy awoke the third day of the breach at his encampment near the road to Bridgedom. He felt reasonably rested as he prepared his horse at daybreak to journey to the Great Bridge. He remembered Thomas's words as he made his way into the village.

Amos's home resided next to the Great Bridge just as Thomas had told him. By midday, Timothy knocked on the door of the modest house where an old man invited him inside. As Thomas, the crier from Wendow, had promised, he found the man, Amos. Timothy told Amos news of the disaster at Stock three days before. Amos, hearing what the young man said, felt it was an impossible story. It wasn't until Timothy mentioned Thomas that he gave the story credibility and his full attention.

"Well, that's a serious matter indeed," Amos said sternly.

"Yes, sir, I would not have intruded upon you with such news otherwise," Timothy stated matter-of-factly.

"Coming from Thomas, I believe what you say. I will get the word out to Bridgedom." Amos looked at Timothy's disheveled appearance. "Tell you what, I want you to stay here, get cleaned up, rest your horse, and have a good meal before you go on." He gave Timothy a moment to consider then continued, "You look terrible . . . if I may be so bold to tell you. What do you say?"

Timothy was in a hurry, but he knew Amos was right. He must look like a dirty vagabond. He turned to Amos and said, "I must get to Vigil, then Emansupass, then look for something that I'm not even sure exists in the northern mountains."

"And what would that be?" Amos asked, intrigued by Timothy's comment.

Timothy looked at the older man who seemed to have no time for foolishness. What he needed to say sounded like such a foolish myth; he was certain Amos would laugh as soon as he heard it. He decided to risk it. "I am to find a mythical place in the mountains that will save Catherine, whom I love with all my heart, and make her immortal," Timothy finished, looking directly into Amos's eyes.

"That so . . ." Amos replied pensively. He looked at Timothy with a degree of consternation then said, "What do you know about the mountains north of Emansupass?"

Sunset Under The Poet's Tree

"To be honest, not much. I've heard rumors and whisperings of events that happened long ago that honestly sound fantastic . . . too fantastic to be taken seriously." Timothy watched as Amos walked to the entrance of his house and rested his hand on the black iron latch.

Amos turned back to face Timothy. "Thomas actually sent you here for two reasons, Timothy. He knew I would help you get word of this disaster out to the villagers. The other reason he sent you here was something only Thomas knew about." Amos stopped for a moment as he raised his eyes to meet Timothy's. "I think I can help you find your 'mythical' place."

"I never asked Thomas to help me that way," Timothy gasped.

"I know . . . but Thomas knew you needed my help . . . my specific help. He could have sent you to any of the criers like Carol or Legrend. They would have helped you as well. But to send you in my direction meant something." Amos watched Timothy struggle with what he heard. Amos knew he would need time to think. He opened the door then turned to face Timothy. "I will tell you when I return. For now, get washed up, get into some clean clothes, and I will be back very soon. We will talk." Amos went out the door and into the crowd to find others who would help get Timothy's news to everyone.

Timothy watched Amos disappear into the crowd. The Great Bridge was the only road to the village of Vigil, and travelers were beginning to gather in large numbers at the entrance beyond Amos's house. Not knowing what to expect upon Amos's return, he went about the business of cleaning off three days of road dust and stubble from his face. His host provided him with everything he needed to clean up. He found a basin with a pitcher of clean water sitting and waiting for him along with a razor, soap, towels, and a clean set of clothes. By the time Timothy cleaned up, Amos returned.

"I see you look more presentable," Amos stated, taking a look at Timothy by circling around him.

"My thanks, sir. I especially thank you for the clean shirt and clothes. I feel much better washing off the dust and the chance to shave. It made me feel normal again, thanks to you."

"You're welcome," Amos nodded. "How about some food while we talk?"

"That sounds good." Timothy smiled back.

"Now it's going to take a few moments to whip something together. What I want you to do is go out the back door to the yard behind this house and take a good look at the Great Bridge. Most people see the bridge a certain way, which is mostly from the top where they are traveling. They don't care how it's put together . . . they're just busy going one place to another. They don't really see it. If you know what I mean."

"I suppose so," Timothy agreed.

"So go out and take a look at her. I always look at it and see something different each time." Amos started getting an iron kettle out of his cupboard, then placing it on the stove, he said to Timothy, "When you're done looking, come back in, and we'll have something to eat while we talk."

Timothy found his way to the back door. When he opened it and stepped outside, the sight of the bridge took his breath away. What Amos had said about the bridge was true! What Amos hadn't told him was the bridge was not only made to be functional but an amazing feat of artistry as well. The Great Bridge spanned an incredibly deep chasm cut into the rock formations by a raging river that wore down the rock for centuries. About three parcels north of the bridge, he had heard, was an enormous waterfall that assured the continued erosion of the chasm. Even from this distance, Timothy could hear the roar of the waterfall echoing through the stone walls. Looking into the deep ravine, Timothy could barely see a rising mist generated by the unseen river below him. The ravine appeared deeper than a parcel, too deep to really see the bottom. The Great Bridge spanned almost two parcels in an arch supported by four stone statues. Legends he had heard said they were carved from stones once cut and gathered from the surrounding hills. The statues represented each of the Four Winds.

To the south was a representation of the South Wind. She was carved in a standing position with her hands just under the southernmost point of the bridge. Carved in pink stone, the statue's feet stood perched on the stony bottom of the ravine. She was unclothed with her long hair stretched just below the bridge. Her wings were folded around her in modest fashion. The ancient sculptors cleverly used colored stone to enhance the reddish color of her flowing hair, and pearl-white stone enhanced her folded wings. There were symbols inscribed on the edges of the wings that were indecipherable to Timothy. He made a mental note to ask Amos about them when they spoke.

Toward the center of the bridge were the effigies of the East and West Winds, with the most distant statue being that of the North Wind. The East Wind was the next rendering closest to where Timothy was standing. The sculpture represented a huge full standing man with his head facing the east. His hands stretched above him, giving the appearance of pushing up the arch of the bridge. His naked body fashioned out of blue stone bore muscular contours consistent with a man pushing up a heavy weight. In contrast, his hair and wings were creatively sculpted using a deep purple stone. It was a menacing rendering, almost a warning of what terrors existed in the east.

The West Wind was fashioned as female, and unlike her sister, the South Wind, she stood fully erect, the wings flowing behind her developed into an integral support structure of the bridge. Her breasts visible as her sculptors positioned the arms fully extended, giving the appearance of supporting the second half of the arch. Her body was fashioned entirely from brown stone. A variegated yellow stone, beautifully chiseled to resemble her hair, crowned the effigy's head. Wings sculpted from gold-veined alabaster swayed behind her. She faced west in a willful way.

The North Wind faced north. He was defined as a muscular being, wings unfolded, with a stern ancient face that exuded wisdom. His face was beardless with long flowing hair that blew behind him in support of the structure above. His arms were bent in a relief, making it appear he was supporting the bridge beneath. His wings spanned in a great sweep on either side of the bridge, unlike any other statue supporting the bridge. His structure was shaped entirely from brilliant white stone that actually appeared to gleam, even at this distance, like a beacon to the north.

Timothy drank in the spectacular beauty integrated into the workmanship supporting the Great Bridge. The ones who made these magnificent statues also made them extremely functional by design. Never before had he seen anything like it in his travels through the villages. The pervasive question he had for Amos was "Who made this?" As each of the villages seemed to have specific trades and abilities that made them unique, none of them possessed such knowledge to have ever created anything like this. This had to be something left behind by the Ancients, the ones who left them the Wall.

From somewhere out of sight, Amos yelled for Timothy to come back into the house. Timothy traveled back through the house the way he had come. He entered the kitchen, where Amos ladled portions of warmed-up stew into two generous metal bowls. Along with the steaming aroma of the hot food, Amos had warmed thick slabs of crusted bread, cut and waiting, onto a large wooden salver.

"What did you think of them?" Amos asked, as Timothy sat in one of the twenty or so wooden chairs sitting around the perimeter of an enormous wooden table. Timothy observed the table's impeccable surface had been polished smooth by years of meticulous care. Though Amos lived alone, there must have been times when large gatherings took place here. Timothy watched as Amos placed a set of spoons and knives beside each bowl. When Amos turned to place the remains of the stew on the stove, Timothy lunged into a piece of the heavy bread, biting hungrily into the crust. As he started chewing, Amos looked at him from the stove and said, "By the Winds, boy, when did you last eat? Take your time. Besides, we must give thinks to the Winds for providing us the food we are to eat."

Timothy laid his bread back on his plate, embarrassed by his hunger, and apologized. "You're right, Amos. I should have realized my manners were not what they should be. Did you want to say the blessing, or would you like me to say it?"

Amos furrowed his brow at the young man sitting at his table and said, "You look pretty hungry, and I need to put some things away, so get ready, and when I sit down, we'll say the blessing together, all right?"

"Sure," Timothy said, as he bowed his head and admitted resolution to the pretext for a moment longer.

Amos finished putting things back as he wanted them and sat down at the table. "Shall we begin?"

"Please," Timothy said in an almost pleading voice.

Together they said the blessing. Then they started the meal. Amos finished a mouthful of food then asked, "So I know I asked before, what did you think of the bridge?"

"It's amazing! How long has it been here?"

"Long before I was born . . . even longer than my parents and their parents before them . . . For all the villagers, the Great Bridge to the Four Winds has always been there."

"Who made it and how did they do it?" Timothy asked, perplexed by the interlacing technology, strange mysteries, and magical aura surrounding the Great Bridge.

"No one really knows, but on a guess, it was probably built centuries ago by our ancestors, the Ancients. Back then, they possessed the knowledge and skill to create such structures. None of us possess that kind of skill anymore."

"But how do the villagers keep it structurally intact? Don't parts of the bridge need repairs from time to time? The bridge sees a lot of heavy traffic."

"We patch and rebuild some of the flat stones on the surface of the bridge, but the understructure—that is, the huge statues that

hold the bridge up—we never touch. So far, we haven't had to do anything to support it. That's what makes it such a mystery to us all. How can a structure that is used every day under heavy loads, mind you, continue to tolerate such use? Every bridge we villagers have made over the solens had needed work almost constantly to keep them running, but not this one. This one was made to endure for an eternity of lifetimes." Amos stopped for a moment and tried to judge how Timothy was processing all the information he had given him. Amos continued, "But I do have another little mystery for you . . . one that, I hope, will help you in your quest."

Timothy stopped eating long enough to stare at his host as a bit of stew ran over his chin. "There is something that supports the message Victoria gave to travel to the northern mountains?"

"I think so," Amos pondered, as he folded his hands beneath his chin and looked in his guest's direction. Almost like the conversation had gone in a direction he didn't want, Amos picked up his spoon and dug into his bowl before he looked up at Timothy again. "Finish eating . . . ," he offered as a gentle command. Then he continued, "Afterward, I will tell you a story that was handed down for many generations, particularly here in the village of Bridgedom."

Timothy finished the meal and helped Amos finish tidying up after. Then when everything was put away, Amos sat down in a large cushioned chair in the corner of his waiting room and had Timothy sit in a chair opposite him. "Now, I must ask you, have you ever heard of a place called Winterland?"

Timothy gave Amos a strange look then said, "Yes, I've heard stories about it. But no one really believes that it exists or if it ever existed."

Amos thought about his response for a second then said, "What if I told you that I think the stories are true?"

Timothy laughed. "Amos, it's just old folklore designed to explain how our villages came to be and why schools and teachers are prohibited. The villages prosper by handing down traditions. We learn what we need by actually doing them. Of course, we have books and stories that we pass around to each other. Our mothers and fathers teach us reading and writing when we are ready for it. We are a well-maintained society with little to want or need throughout our lives. We haven't needed or wanted such a place where everyone was taken out of the fields and shops to sit in a classroom unproductively."

"But I believe there was a time when such things existed in our world," Amos said thoughtfully.

"So if that is true, what became of that world? Why would we need something that, after seeing what our villages are capable of, would lead to our own destruction?" Timothy asked impetuously.

Amos was ready for a discussion, but the path Timothy led him on was argumentative. He would have to be cautious with his words if he was to help the young man. "But what if the teachings made us greater than what we are? What if we could build structures like our Great Bridge? Wouldn't our world be a better place if we could learn to do these things again?"

Timothy was deeply entrenched in the traditions of his times. He would not easily abandon his beliefs. He looked at Amos, aflame with his own sword of truth, and said, "But these things have passed. They passed for reasons none of us really know about. Do we really want to disturb the ghosts of a culture that is gone forever . . . a time and a culture that may simply be childish stories? Isn't our society, where everyone looks out for one another, enough to satisfy us? Why awaken old ideas that have us competing against each other for select places where some have everything and others have nothing? The old stories tell us of poverty, want, malicious crimes, hatred, and wars. We have none of it living as we do. Don't the stories also tell of the teachers at the fabled Winterland giving in to the depravity of setting students on students? Their students' concepts of competition allowed them to rape and murder in order to secure their educated advancement over their fellow human beings. Winterland's legendary history released educated criminals, rapists, and murderers into the world and almost destroyed it under the guise of competition. Of course, we know the stories are just stories." Timothy looked to Amos for a response. "Don't we, Amos?"

"Yes, Timothy," Amos said quietly, *"I have heard the stories too."*

"Then why would I even attempt to go there?" Timothy asked emphatically.

"To save your Catherine," Amos said a little more sternly.

"But how are these old stories about a place known for its cruelty going to help someone as loving and generous as my Catherine?" he said, indignant Amos would even suggest such a thing.

Amos remained resolute. He was determined to have Timothy hear him out. *"I had you look at the Great Bridge for several reasons. One of them being, I think the Great Bridge is a product of the minds that once was Winterland. The other, and more important reason, is something I want to show you when you are ready to go your way to Vigil and Emansupass."*

Amos was his host and a new friend. Though he didn't like discussing the old legends, he now seemed to be ensnared in an old belief system that failed centuries ago. He despised the very idea Winterland existed. The very idea Winterland might hold the key to saving Catherine sickened him. He vainly disguised his contempt by directing the attention of their discussion elsewhere. *"The thing you want to show me . . . is it here with you?"*

Amos saw the old convictions of truths and legends twisting in Timothy's face, so he responded as indiscriminately as he could, *"No, but I believe the North Wind may be able to help you on your quest."*

His response pulled Timothy out of uncertainty, rendering his full attention. *"The quest to make Catherine immortal . . . so she won't die?"*

"Yes." It was the only word Amos would say.

Raining in Paradise

Tell me about regret . . .

I do not look back on this time fondly. The year 2001 was probably the worst year Lois and I experienced. Lois started her field placement at Johns Hopkins by the end of January. I prepared for the long absences, hurried schedules, and silent frustration that would be generated. Our son was seldom home, as he continued his last year of college with a future graduation coming in the late spring. My book was successful on its own. Later in the year, the publisher released an audiobook version, which won the Audie Award for 2001. While these sound great in retrospect, my relationship with my wife was deteriorating. My son would be thinking of setting out on his own after graduation, and my father would need open heart surgery in the early spring. Lois too would have her own version of devastating news later in the year. As January blossomed, I had no knowledge these events would unfold as they did.

As I remember, winter passed quietly, uneventfully. There was the January cold but very little snow. Lois, our son, and I passed one another as each went to our appointed destinations. On weekends, when I was off, both Lois and our son were deep in their studies. During those times, I did the basic household chores of cooking, cleaning, grocery shopping, and whatever it took to keep the household running while they studied and prepared for their classes. I tried to start conversations with Lois but generally was told not to disturb her because she needed to concentrate on what she was doing. Our son was equally busy. When he wasn't home studying, he was visiting his girlfriend of five years. I thought I would see a wedding blossom there at some point, but I kept quiet, not wanting to jinx the possibility. The only thing I heard from Lois was a request for a hot cup of tea from time to time (which was one of her favorite things). I was happy to oblige, since it was the one thing I could do that did not seem to offend her.

February 28, 2001, was Ash Wednesday. "You are dust and to dust you shall return" was what we would be told, as ashes, made from burned palms mixed with oil, would be smeared on our foreheads in tiny black crosses. It would be too much of a foretelling than I could bear, as I remained absent from the ceremony that affirmed my mortality. I would be alone those first five days the following month, since Lois decided to stay in Baltimore overnight to attend a conference lasting two days. When her conferences were over Friday, she would be boarding a train to Washington DC to attend a second conference with the NBCC, ending Sunday night. When she returned for a few hours on Sunday night, I would at least get to see her. I felt the absence, and the time by herself with her friends and associates might be the best thing for both of us.

At the conference in Washington DC, Lois worked with the NBCC to get legislation passed regarding "genetic discrimination" in the workplace. It involved the practices of hiring and firing based on preexisting medical conditions and the insurance industry regarding insuring or not insuring in like fashion. So even with pressures at home, work, and school, she continued to help cancer survivors throughout our nation.

(Editorial dated March 6, 2001, by Lois A. Anderson)

I have just returned home after two back to back conferences and I haven't seen my family in three days. I was pleasantly surprised that no major crisis took place and that the house is in good shape. As for these two conferences, the first one on "Pain and Symptom Management" educated me about what social workers can be doing with patients in pain. To my surprise, there is a lot I never even thought of. From teaching patients in pain relaxation techniques to actually working with physicians on a pain service and making rounds with them, social workers can function in a patient advocate and intermediary role to get the proper pain medications ordered. Pain assessment is one of the keys to this, and I know how to do a good pain assessment. With the addition of pain management regulations by the JCAHO to its inspection criteria, social workers can expand their roles and assess pain on a regular basis in the patients they see.

As for the second conference, the National Breast Cancer Coalition's Team Leader Training, NBCC members will be working on getting a law passed to prevent genetic discrimination in employment and health insurance practices, something that will be very important with the completion of the Human Genome Project. One thing we do not want to have happen here is allowing insurers to use genetic information to determine those they will or will not insure. We cannot let that happen in the United States like it has in Great Britain. More information will follow on this subject.

That's about all for now.

Be on the lookout for that first Robin,

Lois

By March, my mother told me stories about my father's worsening heart problems. He had a cardiac abnormality that caused sudden bursts of atrial fibrillation, which remained undiagnosed a very long time. When it was diagnosed, a workup revealed several blockages in the vessels of the heart. He would need open heart surgery to correct this. My father demonstrated early signs of dementia but still understood what needed to be done. My parents asked me for advice. When Lois heard what they were facing, she came out of her study and spoke with them. She gave them her advice based on what she knew and what she could find out for them. Lois never turned anyone down who asked for her help, no matter how busy she was. This was no different. After speaking with Lois, my parents felt better about having the surgery done as soon as it could be scheduled.

Hearing the news my father was preparing for heart surgery, I couldn't imagine what could happen to top that news. Nothing could have been further from the truth. Shortly after my father's surgery in mid-April, my son and his fiancée came to me and told me they wanted to get married the summer after he graduated from college. Finally, I thought I had some good news to share with Lois. However, when I approached her with it, she was very upset. She wanted to know why the kids had gone through me and not her. To be honest, I never thought the kids meant anything telling me first. I was certainly more available than Lois, as she continued running from one meeting to another, or from work to classes. Her schedule was alarmingly busy, and she did not want to be confronted with anything other than her own business at the time. Lois was upset not only with my many shortcomings but also with her son for not making her privy to his actions regarding his fiancée. I was tired of walking on eggshells around my wife and her sometimes unpredictable and condescending outbursts. I knew the tensions from work, school, and her many activities were exhausting her. Whenever I tried to open the conversation to slow down or take a break from everything, Lois would either ignore me or start an argument. She readily pointed out how she supported me when I went back to school. One time I finally told her, "I give up." She wanted me to explain, but I just walked away. When she started after me, I got in my car and drove away for a few hours.

I was very angry with my wife. I could not believe she didn't see what her schedule was doing to her. I spoke to her father about what her schedule was doing to everyone. Eventually, he spoke with her, but she did not respect or want anything coming from him. I was afraid if she continued this pace, she would have a breakdown either physically or emotionally. Something had to give.

The day I left those few hours, I drove into the state game lands where I could think in the quiet solace of the empty woodlands. I knew Lois's impetuous drive set the momentum, and there was no other way than a major roadblock to stop her. "I give up," I repeated to myself. Even I did not like what I was saying, but at the moment, it was starting to make sense. I was ready to take myself out of the equation . . . the equation that allowed Lois to drive herself into the ground. I decided I would eventually leave the house . . . support her financially . . . but leave. Then from the place where I find my inspiration, remnants of a place my conscious mind cannot resolve, from somewhere the voice of my grandfather came and said, "We don't leave our loved ones behind." I started my car and went home. "I don't know," I said to myself. "I just don't know."

By the time April 2001 expired, I could no longer run the men's support group. I selected two men who came to the meeting since the beginning I felt would make good leaders, but unfortunately, neither wanted to take on the responsibility. I told Lois before our last meeting I could not get off for the support group meeting as I had due to scheduling complications with my employer. Considering how things were between us at the time, she took the news as just one more thing I failed her on, though it was certainly not the case.

Somehow we managed to stay together. I was waiting to see how Lois would be after her classes ended in June. I was hoping she would be in a better state of mind once the stress of schoolwork was out of the way. I thought my news of leaving Lois would be enough to kill my father still recuperating after open heart surgery at home. I did not want to burden anyone with more sad news. Lois continued darting in and out of the house with papers, folders, and schedules without running into me for almost three months. We saw each other briefly, but the conversations were brief and businesslike. Even before her classes ended, she was asked to speak on May 4, 2001, at the Relay for Life. Afterward, she was scheduled for a four-day conference in Washington DC with the NBCC from May 5-8, 2001. She had a meeting in Silver Spring, Maryland, on May 9, 2001, then another meeting in Hershey, Pennsylvania, on May 11, 2001. I was able to be with Lois on May 11, since it was one of the last book promotions she had set up before she stopped promoting the book in December the previous year. I did not let her down as I read excerpts from my book for the conference.

On Monday, May 14, Lois had an appointment with her oncologist. She never said anything, but she delayed getting her CA 27-29 done. Normally done in early March, the delay of two months was not surprising, knowing the commitments she was trying to achieve. On May 15, 2001, the oncologist called her with the results.

I was preparing to leave for work that late afternoon after we had eaten. I was just about to walk out the door when Lois finally spoke to me. She looked very tired, and a grave look washed over her face. It was one of those rare days when she was home before I left for work. We hadn't had a day like this in months. Normally, I would have walked over to her and kissed her good-bye; but under the circumstances, it didn't seem right. She watched as I gathered my things I take to work each night and put them in the car. I came to the door and meant to close it, but something stopped me. Lois just stood at the end of the dining room table and asked meekly, "Don't I get a kiss before you go?"

I was confused by her request. After three long months of not wanting to talk to me, she was asking for a kiss. I stood at the door and wondered what she was trying to do. I asked, "You really want to?"

She nodded yes to me before the tears started flowing from her eyes in torrents. Before I could make the five or six steps toward her, she was sobbing uncontrollably. I wasn't sure I could trust what I was seeing, so I asked, "What's wrong?"

"My tumor markers are up . . . the cancer's back," she shouted through her tears.

I took her in my arms and held her. She was so upset, she was shuddering. "I will call in late if you want me to," I told her.

"You'll probably get in trouble, so just get going. I'll be all right," she said empathetically. "I just wanted to kiss you good-bye. I don't know how many times I will get to do that, and I wanted you to know."

"How bad are the markers?" I asked, thinking she was just overreacting to a minor rise in the markers.

"They are up to 140. My oncologist just called about half an hour ago to let me know."

I was shocked by the number. This was no mistake. The cancer was back, and this time, there would be no remissions. This time, it would be a fight for every day she could manage. I asked her again if she wanted me to stay, but she wanted me to get to work. I told her, "I guess we have a lot to talk about when I get back."

She backed away from me and nodded yes as she wiped the cold tears from her eyes. "I have a lot to think about and research while you're at work. I'll tell you what I find out when you get home."

I gave her a long kiss, said good-bye, and then left for work. My heart was not on my work that night, and I had a difficult time focusing. My wife's cancer was back. Her CA 27-29 readings were never this high in her life, not even when the cancer was fully active in 1992. Just how bad would this recurrence be? What happened in her body to send the tumor markers this high? Then there were the other more-common, mundane questions. How long would she be able to work? What would happen to her schooling? Had she come this far only to be stopped by cancer? What would happen to her support group, to her newsletter? What would happen to all those people who depended on her for her knowledge and expertise? Yes, we had a lot to talk about when I returned home.

What everyone who cared about Lois had tried to do to stop her from running herself to utter exhaustion and breakdown was now stopped by the very thing Lois was most afraid of . . . a recurrence of breast cancer. "We don't leave our loved ones behind," said the voice of my grandfather from the place I called the Poet's Tree. "Sometimes we get the chance to change things," I remembered Lois telling me from a time when things were simpler in our lives. I would need all the strength I could draw to myself for the year unfolding before me. I inventoried the problems before me. We had a grown son graduating in about a month, a wedding to plan for next summer, Lois's mother with dementia and diabetes, her father who would not accept his diabetes and was uncontrolled, my father recovering from open heart surgery, and now Lois with a recurrence of breast cancer from an unknown site.

The next morning, when I came back from my job, Lois was much calmer. She had spent most of her night on the computer doing research on possible treatments and communicating with fellow cancer survivors and researchers. Instead of being emotional, she focused on what course of action she wanted to take. She told me, "First, we have to find where the cancer originates. It could be the liver, the lung, or possibly the bones."

"CT scan, MRI, or PET scan . . . possibly all of them eventually, I would suspect," I replied.

Lois continued to rifle through the collection of paper she printed off the computer overnight. "I think the oncologist will start with a CT scan because he prefers it to other scans."

"But where will he concentrate the scans? Where will he look? You have no symptoms, so we have no place to really start?"

By the end of May 2001, Lois had her visit with the oncologist. Together they decided to check a CT scan of the abdomen and chest and a complete bone scan. Because Lois completed her mammogram in mid-May, the tests would not be allowed until mid-June with the oncologist seeing her the day after the scans. This was done to lessen the effects of radiation exposure. Until these two tests were completed, Lois had the long emotional wait to get through. She spent her time putting together the support group newsletter. Overall, the newsletter for June was much shorter, and the editorial was condensed. It is interesting to note in hindsight that though she was aware cancer had returned, her editorial doesn't reflect what she was about to be going through. It remained upbeat and did not contain any indication she was fighting for her life.

(Editorial by Lois A. Anderson dated June 8, 2001)

Well, the Red Lion Garden Club Tour and Cancer Survivor Day are a thing of the past. Now it's on to other events, duties, and summer courses in school. It used to be that the summer would give some rest before the busy-ness of the summer took over. Now we have barely enough time to take a deep breath during July, only to come out fighting again in August with Longaberger parties. Ah well, such is Life!

One more short paper and a presentation to do for our class and my summer course will be over. That's what I keep telling myself, but I can't wait for this one to end. The trials and tribulations of being a student later in life!

So much for me . . . I hope everyone's summer is going as they planned and that you all get some vacation time in during those lazy, hazy days. Take care.

Watch for the butterflies in your garden,

Lois

The world moved on. Lois still had some classes to finish over the summer, which were not nearly as stressful as her field placement had been on her. Once she completed the courses for the summer, Lois cleared her schedule. She continued to hold her monthly support group meetings, and by July, there was a picnic for her members, which was very well attended. She waited to hear from the oncologist who would determine the point of origin and treatment options. First, Lois needed to know what to treat.

Lois finally slowed down. We took a vacation to Williamsburg, Virginia, where Lois loved to go, especially when she was under stress. It was the first place Lois had been to when we were on our honeymoon, and the memories there were always so positive, she came away feeling better. It was on this vacation that we discovered each other again. Though things between us were never the same as they were before this year started, it was, at least, the beginning of finding our way back.

Our son graduated in July 2001. He and his fiancée wanted to get married the following summer. My mother started coming to my house exhausted by the continued needs of my father still recuperating from his open heart surgery. Lois's tumor markers were elevated and seemed to have no real point of origin. To say the times were tumultuous, in both good and bad ways, would be an understatement. To have dealt with any one of these life-changing events at a time would have been enough. Now we seemed to be assaulted on every front.

The oncologist did call and schedule a CT scan for Lois. Once Lois had the results of the scans, there appeared to be no definite findings. Other than three slightly enlarged lymph nodes near the right lung, the report was deemed not conclusive, since a mild cold or flu may have caused these changes. The only reason the radiologist even reported them was he knew her oncologist was looking for anything unusual. We were told at the meeting with her oncologist, these kinds of findings would not be reported normally.

With nothing else to go on, Lois discussed the findings with the oncologist. Together, they decided to consult a thoracic surgeon to get his perspective on the CT scan. The consult was scheduled for early June 2001. The consult with the surgeon did not go as Lois expected. She thought the surgeon would be as aggressive as she was in treating, or at least exploring, the potential cancer site. The surgeon pointed out that in order to get to the area of concern, he would have to open her chest just below the rib cage, then collapse the right lung in order to visualize the site. It was not a surgery he was willing to attempt until other options were considered. According to the surgeon, the three minimally enlarged lymph nodes could have easily come from allergies. It was early summer, and it was true: Lois did have trouble every allergy season, and this season was no exception. His suggestion was to have her oncologist run another CA 27-29 in three months.

Lois left the surgeon's office emotionally deflated. She felt the surgeon did not take her seriously, and she was convinced there was definitely a new cancer growing inside her. She quickly made a call to her oncologist to order a new CA 27-29 precisely three months from the original one. Meanwhile, Lois and I discussed which physicians seemed to be on the right track. Lois had complete faith in her oncologist, since he was as aggressive as she was with her treatments. The thoracic surgeon, she felt, had problems dealing with a woman telling him what she wanted to have done. She felt she should not have to be subjected to begging the man to do a procedure she was perfectly willing to do. Even before the August tumor marker was drawn, I saw the battle lines forming between the thoracic surgeon and my wife. I knew Lois was not returning to his office without a substantiated plan, which she would reinforce with data, both her own and from some of the leading authorities in the cancer field. In that respect, Lois did not disappoint anyone. Still, even I had doubts about doing such an extensive surgery on a site that could turn out to be nothing, a site even the radiologist admitted he would not have normally reported. It really wasn't much to go on. The other argument we considered were the tumor markers. These were abnormally elevated for Lois, but we both knew the markers could be influenced by almost anything. Colds, flus, allergies, or infections could cause the markers to be elevated. But Lois could be right too. Was it what she suspected? The surgeon was right. We needed a second tumor marker to verify our suspicions. Too many factors could have contributed to this one isolated elevated reading.

Lois had the tumor marker completed in August. The reading was 307.6, more than double the reading from three months ago. The question had been answered. This was cancer, not just an isolated reading. A more-trenchant resolve from Lois, her oncologist, and me would echo in the office of the thoracic surgeon on our next meeting. This encounter, I suspected, would not be as civil as our previous encounter. Lois would go to his office armed with articles, suggestions from authorities across the country, and her own contribution of her CA 27-29 history and medical records. She wasn't going to leave his office without a definite surgical plan, no matter how dangerous her surgeon felt it was to do. Lois felt the risk of finding the cancer was more important than allowing the cancer to completely overtake her and allow her to die any sooner than she wanted. She wanted to fight, and she wanted this unwilling ally to cooperate with her.

The meeting with the thoracic surgeon came on August 30, 2001. Lois asked me to go with her again, as she felt he would ignore her because she was a woman. Knowing this would be an exciting and less-demure meeting, I told her, "I wouldn't miss it for the world." The recurrence of her breast cancer made us draw close again. The fact she needed me again made me feel secure in my feelings toward her. I really wanted to be there to support her, and I wanted to see how she managed with this surgeon. We went to his office and were asked to go back to the exam room where we found the surgeon rifling through his own set of papers on Lois's case. He had Lois sit on the exam table where he did a cursory exam then had her sit in one of the chairs next to me as he stood and leaned against the exam table. He watched as Lois began unfolding the stack of papers she brought.

"You don't need those," the surgeon said, more a command than a request.

"These are my records I wanted to show you," Lois told him, not allowing him to gain the advantage in the conversation.

"I already know what I need to know . . . and I still don't think you have enough to convince me to do this kind of surgery on you," he said with no change in his demeanor.

"Well, I think I do," Lois insisted. "The markers have more than doubled since you saw me. I think that alone warrants investigating the nodes radiology found on the CT scan," Lois told him even more emphatically.

"You do realize this is extensive and dangerous surgery?" the surgeon turned and asked me, dismissing Lois from the conversation as quickly as he could.

I looked to my wife, realizing the surgeon was trying to put me in the middle of the decision, not her. I could see how frustrating this was to Lois, considering how much time and effort she had put into researching her situation, so I responded, "My wife has been right about her markers almost 100 percent of the time. Her oncologist feels this is a risk worth taking, as do we. Lois wants this investigated. So I'm asking you, will you do the surgery?"

The surgeon looked me in the eye and stated as seriously as he could. "If she," he said, pointing at Lois sitting in the chair next to me, "were my wife, I would not want her to go through this procedure. It's painful, dangerous, and we're not even sure we're going into the right place. We could be doing all this for nothing."

"She's willing to take the chance . . . and I agree with her," I replied just as seriously.

I saw the look in Lois's face, and it said she was really angry with this man. She gave me a quick glance, letting me know I did well, but now it was her turn. "But I am not your wife!" Lois was quick to point out to the surgeon. "My husband and I have discussed this, and we both feel this is worth going after. So I am telling you now that I want this done!"

I could see by the surgeon's face, Lois finally struck a nerve. I don't know if it was because a woman contested him or Lois had her facts prepared, but his cool clinical demeanor fell apart as he shot back. "I think this is a foolish thing to do, but if you want to put yourself through this, I'll do it." He walked to the folder containing her records, then turned back, throwing his hands in the air. "Remember, I'm just the mechanic in all this. I'll fix what I can when I'm in there . . . but I'm just the mechanic!"

Lois and I just stared at the surgeon like he lost his mind. I thought I heard everything, but for a surgeon to say this to a patient, under these circumstances, was unfounded. I was upset and angry at the surgeon for such callous behavior with a patient undergoing such an emotional decision. Lois, on the other hand, was in pursuit. She finally had the surgeon at his game and was getting to what she came here for. "Okay then, when do we do this?" she asked while the surgeon stood there with her chart in one hand over his head and the other up like a thief caught in the headlights of a police car.

I could see the resignation his eyes as he knew this woman was not one to be taken lightly. He walked to the door and opened it. Before he left, he turned and finally directed his words to Lois. "I'll have the secretary bring the papers you need to sign. Then this office will call you with a time and date. Stay here, and I'll have her come in." Then the surgeon left the room. Within seconds, the secretary came in with papers for Lois to sign. When the secretary finished, a nurse came, timed with precise continuity, to go over labs, tests, and general preparations needed prior to surgery. The surgeon moved on to his other patients. Lois and I left his office for home. We needed to tell everyone Lois was to undergo major surgery very soon.

Just a few days after meeting with the thoracic surgeon, Lois was giving a speech to a group of women at the Fourth Annual Baltimore Day of Caring held in Timonium, Maryland. The gist of the program is well described in a letter Lois received on October 9, 2001.

Dear Lois,

On behalf of the entire planning committee we thank you for your part in making the 4th Annual Baltimore Area Day of Caring a success. Your contributions greatly enhanced the day and you are to be commended. Because of our combined efforts to provide a day of education, encouragement and empowerment to anyone who cares about breast cancer we have received many positive comments.

Our goal is to devote one day to increase the awareness of the importance of early detection of breast cancer, to encourage self-responsibility, and to reinforce the fact that women who develop breast cancer can and do lead normal, healthy lives.

Your participation as a speaker was invaluable. We hope you feel as rewarded as we do knowing that you reached pout and touched the lives of those who participated in your seminar session. The feedback has been outstanding and we thank you.

Most sincerely yours,

We couldn't have done this without you! (This was handwritten below the body of the letter.)

Lois's surgery was scheduled for September 18, 2001. It was our twenty-forth wedding anniversary, and Lois would be in the hospital fighting for her life. The emotional turmoil going on in our lives would have stopped most people from doing little else than preparing for surgery. Lois looked at it differently and decided to put together the newsletter for her support group. At the time, she was still working a forty-hour workweek fifty miles from home, helping my mother work with my convalescing father, preparing for an upcoming wedding next summer, and making preparations for surgery. She wanted to let her support group know how she was doing.

(Editorial by Lois A. Anderson dated September 7, 2001)

It's that time of year when things move on. Children move on to their next grade in school, adults move on to a more serious intense phase of their work, compared to the lazy, hazy days of summer . . . and I too have moved on.

For those who don't know, I have had a recurrence of breast cancer after 9 years. I am on the verge of making important decisions that affect the rest of my life. I've had to give up school for this semester and probably this year . . . ? Nevertheless, I look at this as a bump in the "Road of Life." I will refer to this as some of the "rough seas" I and anyone who knows and cares for me must travel. For those of you who do not understand this statement, please look at my square on the Breast Cancer Patchwork and you will understand. Anyway, I have decided that I will get through this and then finish my degree in social work.

I have a wedding to look forward to next year and am proud that my son has graduated after an arduous task of getting his education completed.

From all this I guess you could say I'm moving on too! . . . to a different stage in life, one that will be happy and rewarding in new and different ways.

Be well, stay happy and watch as summer fades into Autumn's glory.

Lois

Lois went into surgery on the early morning of September 18, 2001. It was a beautiful day, and we both knew we would be missing it. My son and I stayed with Lois in the admissions area for as long as we were allowed, then went to sit in the waiting room. Lois was very optimistic and told me she was glad the surgeon was finally getting to the site she was concerned about. Before we left Lois, a nurse told me the surgeon would be out to talk to me in the waiting room after he was finished. Lois went into surgery in the very early hours of the morning, and after many stressed hours, on my part, she was out of surgery and into recovery by one o'clock in the afternoon. My son and I waited nervously for the surgeon to arrive with news of what he found. He finally arrived in blue scrubs and said to me, "I have some good news and some bad news."

"I'm ready for whatever you have to tell me," I said, as I conjectured what this man would construe to be good or bad news.

The surgeon managed a cursory survey of the waiting room to evaluate who might be listening, then caught my son paying attention to what he was about to say. He looked to my son and then to me, asking, "Is this your son?"

"Yes, whatever you have to tell me is all right to share with him as well," I said, trying to keep my anxiety in check.

"Well then, I'll get right to it. First, the good news. Your wife was right! The three lymph nodes she wanted checked out were cancer. Two of them were fairly easy to remove, but the third one actually sat on the aorta of the heart. I did my best to remove it, and I think I actually got it all, but as you know, if any cells remained, this could all start up again. I'm thinking with some aggressive chemotherapy, we will clean it all up."

"Well, all of that sounds like great news. Lois would love to hear this all from you at some point." I looked at the surgeon, thinking Lois had problems during surgery. My anxiety level went up a notch anticipating what the surgeon meant as "bad news." So far, everything he told me was wonderful news. He found the enigmatic cancer, removed it, and now we had a specimen of tissue to use to determine which chemotherapy would be effective. So what could the bad news be, other than Lois did not do well during the procedure or something happened during the surgery? I wasn't sure I could take news any worse than that. Very uneasily, I asked . . . "The bad news?"

"I don't know how bad this is really," he said, looking down at his feet. "I'm not an oncologist, but I found the nodes created a lymphangitic spread over the right lung. It appeared like a fine layer of tissue spreading over the lung itself. I didn't know if the lung tissues beneath may have been invaded, so I took what would be called a "wedge biopsy" of the lung. That way, the oncologist and pathologist can tell better how invasive the lymphangitic spread is and give them a better idea on how to treat it."

"That was the bad news?" I asked, relieved Lois made it through the procedure relatively unscathed.

"Oh yes, I did have a talk with your wife before she was sedated, and she decided to have a port placed for chemotherapy." I looked at this surgeon with new interest. He continued, "We had a terrible time trying to get an IV started on her, so I suggested the idea of a port placement to her, and she agreed."

"I think that was a very smart idea. The first chemotherapy pretty much took out any decent veins she had in her good arm. Thank you for suggesting it to her."

Seeing he had smoothed over any previous altercations with Lois and me, the surgeon smiled at me and said, "I'll be in to see her tomorrow."

"Thank you again," I said, relieved that the "bad news" was not nearly as insurmountable as my mind was making it.

Lois had to remain in the hospital for about a week after surgery. She spent the first night in intensive care with a chest tube, IVs, and monitoring devices. I was only allowed about one hour that day to spend with her. My son was able to see her the next time the hour visitation was allowed in the evening. For the week following her surgery, my son and I took turns going into the hospital for visits. I generally took the mornings, and he took the evenings when I was at work. Eventually, we brought her home to begin the long road back to recovery. As anyone who has had chest surgery can imagine, Lois needed weeks of physical therapy to get her right side strengthened again. This was the second major assault on her right chest wall. Muscles, fascia, and tendons were rearranged in the upper chest wall during the right-sided mastectomy nine years before. Now a very similar situation existed for her on the lower chest wall. Lois would again have to retrain the muscles on the right side so she could use her right arm again. Potential problems manifested after this surgery that hadn't occurred with the mastectomy. Lymphedema, decreased mobility of her right arm, decreased strength, increased pain, and muscle spasms were all in the realm of possibilities. Physical therapy was crucial.

Another integral part of her recovery rested in the hands of her oncologist who would prescribe the appropriate chemotherapy. When Lois received her initial chemotherapy in 1992-1993, she was nauseated for days afterward. If her surgeon was right, her oncologist would initiate a chemotherapy protocol that would be even tougher to tolerate. Fortunately, by 2001, the drugs used as antiemetic were much improved. From previous treatments, we all learned that Lois tolerated chemotherapy much better if she was given steroids, like

Decadron, before and after her treatment. Doing so relieved most of her symptoms of nausea and loss of appetite. So it was after her first chemotherapy session on November 1, 2001, that Lois came through it with minimal effects. She prepared herself for the eventual hair loss, which occurred about two weeks before Christmas. She had several wigs, with her favorite being a fashionable red one.

After getting through her first treatment, she felt good enough to go back to work. It had only been six weeks since she had major surgery. She had a final appointment to see the thoracic surgeon before she returned to work. I asked Lois if the surgeon had ever spoken to her about "being right" about her cancerous lymph nodes. She told me, "He will never tell me I was 'right' and he was 'wrong.' He had many chances in the hospital where I asked him about it, but he would always rush in and out, leaving his interns and residents to deal with me. He will never admit that to me."

"You're probably right." I laughed back at her. She smiled and just shook her head. Once Lois determined the source of the cancer and a way to fight it, she continued her fight to help other women combat this disease. Only a few weeks after surgery, she had me drive her to a committee meeting where the members were working on a book *Resources for Cancer Patients*. She stopped in on a project where she assisted, called the Pink Ribbon Walk, and was present for her October meeting of the breast cancer support group. In November, she participated in a telephone conference of End of Life concerns. She stopped going to her college classes out of necessity but had hopes of returning at some point. She made almost impossible strides in her pursuit of her master's degree, it was literally within arm's reach at this point in time. Now, she only had to survive this second assault of breast cancer long enough to finish it. Lois tells of her ordeals that autumn of 2001 in an excerpt from one of her journals.

(From the journal of Lois A. Anderson)

My tumor marker test began to rise in May 2001, and then again in August 2001. I was referred to a thoracic surgeon after a CT scan in June in 2001 revealed an enlarged lymph node in my chest. The thoracic surgeon stated that this kind of finding could come from an upper respiratory infection and since my allergies had been active he attributed the CT finding to those active allergies.

He recommended that we wait three months and repeat testing. This we did even though I was uneasy about it. However, when the second test CT scan revealed the same findings and the tumor marker test went even higher, I knew it was time to do something. I insisted on an excision of that lymph node which meant a thoracotomy, major surgery, for me. The surgery was performed on my wedding anniversary in the fall of 2001 and lo and behold, I was right and the doctor was wrong. When the surgery was done, the surgeon noted a thin gray layer of cells growing over the pleura of my right lung. He performed a wedge biopsy of this area and it came back positive for the original breast cancer. Had things not worked out this way, had I not advocated for myself with this man, had I not been knowledgeable enough to put together the CT findings with the rising tumor marker and come up with something very suspicious, my lung metastasis probably would have gone undiagnosed until it was too late.

Finally, the most tumultuous year of my life, 2001, was almost over. Lois had one final thing to do, and that was her December newsletter. She was two weeks late, and the printing would not come out until January. Still, she wanted to do it. Her editorial that Christmas was almost subdued, almost too serious for her, but it was still hers.

(Editorial by Lois A. Anderson dated December 12, 2001)

Christmas time, and all the hustle and bustle that it brings, is here again. This year I am taking it easy and doing what I want to do, which means that most of the people on my Christmas list are getting gift certificates to a store where I know they can use something. I do not want to take time out of the holiday season to have to worry about whether this person or that person is getting the "right" gift for them, and this change has made such a difference in me. I feel much more relaxed and able to cope with the holiday season so much that I would suggest this to anyone.

For those of you who have not seen me lately, I am now sporting a very fashionable red wig after losing my hair to chemotherapy. The chemotherapy sessions are coming along with three of them finished by the time you receive this newsletter.

Several things I want to call your attention to in this newsletter are the websites, and book list. Many new books out have to do with breast cancer right now. Not only are they for patients, but some are devoted to explanations for other family members, especially children. They may help you to explain some of the words that confound you on these reports. The site is very informative and contains definitions and explanations of terms that I hear every day in my work as a medical technologist.

I hope that you all have a Happy Holiday season and celebrate the New Year with joy. I know I will.

May your Christmas candles, wherever they are, glow brightly, as brightly as the warmth in your heart.

Lois

Melancholy Mile

Tell me about mending . . .

I have been to this place so many times. I find my way here not really knowing if there is anything to find. The burdens of my life seem so heavy. It's almost like each year adds a heavier stone to the ones I must now carry. The Poet's Tree lies in silence, save the rustling of the flowered limbs above me. I look into the bright sky for answers that are not forthcoming. Inside I lie deep in melancholy, while the irony of unimaginable beauty surrounds me.

"Remember a kiss" came the voice of my grandmother interjected into the sweet shuffling of leaves.

"I don't remember," I said, too tired to investigate the source of the voice. Absently, I looked at the sky, cerulean blue and golden with the sunlight streaming through the branches. "I don't remember."

"It takes courage to love," her voice said, as it faded into the rush of breezes blowing against the Poet's Tree.

"How much courage can you expect from a broken heart?" I asked the voice of my grandmother. There was no reply, save the wind in the leaves, as I went into the dream within a dream. Weariness stung me from every side, and I longed for dreams.

On the morning of the fourth day of the wall breach, Leon stood in front of his wagon, trying to find some way to enter the village of Stock from his location. Penny came from behind and laid her hand on his shoulder. She knew Leon was troubled by his failure to get Victoria to Stock before the power of her friend's lifestone faded to nothing.

"Sweetheart, we tried to get Victoria back to her friend before it was too late, but we couldn't do it. No one could have done it." Penny looked out over the sea of orbs and blue mists prevailing before them. "Just look at what the orbs have done."

Leon continued to look at the orbs bobbing in and out of the blue mists. "We still need to get there and make sure Catherine knows the message Amelia tried to get to her. Right now, we have no way of knowing if she knows about the message or not," Leon said, watching the endless ocean of mists, while orbs by the hundreds moved toward the defensive fire wall Stock created to prevent them from overrunning their village.

"But how are we going to get across that?" Penny asked as she surveyed the besieged village of Stock. "I don't believe we could ever make it with all our lifestones put together. There are just too many of them."

No, my dear Penny, the orbs would overrun and destroy us before we even get a few arm's lengths into that mire," Leon said thoughtfully. Leon turned back to face Penny and said, "We may have stranded ourselves here. The way back from the top of this hill may now be as treacherous as the path before us. We could make a stand here, or we could turn back and hope we have a chance of moving either north or to the west . . . someplace the orbs haven't gotten to yet."

"I think you two are giving up too easily," Rand said, as he moved some boxes off the wooden driver's seat of the wagon.

"Well, what would you have me do, Rand? Run a suicide mission through those things?" Leon asked, frustrated by their lack of resources to fight the orbs.

Rand stopped for a moment and looked at Leon, frustrated by what he saw around him. He looked at the boxes stored on the wagon then said, "Leon, when you packed up to leave Glade, you brought a lot of your stuff with you, am I right?"

Leon didn't like that Rand was lessening the value of his wares by calling them "stuff." "Stuff, Rand?" Leon said with a bit of impertinence. "Yeah, we brought along some of our housewares, tools, weapons, and some of my work supplies. What of it?"

Rand knew he hit a sore spot with Leon but continued anyway, "Did you see what they're doing over at Stock to keep the orbs out of the village?"

Leon looked toward Rand with fire in his eyes, "Yeah, they're burning oil and whatever else to keep the mist from getting too close to the village."

Rand looked at Leon like he finally had something to offer, and it mystified him. "Well," he started, "if we set up some of your solvents and burn a path through the orbs, we could possibly make it to Stock."

The thought of using his solvents never crossed Leon's mind. He thought for a moment then turned to Penny. "You know, Penny, I could reformulate some solvents to make them more explosive and longer burning. Rand might be on to something here."

"Well, it beats being stranded here on this hill," Penny replied. She turned her attention to Rand and said, "Rand, how about waking up our sleeping beauty, Victoria? She could help."

After Rand moved to the back of the wagon to rouse Victoria, Leon turned to Penny and said, "We are doing a dangerous thing, my dear. I would not put you through this if there were any other ways." With that said, Leon bowed his head and cried.

Penny understood Leon's tears as she took him into her arms and just held him until his tears subsided. When she looked over her husband's shoulder at the blue misty ocean before her, she understood Leon held all their lives in his hands. There was no way to tell what the orbs had done to the underlying grounds between them and the village of Stock. It was the nature of the orbs, they had learned by experience, to create deep ravines and gullies by which they traveled in hordes. The road that ran before them in the direction of Stock was *only a vestigial part of the road that theoretically still existed under the orbs foggy blue environment. For all they knew, the road was gone within a few arm's lengths of their visual field, replaced by deep cut trenches that would be impossible to negotiate with a wagon and horses.*

Rand walked between Penny and Leon and said, "We are ready, Leon."

Leon faced Rand, then Penny, and said, "I guess if we are going to do this, we better get started. Is Victoria awake?"

Victoria, still tired from their ordeals, rubbed the sleep from her eyes and struggled slowly to her feet. She walked slowly to the front of the wagon where she saw Rand, Leon, and Penny standing near the horses. What got her attention and drew a gasp was the sight of the boiling ocean of blue mists blocking their way off this hill going all the way to the village of Stock that lay before them. Purple orbs by the hundreds assaulted the village. Red tendrils shot out like a hundred red spears from the blue mists attempting to breach the wall of fire created by the villagers. The village of Stock was under siege. What were they burning in the trenches at Stock? What could possibly be on Leon's mind that he would risk their lives attempting to move off this hill? The way before them was an impossible mire. Victoria looked at Rand then to Leon and asked incredulously, "What are you thinking about doing?"

Leon looked at Victoria gravely and said, "We are going to try to get into Stock."

The situation inside Stock was critical in some parts of the village. Catherine made the final decision to sacrifice her lifestone, and Leena was visibly shaken by her decision. "Catherine, you will die if you place your stone in the wall."

Catherine looked at her mother and spoke as gently as she could manage, "Yes, Mother, I know. But if I don't do it soon, we will all perish. Besides, if what Amelia told us is true, my great love, Timothy, may be on his way right now to keep me from dying."

"But we don't even know if Timothy ever received the message," Michael protested, overwrought by the thought of losing his only daughter.

"We have to believe he does know and he is doing his best to help me," Catherine replied, trying to alleviate some of their fears.'

"I don't like this," Jacob said. "There is just too much we don't know. First, we don't know if we can even get to the breach without a fight. Second, we don't know if Catherine's stone will work when we seal the wall with it. We could be sacrificing her for nothing," Jakob said directly to Michael.

"Amelia said my lifestone would save us, and I believe her," Catherine said defensively.

"Yeah, from a voice she heard coming from the wall . . ." Eric chimed in defiantly.

"Suppose she was wrong," Lamin stated, trying to talk Catherine out of sacrificing herself. "Suppose everything Amelia said was done just to make us think we can do something to stop this?"

"Then she certainly sacrificed herself for nothing, didn't she?" Catherine asked with suppressed anger in her voice. "Why would she do that, Lamin? Why would anyone risk their life to warn us like she did if she didn't truly believe in what she said?" Catherine finally had the room's attention, and she continued, "Amelia died yesterday. Her father came by and told me. When Victoria brings her stone home, he would like to place it in the wall himself. If I don't do this, she and many others will have died for no reason . . . no reason at all. I have to place my stone in the wall to stop these things before they kill everyone. The time is now. You can either help me or I will find someone who will."

"If this is truly what you want to do, I will help you," Jakob said solemnly.

"I too will help," Lamin said, his heart breaking from the sacrifice Catherine was willing to make for all of them. "Though I don't know what I will say to Timothy when he returns to find you're gone."

Soon, Eric, Andrew, and Alexis agreed to help Catherine move her lifestone to the opening in the wall. Only Leena and Michael could not bear to say they would help. Yet to look into their solemn eyes, it was deeply evident that they knew it was the only way to save the villages.

Catherine looked to her mother and father and said, "I know you love me more than anything in the world, but I am doing this because I love you all more than myself. It is because I love you that I want to do this. I may not be able to save myself, but I may be able to save all of you, and that is something that should matter, especially to me."

Jakob moved slowly to the door opening to the walkway where the barn waited with its valuable treasure. His hand stayed on the latch as he sadly looked up and over his shoulder. "I'll get the wagon ready."

"I'll be waiting for you at the front door," Catherine said with spirited conviction. She turned to face the room where her mother, Leena, could not look any more distraught. Catherine looked directly at her mother and said, "Mother, I do this for you." Catherine turned to walk to the front of the house then, as an afterthought, turned back and said to those assembled in the room . . . "I do this for all of you." She went outside the front door where she found a chair. She sat alone and cried while she waited for Jakob to bring the wagon.

Amos led Timothy's horse to the last several steps on the Great Bridge. He turned to Timothy and said, "When we get to that last stop point," Amos pointed to a worn stone obelisk at the end of the bridge, "I will take you to a place not seen by many villagers."

"What's there, Amos?" Timothy asked, intrigued but disturbed by Amos's dismissive attitude.

"Perhaps a message . . . perhaps just another puzzle," Amos said, not looking up from his feet.

"And this mystery is going to help me save Catherine?" Timothy asked, sounding unconvinced Amos had anything substantial to offer him on his quest.

"Leave the horse . . . we're here," Amos said over his shoulder. Timothy stopped, took the horse from Amos, and then tethered the horse just off the one side of the bridge. Timothy looked back and saw they traveled the entire bridge. The stone marker, Amos pointed out, all but a few arm's lengths from the end of the bridge, sat but the breadth of a few fingers from the overworn stone railing.

Timothy looked at the stone marker then to Amos. "This"— Timothy pointed to the stone—"is what you wanted to show me?"

"No," said Amos abruptly, "this is where I wanted you to stop. What I want to show you lies off the side of the bridge." He looked into Timothy's puzzled face. "You ready?"

Timothy nodded yes, and the two walked to the edge of the bridge. Next to the stone railings, the brush grew thick and impenetrable. A small path, cut and worn, opened through the overgrowth and led to a clearing just beside the end of the bridge. Over their shoulders, lush ferns and verdant moss grew on steppes of broken stones leading to tree-topped cliffs where the road to Vigil cut through them. Timothy looked to every side and saw no egress leading anywhere. The only path, in or out, was the one leading them to this natural enclosed area. Timothy sighed in disgust, thinking Amos saw something here that had no bearing on his quest. He looked at Amos and asked, "So this is what . . . Amos?"

Amos moved where a thick slab of black rock lay embedded in the side of the ridge. Timothy was surprised he hadn't noticed it when he came into this clearing. To Timothy's surprise, the large rock moved easily at Amos's touch. "Well, come over here. I need some help with this." He moved to Amos's side, and together they slid the large rock to one side. Before them, Timothy saw a stone stairway leading into a pitch-black hole.

"What is this?" Timothy asked, unaware surprise leaped into his voice.

"I think it may be an answer . . . an answer you may not know the question to. At least, not one you ever thought of yet," Amos teased.

"But how are we going to see down there? There's no light, and we didn't bring a lantern with us," Timothy said, surveying the darkness, trying to see further than his eyes would allow.

Amos stood over Timothy as he pondered the dark stairway in the ridge. He stood with arms folded until Timothy managed to control his surprise. "Have some faith, boy," Amos chided with a scowl on his face.

"Faith?" Timothy asked, reeling from the amazing structure that disappeared into the earth. He turned to Amos and asked, "Faith in what?"

"The Four Winds, boy. The Four Winds," Amos said, as he slapped Timothy on the back.

His curiosity heightened. "What do the Four Winds have to do with this?" Timothy asked, pointing to the strange darkened stairway leading into the ground.

"Come along, and I'll show you," Amos said, as he stepped into the hole where the first of many stone steps held their mysterious invitation.

"But how will we see?" Timothy protested.

"That too will become clear as we move down the stairway. Come along, Timothy. What I show you may be important to your quest." Amos motioned Timothy to the stair with a gesture of his hand after taking a few steps into the earth. When Timothy continued to

remain where he stood, Amos turned back and said, "Come on, boy. Have faith!"

Timothy looked at Amos with serious trepidation. "Okay, Amos . . . lead the way. I'm coming," Timothy said with a bit of reticence. Timothy moved to the entryway, placing his foot on the first stone step then the next, with Amos leading the way down into the earth.

As they both moved past the point where light from the open entrance started to fail, Timothy asked, "Okay, Amos, it's getting too dark to see. Are we going to light a torch or something?"

"We won't need it." Amos grinned, seeing the confusion on Timothy's face in the failing light. "Just watch . . ." Amos moved down a few more steps to a flat platform of square stone. The walls around them lit up with a bright green glow.

Timothy was in awe of what he saw around him. The ceiling of the vault, the floor, and the walls around them all emitted the greenish glow. "What is this?" Timothy asked in wonder as he turned his head all around, taking in the subterranean beauty exposed by the green light.

"I wish I could tell you," Amos said. "If you look closely, you will see the light comes from some kind of serpentine structures, like inlays in the rocks . . . Why they glow like this, I cannot tell you . . . just that they do, and by their light, we can get to where we are going."

"This is amazing, Amos. Who made all this?" Timothy gasped, with his inability to understand what he was seeing.

"I think, perhaps, we should go to the place I meant to take you before I try to answer that," Amos said quietly, though even he seemed overwhelmed by the amazing lighting structures surrounding them on every side. "Come on, we have two staircases to descend before I show you what I brought you out here for."

"Lead on, and I will follow," Timothy whispered in awed reverence.

Amos turned on the stone platform and started down another staircase. As they moved, the staircase lighted the strange serpentine inlays embedded in the stones. Amos gestured for Timothy to follow. They arrived at another landing and then went deeper into cavernous regions not seen by many others. As they continued downward on the last winding stairway, Timothy asked, "Amos, how long have you known about this place?"

"I've known about it since I was a boy," Amos said over his shoulder. "My father brought me here, and his father before him. A lot of people in Bridgedom have been here. We are not the first ones to see this, if that's what you're worried about," Amos said, as he came to the bottom of the stairs.

"But it is so amazing . . . How far does it go?" Timothy asked, looking about at the designs created by the glowing inlays.

"Don't really know . . . No one goes much further than the level where I'm taking you. But I do know there are many levels beyond there. There are doors, and doors to other doors leading down, but no one has ever ventured there. We barely understand the level where I'm taking you. I can only imagine what secrets lay beyond this level."

Timothy followed Amos into a large cavernous room. The serpentine inlays wove themselves into thick columns of green light ascending into four columns to support the elevated ceiling. At the ceiling, the glowing green columns unraveled to reveal a domed ceiling covered with multicolored stones. Each stone gleamed with its particular color. Red, yellow, blue, violet, and emerald-green colors glowed and twinkled above them. As Timothy watched, a line formed. Scarlet as blood, it crawled slowly from one side of the domed ceiling to the other.

"What is this?" Timothy asked, absently watching the incredible spectacle unfolding above him.

Amos watched with Timothy as more and more of the ceiling revealed itself. "We call this the map room. None of us are really sure of what it is, but certain things we figured out over the many years we have been coming here."

"A map of what, Amos?" Timothy asked, still looking at the amazing sight above him.

"We think it is a map of all the villages as they existed long ago. It is that which I wanted to show you. Something you might be able to use once you pass through Emansupass, the last of our known villages that exist on this map."

"I don't see a map, Amos. It just looks like a field of multicolored stars. Except for that red line that runs the whole way through everything."

"That red line is what gave it away, Timothy. See how most of the stars, as you call them, are to the one side of the line?" Amos looked to Timothy and realized he understood. Then Amos turned to the ceiling. "See the green-colored stone near the red line about three or four arm's lengths from the end of the ceiling?"

"Yes, I see it," Timothy said aloud.

"That green stone signifies the village of Glade, the village just north of Stock, your home. What concerns me right now . . ." Amos stopped for a moment, then continued, "Right now, I can barely see the stone that represents Stock." He turned to Timothy for a moment then turned to look more closely at the ceiling. "Stock is represented by a very bright yellow stone. I know where it is supposed to be, but it seems to be missing." He continued to scrutinize the ceiling for the location of Stock, concerned by its absence. He strained his eyes looking where he knew the yellow stone should be. Eventually, he found the yellow gem. It was still glowing but very diminished from the times he found it before. "I found it. This rather dim yellow spot on the ceiling is the location of Stock."

"It seems very dim by comparison to the other stones. Does that mean something to you?" Timothy asked as he strained to see the location Amos pointed out.

"Not that I've seen before . . . ," Amos said with some concern in his voice. "But that is not what I brought you out her for. See above the village of Glade . . . the next stone is Wendow, a village you came *through. Then here at Bridgedom is our stone. That is the bright blue one," Amos pointed out.*

"Is there some significance to the stone's color or brightness? I see other stones that are lit up as well, but I know there isn't anything there. What's the significance of those stones?"

"There are some things we aren't sure of, Timothy. We think some of the smaller stones were places where other villages may have existed in the past. But it could also be places where the Ancients left other clues for us to follow. No one really knows what the entire map is. Most of what we know is conjecture . . . we're just guessing."

"Other than the incredible beauty of this room, what else did you want to show me Amos?" Timothy asked, still mesmerized by the enormous lighted ceiling.

"Well, what my father and I found interesting was we thought there was nothing else beyond our last known village." Amos hesitated, looking for Timothy's reaction. "See there . . ." Amos pointed to a large red stone lighted near the lowest point of the ceiling, "that red-colored stone is Emansupass."

"I see it, Amos. It looks like it is the last of the stones to be lighted," Timothy said, puzzled. He looked to Amos for some kind of explanation. If the message he received from the young woman he knew as Victoria was true, and there was nothing beyond Emansupass, then what was she trying to tell him? Did Amos bring him down here to tell him there was no point in continuing his journey? Was he telling him to stop now because there was nothing beyond Emansupass that would save Catherine . . . that she was doomed? He looked gravely at Amos then asked, "There's nothing beyond Emansupass? Nothing?"

Amos was unaware of Timothy's growing feelings of regret and fear. He was studying something on the wall below the last red lighted stone when he turned back to Timothy and said, "Timothy, my father thought the same thing as yourself, that there was nothing but the mountains beyond Emansupass. Then two solens ago, I came down here just to look at this amazing map, and I discovered something . . . something I brought you out here to see. There was more to the map."

Timothy felt a sudden faint twinge of hope that he still had a chance to save Catherine. "So where is the rest of the map? Why don't we see it? There's nothing lighted beyond the stone that's supposed to be Emansupass, right?"

"Some patience, boy," Amos reprimanded sternly as he moved further toward the center of the room. "You see, you and I have been standing at the edge of the map looking up! Once I had a thought, where I wondered why anyone would create such a large map you had to move around the room just to see it all."

"Yes, that does seem strange to make something that you would have little or no control over," Timothy pondered while he wondered what Amos was thinking.

Amos looked at Timothy and saw he was trying to follow his reasoning. "So my thought was, what was in the middle of the room? I looked and saw the four lighted columns holding up the structure of the ceiling . . . but it seemed odd."

"Odd?" Timothy asked. "Odd in what way?"

"Remember how the glowing inlays that lighted our way here twisted and ran together?" When the inlays entered this room, they consolidated to create the four glowing pillars. Why there? Why not run the system of light at the top perimeter of the room?"

"I don't know, Amos . . . I think lighting the room with the four columns is a wonderful feat. Besides, it works, doesn't it?" Timothy asked, trying to follow Amos's logic.

"Yes, that's what I thought when I first came here, but it started me thinking. Why light a room up from the center when lighting it up from the perimeter sheds light on the map more effectively? So why was it done this way?"

Timothy stood back as Amos crossed in front of him as he moved further toward the center of the room. "Should I follow, or stay here?" Amos didn't answer right away. "Amos, what do you want me to do?"

"Stay where you are for now," Amos commanded as he worked his way toward the four columns using a circular path.

"What are you doing?" Timothy called out. "Is there something I can do to help?"

"I'm looking for the way in," Amos replied.

"What do you mean? We can cross the room and walk into the middle of the columns from here?" Timothy protested.

"It was just an accident before, but I found what I want to show you by following a certain path into these columns. My father and I walked through these columns for many solens, and nothing more was revealed to us. But one time I decided to walk around the room. While I was looking at all the beautiful designs and stones, I decided to walk through the columns, and there it was . . . a hidden piece of the map."

"So how did you do it? What's the secret?" Timothy asked, intrigued by the thought he was going to see something only Amos had ever seen . . . a secret that would, perhaps, help Catherine at the time of her greatest need.

"The secret is all about the Great Bridge," Amos called back over his shoulder. "Remember, the Great Bridge is dedicated to the Four Winds. We need to enter the four columns by the north. As I saw it, four columns . . . Four Winds. So by entering the space between the columns from the north sets off a whole other map. A map of places that goes beyond Emansupass."

"So what do we look for, Amos?" Timothy asked, watching Amos scouring the floor.

"I'll know it when I see it . . ." he yelled back to Timothy. "Just stay put and come to where I am without walking through the columns when I say. Understand?"

"Yes, but we better hurry. You understand Catherine may have placed her stone in the wall already . . . It only gives me three days to find a way to save her," Timothy added with some urgency.

"I can tell you she hasn't done that yet," Amos said as seriously as he could. "While you're waiting for me, take a look at the red line that runs through the map. There, where I showed you Stock, is a gap in the red line. If you look closer at that red line, you will see a bluish glow. That's where the wall is open . . . where something is coming through."

"The orbs . . ." Timothy gasped. "Orbs have been coming through the wall since I left Leon and the others behind at Glade. The wall is still open, which means Catherine hasn't been able to place her stone yet. Stock must be under siege by orbs. Stock must be dying or dead already." Panic stuck in his throat.

"Not dead . . ." yelled Amos from across the cavernous room. "If they were dead, then Stock would have faded completely off the map . . . It's still there but only barely. I can tell they're in trouble . . . but not dead."

"But how do you know all this?" he asked, thinking the only reason the wall was still open was Catherine lost her life before she could place her stone there.

"I've watched this map ever since my father brought me here to see it. As a boy I heard stories and rumors passed from tradesmen and travelers making passage over the Great Bridge. After hearing stories of one small village or another growing or disappearing altogether, I made it a point to come and look at the map. By whatever magic or device, the map always showed the truth. That's how I know the breach is still open and that your Catherine has not closed it with her lifestone. It is also how I know Stock is still standing but is in some kind of trouble. That's why I had trouble finding it on the map." Amos watched Timothy from a place across the room, hoping what he told him would give him some kind of peace. Then he said, "Stock still stands, Timothy . . . it still stands."

Timothy looked toward Amos and nodded that he understood. He watched as Amos walked in circles around the four columns, trying to find the true northern passage into its center. Finally, Amos waved Timothy over to where he stood. "Have you found it?" Timothy asked, excited he would be seeing something very few people had seen before him . . . something to help him find what he was searching for . . . a way to save his great love.

Amos looked at the woven green inlays running from the floors, ending in the fantastic illuminated pillars. "This is it. The inlays here curve more toward the center than the others." He watched as Timothy walked quickly to where he was standing outside the circle of the four pillars. "Come this way. This may mean something to you on your journey."

Timothy walked to the side of Amos, and then together they walked through the pillars, presumably north to south. Nothing happened. "What do you want me to see? Nothing has changed . . . nothing moved."

"Nothing will happen . . ." Amos smiled with a devious look on his face. "Until we turn around and face north."

Timothy turned around and faced the direction from where they entered the center between the two columns. There before him was a map beyond the borders of Emansupass. "What am I seeing, Amos?" Timothy asked, even more amazed than when he entered the cavernous room.

"From what I have been able to tell, there seems to be another village in the mountains north of Emansupass. In fact, there appears to be two," Amos told him.

"If one is the lost village of Winterland, which I thought was just a legend, then what is the other one, and why has no one ever spoken about it?" Timothy asked, grasping for any news of where he was to look for Catherine's chance to survive.

Amos watched Timothy struggling with, what he thought, were true answers to his quest. He knew these markers were just more questions to be answered over time, and he didn't want the boy thinking his answers were satisfied. He turned Timothy to face him. "Boy, don't go assuming anything. The one you think is Winterland is marked by a small green stone. Those green stones are markers of places we either know nothing about or, as a borderline conjecture, could be an abandoned village. Now, that might mean it really is the abandoned village of Winterland, or it could be another abandoned settlement that was unable to prosper. It may be nothing, and you should consider it so until you know different. It's the other stone I really wanted you to see. That's the stone glowing green and red." Amos pointed the stone out to Timothy. "I can tell you, no other stones glow in two colors like this one. And before you ask, I don't know what it means, but it may be a mystery you have to solve before you can save Catherine."

All this puzzled Timothy, as it gave no answers, only more questions . . . questions that may or may not need to be answered in time. He turned to Amos and asked, "Does the map show a path or trail I can follow?"

"Not that I can tell," Amos said sadly, seeing this news was not what Timothy had hoped for. "But there is one more curious thing I saw from here . . ."

Timothy looked into the old man's face, "What is that, Amos?"

"If you move closer to the map, you can see it . . . there is something else."

Timothy moved until he was almost in a straight line between the two columns. Then he saw it. The stone with two colors gleamed at the top of an enormous tree. No part of the map had been illustrated this way, and the presence of this magnificent tree made the stone with two colors more of a mystery. Amos looked at Timothy, expecting another question, but he was staring, mesmerized by the presence of the tree.

"I don't know what that means either," Amos said, anticipating the question Timothy never asked. "But it does make me wonder what there is in the real world that would make this map light a stone with two colors. I don't know if it is a village. I guess it could be,

but everything else on the map is predictable, and that"—he said, *pointing to the glowing-green-then-red stone*—*"is not anything like the rest of the map."*

"Could that be where I am to go . . . to that enormous tree?" Timothy pondered out loud.

"Don't think of it as a tree . . . ," Amos scolded. "It could be something else. It's no doubt a riddle of some sort, and your ride through Vigil and Emansupass should give you time to think on it."

"I don't know what to think about. At least, I am going where no one has seen monsters," Timothy said, thinking of the orbs being released into their world while Catherine waited to stop them with the sacrifice of her lifestone. She was waiting for him to come through for her, and he was beginning to think she may have act soon or Stock would not exist when he returned . . . if he returned.

Amos thought Timothy was making fun of him and laughed back, "You ever see a monster?"

"You want to see a monster, Amos?" Timothy asked seriously. "All we have to do is turn around, and I can show you monsters," he said, thinking back to the night in Glade when the purple orbs came within sight of the village. He thought of the friends he left behind when he took this quest to keep Catherine from dying after she placed her lifestone in the wall. Timothy knew about monsters. Amos only knew them from his description. He knew Amos believed because his friend Thomas said Timothy was reliable. Everything Timothy discussed with Amos since his arrival in Bridgedom was conjecture. Now Timothy hoped the story he carried to Bridgedom would become real for Amos. Timothy took one last look at the tree and the map extending beyond Emansupass. "This is a lot to bear, Amos. I don't really know what it is I'm looking for . . . don't know what to do or how I will find my answers. While I'm on my journey for answers, people are dying trying to fight these things. When Catherine's stone is placed into the wall, either by force or willingly, she is certain to die unless I get these elusive answers. I love her, Amos, and I want a life with her. How will I get these things done in three days?"

Amos saw Timothy's concern for Catherine's life made him feel the urgency to complete his task. Amos wasn't sure what Timothy hoped to find at the place where the enigmatic two colored gem glowed on the map. Amos looked to Timothy and said, "We do a lot for love. Sometimes it all works out, and sometimes, everything we do is futile. We always think we have some control over our lives, but 'fate' seems to have a lot to do with our outcomes. But love, Timothy, it can make us go beyond the ordinary and into the extraordinary. I've seen things accomplished for love that were just impossible to do under normal circumstances. Sometimes love can beat 'fate,' and I am certain this is one of those times. You're going to be the one to beat fate, Timothy . . . and you will do it out of love. That's a powerful weapon . . . a powerful tool. Don't you forget it and don't abandon it when it gets too difficult to go on. Remember what I'm telling you, and it will get you through."

"Thanks, Amos . . . I will remember," Timothy said, sincerely moved Amos tried to encourage him. The two men, one young and one old, walked back through the wrought stone passages to the surface where they placed the large black stone over the hidden stairway. Together, they went to where Timothy tied his horse. Timothy climbed up then looked down at Amos. "I think it is time to go."

"Yes," Amos said, as he clapped his hand against Timothy's leg. "I kept you much longer than I intended."

"I will need to stop in Vigil and let them know about the wall. Is there someone I should talk to?" Timothy asked, thinking he had at least another day at Vigil and another day at Emansupass before he ventured into the unknown mountain passes.

"I knew your quest was important when you came to me. Thomas from Wendow sent word after you came to help you in any way I could. I already sent messengers to Vigil and Emansupass to pass on the news of the wall breach. The alarms are already in motion, Timothy. All that's left to do is find a way to save Catherine, and that answer, no doubt, lies in the mystery of the stone that glows with two colors." As an afterthought, Amos called out after him, "When you get to Emansupass, look for a man called Timmerloo. The villagers there should know him."

Second Chances

Tell me about the next battle . . .

In the early part of 2002, Lois had little else she could do except return to work, continue physical therapy twice a week, and follow her chemotherapy protocols. Just after surgery in November 2001, the oncologist wanted a tumor marker done. The result was 464.6. At the time, it was an alarming number; but after several rounds of chemo, the markers backed down to 265 by the beginning of January. In spite of how she was feeling, Lois continued to manage speakers and hold meetings for her support group in January and then started investigating stories for the newsletter on the Internet and professional magazines. By mid-January, she ventured out to teach a class of student LPNs about breast cancer at a local school. She kept in touch with fellow breast cancer advocates from the NBCC, Linda Creed, and DOD by phone or e-mail.

Her oncologist's recommendation was to have CA 27-29s drawn monthly until he saw a definitive decrease in the tumor marker. By the end of February, the marker decreased to 183.7. The chemo was working, and Lois said she felt more like herself. The improved markers gave her hope she would be around long enough to continue all the things she enjoyed doing. However, after several months' treatments, she was starting to struggle with the side effects of chemotherapy. Trying to manage working a forty-hour work week with fatigue, weakness, and attending physical therapy was about all she could handle at the time.

By March, the CA 27-29 had not decreased. The result came back at 186.9, a slight increase over the previous month, which meant the current chemotherapy was probably not going to work. Using decisions based on current protocols and contacts Lois made with scientists working in the field of cancer, she and the oncologist came up with a different chemotherapy protocol. By the beginning of

April, the markers dropped again to 166. What Lois learned from her markers was this cancer was not as predictable as the first one back in 1992. This was more persistent and, if unchecked, could metastasize very quickly to other parts of her body. The other part she had to consider was when certain agents are used to treat a cancer initially, those agents are usually not recommended to use again. In other words, some chemo agents have a lifetime endpoint . . . They can't be used again. For Lois, this would be an ongoing battle that would last from now until the end of her life. Still, her vigilance would be the instrument that would save her time and again.

As with any time since the beginning of her support group, Lois continued to write the quarterly newsletter in spite of how she was feeling or what she was doing. Though her winter of 2002 was relatively quiet, allowing her time to recuperate, she looked forward to the events of the upcoming spring.

(Editorial by Lois A. Anderson dated March 12, 2002)

Well, it is now the end of February with little snow in sight. I am hoping that we soon get some rain or snow so that our water supplies begin to look better than they have over the last several months. Without some increase in water levels, we will be unable to open our pool this summer, and I would sorely miss that. Even though I am not a swimmer, I do enjoy floating around the pool on my big rubber inflatable lounger and relaxing that way. I also find that whenever, I can see a large pool of clear blue water I feel much calmer. Call it imagination or what you will, but I do think there is some connection in healing yourself by using some mind/body techniques.

The Department of Defense Breast Cancer Research Program needs consumer advocates, who will be paid an honorarium for their hard work. You do need to have access to a computer in order to participate as a reviewer. If anyone would like to know what to expect as a consumer reviewer, please call me. I have done this for five years with the Department of Defense. The deadline is coming up fast.

With a presentation to do locally, the Advocacy conference coming up in Washington, and a presentation I am a part of for the International Congress meeting of the Oncology Nursing Society also taking place in Washington, DC, my early spring will go by very quickly.

> *BUT the one advantage this year is that I will be able to see the cherry blossoms since several weekends will be spent in this governmental town.*
>
> *Please check out the enclosures with this newsletter. You may be interested in some of the events taking place. You just never know!*
>
> *Looking forward to those cherry blossoms,*
>
> *Lois*

Even before March began, Lois returned to her advocacy work. She was in Washington DC on March 1 for the NBCC Team Leader Conference, which started on a Friday, after she finished work, and lasted until Sunday afternoon when she returned. I didn't mind, since she was pacing herself better, and it was a way to affirm she was still out there making a difference for breast cancer patients and survivors. She really believed she could stop any woman from having to walk in her shoes. It was her chance to change things for the better. The team leader training she attended was just a precursor for the NBCC's advocacy conference being held in the latter part of April.

Lois completed one of the new chemo cycles on April 5, 2002, a Friday night that year. She did this in case she had any problem with nausea, vomiting, or fatigue. It was a way she could manage her symptoms at home over the weekend so by Monday, she would be able to return to work when she was feeling better. However, Lois was beginning to feel the long-term effects of prolonged chemotherapy. The fatigue was bad enough to consult the oncologist. He made the suggestion to go on Neupogen, which would be given as an injection the week before she had her chemotherapy. The reason for her fatigue was the platelet count was dropping to very low levels during the third week after chemotherapy. Giving the injectable Neupogen would improve her counts, lessen her fatigue, and enable her to take successive rounds of chemo.

It was still the middle of flu season when she needed to go on something to boost her blood count, and Lois had made commitments that put in her large crowds of people. Everyone was concerned that she was predisposed to all kinds of illnesses, which could delay her treatments or possibly put her in the hospital. Somehow, Lois made it through that rough time and continued her quest to improve treatments for people living with breast cancer throughout the country by lobbying senators and congressmen in Washington DC. I think Lois saw this as her last chance at taking part in what many organizations across the country were doing to improve care, improve treatments, and get new and innovative ideas to the consumers quickly through political advocacy.

(Editorial by Lois A. Anderson dated May 29, 2002)

I am finally back home to stay until the end of June when I must return to Atlanta, Georgia. After two trips to Washington, DC and a trip to Atlanta, Georgia within three weeks time, I have decided to rest awhile. The two trips to Washington, DC were for very different reasons.

On the first trip to Washington, DC, I was part of a panel of 4 members from the Consumer Advisory Panel to the Oncology Nursing Society who did a presentation to approximately 1500 attendees at the conference. The session was called, Let's Really Talk-the Patient's Perspective, and it had to do with communication among patient, family members, nurses, and physicians. This was the first time I had ever spoke before such a huge group, and I found it a little nerve wracking. However, things went well for our presentation.

On the second trip to DC, the following weekend, I attended the National Breast Cancer Coalition's Advocacy Conference and led groups of women around Capitol Hill to lobby our congressmen on the legislative priorities of NBCC. This was fun and challenging and by now I am an old hat after having done this for 3 years as a Team Leader.

And from May 8 to 10, I was in Atlanta, Georgia at the national office of the American Cancer Society training as a stakeholder in their Stakeholder Peer Review Program after being selected to participate from the Pennsylvania Division. In this program I will review grants and decide on funding after my training sessions are completed. I must return to Atlanta the end of June to observe peer review panels in action, and that should be fun!

And now for the crowning glory in all this, my son is getting married in about 10 weeks. Yikes!! Lots to do but no time to do it in. So, if you see me without any hair in my wig you'll know what happened.

Here's hoping that life will slow down soon, but it never does . . .

Take it easy in the heat, but enjoy the summer.

Lois

Our son was getting married over the summer, and soon we would be experiencing the "empty nest" syndrome. Lois continued her chemotherapy treatments, and I was giving her the injectable Neupogen at home. Her tumor markers were down to about 100 at the beginning of June 2002. She did everything she describes in her newsletters and held down a full-time job besides. I was busy helping my son renovate an old house he bought in a nearby town. It needed everything, and I enlisted the help of everyone I could think of in order to get it ready by the wedding.

At our own home, I was in the middle of remodeling my bathroom. The general clean-up work was not a problem, but I had to wait on the plumber to remodel the bathtub area before I could move on. I think we were all frustrated by the slow but steady changes going on around us. Eventually, everything was completed. Lois had her new bathroom, my son had his refinished house, the wedding was over, and we all had a chance to breathe again. When Lois said something about going to Williamsburg, Virginia, for a vacation in September, I jumped at the chance. We were exhausted and needed to get away from everything.

The short but pleasant trip to Virginia took us both away from the chemo, the testing, the telephone, the jobs, the impossible schedules, the day-to-day demands on our time, and for that short time, we were just two people enjoying each other's company. Walking the old streets of Williamsburg, Virginia, seeing that simpler time, moving at a slower pace, allowed us time to forget about her cancer. We acted like we had no worries on that special impromptu vacation. But in reality, Lois was clearly not out from under the shadow of her breast cancer recurrence. Tumor markers taken before we left on vacation were only down by twenty points after being on the new chemotherapy for almost three months. The results were not encouraging. We tried to forget about all that, if just for a few days, and we succeeded.

Of course, once we were home, the activity began again. Though Lois was not back into her college program, the activity around our house made it seem like she was. Lois utilized her time to continue the fight against breast cancer with her lobbying efforts. This time she was back in Washington DC with the American Cancer Society. Her newsletter explains her activities very well.

(Editorial by Lois A. Anderson dated September 11, 2002)

I have just finished one of the busiest summers yet. My son was married in August 17 and most of this time has been spent in preparation for the wedding and the rehabilitation of a semi-detached house that he and his wife bought. Besides that the remodeling of our bathroom which was supposed to be finished by now is nowhere near being finished, I guess Mom's bathroom has to take a backseat to this new house. Oh well!

I am preparing to make three trips within the last two weeks of September. The first trip will take me to Washington, DC with a group of Community Ambassadors for the American Cancer Society from Pennsylvania. Most of us were selected based on our past lobbying and legislative efforts or our connection with the Relay for Life. We will be lobbying the Pennsylvania members of Congress along with other Community Ambassadors from all the other states in the nation who will lobby their representatives. This represents a major new effort for the American Cancer Society and puts a face on their efforts to effectively lobby for cancer initiatives. The whole event is called Celebration on the Hill and it links Relay for Life, the signature fundraiser for ACS with legislative advocacy efforts.

My second trip will be a more relaxing one to celebrate both our anniversary and my birthday in Williamsburg, Virginia. This should be fun since I love Colonial Williamsburg. We will be staying in the newly completed Woodlands Inn that the Colonial Williamsburg Foundation has added to its list of hotels.

And my third trip will be for educational purposes to gather as much new information as I can and report back to you about the latest research in breast cancer. I will be flying to Orlando, Florida for the Department of Defense Breast Cancer Research Program's Conference called the Era of Hope 3. This is a free trip for me because I have participated five times on the peer review panels for the DOD, and at it we will learn of what the scientists have found through using the money that we awarded them during the review of their grant applications. One of three presenters is Danny Welch, PhD from Hershey Medical Center and he will talk about the metastasis gene he has located. The money from his research came from this Department of Defense Program. This just shows you what kind of difficult research Penn State is involved in. I will also get to see many of my fellow advocates and we should have a good time.

All these trips should be fun, but each for a different reason. That's what makes life so fantastic!

If you've seen Lake Redman lately, you'll realize what I mean when I say: Conserve your water!

And here's hoping we get rain this fall and snow this winter.

Lois

The year turned the corner from the one before it. Where Lois and I were almost prepared to say good-bye to each other at this time last year, we now embraced. The tumor markers ranging in the upper 400s the previous year were now down to 42.8 by the middle of December. Los was now a full-time chemotherapy patient. There would not be many times from the time she started treatments in late 2001 until 2010 when she would not be on chemotherapy. Schedules to accommodate her treatments with her daily activities were created to keep everything organized. When she had appointments in other parts of the country, she would work with her oncologist to give the chemo before she left on her assignments or shortly after her return. Everything had to be planned, measured, and weighed for effect and consequences of early or late treatments . . . Nothing was certain. These were indeed the "rough seas" she described on a quilt square earlier in her life.

In December 2002, Lois was called to Philadelphia by the Linda Creed Foundation to receive the Suzanne H. Kaye Award for

Advocacy. The award was only given to someone who was a great advocate for breast cancer issues. This was not an award that was given out very often, and until this year, only one other person had ever received it besides Lois. That person was Fran Visco, president of the National Breast Cancer Coalition. In 2002, the Linda Creed Foundation recognized Lois for all the advocacy work she had done voluntarily over the years.

At the luncheon, a speaker came to the podium and recited all the accomplishments Lois made since her diagnosis in 1992. The list was so long, Lois had a hard time trying not to look embarrassed. I watched as she went to the podium with a speech she made up off the top of her head. She sounded like she practiced it all night. She was gracious and humble before her audience as she always was. When she returned to the table, she asked me, "Did I really do all that?" I told her, "Yes, and probably more." She looked at me with tears in her eyes . . . happy tears, but tears. I think it took this award for Lois to realize what an impact she had already made with her life. Still, I don't believe she fully realized what she had done for breast cancer patients, survivors, and caregivers across the country.

(Editorial by Lois A. Anderson dated December 10, 2002)

I just returned from a weekend trip to Philadelphia where I was presented with the Suzanne H. Kaye Award by the Linda Creed Breast Cancer foundation. This award was set up by Ms. Kaye's family to honor her memory after her death from breast cancer. Ms. Kaye so wanted to be able to go to Washington to lobby Congress but was unable to do so before her death. However, she did make a huge difference in the lives of breast cancer patients at both, Abington Memorial Hospital and Temple University Hospital with her counseling and support groups. My selection for the award was based on all the work I have done in breast cancer and the presenter of the award, Suzanne's daughter Judy, listed all of the things I have done. It seemed to be an unending list as I stood beside her on the podium, and I could not believe all of it. However, my husband assured me that ALL of it was true. I was given a standing ovation by almost 200 people, which I really felt embarrassed by because I still cannot believe that this award was really given to me. I thought there had to be someone else more deserving.

Well, my next out of town trip will be to participate as a member of the American Cancer Society's peer review committee for Primary Care Physician Awards in Cancer Prevention and Control. This is truly an honor that I am looking forward to with great enthusiasm. It is one more way I can voice the opinion of the cancer patient/survivor/ advocate and have a real effect on the cancer research done in this country.

I am in the midst of preparing to return to my Temple graduate school program in January and look forward to getting back to studying and school and all of academia. I will be doing my internship work with the Heartland Hospice, part of my overall educational plan of following the experiences of an oncology patient from the beginning to the end.

Christmas will be here before you know it. Here's to one more year of happiness and good health. Hope you have a good 2003.

Be careful on the ICE and SNOW,

Lois

Lois desperately wanted to finish her master's degree in social work. She discussed the possibility with both her oncologist and me. When she considered the CA 27-29 had dropped to a manageable level and the current chemotherapy was working for her, she decided to return. This time, however, she was exercising more caution with her field placement. She chose a hospice unit close to home, which allowed her more time to concentrate on her studies. She cut back on her advocacy work, though to be honest, she never stopped trying to advocate through phone calls, e-mails, and faxes. It was a difficult thing for Lois to drop some of her advocacy work, but I think she realized she never wanted to get to that point of exhaustion again. Besides, the chemo was working, and she didn't want any additional stressors to compromise any recovery she could make.

Magic

Tell me about magic . . .

The world kept spinning while I struggled to keep balance on an unsubstantiated facade. Time was the journey where strategies of forward ventures twisted themselves into byzantine judgments. The imposed journey always displayed ambiguous paths to the lost, guiding them to destinations fertile with choices and insurmountable deceptions for failure. The times I walked in dreams, I found my destination by abandoning the noxious paths to wander the wilderness guided, not by roads and paths but by signs and the powerful charisma of the Poet's Tree.

In dreams, I found my way there. I pressed for answers to guide my life of chaos and looked back at the ruins burning behind me. "Where is hope?" I asked, while the tree stood silently before me. "Where do I find my path? Where do I go from here?"

From behind the tree came the voice of a friend who died too young in a war we never asked for. "Remember when you made the swing . . ."

"I remember," I told the hazy dark figure.

"It was magic. We were children there. We are children here. It is magic."

"But where do I go from here? Where will my journeys take me when all I see about me are the ruins of what was? The journeys of what will be and what is to come are almost unbearable. How do I keep my feet on the ground?"

"You don't," said the voice of my friend, as I watched his visage washing away in the sky behind the great tree. "Get your feet off the ground. Find the magic you once knew on the swing at your grandfather's farm. Remember the magic . . ."

"Magic?" I asked, but he was gone, just a glimpse of a life I once knew. I had no more questions. I could feel again. I put my back against the enormous tree and fell into another dream.

Leon concocted what he thought was his best creation to keep the destructive orbs safely away when they moved from their high ground into the blue mists. While he worked on his solvents and solutions, he had Rand search for the best point of departure into the ominous terrain. He hoped some closer point would give them some advantage to make it into the village of Stock. Even from this distance, Leon's work was disturbed by desperate sounds echoing from the embattled village. Stock was being assaulted incessantly by the killing violet orbs flailing their deadly tendrils through the walls of flame with monstrous consequences. Still the people of Stock fought them, stopping any further egress of the orbs into their village. From Leon's observations, the scene playing out before him confirmed the orbs possessed a certain consciousness of warlike ability. When one orb became scorched by the fires, another moved in to take its place. The orbs behind the main line of offense brought the scorched orbs back into the blue mist, where they went into a stage of immobility, then metamorphosed completely healed, ready to do battle again. Nothing was going to stop them. They were savage and relentless. The only motivation Leon could determine for the orbs' aggressiveness was to destroy the civilization humans had created. They were here to annihilate everyone.

Rand walked to where Leon was blending numerous solvents together. "So how are we going to do this?" he asked, knowing Leon was doing his best to get them all out of this alive.

"I think we should test one of these flasks before we attempt anything," Leon replied, not looking up from what he was doing.

"How are Penny and Victoria doing?" he asked, stopping a moment to give Rand his attention.

Rand looked tired but had a certain amount of excitement in his voice. "Both have changed out of skirts to trousers and light leather shoes. They are presently preparing our belongings into parcels we can carry if we need to leave the wagon and horses behind."

"That's good . . . It may well come to that," Leon stated as he looked out over the ocean of blue mist separating them from the village of Stock. "Well, Rand, I think it is time we tried these concoctions out . . . What do you say?"

"I guess we have to start sometime . . . why not?" Rand stated, watching Leon pick up a flask and insert a wick.

"Some of what I mixed up ought to clear a decent path, provided we are fast enough and if the blast stuns the orbs long enough to make our crossing," Leon stated as he looked around for Penny and Victoria.

"Did you say 'blast'?" Rand exclaimed. "But I thought these were just firebombs!" Rand bellowed, thinking Leon created such volatile combustibles that they would blow themselves up just carrying them.

Leon saw Rand's abject aversion to his creations and said, "They are . . . but did you want to be walking over fire yourself? Can you imagine what the horses will do if they have to walk over fire? I can tell you myself . . . they won't like it, not one bit." He waited for the horror on Rand's face to mellow a bit then continued, "No, I didn't think either you or the horses would want to try to walk through wall of fire either, so I made the flasks in a manner where they should explode away from where they land. That way, the flammable liquids inside will fall in a perimeter, or a large circle, away from the original blast. Basically, one of these," Leon said, as he lifted a flask from a box to show Rand, "will produce a circular wall of flame that will burn long enough to allow us to pass through about a fourth of a parcel before we meet the wall of flame on the other side. We only need to pass through a thin wall of flame to be inside and safe from *the orbs." Leon turned to Rand who was already looking back in disbelief. "Make sense?" Leon asked.*

"Not entirely," Rand exclaimed. "If this fire will burn enough to repel the orbs, how is it we won't burn running through the wall ourselves?"

Leon said, "We need to cover ourselves in wet leather, Rand. Before we leave here, we need to soak the leather outfits that I asked you all to wear this morning. We will carry additional flasks to soak them whenever we move through the fire walls. At the halfway point, there is a modest stream where we can resupply our water before we reach Stock."

"And the flasks you made . . . how will they travel so we don't blow ourselves up?"

"I have them stoppered and laying in a sealed box of water until we need them."

Rand was still unconvinced. They were safe where they were, and he didn't want to move off this hill unless he had to. He knew they had to stop the invasion of the orbs, but certainly there were others trying to do the same. Why should he risk his life? He looked at Leon and asked, "These firebombs . . . are such things possible? Will they do what you say, or are we risking our lives for nothing?"

"I guess we need to try one out, won't we?" Leon said, as Rand's jaw dropped in amazement. Seeing Rand react, he continued, "I just don't do solvents. I also do explosives, and I brought along some of my finest."

"So we have to be careful in how we handle these . . . explosive firebombs?" Rand asked with a distinct distrust and trepidation in his voice.

"Not so much," Leon explained. "The flasks are harmless until the fuses are lit. Then we only have a few moments until the fire hits the accelerant, and . . . poof . . . the whole things goes up. When the wall of fire goes off in all directions, clearing an area big

enough to make some progress toward Stock, we will move through the wall."

Rand remained unconvinced. Leon was either brilliant or a fool, and he hadn't decided which was true. He would have to see to believe. Knowing the wagon had a goodly amount of supplies, he asked Leon, "How many of these things did you make?"

"I had enough materials to make eighteen of them. It looks like there are about two parcels left to get to the village of Stock, which will give us nine flasks for each parcel. That should be more than enough to get us there. We still will need to have one flask left when we get to Stock," Leon said, as Penny and Victoria joined them at the front of the wagon.

"What do we need the last flask for, Leon?" Victoria asked after overhearing the conversation between the two men.

Leon looked seriously at his fellow travelers. He looked to Penny, then Rand, then finally to Victoria. "The orbs are problem enough, as you know. I'm fairly certain my firebombs will service us well as we cross. Our biggest problem arises at Stock where the villagers have set up an enormous fire wall to keep the orbs from overtaking the village. We need to open it . . . if only for a few seconds . . . so we must open their fire wall with an explosion that will take the air away from their fire. That should give us a few seconds to get through"—Leon looked in Penny's direction—"or else we will be trapped between the orbs and the villagers' wall of fire."

"Frankly, Leon," Rand said with a shudder, "that doesn't sound like a position we want to find ourselves in."

Leon looked at Rand and shook his head. "No, Rand, we definitely do not want to find ourselves in that position. That's why I'm hoping we have at least one of these flasks left when we get to Stock . . . or we will be trapped."

"So we are going to test one of the eighteen?" Rand asked, with the realization they were sacrificing one of the firebombs just for sport.

"No, I made one more," Leon said. He looked in Penny's direction and asked, "Could you fetch the white flask there at the end of the wagon?" Penny went to the end of the wagon where she found a white flask sitting alone.

Penny examined the milky white flask as she turned it over in her hands then walked the few steps back to Leon. "All the other flasks are pink, Leon . . . Did you run out of the pink ones?" Penny asked curiously.

"The white one is the one that might send us on our way . . . if it works." Leon paused like he had something else to say. "The one you are holding, Penny, that one is for 'hope,' our hope and for the hope we can find Timothy's Catherine and deliver the message Victoria's friend Amelia died for. Hope was all we really ever had. Isn't that what you told us?"

Penny handed the white flask to Leon then slid her arm around his waist. "So it's down to hope, my dear? I say, let's give these hateful orbs a taste of what an old villager can do."

Rand was impressed by Penny's courage to follow her husband into this quagmire of blue mists. He turned to Leon with a smile and said, "You heard the lady, Leon, let's be at it. What can I do to help?"

Let's light this one up and give it a try," Leon said with the faintest wisp of a smile. Rand lit the wick on the white flask and threw it into the ocean of blue mists before them. For a second, nothing happened. Suddenly, the blue mist imploded, then a blinding white circle lifted out of the mist. First, it exploded into itself then rose in a dome of orange flames, which forced the mists away from its origin. When the dome melted back, a ring of fire remained on all sides with the empty ground before them. Leon's artistry with solvents had to be admired.

Rand stood by the wagon with his mouth wide open, speechless. Victoria reached out and grabbed Penny's hand. Even Leon seemed impressed with himself as his faint smile broke into a big grin. "I think I may have made too many," he said, as he surveyed the huge expanse of ground laid bare before the wagon. "Come on, everybody. Get on the wagon. We are going to Stock."

Victoria was the first to jump into the wagon, followed by Penny and Leon. Rand just stood there impressed with Leon's handiwork.

"So, Rand, are you going to stand there all day? I suggest you join us. The orbs aren't friendly. They will come for you if you stay here." Rand looked at Leon sitting on the front seat of the wagon, ready to engage the first part of their journey. He nodded to Leon, then jumped onto the back of the wagon.

"That was impressive," Rand finally said as Leon forced the unwilling horses through the short fire barrier before them.

When they were through the wall and safely traveling over the cleared path, Leon leaned back and said, "Glad you enjoyed it. Now let's hope our luck holds out. Get another flask ready, Rand. Be ready to throw it as hard as you can in front of us when I tell you."

Rand reached back and drew the first pink flask from the water-filled box and removed the stopper. Penny handed him the fuse he would need to light it. Leon had arranged the flasks, allowing for quick dispersal if needed. Penny had charge over the fuses, keeping them dry so they would ignite when the time came to use them.

As Rand prepared the next flask, Penny lit a lantern to keep a ready flame available. Meanwhile, Leon pulled the horses the last bit of distance they created with the white flask. To the left and right of the wagon, the small band of travelers watched as the orbs hungrily attempted to get past the fire barrier. The path they crossed was rutted by the orbs' constant digging, but it was still possible to travel. Leon watched as the fire ring started to fade behind him, allowing a few orbs to make some progress through the wall. Beyond them, hundreds of orbs prepared to attack. The purple spheres prepared glowing reddish spots, ready to propel their deadly tendrils into the four humans.

"Rand, light a flask now, and hurry. They are coming across the fire wall fast."

Rand had the next one in his hand and, with the ready flame provided by Penny's lantern, lit the fuse. The fuse caught, and Rand threw the first pink firebomb into the blue mists before them. Before the orbs were upon them, Leon plowed the horses through the next fire wall. As Leon pushed forward, he noted the terrain getting rougher. The ground was sliced by random incisions by orbs digging themselves into lower ground. The incline they traveled was going deeper and deeper into a ravine . . . a ravine the orbs created, making an environment they could survive and fight from. Leon's thoughts became uneasy as he considered he may have brought them into a trap they could not get out of. Leon watched as the first of the pink explosions started failing. "Rand, set off another one," Leon shouted. Again, Penny helped Rand light the fuse of the second firebomb. Then Rand threw it into the blue mists.

Leon pushed the horses through the next wall of flames, noting the deeper irregularity of the ground beneath them. The broken earth was so torn up that any road that may have existed to Stock was erased by the orbs' constant digging. Leon was certain they would need to abandon the wagon, making their progress slower than it already was. Leon sensed an intelligence ruling the actions of the orbs. He was starting to understand what they did or how they attacked the villages was not as random or as indiscriminate as it appeared to be at first. The orbs were attacking Stock with a purpose. The orbs were also slowing his progress. While Leon did not see any particular defense mounted against his firebombs, he felt there was something he may have missed in his calculations . . . something that would prove fatal if he didn't fix it fast. Still, he didn't know what flaw laid in his plan. His plan worked to keep them safe so far. Rand still possessed most of the eighteen flasks. Even if they abandoned the wagon, they could still ride the horses faster than they could walk the remaining distance to Stock.

The last firebomb was beginning to die out, and the mists carrying the deadly orbs were starting to flow toward the wagon. "Rand, get another one off now!" Leon screamed, as the blue mists lunged toward them about twenty arm's lengths away from them.

Penny lit another of the flasks and handed it to Rand. Rand pitched the firebomb far into the mists, with the resultant fire ring almost reaching the wagon. Leon hurried the wagon into the fire wall as quickly as the horses could take them. When they made it safely through the wall, the front wheel hit a deep cut in the hardened soil and snapped. The result jarred the horses to a standstill, while the contents of the wagon spilled across the flat boards of the wagon. Fortunately, Penny secured the box containing the firebombs between her feet. They shifted, but the contents of the box were safe. The lantern for lighting the fuses was extinguished. The wheel was beyond repair and, any time they had, could not be used to fix it.

A quick look was all Leon could spare on the broken wheel. He jumped off the wagon and shouted in alarm. "Everyone . . . the time has come to gather the supplies we have and make ready to move. The fire walls will not last long, so we have very little time. Everything else must stay behind. Rand, help me with the horses then come back and help the ladies tie the gear to the horses. We'll use the horses for as far as they will take us. The wagon is gone . . . please hurry. I'll get the firebombs."

Penny looked at Leon and saw the weight of his decision to go into Stock bearing down on him. It was hard to be optimistic, and she felt very discouraged she had to leave her beloved belongings behind. They may never see Glade again, their house, or their friends. It could be they may never be found or what became of them. They may have given up everything just to die here. Penny looked around and saw the blue mists encroaching on the fire barriers around them. She looked to Leon and spoke gently to him, "We may lose each other as we ride. It is very difficult to see anything when the mists draw close to us." It wasn't what Penny had on her mind as she spoke to her husband, but her point was well taken. She looked again to Leon and said, "I have never been afraid in all my life, but I am afraid now."

Penny's tears were proof enough of what she said, as he gathered her into his arms and kissed her. He pulled back and looked into her eyes. He realized they were in a very perilous position, a situation where they may not survive. He left Penny to attend to the matters at hand before the fire ring diminished to the point where they would have to use another one. "Rand, can you manage the firebombs by yourself on horseback?"

"I can still throw them, but I won't be able to light them and throw them far enough away so we won't be caught in the fire ring as it starts up. I'll be liable to light the whole box up at once," Rand told him as he strapped the last pack onto the horses.

"Then we shall put you between Penny and Victoria, while I take the lead," Leon replied. He then turned to Penny and Victoria, "We need a strong rope to run among the horses. We need to do it quickly." Leon motioned to Victoria. Victoria picked up the command and immediately took a rope from the wagon and began lashing it through the rings of the harnesses left on the four horses. While Victoria worked, Leon said to Penny, "I need two lanterns lighted. You and Victoria stay on either side of Rand. Keep a ready fire on both sides of him for whatever what we run into."

Victoria and Penny were afraid of Leon's plan. Penny spoke up, "Leon, do you mean to sacrifice us to get into Stock?"

Leon turned to Penny, distraught that she would think he would allow any harm to come to her. "I will not sacrifice anyone." Then Leon looked to the far perimeters of the fire walls dying around them. "But I look around, and I see killing and hatred, just because we exist." Tears brimming in his eyes, he faced his wife and continued, "I don't think we will all make it to Stock. I think we were walking into a trap ever since we came into the mists." Leon looked over Penny's shoulder, watching the fire walls diminish dangerously. He shouted to Rand, "We need to get another one lit and out, now . . ."

Rand prepared the fuse, but before he lighted it, he said, "Leon, we need to be ready to move when I throw this. Everyone, soak your leathers and be ready. Once this explodes, we need to cross the fire wall quickly before the orbs get through this one."

"I know, Rand . . . I know!" Leon shouted petulantly. He turned to Penny. "Do you have the lanterns ready?"

"Yes, Leon," Penny replied, terrified by Leon's abruptness.

"Both lit?" he asked Penny and Victoria tersely, making sure everything was ready to move when Rand threw the firebomb.

Penny nodded her head and lifted the two lighted lanterns for Leon to see.

"Victoria," Leon screamed, "are you ready with the horses?"

Victoria hurried from Penny's side and ran to the front of the wagon. "Yes, Leon, I have them ready."

Leon shouted, "Soak your leathers. Whatever water you have in your flasks, soak down your horse's legs. Get ready to move," Leon commanded, as he watched the flickering fire wall give way to the mists. The orbs would be certain to follow. Leon jumped onto the lead horse and waved everyone to do the same. Penny and Victoria were trying unsuccessfully to tie the box of flasks onto Rand's horse. Leon looked back at the three still standing on the ground. "Rand, if we can't secure the firebombs on the horses, then put them in your pockets. Victoria! Penny! Whatever Rand can't carry, you two will have to. Hurry, for the sake of the Winds . . . hurry! I see the blue mists starting over the fire walls. We are out of time!"

Rand threw the lighted firebomb into the mists. When the explosion sent out its blinding white ring, driving the mists and orbs back once again, Rand filled his jacket with six of the remaining flasks. He handed four to Penny and four to Victoria. "Here," Rand said, "take these and mount your horses now! I can carry the rest."

Rand settled himself on his horse, while Penny and Victoria climbed the horses on either side of him, positioning the lanterns into a prepared niche hollowed out in the harnesses. Leon looked back at his vagabond riders and shouted, "Now hurry and follow!" Leon pushed his horse through the fire wall and into the other side. The rope binding the riders slackened as Penny and Victoria passed through the wall. Then the rope tightened as they waited for Rand to come through. They all watched the wall of flame as the first horse leg passed through then the rest, as Rand made it through the fire unscathed.

"Rand, what happened?" Leon screamed over the rage of the fire wall around them.

"That was close." Rand breathed. "One of the orbs was almost on top of me when I came through the wall. If they had taken me, most of the firebombs would be gone now!" Rand looked out over the expanse cleared by the firebomb.

It was then Leon realized his deadly miscalculation. He looked at Rand still catching his breath from his near misadventure. "Rand . . . look over to our west." Rand surveyed the western edge of the fire ring and realized Leon's concern. "Our fire wall is dropping down into lower ground. My fire walls won't be high enough to keep the orbs from coming over it." Leon thought a moment then continued, "The walls will hold for now, but we need to be cautious about the terrain. If one of the firebombs doesn't create a wall high enough to protect us, we will have to use another one immediately and change direction."

"That may mean we will use everything we have left just surviving this mire," Rand said, despair pulling his voice into hard edges.

Leon looked back at Rand sitting on the horse between Victoria and Penny. "How many left?"

"We have fourteen left . . . I hope we're at least halfway there," Rand replied.

Leon shook his head. "In these mists, it's hard to tell where we are or how close to Stock we might be." He looked around, trying to see where the next firebomb would do the most good. He spotted an area almost level to the ground where they stopped. "Over here, Rand . . . get the next one ready. We'll try to clear areas that are not so deep."

Rand lighted the fuse from the lantern offered by Victoria. He threw the lighted flask directly where Leon requested. The blast cleared the mists, revealing a shallow area, which deepened on all sides, allowing but a narrow footpath of tortured terrain at the far end of the fire ring. When Rand saw what was revealed, he pushed his horse to Leon and said, "I don't think the horses will take us across that." Rand pointed to the narrow strip of ground leading off into the mists as Leon turned his eyes away from him.

"We don't have the time or the resources to go back now," Leon said. "We have to gather what we need off the horses then leave them behind. Quick, everyone, get what you need and then let's be off before the fire wall dies. These things would have us trapped here if we don't hurry."

Penny and Victoria ran to the horses and quickly pulled parcels from the horses they had attached only a short time ago. They shouldered their packs and ran through the next fire wall, hurrying to the narrow pathway lying before them.

The Edges of the Borders

Tell me about returning . . .

There are no "clean margins" in metastatic breast cancer. The concept of "clean margins" only portends to those who caught cancer in its very early stages. From then on, those people who enter the realm of "metastasis" only hope for remission, which is only a degree of respite from the cancer trying to overtake the body. In 2003, Lois would find she was in such a time, as markers diminished to the comfortable level of 26.6 by mid-March.

Lois was well enough to return to college and her master's degree in social work. I think somehow, she wanted the work she was doing in her work life to coincide with the work she was doing as a breast cancer advocate. In hindsight, I think she realized her chance to change things was becoming unreachable unless she concentrated both her professional life and her volunteer life together. This idea was appealing, and she must have realized her life was going to be significantly shorter since the diagnosis with metastatic breast cancer. I believe she wanted to make the most of what remained of her life. She had no way of knowing how long she had but wanted the tools she needed to help everyone in the time she had left.

(Editorial by Lois A. Anderson dated March 18, 2003)

Wow, I can't believe it. I started back to school this semester and my first semester is halfway completed. What a way to jump in with both feet! My field placement (internship) is with Heartland Hospice here in York and I am having a wonderful time learning and taking care of the hospice patients. A friend of mine had warned me to "leave the cancer thing alone this semester and enjoy yourself," but of course I didn't pay any attention to her and I'm oh so glad I didn't do that. I would have never had the kind of wonderful experiences I am now getting. One thing I hadn't planned on is how overwhelming it can be to be back in school once again with papers and projects to be done. The one thing that keeps me going though is the fact that after this semester I have only 9 more credits to finish. For me that means I will finish my Master's in Social Work by May 2004 and then I will be official.

I am looking forward to the professional conference that is slated for April 25th because, hopefully, I will be able to meet a heroine of mine, Hester Hill Schnipper. I have admired Hester from afar as she is both a breast cancer survivor and social worker, too. I carry an article in my briefcase that has to do with Hester, her breast cancer and how she now practices as a social worker. The article is based on the fact that breast cancer changed her life in ways she never realized until she started back to work after her treatment. Thus, I believe that even though she was a health care professional dealing with cancer patients before her experience with breast cancer, that experience changed her and her practice in immeasurable ways. That's why I will always believe that no matter how close you are to a person who has cancer, unless you actually experience the disease, you can never know what it feels like to be a cancer patient.

Well, it's time for me to come down off the soapbox and finish my project for school. Hope you are looking forward to the sunshine and warmth of spring. I know I am. Now that the snow is gone look for those green blades of grass.

Waiting for the Easter Bunny,

Lois

Throughout the winter, Lois remained in contact with the activities of the NBCC with telephone conference calls. In February, Lois made a trip to Atlanta, Georgia, to work at the national level for the American Cancer Society. In March 2003, she journeyed to Harrisburg, Pennsylvania, to work with the American Cancer Society on the state and local levels. She continued to get speakers for her support group and, as always, continued to write and research her quarterly newsletter. She did all this and still maintained her full-time work schedule at night, making the hour's drive to and from Baltimore. Now, with trying to fit all this together with mandatory chemotherapy sessions once every four weeks, her schedule was filling up.

In addition to her busy schedule, her sister and brothers brought another serious problem to her attention. Both of her parents were diagnosed diabetics for many years. Their lives were in control with regular visits to their physician and their children's interventions, but things were beginning to change. It started with a phone call to Lois's brother. The restaurant owner, where her mother was bussing tables, contacted him. According to the owner, their mother was acting very strangely over the past few months. At first, she forgot things; but at times, she seemed lost to where she was or what she was doing.

When she convinced her father to take their mother to the physician, she was diagnosed with multi-infarct dementia. This was a progressive disease, which would eventually need around-the-clock observation. Lois's father was not equipped emotionally or physically to care for her, but no one wanted to split them up. This would not be the end of her parents' problems.

The physician also contacted one of her siblings and said their father's diabetes was uncontrolled on the current oral hypoglycemic medications. This could lead to more-serious complications and possible hospitalizations. He needed to be on insulin, which he was wildly opposed to taking. Now, with Lois involved in her own chemotherapy treatments, busy with the work involved in her master's degree, working a full-time job at night, and doing her advocacy work for breast cancer, she was also needed in her parents' care. While this alone was another full-time commitment, she made time for the periodic trips to the physician with them.

In the years preceding their father's diagnosis with diabetes, he suffered a slight stroke. This finding revealed the underlying diabetes. The stroke had minimal consequences, with temporary paralysis and recovery after very little treatment. The physician warned him, he needed to be alert to signs of possible strokes in the future. The finding alerted the physician to the possibility that, over time, her father would need to be restricted from driving. Recovering from his first stroke relatively unscathed, his physician permitted him to resume driving. Driving was important because this activity brought extra money to their household. Without it, finances would become borderline poverty level with medications and food becoming enormous burdens.

Lois's father only knew the workings of an electrician from the time he was a young man. He had no concept of what his physician tried to explain about his diabetes. For him, he was taking "pills" to control his diabetes for years and had no intentions of stopping them. Furthermore, he was defiantly opposed to taking any insulin and wanted no parts of learning how to take his blood sugar. Lois's mother was in the early stages of a rapidly progressing dementia, where she couldn't remember to take her medications or provide incentives for her father to take his. When her brothers went to their parents' home, they found bottles of prescription medications for them that were never opened or taken by either one. When Lois was told of the conditions at her parents' home, she went and took charge of the situation.

Since Lois was tied up with many commitments of her own, she suggested the duties of checking their parents be split up among herself, her sister, and her two brothers. Each would take a week and make sure their medications were set up for the week using a special medication tray, dividing their medications daily and times for each day. It would the responsibility of each of them to check the containers to ensure everything was taken properly. In addition to the medication trays, Lois set up a running log for each of them to write their blood sugars so she could monitor them. Lois asked me to educate her father to do finger stick blood sugars properly, which I personally educated and demonstrated. When I felt he was proficient in the mechanics of the meter, I told Lois he could do them.

For the time, everything worked out. Lois, her sister, and two brothers checked in on them. Her father could still leave the house and work delivering supplies for an electrical warehouse part-time. Eventually, her father needed to leave this job for both health reasons and to keep their mother from wandering away. Lois came home one day and told me, "It won't be long before we have to think about nursing home placement for them."

Lois's father always believed in "living in the present." His ideas of saving for the future did not exist. Now, the future came without any security for their impending nursing care, which grew more ominous with every passing day. The obvious lack of planning left very few options. The only things of value were her father's car and the house they lived in. Otherwise, there was nothing of value to help either of them. For now, her brothers and her sister would do what they could for their aging parents. Still, as time wore on, their energies, their time, and their resources would wear thin. When that time came, the decisions they would all have to make would be difficult and heartbreaking.

Lois worked diligently on her studies. Her return to college, coupled with the Suzanne H. Kaye Award given for outstanding breast cancer advocacy in late December 2002, caught the attention of the academics of Temple University. Even before the end of 2002, Lois received this letter from the acting dean of Temple's School of Social Administration.

December 23, 2002

Lois Anderson
York, PA

Dear Ms. Anderson:

It has come to my attention that the Linda Creed Breast Cancer Foundation of Philadelphia recently honored you with the Suzanne H. Kaye award. The award is only given when there is an outstanding volunteer who has excelled as an advocate for women with breast cancer. I want to congratulate you on this wonderful accomplishment. The school is proud to have students such as yourself carrying out work that is highly compatible with our mission.

When you have the opportunity, perhaps you could share some of what you have been doing as an advocate for women with breast cancer. Feel free to contact me via telephone or e-mail.

Sincerely,

****
Acting Dean

Though she wasn't actively pursuing courses at the time she received the letter, it was certainly a tremendous boost to her morale. In May 2003, Lois finally made the trip to Philadelphia to grant the request of the acting dean of Temple's School of Social Administration. In Philadelphia, she addressed a room filled with social work students on her activities regarding breast cancer advocacy. By either coincidence or fate, Lois was inducted into a very prestigious honor society at Temple University by the middle of May.

In spite of all the controversy arising in her life, Lois made no mention of it in her newsletter. She never believed "her problems" were ever insurmountable and simply felt this was just another "phase" she had to go through. Her newsletter remained upbeat and positive, never revealing what was happening in her own life.

(Editorial by Lois A. Anderson dated May 29, 2003)

As I write this newsletter, it is finally sunny and bright after a long period of rain and dismal weather. Bring on the sunshine!

I just finished another semester of school and have only 9 credits to go with 6 of those being for fall semester and 3 for next spring. The light at the end of this tunnel is shining brighter. I had the distinct pleasure and honor of being inducted into the Beta Rho Chapter of Alpha Delta Mu, the National Social Work Honor Society earlier this month. After having gone back to school after all this time, I feel quite accomplished to have been able to meet the standards that enabled me to be inducted into this honor society.

I will not be able to attend our annual picnic because I must go to Philadelphia to attend two conventions, the American Society for Clinical Laboratory Science and the American Association of clinical Chemists. My hospital is paying for this so I cannot say no. The conventions overlap for 2 days in the middle of the week and so to take advantage of both I have to get there by Wednesday of the same week that our group usually meets. So have a burger for me while you're at the picnic.

And anyone interested, please call me. I managed to get a copy of the March 2003 supplement to Oncology News International. It is filled with information from the

San Antonio Breast Cancer Symposium. I can mail you a copy if you would like one.

Cool off and take a dip in the pool!

Lois

By June 2003, Lois began to feel joint pain, which started to slow her down. After consulting her physicians, they concluded chemotherapy treatments were probably behind the increased pain. Lois's oncologist suggested a rheumatologist to help with the annoying joint pains. I thought back to her dream about checking names on the list of people boarding her ship when she told me she was adding another physician to her list. She was indeed loading her ship with many people to help her cross the "rough seas" in her life. Her list of physicians now included her original surgeon, her oncologist, a neurologist, and now a rheumatologist. Making and keeping her appointments was almost a full-time commission. Add to that schedule, a list of classes to attend, a forty-hour night shift work week, a drive of one hour both ways, commitments to her support group and newsletter, commitments of running a household, commitments she kept by telephone conferences for various breast cancer committees and advocacy groups, and finally overseeing her parents' declining medical conditions, you can see how full her combined schedule really was.

By June 19, the Infusaport (a device implanted just under the skin against the chest wall for IV access) placed by the thoracic surgeon in 2001 was no longer functional and had to be replaced. First, the old one needed to be removed. Then the surgeon who initially treated her placed a new one. It was an outpatient procedure, but arrangements needed to be made, physicians had to be contacted, and time had to be taken out of an already busy schedule to accomplish this.

While she recovered from her surgery, we decided to go to Philadelphia to visit the museums and enjoy some of the historic sites the city had to offer. Her oncologist gave her the good news that her CA 27-29 had dropped to 25.6, a level not seen in two years. Lois was encouraged she would get to practice as a social worker and would have the time to do it. She still had to finish school. She took the rest of the summer working on the next field placement for the upcoming year. Her entourage of physicians made her quality of life good enough to function under the treatments and medications. The newsletter she wrote for the September newsletter shows her relaxed momentum.

(Editorial by Lois A. Anderson dated September 1, 2003)

Well another summer has flown by and it is time for school again. The weather is just barely beginning to cool down a bit with few vegetables left in the garden ravaged by the wet spring weather. Our garden performed very poorly this year. How about yours?

My son has now been married just over a year and I am finally adjusted to the idea that he is gone, and may be going even further away if a contemplated move to Iowa comes about. Ah, but first that magical, mystical thing called a better job must be had so I have a feeling this move may be a while in the making. I am also the proud grandmother of a cat that has adopted them by moving into their home one dark, stormy night.

School will start in another few days and this promises to be my busiest semester yet with a trip to New York City's Beth Israel Medical Center for observation of the social work role in the Pain and Palliative Care department there. I am hoping to bring back more, new, and varied information to be put to good use as I change careers to be a social worker in the near future.

It is time for me to close because I can barely see the letters on this page as I write. I have been up all night after working my night shift job and have not been to bed yet.

Watch this space and the updates at our meetings for news about legislation that affects cancer patients because I am now a Legislative Liaison for Pennsylvania, trying to effect change for cancer patients everywhere through legislative efforts.

Take care, cool off, and slow down now that the Autumn leaves will soon be upon us!

Lois

In September 2003, Lois started the last of her field placements. She chose the Lebanon VA Hospital that semester. She always kept in touch with her fellow breast cancer advocates and was named the legislative liaison for Pennsylvania during the time she was back in school. This meant extended periods of time away from home for a while. But with my own busy schedule and the additional chores I needed to do with our son out of the house, we were too busy to be concerned. Besides, when we had the time to ourselves, we made the most of it, and that was a comfort in itself. We both saw the end of her schooling and realized she would be home with more time, which made me feel better about her unbelievable schedule. At the beginning of November, Lois had a few days over a weekend to get away. We picked our favorite place in Virginia and got away from everything.

By the end of November 2003, the stresses of her full-time job, the class work for her field placement, the ongoing chemo sessions, and the management of her parents' medical conditions again took a toll on her. Her oncologist called to warn her that the tumor markers had risen again. He suggested another change in chemotherapy. By December, the markers increased to 124.8, and Lois started to be concerned. Yet again, she did not share her concerns with her fellow breast cancer survivors or her support group. Her newsletter remained upbeat and positive as you can see below.

(Editorial by Lois A. Anderson dated December 7, 2003)

Christmas will be here before you know it and with the snowfall that we just had it makes the season seem more Christmassy so to speak. This snowfall was not a surprise to the meteorologists, but I was surprised that again this year we had to deal with an early snowfall. The official start of Winter is not until December 22. Can someone please tell our weather that Winter and snow go together, not late Fall and snow? Maybe the Farmer's Almanac is right again!

I have to apologize for the lateness of this newsletter but it could not be helped. There are only so many hours in each day and it seems mine are eaten up with my schoolwork. And by the way this was the last semester that I had to do any internship work so you won't hear me complaining about all that anymore. But thanks for listening anyway! I have only one more semester to go and that one means only one class I have to attend once each week, but who knows how many papers, reports, and projects will be required? And then graduation on May 20th in Philadelphia at a ceremony I WILL attend no matter what!

And while I'm still waxing nostalgic, I have to tell you, I never did attend my graduation for my undergraduate degree. Even though I was finished with all my coursework and all by the end of August, York College made us wait until December if we wanted to attend a ceremony and make it official. By that time, I had been working for over 4 months and I could have cared less-that ceremony meant very little to me. However, this one with all the work required and the fact that it happened "late in life" will be a different story. I am already starting up to cloud 9. I think right now I'm on cloud 2 with a finish of all my internships. Knowing I'm almost finished is one of the best feelings in the world. Of course now I'll have so much more time on my hands. I wonder what I can get into. Well, I'm sure some of my friends will figure that one out for me and I won't have that time for long.

Be careful of the ice and snow. We don't need any broken bones. And even though this is late, I hope that those of you who took the chance to come to our December meeting, enjoyed our speaker.

Merry Christmas and Happy 2004.

Lois

Still, the end of her classes was in sight, and then she would graduate in May 2004 with her master's degree. She was hoping the change in treatments would bring the markers down long enough for her to become a social worker and do the kind of work she really wanted to do before metastasis reached levels that could no longer be controlled. By the end of 2003, she was hopeful she would accomplish what she set out to do in 1997. It would take her seven years, but eventually it would happen. Sometimes you do get to change things.

Accepting Significance

Tell me about values . . .

Dreams become uneasy when you have nowhere to put them. The Poet's Tree rustled with anticipation of a waiting storm, abandoned on the far horizon, which longed to be remembered. Voices, hushed and silent, waited in the branches above me for a sign to speak. I saw the glimmer of a man standing in the distance, but he would not proceed. Then like a mirage, he faded into the winds and colors of the sky beset with the shadows of a storm.

"What meaning am I to gather from this?" I asked.

"She will become the dream . . ." an unknown voice whispered.

"Who will be the dream . . . Lois or Catherine?" I asked, knowing the revelations of both worlds. Knowing was not any easier to bear. Was this a prophecy or a conjecture of the obvious?

The voice spoke again, "We will be known by our moments of fire."

"Moments of fire? A way to reveal your soul . . . a way to see truth?" I asked. I looked around at the gathering darkness and thought, *What did this have to do with me or Lois or the fantasy landscape where Catherine lives with her beloved Timothy? The Poet's Tree lives in my dreams. What consequences exist by remaining here? Dreams became real only in the telling. Was this one of mine?*

The blustery winds were mild and deceptively soothing. I stumbled into the long grass and wandered into a long deep sleep. Before I succumbed, I heard the voice say, "This moment of fire . . . perhaps it is one of yours."

Jakob led Catherine, Leena, and Michael past the wagon where Catherine's lifestone was glowing red, resting beneath a tarp designed to look like a wagonload of straw. Jakob had his sons hitch a pair of horses to a second wagon for himself and Catherine's family after he sent Benjamin back to his family. As he checked the harnesses, his sons Lamin and Eric rode their horses to Stock to enlist anyone willing to help move Catherine's lifestone into the breach. Their efforts would be rewarded handsomely as villager after villager enlisted in their impromptu army by the hundreds. By the time Jakob made his way to the southern borders of Stock, his two sons would have an army willing to open the road to the breach with trenches of fire big enough to ward off the murderous orbs.

Jakob moved to the forward bench of the wagon with Michael. Leena and Catherine sat on a smaller bench behind them. The large stone followed on the wagon driven by Alexis and Andrew. They moved slowly from Jakob's farm, not only because of the weight of the enormous stone but also because of the heavy responsibility of sacrificing Catherine's life. The long slow road seemed distant, giving the illusion they would never arrive at their destination. They would never have to sacrifice one of their innocents. Unfortunately, all roads end. Destinations are met, and new beginnings are wrought from the old.

Leena looked to her daughter. The evening sky, burning with remnants of red-streaked clouds, hung over the distant fires burning on the northern borders of Stock. The crimson light made Catherine's blond hair reflect the same elements of fire. Leena knew it would not change Catherine's resolve even if she pleaded with her. She wanted a long life for her daughter. She wanted grandchildren and to watch her daughter grow into a woman, a mother, with all the trials and joys that come in a lifetime. Now, looking at her daughter, glowing in the fires and faltering sunlight, she saw only a sacrifice led to oblivion. She would save them, and for a while, her name would be on the lips of every villager. However, each passing solen, her name would grow to whispers, eventually becoming a fleeting pause of silence as villagers strained to remember the name linked to something that changed a time of doom into a time of renewed survival and joy. Yet reflecting on what would be, Leena was reminded of the mysterious journey she hoped Timothy found . . . to make Catherine immortal.

What did it mean? *Leena thought to herself.* What would Timothy find on his journey to save Catherine's life? *She felt defeated. Leena, for the first time in her life, had no control over the events unfolding around her.*

Catherine turned solemnly to her mother and saw the anguish in her eyes. They looked at each other in the red glow surrounding them and wept for each other. There were no words to explain their feelings as the wagon drew closer to the southern borders of Stock. It was Catherine who broke the silence between them. "I have to do this."

Leena spoke softly through her tears, "I know."

Catherine tried to console her mother. "I won't die tonight. You and father will still have me for three days after the stone is placed into the wall."

"It's still not enough time," *Leena protested through her tears.*

"It has to be!" *Catherine said a little more sternly.* "Timothy, my great love, Timothy, he will come through for me. I know it," *Catherine told her, hoping her resolute decision would encourage and console her mother.*

But Leena was not to be dissuaded from her thoughts and brought them to Catherine's attention. "We don't know what Amelia's message for Timothy really means. What is worse, we don't know if he got the message or if he is just waiting in Glade for all this to end so he can get back. We can't believe in something that may not happen. We just can't!" *Leena ended emphatically, hoping to seed caution in her daughter's mind.*

"Believe in this, Mother," *Catherine said as bravely as she could.* "I can stop this destruction and death by giving up my lifestone. Even if Timothy doesn't find the solution to his journey, my sacrifice will save everyone. That must count for something. The villages will go on with their lives. You and Father can go on . . ."

"But living without you," protested Leena, "how will your father and I do that? How will we move on, knowing every villager owes a debt to us for sacrificing our beautiful daughter?"

"And if I don't . . . everyone, everything anyone holds dear will perish in the destruction and death dealt by this threat." Catherine paused, waiting for her mother's response. When Leena could not answer, Catherine said, "Amelia's message led me here. If we believe we are meant to survive, then we have to believe Victoria delivered her part of the message to Timothy."

Michael and Jakob sat on the front seat of the wagon, while the horses gained steady progress toward their ill-fated destination. Their eyes appeared dark and tired in the reddish glow. Jakob turned to Michael. "I'm so sorry, Michael. I can't begin to understand what you might be feeling." Tears were in Jakob's eyes as he turned his eyes forward, trying to focus the team of horses forward on the rutted dirt road to Stock.

"Thank you, Jakob," Michael murmured. "I can't explain how I feel right now. I'm leading my loving daughter to her death as certainly as I'm breathing. Every beat of my heart takes her further away from me, and I am useless to stop it. If I could take her place, I would do it."

"Any of us would," Jakob said solemnly. "I would do anything to change the way our world has gone, but your daughter is the only one who has the power to change it. I wish it wasn't so, but it seems to be the only way." Jakob could no longer contain his tears as they welled up then ran silently down his face.

Michael could not look at the sorrow on Jakob's face. Instead, he turned his attention to the ground passing beneath the wagon wheels as the forward motion of the wagon pushed them further toward Catherine's obscene destination. The night's sky was opening into a garden of stars, and the glow of sunset passed into nothingness. Only the glowing fires on the northern borders existed to guide them. The time of the fourth day of the breach ended unceremoniously with the fifth day ominously beginning underneath the darkness. Without looking up, immersed in his dark thoughts, Michael said, "I wish

I never gave my daughter that cursed rock. It's my fault she has to make this terrible sacrifice. It was folly on my part trying to keep her close to me."

Jakob looked over at his friend, realizing he wanted to blame himself for all that happened. "It wasn't your fault, Michael." He continued to watch, but Michael would not avert his eyes long enough to look at him. Knowing Michael's thoughts were driving him deeper inside himself, he made another attempt to reach him as he turned forward again to redirect the team of horses. "Catherine is to marry my son. I love her like she is my own. Timothy and Catherine . . . well, they want to make a life for themselves . . . a good life. And now . . . now I feel like I lost something, and my heart is breaking from the weight of it." Jakob again turned to Michael, who continued to watch the rolling wagon wheels, making the journey to Stock shorter and shorter. "Michael," Jakob spoke a little louder, "if you hadn't given your daughter that enormous stone, none of us would even have a chance of surviving right now. This had to be predetermined. This had to be destiny."

Michael finally turned from watching the momentum of the wagon wheels to look at Jakob. He watched Jakob concentrating intensely at keeping the horses on the road. He knew his friend's heart was heavy too. Until now, he had not realized the extent of Jakob's pain. His own tears would no longer flow in this desert of torments. Consolation was too much to expect from either of them. They were well beyond it.

Alexis and Andrew followed in the wagon carrying Catherine's lifestone. "What do you think they are saying up there, Alexis?" Andrew asked.

"I wish I could tell you I don't know . . . but I would be lying," Alexis told him as she watched how slowly her father proceeded in the lead wagon.

"You don't mean you can hear them from here?" Andrew asked with dubious surprise.

"Of course not . . ." Alexis looked at her brother sternly. "I think they are saying good-bye to Catherine."

"Have they no faith in Timothy? Timothy loves her. He will try anything . . . do anything for Catherine," Andrew protested, knowing Timothy's feelings for Catherine.

"I know . . ." Alexis relented, also knowing well of her brother's deep feelings for Catherine. "He would die for her before he let anything happen to her."

Andrew grew silent and somber as he restrained his forbearance of tears. "Timothy will do anything he can to save her . . . you know that?"

"Yes, Andrew, I do." Alexis paused, trying to get Andrew to look at her. "It takes courage to love someone the way our brother loves Catherine."

Andrew looked to his sister, puzzled by her remark. "Courage?"

Alexis wanted to console her brother but had something else she felt needed to be said. "Love goes both ways, my dear brother." Andrew continued to watch his sister, puzzled by her words. "You know our brother would lay down his life to save Catherine . . ."

"Of course he would . . . Nothing would stop him if anyone or anything tried to hurt her," Andrew said, as unborn tears trekked over his cheeks, dropping to an unresolved destination.

Alexis looked at her brother who could not respond. "She's doing it out of love, Andrew. She is putting all of us before herself. She is trying to prevent us from dying . . . keeping her great love, Timothy, our brother, from dying."

Andrew pondered his sister's words. He looked where Catherine laid her head in Leena's lap. He could tell, even from here, Catherine was in pain. She had not relinquished her lifestone, and yet she was in pain. "Some pain doesn't come from sickness or dying, does it?" Andrew asked his sister.

Alexis did not respond. The scene before them seemed impossible. At this time of night, they should be getting ready for bed, not pulling an enormous rock into an embattled village . . . not leading an innocent woman to her untimely death. Timothy should have returned from Glade days ago. He and Catherine should be sitting somewhere, talking excitedly about the wedding. Everyone should be happy for them while their ordinary days passed in comfortable predictability.

Alexis remembered how quiet the day seemed when Timothy set out for Glade. The world she knew changed . . . Nothing would be as it was. Even if Catherine's sacrifice worked, even if the villagers pulled her and her lifestone through the plague of purple orbs, even if sealing the breach worked, no one would be innocent again. The mysterious wall lost its enigma. People died trying to escape the orbs or died trying to stop them. So many lives altered . . . changed irrevocably by a few careless people who were too curious, too willing to change beliefs, and too willing to risk all to gain all, leaving everyone the debt of their folly. It wasn't fair. Catherine should never atone for them with her life . . . but Catherine loved them, especially Timothy. There was nothing anyone could do to stop her from trying to save their world from the certain destruction the orbs determined to exact upon them.

The little caravan traveled all night then came to a hill overlooking the distant walls of fire burning at the northern borders. At the top, Jakob stopped the horses to give them a well-earned rest. Seeing the orange glow painting the black canopy of sky meant their journey would end. Plans, which seemed abstract, became real in the paced moments numbered in the footsteps before them.

Alexis, sitting in the wagon behind her father's, watched Leena hold her daughter tightly against her. She saw Michael's form slumped over to the extent he appeared like a large sack beside her father. She looked to her brother and said, "I think we will have a problem with Leena when the time comes for Catherine to go to the wall."

"I've been watching them too, Alexis," Andrew responded, his well-intentioned seriousness appreciated by his sister. "I believe we will need to be gentle with Leena, or she will become hysterical."

"It's what I've feared since we started. This seemed so distant . . . like it would never happen. But here we are. Now what we feared would come is going to happen. None of this seems real," Alexis said, watching the motionless silhouette of her father's wagon against the blazing landscape.

Against the glowing edge of the horizon, the shadow of a young man grew near the top of the next hill. He waved his arms and yelled, "Hello."

"Hello," Jakob yelled back.

"Father, it's Eric. We are ready to move Catherine's stone to the wall," he shouted breathlessly, running down the hillside to close the distance between them.

Jakob turned to Michael who aged ten solens overnight. Michael stared numbly at the wooden floorboards. His eyes were lined with dust, coughed up from the journey over the dry dirt road. His face was a map of weariness and grief. He had no words left to say . . . Silence choked him.

"It is soon time, Michael. We will arrive, and what we came to do must now be done," Jakob said solemnly as he faced Michael.

Michael broke his attention to address Jakob. He spoke in a chilly monotone, "I know . . ." It was all he said before returning to the empty stare and silence.

Jakob could not imagine what was happening in Michael's mind. He turned from Michael's cold figure, watching Eric run breathlessly to the side of the wagon.

"Lamin is waiting with a hundred or more villagers willing to move Catherine's stone to the breach," Eric said excitedly, catching his breath.

Jakob could not begin to tell his son the sadness he brought with him. He turned, trying to quell Eric's excitement. "You did well."

Eric was deflated by his father's cool response until Jakob said, "Where are we to meet this small army?"

"Benjamin's shop . . ." he told his father. "It lies along the road out of Stock, leading north. Benjamin is there too. It was his suggestion we meet there."

Jakob turned to his friend Michael who maintained a faux surveillance of the wagon's floor. Grief, with its icy fingers, immobilized him. Jakob turned back to his son and said quietly, "Some things we will all have to learn to live with . . . for a very long time."

"Father?" Eric asked, perplexed by the meaning of his father's words.

Jakob looked at his son with eyes so grave, Eric had to turn away. He could not bear the sadness in them. Catherine was going to die. Eric had a feeling that went to the core of his being, telling him a lot happened since his father left their farm. No one knew if Victoria found Timothy. Even Victoria was a mystery. What happened to her? Was she able to get to Glade before the orbs started their murderous rampage? No one knew if Victoria survived. However, Amelia's message was very clear. It was something they could do with positive consequences. Still, though it was heartbreaking, Eric knew it was the only plan they had. It was their last bit of hope to return to the way things were before the breach. Many died trying to keep the orbs away from Stock. He knew many more would die trying to get Catherine's stone into the wall. Somehow in the process, Catherine had to stay alive long enough to push her stone into that gaping hole herself. If she died in the attempt, her lifestone would not work. Eric imagined the orbs would simply break Catherine's stone if it merely existed as another common stone. Catherine had to stay alive three days after the stone was placed to keep the orbs from coming through. After three days, the stone would settle and mold in place forever, sealing the orbs in a world away from the villages. Eric remembered seeing the piles of stones left by families along the road from Stock. They were waiting to place the stones of their dead into the wall, cut off by the vengeful orbs. Hope was thin, but hope remained while Catherine lived.

Eric listened to Leena's quiet sobbing in the darkened bench behind his father. He turned to see his father sigh at the morning air lit by the burning fires and new sunlight filtering through the smoky air.

"Lead on, Eric . . ." Jakob told his son. Resigned to their fate, he whispered, "Lead on . . ."

Eric passed slowly by the side of the wagon then moved ahead of the lead horses. He did not look back as he walked toward the hill where he hailed his father and the sad entourage that followed him. It seemed his every step became a journey of its own. His mind filled with unbearable thoughts, as he retraced his footsteps to the top of the hill. He stopped on the crest, watching a band of villagers approaching with torches. Eric turned, looking back where his father was slowly bringing his team of horses up to him.

"Why did you stop?" Jakob asked him.

"Pull the wagon to the top of the hill and see," Eric said, his eyes fixed on the approaching torches.

Jakob pulled his team to the top and stared in disbelief. It wasn't just a small band of people; it was hundreds, possibly a thousand or more. It looked the entire village of Stock. "By the Four Winds . . . I've never seen anything like this," Jakob said, dumbfounded by what he saw.

Michael, barely able to raise his head, now looked to see the approaching mass of torches. The villagers were arranged in two distinct columns, the torch fires stretched from the distant village perimeter to just beyond the hill where their wagon rested. "What's happening, Jakob?" he asked, like a man waking from a dream.

"It's a procession, Michael. According to the old beliefs, the villagers only do it when an extraordinary event takes place . . . an event that changes the lives of everyone." Jakob watched the approaching torches with deft attention. "I've almost lived a lifetime, and I haven't lived long enough to see one happen . . . until now!" Tears of pride, tears of sorrow, and tears of resignation held in the

corners of his eyes as he turned to Michael. "They are honoring her, Michael. They understand the great sacrifice Catherine is making and . . ." Jakob could no longer contain his emotions as sobs racked him until he could barely catch his breath.

It was Catherine who put her steady hand on his shoulder and said, "Jakob, they have come to honor me. I am not afraid. I am ready." Catherine slipped between Jakob and her father and relieved the reins from Jakob. Grief blinded him. She realized he could no longer keep the wagon on the road when they started. "I will take it from here," Catherine told him. To her father, she said, "Father, sit with my mother. She needs you now. My fate is set. If Timothy has the message, there is still hope for me."

Michael moved slowly, but before he climbed over the bench to sit with Leena, he looked into his daughter's eyes and said, "I love you more than my own life. If I could take your place, I would do it before you would waste your breath to ask me."

"I know, Father" was all Catherine would say before he climbed to the back bench with Leena. He took Leena's hand and held it in the fading darkness, quickly becoming the morning of the fifth day of the wall breach.

As Alexis watched, she was speechless as villagers lined both sides of the road to Stock with their torches. Andrew watched Catherine move to the front bench. His father appeared overwhelmed, and now Catherine moved to the front bench, taking the reins from him. Andrew never saw such courage. He felt weak in the presence of Catherine's great love of everyone. He couldn't imagine how Timothy would not see her in her final moments. He said a prayer to the Four Winds, leading the horses to follow the wake of his father's wagon.

Alexis watched as they passed villager after villager holding lighted torches on both sides of the road. As their wagon passed a torchbearer, each would fall in behind then follow in neat double lines. In the muted light, the road behind them appeared like a moving trail of fire growing behind them. Alexis never saw anything like this before. "Andrew, there must be over a thousand people here!"

"It's the ritual called 'procession,'" Andrew told her, not taking his eyes off the lead wagon.

"I don't know what that is, Andrew. Why are they doing it?"

"They are doing it out of deep honor." Andrew turned momentarily to face his sister. "I never saw one myself, so I can only tell you that it is done for someone who has or had a profound effect on the villages. I would say what Catherine is doing would definitely qualify for this honor."

"She's going to die, isn't she, Andrew?"

"Timothy won't let that happen," Andrew said bitterly.

Alexis watched her brother as doubt stabbed him through the heart. She spoke to him, "Still hope . . . we should still hope." Her voice trailed to nothing when she saw no change on her brother's face. She looked behind the wagon only to see an impossible double line of torches stretching over the hills behind them. "There's no way to stop this now," Alexis said under her breath.

The buildings on the south side of Stock appeared untouched as the small caravan made its way into the village. As Catherine drove farther into the village, the devastation of the insidious orbs was apparent. Within half a parcel, the buildings, still standing, gave way to ones gutted of timber and siding to use in the fiery trenches surrounding what remained of Stock. As they moved to the northern side of the village, Catherine saw the skeletal remains of buildings ravaged by people trying to find timber to burn. Left behind were masonry foundations where homes and businesses existed just five days before. She guided the wagon through the barren streets and wondered how Benjamin fared. Even trees and bushes, assembled as backdrops and hedges against the beautiful streets, were savagely torn away to fuel the fires.

At the south end of Stock, she entered the area where she and Leena shopped for a wedding dress a few days before. The bench where she rested was gone. All around were men with heavy tools, deconstructing the abandoned buildings and loading the torn lumber onto waiting flat wagons. The men were so entrenched in work, they took no notice of the wagons passing through. However, when the huge procession followed, hammers stopped, saw blades stayed embedded in wood, and the moment stilled every villager they passed. The gravity of unfolding events inspired their failing hopes as their industry resumed with renewed fervor. As Catherine passed, calls came from all directions, proclaiming her name. From behind a broken wall, she heard, "Tear them down faster. Catherine is here." Echoes stumbling from another direction announced, "We need to get Catherine to the wall." It seemed her presence improved their diligence, enabling her passage to the breach. Catherine tried to stop listening to their discourse. She concentrated heading the wagon toward Benjamin's shop through the crazed activity and broken debris cluttering the village streets.

As the wheels drove pieces of wood and glass into the cobbled streets with unrelenting crackles, Catherine realized she would not survive. Her sleeping conviction grew into a sharp, bright pain. As much as she wanted to help everyone survive, some latent instinct rose inside her and asked, When I am gone, will anyone understand what I have done for them? Don't I deserve life and happiness too? *It was the moment her heart broke, dropping her into deep despair. She was afraid for the first time since the orbs invaded their world.*

Jakob turned to Catherine when she started sobbing uncontrollably. "Give me the reins, Catherine. You've been strong for all of us. Now it is time we are strong for you. Let me take the reins . . . Let me take you the rest of the way."

Catherine looked where Jakob offered his hands to her. The weight of the world twisted painfully. Accepting Jakob's help over this final part of the journey pulled the little deaths she felt from her heart. When she looked into Jakob's eyes, she found the same kindness she saw in the eyes of Timothy. Knowing they would survive the aftermath was enough to regain her resolve. After giving him the reins, she put her arms around his neck and kissed him on the cheek. "Thank you for helping me."

"How are your parents doing?" Jakob asked, hoping to distract her from the reasons they came to this time and place.

Catherine turned to see Leena sleeping on Michael's shoulder. "We're all right," Michael whispered. "Your mother was exhausted and dozed off. I'll let her sleep until we get to Benjamin's shop."

Looking past her shoulder, Catherine glanced at the wagon following them and waved to Alexis and Andrew. The line of torchbearers continued behind them, beyond the boundaries of Stock, still reaching beyond the hillside where they started. Seeing the support of so many lightened Catherine's heart. Still, if Timothy could not do anything to save her from this fate, she would be dead three days after her lifestone was in the wall. Heaviness settled on her as she faced the desolate streets lying before her.

Benjamin's shop was relatively intact as Jakob pulled the wagon to the front of the building. Benjamin raced down what remained of steps leading from his shop. He surveyed the two wagons, taking a quick inventory of passengers and the load they carried. The torchbearers stopped their solemn procession and gathered on either side of the two wagons.

"Jakob, it is good to see you, but the seriousness of the situation does not give us much time to talk. But we must talk . . ." Benjamin paused, looking first to Catherine, then to the rousing form of Leena, and then Michael, who would not look his way. Finally, he cast a quick look at Alexis and Andrew in the next wagon before turning to face Jakob. "The orbs are not making our passage to the wall easy. Right now, men fight them from the wall with fires made from anything that burns. We need to travel three to four parcels north behind our fires on the Last Road to get to the breach."

"So what can we expect?" Jakob asked out of concern and curiosity.

"Word was sent through the lines of men who kept the fires burning throughout the night. The orbs were treacherous and relentless in their attacks. They have been digging deep ravines against the Last Road, both as attempt to undermine it and to create an access point into Stock. It will be a perilous undertaking to get to the breach. The old trees against the wall where Amelia heard the voices were sent into the fires two days ago. The stone path leading into the breach is *a river of blue mists teeming with purple orbs that attack with their scarlet tendrils as soon as they come through. The orbs don't want any of us close to the breach. They guard it with violent outcomes. We lost over twenty men trying to get close enough to spot the opening."*

"So you're saying this is a 'fool's errand,' Benjamin?" Jakob asked with renewed skepticism, realizing they may be too late.

Benjamin looked to Jakob in exasperation, "The alternative of not trying is far worse to consider." Benjamin paused, waiting for another argument. Jakob stared at him with contempt. "We must try to get Catherine and the stone to the breach. To think we will get there easily is foolish. We have to fight our way out there."

"Fight? With what weapons will we fight?" Michael suddenly spoke up. "Fire seems to be the only thing preventing these things from getting into the village right now. You said it yourself. Fire is what stops them. Is there something else that works against them? If there is, please tell us, and we will bring it with us."

The procession of villagers gathered on either side of the wagons. Their torches still burned, while some lined the streets running from the village of Stock to the north where the warlike orbs waited. Michael watched as men and women randomly entered from the side streets armed with crossbows, swords, an array of sharp bladed tools, and assorted weapons. They watched the melee of villagers joining forces with them. Michael was deeply moved by their show of support, but he was also troubled. "These people may be laying down their lives for nothing. What can any of us do with weapons such as these?" Michael asked, sweeping his arm over the gathering crowd.

"What Michael asks is a valid question. How can we possibly break through the orbs with steel blades and arrows? Only fire stops them . . . It doesn't kill them," Jakob asked, sharing Michael's concerns.

The somber crowd continued to walk through the streets lined with torchbearers. The rustling of footsteps on the detritus-littered street was disquieting. Only distant stray orders, announcing "Stay in line" or "Keep up," broke in echoes, disturbing the otherwise silent reverie.

Benjamin bowed his head then slowly looked into Michael's eyes. "I think we have our best weapons with us already."

Jakob turned to Benjamin. "What are you trying to say?"

"Remember what Amelia said about her lifestone?" Benjamin asked.

Though Benjamin directed his question to Jakob, it was Michael who spoke up, "Jakob never heard that part of Amelia's story, but I did."

Jakob, interested in what Michael had to say, asked, "So what did Amelia tell you?"

"She said she gave her lifestone to Victoria to convince her to take her message to Timothy."

"Yes," Jakob said abruptly, "we've heard this before. What of it?"

Benjamin could not resist the chance to take the lead. "She also told Victoria to use her lifestone for protection. It was the real reason she wanted Victoria to take it."

"So how does this help us, Benjamin?" Jakob asked, irritated by his habit of circling the issue.

"The same way Catherine's lifestone will . . ."

"But how does it do this?" Jakob asked Benjamin, irritated to the point of frustration. "We have the word of a girl . . . a girl who couldn't explain what she meant . . . . telling her friend to use it to protect her."

"We have to have faith in what Amelia said," Leena spoke suddenly, walking behind the men. "My daughter is offering her life to spare you, and yet you waste time discussing theories about

stopping these things. We don't have the answers. We know fire keeps them away and some weapons can use fire to hold them back. If we find a way to use our lifestones, we will. We know Amelia gave her life trying to convince Catherine her lifestone will stop these things. I believed her. Catherine believed her. But nothing happens until we decide to act and move Catherine's lifestone to the breach. We decided to do that much, and my heart is numb not knowing if her sacrifice will be enough."

"I'm sorry to interrupt . . ." a man dressed in ash-soaked leathers called out to Benjamin. Scorch-marked leathers covering his arms and leggings matched the face smeared black with ashes. "Benjamin, we opened a way two parcels north to get you within a parcel of the breach."

Benjamin turned and asked, "Will the road hold, moving a huge stone over it?"

"Not as well as we'd like, but possible," the man replied, his tone of voice reserved.

"The remaining parcel of road," Jakob asked, "how treacherous is it?"

"I've been as far as the next two parcels . . . Beyond it, the fighting has been fierce, with many casualties."

"Will we be able to make the breach?" Catherine asked him.

The leather-dressed man turned to Catherine. "The men who escorted you will continue ahead. They are willing to sacrifice their lives to get you to the opening in the wall. They will fight to the last man if they need to."

His news did not comfort them. Benjamin saw their growing disquiet and quickly dispatched the man, saying, "I will bring them to you. Go and tell your men we will be along."

"Certainly," the man replied, then turned and walked into the crowd of makeshift warriors.

"We must be on our way soon," Benjamin said to Michael and Jakob. "Men are fighting and dying to keep the road open and passable to the site of the breach. Every moment we sit here is paid out in lives . . . We must move."

Catherine looked to her mother and father and told them, "It's my time . . . I must go, but I will understand if you cannot follow me."

"I will go with you, my daughter," Michael said almost in a whisper.

"I too will follow," Leena added. Then with more conviction in her voice, she said, "Let's be off then . . . Let's end this."

Michael looked to Jakob and said, "I'm ready."

The End of a Beginning

Tell me about beginnings . . .

Before Lois started the last of her studies at Temple University, she was confronted by yet another tragedy. By mid-January 2004, our son's marriage came to an end. Lois left for Atlanta, Georgia, earlier in the week to attend a meeting with the National American Cancer Society when I made the call to her. She was very upset but asked me to keep our son's spirits up until she returned at the end of the week. Fortunately, I was off six weeks, recuperating from hand surgery, and stayed with my son until she returned. When she returned, we worked to get his life composed again. It was not a good year for my son. I believe he drew most of his strength to survive from his mother, a natural-born survivor herself. It seemed, no matter what controversy confronted Lois, she always knew what to do. This situation was no different. After speaking with our son, a plan was formulated, a lawyer was obtained, and the slow painful process of divorce was started. The process, in retrospect, would actually take years, not months, to complete.

Lois began her college classes at Temple University at the end of January. She did not allow diversions at home to interfere with her objective—that being, graduating with her master's degree in social work. She had a round of chemotherapy the Friday after her first class. She continued to work full-time and managed the affairs of her support group along with her political advocacy, as she did all along. Her time was precious, and she needed help to make everything work. She started to make lists for me to complete. Her lists, as she called them, looked more like an agenda of where she would be and times she would be there than actual lists. It was during this time she decided to carry a cell phone with her. Until this time, the cell phone she carried was heavy, bulky, and could barely keep a charge three hours. In order to use it, she had to keep it charged constantly and left it to charge in her car rather than carry it. Now cell phones were smaller and could fit easily in her purse. Having her cell phone with her was wonderful. When I needed to talk to her, I could call, and she would answer. It was a great way to keep in touch, and it became a necessity as the year unfolded.

By mid-February, her tumor markers changed slightly for the better with the new chemotherapy protocol. The CA 27-29 was now 120 . . . a decrease of only four to five points. Lois worked with her oncologist, and together, they determined a new course of chemotherapy. When Lois knew a particular group of drugs weren't working, she investigated the new therapies becoming available, utilizing contacts with leading physicians and scientists across the country. After doing her research, she would come to the oncologist's office with information she and her physician would discuss and then decide what protocol to try next. After deciding what they were trying, a decision to recheck the tumor marker in two months was agreed upon. This would give the new therapy a chance to succeed or fail.

While confronting her cancer again, along with her personal battles at home, Lois began to involve herself with her political advocacy role. With college classes held once a week, she had more time than she had for over three years. She visited our state's congressmen and senators at their offices in Pennsylvania or in Washington DC. Her message was always clear. She wanted funding for research and advances for breast cancer so the work she started in 1992, when she helped deliver thousands of signatures to then president Clinton, would not fail. It did not matter if she was in Washington DC; Harrisburg, Philadelphia; Baltimore; or her hometown of York, Pennsylvania; Lois carried her fight, her message, that funding needed to be allocated to a disease that potentially affected the female population of this country.

In spite of the many difficulties of time, care of her parents, college classes, support group activities, her newsletter, and long trips away from home involving both national and local concerns, the March 2004 editorial never reflected all the changes happening in her life. Other than the lateness of the newsletter, there were no clues as to the many directions Lois was being pulled.

(Editorial by Lois A. Anderson dated March 22, 2004)

I'm sitting here thinking about how fast time goes by and I realize that it's now my last semester of school, and I will be so glad when it is complete—senioritis has struck. Not the kind where you get old and crotchety and can't hear, walk, or talk, but the kind of senioritis that hits when you know you are on the verge of the completion of something major in your life. The flip side of this coin is that this is only the beginning. After this comes the licensing exams and deciding which state I really want to work in—PA or MD. Of course the new position has to be somewhere within the spectrum of what I have been preparing to do for the last 5 years—to work with oncology patients. Bill Cosby, and the Philadelphia Temple University Campus—here I come so beware!!!

Two of my friends and me are planning a "girls only weekend" at a spa in Tampa, Florida to celebrate my graduation and to get together for some fun. I can't wait for that weekend to roll around.

And last but not least, I am setting up a new fax and e-mail network for the Calls to Action that I get from the National Breast Cancer Coalition and the American Cancer Society. For those of you who want to do advocacy work, please e-mail me with your email address or fax number so I can add you to my list of those willing to send letters, faxes, phone calls, and emails to our legislators in support of state and federal legislation. And for those of you who had previously told me you were interested, please email me, again, with your interests. It is not hard to participate in this network, and all the information you need is contained in the Call to Action. Thanks for your help.

Hoping this cold weather goes away soon,

Lois

On March 24, 2004, Lois won the Health Care Heroes Award given by *Daily Record* in Baltimore. This award recognized the work she had done with the National Division of the American Cancer Society that year. They also recognized her work with the National Breast Cancer Coalition and their work to advocate for a genetic nondiscrimination bill. The award was given to Lois, a medical technologist at the time, among well-known physicians, nursing professionals, and scientists in the area of Baltimore. It was a very distinguished honor to have received such an award.

As the year progressed, the new treatments effectively moved her CA 27-29 from 120 to 67 by the time she finished her college courses in May 2004. It always seemed when something good happened for her, something equally bad would happen in her life as well. Only a few days after her college courses ended, her father had a serious heart attack, which left him with grave complications that would affect the entire family. Lois made an attempt to get a newsletter together for June but realized she would never do it any justice. While doing her best to address her father and mother's situation, dealing with our son's problems, and trying to prepare for graduation, she managed to write a one-page letter. She graduated May 20, 2004, with her master's degree in social work from Temple University . . . seven years after she started. Lois's letter to her support group followed.

(Letter of June 10, 2004, by Lois A. Anderson)

A new newsletter will be on its way to you in the very near future. However, on the other side of this letter is an invitation to our annual picnic to be held on July 21ˢᵗ.

My MSW is now finished, but I am dealing with another challenge, that of my parents and their medical problems, which have become more life threatening recently. Because of my father's hospitalization and my graduation ceremonies, I have not had enough time to devote to my volunteer activities, one of which is the newsletter. Therefore something had to give and the newsletter was put on hold. I know how many of you enjoy this newsletter and how it keeps you in touch with the world of breast cancer research and what is new in its treatment. I am glad I could fulfill that need for you. However, due to constraints on my time I could not write what I feel is a good informative newsletter. So rather than do a bad job, I chose to wait until later and put the newsletter together.

I am also asking you all for some help. I would like to publish more poems and things you feel may help breast cancer patients. And I could always use help getting speakers for our meetings. The one thing that worries me, though, is that if at least a little help is not forthcoming, this whole newsletter may no longer be published, and I don't like that idea one bit. I have kept the newsletter going in its current format for over 10 years now and that's a long time, but now I need some help from you. Please contact me if you have any ideas. We can talk privately or at our next meeting—whatever you would like.

Thanks for your help and concern,

Lois

Her parents now needed care twenty-four hours a day. The heart attack left her father with congestive heart failure, and his time of watching her mother with increasing dementia was coming to an end. Her brothers and sister had many meetings over the remainder of the year as to what to do for them. Her mother's dementia started to reveal itself in events where she abandoned her house with no way of finding her way back. If not for some benevolent neighbors, the outcome could have been tragic. Her father could not chase her or effectively monitor her erratic behavior with the condition that forced him into a wheelchair. Essentially, his overburdened heart would not allow him a few steps to the front door without being crippled by shortness of breath.

With her parents' declining conditions coming at the end of her college career, a need to change positions from that of a medical technologist to that of a social worker, and the compelling changes happening around her, Lois realized she needed help to continue her newsletter. She wanted to continue her investigations and analysis of the stories she heard from the local and national media on breast cancer herself. However, she needed someone to investigate the burgeoning local events, which had become, over the years, numerous and very time consuming to cover. A fellow breast cancer survivor and friend, who had been with the group from the very beginning, stepped in and helped her. By July, Lois was able to piece together the last newsletter she would ever produce by herself.

(Editorial by Lois A. Anderson dated July 19, 2004)

Well, it is now July and our annual picnic is coming up next week. I am sitting here thinking about the many things that have happened in my life within the last 3 months, and realizing how fast time goes by. I'm sorry that this edition of the newsletter is delayed, but it could not be helped. My father had a heart attack the beginning of May and I along with my brothers and sister have had to take on a greater role in his and my mother's care. At this point, he cannot drive a car and we are their transportation for whatever is needed. He has had to make adjustments because the heart attack left him with congestive heart failure, a condition that unfortunately is permanent and will only worsen over time. But I guess that's to be expected—all part of life.

A bright spot in May was the completion of the requirements for my Master of Social Work (MSW) degree and my graduation from Temple University. Ceremonies were held in Philadelphia and Harrisburg and I attended both of them because this degree means so much to me—a complete change in my life.

And the change in my life was made even more complete by a change in jobs. In my new position, I am now the Bereavement Coordinator for Heartland Hospice in York. Of course I am busy learning the new responsibilities of the new position and studying to take the licensure exam for social workers in Pennsylvania.

Soooo, now it is on to other things and with that I am announcing a campaign that the National Breast Cancer Coalition is conducting stories that have to do with guaranteed access to quality health care for all. The campaign is called "Stop Breast Cancer: Personal Stories, Public Action." The stories can be submitted anonymously or with your name and other information attached— that is what to do. I have submitted a story about the problems I went through for over a year in trying to get one insurance claim paid. I have a stack of paperwork almost 2 inches thick that has to do with that one claim. The whole incident was ridiculous but it shows you what can happen when many people do not perform their jobs properly. If anyone else has a story they would like to submit for this campaign, please call me and I can let you know how to send in your story.

And I'd like to thank Ruth Ann Burke for taking over the writing of the Local News Column for our newsletter. I am still looking for someone with computer capabilities who would be willing to take over some other sections of the newsletter.

Here's hoping you are having a wonderful summer and a good picnic later this week.

Lois

As Lois promised, she met with her friends in Tampa, Florida, for five days of relaxation and just talking to one another. It was a well-needed break for her. Under the circumstances, she just wanted to get away from everything for a while. So many things were changing in her life, with some creating greater tensions than she experienced before. It seemed that Lois was under "fire" ever since she decided to return to college. At times, the pressure seemed insurmountable, but she always managed to come out on top. The new changes coming in her life would soon make permanent markings on her world. There would be nothing she could do except witness the changes and try to live with them.

That summer, the remnants of a major hurricane blew through our area, leaving the ground saturated by the heavy rains. It seemed like a harbinger of the personal storms unleashed over the remaining part of the year. There were tragedies yet to be played out in the lives of both our parents' lives. After my father's open heart surgery, just two years before, it was hoped the outcome would improve his overall condition. However, the confusion he experienced before and after surgery never improved, and his general decline accelerated. Some of his physicians felt the increasing confusion may came from a minor stroke while he was in surgery; others simply felt it was a worsening symptom of his advancing Parkinson's disease. No matter how anyone saw it, or the reasons behind it, my mother was having a difficult time taking care of him. Getting my father to a standing position, with the stiffness and tremors associated with Parkinson's disease, became an impossible task for a 110-pound woman to do. Once he was out of bed and into a sitting position, he could navigate on his own, but getting him to decide to move was another thing. Lois checked with my mother and discussed her needs for help with my father's care. She set up times for both my brother and me to assist her. Now my brother and I had to make daily checks on our parents to help my mother get my father up and about for the day, then later help him into bed.

On the other front, Lois was setting up a network with her brothers and sister to make sure their parents were taken care of. Lois and her sister coordinated their efforts to assure their parents would be cared for safely, but her two brothers were not as cooperative. There was a dynamic in place where her father still wanted to call the shots, and Lois, as a daughter, was overruling the man of the house. Her father didn't want to be told anything, and he enlisted his sons to be his advance guard. He still wanted to be independent of them, and his two sons agreed. Lois and her sister realized caring for their mother and father in their home was going to be a losing battle. However, their brothers did not see it that way. Lois and her sister were disgusted with the whole situation and decided to let their two brothers get a taste of what it would be like trying to care for their sick elderly parents at home. It would be six long months of watching the continuing deterioration of their parents' medical conditions until her brothers finally relented and allowed Lois to start working on long-term placement for them. The whole outcome was necessary, but the repercussions of Lois's decisions with her brothers made them distant for a very long time.

Our son was now truly on his own with only one paycheck to support himself. He had taken the mortgage on his house with the intention there would be two incomes to rely on. Now he had the mortgage and the added costs of the divorce to handle. He came up with a wonderful solution when he accepted one of his friends into his house as a boarder later in the year. He still wasn't through the worst of it, but he found a way to accommodate the mounting financial obligations and keeping the house we helped him renovate. For a time, we helped with loans or some meals; but otherwise, he handled the situation on his own. He was always grateful for our help but never once did he ask to come home or give up being independent.

By September 2004, some of the dust settled; though at this point, decisions to move her parents into long-term care had not been agreed upon. Lois was working in her new position for about four months, and our son settled into an empty house. My mother was happy with the arrangements Lois arranged for my father's care, and we all agreed that all three elderly parents would need more than any of us could give them as time moved on. Nothing was really concluded, but everything was certainly better because of Lois's interventions for all of them. Lois was almost able to get her newsletter out on time this September with her friend's help. All the controversy and turmoil in her personal life did not stop her from doing all she could for her support group and her advocacy efforts.

(Editorial by Lois A. Anderson dated September 12, 2004)

Oh, wow how the summer has flown! I just turned around and saw the flowers starting to bloom and here they are beginning to get brown and die off for the winter. Ivan has blown through our area wreaking havoc with the creeks and rivers in this part of Pennsylvania. We are still waiting for the Susquehanna River to crest which probably won't happen until Monday sometime.

October and Breast Cancer Awareness Month will be upon us before we know it. My time with some of these events will be sorely limited this year because of just starting a new job. Because many of these events are going to be held on Wednesdays, I am very limited in the time I can get away from the office to attend these events— Wednesdays are the most important day of the week for us in this hospice because that means IDT (Interdisciplinary Team) meetings when all of us—case managers, physicians, nurses, aides, social workers, bereavement coordinator, and volunteer coordinator get together to discuss the patient, their family members, and their care. So I guess I'll have to bite the bullet this year because other things in my life need to take precedence and that makes me sad. I'll miss all of those I usually see this time of year at these events.

I am in the process of studying for my social work license, which has proven to be a daunting task because of family problems with my parents that I must deal with. Oh well, sooner or later, that will happen, but for now I just have to be patient.

> *May you have a brilliant autumn, just as bright and inviting as the leaves when they turn crimson and gold.*

Lois

Her new position as a bereavement coordinator for a local hospice consumed the bulk of her time and energy. Her predecessors were not as discriminating to detail as Lois, and much of the groundwork that defined and made the position operational was never initiated. In the physical sense, her predecessors were unorganized and had no sense of prioritizing their work. There was so much filing and cleaning out of ancient papers that many times when I was not working, she asked me to come and move boxes, files, and furniture for her as she cleaned out one thing or another. Many times we would both work until two or three o'clock in the morning trying to get some semblance of order in her new office. Between all this cleaning and refilling the files with appropriate documents, her time was spent helping others, which was not a new thing for her. She still managed to keep in contact with her breast cancer support and advocacy groups via her newsletter and Internet connections.

The stress of taking care of her parents in their home started to weigh heavily on her and her siblings. It took six months of disruptions for one of her two brothers to understand what Lois meant when she suggested they get their parents into a nursing home, where they could get twenty-four-hour-a-day care. Her father's condition was getting unmanageable. His congestive heart failure manifested in intolerable fluid accumulation in his feet and legs. It became impossible for their father to lie down in bed, as his compromised breathing would not allow him to be in a reclining position. To remedy this, he sat upright and immobile in a lounger positioned in the living room. Her mother's dementia deteriorated to the point where she wandered out of the house at all hours of the night, knocking on neighbors' doors and looking for her way home. Many times, one of them had to stay overnight to make sure their mother didn't try to leave. Lois did her best to participate in their care under these conditions and hoped everyone would soon come to the same conclusion she had.

I looked at the accumulating problems assaulting Lois since the year began. She was finally out of school, but constructing the foundations of her new position was very demanding, requiring at times sixty hours or more a week. She maintained her advocacy work with many of the traditional agencies she worked with over the years by phone and Internet conferencing. She was trying to manage the care of two sets of parents with encroaching maladies that would eventually end in heartache for everyone. She finished her last newsletter of the year. She completed it just two days before Christmas. Even with the help of her friend, she barely had time to finish before the year left out.

George S. J. Anderson

(Editorial by Lois A. Anderson dated December 23, 2004)

All I can think about is how 2004 has flown by as I sit here and write this last newsletter of the year. (Yes, you will be reading this in January). We are having a temporary warm-up in the weather after almost a week of unusually cold weather for this time of year. Christmas will be here in another couple of days!

I have some wonderful project underway at work, now that I can concentrate my efforts in York County rather than try and take care of a much larger four county area. As the Bereavement Coordinator, I hope to be able to introduce some new ideas and make available to our hospice families many more resources than what they now have. Another improvement is that I am in constant contact with many more of these families after the death of their loved one than any of my predecessors and that's saying something when you have a caseload of over 250 families.

I am looking forward to Christmas, just to be able to relax and do some things I want to do. Merry Christmas, Happy Hanukah, Happy Kwanzaa, and all of that whatever your holiday favorites are, but for everyone, I wish all of you the best in 2005!

Lois

She was still battling her own stage IV breast cancer with chemotherapy, its adjacent modalities, follow-up testing, and sometimes cruel side effects. So many times I just had to put my hand on her shoulders and tell her things would get better. In fact, by the end of the year, her tumor markers were down to 34. The chemotherapy she and her oncologist agreed upon was working for her. It was, at least, one good thing to end her year.

A Glimpse of Oblivion

Tell me about the darkness . . .

The origins of what "would be" passed into the time of empty yesterdays as I ventured time and time again into my solitary world beneath the great tree. Silent, waiting, and with perpetual patience, it stood with its laden branches, shielding me from the harshness of the rain and truant storms. The dance of foretelling commenced, and neither I nor the dream could bear to see the roots of its weeds grow in our hearts. I listened for wisdom and heard silence, looked for visions and was blinded, and wanted to feel warmth but was offered the winter.

There was no obstacle to prevent the knowing of the things to come. It was the strength to know them before they went from perceived to real. That strength would come from magic, life, and love for all of us. They would not be forgotten. They would get the chance to change things, make it happen, then move on . . . beyond the places where we once knew them. I asked the tree, "Why such short moments to run so long a race?"

It was the wind that answered through the tree's rustling leaves. "From the moment of our birth to the moment of our death, we are given a space of time to show the worth of our being here."

Finality was in our sight. Fear was the cold grasp . . . Courage was the way to break it . . . Wisdom was the way to see it coming.

On the fourth day, Timothy passed through the village of Vigil then pushed forward on the remaining twenty parcels toward Emansupass. Night walked toward him with deliberate steps, making him realize the extent of his weariness. The exertion of pushing forward on his quest forced exhaustion to descend over him like a heavy blanket. He found a bevy of fir trees, which would restrict the view of his camp from unwanted onlookers, and stopped to rest there. He lay his head against a pile of cut limbs and laid his blanket beneath him. The scent of the firs enticed him into a world of sleep and dreams, but before that door opened, he needed to think.

Omar showed him the map room of the North Wind. "Not one village . . . but two villages," Omar told him. "But they may not be villages . . ." he said as a warning.

"So if they aren't villages, what are they?" Timothy shouted to first stars of the night.

Timothy finally collapsed inside the reality of his world, swimming across the deep pool of darkness known to those who sleep, and dreamed of a great tree. He dreamed he followed the wall of stones where a fantastic tree unveiled its presence a great distance away with no way to reach it. Its beauty surpassed anything he saw in the villages. Cloaked in layers of multicolored flowers, it almost glowed in a variegated gown of phosphorescent leaves. It was, indeed, the place where dreams and answers met. As he struggled to move closer, the distance remained constant. He could only admire the sight of a path of white stones that stretched from the wall to the strangely beautiful tree. From behind him, the voice of his beloved Catherine said, "My immortality lies beneath." Timothy longed for a glimpse of her, but when he turned, nothing was there. It was a phantom voice. When he turned back, the tree vanished, leaving a terrain of broken rocks and gray mists consuming the vision. The dream disturbed him, and he awakened, just long enough to see a halo encircling the night moon in her slow-paced dance across the night sky. He woke long enough to understand the pretense of bad weather for the morning's journey to the distant village of Emansupass.

He was tired; sleep poured its opiate nectar over his eyes, and in moments, he dreamed of a desolate mountain ridge littered with withered trees and snow. He looked across the stony ridge where an abandoned village broke through the icy valley with impossible ruined spires and incredibly ornate but broken stone walls. This dream forced endeavors to find a way inside but blocked every attempt with enormous felled trees, brush, and paths ending in unscaled rock formations. He vainly tried other ways, but obstacles blocked his every move. He realized time was growing short, but anything he tried, no matter how tiring or dangerous the path was, he was unable to enter the deserted village. The dream was contrived to be exhausting; the frustration inherent to its untenable purpose eventually woke him just before dawn. He had enough of these disturbing dreams and quickly folded his bedroll and started his way to Emansupass.

It was the fifth day of the wall breach when Timothy rode across the southern borders of the village. He was greeted by the village residents who heard of his coming from Amos's messengers. Everyone was well aware of his quest and encouraged him to find a man called "Timmerloo."

Timmerloo was to be found above the northern borders of Emansupass in a hewn stone house the villagers called "the lodge." According to the villagers, the lodge would not be difficult to find in that its architecture was unique. The lodge was a vision of scribbled carvings featuring the creatures and humans of legends and folklore. This was not the only feature to make the lodge unusual. The lodge was surrounded on all sides with random placement of stone carvings of creatures and beasts not seen in this world since Timothy or his ancestors were born to this world. To the inhabitants of Emansupass, Timmerloo lived with the haunted failings of the ancients. No one ventured there without reason . . . No one sought the elusive and mysterious resident for many solens. However, when the villagers received the message of Timothy's arrival, word was sent to Timmerloo's residence to expect him.

Timothy restocked his provisions with goods from various traders and merchants on the streets of Emansupass then resumed the search for the elusive man the villagers called Timmerloo. He wandered the streets and lanes of this unusually large village, marveling at the unique architecture he found. His travels brought him within sight of a stone arch framing a wide street into the west. The arch was fashioned to allow travelers to pass through the open mouth of an effigy to the West Wind. Another lane was lined on either side by two mountain goats, made of white stone, laying side by side, their full bodies towering the tallest buildings in Emansupass. This village had its share of intrigue and mystery Timothy discovered as he travelled to the northern gate of the village.

Before Timothy left the hospitality of the vendors in Emansupass, they told him to find the Northern Gate. The villagers described it as an effigy dedicated to the North Wind. Timothy supposed the gate would be similar to the western gate. He was not expecting the enormous apparition appearing before him. The entrance to the north was an elaborate carving illustrated by the upper torso of a male body with the lower half buried at the waist. The enormous statue appeared to be lying down, its opened mouth resting on folded arms, lying buried beneath the chin. The way to the north was through the mouth of the ancient statue. It wasn't just a gate. It was a short tunnel opening between the North Wind's unfurled wings. As Timothy passed through this impressive sculpture, he surveyed undecipherable scrawling, written in the hand of the Ancients, inscribed on every surface. Timothy stared in amazement as his horse, oblivious to the history it passed through, walked away from the effigy into the last traveled lands of the north.

The road continued on the other side as it closed against Timothy with foliage, trees, and rugged stone cliffs. In time, the oppressive road opened to an expansive well-tended field. It was here the villagers instructed Timothy to watch for the road to branch in two directions. One continued to the north, while the eastern road ended at Timmerloo's home. Where the road branched, Timothy stopped his horse. He knew the way north would take him closer to the end of his quest, but without knowing what he was looking for, he would risk Catherine's life needlessly. The desire to go north was strong, but his need to understand the purpose of his quest made him turn his horse east.

The eastern road followed the open field for a parcel or more before it disappeared behind a thick dark forest. A weird darkness spread over the road, and the thick scent of pines textured the air. The sky became gray as an impending storm stilled the air, and everything went quiet. Timothy pushed his horse, while the damp air grew misty tendrils and poured them on the road before him. A feeling of dread knotted his bones as mists walked as transparent specters, blocking the view of the road before him. Finally, he saw the gray daylight appear where thick pines framed the road to an open area. He ushered his horse into the graying light where another field opened before him. The icy feeling of dread melted, as astonishment crashed through with amazing discovery.

The villagers of Emansupass warned Timothy of the strange statues occupying the grounds around Timmerloo's lodge. They greatly understated the expansiveness of the carvings. He was surrounded by endless renderings of pale stone animals and creatures, the likes of which he had never seen. The edge of the tree line was marked by the effigy of a bearlike creature, poised to attack, carved with small eyes and curved tusklike teeth. The apparition was larger than three horses, making Timothy consider the work was full sized to illustrate its likeness when this creature inhabited their world. The grounds were a study of irony, as beyond this massive reproduction were carved effigies of tiny horses no bigger than a small dog. He continued staring in wonder at the enormity of stone creatures poised and arranged in random order. He searched for the elusive stone lodge, veiled by the thick mists, still beyond the reach of his eyes. The haze spilled over the grounds like a pale, slow-moving ocean; its waves swallowed the sculptures in eddies washing over the mountings, making each creature appear to be standing or crouched in the growing mass. The silence of this garden of stone was unnerving as he proceeded to a tall black obelisk. It was strange to find such a structure among the white carved stones. It was as tall as ten men covered with the same undecipherable writings he saw in the map room in Bridgedom and again at the northern gate of Emansupass. He stopped a moment to look at the writings more clearly.

"Timothy, I believe," said a voice, coming from behind it.

"Yes . . ." he said, startled to hear his name.

A tall lanky figure moved from behind the structure and faced him. "I've been expecting you for some time. I am Timmerloo."

Timothy took a moment to regain his composure. This man Timmerloo moved like a ghost. He was soft spoken and moved with quick silent footsteps. He was dressed in the long black coats worn by mountain guides. His white wizened locks spilled over the lapels of *his coat like snow. He was clean shaven with stone blue eyes. Timothy did not know what to make of his strange interloper. His voice did not reveal tension, dislike, aversion, friendship, or acceptance. Timmerloo was like a ghost inhabiting a body to communicate with the living. Timothy stared at the old man, trying to understand what disturbed him; but when Timmerloo continued his unmitigated silence, he was forced to ask, "Where do we go from here? I was told you stay at a lodge inside these carved stones, but I have not seen such a structure since I arrived." Timothy surveyed the visible horizons quickly erased by the growing mists. He turned to Timmerloo and said, "The size of these statues would block out the sun, if there was any sunlight to speak of."*

Timmerloo nodded. "I too have seen the signs that foretell of changing weather. By tonight, there should be thunder, lightning, and heavy rain. I think you will do well to stay at the lodge until it passes."

"I know Amos passed word along of my pressing need to finish this quest," Timothy said, hoping to urge the old man to continue.

"I was told to help in any way I could," Timmerloo said, as he turned and walked away.

"Where are you going?" Timothy asked, prodding his horse to follow the strange old man.

"Follow me, and I will help you," he said without turning to face him. "We have much to talk about."

Timmerloo may have been old, but he was quick on his feet. The old man moved so quickly through the stone creatures, that many times, Timothy lost track and called for direction. Timmerloo led them through the arcane, sometimes bizarre, garden of stone carvings. Eventually, the lodge appeared in the midst of the ancient statues. A light rain started by the time they arrived. The unsettled weather did not distract the view of the massive stone structure.

Again, the villagers greatly understated the magnitude of the stone building they called the lodge. The structure was created inside an entire hillside made of solid gray rock. It was cut into multiple levels with steps leading to a large stone landing, where four towering columns held the face of a sculpted wall behind them. Timothy heard such structures existed in ancient times, but all were destroyed when Winterland fell centuries ago. He thought such structures were simply folklore, but here was evidence they once existed.

Timmerloo stopped at the first staircase and stopped. He turned and observed how Timothy stared, mesmerized by the architecture he saw before him. He called to Timothy, "Take your horse to the side of the lodge. There you will find food, water, and a place of shelter for it. When you finish, come back."

The order Timmerloo ushered to Timothy was well received. When his horse was properly attended, he rejoined Timmerloo at the first set of stairs. He found the old man exactly where he left him. The rain picked up pace as Timmerloo continued to sit in the rain without saying anything. "Timmerloo, I've stabled my horse. Are you ready to go inside?"

Timmerloo stood and looked around like he forgot his guest. He ran his hand through his hair and realized his hair was soaked with rain. He looked where Timothy stood and said, "It's raining. We should go inside."

"Please lead the way . . . I will follow," Timothy said, puzzled this man could help him. He didn't have the sense to wait for him out of the rain. Still, Amos believed Timmerloo held the answers he was seeking, so he was willing to learn what he could before he moved on. He followed him up four flights of steps leading to the large landing. They crossed the landing then passed through the columns where Timothy saw the wall covered with carvings. Cut into relief, above two huge wooden plank doors, were the effigies of the Four Winds walking through mountain ranges in abject nakedness.

Timmerloo stopped before the great doors. "Have you ever seen the Four Winds depicted this way?"

Timmerloo raised a hand to direct Timothy's attention to the relief with a pointed finger. Timothy broke his fixed attention on the relief and responded. "I never saw anything like it." Timothy wasn't sure if the artist who rendered the work did it in reverence or defiance. The relief was a huge deviation from what was considered "proper" in the villages. One word came to mind as he observed the relief, "obscene."

"I can see by your eyes you do not approve," Timmerloo said without a hint of judgment.

"All I said was I never saw workmanship like this before . . . that's all. I had no opinion of it being good or bad," Timothy countered, wondering what this strange man had in store for him.

"Words rarely say what is intended," Timmerloo said cryptically over his shoulder, while he unlatched the massive wooden doors. When the doors opened, he said, "Come inside, we have much to talk about."

Timothy thought what Timmerloo said was ironic. First, he says words don't mean anything, and then in the same breath, he says we have to talk about a lot of things. *He followed the old man through the doors and stared at the magnificent hall before him.*

Inside, the foyer expanded dramatically to a gigantic chamber. It resembled a tomb, not a room to entertain guests. A mass of alcoves displaying statues of men, women, and children were methodically carved into a repetitive standing position and rose, stacked in calculated columns around the circular wall. Each figure was clothed in the long robes the villagers prescribed as proper burial attire. Every statue was provisioned with books, weapons, or baskets of flowers. They were exquisitely rendered, each one distinct, yet connected in their creation by the same white marble. When Timothy processed the sight of the entire room, it became very disquieting. The wall of alcoves started at the floor and rose, tier after tier, to the level of eighteen niches where it curved at the top of a domed ceiling. The dome, constructed of clear material, allowed natural light to illuminate the chamber. At the center of the dome was a huge rendering of a single rose, carved from the same stone as the statues living in the niches.

Timothy was overwhelmed by the beautiful strangeness, never looking to where he was walking until the edge of his boot caught something. He looked down quickly and saw the floor littered with shining stars. He looked where he entered the room and saw multicolored stones glowing all over the floor where he walked. He looked around and realized the entire floor was glowing, their light touching the walls everywhere he looked.

Timmerloo, unimpeded by the curiosities of the gigantic chamber, glided over the floor faster than Timothy could walk. Seeing his obvious interest in the peculiar nature of his home, he stopped and turned. "Timothy, you must keep up. Certainly an old man is no challenge for you . . . am I?"

Timothy asked, "What is this place?"

"The answers you need are not in this room, young man . . . Follow me and see," the old man said, as he continued his way across the floor bejeweled with flecks and points of multicolored stones embedded in the floor.

Timothy watched the old man moving away and then started walking quickly to close the distance between them. He had many questions but kept silent, waiting for the chance to ask them. When they traveled the distance across the vaulted room, Timmerloo moved beside a small unimposing wooden door. Light spilled over them as the door opened. Timothy hurried across the threshold, leaving his last footsteps on the foyer behind him.

Beyond the door was a large modest kitchen. The warm light inside was provided by several oil lamps hanging strategically around the room and the remnants of a fire dying in the hearth. It was a sharp contrast from the room they left. The foyer was eloquent, cold, and enigmatic; the kitchen was inviting, warm, and commonplace. There was a rough wooden table running the length of the kitchen's wall with eight chairs so beautifully carved and treated, only a master woodworker could have created them. The remaining walls were adorned with heavy tapestries showing scenes of men hunting ancient animals Timothy only knew from stone reliefs found throughout the villages. At the far end of the kitchen was a stained-glass window made from eighteen sections of pink glass surrounding one white section in its center. The rest of the room was an eclectic collection of wooden cabinets and closets made for the simple function of organizing the many kitchen utensils and cookware.

About halfway through the room, Timmerloo stopped. He turned to Timothy and said, "Sit down. There is much to learn."

He walked to a chair and sat as Timmerloo instructed. The old man did not continue his conversation. Instead, he moved to the hearth and added kindling to the dying flames. He swung a black kettle, mounted on an iron arm, over the remnants of the fire and then pulled a stool near the fire to warm himself. Again, Timothy felt Timmerloo forgot he was there. When the old man continued his silence, Timothy asked, "You say there is much to tell me. What is there to discuss? I feel my time running out, and since I arrived at Emansupass, I have also run out of places to call my next destination."

Timmerloo looked from the growing flames in the hearth and spoke, "Many have come before to this place looking for legends and stories of where they have been and where they are going. Amos sent word of your coming, and your quest is particularly fascinating."

Timothy was impatient. He wanted to know the location of his next pursuit to save his beloved Catherine. He stared at Timmerloo and then asked, "So are there villages in the mountains that no one knows about, or have I come to the end of the journey with nothing?"

"Many journeys come to nothing," Timmerloo said with no emotion in his voice.

"Has mine?" Timothy asked. "Has my journey ended here with no hope of saving Catherine?"

"Have you ever read a book, boy?" Timmerloo asked.

"My father read to me as a young boy," he said, confused by the strange question and growing impatience.

"Then you noticed how chapters began and how each ended as a thought completed. They collectively made a story or taught a lesson. They are essentially a journey of steps leading to a conclusion by the end of the pages."

"So all stories and lessons come to an end . . . Is this what I came to discover? That's pathetic," Timothy told him, his impatience growing to anger.

Timmerloo remained silent, allowing the boy time to understand what he told him.

"I don't understand why Amos would send me here. This seems like an end point. This can't be all there is . . . There must be something beyond this village. How do I find the things that exist beyond this place? Amos said you could help me, so tell me what I need to do to go on."

"You need to listen and learn . . . The things and places existing beyond these borders are like ghosts. They appear and disappear without provocation and rarely, if ever, do they help in any way," Timmerloo told him, trying to stave his insistence to be on his way.

"Who are you? Amos and the villagers of Emansupass told me you are a very wise man. They told me you might be a 'seeker.'"

"A seeker!" Timmerloo said, startled by Timothy's accusation. *"I haven't heard that word spoken in some time. Why would anyone say that?"*

"I don't know," Timothy conceded.

"I'm sure I am a lot of things to different people, but to be called a 'seeker' without pursuing such an endeavor is insulting." Timmerloo's calm exterior was lost. Timothy was definitely something out of the ordinary. Timmerloo needed to consider him outside the realm of his usual guests. Most were hunters, simply looking for good places to hunt, and the superficial explorers, looking for rare ores or treasures supposedly hidden in the mountains by the Ancients. Timothy, it seemed, was looking for something far more elusive, more

magical, and perhaps unattainable . . . immortality for someone other than himself. There was a legend! The legend spoke of a place beyond the mythical village of Winterland. He had only spoken to one person about this in his entire lifetime . . . Amos. He faced Timothy and asked, "What did Amos tell you?"

"He told me you knew how to help me," Timothy exclaimed, thinking Timmerloo was looking to fault Amos for sending him here.

"Did he say how? Did he tell you about Winterland?" Timmerloo asked. His loss of temerity and control of his even temperament departed.

"He told me not to believe in Winterland, though I saw a place on a map where it could be . . . Why? Is it really there?" Timothy asked, excited he finally broke Timmerloo's resolve.

"In a way . . . it is there." Timmerloo paused, then turned to the fire as it picked through the pile of kindling with pointed fingers of flame.

"In what way is Winterland there?" Timothy asked, insisting on a straight answer.

Timmerloo turned from the fire to face him. "I mean, it exists from time to time in the blowing snows and splintered rocks and stones that guard it from outside eyes."

"So it is a real place?" Timothy asked, not getting the answer he wanted from Timmerloo.

"As real as your thoughts . . ." was his enigmatic reply.

"How real are thoughts?" Timothy asked, trying to get to the bottom of Timmerloo's answers.

"Thoughts become real when acted upon." Timmerloo held up his hand to stave off Timothy's next question. "Remember when I asked if you could read?"

"Yes," Timothy answered patiently.

"After I told you all stories and lessons are steps in a journey, you told me all journeys end. Am I correct?"

Timothy nodded in agreement.

"Why is it then, when we get to the end of the story and the lesson, we continue thinking about what we read and what we remember about them? If the conclusion lies in those final pages, then why do we go on thinking about them? Are thoughts just more pages we add to any story, any lesson we ever heard or read? Are they any less real than written pages?"

"Invisible pages? Pages that are real because my thoughts are real?" Timothy asked skeptically. "It is still not something I can see or hold in my hand. It is still not something I can touch or feel if it is warm or cold, soft or coarse. Real is something I can see . . . with my own two eyes."

Timmerloo raised his eyes to face him. "Then the Four Winds do not exist for you, do they?"

The question forced Timothy to his feet. "That's not what I'm saying!"

Timmerloo was insistent. "Think about it. Every day you cannot see the winds. You cannot hold the wind in your hands. They are neither soft nor coarse . . . and though they can blow hot or cold, they are really neither one. They simply carry the cold or warm air along over the places they come from." Timmerloo saw he was finally getting through to Timothy. "Yet they are quite real, are they not?"

Again, Timothy nodded in agreement, not knowing how to answer Timmerloo's question yet retain his belief in what was real and what was not.

"The Four Winds have their way of showing us they are real when we see the clouds blowing across the sky, when a storm moves in and then moves away, when the leaves rustle in the trees, and when they sing through the rafters at night. Just because we don't see them

does not mean they don't exist . . . that they are not real. I think the things that are real need a broader definition, don't you?"

"But I need a direction, the next village, the next cross roads, and the next destination to get the chance to save Catherine," Timothy protested. "This is not taking me any place."

"It will," Timmerloo said, as he bowed his head and put more wood on the fire, blazing in the hearth. He glanced where Timothy was sitting and said, "I've seen Winterland . . . It lies on the unwritten pages."

"What?" Timothy asked, startled by Timmerloo's quick, chopped statement.

"It's what you wanted to know, isn't it?" Timmerloo asked, while he kneaded more wood into the fire.

"And it exists in the real world?"

"Yes, but the treachery of the land and the constant cold weather makes it almost impossible to get to."

"But you've been there?" Timothy asked with renewed interest.

"I've been close enough to see it, but I never made it the whole way," Timmerloo said, as his demeanor returned to its controlled nature.

"What stopped you?"

"Everything . . . drifting snow, wind so strong it pushes against you, splintered rock sharp enough to cut you just brushing against it, and passages leading to blind cliffs and impassable trails," Timmerloo told him.

"But you 'did' see it?" Timothy asked. "It wasn't an illusion or snow blindness?"

"Yes," Timmerloo replied, as if no one was in the room.

"How did you know it was Winterland and not some rock formation that looked like a village in the snow?" Timothy asked skeptically.

"What do you know of Winterland?" Timmerloo asked.

Timothy thought for a moment then said, "Not much. Just what the legends and folklore have told us, as they were handed down over the centuries since the village supposedly fell. The legends tell of horrific crimes committed against the very students who lived and studied there. The teachers forced them to compete against each other. Their sense of competition, where one person wanted to be in that top position, was so ravenous that rape and murder became common occurrences as a means to humiliate, destroy, or remove someone from the contest. Because of the depravity that occurred at Winterland, competition has been outlawed for centuries and continues to this very day."

Timmerloo sat staring at the fire while he considered Timothy's words. He turned his face from the fire and addressed the young man. "Yes, I believe there is a grain of truth to the old legends. But I also believe some of the power in Winterland survived, even after the 'scourge' that forbade the use of the word 'teacher,' a term once used for a person who improved the minds of the young."

"Improved their minds . . . at what cost?" Timothy continued, angry with more questions. "Having one person living their lives in peace with no needs other than each other is not enough? Why would we need to compete to such a level where we would destroy one another just to be better than someone?"

"Please!" Timmerloo said, holding up both hands. "I'm not here to defend or support the alleged legends of Winterland. I'm just trying to explain what I found when I stumbled into that desolate place."

"And what did you find? Was it really the remains of an ancient village?" Timothy asked, calming himself as he pulled a chair away from the table to sit facing Timmerloo.

"I wasn't looking for it . . . that's a certainty," Timmerloo began. *"Three hunters from Emansupass decided to hunt for deer, elk, and other game in the mountain passes and asked me to act as their guide. It started as a simple hunting trip. The sky went gray while we prepared our gear for harsh weather. The mountain passes are rugged, and with snow already on the ground, our prey would be easy to spot against the white background. We traveled ten parcels north when the snow started. At first, it was just a light snow, gentle and easy, but when it started falling in clumps, we could barely see each other. We decided to find shelter until it passed. We found a deep niche, broken out by the weather, in the side of a cliff."*

"I'm sure you were all cold. Could you start a fire to keep warm?" Timothy interrupted.

"We tried, but though the passes are mostly stone, there were enough trees in the area we should have been able to gather wood for a fire. Unfortunately, no one could see beyond the falling snow to find firewood and return safely. Besides, snow covered the dry wood to such an extent we needed to cut branches from the live trees we could find above the snow line. We were completely snow blind. Once we settled into the niche, we covered the entrance with branches we found inside and stretched a woven tarp across them. It wasn't much, but it kept the snow off and stopped the wind from driving the cold snow against us. By morning, the snow stopped. Phillip, one of the men in the hunting party, opened the tarp and found snow as deep as our hips."

"So the four of you were stranded there?" Timothy asked.

Timmerloo looked up from his place at the hearth and continued, *"Yes, we were stranded, and we were afraid. No one knew where we were. Any search party Emansupass sent would never know where to find us. We did not know where we were . . . We didn't recognize our surroundings. Phillip asked me and the other hunters, Bethan and William, where they thought we were. In our need to find shelter, none of us knew where we had come to. We were lost, with little food and no fire to warm or cook what we had. It was Phillip who decided to dig out of the niche to find wood. A few arm's lengths from the opening, he found a tree where he cut some branches and brought them back.*

Inside the niche, we found some dried grass and twigs to start a fire. When Phillip could venture out farther, Bethan and William joined him. Within a short time, we had a fair fire burning at the mouth of the niche. At least we weren't going to freeze. There wasn't enough food to cover us for more than a few days. We knew we needed to find a way back to Emansupass. We knew it had to be soon, or we would all starve or freeze to death on the mountain."

"So how long did you stay in the stone niche?" Timothy asked, wondering how Timmerloo and the others survived.

"We weren't there much past the second night. Bethan found something in the niche none of us noticed because the darkness and the dark nature of the stone from which the niche was formed hid it." *He looked up again, finding Timothy listening intently to everything he said. Seeing he was not wasting words, he continued his story, "For some reason, Bethan watched the smoke rolling out the vent we made in the tarp. He watched the smoke collect at the top of the niche and move to a place behind us. He followed it, taking a lighted branch from the fire to investigate where it was going. What he found was an opening in the roof of the niche not seen without light. It was there the smoke rose up out of sight."*

Timmerloo stopped a moment, collecting his thoughts. Timothy, impatient for the old man to continue, said, "Go on, what happened next? Was the opening large enough to fit a man through?"

"It was better than that. The entire roof was a stone ledge moving in an upward slope. When Bethan found it, he threw the lighted branch into what he thought was just a small hole and realized it was a large stone ledge. It was a way out!"

"How did he know this?" Timothy asked, thinking how odd the whole situation seemed to him.

"It was the smoke. The smoke rose up and away as if there was a shaft leading outside."

"But weren't you all taking a chance? The passage could have ended in fissures in the rocks at some point. You all could have died

trying to find a way through passages blindly ending in cracks no larger than your hand."

"Indeed, we did discuss that possibility. In the end, we decided we would die staying where we were, so it was either take the chance on the shaft or freeze to death in the niche. We decided to take the chance it might lead to a way out. Bethan led us. Each one grabbed the stone ledge in turn and climbed up. The ledge slanted in an upward grade and continued in a spiral."

Timothy interrupted, "The ledge was actually a 'spiral walkway'?"

"Yes," Timmerloo said.

Timothy considered what the old man told him then asked, "The ledge was actually made by someone—it wasn't a natural fault in the rock?"

"At the time, we were more interested in escaping our situation than why the spiral walkway was there. We were just happy to find it. But yes, the questions as to who made it did occur to us when we came out of the passage." Timmerloo stopped and then bowed his head. A tear ran over the side of his cheek.

Timothy watched the old man pause, realizing something terrible must have happened there. He held his questions, hoping Timmerloo would continue.

Without looking up, the journey of his tear ended, and Timmerloo continued, "The top of the walkway ended inside a cut stone chamber. There we realized we entered a man-made structure. Its purpose was not evidenced by anything we found there. But we were not the first people to have found the walkway. Etched in stone were names written in the hand of the villages and, more importantly, words written in the hand of the Ancients. In the center of the room was a square stone table, as high as your knees, piled with small stones. Written on its side, in the writing of the villages, were these words. "If you are friends, please carry our stones to the wall." There were people here that did not survive the perimeters of this chamber."

"But you said there wasn't any danger as you all climbed the walkway to the chamber. Was the chamber dangerous?" Timothy asked.

"No, but seeing those stones heaped on the table made us very cautious. There were, at least, a hundred stones there. We searched around and found nothing dangerous in the chamber. On the other side of the room was another passage leading out to sunlight and a warm breeze. We left the stones where they were and decided to move on.

"The passage took us to a flat stone path running across the top of the mountain. It showed no sign of deviating for as far as we could see. It was barely a footpath, but we saw the stones were interlocking and realized we were looking at something man made. Again we saw the work of the Ancients. However, the treachery of the mountains made us wary of where the path led. The snow we abandoned at the niche was almost nonexistent where sunlight melted what remained off the black stone footpath. None of us understood why the pile of stones existed where we left them. The path before us was well worn and appeared remarkably safe from our vantage point."

Timothy put up a finger to interrupt. "So you were all traveling along the top of a mountain with nothing to stop any of you. Then why the ominous warning from the travelers who left their stones in the chamber?"

"The stone path led nowhere. We traveled a full day before we understood the footpath was something people used at one time to cross the tops of the mountains to unknown destinations that no longer existed. We made the decision to climb down the side of the mountain to go get help. It was almost sunset when Bethan volunteered to make the attempt.

"We had no climbing gear, since our original plan was to hunt. We had weapons but nothing to climb off the mountain. Our journey from the stone chamber led through nothing but sharp splintered rocks the entire way. Based on the direction of the sun, we surmised the path ran south to north, which meant the almost impassable sides were the east and west. Our way to Emansupass would lie southeast *from where we were. We traveled all day northward trying to find a way off the mountain. We were well off course with little food to spare. Nothing grew on either side of the mountain for as far as we could see, which meant any wildlife we might find had no need to venture to this desolate place. Staying here was a poorer decision than staying at the stone chamber or the niche where we could have a fire to stay warm.*

After much discussion, we agreed to sleep on the path then find a way off the mountain when the sun came up. Bethan woke before anyone and found what he felt would be the best way off the mountain. He woke us, and we prepared to make our way off the top of the mountain. Bethan was a remarkable climber, finding ways through the sharp black rocks that blocked the light and making the way through the homogenous stones a safe walkway."

Timothy stopped him for a moment and asked. "I don't understand, Timmerloo. What do you mean by that? Do you mean to say the cliffs and rock faces where you were looked exactly alike? The entire mountain was made of the same kind of stones and rocks?"

"That's precisely what I mean. The mountain was a product of nature, which, at the time we made that first attempt to climb down, masked our progress with the common unchanging character built into its structure."

Timothy put his hand under his chin like he was thinking about something then said, "I can understand why the group had trouble descending the mountain. With the unchanging surroundings, it would be impossible to follow any landmarks as a guide." He then sat up and asked Timmerloo, "Did anyone place marks or signs on the rocks to prevent any circling back or guide where you left the path?"

"Bethan insisted we leave markings on the rocks as we made our way down. It was, as you said, any safe ways off the mountain had us circling back to places we traveled before. Eventually, we realized there was no safe way to simply walk off the mountain. We needed to climb down the sharp craggy rocks with ropes and tackle to escape our fate."

"But none of you were equipped with climbing gear. How did anyone think they were going to climb down?" Timothy asked, curious how they solved this problem.

"Where we stopped, William spotted a flat snowy patch of ground where we could climb safely, if we had ropes. It was William and Phillip who came up with the idea to make ropes, hooks, and rings from the equipment we carried. We knew it was a desperate move, but it seemed like something that might work. We only had enough equipment to lower one man at a time. It would take two of us to keep our makeshift ropes from rubbing against the sharp stone face as each man was lowered. It meant two of us needed to stay behind. We would return to the niche and wait, while the other two made their way off the mountain for help. When all was ready, we decided Bethan and William best suited to make the decent. After we lowered each man to the snowy patch below us, we dropped all the makeshift gear and tackle to them. Phillip and I watched as they waved and then walked through those black spires of stone crusted with snow and disappeared. We never saw them again."

Timothy watched the old man pause and saw the sadness fall over him like a mist. He needed Timmerloo to continue his story, so he asked softly, "What do you think happened to them?"

"I think the mountain swallowed them. They probably became disoriented by the various obstacles the mountain presented, and they either were injured or starved to death. I never wanted to know, and I never did."

"So what did you both do?"

"We found our markings on the black stones and eventually climbed back to the path at the top of the mountain."

Timothy looked at Timmerloo and realized the old man was having a difficult time retelling this part of the story. But Timothy's interest was related to the existence of Winterland. He suspected Timmerloo was getting to that part, but he was impatient to move on to his next destination. Catherine's life was depending on him now . . . he was certain of it. "Timmerloo, how does your story tell me anything about the lost village of Winterland? Everything you have spoken about tells me of wastelands and paths that lead nowhere. If everything is as desolate as you say, why would anyone build such a place there? In fact, why create a place so impassable, a place the villages once sent its young students? Who would have traveled there? The way to Winterland should have been traveled easily from all directions, making it the most accessible place of all the villages."

Timmerloo could see the young man's impatience growing. Yet he knew warnings of what lay before him needed to be said. He didn't want Timothy rushing off to what could be his death. "I understand your questions. I also wondered, if Winterland was not just folklore, then how did the ancient villagers manage to send children there? The place we saw was dangerous, and any misstep could be fatal. It was not a place to send children. I really have no answers as to why it was placed where it was other than to make my own conjectures".

Taking a breath, he continued, "I believe, when Winterland fell, the villagers destroyed all the safe roads and passages with perilous rock falls, traps, and impassable roadblocks. I think the revulsion that festered for the decades after its fall consumed them. They left its ruins ripe with dismembered roads, ingenious traps, and superficial paths leading nowhere, forcing utter, final isolation upon it and assuring its demise. Any family who lost a son or daughter to the corrupt perversion that destroyed lives and suffocated the innocent inside its borders had terrible retributions to exact upon Winterland. Many secrets preventing those from finding Winterland remain silent, waiting to exact their suffering on the voyager. The outer perimeter guarding its clandestine location is more than cautionary . . . it's deadly!"

"Your need to caution me is well intentioned, but you know I will go even if the journey is hopeless," Timothy said with greater insistence.

"Yes," Timmerloo acknowledged with resignation. "I believe I realized you would not stop when I first met you. I knew you would continue to look for a way to save Catherine even if it meant your own life. I will try to be brief, but I want you to know what you are up against."

Timothy turned to where Timmerloo sat and said, "Then tell me, what did happen when you and Phillip got to the top of the mountain again?"

"We split up," he said, as he looked directly at Timothy.

"But why?" Timothy asked, confounded by the thought of why two grown men would risk splitting up in such an inhospitable place.

"We knew the niche was a safe place. One of us could go back and wait for the others. We felt the path had some destination, and as long as the path remained safe, one of us could take the risk to find out. We hoped it would eventually lead off the mountain. I decided to go."

"And Phillip went back to the niche?"

"Yes. If I could get off the mountain, I would return with help. If not, I would return where Phillip would be waiting for the others."

"So it was then you discovered Winterland?" Timothy asked.

"I found something." Timmerloo paused for a moment and then continued, "The path continued as I hurried along the ridge of the mountain. It was endless, with flat-faced stone or bottomless ravines pitted up against both sides of the man-made path. One could not stray from the path without risking being torn to pieces in the razor-sharp rocks or fall to a crushing death from the top of a sheer cliff. At times, the path crossed open places where the mountain fell off to such places on either side. I saw no way down. I followed the path, wandering along a serpentine passage through high rocks that blocked the meager light of the winter's sun. When the path came to a kind of crossroads inside these black monoliths, I was forced to decide which direction I would take.

"There were no markings to determine where each path led. I found some loose stones and piled them up to mark the way I came and used others to show the way I would proceed. With the sun blocked

by the huge stones, I could not determine which road went east. The path turned and twisted so much, I did not think I was still walking north. I suspected the path to the right would be heading east, toward Emansupass. The fact was I could have been heading any direction. I went with my instincts.

"The passage to the east, as I suspected it to be, was narrow with broken pieces of stone covering the cut stones laid by the ancient stonecutters. Unlike the path on the ridge of the mountain, this path descended and opened eventually on a perfectly circular valley. The path continued along the ridge but showed no signs of a way to climb down. The cut stone path had not fared well in the elements, and many times, parts of the stone path lay in slanted positions where water and ice undermined the ground beneath them. But the path was not as curious as what littered the bottom of the valley."

"Was it Winterland?" Timothy asked, intrigued he was finally getting to what he wanted to hear.

"What I saw were the possible remains of a very advanced village," Timmerloo told him.

"What do you mean? What makes you think it even was a village? If it was just pieces, how could you even know how advanced it was?" Timothy asked, skepticism returning to his questions.

"Again, Timothy, you raise good questions. Understand, when I saw it, I was looking for a way off the mountain. The sight of a lost village is not new to me. There are many lost villages and settlements to the south and to the west, where I journeyed in my time. To find one in the north? Well, that was unprecedented. Knowing the legends and folklore surrounding the lost village of Winterland made what I found intriguing, yet like you, I remained the skeptic. I was not willing to make a fool of myself telling, even myself, this was Winterland."

"But something convinced you this was different from what you saw in your travels, didn't it?" Timothy asked.

"Being at the top of a ridge, looking down on something, gives you a sense of perspective. I could make out wide geometrical streets, with a vortex leading to the center of the valley."

"Geometrical?" Timothy interrupted. "What are you talking about, Timmerloo?"

"It's a word meaning there were shapes of triangles, or three-sided figures, squares, and circles, or rounds, as the villagers call them now. All these shapes worked together like a fitted mosaic over the entire floor of the valley. It was not laid out like any village I ever saw. A small waterfall was channeled off one side of the mountain then sent on a straight course through a stone sluiceway cutting through the ruins. Water still flowed and went into an underground aqueduct on the opposite side of the valley. I know many of our villages use this technique when a ready water source is available, though to see it running through the snow-covered stone ruins of walls and streets made me realize the ones who lived here were also knowledgeable of it as well"

"The sound of the waterfall echoed over the entire valley and drowned out the silence that lived there. Yet as I followed the perimeter of the ridge, I started hearing another sound, like stone grinding on stone. I walked toward the sound, and to my amazement, I saw a gigantic round stone rotating on the surface of the valley away from the center. It seemed to be powered by an underground water way that pushed it along like a side-lying waterwheel. For it to have survived those many centuries in working condition in such a hostile environment was phenomenal. The purpose it served was unknown to me, but considering its enormous size, there had to be some reason for its existence."

Timothy, impatient to hear of Timmerloo's find as it related to the fabled village of Winterland, asked, "Were there any structures still standing?"

"Whatever happened laid waste to almost everything. Here and there were parts of elaborate ornate walls that may have been large buildings. What really caught my interest, and not well known by the villagers, was Winterland was marked by a very unique symbol.

They used an enormous tree with branches spreading in all directions ending in points of stars."

"Did you see such a symbol?"

"Though snow covered much of the valley floor, the geometrical forms making the streets, alleys, and lanes made a visible form of the symbol for the lost Winterland."

"But you were tired and afraid . . . Could your mind see patterns in the snow that weren't really there?"

"While I pondered the various forms and shapes I thought made the great tree symbol on the valley floor, I looked at the slow-spinning stone wheel and traced the water moving out of the valley to an underground aqueduct. The small circular opening for the waterway existed near the bottom of a straight flat wall, which extended from the floor of the valley to the top of the mountain. There engraved into the side of the mountain was the massive tree with stars caught in its uppermost branches. It was then I realized I found Winterland."

"And that was everything?" Timothy asked, deflated. Nothing Timmerloo said helped him find a way to make his beloved Catherine immortal.

Timmerloo saw Timothy was losing hope. He wanted what he told him next to relight it. "I thought I would try to make my way into the abandoned village, but as I said before, every pass, every possible place I thought I could leave the stone path was blocked by something. I saw no possible way to get to the bottom of the valley, so I decided to return to Phillip and the niche. Looking back over the valley, I saw the scarlet reds of the sun streaking the violet sky and realized I would be fortunate to make it to the waterfall before the sun set. I knew I would be making my way to the niche in the darkness by the time I arrived.

"The valley was huge, and I observed the waterfall from the opposite side of the valley when I turned back. I calculated the distance to be at least three parcels from where I stood and yet another four from there to the stone crossroads. I needed to travel the rest of the night to make it to the spiral walkway and the chamber of stone. I hoped Phillip made his way, keeping warm beside the fire.

"My calculations proved true as I hurried around the perimeter to the waterfall. Darkness overcame the valley when I stopped to rest and light my small lantern. When I looked back at the distance I covered, the valley floor was dotted with lights."

"Lights?" Timothy picked up. "What kind of lights?"

"If any villager saw them, they would call them 'ghost lights.'"

"And what do 'ghost lights' look like?" Timothy asked, convinced the old man was nothing more than a teller of wild tales

"The lights looked pinkish-red in the mountain air. Yet if you believe the folklore, the lights are actually pink when they appear. The whole place was haunted . . . haunted by spirits that may have existed when Winterland was at the height of its history. It was haunted by those who were destroyed and died by the perverse tortures executed by their tormentors. Whatever is there remains there, untouched by outsiders . . . certainly untouched by me. At the sight of those hundreds of lights, I hurried into the tall black stones from where I arrived. I did not stop until I was back inside the stone chamber. I rested there until the sun was high in the sky again."

"Why didn't you go down the spiral walkway to let Phillip know you made it back?" Timothy asked, wondering why Timmerloo's behavior seemed strange to him at this point in the story.

"The way through the stone walkway was very treacherous. What made it easy the first time was having four of us to depend on to keep our balance, have adequate light, and make sure we made it to the top without injuries. Believe me, I didn't want to make the dark descent exhausted from the overnight journey. I hoped Phillip, who was rested, made the journey safely before me and had a warm fire waiting to welcome me.

"After I rested, I felt I could make the walk down the stone walkway. Before I left the chamber, I remembered the pile of stones *left by those who came before us. I went where so many left their lifestones, hoping some vagrant traveler might remember them and collect them. The stone table was empty. Phillip must have collected the stones and, as an act of reverence for the dead, would take them to the wall. Phillip deserved my respect for doing such an honorable act. With my wits about me, I prepared my descent. I moved slowly and cautiously down the spiral tunnel, stopping finally at the flat stone slab. I found Phillip. The welcoming fire was absent from the old fire pit we used a few nights before, cold with the smell of wet ashes. He was dead. His neck was broken."* Timmerloo stopped. He was lost remembering what happened. Timothy thought he saw a twinge of guilt steel over his face. The old man raised his head from his reverie, looked at Timothy, then continued.

"Phillip miscalculated and slipped off the ledge to the stone floor below. I found his lantern and a burlap sack with the stones folded under one of his arms. I left him. Noting the morning sun peering through an opening in the tarp, I pulled it back to find the snow melted down to the top of my boot. I needed to be quick. Sunlight does not last long in winter. It would be slow going, but I knew I could retrace the way back from where we came. It was a ghoulish thing to do, but I went to Phillip's body and added his lifestone to the bag. I found food within his belongings and took it with me for the journey back. It took three days to journey to my lodge. I never returned to the mountains again."

"You left Phillip's body in the niche for the animals to devour?"

Timmerloo was offended but put the boy's youth and inquisitive nature as reasons for his arrogance. *"I covered the body with any loose rocks and stones I could find before I left. After I returned to the lodge, I made a pilgrimage and placed all the stones we found into the wall."*

Timothy looked at the old man sitting by the fire. His long story concluded. The exhaustion of telling it lay written in graying lines etching his face like a marble bust. There would be no more questions for Timmerloo now. As he watched, Timmerloo leaned back in his chair and fell into a deep sleep.

Timothy would wait. He needed more answers. Timmerloo's story addressed the existence of Winterland, but nothing he said helped make Catherine immortal. It was two days since Amos told him Catherine had not placed her stone. Now, two days later, was Catherine dying? Could Timmerloo tell if she placed her stone into the wall to stop the destruction of the orbs? What were the pink lights he saw at Winterland? Were they spirits as he suggested, or were they people isolated from the rest of the villages either by fear or self-preservation? And how did an outsider get inside the borders of that lost village?

Timmerloo slept as though he had no concerns in the world. While Timothy watched and waited for the old man to wake up, he looked from the window facing the unknown territory of the northern mountains. This strange impossible story filled him with questions and hope. Now . . . all he needed was time . . . He knew it was running out.

Songs We Sing at Midnight

Tell me about redemptions . . .

Lois defined the boundaries her new position as bereavement coordinator for her hospice by the beginning of 2005. Tearing down the old concepts of what was done in the past and restarting the program from the very beginning were more than challenging. The concept of "bereavement" meant different things within the services provided by hospice. Some found a religious significance, some saw a soft hand extended, and some felt it was the finalization of everything hospice stood for. Therein resided the problems she encountered. Until Lois entered the position, the concept of "bereavement" was undefined. She educated herself on all the concepts extended by her facility and the regulations provided by government agencies, then recreated the position as she understood it was supposed to be.

She made the changes, and eventually, the ideas she promoted began to take root in the minds of her colleagues. It was a slow tedious process. When her position solidified, she began to feel more comfortable in what she was doing and the direction she was taking her newfound concepts. With that intention, she could predict, with some certainty, how to manage her position and planned her return to the political arena of breast cancer. She did such a good job with the bereavement position, inspectors who came to audit asked if they could use her model as an example for other agencies to follow.

Already, by mid-January, Lois was planning strategies for the upcoming year with the American Cancer Society in Atlanta, Georgia. After a week in Atlanta, she returned to York, Pennsylvania, to teach an LPN class about breast cancer advocacy and the role she played over the years promoting breast health. She continued chemotherapy treatments the following week. She made contact with the NBCC by conference calls, made arrangements for speakers, and found materials to discuss at the support group meeting in February.

March certainly arrived like the proverbial "lion" when Lois's father was admitted to the hospital for congestive heart failure. Her two unconvinced brothers finally relented, realizing the care their father and mother needed inside their home would be unmanageable. Lois arranged the details for their parents to be admitted into a local nursing home. Her mother would have been in a very dangerous situation without constant supervision, as her husband was recuperating in the hospital, leaving her alone. It was not realistic to leave their mother unattended. Until the arrangements could be made, Lois and her siblings took turns staying with her twenty-four hours a day, until a dementia unit bed was available. Her father would have a placement at the same facility when he was discharged from the hospital.

Her older brother and younger sister understood the need to do this, but their younger brother still envisioned having both parents return to their home eventually. Lois realized this would never happen. Her father's heart was in terrible shape, and only a transplant, which was not likely, would perhaps save him. As for her mother, the dementia was so advanced by this time, she no longer recognized her own children. The fact was, she did not realize she ever had children. In her mind, her children were just "nice people" who came to visit now and then. The whole situation was sad and heartbreaking.

When her father realized what Lois did, he was furious with her. He did not want to talk to her and only wanted to speak with the son who sided with him. Lois realized her father would not accept the progression of his illness very well and steadied herself against the foul language and raging guilt he heaped on her. Though Lois knew what she did was the best thing she could do for them, the bitterness of her father's words still hurt. After a few days, he calmed down and actually accepted where he was and was appreciative of the care he was receiving. During days he felt up to it, he used a wheelchair to go to the dementia unit to see Lois's mother and found she had no knowledge of who he was or their life together. I think he finally came to the realization that Lois did the right thing for both of them. Her father never thanked her, but at least he stopped complaining. Her younger brother would not give up the idea he would get his father and mother back to their home one day. He couldn't resolve what Lois had done to create a safe environment for them to live out the rest of their days.

Lois held her support group in mid-March then went for her chemotherapy treatments the next day. She continued to work, sometimes putting in long hours in the evening and extending into the early hours of the morning, especially on nights when I was at work. When I was off a night, she would stay home with me or have me follow her to work to keep her company. Most times, she just wanted an extra set of hands to help move heavy boxes or do some running for her. I didn't mind, and it was during those times we really got close to one another again.

At the end of March, Lois was again back in Washington DC with the NBCC. She returned just before April began. She was just getting her feet on the ground when her father developed pneumonia and had to be admitted to the hospital in the early weeks of April. Papers needed to be signed at the nursing home in order to get him into the hospital. Her father was not well enough to understand what was needed, and her mother had no concept of what was happening or that she was even married to the man. The nursing home was close to our home, making situations like this easier for Lois and myself to manage. When her father could not sign the papers himself, and no one else was available, the responsibility went to Lois. With so much going on in her life with her parents, she was not able to write her newsletter and publish until April 15, almost a month after it would normally be published. In this newsletter, she finally tells her support group what is happening in her life.

(Editorial by Lois A. Anderson dated April 15, 2005)

As I write this newsletter, we are finally getting some warm, sunny, weather. Bring on the sunshine and heat!

I must apologize for the lateness of this newsletter, but it could not be helped. Family matters have had to come first. My father paid a visit to York Hospital in March and then was admitted to the Manor Care Nursing Home in Dallastown on the same day that we had to admit my mom. As some of you know, my mother cannot be left alone because of her dementia and my father is no longer capable of taking care of her which necessitated the move to the nursing home for both of them. However, as of April 12th, Dad went back in the hospital with multiple infections and fluid in both his lungs because his heart can no longer pump properly. So it has been crazy around my house!

I want to call your attention to the NBCC Advocacy Conference in May and ask if there are any of you who would be interested to participate in the Lobby Day as representatives from Pennsylvania. If so, please call me and I can give you more details. We would like to have more women from central Pennsylvania accompany the Team Leaders to meetings with our local legislators. You don't have to do or say anything, just go along for the visit. Your presence says you care enough to be there, and believe me, it does make an impression. I will be a Team Leader for one of these groups.

I have also had the honor of being invited back to the Department of Defense Breast Cancer Research Program (DODBCRP) as a member of the Integration Panel to make decisions about the funding of breast cancer research. I will be meeting with other Integration Panel members in late April to accomplish the task of deciding who does/ does not get funded under the DODBCRP.

Wondering if life will ever slow down,

Lois

Lois's father eventually recovered well enough to return to the nursing home. He continued on oral antibiotics for his infections, and with the help of diuretics, the flood of fluids building on his lungs was now controlled, enabling him to breathe. Her father was in good spirits when he returned to the home, but we noted an air of resignation about him too. About a week later, the nursing home called, requesting we come to the facility immediately. Fortunately, I was off that evening and drove Lois to the nursing home as quickly as I could. The news was expected, but it was still difficult to hear. Lois's father died in a wheelchair waiting for the assistant to help him back to bed. We were told he had no complaints throughout the day and seemed happy and content just before he rolled his wheelchair to the side of his bed. He had a look of peace on his face when we went to the room to see him. Lois remained resolute in her demeanor and set herself to the task of calling all the family members to the bedside.

Remarkably, Lois was able to maintain control of her emotions throughout the time everyone arrived to give their last respects. Finally, when everyone had gone and the body was released to the funeral home, she got into our car and cried. She told me she wasn't crying for her father, but for her mother, who was now truly alone.

The funeral was held on a Thursday. It was April 28, 2005, when we brought Lois's mother to the funeral. Despite her severe confusion, she knew on some level that she lost someone special. She told us, "I lost my best buddy." Somehow she may have lost everything else in her life, but she did remember she once loved someone. Hearing what their mother said about their father at the funeral made a deep impression on all her children, especially Lois. When the funeral was over, we took her to the nursing home where she returned without her usual protests. Her dementia erased everything that happened that day, but every once in a while, she would look about the wandering faces in the hall like she was trying to find him. Sometimes she would say she missed her "buddy" or tell us "he isn't coming back again." It was heartbreaking to watch her. In time, her memories were erased by dementia. No longer did she search the crowd of faces as they walked by.

Lois's tumor markers were under control, and she was comfortable with her new position. However, she just lost her father, and her mother could barely recognize her or her other children. In spite of her personal gains, the life around her was fading away. Anyone going through these experiences as quickly as she did would be devastated under most circumstances. I'm certain it would be mind boggling to deal with so many losses over such a short period, that even the best of us would have had trouble dealing with it all. Lois was already fighting the fight of her life without these setbacks. She was dealing with chemotherapy every three to four weeks with its accompanying symptoms of hair loss, nausea, vomiting, and fatigue. Yet even in these tumultuous times, she still found ways to maintain her contacts with her fellow breast cancer advocates.

In early May, Lois made a conference call to the American Cancer Society regarding the Reach to Recovery program, where she was a registered instructor. By mid-May, Lois went to Washington DC for a special symposium for "Project Lead" sponsored by the

NBCC. She stayed in Washington for four days, with the final day spent lobbying senators and congressmen for support of breast cancer issues and funding.

After her father died, there was no longer any question as to what to do with her parents' possessions. The unresolved items of real value were their home and her father's car. The belongings remaining in the house they once shared had little value. Lois, with her sister and brothers, did what they could to salvage what they could in their mother's behalf. With everyone's help, they were able to liquidate everything by the end of June. The money would be used to care for their mother who would remain in the nursing home for what remained of her life.

Even under the shadow of her father's death, Lois continued her efforts for breast cancer advocacy, worked to make improvements in her new position, fought stage IV breast cancer, and made arrangements for the settlement of her parents' property and belongings. Even with everything that preceded her June newsletter, Lois continued her treatments and still had enough time to make a four-day trip to Philadelphia, Pennsylvania, for a conference called the "Era of Hope." Her newsletter was late, but considering everything happening in her life at the time, it is amazing she had time to get one together.

(Editorial by Lois A. Anderson dated June 27, 2005)

The hot, hot, hot weather has struck and we are in the midst of it as I write this newsletter. Looking back over the past several months, I wonder how I ever got through all the events that happened.

As most of you know, my father died near the end of April after a long drawn out battle that began with a heart attack in May, 2004 that left him with severe congestive heart failure. However, this all resulted from being a diabetic who did not take care of himself. And now that his life is over I have to look forward to my mother and what her life has become. She can no longer take care of many of her own needs because of her dementia and that is sad. I feel like I really lost her several years ago when the dementia started to be very noticeable. She currently resides in a nursing home, where my siblings and I have already noticed she is on the verge of feeling safe inside this now familiar environment. We have come to realize as many dementia families do that there is nothing we can do about it as things only worsen. So that is my lament these days, but now onto better things.

I attended the 55th Annual Institute for Spirituality in Medicine conference at Johns Hopkins hospital in May and came away refreshed and renewed with new spirit and conviction for the work I do. This international conference was very revealing for the soul.

I was also invited to attend the 2005 Era of Hope meeting held in Philadelphia in June. This meeting is where all grantees of the DOD Breast Cancer Research Program present their findings to the public. There were some very interesting presentations on quality of life issues for all breast cancer patients, treatment of advanced breast cancer and its metastatic sites, and tons of information on the genetic aspects of breast cancer. This conference was a good one that should not have been missed. Our next newsletter will be filled with reports from it. Well, space is short and I must go. Stay cool and I will . . .

See you in September,

Lois

By June, Lois's tumor marker (CA 27-29) would be down to 23. Lois would not see her numbers this low again for the rest of her life. Basically, it meant her cancer was at a very low level and well managed on the chemotherapy protocols she was following. Lois was feeling the best she felt in years. She continued her incredibly busy work schedule, teaching on invitation, a LPN class on breast cancer awareness and advocacy, and managing the breast cancer support group and newsletter. In comparison to past years, Lois was having one of the calmest years she had since her original diagnosis in 1992. However, by the end of August, the CA 27-29 began a modest rise to 30.6, which concerned us both. Yet again, Lois was on treatment, and such a small increase was no reason to be concerned.

By the time she wrote her newsletter for September, Hurricane Katrina and the events occurring in New Orleans became national news. Lois was outraged by the lack of response within the borders of our own citizenry. I think her outrage was really a concern, if the government would not help those with such evident need, what would it do or, more aptly, what would it not do for people visibly needing help? I think the underlying message of this governmental apathy for its citizens caused her to speculate. If the government would not help the least of us in our time of need, who else would it abandon and what other programs would it take away?

(Editorial by Lois A. Anderson dated September 6, 2005)

As I write this newsletter, it has been a week since Hurricane Katrina blew through the U.S. and we are still cleaning up after her in an unprecedented way. This country has never taken such a direct hit to its infrastructure and the lack of preparation for it appalls me. The leadership of our country does not seem to care much about what happened down in New Orleans and Biloxi and that really saddens and, at the same time, maddens me. The leadership of our government is in a sad state of affairs.

After vacationing in Florida in July, I am now looking forward to a weekend in Williamsburg, Virginia to celebrate our wedding anniversary. The anniversary is not until September 18th, but we'll celebrate early because George and I both have to work that weekend.

I have been honored by the Department of Defense to be selected as a programmatic reviewer for the Breast Cancer Research Program again this year. The meeting is to take place in November in the Washington, DC area and I will get to meet some old friends and make some new ones. The time should be fun.

I have been asked to present several sessions at upcoming conferences in the York area during the beginning of 2006 and I am looking forward to that.

Oh, and I almost forgot, the Pennsylvania Breast Cancer Coalition has chosen me to represent York County in its revamped "67 Counties, 67 Women" photo exhibit of breast cancer survivors. The next presentation that is close to us will be in Lititz, PA at the Heart of Lancaster Regional Medical Center from October 27th to November 6th with the opening reception taking place on October 27th at 5:30 PM. George and I are planning to be there. If anyone else wants to come along, let me know.

Busy, busy, busy . . . it never stops.

Lois

One chemotherapy medication Lois received to keep her cancer under control was a bisphosponate. Apparently, the medication had some unusual side effects, which affected a small percentage of the population. Lois, unfortunately, fell into that small population. The side effect was known as osteonecrosis of the jaw. Since the bisphosponate was a relatively new drug, the documentation on this seldom-seen side effect was obscure at best.

When Lois manifested the condition, she consulted her oncologist and her periodontist to follow her progress. The complication appeared as a small bonelike structure on the inside of her lower right jaw. The structure was observed by her physicians several times over the remaining part of the year. The structure eventually grew to a one-inch-long-by-one-eighth-inch-wide brown-white scale. Lois told me her condition was annoying but not painful. This news came as a relief, since almost 75 percent of patients with the condition report pain as a main side effect. Since I was convinced the condition would eventually weaken the underlying structure of the jaw, I told her to understand the situation was very serious. She assured me she was not in pain, and if anything changed, she would get her physicians right on it. It seemed no matter what side effect a drug gave her, no matter how bad things looked, she always remained positive. She was certain her physicians would find a way to arrest the condition, and for the present, she was hoping the physicians following her might learn something from her rare condition to help women using the drug in the future.

Overall, Lois was feeling better than she felt in years. She felt good, in spite of the achiness in her joints from bone metastasis, and was able to lead a normal life. Of course, for Lois, her concept of a normal life was anything but normal. Her feeling of well-being prompted her offer to have Thanksgiving dinner for the entire family. This was something she could not do for several years, due to commitments, illness, and other problems. Having Lois prepare a dinner was always a treat, and the excitement of the preparations was palpable throughout the house. Sadly, it would be the first year her father would not sit at the table with us. Her brothers brought her mother from the nursing home, and with my brother's assistance, we managed to get my father to the table as well. We had a good time, and I think her mother felt a sense of belonging, as did my father, also a shut-in for many years with dementia. My mother tied a bib on my father to prevent him from spilling food on his clothes, and everyone helped Lois's mother to get food on her plate. It was strange seeing two grown adults, who once were our caretakers, treated like small children . . . but it was what they had become.

The songs we sing at midnight are the songs we sing alone. We can share our pain with each other, but in our hearts, they echo in that empty room once filled with dreams of better things. The memories are sweet, and our lost expectations are, many times, the fabric of sadness woven like a veil over our eyes. Not seeing her father at the table, complaining she didn't make the gravy right or complaining about the mashed potatoes, was a song forever silent, no matter what music it followed. We missed him, in spite of his shortcomings, and we did not speak of his absence that day. We would sing those songs at midnight when we were alone and remembering.

We enjoyed being with each other to celebrate Thanksgiving, and when everything was over, we said our good-byes. Her older brother took their mother back to the nursing home. My father returned with my mother to care for him at their home. Lois and I put the dishes away and stored the remaining food we couldn't give away. We felt satisfied, happy we could share the meal and our home with everyone one more time. It would be one of the last times Lois's mother could come to our home. Destiny would come again to take her from us as well.

Lois had the newsletter out early. Usually, her last newsletter was slated to come out in December. However, concerned that the complication of taking a bisphosponate drug might create a busy schedule with her oncologist and periodontist near Christmas, she wrote the newsletter in early November. Her concerns were realized when both physicians continued to monitor her closely, requesting additional office visits and testing, with subsequent changes in treatment and medications.

(Editorial by Lois A. Anderson dated November 19, 2005)

By the time you receive this newsletter, we will be in the middle of the holiday season so I take this opportunity to wish everyone a happy holiday season and hope that 2006 brings with it a better future.

I have been "blessed" (I don't know if that is the word to use or not) with having to cook Thanksgiving dinner. Hopefully all my planning will work out for the expected 20 or more guests. It seems very strange not having my father or mother around for these events and I have a weird feeling about moving into the role of the female that the rest of my family looks to for advice and other things. Guess it just goes to show you how old we really are!

I thoroughly enjoyed being part of the programmatic review panels for the Department of Defense Breast Cancer Research Program held the beginning of November in Virginia. This time there was a very collegial spirit among the researchers, scientists, and advocates, something that has not been present before this. One comment that was made by several people was that laughter was heard coming from each panel's meeting room at one time or another. This was something heard very rarely at these same meetings held in the past. Most of the time what anyone in the hallways could hear was people arguing their point of view about the proposed research under discussion.

I was also able to talk to several of the scientists about a fairly recent event taking place in the breast cancer population treated with a bisphosponate. This event is the development of osteonecrosis of the jaw, which I have. It seems that on rare occasions, osteonecrosis will follow a tooth extraction in a breast cancer patient who has been treated with a bisphosponate for 18 months or more. I had been treated for 22 months when I had a spontaneous eruption of the osteonecrosis in my jaw. This puts me in the category of having an even rarer side effect with only 22% of those who develop this condition. The treatment thus far has been using penicillin and a mouth rinse. So we'll see what happens when I see the periodontist at the end of November.

My case has prompted a meeting of the oncology doctors and the periodontists in this area that is being set up for sometime after the holidays. At the suggestion of some of my researcher friends, I encouraged the periodontist to write up my case and publish it in the dental journals. So I *guess I'll become famous eventually, but only time will tell. In the meantime, I will be watching any sessions about this side effect of a bisphosponate that may be presented at the San Antonio Breast Cancer Symposium and other breast cancer research conferences and reviewing any new articles about osteonecrosis of the jaw.*

Here's hoping that everyone has a good holiday season and that we can all enjoy ourselves and leave our troubles behind, at least temporarily.

Lois

Before the year ended, Lois received a service award from the American Cancer Society for her work on their peer review programs. The award spanned the years between 2003 and 2005 and was awarded following her time with them.

The year ended quietly enough. Everyone gathered at relatives homes for the Christmas holiday. Lois continued her quest to understand the effects of taking the bisphosponate. The tumor markers taken in December showed another modest rise in her numbers to the level of 48.1. I was concerned that the rise might mean her cancer was starting to be resistant to the treatment. We were both reassured by her physicians that such a modest rise may only mean she was having a problem with osteonecrosis. After all, tumor markers are easily influenced, and a slight rise like this could be almost anything, especially a side effect from a medication. We took their advice at face value, but we remained concerned and vigilant.

Listening to the Silent

Tell me about silence . . .

In dreams, I traveled to the tree of inspiration. I saw an afternoon of great peacefulness as a slow-moving river washed against banks of soft earth covered with lush green grass. Even the most troubled dreamer could find solace there. I looked against the waters to the other side and watched the trees blowing silently in the hushed but stable breeze. It was like a silent heartbeat, never stopping, ever flowing, like the pace of time.

If there were answers there, I would seek them in a dream within a dream. I had no questions that wanted answers. I sought peace, and that was what I found there. All was silent, and I put my head against the base of the great tree and dreamed of the wall of stones.

Leon and his fellow travelers retreated from the last fire-walled perimeter and entered the next. Their leathers were steaming from heat, as Penny and Victoria soaked their leathers for the next engagement. The level land was falling deeper into the earth as they progressed, allowing the blue mists to level near the top of the fire walls. Rand put a hand on Leon's shoulder and pointed to the walled perimeter. "The orbs are very clever. See what they have done? The deeper we descend, the higher our fire walls need to be. Our flasks cannot create walls any higher than what they are. Before long, they won't protect us." Rand expected a response but heard silence.

Penny looked where Leon sat and wondered what he was thinking. "Leon, we won't be able to stay here long. What can we do?"

Leon stared ahead; something continued to elude him. He lifted his head and spoke to the empty space, "We need to stay on higher ground."

"To be sure . . ." *Rand was incredulous by his obvious reply. "But we haven't come to the stream. We certainly are carrying enough water to soak our leathers, but we will run out of flasks if we don't find that landmark."*

"The water should run at a low point in the valley before us. I'm certain the orbs excavated a deeper channel after all this happened. They probably changed it to confuse anyone trying to cross their territory. The landmarks have all changed. We will find the stream running a new course at the bottom of one of these ravines," *Leon told them, keeping watch on the fire wall as it showed signs of diminishing once more.*

"We are running out of time to find it," *Victoria shouted nervously, as the walls of flame started to weaken, allowing wisps of blue mist to penetrate their only defense.*

"Leon, we need to move from here soon," *Rand stated.* "I suggest we stay on this ridge at least another time."

"It will buy some time," *Leon agreed.* "The problem we have is we need to move forward toward Stock. The only way to do it is go through one of these trenches."

Penny spoke up, "But if we go deeper, the fire walls will be useless, won't they?"

"Yes," *Leon answered sadly.* "We have to consider another way into Stock."

"What other way?" *Rand said, alarmed by Leon's words.*

Penny looked into Leon's eyes, hoping to stall his decision. "If we stay on the high ground, we stay safe."

"For how long? How long can we outrun these things? We are not even halfway, and we almost used half the flasks. We either go back, which may already be impossible, or go on as we planned," *Leon said, his voice creaking and trembling as he spoke.*

  Penny put her arm around him and told him, "We will go on, my dear husband."

  "I need to say something . . . something none of you want to hear. To get Victoria into Stock, we must split up," Leon said, feeling Penny shiver against him before she melted into tears.

  "But we can't do that!" Victoria screamed. "We must stay together."

  "I know it's what we wanted, but things have changed. The orbs are clever as well as industrious. They have cut us off with an impossible channel lying between us and the village. We need to cross this ravine and find higher ground on the other side before we can use the pink flasks again," Leon explained.

  "Our flasks are no use in the deep channels," Rand repeated, trying to support Leon.

  "I know," Leon said in sad reply. "But our lifestones are."

  "But we can only use them a little while before they weaken. The orbs will be on us before we cross the stream," Victoria rasped.

  "Not if you carry two lifestones each . . . ," Leon said, knowing Penny did not want to leave him.

  "You mean two will sacrifice to give two the chance to get into Stock?" Penny asked, ashen with grief, knowing what Leon was prepared to do to save them.

  "It's the only way to cross the deep spaces between here and Stock. The flasks are of no use. The fire walls aren't high enough to stop the orbs from attacking and killing us. The only thing we have to stop them is our lifestones. Though they only work as long as we have the strength to carry them or stay alive long enough to work, I think they are our best bet," Leon said, as he pulled a leather pouch from beneath his shirt.

  "So what do you propose?" Rand said, reaching beneath his shirt where his lifestone safely waited.

"*If we split the flasks so one group has four and the other five, then both groups may have a chance to survive. The group going to Stock needs the extra flask to break through the fires when they get there. Rand and I are going to draw their attention away from you . . . They like following my fire walls, so we'll let them. The orbs seem stunned when the stones are used, then move on like they have no memory it,*" *Leon said, as he pressed his lifestone into Penny's hand and kissed her.*

"*But we can't do this, Leon . . .*" *Penny protested, with tears welling up in her eyes. Rand walked to Victoria and put his lifestone into her hand, where it glowed with a penetrating red light.*

"*We don't have the time to discuss what is right or wrong, dear Penny. Rand and I will do what we can to get out of these mists and stay alive so our lifestones are of some use to you. Take Victoria and find Catherine. This is what we came to do. We do not do this in vain.*" *Leon embraced Penny as the fire walls deteriorated behind their last kiss. Rand lit the next flask while they said good-bye.*

Leon watched the fire wall fail in thin slivers, the blue mists spilled steadily over the top of the fire ring. Leon had precious moments to explain his plan once more before departing. "*Listen, the orbs have one design for us, and that is our destruction. Use our lifestones as far as they will take you. If they no longer work, use your own. I hope, by the time you find the ground rising on the other side of this ravine, you can use the flasks again.*"

"*But you can't stay here,*" *Penny protested.*

"*Rand and I will try to get to high ground, away from these things. Go . . . you don't have much time.*"

"*I'll do it, but remember, I love you. Keep safe.*"

Rand watched as Penny and Victoria moved through the fire wall into the deeper ravine beneath the halo of blazing crimson. Leon watched Penny's form melt behind the failing flames. He did not believe he would see her again. He looked to Rand and shouted,

"Light it and throw it back the way we came. We need to stay alive long enough to let them pass through the low places."

"I hear you, Leon," Rand shouted as he threw the lighted flask through the fire wall, deep into the blue mists surrounding them. The predictable white ring exploded, forcing the mists and orbs beyond its perimeters. Leon and Rand ran through the formidable wall of fire with nothing more than their wet leather fittings, three flasks, and enough water to soak their leathers more times than they needed.

"I have to ask . . ." Rand said, when they were safely on the other side of the fire wall.

Leon looked to Rand, shaking his head. "No, I don't think we have a chance. I was hoping to give them a chance, and that is what we have done."

"So we stay here as long as the fire wall holds these damned things off?" Rand asked, as he took a seat on the ground and leaned against a large stone.

Leon sat on top of the stone and looked where Rand sat below him. "We are buying them some time."

"Getting out of here was never really in the plan, was it?" Rand asked, a solemn quietness washing over his face. He found a broken stump nearby and put his feet up on it. When Leon held his silence, Rand spoke again, "You almost had me convinced we were going to try to get to higher ground again."

Leon bowed his head, then looked at Rand. "You know, we could actually make the attempt. As each flask moves us toward shallow ground . . ." Leon trailed off, as one thought pushed its way in, another crushed itself to pieces, failing beneath the weight of decision.

Rand watched Leon struggling with their inevitable loss, staring vacantly at one another. "Leon . . ." Rand called loudly, trying to regain his attention, "you said something about trying for higher ground. What of it?"

Leon looked up, unaware how deep his thoughts buried him in the mire of passages where disillusion broke against the last bastion of hope. "We have three flasks. While the fire walls burn, we should look where the ground leads up. When we find it, that is where we throw the next flask when this burns out."

"That's more like the Leon I know." Rand laughed nervously. "Let's circle the perimeter in opposite directions and take our best guess."

"Let's be at it then," Leon said, happy to be doing anything other than awaiting their destruction. "We may buy more time if we actually get out of these mists."

The way through the ravine was a gauntlet of horrors as Penny and Victoria struggled through the onslaught of orbs, stunned into immobility by the power of the lifestones. The ground beneath their feet sloshed with torn flesh and shattered bones. In places, the detritus was piled in riotous hills, making their passage through the broken remains circuitous and confusing. The incredulous sight of bodies torn to pieces, thrown together like heaps of refuse, sickened Penny. At times, Penny was grateful for the thick blue mists, as they provided a curtain that veiled these human dump sites. The lifestones glowed brightly against the cerulean gloom, giving enough light to see through the orbs and the blasphemous destruction generated by their hatred.

"We can't let what we see stop us," Penny whispered, hoping her voice did not draw the orbs to them.

"I know," Victoria whimpered, the silence broken only by their voices and sucking footfalls.

Victoria was crying softly, trying to spare Penny from her childish fears. Penny realized seeing such unbridled hatred must have affected her young friend. When she turned, she saw Victoria's streaked face shining in the red glow. "This is hard, sweetheart," Penny said, taking Victoria's hand into hers. Victoria looked at Penny, put her arms around her, and sobbed uncontrollably. Feeling Victoria's pain, she said, "I'm so sorry to put you through this, child.

If there were any other way to pass through this, I would. But this is our way. There is no other." Tears welled up in Penny's eyes as she continued, *"Rand and my Leon, I'm sure, have given their lives to make sure we deliver your message to Catherine."*

"What if Amelia did get to her? Then what we are doing is pointless," Victoria spoke up, wiping her face on her leather sleeve, leaving the black soot of Leon's fire walls smeared across her face.

Penny looked at the younger woman. She looked pitiful and small against the plethora of atrocities lying in mountainous wet heaps of bone, flesh, and congealing blood. Yet there was courage in her voice, and she posed a valid question. Penny asked, *"What if Catherine did get the message? What if, at this very moment, she is on her way to the breach with her stone? Will she have the courage to place it in the wall? Will she know what she does is right? And more importantly, if Amelia did not get to Catherine, then aren't we the village's last hope to deliver that message? It is that message that will save us, not just Stock, not just Glade or Wendow, but all of us."*

Victoria nodded she understood. *"The weight of everyone's lives depends on us now, doesn't it?"*

Penny looked into the mists, thick with purple orbs, suspended, motionless, in the powerful light of the men's lifestones. She knew Leon and Rand were still alive and strong. If they continued to use them, their light would fade. Eventually, the men would weaken. Unable to fight, they would succumb to the orbs' emotionless dissection, destruction, and ultimate desecration. She looked to Victoria, still searching for answers, and said, *"We must hurry. The price we pay for this time is too heavy for me to bear. Come."*

Penny pushed through heaps of human refuse, trying to find the stream marking the halfway point. Victoria followed closely, holding Rand's glowing lifestone. They would need all their strength and courage to get inside the besieged village.

"How many flasks are left?" Leon asked as he cleared some broken limbs from a large stone near the perimeter.

"We are unfortunately down to the last one," Rand said sadly.

"Then we must make the best of it and wait here as long as the fire wall lasts. It will give them a little more time," Leon said, feeling defeated.

Rand looked above him and saw a patch of sky and clouds break through the blue mists. "I think we are close to high ground." He pointed to the sky shining through an opening in the mists. "See."

"Yes, I saw it too," Leon said, as sunlight pierced the sluggish blue mist surrounding them. "The question is, which way do we go to get there? These damned mists are relentless. Orbs seem to be collecting in droves beyond the fire wall, just waiting for any misstep from either of us." Leon turned toward Rand and said, "It's like they know we are out of time. They seem to know where we are weakest. They can sense our thoughts." Leon realized, "They know what we are doing. We walked into a trap."

"But we are getting out of that trap. Aren't we, Leon?" Rand asked.

"I don't know . . . It seems we made more progress to higher ground than what I hoped for. But we still haven't put these murdering bastards behind us."

Rand turned his head toward Leon. "We have one flask left. If we get to a small hill, or just out of these mists, we might get where we left the wagon and supplies. We could wait them out," Rand said, trying to reassure him.

Leon was beginning to feel the weariness connected to his lifestone being drained of its remarkable powers, yet he said nothing of it to Rand. But as he watched, he saw fatigue affected him as well. When this fire wall faded, he doubted their last flask would get them past the mists. A sense of quiet resolution passed as he realized this final effort would be the last thing he could do for Penny and Victoria. The longer they survived, the better their chances were at passing through the ravine. "Sometimes you get the chance to change things,"

Leon said, loud enough for Rand to hear. "I think this may be one of those times."

"Did we ever have a chance?"

"We came farther than I ever thought we could." Leon looked wearily through the flames; not seeing any signs of rising ground, he said, "I think the higher ground lies west," Leon spoke wistfully, as if he entertained the thought to actually escape the mists thriving with lashing purple orbs.

Rand understood this was the end of their escape. Neither wanted the other to recognize it. They would not accept despair with open arms. Rand watched the perimeter of the fire walls assaulted by orbs unsuccessfully attempting to pierce it with their deadly tendrils. Their persistence to destroy every human would find their goal closer after the last flask was thrown. Rand turned to Leon with reserved confidence and said, "Then we go west."

"We'll wait here until the fire walls start to fail, then we move. Hopefully, we'll see a way out from our next vantage point."

The stink of corrupting flesh and bones assaulted Penny as she led Victoria through the rotting piles of human and animal remains. She continued to search for the stream as they made their way forward to lower ground. "By the Winds, where is it?" Penny hissed into the air.

"Are we lost?" Victoria said with alarm.

"No," she told her, trying her best to be strong, trying her best to keep Victoria from going mad at the sight of mangled corpses strewn in heaps, and trying her best not to succumb to the fear she felt in her chest, making her heart numb with cold. She turned to Victoria. "We are not lost. We need to get past these barriers, find the bottom of this ravine, fill our water flasks, and move up to high ground."

"But we can barely see more than a few steps ahead of us."

"I know," Penny agreed. "But we feel. We feel our steps as we move down. We will find the stream when we feel the cold water running over our feet. It is an advantage we have over the orbs."

"The orbs don't feel anything?" Victoria asked, as they passed a pile of rocks strewn with blood.

"I think they are empty beings with no regrets, with no feeling for what they are doing, and have no regard for life. I think their only intention is to destroy everything in their path."

"But why?" Victoria asked, when her foot splashed in a pool of water. Penny was about to answer when she cried, "By the Winds!"

"What is it?" Penny asked, thinking she walked into a swamp of bloody horrors.

"I'm standing in water. I found the stream!"

Penny moved toward her until she too was standing in the running water. "I told you we would find it," she said, excited by the find. "We need to fill our flasks and then find a way out of here." Penny looked at the men's lifestones and saw, while they still glowed, they were weakening. Rand and Leon were still alive. Penny did not know what she would feel when the stones no longer emitted their reddish glow. The answers to what happened to them would be riddles written on the stones she and Victoria carried for them. Until the red glow faded, there was still hope for them. If their lifestones faded to nothing, she would make sure Leon and Rand would not be forgotten when the world they knew came back again.

Victoria filled the last flask. They would need them to cross the fire walls, created with Leon's pink flasks, when they reached the top of the rise. She looked to Penny and said, "That's the last one. Are you ready?"

Penny looked at the young woman kneeling in the moving water of the shallow stream. "Yes, I'm ready to move out of this place." Penny surveyed the area surrounding them. The blue mists, painted with the red glow of the stones, cast a purplish hue over everything around *them. For a moment, the phenomenon almost erased the sight of the floating monsters hanging in the mists like sleeping spiders. "Seeing these orbs suspended in the mists makes me feel strange. It's like we don't belong here."*

"We don't belong here," Victoria snorted, as she stood and lashed the water flasks against her back.

Penny looked in her direction and said, "Yes . . . we do belong here. The orbs are the invaders. They are the things that do not belong. This is our home, our place to live and die on our own terms, not theirs. We belong here . . . They don't. And while I have the strength to fight . . . I will." Victoria was still standing in the water, looking impatient to leave. "Let's get moving then," Penny insisted.

Victoria did not need to be coddled. She moved from the stream bed quickly to join Penny on the other side. Together they moved past another pile of bones, stripped clean of their flesh, rendering them unrecognizable as human or animal. There were remains of other horrors piled randomly in wretched hills, where they held their breath passing the smell of decay in the fetid mists. Penny watched above them as the purple spheres moved soundlessly through the ravine, darting and diving at the red luminescence of the borrowed lifestones. Penny kept close watch as the distance from the orbs diminished as the lifestones showed signs of failing. Still, the orbs stayed twenty arm's lengths away as they progressed across the bottom of the ravine.

"We waited too long to set off that last flask, Leon." Rand puffed heavily, out of breath. "I almost didn't get through. One of those damned things lashed out right next to my leg as I jumped."

"We are getting slower, Rand." Leon breathed heavily. "If we tire out, the lifestones will not work as long. We need to rest awhile."

"Then we better use the strength we have to find a place above these mists."

Leon looked to Rand leaning heavily against a broken tree. He briefly scanned the edges of the fire ring and saw nothing different in the consistency of the mists. He knew Rand would be disappointed if they didn't take the time to survey the perimeters for a way out, but they were both very tired. Even if they did see a chance to run from this haven, they may not be strong enough to get very far. They would rest as long as the fire walls held then move into the mists as far as the orbs allowed them. It wasn't much of a plan, but it was all they had.

"I caught my breath, Leon," Rand sighed. "You stay here and rest. I'm going to have a look around the edges . . . see if the mists thin out anywhere. Okay with you?"

"If you see anything, call out, and I'll come to you."

"Save our strength, right?" Rand smiled.

"That was the idea." Leon smiled back. "Go on then, see what you find."

Rand walked slowly near the fire wall and started following its edges. Leon watched the flames dance in a solid mass of single flames . . . interweaving, twisting around one another, and keeping the orbs from attacking them as long as they burned. Leon's strength was slow to return, and at times, he felt an emptiness he could not overcome. His eyes glazed with tears as he remembered a moment he had with Penny not so long ago.

It was a warm spring day. Penny finished cleaning the table and dishes. For no reason at all, he swept her into his arms and started dancing with her. She thought he lost his mind, but she responded, and they danced until Penny's giggling got the best of her. She asked, "So what brought that on?"

"You looked so beautiful, I just had to dance . . . that's all."

"I love you, you silly man," Penny said, just before she kissed him.

Leon remembered through bittersweet tears how they walked hand in hand to the porch just to watch the sun go down afterward . . . their innocence clasped inside the hands that touched. Those times passed. Innocence was tested by hardships never seen before by the villagers. Leon looked where Rand waved to him from the far side of the circle. "What have you found?" Leon yelled from his position.

"I don't know," Rand called back. "Maybe it's a way out."

Leon stood on legs so heavy, he wasn't sure he would move, much less walk to where Rand waited for him. When he was certain his legs would support him, he walked slowly where Rand was standing. "So what have you found?"

"This." Rand pointed to a rock formation nestled against the fire wall.

"What is it?" Leon asked, the tiredness in his voice coming out.

"I think it is the entrance to a cave of some sort."

"There could be orbs waiting in there," Leon said, shocked Rand had not thought of the possibility.

"If there were, wouldn't they have come through the other side already?"

Leon considered Rand's evaluation was sound. "We could do this, but what will stop the orbs from following us when the fire wall dies?"

"We can block it with rocks. Set a pile of brush on fire at the mouth of the cave . . . make it more difficult for them to follow us."

"It will buy Penny and Victoria more time . . . but it may not save us, Rand," Leon warned.

"That's true . . . but it's a chance, and it will buy them more time even if it fails," he argued.

Leon looked around and saw heaps of broken trees and branches within the circle of fire. "Let's drag some of the brush and limbs over here before we try to block the way with loose rocks. The fire will keep them away from the entrance for a while, then we better hope for a way out."

"We better hurry. The wall is starting to deteriorate already. We don't have much time."

It took all of Leon's strength to move a dry tree limb to the opening of the cave. Rand seemed to have more energy than Leon and dragged two massive limbs with a fan of dried leaves in front of the opening.

"That's about all I can handle," Rand said, panting to catch his breath.

"I think it will be enough. Let's get into the cave before the fires die down," Leon suggested.

"Wait, we need something to light this with," Rand said, pointing to the pile of brush they set at the entrance. He ran out and broke two limbs off the brush then wrapped the ends with pieces of his shirt. He poured some leftover solvent onto it and leaned one of the makeshift torches into the fire wall where it caught immediately. He ran back to the cave entrance and handed the other torch to Leon. They both watched from the entrance of the cave, while the final circular wall of fire started showing signs it was failing.

"I think it is time," Rand said.

"Yes, light the brush, then pull those loose rocks over the opening. Hurry," Leon shouted over the roar of the fire.

The two men shuffled inside after the brush caught fire, then pushed whatever stones and rocks they could move over the entrance of the cave. Leon lit the second torch and handed one back to Rand. "Let's have a look around." The cave seemed to go on for a long time on a level path then made a steep descent. It wasn't long before the cave narrowed, and the two men realized they walked into a dead end. There was no going back.

"I guess that's it then," Rand stated sadly.

"We gave them a little more time." Leon wheezed as he sat down on the cold stone floor exhausted by their efforts.

"It may take the orbs awhile to find us," Rand said, still hoping they would survive this.

"They could miss us completely . . . if we're lucky." Leon exhaled weakly, as he watched Rand sit down on the cave floor beside him. *"It was worth the risk, my friend."*

"I was hoping the cave would lead to higher ground or allow us to stay ahead of these monsters."

"You did well. It's more of a chance than I thought we had," Leon said, trying to comfort his friend. He leaned his head against the rock wall behind his back.

For a time, the only sound inside the stony labyrinth was the labored breathing of two men. Without warning, a distant sound resonated from the entrance of the cave, echoing against the rocks where Rand and Leon laid on the floor of the cave. Rocks were moved and thrown against the edges of the stone entrance as the two men drifted toward the dreamless sleep of exhaustion. Leon looked to Rand and smiled. Rand was asleep. He would not see the terrifying things coming for them. Leon spoke to Rand, though he was certain he would not hear him. *"Good night, my friend, and good-bye."* Then he turned toward the entrance of the cave and said, *"I love you, Penny. May the Winds be kind to you and Victoria. I'm going to where the Four Winds blow peacefully. I will see you there, and I will wait for you."*

The rocks covering the entrance were crushed and thrown aside, allowing access into the cave. The fire wall protecting them died out long ago. The fire at the mouth of the cave became scattered cinders and hot ashes in the conflagration of flagellating tendrils. With nothing to stop them, the orbs floated on the cerulean mists to where two men lay sleeping. They never felt the violation of their bodies when the orbs laid waste to them.

"The ground is starting to rise," Victoria said, excited to be moving upward and out of the dark places at the bottom of the ravine.

"I noticed it too," Penny responded. She looked into her hand where she held her husband's lifestone. "Leon and Rand's lifestones have become dimmer over the last few moments. They are very weak. We need to switch."

"Yes, I've seen them fading too. They're letting the orbs a little too close to us. I think we should switch now and give Leon's and Rand's a rest before they lose all their strength," Victoria said, searching inside her blouse to find the satchel holding her lifestone.

"Besides, they need their strength to survive. Letting the stones rest should help. I forgot how tired we were when they faded like this. I hope Leon and Rand are still okay."

"As long as they glow, they are alive . . . and they still glow . . . just not as well as they did," Victoria observed.

Penny and Victoria gently removed their lifestones and reverently placed Rand's and Leon's into satchels hanging around their necks. The lifestones blinded the lecherous orbs back forty arm's lengths when they exposed them together. Neither Penny nor Victoria realized how many teeming orbs laid in wait to destroy them until the reddish glow immobilized them in midair. Penny gasped at the sheer numbers of them. There were hundreds, immobilized by the crimson light, frozen like a solid wall of purple spheres around them.

"We need to keep moving while we have the strength. These orbs will drain our strength quickly. We need to get where we can use the pink flasks again."

"Come on," Victoria pointed, "this way is leading up."

The two women no longer walked up the slope but moved at a quickened pace with Victoria in the lead. They passed by more of the orbs' handiwork piled in hills of corrupted meat and bone. The steady horrors turned them cold to what they were seeing, and their attentions pressed them to clear as much ground as they could. When Victoria saw the sky shining through the blue mists, she shouted to Penny, "Light a flask and throw it now . . . We're high enough for the flasks to work."

Penny pulled one of the pink flasks from beneath her leathers and lit the fuse. She threw the flask as far as she could, then steadied herself for the white fire ring to emerge from the blast. "Victoria," she shouted, "we need to soak our leathers again."

After the white ring fulfilled its purpose, Victoria pulled water from her supply and soaked her and Penny's leather outfits. When they finished, the two women ran through the singeing heat of the wall into the safety of the ring of fire.

Penny looked to the sky above them for the first time since she and Victoria left Leon and Rand behind. It felt good to see it again. "I am afraid to know, Victoria, but can you pull Rand's lifestone out and look at it?"

Victoria's look of elation, fueled by their finding a way out of the nest of orbs, melted as she pulled the lifestone that once belonged to someone she knew. She looked at Penny with a look of foreboding then put the silent stone in her hand. Penny came over to see if the red glow still existed, but both women saw the lifestone had run its course. It was merely a common stone once again. "We will put it into the wall someday," Penny said sadly as she pulled her beloved Leon's stone from her leather satchel to find it too had lost all its powers.

Victoria watched the older woman fall to her knees. Grief seized her heart with an icy hand. She saw unimaginable pain creep into her tired, soot-covered face like a sickness. She went somewhere beyond sorrow as she lay on the ground at Victoria's feet. Victoria knelt beside her and pulled her hand into her own. "We will put Leon's stone in the wall together, beside Rand's, someday when we have won this fight. I miss them too." She sobbed. "But it would be disrespectful to stop now. They did this to save us. If we don't survive, then their sacrifice was for nothing. We need to go on."

Penny looked into Victoria's eyes and saw kindness tempered with courage, and it gave her strength. Looking past her shoulder, Penny saw something else. She observed the perimeters of the fire ring and saw another fire blazing in the distance to their east. "Victoria . . . look," Penny said, as she pointed to the wall of flames burning in the distance.

"Is that where we are going? How are we going to get through that?" Victoria gasped.

"With one of these," Penny replied, pulling one of the pink flasks from beneath her tunic and held it in front of her face. "Leon told us to save one. He said it would suffocate the fire just long enough to get through the fires they set at Stock. Remember?"

"Did Leon realize how big the fires would be when we got to them? Those fires are almost forty arm's lengths high," Victoria disputed, seeing how impossible their task seemed against the violent walls of flame.

"All I can tell you, Leon felt one of these flasks would give us a passage through. I'm willing to try. Besides, the other choice is to wait for the orbs to attack," Penny said with renewed conviction as she waited for Victoria's response.

Victoria turned to Penny with a wry smile and said, "Of course we go on. I still have hope. One flask will be enough to get us through." Victoria turned away and looked in the direction of the inferno crackling in the distance, then turned to Penny and pointed to a spot in the ring of fire protecting them from the onslaught of the orbs. "I think we should throw the next one there."

Penny lit the flask and threw it where Victoria pointed. Together they waited for the circular blast to touch the perimeter of their enclosed ring. When the new ring developed fully, Penny looked to Victoria and asked, "Are you ready?"

She nodded to Penny, and then together they jumped through the fire wall. Left behind were the hissing sounds of their fire-singed leathers passing through the roar of newfound flames. When the flames of the first ring failed, the orbs rushed in, intent on finding another life to take and destroy. They found nothing, becoming more frenzied and dangerous.

The villagers wasted no time to build stationary towers along the Last Road, which wound randomly against the edges of the "wall." When the threat of purple spheres they called the "orbs" became too obvious to ignore, several villagers suggested building them to observe the movements of their adversaries. The fires were built a parcel away from the wall, but over time, they lost ground. In places, the fires were almost backed against the wall. There were four towers; the last was built less than a half parcel from the breach, where the hated orbs moved at will through the opening.

"Look at that," a lookout called from the last tower.

"What was it?" a soot-covered man yelled from the ground beneath him.

"I don't know, but I think I just saw a flash of white light just beyond our fire wall." The lookout continued to observe the direction where he saw the flash. He yelled to the man standing below him, "There's a ring of fire burning there now. What do you think caused that?"

"Probably some dry brush caught off the fires we are feeding. I don't believe it's anything to worry about. Are the orbs staying away from the flames?"

"Yeah, they keep teeming up like a purple tide then wash back as they get closer to the fire."

"We're holding our own then," the man yelled back as he turned to leave.

As he started to walk away, the lookout called again, "Hey, I just saw another one light up just outside the fires. Now there are two rings burning." As the man watched, he saw the first ring disappear. "The first ring is gone now. It's weird. It's like something trying to make its way here. You don't think the orbs have come up with something else?"

"That's not possible. The orbs hate fire. They wouldn't be able to manipulate it that way," the man called back from the ground. He stood there thinking for a moment then said to himself, "Stock is under siege. Nothing made it in or out since this thing started." He looked up at the man in the tower and yelled, "I'm coming up to take a look." The soot-covered man pulled up the makeshift ladder quickly just as another fire ring went off against their own blaze.

"Did you see that?" the lookout asked, as the soot-covered man steadied against the railing.

"You're right. Something is coming this way. We better be ready to fuel the fires in case it gets through. Even one of those damned monsters would be deadly. Sound the bell . . . now!"

As the lookout sounded the bell at the top of the tower, the man descended the ladder quicker than he went up. At the base of the tower, twenty men gathered to await instructions. "I saw something in the mists making rings of fire that seem to clear an area of the orbs then lets them back in again. I don't know what powers the orbs have, but from what I've seen, they are clever enough to do anything. I need you to bring as much wood, oil, and tar to reset the blaze if these things try to come through."

The men looked at him like he had gone mad; hesitating a moment, they turned and ran in all directions, looking for the items he called for. "And hurry up . . . Our lives may depend on how fast you all get back here."

Before any of the men could get back with the combustibles, another white flash went off near the tower. He saw the lookout was shocked by what he saw and was ready to bolt off the tower. "Stay up there," he called to him. "I'll go see what is going on and stop it if I can. Send the men there," he pointed, "when they get back."

The soot-covered man walked stealthily behind rocks, fallen trees, and broken debris. He looked where the white flash had gone *off and saw a circle of fire intersecting with the wall of flames created by the villagers. He reached to his back where his crossbow rested and pulled it into his hands. The villagers had sent lighted arrows into the bodies of the orbs in the past with some success. He hesitated, waiting to see what might try to come through the wall of flames. In the orange, red, and white hot flames, he saw the figures of two shadows moving, as if running, in his direction. "The orbs can't move like that," he said loudly to himself.*

Two men rushed to stand beside him. "What is that?" one of them asked fearfully.

"I don't know, but I don't think the orbs have anything to do with this," the soot-covered man appraised, carefully watching the approaching shadows.

"Even so, we should be ready for trouble if the orbs found a way to break through," one of the men contradicted, knowing how careful they had been trying to preserve what they could from the onslaught of the avaricious orbs.

About a dozen men had returned with buckets of tar and oil. The rest continued to gather what wood could be found in the vicinity. They all watched the two shadows running behind the cover of the flames in wonder and in fear. "What should we do?" one of them asked.

The man in the soot-covered clothes commanded the men to ready their crossbows with lighted arrows. "Prepare to fire at whatever comes through these flames on my command." Twelve men with lighted arrows waited as two human figures ran through the wall of flames.

"Hold up . . ." the man shouted to the men with readied crossbows. The man walked to the two figures kneeling and holding each other on the ground just outside the failing fire ring. As he approached, he could hear them crying and praying to the Winds that allowed them to come this far. They were clothed in soot-covered wet leathers, still steaming from their passage through the fire wall and burning hot before him. He could not imagine the story they would

tell him. He needed to move them back from this place so his men could reignite the fires when the circular ring of fire faded completely. He thought these were women after overhearing their voices, and he addressed them as such, "What are you women doing here? How did you get here through the orbs and the mists? What are your names?"

The older woman threw back her leather hood first. Then the younger one did the same. The older woman spoke first, "My name is Penny. This is Victoria."

"Where are you both from?"

"Glade . . . I'm from Glade. Victoria is from here. We were trapped by the orbs between Notting and Stock," Penny said, while she tried to get her bearings.

"But how did you get through the mists and the orbs? It was a foolhardy, dangerous thing to do," the man said, shaking his head in disbelief.

"Can you get us someplace where we can get out of these filthy leathers? Perhaps there is a place we can clean up and into some clean clothes before we talk?" Penny asked.

The man looked at the steaming dirty clothes and thought it was perhaps best to allow this. He looked at Penny and Victoria standing before him in filthy soot-drenched coverings and faces smeared black and streaked red from things he was certain he did not want to know about. "We have a camp near the wall where some of the village women have been keeping goods for the villagers who come out to keep the fires going. I think you will find everything you need there. I'll send word you both are on the way."

"Does anyone know a girl by the name of Catherine?" Victoria spoke up before being led off to the encampment.

"You know Catherine?" the man asked, amazed a girl who walked through the most treacherous threat that ever existed and a fire that should have killed her would still have the sensibilities to ask a pertinent question.

"I'm looking for her . . . Do you know where she is? I have a message I must get to her," Victoria said, emphasizing the need to speak to her as soon as she could.

"She is on her way here," a man standing behind them said.

"We have been keeping the orbs out of the area as much as we can to allow her to place her lifestone," another man told her.

"Then what I have to tell her won't matter," Victoria said dejectedly. *"I've done nothing, and we risked everything to get here,"* she whispered almost unintelligibly, tears welling in the corners of her eyes.

The men listening to the two women seemed concerned, but none understood Victoria's response to the news of Catherine's imminent arrival to their camp. *"Will she be all right?"* one man asked.

Penny looked at the man who spoke. *"I will take care of her. Just point me in the direction of the encampment."*

Penny saw the effect this news had on her young friend. They walked through horrors so unspeakable they might never sleep peacefully again. They lost Leon and Rand trying to get here. All done to get a message to Catherine that was already delivered. Even she was demoralized.

The men directed the two women to the provisional encampment where they were given food, water, fresh clothes, and a place to clean up. They were well taken care of, but both women seemed to have lost their purpose. Catherine would be here by nightfall. There was nothing left but wait for the inevitable to pass. The battle to the breach still needed to be won. Perhaps something they experienced would help get Catherine there. As for what Penny and Victoria could see, the breach was never secured. No one was able to stop the steady stream of blue mists coming through it. They would rest then try to help the villagers in some way. They had not sacrificed everything in vain. Catherine would need them very soon.

Slipping Away . . . Moving On

Tell me about the writing on the walls . . .

Lois was concerned the osteonecrosis occurring in the lower right side of her jaw would cause permanent damage. The bonelike structure did not seem problematic for her other than the extremely fastidious mouth care she needed to do. She was particularly careful not to disturb the site and carried dental supplies with her at all times. As a matter of protocol, she needed toothpaste, a toothbrush, and special oral rinses to use after eating. The troublesome area did not grow any larger, and her physicians watched for changes every week or two to observe its progress.

As Lois always seemed to do, she turned something negative into something positive. I would have to say, in hindsight, she actually enjoyed the notoriety the bony structure gave her. Her physicians proposed to study the unusual phenomenon in earnest, beginning in February, with scientific interest, when the peculiar structure simply fell off on January 31.

Lois and I were watching television when she looked over and said, "Oh my God, I think it came loose." She reached beneath her tongue, and there it was. The troublesome bony structure fell out on its own accord, just like a child losing a "baby tooth." Except, this was like no other tooth I ever saw. The structure was an inch and a quarter long, tapered on both ends to rounded points. It was about an eighth of an inch wide and as thick as a piece of paper on the ends, thickening to almost a sixteenth of an inch in the center. Yet overall, it was as hard as a real tooth. It was light brown and had a stem where it attached to the gum line, where the structure broke off. Lois had me check the site where it came from. The gum line was reddened, showing the outline of the structure. There seemed to be no identifiable sites where the stem originated. In truth, other than the redness where the structure rested, the gums and teeth in the area looked exceptionally healthy.

Of course, other than my cursory evaluation, Lois wanted the two physicians following her to know what happened. We put the strange structure into a specimen cup, which Lois kept just for this situation, and closed it. Lois's background as a medical technologist made her realize this was evidence she wanted to preserve.

The next morning, as soon as the physician's offices were open, she told the bizarre story to each of her physicians. It was her oncologist who indicated interest in the strange specimen. He explained what he wanted her to do to preserve the specimen for analysis and then had her take the specimen to the laboratory. When the report came back, the results were what had been suspected all along. The fragment was consistent with osteonecrosis.

The report, as she received it, went as follows: "Bone, right side of mandible, fragment removed region of healed oral mucosal ulcer: Sequestrum infiltrated by sheets of fibrillar material containing branching, filamentous Gram positive rods, consistent with actinomyces branching, filamentous Gram positive rods, consistent with actinomycosis." In plain language, "sequestrum" means it was a dead fragment of bone that detached from the surrounding adjacent healthy bone. "Fibrillar" corresponds to the filamentous structure the structure appeared to mimic. "Filamentous" also refers to the structure as being one that is threadlike, drawn out into a threadlike structure.

The report went on to discuss the structure indicated bone necrosis (or bone death). The report indicated the presence of "shrunken osteocytes," which indicated it was a bone cell or something attempting to be a bone cell. There were "empty lacunae" or, as we might understand the terminology, pits, depressions, hollows, or spaces where these shrunken osteocytes were found. Over the entire structure was a thin layer of "neutrophils," which, to any of us studying the marvels of the body, are the white blood cells that are the destroyers of foreign bodies and infections. So it was Lois's marvelous immune system that eventually removed the peculiar structure that caused so much concern. Of course, Lois was excited to share the news of her experience with her fellow breast cancer survivors and wrote about it in her newsletter.

(Editorial by Lois A. Anderson dated February 18, 2006)

Wow, life does get interesting when you have a very rare side effect from a drug that is being used much more often than in the past. Everyone wants to know what's going on and how things are progressing so much so that one gets tired of hearing the words, "How are you?"

Anyway, now that I ranted, I can tell you that the osteonecrosis in my jaw is almost completely healed. There is one very tiny pinpoint area that I can still feel with my tongue. So let me tell you what happened during the healing process.

On January 31st, while watching television, the fragment of bone in my jaw simply popped off, like a bottle cap on a soda bottle revealing healthy gum tissue underneath. I didn't know what to do and I called both the periodontist and my oncologist. The periodontist told me to throw the piece of bone away and not worry about it, BUT the scientist in me, and yes, after 30 years of working as a Medical Technologist that part does not go away easily, wanted something more.

I called the oncologist to ask him if we could send this bone fragment to the pathology laboratory for analysis, just to see what was present microscopically. Well, that opened another can of worms because the pathology report on the bone fragment came back as osteonecrosis, but Actinomyces were present. Actinomyces is a type of bacteria normally found in your mouth. However, when this bacterium gets into the bone, it can cause big problems. That finding meant a trip to an infectious disease specialist and consultations among all of my treating physicians, my periodontist, and me. After discussion with the infectious disease specialist, the decision was made to reevaluate me in 3 weeks and go from there to determine whether to treat or not. Treatment would be penicillin for a long period of time, possibly a year.

Then in the meantime, another meeting was held among a group of dentists in the area and principals of the York Cancer Center to discuss not only osteonecrosis, but dental concerns about oncology patients. Compliance with dental visit schedules was another problem discovered during the meeting about osteonecrosis. At the first meeting with the York Cancer Center personnel, the medical oncologists, the radiation oncologists, and others (mentioned in my last newsletter) the fact was brought to light that not all oncology patients are encouraged to keep up their dental visit schedule, an obviously very important matter when it comes to osteonecrosis of the jaw. BUT one can keep up the dental visit schedule and still develop this side effect because no one knows for sure what the cause really is, only that bisphosponate drugs play a part in setting up the environment in which osteonecrosis can take place.

The point is that oncology patients still need to see their dentist regularly, but should probably consult with their oncologist as to the exact timing of those visits if they are receiving chemotherapy that lowers their white blood cell, red blood cell, or platelet counts. This is important for everyone to realize because even we cancer patients get tired of seeing doctor after doctor after dentist and will use any excuse to not see one or the other. The dentist is usually the one we don't see.

Also, it is important that during the dental visits we undergo the recommended dental x-rays to check for hidden conditions that are not necessarily evident on the surface. Just because one has been through radiation therapy for breast cancer is not really an excuse for foregoing bite wing x-rays at the dentist. The radiation received from a bite wing x-ray is very minimal when comparing it to any radiation therapy for a tumor or even a chest x-ray.

I hope, too, that my case illustrates the fact that all patients need to be informed about their conditions and the drugs they are taking. They need to be able to intelligently weigh the risks and benefits of the drugs, and the physician and all the dentists and specialists need to communicate these risks and benefits so that the patients understand what the statistics and studies may mean in their case. Patient should not be afraid to ask questions and to communicate their thoughts and reasoning to those who treat you. Had I not done that, I would not know all that I do about osteonecrosis. And just maybe my case may help in the treatment of this side effect and the development of more guidelines on long-term treatment with bisphosphonates.

I also have to thank two people who were instrumental in setting up the two meetings we've had *so far about osteonecrosis and its concomitant problems among oncology patients after I insisted that my case needs to be reported in the dental journals. Thanks to both of you.*

So stay tuned folks, the story is not yet complete. I still have to see the infectious disease specialist again and then we'll decide what to do. Ah, the life of an advocate . . . just look at what can happen!

Lois

Although Lois was showing signs of fatigue, she continued her work with breast cancer advocates by e-mail and phone conferences. A tumor marker taken in January showed a modest decline to 44.8. Results from various studies showed metastasis settling into the thoracic spine area. She was relatively pain-free from the metastasis except for an unsettling sensation of electric shocks she experienced when turning or twisting certain ways. An MRI was eventually completed, which concurred there was metastatic activity on several levels of the thoracic spine. This finding, along with the new symptom, urged her oncologist to proceed with palliative radiation therapy to the area.

In late March, the radiation oncologist evaluated the various studies and rejected the idea of radiation therapy at this point, explaining radiation could cause bone damage that could be spared by using a new chemotherapy drug called Xeloda. The choice to change Lois's chemotherapy protocol was warranted by another quick rise in her markers to 64.2. The marker, taken in mid-March, was more than double her values at this time the previous year. It was decided to forgo radiation therapy and begin the new protocol using the new agent. In a few months, she was to repeat another MRI to evaluate progress or deterioration.

Despite the ominous future presented to Lois, she looked forward to upcoming events and possibilities. She continued to work long hours at her position in hospice. She traveled to Washington DC to act with members of the NBCC for their annual Team Leader Conference over a weekend in early March. The conference was set in preparation to lobby members of Congress to support breast cancer research and legislation concerning breast cancer. One of their concerns, the Genetic Nondiscrimination Act, was fought for many years before the legislation known as GINA (Genetic Information Nondiscrimination Act) was signed into law on May 21, 2008, by then president Bush. It was at meetings, such as this one, where progress on such legislation was offered and then lobbied for by advocates like Lois and many breast cancer survivors. As Lois told me many times, "Sometimes you get the chance to change things"; and this, once again, was one of those times.

Lois told me living with metastatic breast cancer was like living with any chronic disease. She believed there would be good times when the cancer would be well controlled, allowing her to live her life in the way she wanted, and then there would be times when she would have to stop and accept treatments, whatever they would be, in order to feel better again. There was never a day when she came to me and said, "I feel bad, feel sorry for me." Instead, I always heard, "Well, we may not be able to toboggan down the hill, but we can walk in the snow." She always seemed to find ways to do things with people rather than exclude herself because of her cancer metastasis. She spent less of her life surviving cancer than living her life with it. She always kept friends and family close to her, but she kept her enemy "cancer" closer.

In the early days of April, I received a frantic phone call from our son. I just settled into a deep sleep from working the night before and felt a little disoriented when he called. He told me Lois was involved in a serious accident, and he was coming to take me to the hospital. He said she had not regained consciousness when he spoke to the hospital. I thought back to the morning when I saw her for a few moments to say good-bye. She left with a hurried kiss, thinking I could get some rest before my next shift when the house was quiet. As I stumbled through the numbing sting of wakefulness, with sleep clinging to my eyes, my sluggish movements dragging like thick heavy seaweed clung to them, my thoughts and sensations a step behind where I left them, I found a way to get dressed and ready for my son to arrive.

Our son had a way of knowing what to do in emergencies that must have more to do with instinct than pure thought because he knew when he called that I was incapable of driving. He came straight to the house to get me in spite of the impulse to see his mother first. He helped me make my way into his waiting car as I soundlessly allowed this reality to take hold then dropped into an introspective preoccupation. He tried to speak to me, looking for solace and encouragement, but thoughts kept finding realms of what might be waiting at the other end of this short journey to the emergency room. Was I expected to make life-and-death decisions? Would this be the way Lois made her departure from this life, leaving me with fleeting memories of that last hurried kiss as she rushed out the door to her next meeting? I tried to keep my emotions away from my thoughts because I knew I would be expected to make hard decisions that would affect many people, not just myself, not just Lois or our son. She was expected to be present for many conferences and meetings that would affect the lives of many people living under the threat and nuances of breast cancer all over the country. Her absence would be felt on many levels.

We arrived at the emergency room and were told an agent of the hospital had tried several times to contact me. When I had not returned their call, they tried our son. They did not want to leave too much information on my answering machine, just a message to call them back. I told them contacting our son in her behalf was much appreciated then proceeded with the question of what happened.

The accident must have happened late in the morning, and our vehicle, an enormous SUV, had been totaled. The nature of the accident was grave. Lois lost consciousness at the site of the accident and had to be pulled from the vehicle. From the reports the emergency room had received, Lois had at least one broken rib and had not regained consciousness by the time we had arrived. The news was grim, knowing Lois fought bone metastasis before this; she was now unconscious, with broken bones, which made the news even more devastating. It was challenging to proceed any further, but circumstances made it necessary. With less than three hours' sleep, faced with portentous losses on another side of a closed door, our son led me through the portal to discovery.

We were led inside by a nurse who led us where they were caring for Lois. An IV was running into the port in her left chest; oxygen was delivered by a cannula beneath her nose. She resembled someone sleeping peacefully. I knew this was the sleep of a dreamless dreamer, the breathing too paced, too deep, too dimensional and measured for someone who might still have control over the machine works of their body. Still, she looked remarkably good, considering the report we were given on her condition. There was no one working near her as the nurse led us to her side. She left us with Lois and then excused herself as she walked quietly to one of the physicians working on another patient near us. When I was close enough for Lois to hear me, I called her name, and her eyes fluttered open, struggling from a deep sleep that she just couldn't wake from. When her eyes opened, the confusion to her surroundings was shockingly apparent. She looked at me, to our son, and then the mechanical, digitally electrified surroundings that becomes the personality of any hospital emergency room and asked, "Where am I?"

"You're in the emergency room," I told her, relieved that she was awake and talking. Seeing she was awake, the physician speaking with the patient nearby quickly stopped what he was doing and joined us. He did a quick neurological assessment on her and asked many questions. Apparently, it was the first time he found her awake since she arrived from the site of the accident. Had I not seen the amazement in his eyes, I would have believed she had been awake before this.

The physician told us she had been unconscious for over an hour, unable to comprehend or give any information. From what he said, she woke up coherently for a moment to give them our son's phone number and then lapsed into deep sleep again. They were afraid the phone number she gave while she was semiconscious was incorrect, considering her mental state. At first, they were reluctant to try it; but with no other options to try, they contacted our son using that number, and he was able to help them. Her physician told me it was amazing she could remember a number correctly after suffering a blow to the head, which left her unconscious for so long. "She's been asleep and mumbling, but this is the first time she said anything coherent," the physician told me over his shoulder.

"Does she know anything about the accident?" I asked him.

"It's the first she's been awake. Why don't you ask her? Then I'll come back and tell you what I know about her condition," the physician said, excusing himself as he walked back to another patient arriving in the room.

When he made his way to the other side of the room, I asked Lois what she remembered. Unfortunately, all she remembered was sitting at an intersection waiting to cross, then nothing, until she woke up with us at the hospital. Everything else was blank. She asked for her pocketbook and whatever personal belongings the ambulance crew found at the scene. When she had her belongings, she rifled through her pocketbook for her cell phone. She had barely regained consciousness when, to my amazement, she started making phone calls to people who needed to know she could not make her meetings for the rest of the day. She called her workplace then several friends who would make calls for her. One call she had to make was to one of our state's congressman where she was expected to appear. Lois was well known in the state's political circles, and one of her friends from the NBCC made arrangements to have someone fill in as her liaison for the congressman within the hour. While Lois completed the phone calls she deemed necessary, I sent our son to our house to retrieve clothes for Lois to travel home in. The suit she had left home in that morning had to be cut off by the ambulance crew at the scene of the accident, leaving her nothing to dress in except the hospital gown. I think there is always a loss of modesty when you enter a hospital, but Lois was losing none of it. If she was leaving, she was leaving in her own clothes, no discussion!

While we waited for our son to return with her clothes, her physician returned to give both of us a report on his findings. He told me Lois had a broken rib on the left side near the port where her chemotherapy drugs were administered. The port was checked, and they were administering IV fluids through it at the time I arrived. When Lois threw back the covers, she was covered in large ugly red bruises that would no doubt get uglier as time went on. A CT of the head did not show any hematoma, with no injuries noted by a CT of the head, neck, abdomen, and pelvis. He felt I could safely take her home with pain medications and close observation for the first night. When I discussed the possibility of a concussion, I was told she could go home, provided someone was there to keep watch over her, which was certainly no problem from my standpoint. To further his resolution to allow Lois to leave, Lois herself did not want to stay. The nurse in me said this was not a good idea, but I had both the physician and the patient opposing me as well. The decision to take her home was finalized when our son arrived with her clothes. The time of dismissal was only what it took Lois to get dressed to separate her stay at the emergency room from her time to get home . . . believe me, it wasn't that long.

When I got her home and into a nightgown, I observed a large bruise developing on her left hip and over her left knee where the impact must have been. From what I could tell, she must have been hit on the left side of our SUV, and the impact had thrown her head into the closed window, causing her to go unconscious. Other than the large bruises on her hip and left leg, she seemed to be all right. She had a horrible headache that first night, and eventually she had a really good shiner over her left eye. I was glad I brought Lois home that night because I would have been worried about her all night long if I hadn't.

Overnight, I had to wake her about three times when her respirations went down to eight breaths per minute; and one time, I almost fell asleep myself. When I caught myself drifting off, I observed she dropped to six breaths a minute. When I woke her for the fourth time that night, she wanted to know why I kept disturbing her . . . She was getting irritated, and she wanted to sleep. I explained I suspected a concussion, and she seemed to be displaying some symptoms of having one. When I explained what I observed when she slept, she assured me with a stiff resolve she was okay and hastily went back to sleep. I think it was more to my benefit than hers that her respirations never went below ten after that.

She woke up the next day very stiff and sore. Some places, where there was only redness, now blossomed into large black bruises over her left hip and left leg. There was a bruise extending twelve inches above her left knee to just below displaying potential problems. Unfortunately, years ago, when Lois delivered our son, she developed a DVT (deep vein thrombosis) or blood clot in the saphenous vein at that very site. The condition left the vein tortuous and swollen on any given day. Lois wore support hose every day to prevent any further complications. Now, a large angry bruise covered the site, the vein was bulging, and it was tender to touch. The knee pain now took precedence over the pain of the rib fracture, which, from experience, I knew had to be painful. She could not put weight on the left leg, and the pain medications were not effective against the archetype structure of this pain. The pain in the left knee and hip were so bad, the normally stoic woman I knew disappeared beneath waves of intense pain. She asked me to bring the phone to her, and she called the emergency room physician who had treated her after the accident.

As subsequent weeks went by, Lois had to delay chemotherapy for her bone metastasis. She eventually needed to go on anticoagulants for a DVT of the left saphenous vein. In time, the first rib of the left chest wall mended. All things had their eventual consequences. The DVT of the saphenous vein recurred many times over her remaining lifetime, requiring her to go on anticoagulants. At one time, she went to a vascular surgeon to evaluate the possibility of doing laser surgery on the troublesome vein, but it was simply another blind avenue of pursuit. The surgeon would not consider it because of her extensive history of breast cancer, chemotherapy, and metastasis.

Eventually, the port, usable after the accident, was now unreliable and needed to be replaced. The many plans she made to go to Washington DC to lobby, an outing with some of her fellow breast cancer survivors over the summer in Florida, and being present at her own breast cancer support group, all had to be cancelled for several months while she recuperated from her injuries.

(Editorial by Lois A. Anderson dated June 5, 2006)

> *This will probably be one of the shortest columns I've written in a long time. As most of you know, I was involved in a motor vehicle accident in April and have been struggling ever since. When you already have bone metastasis from breast cancer and your bones get broken in an accident, a double whammy effect occurs. It becomes much more difficult for any treating physician to say definitively that certain effects are due to the bone mets of the cancer and certain effects are due to the broken bones of the accident. So here I am trying to heal up broken ribs and shoulder problems and phlebitis, but at the same time attack the cancer that is putting holes in my bones, and I have to be very careful of the medications I take and when I take them.*

I guess this event was supposed to happen to make me slow down, but then again I think that I am still here for a reason. From the amount of damage done to my SUV, the insurance adjuster told me that if I were in a smaller vehicle I'd probably be dead. So who knows really when it comes right down to it??? I'm still wondering. All I can say is that I will continue to plug away at all I do, and hopefully make a difference for all women with breast cancer.

Here's hoping we all have a good summer,

Lois

During the time she recuperated, she spoke with me about how the attendance of her support group had diminished over the years. She noted how her members seemed to be less inclined to come to the meetings, which she set up with important speakers and topics. Conversely, the numbers of people who wanted copies of her newsletter kept growing. Many times, potential new members made just one contact with the well-established support group to get the newsletter started. It made Lois question herself as to how long she would be able to continue to hold meetings. She suspected meeting times may have been a problem, so she considered changing them to suit her members. She went to the Cancer Center with her concerns but received no definitive answers. She told me several times, the support group for breast cancer survivors, which she loved dearly, would eventually come to an end. I told her I knew in 2001, when the men's support group lost me as their leader, that it would have a certain impact on the group; but even afterward, her support group continued to thrive. The times were changing. Having computers, cell phones, and other electronic equipment to communicate was making face-to-face communication obsolete. Still, as Lois believed, standing side by side with other breast cancer survivors had value and was irreplaceable, though not popular, with the newer, younger breast cancer survivors. She felt something valuable would be lost if she did not, at least, try to revitalize the support group.

Of course, like any life, there were changes to be done at our home, and the greatly anticipated kitchen remodeling was started in the latter days of August. The entire job was to take six weeks from the time the current kitchen was removed and the new one set in place. But like any good intention, there were setbacks. Despite all the planning we had done over the past year, there were many delays. Cabinets ordered for the new kitchen were missing when the final order was delivered. People who had been set up to consecutively do parts of the job were delayed, causing setbacks in time and availability; jobs that could be done were started but left incomplete because other things needed finished before they could complete what they were doing. We managed to set up a temporary kitchen in our basement, utilizing our microwave as our main cooking device. It was adequate for a short time, but we really needed to have our stove and oven back in place to make decent meals. We were able to have the stove back in about three months. It would be almost six months until the kitchen was finally in place and functioning again. The kitchen was incredibly beautiful when it was completed, a prize worth the wait. However, neither Lois nor I was willing to go through an ordeal like it anytime soon.

As it came to the end of the summer, Lois had the time to think things through. She made no mention of her intentions in her editorial. Instead, she seemed more introspective in this editorial than at any other time. The newsletter appeared like any other, eight pages, beautifully written, accepted by professionals and patients alike, but the newsletter after this one would be more informative, with changes, she thought, to help new members get interested in attending the meetings.

(Editorial by Lois A. Anderson dated September 4, 2006)

Wow, Summer certainly has flown, and here we are with the kids back in school and the seasons beginning their changes. I have had so much to do that I have been unable to stop and take a rest . . . what with trying to lobby Congress and still get everything else done, I've had to rearrange my schedules so many times, I begin to feel like I don't know where to go first. I am looking forward to having things slow down over the winter months.

With a change in chemo drugs, too, I spend more time at the doctor's office than I really prefer, but then the drugs are what keep me going so I have to make the time for all of the treatment. And then with having problems in getting our kitchen remodel job completed, it seems that it should be time for all this worry and other stuff to stop.

No matter what happens, a trip to Williamsburg to celebrate our 30th wedding anniversary will be a welcome break, and I can't wait!!!

Well, that's about all for now. Be sure and read some of the articles about the new drugs that some of you may find helpful.

And make sure you take some time to relax. I know I will.

As the frost comes over the pumpkins, enjoy the fall.

Lois

The delay in treatment, caused by the accident, allowed her tumor markers to rise to 77.7 by the end of June. The new chemotherapy protocol had not been started, as it was intended. It was almost the end of July before she was well enough to attempt her first session. By that time, most of the bruising and soreness had disappeared. Part of her summer was spent in the hospital with a DVT. With anticoagulant therapy at home, the clot was gone and no longer presented a problem. She needed no pain medications other than the nonnarcotic medications her rheumatologist prescribed for bone metastasis and arthritic changes in her joints. She looked and felt remarkably well in spite of the increasing tumor activity. She was back to work full-time and back in the midst of her political advocacy work for breast cancer patients and survivors. She wrote several articles for many national groups during this time, one being with the American Cancer Society. She continued to have concerns about the efficacy of her own support group. She still ran our household and used her time to its best advantage.

My father was deteriorating with advancing stages of Parkinson's, and her mother's dementia disintegrated to the point she barely recognized Lois when she went to visit her. Even with Lois's busy schedule, she made time to visit both my father and her mother during those times, making sure everything went smoothly for them. My mother was still managing my father's needs at home, but the effort was taking a toll on her physically and mentally. Lois could see what the stress was doing to her and spoke with my mother at length about what she needed to help. Together they thought putting hand rails through the house for my father to assist himself might be helpful. It took my mother some time to find a carpenter willing to do the job, but when the railings were in place, my father could put his weight on the railings, which was a great relief to her. On the other front, her visits to her mother always seemed to be happy, and she felt secure her mother was well taken care of in the nursing home. Whatever needs her mother had, Lois made sure they were attended to.

It would be our thirtieth wedding anniversary that September, and with everything finally in a state of moderate control, we felt safe in taking a few days for ourselves. We decided to spend our time at the place where we were newlyweds with the world before us and few cares to worry with. The idea was so nostalgic, and though we had been there many times over the years, we just felt the comfort of a place we knew and loved would renew us somehow. We both looked forward to going. We both needed to get away from the problems that wanted to suffocate us. We enjoyed the traveling, the old streets, the taverns, the walks on the brick-lined sidewalks, and having a cup of coffee on an open terrace. We came back renewed and in good spirits.

Though Lois had to miss out on the lobbying efforts over the summer, many of her friends carried the letter *L* on their lapels when they went to Capitol Hill that year. I can tell you, Lois was very moved by this display of concern and affection afforded to her by her fellow advocates when they visited their congressmen. Furthermore, it enlightened me to know that many members of congress drew immediate recognition of the significance of the *L* insignia, showing Lois was absent from their meetings that year. Lois had made an impression on our lawmakers and policy makers in the past, and the letter *L* let them know she would be back to see them in the future.

Lois had a whimsical side to her that everyone loved, and as I've said before, she always took something negative and turned it into something positive. The new chemotherapy again caused her hair to fall out, for possibly the third or fourth time in her life, so she decided to have some fun with it. When the possibility of hair loss arose, she went shopping for various wigs, adding to the already growing collection. She knew about a woman who just opened a shop that dealt exclusively with wigs. She was reputed to have a display of wigs that was phenomenal. Lois had me go to her shop where she bought two red wigs, one short, the other medium length, then a medium length blond, and finally a long locked black one. She told me she had an idea.

At home, she modeled each of the wigs, showing me how they looked on her. Each one seemed to have a personality of its own. Mischievously, she asked if I could get a head shot of her wearing each of the wigs with our camera. After she was satisfied with a set of pictures, she e-mailed a friend who wrote news stories for the local paper and asked her to help set up a contest as to which wig she should wear. Each vote cast would cost a quarter, and the most votes would dictate which wig people liked best on her. The whole project was put together over a weekend, and she got enough votes from all over the area to give the American Cancer Society almost $300. Though it was not the biggest donation the American Cancer Society had ever seen, it certainly was the most novel idea they ever saw. The newspaper, of course, did a follow-up story, indicating that her short red wig was the winner . . . It was her favorite!

There were just some things that could be made light of as Lois and I considered how to manage our aging parents that coming Christmas season. It would be especially difficult if we had to handle both of them together at any relative's home. Both her mother and my father had such advanced stages of dementia that we could not envision any good situation where we could safely supervise them. When we met with our siblings, we elected to visit each parent at their residence, where they, at least, felt safe in familiar surroundings.

My father's Parkinson's had reached the state where loss of mobility and loss of fine motor skills were an everyday problem. My father was still capable of opening his presents, but after the third one, the Parkinson-like tremors started, and my mother had to help him open the rest. Most of us bought shirts, pants, and socks that year, not knowing what he truly wanted. Though he expressed thanks for everything, he said he was just glad that everyone came to see him. Perhaps, after all, that was what he really needed from us, to be there and let him know he was not forgotten. Illness has a way of separating those who can no longer keep pace with those who run, but this year, we all made sure we stopped and walked awhile with my father. While the dementia blocked out many new thoughts and memories, I believe something in my father still realized we came home to see him that Christmas, and this was all he needed to put a smile on his face.

The visit to Lois's mother did not go as well. When she was given her Christmas presents, she smiled from ear to ear and thanked her children for the lovely gifts, which remained unopened. When Lois's sister asked, "When are you going to open your gifts?" her mother looked at her, perplexed as to what to do next. Lois took the lead and explained the process of unwrapping a box, then eventually had to unwrap one of the gifts herself so her mother would understand there was something beneath the wrappings. Her mother seemed to understand as she picked one of the presents up and then touched a bow, only to sit the box down again. She sat quietly looking at all the beautifully wrapped boxes, unable to tap the thoughts and feelings each of her children brought with them as presents that night. Each of Lois's siblings, and Lois herself, unwrapped their mother's presents and placed them into her chest of drawers at the bedside.

It was the saddest Christmas any of us ever celebrated. The inevitability of what would happen as time proceeded was like watching a flock of carrion birds waiting for each one of them to fall. We could not stop it. In some ways, it was best not to try. We each owe a death. No one gets out of here alive. Sometimes, you can't get out even when you're not really living.

The sadness we all felt this season seemed to put Lois in the mood to look back at all the things that happened over the past. She prepared her newsletter and had it distributed at the proper time. With her eloquent style, she used the newsletter to show everyone reading it what had been achieved before, during, and after her diagnosis with breast cancer. All in all, I suspect it was one of the best newsletters she ever wrote. It was truly one of her moments of fire.

(Editorial by Lois A. Anderson dated December 11, 2006)

This past year has flown and we will soon be looking at the start of another year. I don't know about you, but the longer my life goes, the shorter the years seem. So let's look forward to a new beginning of sorts in 2007—more breast cancer research and more innovations in treatments and detection.

And with that last statement about treatments in mind, following is an article I wrote for the Reach to Recovery Newsletter that gives a short synopsis of the advances in breast cancer treatments since 1992, using myself as an example. I hope you like it and that you learn a little about the history of breast cancer treatment. Most certainly, you will learn about what I have seen within my almost 15 years as a breast cancer patient and survivor.

Have a Happy New Year!

Lois

Treatments, Side Effects, and Changes—Now where do I fit in?

By Lois Anderson, MSW, South Central Area

Over the past 14 and a ½ years I have seen the breast cancer world from several different angles—that of a breast cancer patient after having been in some form of treatment for 11 and 1/3 of these years, that of a breast cancer survivor after having been diagnosed in 1992, and that of a breast cancer advocate and activist who participates in the research and policies that affect breast cancer patients. And I've seen so many changes in the world of treatment, that without those changes, I certainly would not be here today.

In 1992, when I, as a 39 year old going on 40, was diagnosed with breast cancer, there were two widely used chemotherapy regimens available to breast cancer patients. These were the CMF and FAC protocols. So what do these letters stand for? Well, the C stands for Cytoxan, the M stands for Methotrexate, the F stands for 5-Fluorouracil, and the A stands for Adriamycin. These four drugs were all that the FDA (Food and Drug Administration) had approved to treat breast cancer, and were in common use by oncologists. I was deemed able to take the FAC protocol of drugs. This treatment lasted for 6 cycles, with each cycle lasting one month.

I considered myself lucky because only 8 years earlier, my only aunt who had breast cancer, succumbed to the disease because she had no chemotherapy treatments available to her. That was in 1984. She had been diagnosed in 1976, the same year I wed my husband, when only surgery and Cobalt radiation treatments were available to treat breast cancer. In fact she was one of the pioneers in the use of Adriamycin because she had a physician smart enough to get her into a clinical trial using this drug. Unfortunately for her, because the Cobalt radiation had severely damaged her heart, she succumbed to congestive heart failure brought on by the combination of the Adriamycin with her heart condition. And that is how the scientific researchers discovered that Adriamycin could only be used in a limited fashion, and that every breast cancer patient, who is given this drug, has a lifetime limit on how much of the drug they can receive.

Along with the chemotherapy drugs there were side effects, especially nausea and vomiting. Zofran was available as an intravenous drug in 1992 and became available in pill form just as my chemotherapy treatments were ending in 1993. The only drugs my oncologist could use for the nausea and vomiting after I left his office were Decadron, Compazine, Torecan, and some of the other older anti-emetic drugs, all of which did not work very well for me. I received Zofran intravenously with my treatments but after several tries with Compazine and Torecan, that did not work, Decadron was prescribed for the nausea that came when the delayed nausea kicked in. Decadron worked well for me, and I was glad I was finished with these treatments in May of 1993.

Because my tumor was estrogen receptor positive, I was deemed able to be treated with Tamoxifen, the first of the hormonal agents, which I began taking in 1993 and continued to take for 5 years. I experienced two very different side effects from this drug—hot flashes and menstrual bleeding irregularities. The hot flashes were not too terrible, and they only disrupted my sleep from time to time when I would yell, "Hot flash!" and throw the covers at my husband. However, the menstrual bleeding irregularities eventually made a hysterectomy essential. That happened in early 1996 and the Tamoxifen continued until 1998, when my treatment with it ended.

I was deemed to have no evidence of disease until 2001 when my tumor marker test, a blood test commonly used with breast cancer patients fitting certain criteria, began to rise. A metastasis was found in one hilar lymph node and on the pleura of my right lower lung. This necessitated surgery and more chemotherapy. This time I received four cycles of Xeloda and Taxotere, one of the taxane drugs. Xeloda is a form of 5-fluorouracil that is available as a pill instead of intravenously, and Taxotere is the newest of the Taxane drugs, released by the FDA in 1996 for use with breast cancer patients. Taxol, the first of the taxane drugs, was introduced in 1993. Both of these drugs are now produced synthetically, but were first discovered in two different plants from the yew family of trees. Side effects with these drugs included some nausea, but most of the time I was dealing with diarrhea caused by the Xeloda. This was controlled by careful observation and the use of the anti-diarrhea medications, like Lomotil, when needed.

After finishing the Xeloda and Taxotere, I was started on treatment using Arimedex, another of the hormonal agents for treating breast cancer. This drug is one of the aromatase inhibitors and considered a second generation drug to treat estrogen receptor positive breast tumors. With the Arimedex, I experienced very minor hot flashes from time to time that were nothing like the cover-throwing Tamoxifen hot flashes. These were much easier to handle, and I was happy.

Then in 2003 I was hit with bone metastases, which I am still dealing with to this day. Treatment for these has consisted of Faslodex, the third generation hormonal agent for estrogen receptor positive breast cancer, and Zometa, a bisphosponate. Faslodex is an injection given once a month in the hip. Zometa is a second generation bisphosponate drug, which seems to have some anti-tumor effects, used to strengthen bones. Aredia, its cousin, is a first generation bisphosponate drug used for the same reasons. However, Aredia does not seem to have the same anti-tumor effect that Zometa has shown.

Along with Zometa comes the risk of osteonecrosis of the jaw which developed in my right lower jaw after a tooth filling, and completely healed after 5 months of treatments with antibiotics and special mouth rinses. Unusual to say the least is what happened to me because most of the time osteonecrosis heals very slowly if at all and is very painful. I experienced none of these symptoms, only a nice surprise when the necrotic piece of bone popped off my jaw one evening while watching television. Miracles do happen and this was one. However, what came next was unanticipated to say the least.

The Faslodex stopped working after almost 9 months and Xeloda was tried again. However, the tumor cells responded weakly to it. Another change in drug regimens took place in June, 2006 and I began treatment with Abraxane, a liposomal encased form of Taxol, and Aloxi, a fourth generation anti-nausea drug. Abraxane is an intravenous drug which looks like skim milk because the Taxol part of it is coated with a form of fat. Abraxane's major side effects are nausea and vomiting. Aloxi controls these symptoms very effectively for me. The nice part of Aloxi is that because it is a fourth generation 5-HT3 receptor antagonist drug, the improvements have made if it very useful to control the immediate and the delayed nausea that can take place with any chemotherapy regimen. However, constipation is a major side effect of Aloxi, but I find constipation is much easier to deal with than nausea.

And that brings me to today and my observations as a peer reviewer of grant proposals for several different breast cancer research agencies, among them the Department of Defense and the American Cancer Society. I am hopeful that all forms of breast cancer will eventually be curable, but that will probably not happen in my lifetime. The more published research I read and the more grants I review, the more I realize how much we still need to know about breast cancer's causes. This alone has made me into an advocate for research monies from any and all resources.

Changes in policies that have to do with this research and changes in the treatment of breast cancer patients are always at the forefront for me. After all, it is this research that has kept me alive for over 14 years and allowed me to beat the statistics and the prognostication I was given in 1992 for almost 3 times longer than what the doctor originally told me. I have seen so many changes for breast cancer patients since my own diagnosis that I am amazed how far medicine has come in the treatment of breast cancer. In 1992 most of what we now have was unheard of! The changes in treatment and symptom management have meant that women with breast cancer must participate in their therapy decisions. If I could give only two pieces of advice to women with breast cancer these would be that one must be willing to work with their doctors and nurses to establish a treatment and symptom management regimen that works for the individual, and keeping a sense of humor about everything is always an essential asset in the face of surviving against the odds.

It was all there in illegible scratches only the most discerning eye could see. Words assembled in parades of sentences, where scribbled lines of future events could not be changed. We saw the writing. Some chose to ignore it, some pretended it wasn't there, and some, like Lois, wrote the words "how much shorter the years seem." No matter what we saw, we all felt the tides rising against us. Small miracles came every day. By the time 2006 ended, Lois's markers held at 65.4. It was a small miracle. Her mother and my father, though very debilitated, still survived the remainder of 2006, another small miracle. But miracles, though appreciated, are short lived, requiring bigger miracles and bigger leaps of faith to span a void growing steadily wider as we grow weaker. The illegible scratches, unseen by the obtuse, would become clearer to everyone as time moved on, and we ran out of miracles.

Between Fire and Stones

Tell me about the places between . . .

As my wife slid between the realities of life and death, I also walked between the worlds of the real and the dream. Inside I could feel the rage that festered like a sickened wound, poisoning my heart with bitterness. Here I could cleanse the rage in dreams that offered escape from the world I often found to be more painful than I could imagine.

Beneath the Poet's Tree sang the low hum of a late summer day. I was older now than when I first recognized the great tree as a small child. It was, as I grew, that I came here again and again to find a piece of myself that I thought I left behind. It was my place of miracles, however small, that seemed to show wisdom in the face of ignorance, honor in place of irreverence, and courage in place of cowardice. No voices came to guide me; their lessons were either a part of me or never were. Still I watched, I listened, and I hoped for council, though none came. I was alone now, and it was my solace and the silence that led me to dream about the wall of stones.

At times, the Last Road was only a narrow passage between the wall of stones and the enormous fires the villagers maintained to keeps the orbs from attacking. There were times Alexis felt the fiery heat scorch the threads of her garments. There were places orbs tore at the foundations supporting the Last Road, where villagers shored makeshift bridges with planks, packed dirt, and stones, enabling the wagons to proceed over the ravaged pathway. Everything was a strained collective effort to keep the passage open to transport Catherine and her lifestone.

As she looked through the smoke-filled daylight, Alexis realized the patterned damage showed an intuitive plan of attack.

The crossing points, taking the most damage, were not well protected by the futile efforts of the villagers. The orbs understood or sensed that Catherine's lifestone was a threat to their survival in this world. The signs written into the destruction around her displayed intelligence intent to stop Catherine. Alexis was certain the orbs would kill her if the chance offered itself. She turned to Andrew, who was guiding the horses through the rugged terrain, and said, "This is incredible! The orbs have been attacking the Last Road to make it impassable."

Andrew turned quickly to his sister, not allowing his attention to stray from the road. "I've seen it too. It seems these things have a single-minded purpose to stop us from sealing the opening through the wall."

"I think once the breach is closed, the orbs won't be able to go back. The mists they follow and allow their survival in our world will disappear, forcing them to die."

Andrew pulled the horses left, correcting their direction, then said, "I never really thought about that moment, but you could be right." Andrew's attention returned to the team of horses as they rimmed a deep pit where fires burned almost thirty arm's lengths high. When he negotiated the area safely, he directed his attention to the wagon carrying Catherine. She appeared like a lifeless form, while the lead wagon creaked across a makeshift bridge, floating inside the thick slow-moving plumes of smoke. The wagon was swallowed entirely by thick gray tendrils, making it disappear before Andrew's eyes. Andrew kept his attention on the team and said, "You better get ready, Alexis . . ." Andrew pointed to the approaching bridge. "I hope this bridge is strong enough to support us!"

Alexis appraised the structure with concern, thinking she needed to get on the ground and lead the horses across it. "Do you think I should lead the horses over this, Andrew?"

"No, I think the horses know it will be okay." He looked into his sister's disbelieving eyes and added, "If the horses get skittish, I'll have you get down . . . okay?"

Andrew aligned the wagon wheels with wooden planks lying parallel with the road and skillfully directed the heavy wagon over the narrow bridge. Andrew beamed at his sister when they were across and said, "There, you see, the horses aren't afraid. They did it without a hitch."

Alexis thought her brother was too cavalier in his handling of the wagon's contents. If they lost Catherine's lifestone over foolish gambles like this, the villages would fall to the treachery of the orbs. They would perish. They may not be able to recover it if a bridge or a shored-up shoulder didn't hold. They needed to be extremely careful. She turned to her brother to make a point. "If we lose Catherine's lifestone, we will all die. You do realize that, don't you?"

Andrew hung his head, ashamed of the foolish risk he made to prove something to his sister. "I'm sorry, Alexis. You're right. If we come up against something like that again, one of us should lead the horses." He shook his head, turned back to his sister, and said, "I just wasn't thinking. If the horses bolted, I would not want to think of what would have happened."

The walls of flame burned high to the west of the Last Road. Catherine and her family rode the lead wagon through flatlands where the road rounded bends and curves created to keep them away from treacherous drops and ravines that endured long before the orbs were known to exist. Catherine watched as the Last Road wound away, then almost rubbed against the wall of stones. This was where she would eventually place her lifestone to end all this and, doing so, end her own life as well. "Timothy cannot know this is happening. He would have found a way back if he did," she whispered to herself.

"Were you saying something, Catherine?" Leena asked.

"No . . . not really," Catherine said, and she gave Leena a weak smile.

Jakob stopped the wagon and then called back to his passengers, "I think there must be trouble ahead. I see a group of men running toward us, waving their hands."

Michael stood up, trying to see over the rider's bench, then turned to Jakob and said, "This doesn't look good."

"That's what I thought," Jacob pondered what they would do if the way was blocked before them.

Alexis saw her father stopping the wagon and called to him from the second wagon, "Why are we stopping, Father?"

Jakob yelled back to her, "I think there may be trouble ahead. We stay here until we hear what news these men bring us."

One of the men, out of breath and unable to say anything, reached Jakob. The terror on his face spoke more to Jakob than any words ever could. When he caught his breath, he told Jakob to "stay where he was."

"But we are to take Catherine's stone to the breach to stop these damned things," Jakob responded angrily. "We have traveled a very difficult road. Catherine has made a very difficult choice, which will very likely take her life, and now you tell me I have to stop."

"I'm sorry. These monsters have all but broken through the fires about half a parcel ahead of us. We were sent back to stop you and warn you not to go any further."

Jakob was frustrated by the news and shook his head violently at the man. "By the Winds, what's going on up there? Benjamin said everything was ready. We could have stayed in Stock where it was safe if the road wasn't secure."

"I'm sorry, but the road isn't secure up ahead. In fact, it's impassable right now. It's almost like the spheres know where to hit. The road is but a bare sliver of ground, hardly a footpath anymore."

Jakob tried to calm down. He knew Catherine and her family risked everything to stop the hideous loss of life from getting any worse than it was. He could tell Catherine's resolve was dissolving. Leena was bordering on the edge of hysteria. Michael was practically immobilized by the idea of losing his daughter, and now, this idiot was telling him they needed to wait. "What is your name, son? I really want to remember it."

The younger man looked at Jakob warily, wondering why his warning made him so angry. "My name is Collin."

"Well, Collin, I hope you have a plan as to what we are to do until the road is secured." Jakob looked ahead at the men still running toward them. It seemed he may have been too hasty unleashing his anger on the young man. There did seem to be something most severely wrong in front of them. The men following Collin slowed down near the two wagons, but most continued walking past or fell into the long grasses beside the Last Road to catch their breath. Some slowed to a walking pace but continued moving south toward the village of Stock.

Collin called after them, "Christopher, Jeanne, Will . . . get over here. I need your help."

Three men resting in the grass sat up, still heaving to catch their breath. Collin asked, "Can you three gather the others? We need to get the wagons to a safe location near the wall for the night."

The one named Christopher responded first, "Can we at least catch our breath?"

It was the man they called Will who finally stood up. "Collin, the men are spooked. Stopping them will not be easy. Especially after what we just went through."

"I know," Collin agreed, "but the sooner we get Catherine to the breach, the sooner this ends."

"You're right, Collin," Jeanne spoke up. "We need to keep them safe until the road is passable."

"I'll go," Christopher said, frustrated by this interruption from a well-needed rest. "They'll listen to me. Just get them"—pointing at the two wagons—"back against the wall. The orbs don't seem to get very close to it. I think they will be safer there than on the road."

Collin looked to Jakob and pointed to a spot near the wall of stone. "There's a big tree that grows about twenty arm's lengths from the wall over there. Pull the wagons beneath the tree and wait for us. We'll make an encampment for you there. I'll try to get a messenger off to where the men are still fighting and instruct him to return when the road is passable. Is that possible for you to do, sir?"

Jakob watched the young men working together to make the situation better for them. He realized they were sitting in the midst of a very dangerous situation. It would take all their cooperative efforts to survive. They needed to work together, but for now, they were safe—thanks to the young man he knew as Collin. Had he not stopped them from pushing on, they would have fallen into a trap.

Catherine overheard the conversation between Jakob and Collin as she jumped to the ground. Collin and his followers were keeping the fires burning, which were keeping the monsters desperately trying to break through their fires from doing so. The fires were just another wall, and she was trapped between them. She was the life that would stop all the death, and she was the death that would start life again. She was afraid. Would anyone remember what she had done, and what would any acclaim matter to her when she was gone? Everyone expected her to offer herself up to stop the killing. It was too much to bear alone . . . too much. And what of Timothy? Was he really on his way to a place to ensure her immortality? Why did no one speak of this before? It was probably just another myth. She was walking the path to hysteria when a familiar voice jolted her from her thoughts.

"Are you all right?" Alexis asked as she put an arm around her shoulder. "You're shaking."

Catherine turned to her and said, "I don't think I can do this. It's too much. I have to stop this now."

Alexis pulled Catherine around so the two of them faced one another and said, "This was never going to be easy. You know that, don't you?"

Tears welled up in Catherine's eyes, but she wouldn't allow herself to cry. She was much too strong for tears anymore. She nodded yes to Alexis but did not speak. She merely looked into her eyes and saw the kindness there along with something she couldn't quite understand, trying to form itself in awareness. This was Timothy's sister, and she had his eyes. There was comfort in them.

"Catherine . . . Alexis," Jakob yelled, as he moved the wagon to a small rise near the wall where they would remain for the night.

"We better get over there," Alexis emphasized. "It sounds like something's wrong again."

Jakob watched as the two young women hurried up the rise to reach him. He wanted to move on, but Collin reported heavy fighting and a choke point where they would not be able to get through. Collin and his followers were sent back to stop Jakob and the wagons from advancing into the trap. However, Jakob had gone further than expected, which landed their little group here, close to the battle. As Catherine and Alexis moved to either side of him, he surveyed the Last Road as it wound between the flames and the wall. At its most distant point, it disappeared into an impossible contrast of flames and stones. He turned first to his daughter Alexis, then to Catherine. "I believe we will be in for a very violent night, girls. We should be ready to attend the dead and wounded."

"But, Father, I never did anything like that. I'm not sure I can do it," Alexis protested.

"It needs to be done . . ." Jakob commanded, stronger this time and with less patience. "Catherine, I know you need to get your mind off what is happening, but tonight, we need to help these men and women. Can you manage it?"

Catherine looked at Alexis still standing in rigid fear of Jakob's command, then turned her attention to back to him and said, "I'll try."

Andrew listened in on the conversation between his father and the two young women while he was securing the wagon with Catherine's stone. When he finished, he walked where they were standing and confronted his father. "I will help," Andrew told him as he moved to Catherine's side in a protective stance.

"I was counting on you. Can one of you get Michael and Leena's attention and tell them what is needed?" Jakob asked, as the three young people banded together.

"I'll do it," Alexis piped up. "Leena is so upset by all of this. It may be better to let me talk to her."

"And Michael?" Jakob asked his daughter.

"I think if I get Leena to help, Michael will follow," Alexis told her father as she looked to Catherine for her approval.

Catherine turned to Alexis and nodded. "I think Alexis is right. She is the best one to talk to my mother right now. I can't deal with an argument or any more of her pity. She will be your best chance of getting their help."

"Go on then," Jakob told Alexis. "Tell them to be ready. Collin took six of his men back into the place where they have been trying to regain the Last Road. He knew of many casualties there, and they are bringing them out."

Alexis hurried off to speak with Leena and Michael, while Catherine and Andrew pulled shovels and picks from some supplies Collin and his men left there with them.

"This will be a long night," Andrew told Catherine as she turned down the canvas wrappings over the remaining supplies.

Catherine did not speak but turned, slowly facing the direction of the vanishing road. Her thoughts were too raw to put into words, the pain of the words too cold to illicit any feeling from them. She wanted to feel good again. She was surrounded by so much death and pain. She wanted an end to it. She could run to the south where the orbs did not attack and no one cared about her lifestone or her. But she couldn't run; the huge lifestone was connected to her survival.

Within three days of running, she would die of the stone sickness just like Amelia. There was no way out.

Catherine dropped into the long grasses still standing green and strong against forces that should have ruined them with fire and smoke. She felt empty. She felt nothing, thought nothing. She was pulled like a lifeless piece of wood drifting on the water. She lifted her head long enough to see two torches moving toward them from the north. She felt a hand touch her shoulder. Looking up, she saw Andrew staring in the direction of the approaching lights.

"Some of them are coming back. We should get ready."

Catherine pulled up to a standing position, balancing her weight on the shovel Andrew gave her. "What are we to do for them, Andrew?"

The voice of Jakob sounded over her shoulder, "For the wounded and burned, we bandage, apply ointments, and pray to the Winds they survive until morning. For the dead . . ." Jakob paused. "We bury them along the shadows of the wall to the edges of the Last Road. In the morning, we will place their stones in the wall as we always have."

Jakob looked where Catherine stood, leaning against the shovel, then turned to Andrew. "Take the shovel from her."

Catherine scowled angrily at Jakob. "I am not good enough to use a shovel?"

Jakob was in no mood for petulance, but he understood her anger. "I mean no offense. The women of the villages have always been taught to be healers. Right now, other than you, Alexis, and Leena, I have only two other women able to do this. I need you all to be ready at the top of the rise to care for the injured. The men going to the bottom of the rise will care for the dead."

Catherine was not to be silenced and protested, "But with so few of us to care for the injured, we will be overwhelmed. Can some of the men help us?"

Michael walked up to Catherine. He looked at her with sadness. "You won't have much to bandage and heal, my daughter. Two messengers told me they are bringing fifty dead to us . . . no survivors."

"Andrew . . ." Jakob insisted, "there is no time for this now. Take the shovel away from her. We need it to bury the dead." He turned to Catherine and said, "I don't want you to see all this. It's heartbreaking enough for me. You don't need this right now." Jakob turned to Michael and Andrew, telling them something about the two torchbearers, and then turned back to Catherine, gave her a nod, then led Andrew to the bottom of the rise bordering the Last Road.

Michael stayed behind a moment with his daughter. "I don't know how all this will turn out, but I want you to know I love you and am so very proud of you."

"Thank you, Father," Catherine whimpered, finally feeling something she thought she had forgotten. "I love you too."

Michael took his daughter into his arms and kissed her forehead. He pushed himself away from her to an arm's length and said, "Now go . . ." He pointed to the top of the rise. "Go and help the other women waiting for you. They will need your help if we get survivors." Then Michael turned and walked away, throwing a shovel over his shoulder, as he made his way to the bottom of the rise.

Catherine turned and walked slowly to the top of the rise, looking over her shoulder from time to time and watching her father vanish into the group of men waiting near the road. Near the highest point of the rise, she was met by her mother and Alexis, who acquainted her with two women delegated to help with survivors. When the perfunctory greetings were out of the way, the group of women stood silent, listening to the sound of shovels working their way into the dirt.

From the south, Alexis spotted a line of torches moving toward them, stretching as far as she could see. "Catherine . . . look!" pointing to where she saw the torches moving.

Catherine realized a new influx of volunteers was coming from the village of Stock to fight the orbs with fire and death. She couldn't bear the thought that they were coming to help her get the lifestone to the breach. She didn't see a new line of warriors but rather another pointless sacrifice of life on her behalf. "Why are they coming?" Catherine shrieked. "They must stop. They must go back."

"Catherine . . ." Leena shouted, "what is wrong?"

"They . . . are . . . all . . . going . . . to . . . die!" she screamed at her mother.

Leena and Alexis looked at each other then watched as Catherine screamed at the approaching line of men and women coming to give their assistance at the breach. "Go back . . . go back!"

"We need to help her," Leena told Alexis, while the other two women stood by, looking horrified by Catherine's outburst.

Alexis pushed her way to Catherine's side and grasped her arm. She turned to Leena, shouting over Catherine's hysteria, "All the things happening around us have broken her determination to finish this. She is afraid. Seeing these horrific events stole whatever strength she still had left. We need to get her to sleep. She doesn't need to see any more of this." Alexis motioned the other two women to come and help them with Catherine. Together the four women were able to get her into a makeshift bed. While Leena calmed her daughter, Alexis brewed a tea from herbs she found nearby known for their sedative properties. Before long, they were able to get Catherine asleep.

"I'll stay with her," Leena offered. "If any injured come to us, call me, and I will come. Right now, I must keep watch over my daughter."

"I understand." Alexis nodded. She had almost turned and walked away but stopped, thinking of something she wanted to tell Leena. "I've known Catherine a long time. She and Timothy would take long walks, and she would always come to talk to me before she went home. Timothy loves her because she is as fearless as he is. Whenever he decided to climb to the top of the hayloft and jump off

into the hay below, she would follow him up there and do the same. If he decided to jump off that high rock cliff near the deep part of the river that runs to the south of Stock, she would be right up there with him and do the same. I could never do that. Even some of my brothers would never do that. They are both fearless. To see Catherine this way must mean she is terrified. Without Timothy being here, and not knowing what has become of him, I'm sure she is being tormented by forces and thoughts we can't possibly understand."

"Thank you for telling me, Alexis," Leena whispered, not wanting to wake her daughter. "I never really understood the attraction the two of them shared. It certainly explains a lot."

Alexis looked where the other women stood waiting for her to join them but stayed with Leena just a bit longer. "I have never seen Catherine so afraid. It scares me, you understand?"

"Scares you, Alexis?" Leena's creased brows betrayed her. "Scares you in what way?" Alexis was motherless for a very long time. In a way, Leena felt she was the mother of both girls. She looked at the fires burning all around them, then to the line of men marching past them from the south, moving into the place where others removed the dead. She looked into Alexis's eyes and pointed, sweeping her arm across every horizon. "Look at all these terrible things happening around you. Why wouldn't some of it make you afraid?" Leena asked, fearful she might soon have two hysterical girls to take care of.

Alexis looked around her. "These things have been with us for days. They are bad things that have no right to be here. People have died because of a careless, thoughtless act, and the innocent are paying dearly for it now. I know these things should terrify me, but they didn't, because Catherine believed she could stop them."

"She still can. She's still here, and she will move on when she can," Leena said, looking at Alexis a little more seriously.

"Don't you see? Can't you feel it? I think Catherine may be giving up," Alexis said. as she dropped her chin into her chest.

Leena looked at Alexis, weighing the young woman's concern with a mother's instincts. Alexis could be right. If Catherine gave up before they got to the breach, she may not be able to place the stone. She might die before it could do any good. If the worst happened, she might be so terrified, she would slip into catatonia where no one could help her. If Alexis was right, this could be the end of the villages. It did scare her. She looked again at Catherine then turned her gaze to Alexis and asked, "What can we do if you're right?"

Alexis lifted her head then said, "I don't know . . . I hope I'm wrong." Leena watched as Alexis turned and walked where the other women waited for the first injured villager to arrive. As all waited, the sound of a hundred shovels splitting the earth echoed against the little rise where it joined the wall of stones.

All the Queen's Horses . . .
All the Queen's Men . . .

Tell me about falling . . .

The meaning of her markers was becoming less clear as the first reading of the New Year moved slightly higher to 69.3. We were assured it only meant the chemo was keeping the cancer stable. Otherwise, Lois felt fine and continued to work full-time for her hospice unit. She met with families of hospice patients and made numerous trips to the homes of the dying. The irony of what she was doing could only be ascribed to the thinking of a madman. In my own mind, I saw her slowing down, showing signs of being tired. I noticed she was starting to sleep deeply when I was home with her. When she awoke in the mornings, I could see how difficult it was for her to be truly awake and moving. Some of her tiredness was explained when the oncologist called one morning and told her she needed to go on Neupogen, a medication designed to support the creation of new blood cells. While the protocol was working to keep the cancer static, it was also making her immunosuppressed. The lowered blood counts explained why she was feeling so tired. By February, she was unable to take the chemotherapy until her counts were back up. However, her tumor markers dropped to 60.5, which meant the protocol must be working.

While she battled her own war on breast cancer at home, she proposed to do battle on a national level with the NBCC in March. It was about this time a new enemy emerged on the horizon . . . "pain."

The medication used to improve her blood counts was beginning to give her intense joint pain after about five days out on a seven-day cycle. By the time I would give her the fifth or sixth injection, she would tell me her joints were so painful, she could cry.

She spoke with her oncologist who agreed to allow her to take as many injections as she could manage until the pain started. We were then to stop and get a blood count. Most times when the counts were done using this arrangement, there would be no problem in giving the chemotherapy within a few days.

It seemed skipping the February chemotherapy was not a good choice, but under the conditions, there was little else that could have been done. The March tumor markers were at a new high of 90.2. Lois would never see her tumor markers this low again for the rest of her life. None of us knew this at the time, and if we had, there was nothing we could have changed to stop it. With the help of the Neupogen, and stumbling with chemotherapy, as it was, allowed Lois to continue, relatively pain-free, with her work with hospice and her advocacy work. She did not want any woman to have to walk in her shoes ever again, if she could help it. She wanted an end to breast cancer in her lifetime, even if she didn't benefit from any new advances.

In early March, Lois went to Washington DC; and with the NBCC, they lobbied the congressmen and senators she missed out on the year before. They were all happy to see her again, sporting her new wigs from alopecia (baldness) caused by the new chemo drugs.

(Editorial by Lois A. Anderson dated March 4, 2007)

Wow, is spring ever going to get here? Will the snow ever go away? These are two questions that many of us are pondering right now. However, me, I don't have time for that. There is too much cancer advocacy work to be done, even though it isn't even spring yet. The Lobbying season has started with a vengeance, especially because we have so many new members of the legislatures on both the state and national levels.

I am writing this in between my return from lobbying our new Pennsylvania congressional representatives in Washington, DC and my getting ready to deliver daffodils to our York County legislative partners in Harrisburg. This promises to be an interesting week as I get all this work done in addition to my regular duties at hospice. But first, you may wonder how you can help in all of this, and that I can tell you . . . All you need to do is call or e-mail me and become a member of the Central Pennsylvania

Breast Cancer Advocate Network e-mail list. The only requirement for this is that you have access to a computer and are familiar with writing e-mails. In return for becoming a member of this group, you will receive e-mail updates from me about important legislative efforts and what you need to do to help get these bills for breast cancer patients passed. I am looking for a few good women and men to do this.

Now to take you back to what we accomplished in Washington DC on Friday and Saturday. We were able to meet some very fresh, young legislative aides who promise to work with us as breast cancer advocates and help us in our quest to get certain pieces of legislation passed and money appropriated for the Department of Defense Breast Cancer Research Program. Our local Pennsylvania Representative is one of the few legislators in Pennsylvania who really understand breast cancer issues primarily because of direct experience with it in his family. One of his legislative aides in the Washington office had a relative with breast cancer, too. Because of that connection, both of them "get it" when it comes to breast cancer.

What really impressed me, though, with all the new members of congress that are from Pennsylvania, so many of them were eager and willing to talk to us. In fact, several made it a special point to be in their office and speak directly with us. In one office, we ended up speaking to not just the aide handling health matters, but the legislative director and chief aide. This is highly unusual for Washington because most of the time you are lucky to get 10 minutes with just one person. What we heard so many times though was that because the power of the National Breast Cancer Coalition, our letters, our e-mails, and our comments are taken much more seriously than some other groups. That in itself is nice to know. All in all, Friday was a good day to talk to the people in Washington.

Then on Saturday our annual Team Leader Training session was held. We learned about the political strategy that the National Breast Cancer Coalition will use to get their legislative agenda fulfilled for this year. I will lead another small group of women up onto Capitol Hill to lobby our congressional delegation from Pennsylvania when we return in May. At that time we'll see how much time the newest legislative aides will have for us. It will be interesting to see how quickly they can become jaded by the Washington rat race.

And on Tuesday of this week, I will be delivering daffodils to our York County representatives in Harrisburg along with the message about the legislative priorities of the American Cancer Society. One of these priorities is about colorectal cancer screening since a financial study has been completed that shows the dollar advantages of performing its kind of testing. Another priority is clean air throughout the state.

Both of these priorities should be of interest to all breast cancer patients/survivors/advocates for different reasons. First, the colorectal cancer screening should be of interest because once one has a diagnosis of breast cancer that individual is at increased risk for colorectal cancer. Secondly, for those who are smokers, the risk of breast cancer is higher because smoking makes one more susceptible to not only breast cancer but in addition, lung cancer.

Probably some of the most important information to come down the pike about breast cancer recurrence is the results of the WIN study. That study shows how diet affects breast cancer and its recurrence. For those interested, the National Breast Cancer Coalition will have a special plenary session devoted to diet and its effect on breast cancer at their advocacy conference. This session promises to be a very interesting one since the researchers involved with the WIN study will present their information as part of a panel discussion.

Okay so enough for the rant. For those interested, I will have the honor of being profiled in the Advanced Breast Cancer Section of the "Living Beyond Breast Cancer" website. Go ahead and take a look at it. You may be surprised at all the information there.

Daylight savings time began earlier this year, but now the weather has to catch up. Will the snow ever stop? Here's to spring. I hope it soon starts.

Lois

Lois was fighting battles on many fronts. She was trying to get more people to attend her breast cancer support group. Many times she would get unpaid professional speakers to come, and very few people would show up. It was very frustrating and embarrassing to have a speaker come to speak with just five or six people, especially when, at its height, the support group census could have been as high as thirty to forty people. Many times she would return from the meetings frustrated by the poor attendance, upset no one came to acknowledge the amount of time and effort she put into getting speakers.

At the same time, she was battling fatigue from the chemotherapy with poorer and poorer progress seen with each treatment. She had to include additional medications to her daily routine to hold the joint pain at a level where she could function. She remained active in spite of the fatigue and continued to take her "on-call nights" at work, which could, and did, call her out at all hours, having already put in a full day's work. When she did have some days off her regular job, I would let her rest. But even then, she insisted on waking up and working on the computer, and on the phone, with advocacy groups and legislative officials, promoting breast cancer legislation and funding.

She also continued to check in on my father and her mother on her way back from work several times during the week to be sure everything was going smoothly. By May, Lois's markers were up to 118. We were certain either another protocol needed to be tried, or her time with us was much shorter than she expected. We all needed her, especially Lois's mother, who had no concept of what was real anymore. Finally, on May 19, Lois received a phone call from the nursing home informing her that her mother just had a major stroke, which paralyzed her entire right side.

We left immediately to see how bad the stroke really was. After we saw the condition her mother was in, we certainly agreed their analysis was correct. The doctor was called with appropriate measures and medications in place by the time we arrived. Lois's mother was still cognizant and still had the faculty to speak. She looked up at Lois and asked, "What happened to me?" Lois tried to explain and reassure her, but her mother had no way to process what Lois was trying to say. Lois took my arm and said, "I don't feel good about this."

"This is not good," I told her. "I'm afraid she will just get up and fall again. She doesn't know what she's doing or that the right side of her body is not functioning. It won't support her anymore."

"I believe it is time for hospice to come in to see her," Lois told me.

"Well, I don't believe the event is fatal. Many times rehab can do a lot with stroke patients that can improve their functioning," I said.

"Even so, I think I will at least put that 'bug' in their ear for future reference. I'm thinking this is probably the beginning of something that will not end well," Lois told me, as she walked to the nurse's station to speak to one of the nurses.

Her siblings arrived, going to visit their mother who didn't recognize any of them as her children. After they had the chance to see and speak with their mother, they spoke with their sister Lois. They believed the situation was very much what Lois told me earlier that evening. They agreed, should their mother not do well with therapy, she should be placed on hospice. They wanted Lois to make the arrangements should they be necessary, and she agreed to do so when the time dictated.

Eventually, everyone left except Lois and me. Lois went to the nurses' station and told everyone there that we were leaving for the evening and to call if there was any change in her mother's condition. She also gave her permission to use whatever means were necessary to keep her mother from injuring herself. We left for home feeling very uneasy about what the future held for her mother.

Even with all that was happening in her personal and professional life, Lois found the time to publish the newsletter in early June.

(Editorial by Lois A. Anderson dated June 6, 2007)

> *Okay, so now I guess we can complain about the heat—seems like another year with no spring or very little time to adjust to the heat. At any rate, our annual picnic will be coming up in July. I have to apologize to all because I had intentions of having the picnic at my house so everyone could see the new kitchen, but due to circumstances I could not control, we'll have to wait until next year for that to happen. My mother had a stroke on*

May 19th so I've had to pay more attention to her and her care at the moment. She seems to be doing very well as of this writing, trying to do many of the things she previously did even though her right side is paralyzed. She is working with the physical therapist, the occupational therapist, and the speech therapist trying to get back what she has lost. She even walked about thirty feet in the parallel bars this week, quite an accomplishment. But with the dementia, you can't explain to her not to do something—she doesn't understand. And so we work with her and try to keep her safe as best we can right now.

Just before mom's stroke, I returned home from two very important events—NBCC Lobby Day and the DOD Breast Cancer Research Program Integration Panel Grant Review. First, on Lobby Day, May 1st, I had the honor of presenting Representative Todd Platts with his second certificate recognizing him as one of the few members of congress who consistently showed his support of the National Breast Cancer Coalition's legislative agenda. And yes, there is supposed to be a picture published in the paper sometime soon of myself and Representative Platts.

All in all, Lobby Day went very well for our PA delegation and we were able to get all of our senators and representatives except three, to cosponsor legislation that was a part of our agenda. These pieces of legislation include the reauthorization of money in the U.S. Defense Department's budget for their Breast Cancer Research Program and the Breast Cancer and Environmental Research Act, which would appropriate money to study environmental links to breast cancer.

And then there was the meeting of the Integration Panel in Baltimore, MD. I had the honor for the 5th time as being chosen as an ad hoc member of the Integration Panel to review the grants and fit them into the categories that the Army determines for its breast cancer research agenda. I was glad I could be there this year since last year I was unable to participate due to the auto accident. I was able to meet some old friends and make some new ones and learn about some new breast cancer research projects. This meeting always tends to deepen my faith in the medical research system in this country. However, one of the topics discussed during the off hours was how the political agenda of this country has affected the money available for research and how some of our researchers may not be able to do the kind of basic biologic research that needs to be done to answer questions about cancer and its origins. It is a very scary time. The NIH is facing some *serious cutbacks that will have long term ramifications and may lessen our ability to remain as a world leader in medical research. All I can say is be sure to vote in 2008.*

Stay cool in the pool or the air conditioning whichever one works for you.

Lois

We pray for a lot of things . . . good weather, good kids, good jobs, and good health. Sometimes we pray to an entity that many of us do not believe exists. But when fear becomes the god we pay homage to, it is when I think we give up. Lois was facing death and thumbing her nose up at it. The tumor markers were still rising, and she faced more chemotherapy, radiation, endless tests, and endless office visits just to remain standing. And standing up she did! When everyone else went finger pointing as to what or who was to blame for her mother's stroke, she took the lead, gathered her siblings together, and presented them all with the inevitable . . . Their mother was very ill and was poorly equipped to handle the losses the stroke had dealt her. It was really only a matter of time before she fell and injured herself so badly that she would be unable to ever get out of a bed again or the thing that caused this disabling stroke would be back and either severely disable her or take her life. Her brothers were slow to accept what she had to say. Only her sister seemed to be listening.

I went to stay with my father one afternoon while my mother went out with some of her friends. It was a strange visit, but strange in a way that said my father was still here, still clinging on to reality by the most gossamer tendrils. Unlike Lois's mother, he still had moments of clarity that challenged all of us to remember what he still retained. My father was sleeping, and I somehow woke him when I sat down on the bed next to him. He looked over to me and said, "George, you look tired. Just stretch out on the bed and rest." It was one of his moments when recognition and purpose met. He surprised me when I engaged him in a conversation. He told me stories about when I was growing up, stories I had honestly forgotten or never knew about. It was amazing. He spoke with me for perhaps an hour, and he finally got tired and dozed off.

The room was so quiet that I too gave into sleep only to be awakened by a tap on my leg. I looked down at the foot of the bed, and there was my father, pushing his wheelchair into the room. He told me he had to go to the bathroom, got up, and brought back a chair for me to sit on. I looked at him, concerned on how he had accomplished all this by himself. The Parkinson's had made his muscles so rigid, there was only minimal flexibility to any of his joints. I got up and helped him get back into the bed so I could have a quick look around the house. As I suspected, there was toilet paper, towels, and an overturned chair where he brought the wheelchair through the house. It looked like a two-year-old had done this. But I wasn't angry. He was my father, and the effort he must have gone through to bring his wheelchair back to me must have been herculean . . . as was the thought to do this for me. I cleaned up the house and sat in the wheelchair as he wanted me to. Then he fell asleep again.

It was the last clear conversation I ever had with my father, and I was happy to have had the chance to do this for him. Of course, it had been Lois who encouraged my mother to get out of the house and get away for a while. It was also Lois who set up my babysitting assignment so my mother could leave. Lois always made sure everyone else was taken care of. She never asked anyone to take care of her . . . that she would do for herself.

The focus of Lois's activities became less based on national affairs as the year moved on and more on the domestic. It wasn't long before she came up with a plan to have the entire first floor of our home refitted with new airtight windows. The many cold winters over the years caused air leaks to grow around the original windows. When the winter winds blew off the lake at the bottom of our hill, the cold air seeped in and around the bedroom windows where we slept. As her bone mets progressed, Lois's intolerance to cold grew to where any cold air caused her joints to ache. With a little planning, she got a window designer out to our home within a week; and within a day, all the upper floor windows were replaced. At the time, I thought her reasoning was inspiration based on the moment; but in hindsight, I think she realized she was losing ground, and she was making preparations not only for herself but also for me.

One thing that Lois always loved to do was gardening. For some reason, that summer she really wanted to fix up the gardens around our home. We had a few small beds of daylilies started at one end of our home that she was very pleased with. She told me she had been studying various flower catalogs and discovered there were hundreds of varieties of daylilies that were indigenous to our area. She wanted to go on a kind of scavenger hunt that summer to find rare and unusual daylilies to place into our gardens. By the time summer was over, we procured almost eighty varieties of daylilies. As of the writing of this book, Lois had accumulated over one hundred varieties of daylilies. They were one of her greatest joys, and to this day, they stand as a kind of living memorial to her.

By July, her tumor markers were up to 149; and she continued on the same chemotherapy protocol, hoping the numbers would turn around. Life would not wait for her to recover, and finally one night in early July, we received the phone call we had been expecting for some time. The nursing home called to tell us that her mother had suffered a very severe stroke. She was still alive, but the stroke left her completely paralyzed, except for some decorticate posturing that appeared as a kind of involuntary grasping of her hands over her chest. When Lois and I saw the posturing, we knew she didn't have long to live. We called the family to the nursing home where they came and stayed long enough to say their good-byes then left. It was Lois who stayed with her mother until she passed. Lois was very emotional at the time, very unlike the time when her father died. This event made her the caretaker of the family. It also made her an orphan for what remained of her own life. It seemed she took on the weight of the world after this.

To have seen her during these times, most people would not have known anything was different about Lois. She continued to work long hours, sometimes staying at work until two or three o'clock in the morning to get everything she wanted to accomplish completed. Again, many times when I was not working, I would go along with her to keep her company or simply act as an errand boy, carrying things around the office for her. As I watched, I began to see her becoming more introspective, looking deeper into herself than she ever did before. She was always positive, looking for the next door that would take her places where she had not been to before. Many times we talked about the chance that she would not win this battle with cancer this time around. We spoke of the future in months, not years. In retrospect, I believe she knew in 2007 that her life would be over very soon. Still, I told her she was still here, still able to do the things she loved doing, and would continue to do until that time came. Our conversations were profound and painful . . . as a conversation with someone you truly love can really be. Sometimes our moment of fire burns unseen by anyone's eyes except the one who is really looking. Her desire to live and make things better for breast cancer patients everywhere was her flame, burning white hot.

As September came around, Lois's markers stayed down to the level of 141. She felt good other than some minor joint discomfort caused by the chemotherapy. She managed to make plans to travel to Charleston this year and wrote the newsletter for September.

(Editorial by Lois A. Anderson dated September 3, 2007)

As many of you already know, my mother died on July 15th making it impossible for me to attend our picnic this year. I missed everyone and I'm sorry I couldn't be with all of you. However, I had other things to do. I am now busy with trying to get her estate settled and working with the lawyer on all of that. I want to thank everyone who sent their expressions of sympathy. It is always nice to know how much support you have at a trying time such as this.

Renovations and fixing things up seems to be the order of the day around our house this year. We started with a new pool liner and several steel panels that needed replacement, something we had been contemplating since last summer. Then we added bunches more daylilies around the house. We have over 100 plants now and George came up with a total of 78 different varieties, but I still keep collecting them and he still keeps planting them for me.

Then the tractor went on the fritz and we had to get a new one just last week. Of course it couldn't wait another week when the mowers went on sale.

So this week it's the replacement windows that will be put in. I just can't wait since it means there will be a lot more clean up that has to be done after the crew gets finished tomorrow or Wednesday.

But the biggest thing I am looking forward to now is a vacation in Charleston, South Carolina. After taking several weekend trips this summer and not really knowing where we wanted to go for a weeklong trip, I made the decision for us to go to this beautiful historic city based on what I saw on the "Today Show" and its summer travel plans segment.

Of course after this vacation it will be the gearing up for October and Breast Cancer month and more lobbying activities in Washington, DC and in Harrisburg, PA, but I do hope to relax and take some time out of this schedule just for me. I still want to see "Cabaret" over at the Dutch Apple Dinner Theater this fall and that's another thing on the agenda.

So what are your plans the rest of the year? Keeping busy is never anything new to me. Enjoy the cooler less humid days and I hope to see you at one of our meetings this fall,

Lois

Lois's work as a bereavement coordinator was so successful, her client list grew to over three hundred clients. The numbers were almost too much for one person to keep track of. She asked for an assistant to help organize and get her mailings out in a timely manner, but the best her organization could do was allocate some volunteers from time to time to help her. When her client list grew to 350, her manager hired another social worker to help with calls and other duties. She still continued into the early morning hours to finish what needed to be done. She continued her work with the NBCC and other breast cancer organizations with phone calls to legislators and mailings to congressmen. She was in contact with her political constituents and encouraged those members of her breast cancer support group to write letters, make phone calls, and send e-mails showing either support or disapproval of legislation pertaining to breast cancer. After the death of the mother, she was involved in the settlement of her mother's estate. At the time, she was running about almost nonstop among doctors, lawyers, and politicians.

When her tumor markers rose to 216 in early November, it was decided to change the chemotherapy protocol once again. In spite of the increasing tumor markers, Lois's main complaint was some discomfort in some of her joints. Otherwise, she felt pretty good. One condition giving her problems was her nails. The previous chemotherapy caused the nails of her feet to grow thick, discolored, and misshapen. She was fastidious in the care of her nails, but their bizarre growth made them impossible to manage with the kinds of manicure tools she could buy. The nails were beginning to give her foot pain when the nails turned inward, causing ingrown nails with subsequent foot infections. The chemotherapy agent she left behind was the last traditional medication reserved for bone metastasis. Lois would now start on a new chemotherapy drug that appeared the year she needed it. Trying to stop the tumor markers from rising was like chasing the wind. It seemed no matter how fast she tried to arrest the cancer, the further from her grasp it moved away. Still, she hoped the cancer remained relatively asymptomatic, which it did for the rest of the year.

Even as her markers rose and the inner cry of alarm went off again and again, Lois found time to work with the American Cancer Society as a trainer and as an advocate. She went to one of our local schools twice a year, speaking to new classes of LPN students about breast cancer. She continued the work she started in 1992 and stayed true to her vow that no woman should have to walk in her shoes with breast cancer. It was during these times when she was most tested, when the urge to turn and run seemed like the right thing to do, that she rose above her diagnosis and made a difference with her life. Just being around her, you knew you were in the presence of someone unusually unique and special. People always told me she made them come away from her feeling good about themselves. What made this interesting was not everybody who told me this ever had breast cancer. Some were surprised that Lois had it.

She eventually got around to writing her newsletter for the end of the year. In it, she expressed concerns, not for herself but for her friends that lost the battle. She tells of her struggles with her mother's estate and the changes she found herself up against.

(Editorial by Lois A. Anderson dated December 21, 2007)

By the time you read this newsletter, the holidays will be over. I hope all of you had an enjoyable time celebrating them. Several of my friends died recently from breast cancer complications and that saddens me as I think of them and their families, especially at this time of the year. Even though their journey on this life is over, I know they are still with me and this thought provides peace.

It is at this time of year, too, that we traditionally tend to take stock of things and look into the new year to decide what to change or do differently, but me, I'm satisfied and I don't really want to change my life in any major way. However, there are several things I want to put on my "Bucket List" to do sooner rather than later.

For those of you who don't know, I am now on a brand new chemotherapy drug called Ixabepilone, which was just approved by the FDA in October. I am only the second patient in this area to receive the drug and that makes me much more cautious with the side effects that it can produce. Because there is little experience with the drug in this locale, I feel a little like a guinea pig of sorts. As I write this newsletter, my blood tests which are due to be performed next week will tell whether it is or is not working. So we wait and see!

Work still keeps me busy. My mother's estate still has to finish its settlement, which has a timetable all of its own anyway. I can empathize with my clients who voice their frustrations over this process. I think there has to be a better way.

Hope to see each of you sometime in 2008. Take care and let's not get into too much snow.

Lois

And so the year 2007 ended, not with a loud roar but with a hush. It was like a breath drawn yet reluctant to exhale. It was a silence waiting to be broken by a sigh of air, freed upon the stillness.

A Path of Ghosts

Tell me about ghosts . . .

"We don't leave our loved ones behind," whispered the words of my grandfather, a man long dead since I was a boy. They were words with wisdom so intense that only his ghost in its otherworldly form could have uttered them. I used the words in my life so many times that I believed his ghost still lingered there beneath the Poet's Tree where I found my inspiration. His restless spirit does not visit me now that I am older. His lessons were to be learned and lived or never learned at all. All I ever needed to do was listen even if I didn't believe in ghosts.

Now there were other voices to be heard. Most of my elders were gone. Their voices were growing more distant and less intelligible as I grew into manhood. It was now the time to listen to the wind rustling through the branches of the great tree. A storm was coming . . .

Timmerloo spent the following day continuing the strange stories and tales he experienced traveling the mountain passes in the north. Seven days after the wall breach, Timmerloo finally had Timothy prepare two horses for them. Starting at the Stone Lodge, they would begin their travels into the treacherous paths leading them to the place Timmerloo knew as the "stone chamber."

Timmerloo had Timothy prepare most of their equipment for climbing purposes. He knew they would have trouble scaling the steep rock slopes surrounding the abandoned village without it. Other than some parcels of prepared meats, cheeses, and bread, there was little room for any quantity of food to take with them. They filled several skins with water but saved most of their space for getting a fire started, dry wood, some skins of oil, and flints to spark a fire to *life. They knew the freezing conditions in the mountains would freeze the water they carried with them within a short time. Even without a water supply, they could melt ice and snow in a small iron kettle stored inside the canvas wrappings. When all was ready, they walked the horses laden with supplies from the security of the Stone Lodge into the lonely mountain passes.*

Considering how talkative Timmerloo was at the lodge, he was strangely quiet as he led Timothy through the staggered, sometimes nonexistent, trails leading to the chamber he so aptly described in his stories. Several times, Timothy tried to engage Timmerloo in conversation, but Timmerloo's attention focused on the markings and signs in the terrain he used to divine their way to his remote, hidden destination. They traveled until nightfall dropped its curtain of darkness around them, forcing them to stop and make camp for the night.

Timothy made the fire using some of the wood they brought from the lodge then went off to find dried limbs and larger firewood from the broken trees surrounding them. Within a short time, he gathered more than enough wood to keep the fire burning through the night. While the flames licked the shadows from their stony perimeter, Timmerloo stayed near the warmth of the flames almost mesmerized by the crackling light.

"We need to eat, Timmerloo, or have you forgotten about that?" Timothy asked, frustrated the old man had not done much of anything other than lead them here.

"Give an old man a chance to rest," Timmerloo said, none too happy by Timothy's innuendos.

"Then keep the fire attended, while I pull some food from our satchels. I don't know how far we have to go, but I have no intention of starving until we get there."

Timmerloo looked where Timothy was standing near the horses then pulled some branches from the pile of wood and threw them into the steady blaze. "The way we must go is hard. We must rest," Timmerloo said.

"After we have some food in our stomachs, we can have a night of peaceful sleep without your stories," Timothy said, frustrated by Timmerloo's lack of effort to have a meal and a comfortable fire to sit next to. Timothy glared at the old man a moment, then dug out some ironware to heat some meat and wild carrots he found while searching for firewood. They were just below the snow line, but the air was cold, and the heat of the fire felt good on his skin. Some of the meat he used like a stew in the iron pot, and some he placed on sticks to roast near the fire. While he waited on the food to be done, he turned his attention to the early night sky filling up with stars.

"I see them almost every night and wonder what those white specks really are."

"What are you talking about?" Timmerloo suddenly perked up, not understanding what Timothy was looking at.

"Up there . . . in the sky . . . the points of light we call stars," Timothy said, as he turned back to turn the meat roasting near the fire.

Timmerloo's eyes reflected the light from the fire as he raised his head. "The Ancients believed them to be little suns burning like our own, but, so far away, they appear only like tiny specks of light."

"Catherine and I would lie at the top of the hill near her father's home and watch them." Timothy remembered then turned to Timmerloo and asked, "Do you know what she told me?"

Timmerloo watched as Timothy turned back to reflect on the starry sky. "What did she say?" he asked.

"She told me the Four Winds scattered them so they could find their way here. It was their map . . . a way to find us and help us while we lived and raised our families."

"Catherine sounds like a poet, my young friend."

"A poet?" Timothy asked, pulling a stick with cooked meat from the fire.

Timmerloo realized he didn't understand, so he continued, "A poet is a word to describe someone who looks at something ordinary and sees something no one else seems to see. It is a person who makes us look at something differently that changes the way we do or see or even feel something. It is a good thing, Timothy."

"Catherine seems to see a lot of our world through a different set of eyes than most of us."

"So what do you see when you look at the stars?" Timmerloo asked him.

Timothy took a bite of meat then turned his eyes to the darkened sky. He turned back to Timmerloo, staring at him with a stick of meat in his hands. "I think they are the ones that are no longer here looking down on us while we sleep. I think one of them could be my mother looking down, keeping me safe."

"It's a good thought, Timothy. Perhaps your mother does see you from somewhere up there. Perhaps they all do." Timmerloo took another bite of meat.

"I need to rest now," Timothy said, as he finished his food. "I'm going to put some of the larger pieces of wood on the fire to burn through the night." He placed some large slabs of wood on the fire then went where the horses were tied to some nearby saplings and removed his bedroll. "I'm going to bed down here. You want your sleeping gear?"

Timmerloo grunted yes as he swallowed his last piece of meat. "Put it there next to the fire. An old man needs to keep warm."

Timothy placed his bedroll on the level ground near the horses as Timmerloo settled in near the fire. The two men laid there with the night sky looming above them. Timothy looked at the stars and wondered if Catherine was thinking about him tonight . . . He was thinking of her. He tried to sleep, but it remained elusive. He looked to the fire where Timmerloo had fallen fast asleep then turned back to look at the stars. "How far do we have to go?" he asked the heavens.

In the morning, Timmerloo was awake and had the fire in a roaring blaze. He heated water in a kettle and made a cup of tea for each of them. "Nice to see you awake. I made something hot to get your day going," he said, as he handed him the steaming mug. "We will both need our strength today. We can take our horses as far as the snow line. Then after that, we must go on foot. We will carry what gear we can and unload the rest there where we can find it again for our way down."

"And what of the horses?" Timothy asked.

"We must let them wander back to the lodge. They know the way," Timmerloo replied dryly. "If we tied them up, they would starve in the snow. It is better this way."

Timothy took a long drink of warm tea then turned to watch Timmerloo tying parcels to the horses. "What do we have ahead of us?"

Timmerloo turned back to Timothy as he picked up his bedroll and tied it to one of the horses. "After the snow line . . . another three or four parcels before we come to the niche. We move from here as soon as we can . . . we can be there by midday."

"We should get moving then." Timothy finished his tea in another long gulp then found some hard bread to eat along the way in one of the satchels. He put a few pieces into his pocket and then turned to Timmerloo still tying his bedroll to the horse. "I'll have my things ready as soon as you put the fire out."

While Timothy gathered his belongings and tied them to his horse, Timmerloo shoved stones and dirt over the fire. As promised, by the time Timmerloo had the fire out, he was ready to leave. "Which way?" he asked.

"Do you see those two pointed rocks sitting just above this line of pines?"

"That doesn't look too far away," Timothy said, surprised that they were so close to the niche. "That's not even the snow line, Timmerloo . . . are you sure?"

"When we pass between those two rocks, we will leave the horses behind. The snow line starts just behind them."

"From there?" Timothy asked, as he looked from Timmerloo to the two mammoth-toothed rocks rising from the thick stand of green pines and fir painting the side of the mountain.

"From there, the path is snow covered, narrow, and barely passable, even this early in the season." Timmerloo watched as streaks of fear, courage, and conviction wrote lines of worry over Timothy's face. The young man stood transfixed by the ominous destination before them. Timmerloo realized he lost his attention. "Timothy . . ." he called loudly, "are you ready?"

"Let's go then," Timothy said, never allowing his eyes to stray from the two projecting stones.

Timmerloo took the lead, while Timothy paraded the two horses laden with supplies behind them. They made the tree line faster than expected because of Timmerloo's surefootedness and experience. There was a worn path leading into the pines, and Timmerloo guided their small envoy through them. The shadows of the stones blocked the sun, and the light dimmed, making the path before them difficult to follow. Just when it seemed the absence of light would overtake them, the tree line thinned, revealing a dirt path that passed between the stones.

"Quite a landmark, Timmerloo. I see why you use it . . . very unusual," Timothy gasped, looking up at the impossible height of the stranded rocks.

"It's true. It is one landmark that you won't ever forget. I've traveled here many times in the past and used it as a way in and out of the mountains . . . especially during the snowy season when all this looks the same. It's a good thing to have one true landmark to guide you. But as you will soon see, there are others," Timmerloo said thoughtfully, as he pointed the way for Timothy to follow.

The way through the two stones was like walking from one solen to the next. They left the solen of "Harvest" behind and entered the solen of "Ice" on the other side. The change in the air was sudden and dramatic. It was two different worlds in a matter of steps. Timmerloo watched as Timothy reacted to the sudden change and said, "This is where we leave the horses." He pointed to a ledge jutting out about twenty arm's lengths to their left. "That is where we are going. The climbing gear needs to come with us and whatever provisions we can carry. When we are ready, we let the horses go. Understand?"

"Yes, we spoke of this before. I understand. I just don't like the idea of leaving our best and quickest way off these mountains run off," Timothy argued.

"The alternative will be to let the horses starve, freeze to death, or have predators kill them where they stand. I want them to be let go. We will walk off these mountains, and if we don't . . . well, at least the horses won't have to suffer for us."

Timothy was shaken by Timmerloo's remark as he realized this journey placed both their lives in peril. "Are you saying we may not be able to get back?"

Timmerloo gave Timothy a strange smile then motioned him to shoulder the supplies and follow him onto the stone ledge he pointed out earlier. The ledge was reached by climbing up a series of flat rocks and ended on a path of stone wide enough for three men to stand shoulder to shoulder. "As you can see, the horses would have spooked and thrown the supplies by this point . . . even if they could have made it this far," Timmerloo said, steadily leading Timothy forward.

At the end of the stone ledge was a snow-covered trail leading higher into the mountains. Timmerloo didn't stop to rest, continuing the climb through the splintered rocks and stony ravines rutting the side of the mountain. The air was getting colder as the sun moved higher in the sky, which Timothy thought was impossible. Eventually, they crested the mountain and saw where the descending path wound like a pale serpent, frozen fast between the stony surfaces and clotted rocks. Timothy watched Timmerloo as he stopped several times to catch his breath in this unnaturally cold mountain air. The old man was getting tired, and at times, it seemed he was uncertain where he was going.

"Everything all right, Timmerloo?" Timothy asked when Timmerloo stopped for the fourth time since they came through the two stone pillars.

"I'm trying to remember things. When I last traveled here, it was snowing and the footpaths were covered in white. I'm trying to imagine how it looked then and make our way there. I remember the snow kept forcing us down when we wanted to get to the top where we could see the two stones leading off the mountain. I remember not wanting to drop down off the mountain, and since we couldn't move to the top, I tried to stay alongside and move to the south. However, in our case, we are doing this in reverse, going north. In about half a parcel, we will know."

"Know?" Timothy asked, unsure Timmerloo's logic was sound. The old man was acting strangely ever since they passed into this frozen wasteland.

Timmerloo looked back, knowing he had to explain something to the young man. "When I came down off the mountain the last time, the horses were dead where we left them tied up. I left their bodies stay where they died. When we get to that place, their bones will lead the way." Timmerloo nodded sadly, asking Timothy for his understanding. Timothy looked at the old man in both sadness and horror as Timmerloo turned to the path and started walking. Over his shoulder, he said, "This is why I left our horses free to find their way back. The last time . . . by the time I got back to them, they had frozen to death. I will never do that to any animal again." Sadness washed over the old man as he pointed to a narrow passage leading through some broken stones. "This is the way."

Again, Timmerloo took the lead. The remote passage was unlike any they had traveled. Some of the stones had markings like the ones he saw etched into the tunnel walls at Emansupass and the map room at Bridgedom. When he pointed out the strange markings, Timmerloo simply remarked that he had seen them and declined speaking of them. "This is the way, isn't it?" Timothy asked, wanting to be reassured.

"You have seen the markings . . . Yes, we are on the right path. The niche should be close now," Timmerloo said, struggling for breath.

"You don't sound too good, old man. Perhaps we should stop and rest," Timothy said, concerned Timmerloo would fall over in exhaustion if he didn't stop.

"We are close now. Soon we will rest," Timmerloo grated, as the vapor of his breath colored the air.

Timothy followed as Timmerloo struggled with every footstep he took. The path leveled out when they entered a small plateau covered with withered, malformed saplings. Beyond the plateau was a smooth solid rock wall, unblemished by any visible foothold, crevice, or crack that could be used to climb it.

"There is nothing here, Timmerloo," Timothy protested. "It's a dead end. There are no bones, no niche, and no way off this flat piece of rock."

Timmerloo stopped and found a stone big enough to sit on. He was out of breath, but he was not discouraged. "This is the place. I know what you are looking at looks flat, but it is just an illusion. Give me a moment, and I'll show you."

"You need to stay here. I'll move on as far as I can then return and tell you what I find," Timothy insisted, eager to show Timmerloo that they needed to turn back.

"I'm getting my breath, but I need a few more moments . . . then I can move on," Timmerloo pleaded.

Though Timothy felt this was a waste of their time, he waited until Timmerloo felt he could move on. "I think I can get there now. Just as it looks like the plateau ends, it drops in a slope that ends at that rock wall." Timmerloo pointed at the sheer wall of black stone that faced them. It was an insurmountable face of stone rising straight into the sky, the top lost in the low-riding clouds.

Somehow, the stone obstacle before Timothy didn't seem natural. The rock face looked as though it was made, created by stonecutters of unnatural abilities, with skills that were never known or so old they were long forgotten. Timothy was ready to follow the old man, but something stopped him. "It was snowing when you were here before?"

"Yes, that's right." Timmerloo wheezed as he stopped and faced him. "Why do you ask?"

"Stand by me for a few moments and take a look at this." Timmerloo turned and looked at the rock-faced wall before them. "It's more of a structure than a natural rock formation, don't you think?"

Timmerloo pondered the straight smooth wall before them and realized Timothy could be right. "Yes, I see what you mean. It's like another landmark. It's hard to miss. The face of the rock almost looks like it was ground smooth at one time."

"It was one of the paths into Winterland, Timmerloo. You found one of the paths," Timothy said, excited by the discovery.

"Shall we go?" Timmerloo asked, picking up on Timothy's excitement. Again, the old man led the way to the flat wall of stone before them. As predicted, the level plateau slanted down to the base of the wall when the plateau appeared to stop. It was a carefully calculated mirage meant to obscure the inconspicuous opening, appearing only after they started down the incline. Just beyond the opening, Timothy saw the remains of the horses Timmerloo and his hunting party abandoned many solens ago. It was the right place. They approached the opening Timmerloo discovered with the ill-fated hunting party so long ago. Timothy stood outside the niche, looking at it in awe and knowing it was the doorway to Catherine's survival.

Timmerloo was wheezing and coughing as they stood outside the niche. Timothy looked over to his older companion and realized the long journey had deleterious repercussions. Timmerloo was ill.

He had to get him out of the cold and get him warmed up. "I need to get you inside and get a fire started. You don't sound good," Timothy said, as he led him inside the niche. "Stay here while I gather some wood for a fire." Timothy removed his gear then helped Timmerloo undo the straps and bindings that held their provisions in place. When Timmerloo was settled, he left. Gathering armload after armload of firewood, Timothy stashed enough firewood to keep a fire going for days.

When he felt he had enough, he found the fire pit Timmerloo and his hunting party made long ago and started the fire. He brought the old man close to the fire and bundled him up in his bedroll. The effort of moving caused the old man to go into a spasm of coughing and wheezing. "I'll make the climb tomorrow. You're sick," Timothy told him.

"You need to go on." He wheezed. "Catherine may have placed her lifestone in the breach. You now have a direction, but you are not even sure what you're looking for. You need to buy all the time you can. You need to get to the stone chamber at the top of the spiral shaft. All the equipment you can carry needs to go with you so you can make your way into that abandoned village." Timmerloo stopped to catch his breath, while Timothy listened to the rattle coming from the old man's chest.

Timmerloo's argument was sound. They came here to find the way to save Catherine. Though he did not want to abandon Timmerloo, there was enough food and provisions here for him to take care of himself until he returned. And he was right, how much time did he have left? Catherine may have put her lifestone in the wall already. Today . . . tomorrow . . . might be all he had left. He bowed his head and asked sadly, "Where is the opening to the shaft?"

"It's there in the back wall." Timmerloo pointed. "I won't be able to go with you." He wheezed.

"I know," Timothy answered. "Thank you for getting me this far."

"It's what I came back here for," Timmerloo rasped. "Now, get these things up into the shaft. You have a long road ahead of

you, and climbing the shaft is no easy thing . . . even without all this equipment."

Timothy gathered what he could carry and set it inside the stone ledge. "You will need one of the lanterns we brought along to see where you are going," the old man told him in a whispery voice.

Timothy pulled a lantern from their supplies and lighted it. He placed it on the stone ledge with his other supplies. "I left a couple of day's food and supplies for you. There should be enough firewood to keep you warm for days. Rest and stay warm. I'll be back as soon as I can."

"You need to go. May the Winds be kind to you and help you find your way." Timmerloo smiled at Timothy as he waved him on his way.

"And you will be okay?" Timothy asked, concerned the old man was too sick to get out of this place on his own.

Timmerloo smiled then said, "I have brought you here, and that is what I wanted. Be off now. When I feel better, I'll make my way back down the mountain. You know the way now. You will find your way back. Just follow the landmarks I showed you."

"I will, and may the Winds be kind to you as well," Timothy said, as he pulled himself onto the ledge with his provisions.

"They already have, Timothy . . . they already have," the old man whispered after Timothy climbed into the darkness beyond the opening of the ledge.

The spiral shaft was dark, but the lantern kept the way well lighted as he moved forward into the steep incline. Several times, he stopped to remove the heavy equipment from his back, allowing the cramps in his arms and legs to relax before he moved on. When the feeling passed, he picked everything up, and then moved slowly and steadily through the dark shaft. The shaft was so uniformly excavated from the black stone that Timothy felt a cautionary sense of claustrophobia lingering like a presence. The feeling of being in a closed space was almost suffocating as he made his way through the narrow passage. As he continued, he felt the air getting colder. There was a draft. He was almost certain he felt movement in the air around him. He must be getting to the top, but the crushing weight of his gear again sent stabs of pain through his shoulders and back.

The exhaustion of the climb and the thin air in the passage made him feel weak. He had to stop, catch his breath, and regain some of his strength. He lay there in the dark with his equipment at his feet and the wall propping him up from behind. He breathed thin air that filled his lungs but wouldn't sate his desire for more. He felt lightheaded as he kept telling himself, "Breathe, just breathe . . ." The flickering light of the lantern sent patches of yellow light against the black walls like a tide washing the shore. The darkness blurred the light, and he felt he was going to give in. But there, in the longest reaches of the lantern's light, was something else. It was a dim light coming from somewhere ahead of him. Timothy grappled for several deep breaths, which helped clear his head. If there was light up ahead, then he must be near the top of the shaft.

When he felt rested and the pain in his back and legs calmed to a tolerable level, he moved on. He saw the dim light growing as he progressed. Every step became brighter as he moved up the stone incline. At the top, the sun stabbed the far end of the stone chamber with blinding brilliance. Being in the dark, with just the lantern as a light source, forced Timothy to sit and allow his eyes to adjust to the bright sunlight. When his eyes could focus on the surroundings, he looked around and found the stone table Timmerloo spoke of, sitting at the center of the room.

Timothy continued to allow his eyes to adjust. He looked around the walls of the stone chamber and saw the remarkable carved writings. As his eyes adjusted to the light, his attention returned to the stone table sitting at the center of the room. There was a single stone sitting there, which meant someone was here since Timmerloo left this chamber many solens ago. Could it have been one of the men who returned after being unsuccessful in climbing down the mountain from their hunting party? Could it have been another hunter who accidentally stumbled onto the spiral shaft just as Timmerloo had done? When Timothy was fully rested, he walked to the stone table and looked at the writing Timmerloo told him would be there. There was writing on the side of the table, written in the scribe of the villages. He fell to his knees as he read it, "If you are a friend of Timmerloo, please take this stone and place it in the wall."

"You never got off the mountain," Timothy cried out, as the cold drove its stone nails into his heart. The world enclosed him in a sea of tears as the echoes of his weeping resounded on the surrounding dispassionate stone and frightened him back to the reality of the stone chamber. "It was Phillip who actually got off the mountain with the bag of lifestones. You never got past this chamber, did you? You never made it back."

Timothy turned and looked out the doorway of the stone chamber where the sunlight poured through with such intensity, it blinded him to what lay beyond it. "What happened to you, Timmerloo? Were you just a ghost? Is that what will become of me?" For the first time since he met Timmerloo, Timothy understood he had been alone all along. He was alone, facing something he knew nothing about, with no guidance, no clues, only the direction a ghost had pointed him to. What would he find at the end of it all? An abandoned village with no name, or an abandoned village called Winterland? He was facing a world of ghosts.

Ships

Tell me about the rough seas . . .

She filled her ship with all the people who would help her cross the rough seas. There was really nothing left but ride out the storm, or be consumed by it. She was in a struggle unlike any other in her life. I didn't want to put any burdens on her, but fate would not allow it.

Early that year, I caught the flu, giving me three days of misery and dehydration. The worst of it was, after three days, I could not walk on my right leg. I stepped out of bed that third morning in exquisite pain, unparalleled to any I ever experienced, which acquainted me with hellfire in my hip running to the knee of my right leg. The concentrated pain was so intense, a cold sweat forced me back into bed. When the faintness passed, I hopped on one leg to the medicine chest, pulled out some pain medicine, and then hoped the over-the-counter remedy would settle the problem to the point where I could resume work that evening. The pain never went away. It was the beginning of an ordeal lasting almost three months. In spite of her own problems, it was Lois who came to my rescue.

Through a series of physicians and a series of tests, we discovered that one of the facets in my spine that allowed a nerve to run to my right leg had narrowed over the years, closing the nerve in a bony grasp. The pain this nerve could generate cannot be put into words, so I won't make the attempt. No pain medication was effective. I didn't like the dead feeling I got when I took them, so I didn't try. Eventually, Lois suggested sending me to physical therapy, where I could do stretches and exercises to open the facet and release the nerve. The whole process took almost three months to solve, and Lois was by my side the whole time. I was grateful she was there for me when I needed her. I knew, when I looked at her, my time with her was running out. It would be me, eventually, taking care of her.

We always had an unspoken bond between us. If one of us were sick or in trouble, the other would be there for whatever was needed. Our bond was so strong that once when I was thirty years old, she saved my life. As an outpatient in the recovery room, I went into third-degree heart block as she was leaving the room to get my prescriptions filled. I don't know what it was, but she told me she knew she had to turn back. When she got to my side, I stopped breathing. She told me later, she just felt "wrong" and came back. I was put on a monitor and eventually came around. She spent the whole day with me, and I was allowed to go home. It was also like that for me when she had her accident and her breathing slowed down to almost nothing. It woke me up, that "wrong" feeling, and I made her wake up to get her to breathe again. Our bond was like that . . . very strong . . . each tied to the other in some kind of psychic knot, letting each other know when something was wrong. For some reason, our connection was not as strong, it seemed, when it came to breast cancer—that is, until almost the end.

By February 2008, Lois was recovering from a case of bronchitis, had severe neuropathy of her hands and feet, and the tumor markers continued to rise. The protocols she was on in 2007 caused an overgrowth of the nails on her hands and feet. She secured a podiatrist for the conditions called "onychomycosis and onychodystrophy": two terms meaning a fungal infection of the nails and thick, twisting, and discolored nails. The condition was very painful, and the measures Lois attempted at home were only cursory remedies. Regular store-bought tools for nails were completely ineffective against the almost quarter-inch thick nails the chemotherapy produced. In addition to the much-needed podiatrist, her list of passengers now included a neurologist and a rheumatologist to help with the neuropathy. They were all there, helping her cross the "rough seas," each making recommendations and adding medications to her growing list.

The respiratory infection caused her oncologist concern about her blood counts. After careful study of her labs and consideration of how easily she picked up infections, he decided to prescribe Neupogen to boost her counts and prevent further immunosuppression from the new protocols. She had some chronic and some transient numbness of her hands, which made it difficult to use a pen or type effectively at work. The rheumatologist and the neurologist again prescribed either new or increased medications, which began to effectively treat this plaguing symptom. Overall, she was able to function on a normal basis once everything was in place. Other than a day or two off work for the bronchitis, she went to work every day. I was relegated to giving the seven- to nine-day protocol of Neupogen at home preceding her chemotherapy. For many months afterward, she remained stable and functioned on a somewhat normal basis.

Over the winter, my father, now very debilitated, came down with pneumonia and needed hospitalized. Though Lois was not feeling well herself, she made sure he was admitted. When the time came for him to be discharged, she made sure he was temporarily admitted to a nearby nursing home for rehabilitation. My mother, unable to care for him by herself in his weakened condition, worked with Lois to make all the arrangements. He eventually got home under the care of hospice, which Lois arranged for my mother before he left the nursing home. Lois recognized the burden his decreased capacity created for my mother over the preceding year. She was concerned my older mother would hurt herself trying to move him alone. Hospice was one of the best things Lois could have done for my mother. My mother was delighted the nurses could help with bathing, walking, and generally taking care of my father's needs. Even in his debilitated state, my father told my mother to thank Lois for helping him and helping her. It wasn't long after he came back from the nursing home when he developed dysphasia (trouble swallowing food). Lois and I understood he would not recover from the effects of the respiratory infection without eating. Lois spoke with the hospice nurse about my father's dysphasia, and then they instructed my mother how to prepare food he could swallow. Lois and I visited them whenever we had the chance. However, we observed the palpable deterioration occurring before us. We anticipated the worst, making Lois's decision to involve hospice at that point a foregone conclusion.

As one can imagine, with all the unprecedented illnesses, changes in chemotherapy protocols, and medication changes, Lois was occupied with more crises than one person should be asked to juggle at one time. Still, she enjoyed helping others and being there for me, my father, and my mother, which took some scrutiny off her problems at the time. By the end of March, Lois's tumor markers were at 281. The markers had not stopped rising since the beginning of 2007 when they were only 61. The cancer was active, and any treatment she took only seemed to allow it further gains. Though her symptoms were slight, the pain in her hips and spine was getting increasingly difficult to bear. Even before she released her newsletter at the end of March, Lois had the oncologist working on having radiation therapy.

(Editorial by Lois A. Anderson dated March 31, 2008)

Well, first of all I must apologize for the lateness of this newsletter. It should have been out a month ago. However, I got caught in the caregiver act and had to let some of my volunteer work alone for the time being.

My husband had to go through a series of tests and 3 different specialist visits only to find out that the nerve and some of the muscles are not functioning properly on his right side in the hip and back area because of entrapment in scar tissue from 3 old hernia surgeries. After x-rays, 2 MRIs of the back and hip, and nerve conduction tests, the rehabilitation doctor pinpointed the real problem. However, the MRI of his back did show a narrowing of one of the spaces where the nerve exits the spine at the L5 vertebra and this may pose a future problem which will have to be watched for now. Anyway, he is now undergoing physical therapy and things seem to be very much improved.

So then we followed this up with my father-in-law who came down with pneumonia and landed in the hospital. He is now in a local nursing home for rehab, and if he successfully completes his rehab will return home to be cared for by my mother-in-law. If he doesn't then we have to decide what else to do since one person may not be able to handle his care any longer.

And because of all this, I had to reschedule the radiation on my spine to the beginning of May. So we'll see what happens.

Once again I know what the meaning of the sandwich generation is. And I thought that would all be over with the passing of my parents, but it seems it doesn't stop there when you work for a health care organization and your spouse is not as well up on elder care as you are.

But now I am looking forward to trying to take some kind of break and go away for a weekend somewhere, just to relieve some of the stress with all this.

With warmer weather just around the corner, it's time to get out in the garden again so go for it!!

Lois

By the end of March, Lois was more my caregiver than I was hers. She called our son to take me to the various appointments she could not manage herself. By April, I was in physical therapy, where the long road of getting me back to work began. By the end of April, I was back on my feet and working part-time to build up my stamina. It would be the end of May before I would be allowed to go back to work full-time.

A CT scan taken in March revealed Lois's cancer metastasized to regions of the cervical and thoracic spine, and the number of lesions increased since the last CT scan of 2007. The flu symptoms I had before all this happened moved to Lois, and she presented similar symptoms. The respiratory symptoms were more intense for her and slower to relent. When the symptoms of the illness finally passed, Lois noticed a change in her respiratory symptoms. She was increasingly short of breath and progressively more fatigued than she had been in months.

Finally, in April, Lois received the first radiation treatment to her spine. Within days, she noticed a remarkable improvement. However, another evaluation of her tumor markers showed no improvement as they again increased to 421. It seemed to Lois, and myself, the cancer may have taken another turn and was actually somewhere besides her spine. In June, she, in agreement with her oncologist, decided to repeat a CT scan. This time, they would look more intently at the chest area, since Lois showed symptoms of increasing shortness of breath. The report was very ominous when it showed a density in the right lower lobe of the lung with a possible accumulation of fluid. Lois asked the oncologist for a pulmonary consult to follow this finding. She told me later, she was concerned the lung mets could recur, since it was there when the cancerous lymph nodes were removed in 2001. All studies after 2001 showed the area to be clear, but with rising markers and symptoms lending themselves to a respiratory condition, she had to consider it.

Throughout her battles with breast cancer, Lois maintained she would continue to live a normal life, as if anyone would consider what she did as normal. In spite of the symptoms of pain, shortness of breath, and the increasing barrage of tests and treatments, Lois continued to work almost forty to fifty hours a week at the hospice she loved without complaint. She negotiated her treatments and appointments around her job and other outside commitments. To most people, she seemed like a healthy positive woman doing what was important to her.

So many times I asked her to slow down but was always told she would slow down when she was dead. I had to ask if she was certain that would even slow her down. She would laugh and say, "I plan to live every day until I die." At the time, I thought she was being facetious; but when I think back on what she was really saying, it made a lot of sense. Too many times, in my own life, I see people attempting to justify their absence from the world of living on their illness. Lois took it the other way; she justified her right to be alive and productive against a cancer that assaulted her in every way. Her sense of being alive meant she would continue to fight breast cancer to her last breath. It was a commitment seen when she went to Harrisburg in late April to the American Cancer Society's ACT summit, then turned around and headed to Washington DC the next day to spend three days with the NBCC and lobby day on April 29. She returned home Sunday afternoon then went to work the following day on her hospice unit.

My father was recuperating at the nursing home, regaining his strength. He started voicing he wanted to come home to my mother on her daily visits. When my mother approached Lois about getting him home, she did her best to discourage her. When Lois checked with the nursing staff as to what would be involved in taking him home, they explained they were having a difficult time taking care of all his needs. Lois felt my mother would be overwhelmed and would hurt herself trying to move my father by herself, so she asked my mother to consider home care. My mother was a tough sell, but Lois was willing to make all the arrangements, and together they decided he would be able to return home.

With home care in place, my father returned to their home in early May. My mother may have been skeptical at first, but when she saw how well my father worked with the home care nurses, she was happy Lois talked her into it. My mother was delighted her daughter-in-law was able to help them both. The arrangements allowed my mother time to get groceries, wash the laundry, and finish other household chores, while the home care aides worked with my father. Even to this very day, my mother tells me how grateful she was to have had this kind of "good" time with my father.

Parkinson's has a way of taking you apart a little piece at a time. By early June, my father again had problems swallowing food. The nurses were fearful he would aspirate something, forcing him back into the hospital with "aspiration pneumonia." It was the home care nurse who called Lois at my mother's request. My mother could not understand the problem but trusted Lois to explain it to her. It was Lois who again took charge. She went to my mother and explained the situation and the causes behind the nurse's concerns. The problem with not being able to swallow would eventually leave my father dehydrated and malnourished. The only solution would be to place a feeding tube.

This was a topic my mother had with my father while he was of sound mind. He did not want to have a feeding tube if that time ever came. However, the time did come, and their discussion made it easier for my mother to say no. That left the alternative, IV therapy, which my mother agreed to on a limited basis. The inevitable loomed before them. Lois spoke with my mother about getting my father into hospice. Since my mother had such a good experience with the home care nurses, she was more than willing to allow hospice to come in. She considered hospice for a few days then asked Lois to set it up for her. Lois was happy to do this. From here, it was only a waiting game. The days where my father was awake a few hours a day became less and less.

Our son was not blind to the events occurring around us and asked if he could move back into his old room at our home. Lois and I took his request under serious consideration. Since Lois wasn't certain her own outcome would be positive much longer, and she was certain she needed help with my mother when my father died, she thought his help would be immeasurable. Our son told us he had an alternative reason for coming back home. He wanted to sell his home and use the money to return to college for a degree in nursing. When we understood his motives, neither of us had a problem with it. "Besides," she told me, "he may be there when you need help with me." She laughed when she said this, but thinking back, I think she knew the "inevitable" was closing in on her, though she had the symptoms of her metastasis well under control.

Chemotherapy, radiation treatments, a dying parent, and an adult child returning home, coupled with obligations at work and keeping our household running, I spoke to Lois and said, "We need an early vacation." We traveled to New York City and enjoyed a three-day vacation where we parked the car, turned off the phone, and just relaxed. We had a lovely dinner then to the theater and saw *Wicked*. Neither of us knew what to expect, but the production was incredible, and the message of the play was insightful. Those three days could not have been more perfect. We spent another day just window shopping then found our car and made the journey home. Lois had one more day off work and used it to get her newsletter started. I had to return to work later that night.

By Tuesday the following week, New York City and the wonderful time we had there seemed like years in the past. There were so many issues to contend with when we returned, we were almost sorry we left everyone on their own. It seemed everyone needed Lois's advice for one thing or another. While it made Lois feel needed, it also wore her down. The flood of requests did not dissuade her from helping anyone who needed her in spite of how she was feeling herself.

My father's health deteriorated to the point where hospice was helping my mother almost every day with his care. He was bedridden by mid-June, and Lois stopped every day to check in on them.

By the end of June, Lois went to a five-day symposium held by the Department of Defense called "Era of Hope." There she attended seminars given by the top researchers of the country on the topic of breast cancer. She brought back her findings and shared them with her colleagues and her fellow breast cancer survivors in the body of her newsletter. Her editorial at the end of her newsletter gave no indication of the amassed tragedies facing her.

(Editorial by Lois A. Anderson dated June 7, 2008)

Hello again to all—Wow it's that time of year again—summer is here although as I write this newsletter we are having a cool spell. Hopefully it will be nice for our picnic in July.

This year our picnic will be held at my home. For those of you who have never been here it should be interesting and for those of you who have been here before, you'll get to see the new kitchen. Tours will be given. Yes, we have done some remodeling with more to come. Both indoors and outdoors, too.

We have a pool and if anyone wants to swim-it's okay with me, but remember to bring your swimsuit and towel.

MY latest craze for about the past 5 years has been daylilies and they are now everywhere. Some of them should be blooming by the time of the picnic although they are about 2 weeks ahead of schedule with the hot weather we had in June.

My son is moving back home so he can return to school. And guess what he has decided to pursue—Nursing. So I'll apologize in advance for the boxes that you may see everywhere. That's about all this space allows. Come and have a good time on the 16th. Call me if you have any questions. Check the invitation on the next page.

Lois

By the beginning of July, Lois could tell she was feeling different. She told me she had a hard time recovering from her work schedule and everything she did. She felt chronically tired but with no real pain or shortness of breath. Results of a CT scan taken in mid-June showed extensive progression of her bone metastasis and a new finding of atelectasis (fluid) collecting at the base of her right lung. By July 2, she had a pulmonologist consult. Her new pulmonologist suggested additional studies to follow up on the CT scan and then referred her to a cardiothoracic surgeon. We went to the cardiothoracic surgeon later in the day where we found he wanted to wait until the studies came back from the pulmonologist before he would suggest anything. As we left the cardiothoracic surgeon's office, Lois looked over at me and smiled.

"What's that for?" I asked her.

"I'm still filling up my ship," she said, still smiling, as a tear built up in her eye. I looked at her, puzzled. I then remembered her dream about the ship sailing over the "rough seas." "You know, the ship where I'm checking off passengers."

"I remember," I told her sadly. We took each other's hand and walked to the car. "How bad are you feeling?" I asked.

"Actually, other than being more tired than usual, nothing seems any different!" she told me inside the car.

I stated the car and pulled out of the parking space. "Is this just another bump in the road, or should I get concerned? None of this sounds very good to me."

Lois looked at me, seeing how seriously I was taking the consult. "You know I've been through worse situations and came out all right. I plan to be around, at least, into my sixties. You don't get rid of me that easy." She laughed. "Besides, I think my son wants me to be around to see him graduate."

I had so many arguments I could have brought up, but at the same time, I knew Lois had beaten the odds so many times in the past, when it didn't seem possible, I began to feel she probably had the strength to do it again. Still, the idea of the metastasis settling into the base of the right lung made me feel very uneasy.

Lois had to return to work later that evening when she was "on call." She left in the late evening and did not return until the sun was rising the next day. I was home and waited up for her. I stayed awake writing a story about a dream where people carried a stone around their whole lives, and someone would place it in a wall when they died. It was a strange profound dream, and I had no idea of where I would be going with it and put it aside. I thought over all the situations facing us. Our son was selling his home and moving back, and Lois was now confronted with the fight of her life but would not let it interfere with any of her obligations any more than it had to. It was a strange tumultuous world where we walked. Nothing was safe. Nothing was certain. We stood, poised on a tightrope between fear and hope.

A few days later, Lois's oncologist received a letter from the cardiothoracic surgeon. The studies showed a nodule spreading the cancer over the right lung again from the vicinity of the site found in 2001. There was a discussion about doing another thoracotomy to correct this. However, with such extensive scarring covering her entire right side, the surgeon felt the surgery would most certainly make her an invalid the rest of her life. Lois could not allow this and believed using chemotherapy would again stop the progression of this new metastasis. She worked from the rationale, chemotherapy worked before, and she had faith it would work again. Even the surgeon stated at the time, "She has no symptoms attributed to this nodule."

Lois's metaphoric ship now contained her original surgeon, her family doctor, an oncologist, a pulmonologist, a neurologist, a podiatrist, a rheumatologist, a radiation oncologist, and now, a cardiothoracic surgeon. She had graduated to a list of over twenty-plus medications designed to keep her on her feet and functioning on a normal basis. The time consumed to make and attend all her physicians' visits, maintain and allot pharmacies with prescriptions requiring authorizations and forms from both my insurance company and hers, and make a schedule allowing her to work a forty- to fifty-hour week was a full-time job itself. Somehow, she managed to do all this while metastatic bone cancer and lung cancer took up residence and attempted to stop her.

Out son sold his house in early July and needed to be out by the end of August. He gave me a quick appraisal of how much room he needed to store his belongings. To accommodate him, I decided to finish the flooring in our attic. Lois and I had been content with using only a third of the total attic space and had done so for our time together. However, with our son's return, I needed to utilize all the space the attic could provide. So on what was possibly the hottest

July on record, I climbed into the attic and carried as much plywood as I could for the task before me.

My father was not doing well, and Lois suggested when I had time off, I should go and visit him. She suggested I stay with him to give my mother a break. I had no problem with the idea, but I wasn't able to get time off until late July. I was concerned his condition would not avail itself, allowing me to be off soon enough to help.

My father died in mid-July when I was at work. When Lois made the anticipated call, she quietly and firmly asked me to come home. Just after midnight, I started the engine of the car that would carry me across the hour's journey to my parent's home. In the dark silence, with the car floating over the asphalt, I had a feeling of numbness that infects you when you can't quite get your mind around something. With her call, Lois told me she gathered everyone together, and they would wait until I arrived before notifying the funeral home. Somehow, knowing this inevitable event would happen didn't make it any easier when it did. My thoughts pushed me into a place where I would be walking into a horrible scene of emotional turmoil. When I arrived, I found Lois had everything and everyone under control. She was the stone that doesn't break. She was my port in a storm. She was the support for everyone around her.

In spite of my father's death and subsequent funeral, we still kept our plans to have the support group picnic at our home that summer. Lois told me she felt it would probably be the last time she could get the support group together at our home for the annual picnic, and she wanted to do it. For me, it was a good diversion from the preparations for my father's funeral the following week. Lois told me later that evening, the only person left from her parents' generation was my mother. Otherwise, all our parents and grandparents had died. In the past four years, we had three funerals for our parents. It was depressing for me and had ominous undertones for Lois.

The unfolding events in our lives made Lois realize how quickly time was slipping away from her. She asked me to take some time off to make a trip to a place neither one of us had been to before. I told her that I would get some time off, and she could surprise me with the arrangements.

Later that night, while I was at work, she called at three o'clock in the morning to tell me she made arrangements to go to Martha's Vineyard and Nantucket. I thought it was a great idea. By mid-August, we did go and spend a week there. By the time we made the trip, chemotherapy had taken most of her hair. Though she could have used many of her assorted wigs, she decided to simply use a hat for this outing. Over this vacation, I noticed how much she slowed down. I noticed her struggling to keep up walking the narrow streets of Nantucket. I was concerned when I saw her out of breath or simply wanted me to slow down or sit on one of the benches with her.

When we returned, her oncologist arranged for Lois to have a bone scan, an MRI, and a CT scan. He was concerned about brain mets after Lois described a considerable shift of balance to her left side when she was walking. It was of grave concern, since a previous study indicated the existence of extensive vertebral metastasis throughout the cervical and thoracic spine. The question was "Did even a single cancer cell get into the spinal fluid and find its way into the brain?" The studies her oncologist ordered found brain metastasis had not occurred. However, all the studies performed on the chest area indicated right-sided pleural fluid sitting at the base of the right lung. The chemo had not been effective against it. Again, it was an area of great concern. Lois's oncologist sent a detailed letter to her family physician informing him of her status and disease progression.

(Letter dated August 28, 2008)

I saw Lois Anderson for follow up of her metastatic carcinoma of the breast. To recap her history, she was initially diagnosed to have a poorly differentiated carcinoma of the right breast in 1992. The tumor was 1.9 cm. in size and five regional lymph nodes were positive for metastatic disease including micrometastases. She had a right modified radical mastectomy, and this was followed by six cycles of adjuvant FAC chemotherapy followed by local regional radiation. She had five years of adjuvant Tamoxifen from 1993 and 1998. She felt well until 2001 when she developed recurrent disease with evidence of pulmonary and bone metastasis. She has been on various systemic treatments over the past seven years including initially Taxotere with Xeloda followed by Arimedex followed by a trial of Faslodex followed by oral Xeloda from March to June 2006 without much response, but she had subsequent progression. This was followed by Gemzar and Carboplatinum from September to October 2007 with no response followed by seven cycles of Xeloda and Ixempra from December 2007 to July 2008.

In the past few months there has been gradual progression of her tumor marker, CA 27-29. She had a follow up MRI of the spine as well as bone scan and CT scan of the chest recently. These studies, unfortunately, showed progression of her bone metastases, particularly on the MRI studies. She is relatively asymptomatic from her disease with no major pain issues, and her overall performance status is still excellent. Earlier this year she also had a course of radiation to the thoracic spine area because of metastatic involvement in that region and concerns about progression of disease and potential spinal cord issues. There was no evidence of spinal cord compression at that time. She has some neuropathy symptoms from her previous taxane therapy and more recent Ixempra therapy. Overall, this has not progressed. The neuropathy is affecting her hands and feet. Weight is stable at 130 lbs.

I reviewed with the patient over 20 minutes or so the clinical situation and the various options at this time. She last had anthracycline therapy back in 1993, and one option would be consideration of Doxil therapy if her ejection fraction is still satisfactory. Another option would be Navelbine, but there is some concern about the potential neuropathy side effects. A third option would be a consultation at Hopkins to see if there are any protocols that the patient may be eligible for. The patient has failed previous hormonal therapy with Arimedex, adjuvant Tamoxifen and Faslodex. Her last hormonal therapy was over two years ago, and another option would be a trial of Aromasin hormonal therapy with a small chance of some stabilization of her disease.

After reviewing the situation, she would like to proceed with a consultation at Hopkins. In the meantime she will start Aromasin hormonal therapy. I have given her a prescription for this. We will continue with plans for Zometa once every 4-6 weeks. I plan to see her again after her Hopkins consultation.

The tone of the letter offered only the slightest chance of turning the metastases around no matter what therapy was used. While many of us would have been paralyzed by such devastating news, it only made Lois more determined to reach out to other breast cancer survivors and those who wanted to understand more about the disease.

In July, with all that was happening around her, she found the time to put together about thirty packets of information on breast cancer to take to a lecture she was giving to a class filled with LPN students on July 22, 2008. On July 29, she made her monthly conference call with the NBCC as a participant in their advocacy struggles.

Lois continued to work full-time and take on call for her hospice unit in spite of the diagnostic findings. Our son finally finished moving in. Lois continued with some moderate feelings of shortness of breath, which did not concern her. However, it was the sheer feelings of exhaustion she was feeling by the end of her day that began to concern her openly. She had her oncologist schedule another CT scan of the thorax. This scan showed abnormalities in the lower right lobe of the lung and the upper right lobe. The impression given on the scan was pneumonitis versus pneumonia. By September 19, 2008, her tumor markers were elevated to 525, a level not seen before. Lois realized she needed measures to turn this marker around, or she might not survive another year. Lois managed to put a newsletter together for September that year. She told her support group of her battles but never shared the severity of her situation in her editorial.

(Editorial by Lois A. Anderson dated September 15, 2008)

Hello everyone. It has been a while for this newsletter, and I apologize for that. However, the newsletter had to go on an enforced holiday due to some problems that I've had recently. For those who attend our group, you already know that my disease has progressed and that I have been having some problems in my lungs again.

As of this writing, the lung problems are still being evaluated. A consult with one of the oncologists at Johns Hopkins has been finished, too, and it means that I am in for treatment changes. So for those of you with more questions, give me a call please. I would be more than happy to catch up with you. And we can go out to lunch and catch up with each other.

Now for some of the other changes around our home . . . My son has completed his move back in with us and is doing quite well in school. He actually enjoys school more this time around and finds much to discuss with his "old" parents. It's funny how time changes things. Of course, I guess it does make a difference that he is in the RN program.

And what with the big changes in the weather recently, it seems as if we've had an extended summer. But that may be coming to an end as the temperatures go back to more seasonal levels. This beautiful weather has even allowed George and me to do a little more travelling that what we usually do this time of the year, what with several weekend trips lately.

Well, that's about all from me. Hope that each and every one of you are doing well as we look forward to the changing leaves and the real beginning of autumn. Be sure to check out those beautiful colors we have outside this year.

Lois

Our thirty-second wedding anniversary was coming up. For whatever reasons, we wanted to go someplace where we were comfortable with the surroundings. We wanted to relive part of what we were at one time in our lives, carefree and unencumbered by the worries and terrible decisions we needed to make in the not too distant future. I believe Lois was starting to feel like she was being backed into a corner with no escape. She wanted to be somewhere where cancer and its treatments were not spoken, at least for a little while. Again, Lois chose to go to Williamsburg. Before we left home, we set up our itinerary with a dinner at one of the best taverns in the historic area. We found tours we could take while we were there and ways to be entertained that were slow paced enough to allow Lois rest periods.

Before we left for Williamsburg, Lois's oncologist wanted to follow up an abnormal x-ray report of the chest with a CT scan. Again, the report showed right lower lobe atelectasis (or fluid) along with a "ground glass" opacity in the upper right lobe of her lung. In spite of the numerous medications to keep her symptoms under control, Lois was starting to feel more pain in her low back, breathing was getting more difficult, and she tired out very easily. But Lois never focused on her symptoms; she continued to look forward to the simple joys that were in her life. Whatever the findings meant to her oncologist, they would wait until she returned from a well-needed vacation in Williamsburg.

We spoke very little of her cancer on that vacation. It was almost like we both wanted to pretend it didn't exist. To see Lois, she didn't look or act any different than she ever did. The cancer had slowed her down, but it had not stopped her. I think she wanted me to feel she was not worried about her prognosis, and for three wonderful days, the topic stayed out of our conversations. We spoke of the experiences we were having on this trip to Williamsburg. Instead of speaking about what the future held for us, we talked about the things we did in the past. We remembered the first time we traveled here when we were first married. We walked all the brick-laid sidewalks again, enjoying the well-manicured gardens strewn on every street. The real appeal Williamsburg held for us was, not that it changed every year but that it remained the same. It was the colonial town's unchanging consistency that kept bringing us back over the years. Our memories of the good times we had here stayed locked in place. It seemed here, in Lois's favorite and first vacation destination, she could exist in a place where cancer did not exist for her at one time. It was a resolute peace.

Our little three-day vacation was over before we could allow our dreams to become nightmares. Reality moved in on thunderheads when we returned. On October 6, 2008, Lois's fifty-sixth birthday, she went for a consult at Johns Hopkins. After the oncologist thoroughly went over her records and did an exam, he made his recommendations for her oncologist to follow back home. However, when the recommendations came, her oncologist was already following them. In other words, the specialist had no new recommendations to offer Lois's oncologist. This left both of them in the dark as to what to try next. Her oncologist decided to follow his plan of attack on the persistent cancer.

Lois's hospice unit was busier than ever after they did some reorganization. In addition to her other duties, Lois was in charge of an all-day class for the entire staff, which needed to be completed early the following year. The reorganization increased their patient load for social workers and nursing staff alike. Her long hours were getting longer with increasing staff meetings and classes to prepare for. Even with all the events surrounding her personal life, she managed to keep in touch with her advocacy constituents and breast cancer support group.

By mid-November, Lois's tumor markers rose again to a new high of 676. The number grew more alarming every time they were taken. Her oncologist wanted to attempt another round of anthracycline therapy, which was a cardiotoxic agent. To take such a medication required Lois to undergo a MUGA scan to evaluate her heart function. But before Lois decided to do the scan, she wanted to continue on the current treatments and do further studies on her chest and spine in early December. Between her appointments at the various physicians and the increased workload at her job, Lois was unable to complete a newsletter for December of that year.

We both felt like we were adrift on a boat with no means to propel us anywhere. Lois was in a kind of limbo with no new alternatives to try and only an old treatment that could be risky . . . with no guarantee it would work. The slight pains she felt earlier in the year grew to almost debilitating levels, though she continued to work for her hospice on days when the pain was more controlled, or at home when it wasn't. Either way, Lois continued to work full-time. She wanted to escape the reality she found herself in. We both looked for activities to help remove us from the helplessness we both felt. We attended plays, special events, and became more involved in the upcoming Christmas season by attending the performance *The Nutcracker*.

The studies done in early December continued to show the same stubborn bone metastasis and the two troublesome areas on the right lung. Though she religiously followed her oncologist's suggestions and stayed on the protocols prescribed, I know Lois felt she was in a losing battle. She was losing ground, but somehow, she was still able to function on a day-to-day basis. The whole situation seemed surreal, like it was happening to someone we knew, not Lois. Lois looked and felt, at least, well enough to get everything done she wanted. It seemed the world was ending, and we were just spectators. The waters grew dark and ominous; the encroaching storm was almost upon her. The three-masted schooner named *Hope* needed to make sail with all her passengers or be bashed to pieces at the dock.

The Bridge Between

Tell me about the way to the other side . . .

The world swirls around me like a cyclone that will never cease. The world where my wife Lois survives in day to day is so tumultuous, I've retreated to the only place left for solace, the place beneath the Poet's Tree. Here too, my thoughts of Catherine and her family struggling to get to the place where they will end her life seem sad and desolate. And like Timothy, I feel lost while searching for answers that may or may not exist. It is a time of questions and dubious answers, yet we move on and try to prevail over the bitter winds that encompass us.

I listen as the Poet's Tree shrieks its warning in the strong incessant winds and wait for answers likely sent in the form of dreams. While I listen, a magnificent bridge appears on a distant horizon; and the voice of my father, now gone from this world, tells me, "It is merely the bridge between, my son. Do not be afraid. I will watch for you. Be at peace." Afterward, the wind subsides to a gentle breeze, and the voice of my grandfather whispers, "We don't leave our loved ones behind. You are the rock that doesn't break."

"Leena . . . Alexis . . ." a man called as he walked quickly up the rise where the women attended the few injured brought to them during the night.

"Who calls us?" Alexis shouted back.

"It's Collin, ladies. We made a passage to the breach, but you must gather everything and hurry. The price we paid to prepare the way was very high. We pushed through, but it is still dangerous in the places we fought the orbs back. We control the ground, but you must hurry. We may not hold the Last Road very long."

"Thank you, Collin," Leena replied, stepping next to Alexis. Putting a hand on her shoulder, she told Alexis, "I will awaken Catherine." Collin just started back toward the Last Road when Leena asked, "Do you know where my husband and Jakob are?"

"I found Andrew at the edge of the Last Road helping to bury the dead. I told him what I told you, and he understood our urgency. He left to find Michael and Jakob. He told me they were carrying the lifestones of the dead to the wall. He knew where to find them."

"Where are they to meet us?" Alexis asked.

"Andrew hoped you would get the wagons loaded and prepare to leave. When they get back, they will meet everyone there," Collin told them, eager to return to his duties.

As Collin hurried down the rise, Leena turned to Alexis and said, "Gather what belongings we have and take them to the wagons. I will get Catherine."

Alexis nodded she understood, then hurried to make preparations to leave. Leena walked to the top of the rise to get Catherine.

Inside the crude canvas overhang, she found Catherine sleeping so deeply, she appeared dead. Leena approached her and watched a light breeze blow strands of her blond hair over her face uninvited. Inside her deep sleep, Catherine made no gesture to stop the advances of the light breezes. "Catherine . . . Catherine . . ." Leena called, hoping her voice would waken her.

Catherine remained still, lost in the fabric of dreams. She made no motion, no sign, she heard Leena calling her back to the land of waking. Leena knelt beside her daughter, taking her by the shoulders, and lightly shook her. "Come on, Catherine, we need to get moving. The passage is open. We need to move now!"

Catherine's eyes fluttered open as she struggled to awaken to her mother's voice. It sounded like she called to her from a distant hillside. She felt confused by the smell of smoke, the loud hurried voices coming from the bottom of the rise, and the memory of dim morning light. She was awakening from a dream. The dream was so vivid, it felt like it happened a few moments ago, yet she knew those times existed in a past that would not be remembered by anyone but her. The dream was a time when Timothy took her into his arms and kissed her. She remembered how he gently pressed her into the long soft grasses growing by the waterfall. It was a place where they jumped from the high rocks and swam to shore. They were alone. Their wet discarded clothes were spread over a sun-drenched rock, waiting to dry. The sounds of water splashing in the enclosed lagoon drowned the sounds of their fierce lovemaking. It was the day Timothy asked her to marry him. She could not get the vision out of her head. The time had been sweet, intense in its memory, and out of context with what was happening around her.

"Catherine . . ." Leena called again, "we need to get going. The villagers have the road open for us. We need to hurry."

Catherine rubbed the sleep from her eyes and looked directly at her mother. "What is all this, Mother? I can't seem to remember what we are doing."

Leena looked at her daughter with concern and sadness. Catherine finally sat up, giving the appearance of being alert and ready. Smoke, people running and shouting, and the wall of stones lying behind her made her feel disoriented. She turned to her mother and said, "I was dreaming of Timothy and the day he asked me to marry him. It was a beautiful day, and the memory was so vivid, I felt I was back there again. When I awoke, I saw all this pain and fear." Catherine pointed to the slope descending below them. "Is this really happening, or is this another dream?"

Catherine was awake, but her eyes were dark and hollow. Leena felt her daughter was traveling on a plain between dreams and reality. She never saw her daughter like this. She didn't know what to say and simply pulled her daughter to her feet. When Catherine was standing, she told her, "This is not a dream. This is the place where we don't want to be but where we exist, with dimensions, with problems, and with consequences too grave to consider inside the kindness of words."

Catherine struggled to be fully awake, trying to remember what she was doing at the top of a rise so far from home. She turned to Leena. "We are going somewhere . . . to a place I can't return."

"Leena . . . Catherine . . ." a voice called from the cacophony of confusion occurring at the bottom of the rise. It was Andrew calling them, emerging from clouds of smoke floating up the rise as he approached. "Alexis has the wagons ready. Why do you both delay?"

"Catherine hasn't regained her senses. She's been asleep a long time, and she hasn't been able to recall why she is here," Leena told Andrew as empathetically as she could.

"But we must leave here . . . now!" Andrew implored. "The men fought all night to get a passage through the orbs. The price they paid to do this is more than I can bear to tell you. The ones still fighting, still keeping the wall of flames burning for us to get through, are exhausted and will probably let the wall fail when we pass through. We must board the wagons now."

Catherine did not have the awareness to acknowledge Andrew's presence or the urgency in his voice. It was up to Leena to get her daughter moving. She took her hand and gently but firmly got her daughter walking toward the wagons waiting below them. Andrew led the way. When Jakob saw the approach of his son leading the strange procession, he called out, "Catherine is walking like she is in a daze. Is something wrong?"

Andrew walked to his father's side as Leena helped Catherine into the wagon. "It's like she can't wake up . . . almost like she's hallucinating with her eyes open," Andrew told him.

"We have to get her to snap out of it. The road before us is treacherous and filled with dangerous crossings. We need everyone to stay alert, ready to do whatever is needed, especially Catherine," Jakob said, as he sat ready to move from the driver's bench of the wagon. Andrew stood by the wagon waiting, as Leena led her daughter beside him.

"Andrew, would you please help her into the wagon?" Leena pressed Andrew. She turned to look Jakob squarely in his face. "Have Michael and Alexis been here yet?"

Jakob turned back to the team of horses, steadying them from moving. "Alexis went to find Michael and bring him back. Why don't you and Catherine ready yourselves in the wagon until they get here?" Jakob turned his attention to his son Andrew still standing beside the wagon, waiting for instructions from his father. "Help them in then bring the other wagon with Catherine's lifestone up behind us. When Michael and Alexis get here, we should be ready to move out."

Andrew helped Leena into the wagon, and together they moved Catherine into the bench beside her. Catherine's eyes were wide open, yet she remained despondent, seeing nothing of the world crumbling into ruins around them.

The wind was changing direction, and the plumes of gray-white smoke shuffled around the wagon wheels, drowning out the solid appearance of the wagons. Within moments, the wagons were engulfed like square boats sitting on a foggy lake. Finally, Michael and Alexis emerged from the thick smoke, running as quickly as they could through the blinding haze. Jakob called out to them, "Alexis . . . get in the wagon with your brother. Michael, I need you up here with us. Leena needs help with Catherine. I think something is wrong with her."

Alexis ran back to where her brother was waiting and climbed into the seat beside him. Michael moved cautiously into the seat facing Leena and Catherine. Michael looked into the vacant gaze of his daughter then looked to Leena for an explanation. "What's going on, Leena? She was fine last night when I left you both." As Michael assessed the situation, Jakob started moving their wagon through the thick billowing smoke, wallowing in slow tides around them.

"She woke up like this. She acted disoriented at first. Then she went into this. When I could talk to her, it seemed she couldn't remember what she was doing here," Leena told him, with mounting concern and fear in her voice.

Michael put his hands on either side of his daughter's face, forcing her to look at him. "I know this can't be easy for you. I know you told everyone you are willing to place your lifestone in the wall to stop these things. If you are having second thoughts about doing this, tell me now, and I will put a stop to all of it."

Catherine's glazed eyes looked straight through him to something beyond everyone's sight. Her skin was sallow and cold. She tried to focus on her father and failed as she watched Timothy chasing her through a meadow of spring blue flowers. She was safe here with the memories of her love. It was here she found a way to hope again. If she left this place, she would perish . . . She was certain of it. From the dreamlike mist, she listened to her father calling her from an echoing distance. She wasn't ready to go back. She would stay here with Timothy. He loved her, and she knew she loved him.

"She just stares right past me," Michael shuddered in horror. "It's like she's not even here. Her body is with us, but the person who is Catherine is gone."

"What can we do?" Leena wailed. "All these people have died to get our daughter to the breach. With her in this condition, putting her stone into the wall may not work. It's almost like she has died already."

Jakob was busy keeping the horses on the road but managed to turn around and take a quick glance at Catherine. The girl looked as though her mind left her body behind. "Michael, I need you to know that I will do everything in my power to get all of us to the breach. But it's all that I can do. I do know Benjamin said Catherine must place her lifestone in the wall of her own free will. If she is unable to do that, Leena may be right . . . it may not work. Just closing the wall with a big rock won't stop these things. She has to know she is placing her stone in the wall for it to work."

Michael glared at Jakob from the back bench of the wagon. "What do you suggest we do, Jakob?" Michael asked him angrily. "She's my daughter. She is under unimaginable pressure to do something that will probably end her life. Timothy is not here. No one has seen or heard from him from the day he left for Glade. He could be dead already with no hope of saving Catherine whatsoever. He's certainly missing. He is certainly not caught up in this horrible situation of having to make decisions over life and death. Where have the Winds swept your son? Holed up with Penny and Leon in some safe place until this all blows over?"

Jakob heard enough. He coaxed the horses to a stop then turned around to face Michael. *"I don't know what you have been thinking, but you and Leena . . . and Catherine are not the only victims here. My sons Lamin and Eric are out in front of us keeping the fires going to hold off these bloodthirsty creatures we call orbs. They are risking their lives and the lives of many others trying to keep the road open so we even have a slim chance of success. Right now, I don't even know if they are alive. And Timothy, I worry that he may already be dead or worse. Don't you remember what we did last night, Michael? How many dead did you bury . . . twenty . . . thirty? And that was just you. I had to have put that many to the ground myself and any man who possessed a shovel last night did the same. There are hundreds of lives that no longer exist, lives lost in the shadows, lives that never wanted any of this to happen but believed they could make a difference somehow. Don't ever forget that. You still have Catherine . . . and it is still her choice!"*

"She never asked for this!" Michael fumed. *"All this didn't happen because of her."*

"Jakob knows, Michael," Leena said in a soft, pained voice. *"We all understand Catherine has a difficult road ahead of her."* Leena put a hand on Michael's hand. *"Catherine is not the cause of all this dying either, Jakob. I think we are all fighting to stay alive because Catherine is our last real hope we can ever come out of this. Without her, without something to hope for, I believe Stock would have been overrun by orbs days ago."*

Leena had Catherine propped against her, where she stared blindly into the smoke-filled air surrounding them. Catherine stayed in her world of memories where she was safe in the arms of her lover, her friend, and a man she may not see again in the last moments of her lifetime.

"She doesn't even know what's going on," Leena said. "I understand the sacrifices being made to get Catherine to the breach. I also understand how you both feel about what is happening around us. I would be blind to ignore it. But we are here to get Catherine to the breach. The men and women fought hard to get us through. We are not going to disrespect their sacrifices nor will we soon forget them," Leena spoke to Jakob, with silent tears running from her eyes. "Move the wagon, Jakob . . . move on."

"You're right, Leena," Jakob said in a calmer voice. "It is best we move ahead." Jakob turned back to the team of horses and coaxed them to move on. The wagon jerked forward as wagon wheels rolled over the ashes of another time that seemed to be centuries ago. Alexis and Andrew followed with the wagon carrying the lifestone of Catherine. Unseen, beneath the heavy canvas tarp, reddish light pulsed with unrealized power.

☗☗☗

Many parcels from where Catherine traveled, a shout resounded from the breach, "If we have to tear them down, then we will." The shouting and noisy rabble woke Victoria from her troubled sleep. She opened her eyes to the sting of the acrid smoke-filled air and saw Penny standing against one of the tent poles holding up the canvas tarp. She was still in the place the villagers brought them to during the night.

"Did you get any sleep?" Victoria asked her.

Penny turned to face her, still leaning against the post. "Not much."

"What's going on? I heard shouting."

"The men are running out of things to burn." Penny pointed to the huge wooden tower where the men spotted them from overnight. "They are thinking about tearing it down for firewood."

"But that will leave us blind to the movement of the orbs, won't it?"

"I would think so, but if they don't use it for the fires, the orbs will overrun this area, and Catherine will never get the chance to get this close to the breach. You heard what happened during the night?"

"I was exhausted. I was asleep as soon as my head hit the pillow." Victoria looked at Penny with a question in her eye. "What has happened?" Then thinking the worst, she reluctantly asked, "Did Catherine die on the way here?"

Penny brushed the alarm from Victoria's face with a gentle hand. "No, she was delayed a few parcels from here. The orbs found a weak spot in our wall of flames and tried to break through. We lost so many trying to push them back. They couldn't allow Catherine to pass through the area. They were stopped about a parcel to the south of the fighting and held there until the pass was cleared. They were able to push them back far enough to allow Catherine's envoy to make the attempt this morning. They are coming." Penny turned back to watch the activity unfolding below them.

Victoria's memories of Rand and Leon were still raw and new. The reason for making such a dangerous journey, where they put their lives in terrible danger, seemed insignificant at the moment. "Is there anything we can do to help them?" she asked, feeling useless and saddened over losing her two friends.

"Just stay out of their way for now," Penny said quietly, as she turned her attention to the sounds of the battles and activity below her. "If they need us, someone will, no doubt, come and find us."

𝄃𝄃𝄃

As Jakob rounded the second curve of the Last Road, he saw the devastated area of the previous night's fighting. The passage was clear, but the narrowed road had to be bolstered with logs, soft dirt, and loose stones. The men brought thick wooden planks to surface the entire structure, hoping it would support the enormous weight offered by the lifestone Andrew and Alexis carried on their wagon. The structure spanned almost fifty arm's lengths, with the stone wall running tightly against it. The area was rigorously fought over, yet so *untenable, the villagers decided to surrender the area when Catherine and the lifestone safely traveled through.*

The unstated repercussions of losing this regained access point meant the army of villagers still guarding the breach would be cut off from the southern flow of supplies and combustibles keeping the orbs from overrunning them. When their resources of wood, tar, and oil ran out, everyone caught north of this checkpoint would be in danger of being destroyed by the purple orbs and their poisonous tendrils.

Michael and Leena watched the events passing before them, while Jakob moved the team of horses closer to the embattled makeshift roadway. Alexis and Andrew followed in the wagon behind their father in astonished silence as they surveyed the incredible loss of life and the impossible efforts to make the way passable. Villagers carried the dead to the side of the road, preparing them for burial. They passed piles of stones to place in the wall when the bodies were buried. Bodies lined the edge of the road, making it easier for families to identify the remains of their loved ones. Alexis looked at their faces and recognized two people she met from the previous night. She touched Andrew's shoulder, as she pointed to the faces of Will and Jeanne, two young men Collin enlisted to stop the wagons and make camp. Alexis said nothing, but Andrew understood the implications his sister showed him. If these two strangers surrendered their lives for Catherine, then carrying her stone to the breach would be an honor. They would do whatever was needed to help Catherine survive and seal the breach, even if it meant sacrificing themselves.

It sounded like a loud "churring" sound, like thousands of locusts approaching from a distance. The sound became unbearably loud as hundreds of red tendrils shot up and over the fire wall, piercing the ground in front of them and landing in a hiss. The marauding orbs pierced the air over the wall with their red tendrils, blindly trying to engage the hapless villagers in their deadly embrace. Fortunately, no one was close enough to these blind shots, causing their killing attempts to go empty with their first barrage of projectiles.

One man screamed, "Get them back. The damned things are going to try it again."

"We have to get through!" Jakob countered angrily. "We have to put an end to this," Jakob yelled into the crowd gathering behind Andrew's wagon, just as a tendril stabbed the ground beside him.

Michael yelled, "Jakob, look out!" as another venomous tendril shot below the bed of the wagon. The red tendril slid away, making the ground hiss as it retracted over the wall of flames. The orbs were either searching for them blindly or sending a warning not to advance any farther. Michael recollected the horrible scene where his horse was torn to pieces in front of him. The memory sent fear into his heart like a frozen dagger. He looked up to Jakob and then, with a tremble in his voice, said, "You're right, Jakob. We have to do this . . . now. These things are going to do anything to keep Catherine from the breach. We need to keep moving. We need to do it now, or we may never get another chance."

Jakob pushed the reluctant horses forward as a dozen red tendrils shot into the ground in front of them. "You have to come back . . ." one of the men screamed.

Michael reached beneath the bench and brought out a sharp two-headed ax Jakob showed him earlier. He jumped off the wagon, swinging the ax at the wanton tendrils as they stabbed the ground on either side of him. He swung the blade, neatly severing two tendrils blocking Jakob's progress onto the makeshift passage. "Now . . . that's how it's done," Michael said, pleased he could finally take out his anger on something. Some men holding back saw what Michael was attempting and came forward with swords and axes, screaming a bloodcurdling battle cry. As every tendril was cut, the orbs appeared to stop their assault, though their incessant churring became louder.

"You better get back up here," Jakob said, as he managed to get the horses moving again. "They sound like we angered them. They're sure to strike again, and I don't want to be here when they do."

"I'm more help to you on the ground," Michael shot back. "If even one of these things manages to hit the wagons or one of the horses, you'll need someone down here to cut the damned thing off."

Though Jakob feared for Michael's safety, he felt Michael made a good argument. If they were hit, nothing less than a solid blow to the tendrils would stop it from tearing one of the wagons or horses apart. He looked down where Michael was walking alongside the wagon. "Okay . . . okay . . . just be careful."

Michael looked up at Jakob driving the wagon and smiled. "Some of the others have joined us and are walking just below us Jakob. They saw these things are not as invincible as we thought they were. We just needed a way to fend them off. We are going to make it to the breach with Catherine. I just hope she snaps out of it before we get there."

Suddenly, the loud churring stopped, and the air went silent. "By the Winds," Leena cried out, "what are they doing?"

Michael walked to the side of the wagon and took Leena's hand. "I don't know, but I think we should all be ready for another strike." He gave Leena's hand a squeeze then walked up to Jakob struggling to keep the horses moving over the scorched earth and rebuilt passages. "I think these things are getting ready to hit us again, Jakob."

"I don't know what they are doing, but this wagon is going through," Jakob shouted, as he got the horses moving at a slightly faster pace. He saw Michael was now doing a slow trot to keep up. "Michael, drop back and tell Andrew and Alexis to keep up with me. We are getting through that bottleneck as fast as we can . . . Tell them!"

Michael nodded as he slowed his pace, allowing Jakob's wagon to pass him. He stopped and waited while Andrew and Alexis brought their wagon close to him. "Your father wants you to keep your wagon close behind his. When he gets to the bottleneck, he plans to push through as fast as the horses will take him."

"But the stone is very heavy, and the horses are spent just trying to keep up as it is. How are we going to move any faster?" Andrew argued.

"I don't think your father realizes that. I think he believes you have been pacing the horses to keep the wagon steady. I, myself, didn't realize how hard the horses were working just to pull the stone."

Alexis spoke up, "You better run back and tell him to slow down. He already has a big lead on us as it is. We just can't push these horses any faster."

Michael looked up at Andrew then to where Jakob was proceeding quickly, leaving a wider gap between the two wagons. "Keep this wagon moving. I'll catch up to Jakob and have him stop."

Michael started running toward the wagon carrying Leena and his almost comatose daughter, Catherine. He made half the distance when the churring started again. "Jakob," he screamed, "wait!"

Jakob turned his head as a slender red tendril whizzed by his head. Leena screamed when the second tendril pierced his chest, lifting him out of the wagon. Blood sprayed over her and Catherine. Michael pummeled his feet into the ground as fast as he could, in horror and fear for his family. Leena was immobilized by terror when Michael jumped up and assumed Jakob's place and quickly gathered the reins in his hands. "They killed him . . ." Leena screamed uncontrollably. She held Catherine who continued to be transfixed on something no one could see. In spite of the distance Jakob put between their wagon and the one with Alexis and Andrew, Michael pushed the wagon through the narrow passageway as red tendrils stabbed the ground both ahead and behind them, blindly searching for a mark. Villagers, seeing what happened, came rushing to Michael's side, slashing and hacking the tendrils that fell near them, finally decimating the second onslaught.

When the churring stopped, there were more dead lying on the ground beside them; torn bodies littered the ground behind them. The carnage was unlike anything Michael ever saw. He stopped the wagon and waved to the wagon pulling closer to them. One villager walked up and asked him, "Why are you stopping? We can't keep holding them off like this . . . You have to move on."

"We need that wagon"—*Michael pointed to the second wagon carrying Catherine's stone*—*"to stop all this. Without it, we don't have anything to fight with. We need that wagon here behind us, or all is lost. So for now, we stop and wait, unless you have a better idea,"* *Michael roared at the villagers collecting around his wagon.*

"Jakob is gone," Leena said, weeping in the seat behind him. "Those things . . . they just took him like he was a piece of meat and just killed him," she said hysterically.

"Listen," Michael said sternly. "I need you. I need you to stay calm, stay alert . . ." He looked at his daughter splotched with Jakob's blood then said, "Catherine needs you. I can't have you falling apart now. I need you to be a warrior, Leena. I need you to stop feeling and start watching. Can you do that for me?"

Leena looked up at her husband, her sobs shuddering to a close. "I will try . . . I will try . . ."

Andrew and Alexis finally pulled their wagon behind Michael. Jakob's son and daughter appeared ashen as tears they spent traveled and dried on their dust-covered faces. Michael spoke loudly enough for everyone to hear, "Jakob was your father and my friend. I wish we had the time to grieve for him, but we don't. He believed in what we are doing, and out of respect for him, we need to move on. It will be hard, and all of us may not get to see the end of this . . . but we need to try."

Alexis was too grief stricken to talk, but Andrew managed to say, "Move on. We will try to keep up."

Michael pulled on the reins and ushered the horses forward, while Andrew did the same. The passage before them was rugged and narrow. They hoped they could make it through before the next attack.

Lamin ran to the tower near the breach and called to the man keeping watch, "I just heard two wagons were making their way through the bottleneck."

"I'll keep my attention directed there," the man called back. "The activity at the breach is more frenzied since the wagons entered the narrows. I hope they get through soon. I think these things know they are coming."

"I believe you," Lamin shouted back over the din of men rushing to and from the battlements.

Penny turned back from where she stood, looking at the increasing activity occurring within the encampment. She looked at Victoria fumbling with some buttons that were coming loose on her tunic. "I think something is happening down by the tower, Victoria."

"What do you think it is?" she said, looking up from the loosened buttons.

"I think Catherine and her lifestone must be on their way here."

"This may finally be over," Victoria gasped. *"I wished Rand and Leon could be here to see this finally drawing to an end."*

"Me too," Penny said sadly.

"They gave their lives for nothing," Victoria sobbed, thinking how little she had to offer from their sacrifice.

Penny saw how profoundly Leon's and Rand's death had on her. She considered what to say to Victoria then said, "They saved us, Victoria. They did not die for nothing. They saved us. It wasn't the reason they wanted, but they kept us alive. Just remember that."

"I know," Victoria said, as she wiped the stray tears off her face with the sleeve of her shirt.

Penny looked at the young woman and thought how brave she was to have endured so much in such little time. She looked around at the makeshift tent where they were told to stay then said, "I think I've been in here long enough. Why don't we go down and find out what's going on?"

"Let's go," Victoria said without hesitation.

Penny led the way to the bottom of the rise, with Victoria following closely behind her. Before long, they were immersed in the humming activity taking place at the base of the tower. Penny stopped a man hurrying toward the breach. "What's going on? Why is everyone rushing around?"

"Haven't you heard? Catherine made it through the narrows and is on her way here now. The villagers are setting up a blockade to keep the orbs off the breach right now."

"How are they going to do that?" Penny asked, concerned that many villagers would lose their lives in the attempt.

"We're going to do it with fire, just like we have been doing."

Victoria looked first to Penny then to the young man speaking to Penny. "There is a better way."

"Really?" the man asked skeptically. "What do you know of it, young woman?"

Victoria looked to Penny. Penny looked to her and said, "Go on, Victoria, tell him. We have a weapon against the orbs that will stop them."

The man looked at Penny incredulously then said, "What are you two talking about? What weapon works better than the fires we set up?"

"We are the weapons . . ." Victoria said with conviction. "Our lifestones will stop them in the same way as Catherine's lifestone will put an end to all this."

"What do you mean?" the man said in total disbelief.

"She means we always had the power to protect ourselves. We all carry a weapon to stop these things," Penny added.

"But how?" the man asked, stupefied by the insolence of Penny's response.

"This is how . . ." Victoria said, as she pulled her lifestone from the leather pouch around her neck, revealing the reddish glow emitted in the presence of the orbs.

"By the Winds . . ." the man exclaimed, "what did you do to it?" he said, as the reddish light spilled almost thirty arm's lengths away from them.

"It doesn't matter what our lifestones do. It's just we know they are effective in slowing the orbs down almost to a stop," Penny said, watching the man gasp at the red dome of light emitted by Victoria's lifestone. "We used them to pass through the orbs about a day ago. The strength of the lifestones was almost gone when my husband and our friend sacrificed their lifestones to get us here. We rested, and now our lifestones are recharged. None of you have even tried to use them, so I believe, collectively, we could force the orbs back from the breach long enough to allow Catherine to place her lifestone in the breach."

"Show me . . ." he challenged.

Penny drew out her lifestone from beneath her tunic and held it next to Victoria's. The light it emitted doubled in size and strength.

"It's a good trick if you want a red light to see with, but it certainly doesn't look like any kind of weapon to me," the man said, his voice flavored with skepticism, as he addressed Penny.

Penny looked at the man indignantly and then spoke to Victoria, "Put your stone away for now, Victoria. We obviously need to show these men how to use the stones."

Victoria spoke up and asked the man staring at Penny, "Is there someone we can speak with that is in authority?"

"Do you know the man they call Benjamin?" he asked them both.

"*My husband knew him. I never met him myself,*" *Penny said sadly.*

"*Where do we find him?*" *Victoria pressed the man for information.*

"*He's the big man giving orders down there between the tower and the breach . . .*" *The man pointed to a large harried man who hurried from one side of the tower to the other barking orders and pointing to weak spots in the wall of flames constantly fed by the villagers.*

"*I see him,*" *Penny said, grabbing Victoria's hand and leading her through the broken rocks littering the slope. While they moved down the slope to where Benjamin stood, a sound unlike anything the two women ever heard started coming through the wall of flames.*

"*What is that?*" *Victoria asked, while the churring sound crescendoed to an almost unbearable level.*

"*I don't know . . .*" *Penny shouted to Victoria, as hundreds of red tendrils shot out over the wall of flames like a bloody curtain of death. Victoria ran into the high grasses, while Penny tried moving toward a small ravine. The blind attack missed most of their marks as they hit hardened earth littered with ashes and splintered wooden fragments. Penny screamed and then fell to the ground. Victoria saw where Penny dropped and thought it was a way to hide herself from the killing orbs. Victoria dropped to the ground as well.*

After some time passed, the loud churring sound droned to nothing, and Victoria watched as several bodies laid before her, strewn about the site, discarded, broken, and torn to pieces by the onslaught of the orbs.

"*Penny . . . ,*" *Victoria whispered, afraid to reveal herself amid the tall grasses where she hid, "where are you?*" *Penny did not answer. "Penny . . . ," she managed a little louder. To her left, Victoria heard a muffled voice calling her name.*

"*Victoria, over here.*"

Victoria crawled through the thick grass to a depression in the earth, where a tree had been uprooted. There she found Penny lying in a pool of blood. Her arm was wrenched from its socket and was barely held in place by torn skin and sinew. Penny was fatally injured. She was dying. "Come here quickly, child. I don't have much time. I lost a lot of blood, and it's getting hard to see you."

"I'm here," Victoria said, as she was assessing Penny's chances of getting through the next assault. When she got to Penny's side, she saw the gaping wounds and tried vainly to stop the bleeding.

"You can't save me, child. It's over for me. I need you to tell Catherine, Timothy is searching for her immortality."

"You can't die," Victoria stammered through her tears.

"Promise me . . . promise you'll tell Catherine . . ." Penny was finished. Her color faded, and her eyes were vacant.

"I promise, Penny . . . I promise!" Victoria wailed. "Don't go . . . You can't leave me alone to do this," she said, as the turmoil of what she must do churned in her heart. She stayed near Penny, trying to understand why the world was ending; but when she saw Penny's empty eyes, Victoria knew she was gone. She closed Penny's eyes then stood, revealing her small stature in the tall grasses, and then walked with staggered steps toward the wooden tower. There were two wagons arriving with passengers. They must have arrived after the attack from the breach. Still in shock from seeing her friend Penny die in front of her, she pushed forward.

Benjamin continued shouting orders to the villagers. He had them build enormous fires in an attempt to push the orbs away from the breach. While the fires were effective at keeping the orbs from gaining ground, it did very little to drive them away from the opening in the wall.

"We've got to get fires burning around the opening of the wall, or Catherine will not be able to move her stone there," Benjamin informed one of the men standing nearby.

"We are running out of things to burn, Benjamin."

Benjamin looked at the wooden tower and considered the possibility of using the wood to fuel the dying flames. Even before he issued the order to tear it down, two wagons emerged from the smoke.

"They're here . . . They're here!" cries shouted over the crackling blaze of newfound tinder set ablaze to make an ingress into the breach.

"What is it?" Benjamin called out, missing the wagons moving through the thick smoke.

"Catherine and her lifestone are here," a man called out.

"By the Winds," Benjamin exclaimed, "they finally made it." Then in a whisper to himself, "I was beginning to lose hope. I thank the Winds for getting them here." He hurried to where the wagons stopped on the small rise near the watchtower, unaware of the young blood-spattered woman emerging from the tall grasses behind him walking in the same direction.

Alexis's brother Lamin was the first to arrive at the wagons. As he approached, he saw the prevailing hollow look on the expressions of the wagon's passengers. He walked where Andrew hung his head, holding the reins. "What happened? Where is our father?"

"Gone," Andrew sobbed.

"What do you mean . . . gone?" Lamin insisted.

Their brother Eric ran to a spot near Lamin and saw the washed complexions of his younger brother Andrew and sister Alexis. He looked at Lamin with concern as Lamin continued his questions.

"Do you mean our father is dead?" Lamin spoke in measured tones, trying not to alarm his brother Eric.

"Our father died trying to get here?" Eric shrieked the question to his brothers and then gasped in disbelief.

Both Lamin and Eric watched as the only affirmation coming from Andrew were tears running down his face. "Oh, Father . . ." Lamin shuddered, as Eric kept him from falling to the ground. Using his soot-covered arms and solid build, Eric managed to hold him.

Alexis, silent until now, said sternly and compassionately, "Father wanted to get Catherine here to save us, but he could not save himself. He died because he believed in Catherine's great sacrifice. We have to make this happen so his deed does not vanish because we were not strong enough to see it to the end."

"Agreed . . ." Lamin spoke angrily, tears welling in his eyes. "We must do what we set out to do . . . for our father's sake." Eric still held Lamin in his powerful grasp. "Let me go, Eric. I can stand on my own." Eric released him then knelt on the ground and wept for his father.

"What's going on here?" came the stern voice of Benjamin.

"Our father was killed in an attack coming here," Alexis spoke up.

"Jakob is gone?" Benjamin asked, feeling his heart sink in despair from what he was hearing. "It can't be . . . I just spoke with him." He sank to his knees beside the two wagons silhouetted by raging walls of fire. Other than the crackling fires and the villagers rushing around the huddled group, silence fell like a blanket reverently placed to keep them from the devastation surrounding them.

From behind them, a small voice called, "We have to stop this. Does anyone know a girl named Catherine?"

Benjamin got off the ground and turned to see a young woman spattered with the blood of her friend. "Who are you?" he asked. "What do you want from Catherine?"

"My name is Victoria," the young woman said. She looked at the group of strangers as they responded to her name in gasps of surprise and the occasional response, "It's her . . ." Victoria paused a moment and collected her thoughts. "I met Timothy in the village of Glade. We stayed at the home of Penny and Leon before Leon sent him north to the

villages beyond Glade. He was riding with news that Stock was under siege, and he was looking for something that would make Catherine immortal." She turned her head, looking at the small assembly of people before her and trying to evaluate how her news affected them.

It was Leena who spoke first, "Did you know a girl named Amelia?"

"She was my friend," Victoria said sadly. "I still carry her lifestone with me. It was just about here, on the Last Road, where we said good-bye to each other. She gave me her lifestone to protect me from the orbs."

"We took care of her until the stone sickness took her. Benjamin and I found her father and carried her to him," Michael told her.

"I still have her lifestone . . . I want to place it into the wall next to Catherine's," Victoria told them.

Benjamin looked at Victoria in awe and sorrow. "You have come to us at a good time. But we haven't been able to secure the breach. Trying to move Catherine's lifestone there"—Benjamin pointed to a fiery wall where the red tendrils of the orbs looked like a field of thick red grass—"would be suicide. We lost so many. I find I cannot give orders for more lives to be spent frivolously."

"We don't have to. I know how to stop them long enough to get Catherine and her stone to the breach without spending any more lives. Our lifestones will protect us. Penny and I used Leon's and Rand's lifestones, and then our own, to travel through low terrains too deep to use fire."

"How is that possible?" Leena asked, shocked they possessed a powerful weapon that was in their hands all the time.

"Watch . . ." Victoria said, as she drew her lifestone from the leather pouch. They all stood transfixed by the small girl holding a glowing lifestone spreading rays of red all around her.

"By the Winds . . ." Lamin exclaimed.

"Why does it do that?" Alexis asked, mesmerized by the reddish emanations.

"I don't know," Victoria stated. *"But I know the orbs stay paralyzed when these red rays hit them. They cannot move. They cannot strike at us. The only problem is, as we get tired, the red rays shrink. If they shrink too far, we become too weak to do anything. This was why Leon and Rand gave Penny and me their lifestones, to get us through the ravines."*

"What happened to them?" Andrew asked.

"I don't know," Victoria said sadly, as she placed her stone inside the leather pouch. *"But before we made it through the deep places, their stones faded completely. I'm certain they both died."*

"But the lifestones worked?" Benjamin asked coldly. *"How do we know this?"*

"It was Amelia who told me. When I left Stock to deliver her message to Timothy, she told me to use her lifestone to protect myself. I didn't understand at first, but when one of the orbs attacked, I pulled out her stone, and the red rays stopped it. I was able to get away."

"A message for Timothy . . . is that what you said?" came a voice not heard from for days. Catherine was trying to wake from a dream she couldn't escape until she heard Victoria speak her Timothy's name. *"You saw him . . . you spoke with him?"* she asked, frantic to hear news of what happened to him.

"Catherine, you're back!" Leena cried, as she put her arms around her daughter.

"What can you tell me of Timothy?" Catherine pressed, leaving her mother's arms to get out of the wagon. She moved to Victoria's side and asked again, *"What has become of my Timothy?"*

Victoria felt unguarded, yet she knew she had to tell Catherine everything she knew. She started her story meeting Timothy on the hill outside the village of Glade and ended by telling everyone Leon sent *him someplace where he could make Catherine immortal. Everyone's eyes and ears were on her as she told her story. When she finished, Catherine said, "Then I must get my stone into the breach and hope, mustn't I?"*

Victoria nodded, "Yes, if we are to stop these things, it is what must be done. Timothy, I know, is doing his best to save you somehow. No one has told me where he is since he left Glade. I wished him well for all of us and for you, Catherine. He loves you very much. I know he will find a way if it is possible."

"I know that too," Catherine said, as she smiled at Victoria. She turned to her father and mother and said, "We must begin."

Benjamin started calling the villagers together, "Listen up. My young friend here has a way to get Catherine's lifestone into the breach." He turned his attention to the small girl standing beside him. "Go ahead, tell them, Victoria."

When the remaining men and women were assembled, Victoria explained how the collective power residing in their lifestones would stop the orbs from attacking while Catherine's lifestone was rolled into the breach. The villagers were amazed by what she said. She told them of Leon, Rand, and Penny's sacrifice to get her here. As she spoke, various people pulled out their stones and saw there was some kind of power residing in each of their lifestones. It filled them with awe, and it filled them with hope. When Victoria finished, she turned to Benjamin and said, "We should begin."

"I agree," Benjamin said. He turned to Catherine and what remained of Jakob's family and said, "How many men will be needed to move her stone?"

"About twenty men should manage it nicely," Andrew told him, thinking back on the elaborate system of pulleys and ropes their father had implemented getting the stone into his wagon.

Benjamin quickly ordered the entourage of villagers and wagon carrying Catherine's lifestone to be moved close to the dying fires near the breach.

The churring began immediately as they approached the site. Orbs sent their poisonous tendrils flailing over the wall of flames as Benjamin led them where they would make a stand. Before he could give the command to pull out their lifestones, a tendril ripped through his right arm and pulled him into the air. Before he died, he screamed . . . "Get the stone to the wall . . . Pull your lifestones out now." There was a sick wet ripping sound as his body was carried over the failing wall of fire.

Michael saw the villagers hesitate, shocked to see Benjamin killed in front of them. This was their only possible chance. Too many lives were sacrificed to bring Catherine and her lifestone here. "Get out your lifestone now before they attack again. We won't get another chance. We need to do this now," Michael screamed.

About a hundred villagers assembled on the ridge near the breach. When they brought their lifestones out of their secured hiding places, a horrible growling echoed against the wall as a growing brilliant red glow emanated as each villager continued to unleash the power of the lifestones. The light reached measures of parcels, not arm's lengths, and it forced most of the hideous purple orbs back inside the breach where they came from.

"Alexis . . . Andrew . . ." Michael commanded, "pull the wagon here as close as you can." Michael observed the twenty strong men Benjamin chose and said, "You men there, get Catherine's stone off the wagon and prepare to move it into the breach." The men responded as Alexis and Andrew pulled the wagon closer to the breach. Michael turned to his daughter Catherine. He had no commands to give her, only his tears.

Catherine looked at her father and said, "It is what must be done, Father. I know I must be the one to place the stone. I will follow them." She reached her father and kissed him on the cheek. She hugged her mother and said, "I will be back after I place my stone. Timothy will succeed, Mother. In some way, I will live forever."

Leena looked into her daughter's eyes and said with a choked sob, "You already will. No one will forget this day."

Michael needed to stay strong for all of them. *"Okay, men, let's get the stone off the wagon."* When the canvas wrappings came off the enormous stone, a beam of red light like no other shone from Catherine's lifestone. A sound like a tornado twisting screams into a frightening roar went out from the orbs clustering about the opening in the wall. Many smashed to pieces in the waning blue mists, trying to retreat through the opening. It was the first time since the day of the breach where the villagers felt they had the upper hand.

"Let's move . . ." one of the men shouted. Twenty men pushed the enormous rock to the ground as more and more orbs either smashed to pieces or fled as the group pushed the stone up the incline to the breach. In the reddened light, the mists stopped, and the orbs backed away. The men pushed the stone about fifty arm's lengths before they stood before the breach.

Catherine recognized one of the men helping move her stone was Collin. Collin looked toward her and said, *"It's time, Catherine. Put your hand on the stone, and we will place it for you. When it's done, all this will be over."*

"I know. Thank you, Collin." Catherine looked about at everyone surrounding her and said, *"Pray to the Winds for me. Do not cry for me. I am doing the best I can with a life . . . giving all of you one. I do this with a full heart. I do this with the hope Timothy will find a way to make me immortal."* She looked back to Collin. *"I'm ready. My hand is on the stone."*

With Catherine pushing on her stone with the rest of the men, it fit neatly and securely into the wall. A wail went out across the valleys and trenches and deep ravines as the source of blue mists cut off. The fumes died around them. No orbs attacked. It was over. Most of the orbs retreated. Whatever and wherever any orbs remained died and disappeared even before Catherine returned home with her parents. Victoria walked to where Catherine's lifestone now sealed the breach and placed Amelia's lifestone next to it. The ordeal was over for everyone. For Catherine, it was her first day of the stone sickness. She was weak but alive. It was up to Timothy whether she lived or died.

The Day before Sunset

Tell me about the time before sunset . . .

The last week of December 2008, Lois became profoundly dehydrated. I needed to take her to the infusion center for outpatient IV therapy. Her dehydration manifested with severe nausea and vomiting coupled with intense pain to her back and joints. She cried when I carried her to the car. However, I knew IV fluids would make her feel better. At the infusion center, the IV fluids took most of the day to complete; and when finished, she looked and felt more like herself. I knew she was moving further down the spiral. Whatever hopes she and I had for recovery grew dimmer as time progressed.

The intense pain Lois experienced at the end of December 2008 and into the first week of January 2009 repeated itself on January 22, 2009. This time, Lois had to be admitted into the hospital for treatment. A series of tests were completed to evaluate the extent of bone metastasis. The tests showed the usual metastatic sites. However, there were increased erosions in the metastatic sites, causing bone weakening and irreparable damage. Still, nothing pointed to a definite reason to have this sudden change in pain level. Nausea and vomiting became a daily occurrence, always preceding bouts of intense pain. While hospitalized, she received three days' hydration and a change in pain medications. Her pain regimen now included transdermal pain medications (or skin patches), which she found to be very effective at keeping her pain to a minimum. Lois was to take antiemetics every eight hours around the clock to stave off the nausea. Everyone hoped she would come off the antiemetics when she started eating properly again. Unfortunately, a common side effect of constant use of antiemetics was constipation. Lois made every attempt and enlisted my help in instituting a program to maintain her bowel health. As was Lois's style, she maintained records of her daily habits to track problems and changes. She was released from the hospital on January 25, 2009.

The next day, January 26, 2009, Lois returned to the hospital with a blood clot in her left leg. After a few days of anticoagulant therapy (blood thinners), Lois was allowed to come home, with the understanding she would be on a long-term anticoagulant. Lois was required to follow up with lab work every three days. Her physician would evaluate the lab work then prescribe the appropriate dosage. Finally, after almost five weeks, Lois felt better about returning to work. While she worked from home during this time, the physician considered allowing her to return to her office within a few weeks.

Between February 2, 2009, and February 16, 2009, Lois completed two weeks of radiation therapy to her back. She had not received any chemotherapy for almost two months. I was concerned what the metastasis was doing to her spine and joints. I was grateful she managed to tolerate radiation therapy. I felt this intervention made the pain she experienced in late December to the end of January to be eliminated. Now the clot in the left saphenous vein seemed to be the last part of the equation to be solved.

Things appeared to lend themselves in Lois's direction once again. Everything was returning to normal, other than lab visits to evaluate the anticoagulant therapy. In that regard, I was certain Lois would need anticoagulant therapy for the rest of her life, considering how quickly and easily the clot formed.

Knowing everything was under control, and with our son with her to help, I decided to go to work. Lois had her coagulation studies done around the time I left that evening. About midnight, I received a call from Lois, explaining how our son had to drive her to the emergency room because of the lab results. Apparently, the INR (normally 1.2-2.5 on anticoagulants) rose to 19.2 on the results taken at 6:00 p.m. By the time her test was repeated in the emergency room, the INR elevated above 20, or almost ten times a safe level of anticoagulation. Her chances to have spontaneous bleeding were critical. When she called, she told me she received the medication to counteract the effects of the anticoagulant. However, an alternative treatment needed to be pursued, since the oral form was too dangerous to continue.

Lois suspected long-term use of chemotherapy had altered the effects of this particular anticoagulant. As Lois would always do, she investigated the effects of chemotherapy on the particular anticoagulant she used after she returned home. She called again at three o'clock in the morning, informing me of a connection between the two therapies that would cause a problem like the one she experienced. Eventually, she consulted her oncologist; and together they decided on an injectable low molecular weight heparin, which she started the following day.

Lois was frustrated by the problems facing her. She could not go to her job and asked her hospice unit for work she could do from home just to keep up on her records. The clot was diminishing, but another anticoagulant was used to prevent another clot. She could not get to chemotherapy treatments, and in spite of the radiation therapy, which greatly assisted in alleviating the pain, her tumor markers rose to 745. With pain well controlled and beginning to feel like her old self, she faced the possibility her markers would never go down. The portentous future these numbers predicted made her feel cancer would take her life very soon. The magnitude of their implications weighed heavily on her, and the days she spent at home were times she just wanted to be alone and sleep.

In early February 2009, I went to our mailbox and brought back an innocuous envelope addressed to Lois. She was lying down in the bedroom about half asleep when I brought the mail to her. There were the usual magazines, bills, and advertisements. Lois asked me to bring her letter opener, and she proceeded to open everything. Opening the mail over this time helped her feel connected to the world and felt she contributed something to help around the house. Her activity was very limited because pain increased again by February, and she had not adjusted to the new pain medications. Her days consisted of six to eight hours of work on the computer for her hospice, then the rest of the day sleeping. Any diversion, like opening the mail, was a treat. But this day was different. The innocuous envelope held something neither of us expected.

To this day, the mystery of who initiated the nomination remains cloaked and elusive. No one came forward to admit their involvement, though Lois had many suspicions. The envelope held news she was nominated and won the 2009 Distinguished Alumni Award from York College of Pennsylvania. The honor would be presented on May 2, 2009. Lois still had time to recover and be able to accept the award. Inside the envelope were forms and agendas for her to fill out. She had calls to make and people to contact in order to give information about her activities to be used at the awards ceremony.

The odds were stacked against her. She still had pain, the clot wasn't completely resolved, and her tumor markers were climbing. Yet the very idea the college noticed her contributions in the area of breast cancer awareness over the years made what she was doing all that more important. She made arrangements for a telephone interview with a college director about the middle of February. In spite of how she felt, she was very excited to be part of something again. Before, where I found her quiet and reticent, I now found her busy and excited. She prepared her resume for the college and a speech, which she revised several times, for her presentation on May 2, 2009. Thinking back on this dark time, knowing someone understood the value of what she did over her lifetime, made Lois realize her own value. Just that little bit of incentive and recognition made her feel she could go on.

By the week of March 9, 2009, Lois returned to work full-time. She had an enormous amount of work to catch up on. I sensed the award at the college gave her the enormous strength I missed seeing since the end of 2008. By the middle of March, her tumor markers were checked again. The only treatments since the end of 2008 were the radiation treatments to her spine. We can all speculate on the effects of radiation therapy, but the markers indicated tremendous success when levels dropped to almost half of what they were. Her markers were down to 364 from 745. The combined effect of seeing progress in the right direction and the upcoming awards made her feel on top of the world. She told me later, "Had you worried, didn't I?"

I looked at her rather sheepishly and said, "Yeah, this time was pretty bad. I wasn't sure I would have you around much longer."

"Don't worry," she told me, "I'm going to be around for a while yet." She gave me a quick kiss, then hurried off to her next appointment.

As amazing as Lois was, during the times she was in significant pain, she managed to go to our local school for LPNs in January and spoke about breast cancer issues and her advocacy activities. She managed to keep in touch either by e-mail or telephone conferences with the NBCC, ACS, and her many breast cancer survivors and advocates during January. Finally, in March, she was well enough to drive to Washington DC to participate in the team leader training on March 14, 2009. She coordinated all her treatment, physician appointments, work appointments, and advocacy efforts with such precision that she literally accomplished all she could have on a normal daily basis. In a time when most of us would be concentrating on what it would take to survive metastatic breast cancer, she was helping people from her position as a bereavement coordinator, teaching locally on everything she knew on breast cancer, and being an advocate for any breast cancer survivor in need of her help or influence.

Lois was absent from her breast cancer support group meeting in January and February because of health reasons. When she returned to the group in the middle of March, she was very disappointed. In spite of getting back on her feet in early March, Lois managed to get a late newsletter together for her support group.

(Editorial by Lois A. Anderson dated March 18, 2009)

I will have to admit to everyone reading this that this copy of the newsletter has been the hardest one for me to write for two reasons. Due to my own health complications that began the end of last year and because I feel we really need to look at our group, I have had very much trouble completing this newsletter.

First of all, I will deal with the health complications I experienced. These included an outpatient visit to the infusion center in late December followed by an admission to the hospital for pain management in mid-January when pain control was too difficult to accomplish at home. Because I have metastatic lesions and arthritis in the same areas of my spine, it has been difficult to get this all under control. There are two competing interests here that must be considered and both do not necessarily respond to the same medications. By January, I ended up getting into a cycle of pain, nausea, and vomiting that meant a hospital admission because I could no longer keep food down.

Following that hospital admission, I developed two more complications—a blood clot in my leg and bronchitis while undergoing radiation therapy. And to top it off while trying to convert from heparin injections to Coumadin pills (because of the blood clot), my bleeding tendency went sky-high and a visit to the emergency room was in order. So now I am on the mend and looking forward to returning to work and receiving the 2009 Distinguished Alumni Achievement Award from York College on May 2nd.

I received notification of this award the beginning of February and was really taken aback by this honor. I was completely unaware of being nominated for such an honor, but I appreciate the fact that I was selected. However, I do not know the criteria that were used. I cried the evening I opened the letter announcing the award. Such an honor was truly unbelievable for me and really shocked me!!!

Now for the second reason I had trouble writing this newsletter. It seems the attendance at our group has been lacking lately. Is it because we do not have a speaker at every meeting or is everyone just bored? What can we do to improve things and make this group and newsletter better for all? At our June meeting, we will discuss what we can try. We will also discuss the annual picnic which is usually held in July. I cannot host this event and we are looking for someone else who would like to take this on. I also ask that those of you who only make yourselves available for the picnic strongly consider coming to at least one of our other meetings. Come on, you usually have the newsletter telling you what's going on at the meetings so come and talk to your old friends. We love to have you join us and let us know that you really care about and appreciate this group.

So that's my spiel for this time around. I hope to see all of you at our June meeting to help plan the future of this group. If you really cannot come to this meeting, your *ideas can be e-mailed to me or sent to me at my home. Thank you for taking the time to read this.*

Looking forward to spring,

Lois

Lois continued her advocacy work through March, participating at a conference in Hershey, Pennsylvania, on March 18, 2009, for the ACT meeting for the American Cancer Society, where she worked on issues pertinent to all types of cancer. By April, she was back on track and updated all her work at the hospice unit.

Lois's oncologist prepared to start anthracycline therapy, which was delayed since January. He needed tests completed to evaluate her cardiac functioning before he started. Her radiation oncologist was very pleased with her markers and followed up with a CT scan to evaluate whatever positive progress was made by treating her. The CT showed stable bony abnormalities, which was good. What wasn't good was an area on the lower right lung base. The right lung showed an increase in fluids. While radiation therapy could stifle bone metastasis for a long time, it could do nothing if the right lung was affected. Any improvement to the right lung would need surgical intervention or chemotherapy. The MUGA scan (a test to evaluate heart function) was completed on March 14, 2009, which concluded she had a very healthy heart. Since shortness of breath on exertion continued to be a problem, her oncologist scheduled a pulmonary function test, which she passed without difficulty. With the testing completed, her oncologist considered starting another chemotherapy protocol using anthracyclines.

Lois resumed her first chemotherapy of 2009 on April 23. A tumor marker taken just a few days before this treatment indicated the markers were again rising, as they went to 421. We were hoping, at least for a while, the markers would stabilize and give her a chance to gather her physical strength again. Lois's emotional and spiritual strength rarely faltered. I often told her if she could survive on her spirit instead of her body, she would live to be one hundred. She always laughed when I told her this.

May arrived, and Lois was presented with the Distinguished Alumni Achievement Award on May 2. The event started at eleven o'clock and continued through most of the afternoon. Lois gave her speech to about two hundred people gathered there for the various awards. Afterward, it seemed everyone, from the president of the college to the college students who attended, wanted to talk with her. Lois was having one of her good days, so the long day did not seem to affect her. When she got home, I helped her pack to leave for the NBCC in Washington DC to help with lobbying efforts. She returned on Tuesday, May 5, very tired but optimistic she would return for a full day of work the following day. By the following Monday, Lois was in Harrisburg with the American Cancer Society working with the ACT program. She had a conference call with her advocates by Thursday the same week.

Not everything in Lois's life revolved around advocacy and breast cancer treatments. She also attended her friend's wedding, went to birthday parties for our family members, and rarely, if ever, did she ever miss sending a card out to anyone having a special occasion. In fact, in 2009, Lois wanted to make her presence known both in small groups and in big ones. I think she realized this year might be her last hurrah. It wasn't obvious at the time, but even then, I could feel something in Lois changed. Though she still acted and appeared to be functioning normally on the outside, something was different on the inside. I think she realized my concern, and when the time came, she did not try to hide it.

In mid-May, the tumor markers remained down at 426. This was a reason to celebrate because it meant the chemotherapy was working. Lois filled her time with advocacy calls, family, and many activities we had in our area. We made many small day trips on weekends and enjoyed the time we had to spend together. Somehow, in all of this, she managed to get a nine-page newsletter together for her support group. Her appeal to the support group members did not go unheeded as you will read in her editorial.

(Editorial by Lois A. Anderson dated May 18, 2009)

> *Wow, what a response we've had the last several meetings. I hope it continues. Our June meeting will be a planning meeting to see what everyone would like to*

do over the next year. If you cannot attend and you have some ideas, please call me and let me know about them. So far I have heard yoga, Dr. Bauer, someone on osteoporosis after treatment, and the Curves philosophy on exercise.

As I write this newsletter, my health remains stable—yeah!!!! All things are under control. My son is completing his second semester of classes in his RN program and looks forward to finishing these prerequisites in the fall before starting his clinical rotations. My husband, George, well he's still there, but busier than ever—sometimes it's ships passing in the night or maybe I should say daytime at our house.

I am also happy to announce that I recently presented Representative Todd Platts with an ACE award for his commitment to breast cancer legislation to help all women. I have a picture that I can bring along to our next session for anyone interested.

The 2009 Distinguished Alumni Achievement Award will come along, too, so you may all share in it. The award was based on all the work that I have done with breast cancer patients/survivors. Because I made a vow to myself 17 years ago that I would do whatever it took so that any woman did not have to walk in my shoes as a breast cancer patient, all of you have had some part in this award, and I think you deserve to see it. It is a strange kind of award though—you'll see what I mean when you look at it in person—a picture doesn't do it justice.

So that's about all for now from here. Don't forget our picnic in July at Diane's residence. Please call her and let her know what dish you'll bring.

Summer heat and humidity are on their way. Be careful outside.

Lois

I could tell Lois was weakening as her energy levels fell off once again. She continued telling me I just imagined it, continuing long hours for her hospice unit, following up on clients, and keeping track of everything with a paper trail. When the tumor markers came back for June, the numbers rose over two hundred points. There were changes in chemotherapy and changes in pain medications.

Our outside mini vacations became shorter, and with her decreased stamina, many times we simply went out to dinner or the movies.

When July finally arrived, Lois wanted to go to Williamsburg for the Fourth of July celebrations. Somehow, I think she knew it would be her last time to see them again. The evening of the Fourth, we went behind the Governor's Palace where they set off the fireworks. We usually laid out a blanket and watched the fireworks lying on the grass, but Lois could no longer sit on the hard ground, so I brought two canvas chairs to sit on.

The next day, we retraced the steps we made in Williamsburg when we were first married. We walked slowly, but she managed to do everything in the style that was uniquely Lois. I loved to watch as she went into the various vendors to see what they were selling, excited to show me something she hadn't seen before. As I watched her, I still saw the vibrant twenty-three-year-old woman seeing Williamsburg for the first time. This place was magical for her. She loved being here. Again, this place seemed to take her cares about cancer away. Though she was definitely slowed down by cancer, she certainly did not allow it to affect her here. When we had to return, she slept the whole way home. I think, in some way, she knew she would never return to her beloved Williamsburg.

We returned home at the end of the first week of July to a barrage of work-related activities and new changes in her chemotherapy. Lois was asked to assist the American Cancer Society with lobbying for their cancer agenda, but she was too involved in the activities of her hospice, which took precedence. By mid-July, she went to the local school for LPN students and spoke to them about the various issues surrounding breast cancer. By the end of the month, Lois needed to be present for further testing and scans to continue her therapy. Her tumor markers had risen to a disappointing 813.

In spite of the ominous findings, the protocols for chemotherapy didn't change. Lois didn't feel any different and continued to work full-time, though, I feel, she proceeded with much more caution than before. She limited herself to a forty-hour work week, and her advocacy role was limited to phone calls and Internet contacts. I could tell she was worried, as I would find her on the computer at two and three o'clock in the morning, still awake. Many times when I found her there, I asked why she was still awake. She would tell me she was tired but could not sleep. Many times I made her a cup of tea and sat with her until I started to fall asleep myself. I think she just wanted to be awake because, in her world, being awake was the same thing as being alive. I also believe she was starting to have trouble breathing when she was lying down.

On the nights I was off from work, Lois and I would talk about how she was doing. Many times she would ask me to lay my hands on the right side of her chest where the right breast had been removed in 1992. She told me the chest wall was tightening up and cramping. Whatever was happening in that location tightened the muscles to such an extent, the bottom three ribs turned up like a ridge and caused significant pain. Years before, when I attended physical therapy sessions with Lois, the therapists taught me myofascial release. The technique involved putting gentle pressure on either side of her old incision. Then while I left my hands on the tightened muscles, the muscles would release, the ribs would flatten out, and this would relieve her pain. Many times I could coax her back to bed if I promised to do this for her. Many times I fell asleep with my hands still in place on the relaxed chest wall, and she would have to wake me up and chase me into bed.

All through August, I could tell her pain was on the rise again. Her tumor markers always seemed relatively accurate. I noted, as did Lois, as the markers increased, her pain increased. In addition to her pain, there were the ubiquitous side effects of taking pain medications. Mouth dryness, thirst, headaches, and constipation seemed to be the most annoying and persistent problems. Though not a commonly discussed symptom, her bouts with constipation caused the lower three ribs of her right chest wall to curl up every time she strained. Many times I put my hands on her chest wall to stop the ribs from turning up. It was like a kind of torture over which I had little or no effect. So many times, she would scream. So many times, she would cry out. It broke my heart to hear her struggle. When I could get her back to bed, I would lay my hands on her chest wall in an attempt to flatten the lower three ribs. Most times it worked, but now with the markers climbing, my attempts to actually do anything for her became less and less effective.

At the end of August, Lois made three calls. One was for the Reach to Recovery Program for the American Cancer Society, another to the National Breast Cancer Coalition (NBCC) for advocacy, and another to the American Cancer Society regarding the ACT program. In spite of how she was feeling, Lois continued to work for the betterment of cancer patients. On August 19, 2009, Lois managed to attend the American Cancer Society's Breast Cancer Advocacy Training in Baltimore, Maryland. The proctor of the training session had suggested to Lois she would be a wonderful volunteer to speak at future events. Lois, however, did not volunteer. This was a change in the way Lois worked. Somehow, I believe she knew her time was waning. She was losing the battle, and she did not want to disappoint anyone. She kept her contacts, but, I knew, she wasn't making any new ones. She was to have a newsletter completed by the beginning of September, but between the pain and exhaustion, she never had the time to write it.

By mid-August, the tumor markers rose to 971. The number concerned Lois's oncologist, so he repeated it in early September when Lois reported episodes of increased shortness of breath and increased pain. The markers returned with an alarming 1,213! No one had any doubt the chemotherapy was no longer working for Lois. Lois again submitted to further tests with a focus on the right lung.

Lois managed to go to a family picnic on September 6, Memorial Day that year. She continued to work and somehow managed to cope with the increasing pain and anxiety that went with not knowing what to do next. She frequently consulted her fellow breast cancer survivors on the Internet or colleagues who were researchers in the field of breast cancer, but this time, it seemed everyone was coming up dry for any ideas on how to proceed.

Fortunately, I was off a few days to take classes during the day when the first wave of intractable pain hit her. She got out of bed crying because her pain was overwhelming. She usually kept a glass of water by her side of the bed, which she would empty several times before she went to sleep. I noted several nights where the glass remained full and untouched, which meant she had no desire to take fluids. I knew it would be a matter of time before she became dehydrated. For Lois, dehydration and pain were close companions.

On September 15, 2009, after consulting an oncology nurse at the infusion center, it was determined I would call an ambulance and get her to the emergency room. We were met by an oncologist who admitted her with nausea, vomiting, and uncontrolled pain. It was several days before her oncologist felt she would be able to eat anything. It was almost the end of September when I could finally take her home. Before she was released, she received two radiation treatments to her spine. She would continue these treatments for the entirety of two weeks, the last ones finishing on October 2, 2009.

Lois's birthday was coming up on October 6. We missed our anniversary on September 18 because of her hospitalization. To make up for it, I brought a huge bouquet of red roses the night of our anniversary and spent the best part of the night watching videos in her room. The hospital nurses knew I was there with her but didn't mind I was there after visiting hours. Lois told me she made arrangements with the nurses to overlook the fact I was there, since it was the night of our anniversary. We just acted like two teenagers who thought they were getting away with something, though we knew we really weren't. The night wasn't exactly what we planned, but we had fun, and it took her mind off cancer when I was there with her. We got very close to one another over this time.

Though we did not know it at the time, we were taking our last adventure away from home. Over her birthday in October, Lois wanted to see the pandas at the Washington zoo. It was a time when the October weather blew a fair wind and cool temperatures as we arrived in Washington the night before. Lois made arrangements for a hotel and a place to park in the congested Washington area before we left. When we arrived at the hotel, Lois was exhausted.

We went to sleep almost immediately. Though I was awake by nine o'clock the following morning, Lois was so tired she could not wake up until one o'clock in the afternoon. The zoo closed at five o'clock. I woke her so we could see the pandas. She got ready as quickly as she could. We took a cab and arrived at the zoo by three o'clock.

The cold air really affected her. She needed to sit and rest several times to catch her breath as we made our way into the park.

Lois really wanted to see the pandas, and her resolve to get there made it possible. I found an attendant and asked for the shortest way to the pandas, then went back and had Lois lean against me. I put my arm around her and guided her to where the pandas stayed. When Lois saw them, she fell in love with them immediately. There was a whole zoo beyond us, but she only wanted to spend her time with the pandas. We took lots of pictures, and with only an hour left to leave the park, we made our way to the front entrance. Halfway back, Lois became too short of breath to continue. She sat down on a bench, and I sat beside her. We didn't talk about her breathing, other than she needed to rest, but we knew the symptoms were not good. We still wanted to pretend everything was going to be all right.

We looked over the path leading to the streets outside the zoo and saw a small shop. We decided to go there before we left and find something to mark the occasion. It was a tradition we began when we were married. We looked for a Christmas ornament to place on our tree, something we did at every place we visited over the years. It was our way to commemorate a time and place we visited as we traveled and remembered the times we had together.

Inside the shop, we had thirty minutes before they closed for the day. Lois looked for ornaments with pandas but never found anything she liked. We did find a stuffed animal, a panda, which would suffice. We paid for the toy panda then made our way to the front of the zoo. Lois needed to rest two more times before we made it to the entrance. We caught a cab then returned to the hotel where Lois immediately went to sleep. I knew this would be our last trip anywhere.

We returned home, knowing our short respite from cancer was over. It was time to rejoin the battle again. I took the week off to take her to her appointments, since she was too weak and exhausted to drive herself. Tumor markers taken on October 13, before her appointment with the pulmonologist, revealed a treacherous level of 1,644. The only answer to the rising numbers was cancer invaded her right lung. Studies from earlier in the year suggested the same finding. A chest x-ray, recommended by the pulmonologist, showed fluid pressing on all sides of the right lung, collapsing it to only one-third of its capacity. It was the pulmonologist's recommendation to do "thoracentesis" as soon as possible. Lois agreed to have the procedure on October 20, 2009. Almost 250 cc (or about half a pint) of fluid was extracted from the floor of the right lung.

Lois told me she felt better immediately after the procedure. She was short of breath many weeks preceding this procedure, and removing the fluid improved both her breathing and her energy levels. She returned to work on October 16 and was working full-time up to the Friday before the procedure, and then every day afterward while undergoing treatments, tests, and chemotherapy. Her oncologist continued to be concerned about possible brain metastasis, recommending Lois get both a PET scan and CT scan to rule out this condition. Again, the results showed no involvement in that area. By the time the next tumor markers were done in November, they dropped slightly to 1,453.

In early November, Lois received a letter from the Linda Creed Foundation in Philadelphia. The letter stated their board of directors had chosen to award her the 2009 Elaine M. Ominsky PhD Humanitarian Award. Lois's work in advocacy and in hospice care was inspirational. They were also recognizing Lois's struggles to obtain her master's degree while undergoing treatment for metastatic breast cancer. The event would occur on December 5, 2009. Lois's story was out there, and people recognized the advances her advocacy made over the years she fought for breast cancer patients. She told me, "Sick or not, we are going." I took her at her word. Lois received one prestigious award in May, and this award was an even bigger, more-prestigious award. I was very proud of her but had concerns she would not tolerate the journey to Philadelphia to receive it.

It turned out Lois was more than ready to make the journey to Philadelphia for her award on December 5. We decided to have an overnight stay at a hotel near the location of the awards ceremony. Lois had not driven our new car, which had six forward gears and a lot of power. We bought the car over the summer when my old car had too many problems to fix. Lois was so nauseated at the time I searched for a new car that she only came along once to see the one we bought. Without seeing any other cars, she told me she wanted this one. Now, she had the chance to try it out. Lois always had a problem with "car sickness," which extended back to her childhood.

The problem persisted into her adulthood but overcame it when she was the one driving the car. Nausea was always a problem when she was a passenger.

So on the night of December 4, Lois got into our new car and drove us to Philadelphia. Lois always enjoyed driving, and this night was no exception. We drove to the turnpike and headed east to Philadelphia. It was after ten o'clock, and the traffic was light. Lois had to try all the new devices in the car like the navigation unit, the stereo, and the cruise controls. She was delighted by the smooth easy feel of the car as opposed to the heavier large SUV she drove every day to work.

We came to a stretch in the road uninhabited by any vehicles. She looked to me with a mischievous grin and asked, "Can I let it out?"

When she asked, I knew she had the car moving about seventy miles an hour most of the way. The car wasn't even slightly stressed, so I told her, "As long as you're not having problems keeping the car on the road."

She looked over with one of her peevish grins and told me, "This car is fun to drive. I'm going to see what it can do." That's when she slowly pushed the accelerator a little more. The car flew like it was gliding on air. I could not see the speedometer unless I leaned in her direction. So while I never saw how fast we were going, I suspected we were traveling about ninety, and the car still hadn't kicked into sixth gear. Lois's smile gleamed from ear to ear as she said, "Hey, I made it to 110, and there's still more left in it."

"What?" I asked, alarmed at what she told me. "I think you better slow down a bit before we get to any curves in the road or end up in traffic."

That's when she pouted and told me, "Come on, this is fun. Besides, we'll be in Philadelphia in no time."

"Yeah, but I think we would be better off without a huge fine for speeding or ending up in a ditch some place," I told her, speaking as calmly as I could.

"You're no fun," she told me, as she left off the accelerator. "Okay, I'll try to keep to the speed limit," she told me with feigned resignation then added, "I think I can get us there in about an hour even keeping to the speed limit."

"That should put us there about eleven thirty," I calculated. "That's not bad, considering our late start."

We arrived at the hotel at a quarter past eleven. We were in our room just a little after midnight. Lois washed up and went to bed, falling asleep almost immediately. Her little adventure of driving to Philadelphia in our new car was over. Some of the old Lois reappeared on the drive here. It made me smile to know the girl I loved and knew still existed in the ravaged body that now slept beside me. Exhausted by her own admission, she was still alive and vital.

I awoke the next morning to a ringing phone, our prearranged wake up call. I tried to wake Lois, but she just smiled, rolled over, and told me to get ready. She wanted to get another half-hour sleep before she got up. It took about thirty minutes to get ready. When I went to wake her, she was still groggy and asked for a cup of coffee to help her wake up. She finally got out of bed and went into the shower. I called into her and told her I was going downstairs to see what I could find. I returned to the room with two cups of hot coffee, only to find her still in the steaming shower. I yelled in, telling her, "You better get done. We have about an hour and a half before we have to be there . . . and we still have to walk two blocks."

"Don't worry about me," she chided. "I'll be ready in plenty of time. Did you get my coffee?"

"Yeah, and I brought some pastries for you too," I said, thinking she would like something to eat. After I replied, I thought back over the past four months of nausea, vomiting, essential dehydration, and pain she experienced and wondered how she managed to seem so normal, like none of it ever happened. Her life was the life of hope. She never believed looking behind her would accomplish anything. Yet I looked behind at these past four months and tried to be blind to the obvious. Lois would not be with us much longer.

Lois came out of the shower with cramping over the right side of her chest. She dried off quickly and crawled back under the covers in the bed and tried to get warm. "'Can you put your hands on my chest?" she asked, as I watched pain mist up in her eyes.

"Sure . . . I'll warm up my hands so I don't make the cramping worse." I went into the bathroom and ran warm water over my hands so they would be warm enough to touch her. I went back and put my hands on her arm to let her feel if they were warm enough to touch her right chest wall where the cramping already curled her bottom three ribs.

"That's good . . ." she told me. "Go ahead."

When I put my hands on the right side of her chest, I found the lower three ribs turned up like a ridge. As I laid my hands on the site, the ribs flattened down as I felt the muscles twisting settle and then relax under the light pressure I kept there. When the area flattened, Lois told me to get her clothes. She stayed under the blankets and put on as many of her clothes under the covers that she could.

"Well, this is certainly a new way of getting dressed," I said, shaking my head and smiling at her.

"Shut up." She laughed back. "This isn't funny." She giggled.

She finally crawled from under the covers and finished getting dressed. I said, "Better dress warmly. It's cold outside."

She dressed in gray corduroys, a long-sleeve shirt, and a warm blue blazer over it all. When she was finished, she asked, "How do I look?"

"Pretty good," I told her, considering all she went through to get ready this morning. I looked at the time and saw we had about a half hour to get there. It was only two city blocks, but it was cold, and Lois was already cramping up just getting out of bed. The cold air on her could cause her chest to spasm again if I wasn't careful with her in the cool December air. She drank her cup of coffee and had a part of the Danish I brought for her. I didn't want to rush, but I looked at the time and said, "We better get started."

We made our way to the Crystal Tea Room in Philadelphia where the program was being held. The program started without a hitch, and before long, Lois was called to the podium. She delivered a speech before an audience of almost 150 people, the elite of Philadelphia, with grace and good humor. Her award was a beautiful sculpture of two women mounted atop a heavy slab of hard wood. The award weighed about twenty pounds, much too heavy for a woman of only 120 pounds with spine metastasis to carry off the stage. One of the presenters asked me to help carry the award for her to our table. Lois was very proud and appreciative to be chosen to receive this award. It was one of her proudest achievements, and I was grateful she was strong enough to make the journey to get her here.

On the way home, Lois drove out of Philadelphia but tired out and stopped at the King of Prussia shopping mall. She just wanted to rest, then walk around the mall for a while. For a few minutes, we remained inside the car with the heater running, allowing her to rest. Eventually, when she felt strong enough to make her way into the stores, we exited the car. We made it halfway to the entrance when she stopped and told me, "I don't think I can make it. Let's go back to the car. You can drive."

I helped her back to the car and put her into the passenger seat. "What's wrong? Are you feeling sick?" I asked, concerned the drive out of Philadelphia and the movement from walking made her nauseated. If she needed the nausea medications we brought with us, I was ready to get it before she couldn't get it down.

"No, I'm just too short of breath to keep going. I need to rest."

"I figured you had to be feeling pretty bad. You never pass up a chance to go shopping," I told her with a smile.

"Come on," she laughed, "I just saved you a lot of money."

I started the car and made our way home. Lois was asleep fifteen minutes after we left the parking lot. She stayed asleep for the two-hour journey back home. I woke her when we arrived at the house. I got the car door for her, and she bolted to the bathroom to vomit. Her old symptom of car sickness was back with a vengeance. She cried as each wave of nausea and vomiting hit her. When there was nothing left in her, the retching started. When she was able to settle down, I gave her an antiemetic, and she crawled back under the covers on our bed and went to sleep.

Lois made it to work the following Monday, telling her associates of the award given to her in Philadelphia over the weekend. Her friends at work encouraged her to share her good news with our local newspapers, which she did. However, her small victory was short lived when Lois was readmitted to the hospital on December 16. In spite of her being on a subcutaneous injection for anticoagulation, she found a painful spot in her left leg, which turned out to be another blood clot. The stay was short, but again, Lois had to take off from work at the end of the year. After the clot was treated, Lois was sent to a vascular surgeon with the intention of getting the troublesome vein lasered so it could not happen again. However, when the vascular surgeon realized Lois was on chemotherapy for breast cancer, no studies or no recommendations would ever convince him to do such a procedure. His recommendation was to increase the dose of the anticoagulant and remain on it the rest of her life.

In the meantime, Lois's oncologist changed the chemotherapy protocols, with the first dose given before Lois was hospitalized for the recurring blood clot. The labs drawn on December 18, while hospitalized, were done to evaluate her clotting factors, her overall blood count, and the inevitable tumor markers to evaluate the new chemotherapy agent. When the results returned, the tumor markers showed an exceedingly optimistic result of 881. They were almost cut in half from the previous result. It was perhaps the best Christmas present either Lois or I could have hoped for. It meant, finally, there was still a chemotherapy agent out there that could turn this situation around.

There was no December newsletter. Lois was assaulted on all fronts trying to find a way to save her own life and did not have the time to write one. The year ended with guarded optimism. There was pain, shortness of breath, nausea, vomiting, repetitive episodes of dehydration, moderate to severe constipation, and a clotting mechanism in place causing spontaneous clots. There were too many problems with no real solutions to fix them all. Though Lois and I felt a little better about the prognosis, we both believed our time together would soon be over no matter what the future held and whatever future remained.

Journeys of the Heart

Tell me about your journeys . . .

I sit beneath the Poet's Tree, in the dream within a dream, waiting for answers that never come. I have known the answers for some time as they stare at me in flashes of reflected glass, follow me in the mirrors of my life, and watch me in the polished surfaces of the tables and counters I walk by . . . I don't wish to hear their council. My wife, Lois, is nearing the end of her life, and I can't bear it. Escaping here to finish the journey with Timothy gives me a strange solace. The feelings I have for my wife, Timothy shares with his Catherine. We are brothers and sad travelers in the journeys of the heart.

Are we preaching to the dust? Each day we have with our loved ones is a gift, not a right. We need to treat each day, each moment, and each pondering breath as more precious than the all the sad jewelry residing in the caches of our armoires.

I have seen the devil . . . and he is dancing. Yet it is I who has written the song he dances to, tormenting me with his gesturing. Though he dances to the music I sing, my song may still hold the power over my fate and Timothy's.

Timothy looked through the broken stone doorway beyond the room. The passages beyond the stone chamber were just as Timmerloo described them. Timothy hesitated, feeling cynical about his choice to follow the path a ghost had shown him. Somehow, he needed to continue and find a way to save his beloved Catherine no matter how impossible the journey might become. How long did he have? Had she placed her lifestone in the wall, or had the murderous orbs overrun the villages, making it impossible to get to the breach? He needed to look for the markings Timmerloo spoke of. Resigned to *following the instructions that would reveal the abandoned village lost in these mountains, Timothy moved from the sheltered stone chamber to embark on the journey the path directed beyond its sturdy walls.*

The air was getting colder, and Timothy pulled a heavy coat from inside the collected parcels on his back. Flakes of white surrounded him like butterflies, landing on the sharp black rocks. "I must hurry, or I'll miss the markings Timmerloo spoke of." He walked quickly, disturbing the new fallen snow with every footstep. Every sense was alight with cautious overtures, observing the passes as he moved from one sheltered corridor to the next. Eventually, the crossing that Timmerloo told him would be there revealed itself when he scurried past a large dislodged rock on the path.

The falling snow covered the telltale footprints of his journey, leaving the trails he ventured covered in his wake. At the crossroads, he carefully brushed away the accumulating snow, looking for the stone-formed markings Timmerloo said he made here. Instead of an arrow, Timothy found scattered stones in the crossing, victims of the inclement weather, winds, and torrents of rain afflicting this mountainous terrain. It was then he remembered what Timmerloo said at the time he encountered this crossing. He said he was looking for a passage off the top of the mountain. It meant he would have chosen a way that appeared to move downward. Timothy dusted the accumulating snow off the pile of stones and found most of the dislodged stones sat to the passage to the left of his location. He looked into the sky where the snowflakes floated on a light breeze like a whitened veil and asked aloud, "Is this the way, Timmerloo? Is this the path you have chosen for me to follow?" He expected no answers, and no answers came. He sighed while he watched the snow fashioning itself in deep swells then said, "This could be turning into a blizzard, Timmerloo. I should find shelter."

Timothy moved into the passage leading to the left. He walked with intentions of finding a place to get out of the winter storm approaching him on all sides. He walked with caution and trepidation, not knowing if this path was the one Timmerloo had taken, not sure he would eventually find the abandoned village at the end of his travels. The snow obscured his sight, and the black rocks surrounding him were so homogenous, he was unable to calculate if he was still on the right path. Timothy pressed on, thinking the next landmark was the waterfall near the lost village. He traveled through the black rocky corridor dusted in a powdery white, the snow filling the lines and breaks in the rocks. Any sound the mountain could have made was muffled inside this mountain passage. It was this silent world that Timothy walked, keeping vigil and watching for the signs Timmerloo had given him.

He traveled almost three parcels through the rugged passage then leaned against a straight-standing rock to rest. Panting, laboring for breath in the frigid air, he leaned against the stone that seemed to watch him; he saw the snow settling on the ominous black stones. As the snow dusted his face and clothing, he observed something Timmerloo would not have found on his journey through this place.

The falling snow salted the cracks and breaks, exaggerating the lines in pale shapes like a faded tapestry. This tapestry, written in the stones, revealed a hidden story. Forgotten hands, and powers that were merely legends to the people of the villages forged the illustrations he saw there. What once looked like cracks and breaks bared themselves in a kind of map and history of the lost village of Winterland. The snow-filled etchings and breaks in the black stones became pictures and diagrams. They revealed another passage into the obscure village, a passage falsely masked by impenetrable stones, truth besieged in lies by the vast passage of time.

At first, Timothy regarded the strange phenomenon as some trickery brought on by weariness and distorted vision; yet as he continued to move slowly through the stones, turning first one way and then the other, he discovered the breaks in the crannied rocks were more than simple flaws. Within the strange snow-filled etchings was a map showing a passage into the lost village of the Ancients. Glyphs depicting eyes peered down from the uppermost ridges with lines that resembled waves of water, and still others showing parts of a tree pointing to an undiscovered path inside a wall of stone.

Timothy stopped and gasped in amazement of his discovery, as the falling snow unveiled secrets hidden for a century of centuries. He considered exploring this new discovery, but hesitated, remembering Timmerloo suggested a way into the lost village, which ultimately failed him. The snow was falling harder, forcing Timothy to decide quickly. Still, he had to consider Catherine in all this. If he lost his way or died trying to find a way into the village, her fate would be sealed along with his own. Timmerloo did not make it to the village, so there had to be another way . . . perhaps this was it. He had to try. Somewhere in the recesses of his memory, he remembered the dream of standing before a stone trying to read indecipherable writing in a winter's storm. Was it just a dream or a warning?

He looked again where the branch of a tree, outlined in white, seemed to point to a wall of broken stones covering a passage. The way looked rugged but not impossible. "Timmerloo never knew about this . . ." Timothy said aloud, though no one would hear. "The path he spoke of never got him any closer to Winterland. He died trying to get there. This is might be the only passage left by the Ancients to get inside the village."

Timothy knew the only way to save Catherine was to get to the heart of this mysterious lost village. Everything he accomplished and everything he conquered led him here, this time out of time. "This must be the right thing to do," Timothy said, trying to validate his decision to follow this new passage. He looked toward the road Timmerloo said would lead him to the perimeters of the lost village, then to the rugged passage littered with broken stones. Knowing Timmerloo's ghost never found an entrance into the valley of the village infected Timothy to choose the way the glyphs directed him. From this point, everything Timmerloo told him about the lost village would be useless. He was completely on his own. It was a terrible leap of faith to hang his hopes on, but he had to try. Even if he made it into the lost village, there was no certainty of what he would find there. It might be an assorted collection of old ruins, nothing more. He knew if there was a chance, any chance at all, he would have to take the passage where the glyphs directed him.

He stood in the falling snow, studying the isolated glyph whose shape was like a broken tree. Its mysterious branches, hewn into the rock walls, still pointed the way into a passage of stone, disappearing into a cleft of rock just beyond his sight. The wind was picking up. He would have to find shelter somewhere along the way. The storm was worsening. The light butterfly snowflakes no longer fluttered lightly to the ground. They bounded in straight flight, bashing themselves to pieces on the rocks. It was difficult to see the surroundings, and Timothy realized his every footstep could end in tragedy. He looked at the path Timmerloo instructed, then to the rock-strewn rubble that might be a path and made his choice.

When he made his way to the rugged pass, a kind of peace entered his heart. Somehow, knowing this might be a true passage into the old world village gave him courage to move on. He climbed over the pile of broken stones and found a smooth-cut passage on the other side. It looked narrow and was cleverly obscured by the rise of stones bordering it on either side. There was barely enough space to pull his heavy burden of parcels through the narrow cleft of stone. As he pressed on, the passage opened into a wide road where walls of rock ran straight up, hiding their uppermost borders in a flurry of snowflakes. The walls he could see were covered with writings and glyphs, the like of which Timothy had never seen.

Timothy continued observing his surroundings, his attention on the mysterious glyphs and indecipherable writings, which grew ever more incessant as every step took him farther to the north. There was evidence written in the stones of a very sophisticated culture, not seen by the villages in centuries. Every turn in the passage was met with ever increasing glyphs, inscribed pictures of machines with gear workings, and strange indiscernible devices that emitted beams of light cut in the stone walls as reliefs. The stone cutters who did this were attempting to illustrate lessons, forgotten like the seekers who once taught them. Timothy was certain no villager ever saw a passage like this one as he continued to struggle through the rising snow.

Timothy walked until the roadlike passage opened to a flat terrace where an enormous stone hand kept vigil, extending from the ground to the sky. The terrace, closed on all sides by sheer rock walls, enhanced the stone hand, making it the only focus. The structure was at least a parcel high and appeared to be littered by embedded glyphs and writings he didn't understand. The meaning of the extended stone hand eluded him, while he cautiously approached the structure, considering what the stone hand was trying to tell him. He circled the structure, trying to find another passage away from this confined plateau. When he returned to his point of origin, he was frustrated and afraid. Was it a warning . . . telling him to go no farther? Or was it really saying, this is where you need to stop and ponder the meaning of what is there before you? Timothy looked around the flat open spaces around the structure and saw a deep recess broken into the palm of the stone hand where he could get out of the snow and think what to do next. As he moved closer to the deep fissure in the blemished stone hand, the ground beneath him shifted, knocking him into the snowy ground. He pushed his face out of the snow and looked about, alarmed by the deep resonating sounds coming from below him. Did he set off a trap while walking around the perimeter of the gigantic stone hand?

He watched in disbelief as the gigantic stone hand slowly twisted, then descended in a cacophony of thunderous spasms into the ground beside him. The chasm, formed in the wake of its descent, revealed a spiral stairway winding into the darkness as the stone effigy plummeted into the abyss, leaving just the fingertips of the stone hand above the snow-covered ground. Timothy peered into the vast hole. Seeing the clandestine staircase neatly inscribed in deep angular cuts, traveling to a place beyond his sight, brought questions to his mind. Was this some kind of trap left behind by the Ancients to keep wayfarers away from Winterland's threshold or was it the way into it?

Timothy sat there, knowing to go back would condemn Catherine to death and going forward might destroy them . . . or save them. A gust of wind whipped around him, blowing freezing white crystals into his face as snow started drifting into the chasm, dusting the steps with every hollow breath. Timothy was expecting something else to happen as he watched the snow filling the deep chasm. When nothing happened, he went to the top of the spiral staircase and started down.

The uppermost stairs were slippery with the new-fallen snow as he made his descent. He noticed that the air became warmer as he moved increasingly downward. His eyes adjusted to the darkness as he neared the bottom of the staircase. The light from the snowy sky still managed to find its way to the bottom of the enormous shaft. At the bottom of the shaft, he vaguely surveyed dark engravings he could not determine in this light. Without warning, a thunderous whelp screamed, echoing in the hollow rocks. The huge stone hand started ascending back to its original position, closing Timothy in the dark subterranean room. Before the stone effigy blocked off the light, Timothy managed to get one lantern out of its wrappings and lighted the wick. The stone slab seated itself into the ceiling with a loud clap . . . then all was darkness . . . all was silence.

Timothy opened the visor on the lantern and allowed a wide beam of light to escape. He found another stone chamber filled with writings and reliefs insinuating a way to an entrance out of the chamber. The forms of the Four Winds were carved into the walls with each one's simulated breaths etched like waves on the walls, all leading to some point in a wall that remained obscure in the darkness. Timothy moved forward to that dark place where he suspected the engravings were leading him. The light from the lantern cast warm yellow rays on the black walls that swallowed them, giving him the illusion he wasn't moving. The vast stone chamber where the gigantic stone hand deposited him seemed so incalculable that time and motion seemed to remain still. At his feet, he found stone blocks fitted together, comprising a mosaic that could not be seen in its totality with the light provided by the lantern.

As he moved across the fitted stone floor, he could feel vibrations rising against his feet. "What kind of place is this?" Timothy asked aloud. The dimensions and acoustical qualities of the chamber twisted his statement into a hundred echoes. The sound of his voice became a cacophony, heightening to an almost discernible language, and then dissembled into fractured words before fading into unnerving silence.

"This is a place of ghosts . . ." Timothy said, his voice hushed, trying to keep the echoes from resurrecting.

"Where will this place lead me? What is at the end of this journey?" he asked in silence, as each footstep endured ever harder vibrations on the soles of his feet. He realized it was becoming more difficult to keep his footing as the vibrations grew in intensity. He continued moving where the breath of the Four Winds directed him. Still, no entrance was revealed. He stopped then moved his lantern to the left, then right, and then raised it as high as he could reach,

trying to get a glimpse of the mythical entrance. Just to the right of his position, Timothy caught a reflection of something. He moved to the right, barely capable of standing, falling down twice, before he discovered a giant face engraved in the side of a straight wall. The face depicted a screaming man, mouth agape, as if he was in constant pain, almost an illustration of the irony of his predicament. The opening, created by mouth of the screaming effigy, was the entrance from this vast chamber.

"I must get out of this place," Timothy whispered to himself, hoping he would not hear the resonating echo of his voice again. However, the amazing acoustical qualities of the vast stone room picked up his voice and shattered it into a hundred voices. "Get out . . . get out . . ." the voices said, tripping and leaping in resonating echoes over the silent stones. The vibrations coming from the floor were intolerable, causing his legs to buckle up in pain. He had to get to the opening leading out of this ancient stone chamber.

Timothy struggled to reach the opening, crawling on his hands and knees, unable to stand on the unstable floor, and quickly climbed inside the yawning stone mouth. The vibrations stopped ripping at his feet as soon as he was securely inside the stone effigy. As he looked over his shoulder at the floor behind him, he saw the tiles lining the floor in constant motion. He turned to the way before him and saw a dark tunnel besieged by cobwebs and decaying debris. By the light emitted by his lantern's limited penumbra, he realized centuries had passed since anyone had come this way. Timothy tore off a piece of his shirt, found the flask of oil he used to refill his lantern, and soaked it down. He found a vagrant root that survived the journey to these silent stone walls and broke a piece big enough to make a makeshift torch. When he finished tying the soaked material to the end, he lighted the oil-soaked cloth.

With a lantern to light his way and a makeshift torch to burn away the cobwebs, Timothy started into the unknown darkness, both inviting and terrible. As he moved through the passage, he noted etchings and depictions of women in all states of undress . . . with roses scattered at their feet. A closer examination of the walls showed women depicted with only one breast, a scar inscribed where one had once been. Timothy looked on the etchings and carvings in horror, thinking, What kind of barbaric people lived here, illustrating these crude acts upon women? These creators of anguish certainly had to be confined to the North Wind's frozen mountains, left there to wander in the frozen wastelands for eternity, cursing their misfortune to have lived at all. *Timothy moved on, observing the subsequent depictions with ever more grievous, disturbing images.* What horrors did the Ancients inflict on the women who lived and died here? To what possible purpose did they inflict this agony? *he thought, hurrying to get past these stone reliefs as quickly as possible.*

The piercing outposts of the lantern's light searched over rough stone etchings and realistic reliefs carved into the walls in every direction. Each depiction revealed more and more atrocities to Timothy. As Timothy progressed through the darkness, he found the narrow stone path forge into a towering hall. The pathway remained a narrow walkway, while the walls towered to sometimes a parcel high above him, curving slightly like a bowl as they grew above him. Yet even here, the walls were covered by carvings of people being tortured by other men in masks and cloaks, holding knives and despicable sharp instruments that could only be used to inflict the most unspeakable pain. He saw a man depicted with no legs sitting in a chair with wheels. Dozens of other carvings showed people being stabbed by needles, being sewn into with needles and thread, bottles of beads, or possible small pebbles, being swallowed by the effigies of humans depicted on the walls, and people tying cloth to people who had their flesh torn away. Timothy never saw anything like it . . . the horrific tragedy and torments the Ancients put upon their people was unconscionable. He was glad he lived in the time of the villages. This was a place where they tortured their women and children. "There must have been madness here. But what happened to all of them?" *Timothy asked himself.*

The path flattened out, widening into a manicured road where it led Timothy through a garden of stone carvings and statues. Some creations were as small as his hand, while others were so gigantic, they reached from floor to ceiling. Some humanlike statues bent beneath the stone ceiling as though structured to keep a roof from collapsing. As a conglomerate composition, the gathering of statues and stone workings depicted a story of horrific suffering, whose outcomes were never answered in the creations that surrounded him. Timothy hurried through these structures, quickly trying to get the images behind him. "Surely these were the works of the Ancients. But what were they trying to tell me? Where did this road lead?" he asked himself.

Timothy felt exhausted; the strange clandestine road was filled with paralyzing revelations. The mystery of why men would depict such horrors in statues and reliefs evaded him. Though the underground road was easy to travel in comparison to the snow and ice on the mountains above him, he needed to rest soon. He was hoping to continue, but hunger and exhaustion won the battle. He finally rested beneath one of the large statues near the road.

He looked back at the way he came, where the cobwebs and debris cluttered his way for almost half a parcel, then opened like a great cavern littered with sconces, reliefs, statues, and strange writings depicting all kinds of human suffering. He looked before him as far as the lantern's light would allow and saw even more of the same tragedies depicted in the carvings of stone. He felt abandoned and frustrated by the long journey that led him here. "Even now, Catherine may still be alive if she hasn't placed her stone into the great wall," Timothy prayed. He turned to the heavy satchels he carried, rifling through for some food and water. For now, he would eat and rest, as he listened to the abject silence that walked behind him.

As he rested, listening to his breathing, another sound wavered in the distance. The sound was subtle, so low and distant, he held his breath listening for it. It was no surprise he missed hearing the low and constant sound. It was the unmistakable sound of moving water.

Though he had not rested, Timothy stood up, held his breath, and listened to the distant sound that came from in front of him. He knew a waterfall was another landmark near the entrance of the abandoned village. He holstered his satchels and hurried toward the distant sound. What will I find there? *Timothy thought, the noise becoming incessantly clearer as the sound of thundering water drowned the echoes of his every footstep.*

The sound was a soothing melody. It meant he was on the right track, getting closer to the purpose he set for himself. In his excitement, Timothy ran, dropping most of his belongings on the road. The sound, discovered like a faint whisper, soon reverberated in thunderous peals, echoing against the hollow walls of the man-made cavern. Timothy's footsteps followed the carved road as it wandered through the strange cavern formations, looking for a way to continue when he made it to the end. However, the edge of the stone road fell away into an opening where the waterfall had frozen over like a crystalline window, obstructing the landscape of what lay beyond it. Still, beneath this frozen spectacle, the waterfall continued to purge itself with thousands of gallons of freezing water flowing freely from some source above.

He looked around and saw no stairs, no further passages, and no way out other than the way behind the frozen waterfall. Timothy went to one side of the open wall and found an ancient stairway carved into the stone and washed out by the incessant falling water. It was here. There must have been a way down centuries ago, *Timothy thought to himself.*

"How will I get down now?" Timothy yelled, frustrated at the uneven prospect before him. "There must be another way out of this tomb," he said, thinking he must stay calm, using reason to guide him, not fear. He walked to the opposite side of the opening, hoping to find another staircase undamaged by the relentless waters. He found nothing that suggested there was ever anything more than the broken stones that confronted him on all sides. The only way down was through the freezing waters that led to some unseen passage, washed away long before he was ever born. He tried to reassure himself something awaited him at the bottom of the watery ravine, but the thought of steeling himself against the frigid water filled him with caution. It is Catherine who is depending on me now. I have to make a decision and keep moving. If she was able to place her stone into the Great Wall, she will only have three days until none of this will matter. I cannot falter here anymore. There must be answers and actions I will discover whenever I find the end of this puzzle, *Timothy thought to himself.*

Timothy pulled the remaining satchels from his back and removed a length of rope along with metal links and clasps used for climbing. He found a formation of stone where he secured the rope as close to the raging water as he could. He looked into the thunderous water dropping from above and then threw the loose end of the rope into it. He watched the powerful current yank the rope taut as the water swept by the cavern's open wall. There was no other way down. Timothy looked at the worn steps eroded by time and the elements, and decided to make his way from there. Whatever mystery hid beyond these worn steps would only be found by navigating these treacherous waters. It was not only his life that concerned him but Catherine's as well. For all he knew, he might already be too late to help her. Still, if there was a chance, he wanted to make some attempt to save her and a part of himself in the process.

He put one hand on the rope, pulling it in front of him and fixing a metal clasp he would use to lower himself into the icy water. He was afraid of dying . . . he was never confronted by a decision like this in his life. He looked for comfort in the cold stones and found none, as he pulled a pair of leather gloves over his hands. It was only in his thoughts of Catherine where he found the strength and resolve to move on. Resigned to his perilous task, Timothy looked back into the darkened stone chamber and said, "Guide me Four Winds; I accept your guidance and your judgments. Take me to whatever end you have for me. Take me back to my beloved Catherine. Blow my restless spirit upon your breath. Tell my family, I love them."

Timothy put a gloved hand on the descending rope, feeling the intense pull the waterfall exerted upon it, and left the safety of the stone ledge. He lowered himself an arm's length; the frigid water numbed his face. The waterfall echoed around him in a thunderous roar, drowning all sounds that could have been, but Timothy knew the only sounds existing here were his heartbeat and the sound of his terrified breathing. He lowered himself a few arm's lengths until he could no longer see the stone ledge he abandoned. The cold water paralyzed his hands and feet. He knew he had to get away from the freezing water before he lost feeling in his hands.

Timothy was suspended just above a place where there was no choice but to pass through the waterfall. An outcropping of rock forced him outward and into the raging water. He had no choice but to make the descent through it. Catherine was depending on him to *find the end of this quest. He had to go on. He would not abandon her even if it meant dying for her.*

Though all the warmth and feeling was gone from his arms and legs, Timothy lowered himself into the freezing water. He cried out in pain as the forceful current swallowed him. Water caught in his leather boots, filling them with cold liquid fire. His last conscious thought, screaming to the Four Winds to protect him, evaporated as he slid uncontrollably into the watery darkness.

In the darkness, he dreamed again of the faceless bride as she stood standing on the sunset-colored ridge beckoning him to follow. He tried to move, but a heavy veil of shadows fell over him, blinding whatever visions and memories existing in his world in a miasma of blackness.

Deep beneath the lost village, where the frozen river was forced underground, in the place where an enormous waterwheel turned for centuries, a glow of light grew inside the enormous chamber housing the mechanizations below, ebbing with a faint light. From another direction, another glowing light pulsed, and the chamber grew brighter still. Soon a hundred lights pulsed awake, bathing the chamber in a pinkish light. A sound emerged, like a low whisper. It was almost lost within the noise of the smooth mechanical rotation of the enormous wheel turning in the flow of the underground river, and spoke.

"What has happened?" a voice sounded from a stone ledge near the water wheel.

"A visitor, I presume," another voice answered.

"But we are cut off from the villages . . . No one can get to us . . . We are best to be forgotten," a discordant voice stated in another part of the chamber.

"Where is this visitor?" chimed another voice.

A green light glowed near the edge of the river where it entered the circular domed chamber. A voice cited, "I have found him. He is not breathing."

"He cannot be dead . . . ," another voice from another part of the chamber echoed. "This visitor has awakened us."

The voice coming from the direction of the green light spoke, "He is not dead, but he soon might be if we don't get him warm and out of the water. I will need some assistance."

Timothy was dreaming. He was running toward Catherine's laughter. He could not see her but knew she was close. He called to her, asking her to stop running away from him; but when she laughed and called his name, he knew she was getting farther away. "Let me catch up to you," he pleaded with her.

"Can't keep up? Can't you find me, Timothy?" Catherine's voice taunted, laughing and telling Timothy to hurry.

"I'm trying, my love, but I can't see you. Where are you?" he cried out, beginning to worry she would be lost in the darkening backwoods forest.

The light of the sunset was fading, giving way to shadowy blues and mysterious purples. The evening mists formed thick clouds at his feet as her laughter drifted toward him once again. "Catherine, please stop. It's getting dark, and we need to go home now."

"Come on, Timothy. You can find me if you want to." She laughed, as the sound drifted away on the evening mists.

"You're getting too far away . . ." Timothy shouted after her.

"I'm only as far away as your dreams, dear one," Catherine said, her voice drifting from the top of a ridge where the last rays of sunset still survived, waiting for the suffocating presence of the pressing darkness to take them.

"But I'm trying to come to you . . . Will you not wait? I can't see you. I don't know where you are. Please wait. Call . . . and I will

follow your voice. It's getting too dark to find you," Timothy pleaded with her.

"I am with you always . . . You can find me at your sunset. I will be as close as there and as far away as here." Catherine's voice faded away when the light of the last penumbra of sunlight disappeared into the waiting darkness.

The darkness swallowed Timothy like a starving beast then heaved him up like a sickness upon a cold wet shoreline. From the lightless dream, he struggled to breath, only succeeding to heave up a burning lung full of water. With his lungs cleared, he choked on spit and saliva then breathed in the warm air in short rasping gasps.

From his semiconscious state, Timothy's awareness evolved. He was finally waking up. He realized he was no longer submerged in the icy waters of the river that swept through the abandoned village. His eyes burned as he rubbed them open to discover he was lying on a flat slab of stone, face down. Instead of the freezing air he had breathed, the air here was warm and dry. His clothing was gone, and he felt the summer heat penetrating his skin, warming him from the icy death he was certain must have happened to him. He had made it to the place where the Four Winds blew their eternal breath, breathing life into all things. He was in heaven. He lay on the stone tablet, basking in the sunset colors of pink and feeling too weak to turn himself over.

I have failed, Catherine, *he thought . . . grieving tears welled in his eyes.* I will see her here soon. I am now with the Four Winds, and she will be here with me before long . . . I am certain.

A voice came from inside his head, "You need to wake up, Timothy."

Timothy opened his eyes, still seeing the warm pink colors of the summer's sunset bathe over him. His throat was still raw and sour. For the first time, he understood he was still alive. Why would he be in the place where the Four Winds blew and still feel this sick and weak? Actually, why would he feel anything? He pushed himself off the flat rock with arms that felt too rubbery to support him. A new wave of nausea hit him, and he gagged, unable to bring anything up. "Where am I?" Timothy asked, choking on every word he could enunciate. When no answers were forthcoming, he twisted his head to the left and then to the right, still bent over with his back to the sunset sky warming his naked body. "This can't be real . . . It's winter when I fell into the water. Who took my clothes?" he asked, grateful but angry at the oppressive silence. With his strength returning with every raspy breath, warmed by the lingering pink hues of the setting sun, Timothy turned himself on his back and looked into the pink sky in horror.

The sky of pink hues was not sky but a dome of an enormous vault covered with glowing pink orbs. He let out a gasp, unable to form a scream. He looked furtively for a place to run, but he found the slab of stone he lay upon was sitting on top of a stone plateau atop a pinnacle of stone. He was certain he was going to die here. Yet as he watched, the orbs made no sign they would attack him. They remained constant, unmoving as a collective entity. Why did they put him here? What measure of torture and destruction did they intend for him?

Timothy sat up on the stone slab and dangled his feet over the side. He found his clothes on the polished stone plateau below the slab and quickly put them on. He felt violated, vulnerable, and exposed by his nakedness. When he was dressed, he looked for a way off the plateau. He was perhaps a full parcel above the cavernous stone floor where the river washed through the chamber. He stood, looking down in disbelief and wondering how he got up here. Who put him here, and why did they allow him to survive the icy river that certainly should have killed him?

Timothy walked most of the perimeter of the plateau, looking for a way down, when a familiar voice spoke from somewhere behind him. A green glow, unlike the light given off by the pink orbs, grew around him and bathed him in a verdant haze. "Do not be afraid, Timothy . . . You are safe among us."

"Timmerloo?" Timothy asked, with both surprise and utter disbelief. "But you can't be here . . . I found your lifestone on the table of the stone chamber." Timothy turned, not knowing what to expect,

and saw a single green orb floating before him. He prepared to run, knowing the treachery of the orbs he saw in his travels.

Then the orb spoke again, "It is I, Timothy . . . Timmerloo."

"It can't be . . ." Timothy said in disbelief, fearful this was a trick of some kind. Then collecting his wits, he turned back to the radiant orb and said, "If you are who you say, give me some sign that only Timmerloo would know."

The green orb hovered about an arm's length above the ground before him. When it spoke, the words seemed to be heard with his mind and not his ears. "We met at the Stone Lodge on a foggy, wet day. You asked me to show you the way to make your beloved Catherine immortal. We came to the mountains in a search for the truth, but I could no longer follow you in the form I had taken. You suggested I was a 'seeker,' and that much is true, but I had to bring you to this place in a way only you could have taken, or you wouldn't have been able to understand what I am to impart."

Timothy leaned against the stone slab where he had awakened. "Are you really Timmerloo? And if you are, how did you get this way?"

"Centuries ago, when we felt we could conquer everything, even death itself, the elders met and discussed a need to keep our base of knowledge intact. In a way, they found each of us could be saved from the future by creating the form of one of these orbs just before our physical body died. In that way, whatever knowledge, whatever life lessons we experienced, would be passed along and exist for all time."

"It looks like more of a prison than a way to be immortal. Is this what you have in store for Catherine?" Timothy asked skeptically.

"No . . ." the orb calling himself Timmerloo imparted. "The path to Catherine's immortality is different than the path I have taken."

The green orb glowed brightly then spoke, "Stay where you are. I can show you." The orb hovered for a moment and then floated to the edge of the plateau. It rooted itself into the fabric of the stone with sinuous red tendrils then rose another three arm's lengths into the air before ushering a silent command to the orbs lining the dome of the stone vault. Silently, each one fell away until the floor of the vault was covered with a teeming pink mass of light. The stone dome above them glistened with multicolored lights. Timothy remembered the great map room Amos showed him at Bridgedom, but this was massive. It was like looking at the night sky full of stars.

"Is this what I think it is?" Timothy asked, aware he was speaking to a green orb, not a human being. The bizarre situation made him feel uneasy; he weighed his words carefully when he spoke. When the ceiling of the stone vault cleared, and the locations of all the known and unknown villages were disclosed, a thin red line spread across the room. "Where are Stock, Glade, and the other villages?"

The green orb withdrew its tendrils from the stones and floated high toward the ceiling, traveling toward the areas Timothy had asked to see. It first landed on the glowing light that indicated the village of Stock and then moved on to the village of Glade.

"And the wall?" he asked, straining to see the thin red line.

The green orb floated to a faint red line that bisected the map and traced it in its glow. Where the red line had been broken at the village of Stock, it now showed continuity. The breach was secured. Catherine had placed her stone in the wall; the villages were safe. Though the thought that all his friends and relatives were safe, the news that Catherine had sacrificed herself to do this broke his heart. He felt unable to move forward. Was he out of time? Was all this done in vain? He looked up to where the green orb sat on the dome of the map room; a tear swelled in his eye. "How much time do I have left?"

The green orb floated to where he was standing and hovered beside him. It spoke, "Perhaps a day . . . maybe less."

"Will that be enough time? Will you show me what has to be done?" Timothy asked, not knowing what would be expected of him.

"There is a place you need to go. You must travel to the Great Tree . . ." the Timmerloo orb said.

"And how do I get there from this plateau? There does not seem to be any way off," Timothy protested.

"I see you have still not learned patience, have you?" the Timmerloo orb said dryly.

"I'm here provoking a ghost . . . Is that what you believe?" Timothy asked, feeling a little better with just the green orb in his company. Seeing the hoard of pink orbs crawling over the walls was disconcerting, he still felt that his life was in danger from these things. After all, the orbs released from the other side of the Great Wall destroyed every living thing they came in contact with. "What were these orbs? Why were they here?"

"You worry yourself without cause, Timothy. I and the others have no desire to end your life. In fact, they would do everything they could to preserve it, rather than take it."

Timothy was not convinced. These things murdered everything they touched. How could he trust them? He was certain he was going to be just another victim of their folly. He was prepared to fight and searched the empty plateau for some kind of weapon. He would not make it easy for them.

"You have to understand what really happened here to trust us," the Timmerloo orb said.

"I know what happened here . . . rape, murder, lies, deception, and slander that destroyed reputations and lives . . . all in the guise of bettering one person over another. According to the stories handed down over the centuries, at the time, only the most corrupt, diabolical people were allowed to be their leaders and dictated what was to happen to those they ruled. They either subjugated their opposition with lies or destroyed them by either raping or murdering their family members, sometimes both. Am I that far off?" Timothy asked defiantly. He was not going to abandon

his beliefs just to save his own life. Let the orbs do what they want to him. He would die with a clear conscience.

For a long time, the green orb, claiming to be the embodiment of Timmerloo, floated before Timothy with nothing to say. Timothy watched intently, thinking how easily it could summon the other orbs to destroy him. Timothy thought, Had he taken the discussion too far? Was the orb deciding to kill him like so many before him? *His father once told him, "You have to be afraid before you get the chance to meet courage." If what his father said was true, this was that opportunity, though he didn't feel very brave or courageous. This place was a harbor of death and ghosts. Any hope of saving Catherine sat in the balance of the entities that existed here. He needed to walk quietly, learn what he must, then move on. The thing posing for Timmerloo hadn't proven itself to him. When the chance to remove the cloak of deception presented itself, he would do so and show it he knew its deceit. This was, indeed, the Winterland of his disenchanted fears and his highest hopes. The green orb, whatever it was, betrayed him with the voice of Timmerloo and inflections of the man he once met. However, he knew Timmerloo was gone. Information given by the green orb could have been guessed, using the common knowledge of the land and village legends of Timmerloo. These orbs could easily create this version of the man to deceive him. But for what purpose?*

Without warning, the green orb grew ridges, then tendrils. The tendrils moved around the sphere then locked into locations at the top and bottom of the sphere. Timothy was afraid to watch and turned away, waiting for the tendrils to wrap around him and tear him to pieces much like the behavior he saw exhibited by the orbs he saw before this. A green glow of unimaginable intensity grew around him and then disappeared. Two lines of pink orbs made their way across the stone dome, intersecting at the apex of the vault. Their glow lighted the plateau. He waited for the green orb to kill him.

"Turn around and face me, Timothy," the Timmerloo thing said.

Before Timothy moved, he asked, "Is this how you like to see us die? You want me to face you to watch as I scream?" Timothy was defiant. He knew he was going to die . . . Why make it easy for these things?

"Turn around and see me . . . see me as your friend," it said. "Your fear is unfounded . . . I am here to guide you, not destroy you."

Timothy turned around to see his friend Timmerloo in full human form, clothed in green and black vestments. The orb was gone. The man returned, it seemed, from the grave. "You cannot be here," Timothy stammered, as he fought to keep himself upright, knocked about by fear and shock. He fell to his knees as Timmerloo held out his hand. At first, Timothy thought the hand before him would disappear like a whisper of smoke, but the hand that touched him was warm and solid. "You are real!" Timothy exclaimed in disbelief. "You are here."

"Of course I am. But such discussions must wait. There is much to tell and much to explain." Timmerloo studied the questions written on Timothy's face. "You want to know why these orbs are not intent on destroying you like the ones you've seen. Isn't that true?"

Timothy stared at the man standing before him in awe. How did he know this? He never told the green orb his thoughts. "Yes . . ." Timothy responded with skepticism and then with less sincerity, almost scoffing, "These orbs . . . they want to help, rather than destroy?"

"We saved your life. That should say something about us," Timmerloo said gently.

Timothy watched as Timmerloo walked slowly to the stone slab and sat down. He still didn't understand why the orbs didn't attack as he expected.

"We are not like them, Timothy," Timmerloo said when he looked at him.

"Then what are you, what are they?" Timothy asked, as he pointed to the stone ceiling covered by pink orbs.

"*Sit down beside me, Timothy. My story is tragic, magical, and full of sadness.*" Timmerloo watched as the young man slowly made his way to his side and sat beside him on the stone slab.

"*We do not have much time. You told me this yourself. Catherine is dying, and I have to get to whatever destination I must, and quickly,*" Timothy told him, aware any time he had to save Catherine was waning in the precious moments Timmerloo took to explain himself.

"*I will be quick. Yet you need an explanation if you are to trust us with this final journey.*" Timmerloo leaned his head back and left out a great sigh. "*As you suspected, we doomed our saviors and celebrated our atrocities. The ones most likely to destroy what was good and sane in our world were elevated to the positions of control and governance. Laws were made and enforced to cover up their cruelty, and absolution was given to those with the power to administrate further atrocities on the villages.*"

Timothy interrupted, "*But how did the orbs come to be?*"

Timmerloo looked over a shoulder to face him then explained, "*The orbs, the ones you are referring to, were created, like these.*" Timmerloo pointed to the ceiling where thousands of pink orbs hovered, creating a dome of pink light. "*The ones you see here are what is left of the permanent record of knowledge of the ages and the enlightenment of the future . . . whatever it may be. They will be here, waiting until someone who seeks the knowledge we have wants to learn it and use it for the betterment of their world. We are what is left of the 'seekers.'*"

"*These were people at one time?*" Timothy asked, unable to understand.

"*In a way, they were human, but our technology was so advanced and avaricious, they deemed it necessary to retain every bit of knowledge every 'true seeker' had. They found a way to retain their knowledge and embodied it as a living entity in these orbs.*"

"*So they are alive?*"

"In a way . . . their knowledge, feelings, and their judgments still exist. They remain here because they hope."

"Hope for what?" Timothy asked, puzzled by Timmerloo's sudden aversion of his eyes upon him.

Timmerloo paused for a moment. His face was a riddle of emotions, a tear sliding from his eye; it touched Timothy profoundly. When he looked up at Timothy again, the tear was gone but not the sadness. "We have been waiting for you. Sometimes you get the chance to change things. This is that chance to do something."

Timothy tried to understand what Timmerloo was telling him then averted his eyes to the massive stone ceiling where the pink orbs congregated. He turned back to Timmerloo and asked, "What of the other darker orbs? What is their purpose, what are they here for?"

Timmerlootookadeepbreaththenexhaled,tryingtokeepfocused on what he was telling Timothy. "Like you, we had dreams. But . . . we were arrogant . . . We believed we could control the elements of life and death. We believed we could control the Winds. We were successful, you see . . . in a way. But with all things, there were consequences to be paid for such arrogance, even though we believed we were working for the greater good of all. Things we never saw or ever considered happened, which we had no control over. In the end, we realized the Winds always had the final say."

Timothy, confused by Timmerloo's explanation, looked to him and asked, "Why do the purple orbs attack us? Why are they intent on our complete and utter destruction? We are not food to them. They destroy every living thing in their path and let it lay to rot. I don't understand. What are they?"

"They were our greatest discovery and our greatest fear. They are the pinnacle of our dreams and the darkest nightmare in our existence. We found a way to eliminate every disease that ever existed. Every sickness imaginable, cancer, diabetes, heart disease, hypertension, Parkinson's, Addison's, even madness, was extricated from the population and placed in stasis inside the purple orbs," Timmerloo explained.

"I never heard of such things," Timothy said, perplexed by the words Timmerloo had spoken. "Are such things even real? There are no such sicknesses. We villagers die of injuries, infections of wounds, which the healers keep as best they can, and old age where the body just wears out. When those of us are too weary to go on, they have someone place their stone in the wall. Then it's just a matter of time. But to tell me such things exist, or ever existed, is just some sad fairytale."

"THEY DO EXIST!" Timmerloo shouted at him, eyes blazing with anger. "Do not become so arrogant yourself, young Timothy, that you do not listen to the truth." Timmerloo paused, composing himself, then continued, "We developed ways to contain each and every disease. There were thousands of them, hundreds of thousands. We contained them in orbs, which curiously turned violet, then stored each in an enclosed vault. As we were soon to discover, neither life nor death could be contained. They wanted to be left out . . . free to roam. As it was in life, to continue and prosper . . . so it was in death, to continue and destroy.

"We categorized and identified everything. When we found the first purple orb lying in wait, floating in a pool of blue mists, we didn't understand the extent of what we had mastered. As it ripped apart the body of one of the attendants in a conflagration of reddish tendrils, we understood the orbs were not inert as we hoped but living sentient entities, self-designed and intent on our destruction. We realized, in time, they would break free from their confinement and destroy us.

"We devised an ambitious plan to release the purple orbs to an uninhabited area of the villages. We designed a wall that ran from the northern regions of the land and put the other end of it to the south. Like most living things, they thrived in warmer environments, keeping them away from the most northern and southern land masses where coldness thrives through all the solens kept them from moving around the wall at its most northern and southern tips. The wall was built, and the orbs were released to the other side where they immediately ravaged whatever life was there, turning it into a desert. To maintain the wall, word was sent to all the villagers to maintain it for as long as there were 'villages.'

"The orbs represent all the physical illnesses the villagers were subjected to over a lifetime. It is no surprise the orbs want to destroy the humans inhabiting the villages. It was the destiny of the purple orbs to destroy every living thing. All the villagers had to do was maintain the wall. The breach changed everything, and the orbs came through with deadly vengeance. Causing pain and death are their sustenance . . . your fear and terror are like food to them. They are made from what you all were, and they are soulless. Catherine ultimately sacrificed herself in a way that should appease the breach, allowing the villages to come back to life again."

Timothy sat on the stone table at the top of the pinnacle, wringing his hands. He looked where Timmerloo stopped talking, and yet he could not completely understand what he said. "I have so many questions. But they must wait. Catherine needs me to finish this journey. What am I to do?"

"This night, there will be an eclipse of the moon during our winter solstice. It hasn't happened in over four centuries, well, before your time. Though we are spirits of science, there is a kind of magic associated with a night like this . . . powerful magic," Timmerloo said.

"What does this have to do with my journey?" Timothy asked, now suspicious of Timmerloo's intentions.

"You will only get to the place you need to be through dreams."

"I need to go to sleep?" Timothy exclaimed.

"To find the Poet's Tree . . ." Timmerloo explained. "It is there you will find the poet. He will make Catherine immortal."

"I don't understand," Timothy stated. "Where do I find it?"

"You will find the Poet's Tree in the place between dreams and waking . . . between the starry darkened sky and the first gatherings of light. It lies in the place of inspiration and is only reached when you understand you are already there. Some will never find it. Some will think they have. And others will never believe it exists."

When We Danced

Tell me about the dance . . .

     She was a bright star shining in a dark world. Lois would remain at home during the intervals she was healing from her continuing battles . . . this time for blood clots in her left leg. She would maintain calls to her workplace to continue the schedule she was still keeping there, instructing staff how to maintain the records she created, and to assure everyone of her intentions to return to work when the physician released her from his care.

     Lois could not return to her office for the remainder of January 2010. She was restricted to bed rest. Following the advice of her physician and continuing the prescribed medications, she was back on her feet by the end of the month. Her oncologist was being conservative when he asked Lois to delay going back to work until he tried a course of chemotherapy. He wanted to evaluate the potential side effects she might experience before he allowed her to return to her busy office.

     The finding of lung involvement at the end of 2009 was foreboding. Lois and I spoke of the consequences of the finding, but somehow, we believed the course of events would eventually allow her to overcome it. After all, we saw a dramatic impact in the tumor markers, concluding the chemotherapy protocol was effective. If the lung metastasis could remain static with the current chemotherapy, there might be a surgical intervention to remove it entirely. Lois, even under such heavy turmoil, still looked to the future . . . She still made hope a priority, not just for herself but for everyone.

     While she worked on continuing her life as best she could, her oncologist determined the best course of treatments to get through this set of problems. The oncologist had a handle on the chemotherapy protocol, which was working to keep the cancer static. But the side effects of nausea, vomiting, constipation, and pain were still major problems. Lois had a barrage of specialists treating the symptoms of nail overgrowth and mutations, dizziness, vertigo, imbalance, nail discoloration, tooth discoloration, and a plethora of associated problems. These incredible people worked together to keep Lois on her feet and functioning at an almost normal capacity.

In spite of the consequences of trying to stay alive and productive, she managed to find time to drive to the American Cancer Society and other local agencies to gather materials on breast cancer survivorship and advocacy for a class of LPN students on January 21, 2010. She continued contacts with the support group and the many advocates fighting for breast cancer legislation to improve breast cancer care and treatments. Even on bed rest, she would have our son bring her cell phone, land phone, a laptop desk, paper, and writing materials to work from the bed. By the end of the month, when she was off bed rest, she was in our home office working on the computer and making calls from the office telephone. She was constantly busy, trying to improve the lives of others and advocating for change. She was tireless, never feeling she could not be productive in some way. Lois was feeling so well by the end of January, I was able to get her out of the house to see a play on January 29, 2010.

While recuperating in January and February 2010, she continued looking forward. Making plans for vacations with family and friends, anticipating times when she could work with her fellow breast cancer survivors and associates, and keeping in touch with her colleagues and friends at work were the kinds of activity she accomplished while confined by the boundaries of her illness. She planned an ambitious vacation to Las Vegas, where we could see some shows, visit the Hoover Dam, and enjoy other sites of interest. She made arrangements from our home, utilizing phone calls and the Internet to set everything up. She had the vacation fully planned and paid before she ever returned to work. The vacation, planned for late July, was arranged so I would have enough vacation time to take off with her. When she explained her plans, I was skeptical, considering the enormous set of barriers she had to overcome. However, I was also reassured . . . She sincerely intended to be well enough to make the trip when the time came.

While at home, pain remained problematic. She worked with a variety of medications that maintained pain control without affecting her attention span or her ability to think clearly. This was a requirement she demanded before she took anything prescribed for pain. If there was even a chance the medications would affect her cognition, she would tolerate the pain until she could take the medication, lie down, and then sleep off the sedative effects. She refused to take anything affecting her judgment or responsiveness when she was out in public. The side effects of her pain medications continued to give her nausea and, at times, severe constipation.

Tumor markers taken on January 18, 2010, showed improvement when the results returned at 440, half the result of 881 taken in December 2009. But with persistent nausea dogging her, she was reluctant to continue another round of chemotherapy using the same protocol. Her oncologist agreed and decided to pursue an old protocol called CMF (CMF stands for Cytoxan, methotrexate, and 5-fluorouracil). The oncologist felt this protocol was one that was well tolerated by many of his patients. He felt Lois would be able to tolerate the CMF, since she once had its sister protocol, CAF (Cytoxan, Adriamycin, and 5-fluorouracil), and tolerated it quite well in 1992. The first treatment would be given on February 4, 2010.

Though Lois wanted to return to work at the end of January, her physician would not allow her to return until February 22, 2010. Through previous experience, we learned Lois needed fluid replacement after a round of chemo because the incidence of nausea and vomiting afterward created an environment for dehydration. To keep ahead of any dehydration, her oncologist scheduled times with the infusion center to get fluids. At this time in her treatments, she received a daily injection to stimulate the bone marrow to create new blood cells, enabling her to take the next treatment. The injections were helpful, and she was expected to stay on a two-week course prior to her chemotherapy treatments. However, when she needed to be on medications for neutropenia, she experienced severe joint pain by the seventh or eighth dose and never tolerated the entire protocol. Because this side effect interfered with the protocol, chemotherapy treatments were often delayed or cancelled because of low white counts. Low white counts (neutropenia) also meant she would be defenseless against any virulent strain of infections emerging during the cold winter months.

Her white counts were adequate, and she received the chemotherapy treatment on February 4, 2010. But the world was not kind to her. Just after treatment, with white counts lowering from chemotherapy, both our son and I came down with terrible colds and laryngitis. The winter of 2010 was relentless, with a severe snowstorm at the end of January, leaving us with ten inches of fresh snow, to be followed by two additional snowstorms on February 5 and 6, and again on 9 and 10. The snowstorms were terrible, stranding me at work for almost a week, leaving our son and Lois stranded at the house. By the second week of February, Lois was battling the same infection our son and I had. While our son and I managed to get over it in three or four days, it took Lois about two to three weeks with lingering effects. With the accumulating snow, coughs, fevers, and congestion, Lois became depressed. I was beginning to see how this disease could easily take her life. I knew in my heart of hearts if someone or something crushed her spirit, she might not get back up again.

Though she was not quite over the effects of the infection, Lois started back to work February 22, 2010, the last full week of the month. She started with four-day work weeks, but she still put all the time she could into those four days, almost forty hours anyway. By the first week of March, she managed doing forty hours work in spite of her limitations of a four-day week. She was happy to be back with her associates and friends at hospice. She always managed to carve time in her work schedule to make her physicians' appointments. Though she was not back to work very long, she worked a way to get time off to go to the Department of Defense for a meeting in Washington DC on Wednesday night of March 10, 2010, after finishing at work, and then stayed until Saturday March 13, 2010, for the NBCC Team Leader Conference.

What was remarkable was she overcame blood clots, pain, nausea, vomiting, a first round of chemotherapy, neutropenia, and a cold enduring almost three weeks, and then managed to drive from southern Pennsylvania to Washington, DC herself. Of course, she was very tired when she returned, but she was full of stories and adventures she shared about people she knew or new people she met at the DOD conference and the NBCC Team Leader Conference. This activity worked as a stimulus to make her feel part of the world again. In fact, with her strength returning and her visions of keeping breast cancer advocacy a top priority, Lois managed to write an eight-page newsletter for her support group members. This was the first newsletter Lois produced since May 18, 2009, when she applauded her group members for coming to the meetings. But things changed, since she was unable to get to the meetings herself. Though this was one of her more extensive newsletters, Lois wrote of her disappointment in the turnout for the support group meetings during this time.

(From the newsletter by Lois A. Anderson dated March, 2010)

Okay Ladies it is up to you—do you want our group to continue or not??? We are on the verge of making that decision, one that if you remember correctly, I mentioned a year ago. Our meetings have been so poorly attended that those in charge can only reason that your needs are met without attending the face-to-face gatherings we have. Is this true? It seems to be since on average we have had anywhere from one to three women at the past several meetings. With that few in attendance, we can only assume that these meetings are no longer necessary. With that in mind, we will not be meeting in August, or September. We will decide later in the year if meetings will be held in November and December, but at the moment that looks to be highly unlikely. This newsletter, in the format you see here, will most likely go the way of the meetings, too, but that remains to be seen. We need your opinions, but most of all we need your attendance at the meetings. If attendance should pick up we will look at revamping the sessions and bring in speakers, etc. to make the meetings more enlightening. However, at this time we cannot ask any of our local health care providers to take the time out of their busy day to prepare a slideshow for us on a topic related to breast cancer. It's just not feasible for them and it's embarrassing for this group's leaders to have such poor attendance when these speakers are donating their time freely. We do not pay any of our speakers. It is up to you to decide group or no group, newsletter or no newsletter, and I'll be there unless I'm not feeling well. I'm asking you to bring your opinions along, please.

As for me, my health is stable again after chemotherapy and six months off work to recover from side effects and other maladies. I have to say this last chemotherapy drug I had was the worst in all of the almost 15-16 years worth of treatment that I've had since my 1992 diagnosis. I just returned to work and will be working only four days a week for the time being. I am gradually getting back into the swing of things and I hope to be at our next meeting in April to see all of you there. I'll detail all of what happened when I see you. It's too much to write every detail here.

I also want to thank everyone who attended the tea party in December at my house. It was such a great idea and I have to thank Diane for coming up with that idea. It was wonderful to be with all my friends again, even just for such a short time. I can truly say that I missed each and every one of you while I was out of commission.

So come to our April meeting to decide what the future holds for Surviving Breast Cancer Support Group and Newsletter. If another event prevents you from attending please call and leave a message on the answering or tell Lois directly your opinions. We want to know!!! If you don't voice your opinions, then please don't complain about the changes made.

Happy Spring,

Lois

This was the last newsletter Lois wrote. I drove her to the last meeting of the breast cancer support group in April. The room was quiet. I suggested we turn on some lights and display the brochures we had on hand on the tables, but Lois asked me to wait. At first, no one came. The meeting was to start on the hour. At ten minutes past the hour, one group member came through the door and hugged Lois. She looked around the empty room and realized what Lois had come to suspect . . . The support group had run its course. The two women talked about what Lois had been through over the past six months for about a half an hour. The room darkened as the sun faded. No one turned on the lights. When the three of us left and the door shut behind us, we knew it was closed. It was done!

Lois continued to put in her four days at work. She continued to have shortness of breath at times and would come home very tired. Many times she would go back to bed and take a nap or continue with activities that were not physically stressful. She consulted her oncologist, who suggested she make an appointment with her pulmonologist as soon as possible.

The history with the pulmonologist consisted with one attempt to take fluid from her right lung in October 2009. This attempt yielded 200 cc of yellow fluid, showing metastasis to the right lung on analysis. The same procedure, attempted in December 2009, failed when the fluid proved to be too thick to be extracted with the customary equipment. The pulmonologist wanted to place a thick plastic catheter into the base of her right lung to extract fluids from the base of the right lung. However when the fluid extractions became less than 20 cc, the decision to remove the catheter was made, hoping to stave off any infections that might be introduced at the insertion site. Lois was back at work, keeping the catheter curled against her chest wall under her clothing. She was relieved when the surgeon removed it, and she could resume her activities without it. For almost six weeks, she felt she was on the way to recovery. But when a CT scan taken in late February revealed increasing densities in the right lung base, and the ever-increasing shortness of breath, she knew it was time to do something. An appointment was made to see the pulmonologist once again.

On March 25, 2010, Lois and I drove to the physician's office in the still-melting snow and icy cold rain. She was not encouraged by the weather and said as much. I brought two umbrellas to keep the rain off as she moved to the entrance of the facility. She was unusually quiet until we got to the entrance.

"What do you think will happen?" I asked, trying to get her to talk.

"Don't know what they'll be able to do," she said quietly, uncharacteristic of her usual boisterousness.

"I know you feel pretty good at the moment, but with fluid collecting at the base of the lung, you will be too short of breath before long to do much of anything," I offered, as a way to draw her out.

"I know . . . but what can we do about it? Chemo seemed to work the last time. My oncologist will most likely be able to do something like it again." Then she paused, thinking to herself, then said, "Just so I don't get sick again . . ."

I nodded my appreciation that I understood the horrific side effects of the previous chemotherapy at the end of 2009, where the chemotherapy protocol brought her tumor markers from a high of 1,633 in October 2009 to a level of 440 by mid-January . . . a feat accomplished in four months! Still, the side effects of the agent used were so spectacular, Lois ended up in the hospital by December 16, 2009, with a blood clot and dehydration caused by severe nausea and vomiting. She just returned to work and was understandably concerned about returning for another surgery. Even before we walked back to the suite to the pulmonologist, Lois turned to me and said, "I'm not ready to go through anything at this point. I just want to get my feet back on the ground for a little while. Then if I need to go for surgery, I will."

I looked at her, pleading me to understand her position. "A lot will depend on how you feel and what this guy has to tell you," I said, understanding her reluctance to do anything more at this point.

Dismissing what I said, she replied, "Right now, if I take it easy, my pain is under control. I'm not as tired as I was. I'm breathing better. I just want to get out and do something for a while." She stopped walking and made me look at her. "Is that too much to ask?"

I looked into her eyes, trying to show her I sincerely understood how she felt. Everything she said was true. She was pent up in either the hospital or the house for almost six months. She finally had the chance to get out and do things on her own independently. She did not want to be stuck right back in the hospital when she just got out.

"Let's see what the physician has to tell you. Then you can decide whether or not there is something he can do for you," I told her, hoping to keep her mind open to any possibilities.

We entered the domain of the pulmonologist. He examined the CT scan and the chest x-ray results. He asked many questions, evaluated Lois's lungs, and then asked what he could do to help. Neither Lois nor I could imagine anything outside the parameters of chemotherapy or surgical removal of all or part of the affected right lung . . . both considerations of what we thought possible. However, the physician proposed something called a "talc procedure (pleurodesis)." The procedure required another hospitalization and another chest tube. The fluid collecting outside the right lung would be removed by the surgeon, and then sterile talcum powder would be mixed with a sterile solution, creating a "slurry." This solution would be flushed into the area surrounding the lung. The talc would act as a mild abrasive that would create scarring on the outside surface of the lung, eventually sealing the lung to the wall of the plural sac and stopping fluid from building around the lung again. He hoped this would allow Lois the ability to have maximum lung capacity until chemo could effectively control the lung cancer. He told her he was trying to buy her some time.

The procedure was not without risk and would not be accomplished without a tremendous amount of pain. Understandably, Lois did not want to give an answer right away. We both retreated from the visit with renewed concerns. How bad was the involvement of the right lung to suggest such a procedure? Lois wanted to consult her contacts over the Internet and her oncologist before she made such a drastic decision. But the procedure was offered. We knew it would not have been offered unless it was needed. The physicians must have suspected a major involvement to the right lung to have suggested it.

Lois went right to work finding information on the talc procedure and the indications to offer it as a possible treatment. She engaged several experts online about the procedure . . . They told her the same thing . . . her lung involvement must be extensive. She could barely get her mind around the sequence of events leading to this moment and the extensive draft of information she found about the procedure. The talc pleurodesis looked like her best chance to survive. Lois realized "survival," at this point, might only be measured as a year or two. After that, no one was willing to make a prediction. Several nights later, when she exhausted all the information she could digest on the subject, she told me she made the decision to have the procedure done.

As was Lois's way, she may have needed to have the procedure done, but she would do it on her own time and have it done in her own way. The surgeon wanted to do the procedure as soon as he could, but Lois wanted to get some things she felt were important to her out of the way first. Though the appointment to discuss the talc procedure occurred on March 25, 2010, Lois would not schedule the procedure until April 26, 2010. She wanted to give a speech, as she did every year, to the families that lost a loved one over the previous year. She also wanted to attend several meetings in April she had not attended since January and February. She expected to have a six-week recovery period and then return to work feeling much better than she did at the time.

Two weeks before surgery, Lois went to the American Cancer Society's conference in Hershey, Pennsylvania, on April 16. She still believed in helping other cancer patients survive the odds, as she was doing. As she neared the day of surgery, she noted symptoms of being tired, increasing pain, and shortness of breath starting their crescendo. The day before surgery, she gave a speech to over one hundred people attending her hospice's annual memorial service. Lois related to her audience that as a breast cancer survivor of almost eighteen years, she had a dream where she was going to be sailing her rough seas on an old-style sailing ship. From somewhere, Lois found a sympathy card that illustrated a similar allusion. The writer described a ship, like hers, sailing away, how large and how majestic it was as it sailed before him. Then it disappeared over the horizon, lost from his sight. Then the writer explained while the ship was gone from his sight, on some other horizon, the ship would appear in all its splendor and majesty, greeted by others waiting to see it, as the writer believed the transition from this life to the next would be. It was ironic Lois's dream was only about loading her ship for the rough seas. She never spoke of the time when she would have to push off from the pier. But her time to do so was coming fast.

April 26 arrived on the last Monday of the month. Lois tolerated the procedure much better than anyone anticipated, and she expected to be home by Friday evening. But before Friday came, Lois developed severe pain with intense nausea and vomiting. She could not tolerate food or fluids and relied on IV fluids to prevent dehydration. A consult was ordered for dietary to work with her, and very slowly, Lois tolerated food and was able to leave the hospital on a soft diet on May 11, almost two weeks later than she expected.

Her stay at home was short lived. Lois returned to the hospital two weeks later on May 25, for nausea, vomiting, and dehydration. I finally brought her home on May 28. She was showing signs of weight loss. Lois managed to keep her weight around 120-130 pounds throughout her adult life. Now, a hospital scale weight betrayed her weight to be 118 pounds. I was concerned, as was she, about losing seven to eight pounds in two weeks. Again, before she left the hospital, a nutritionist stopped by with ideas on how to gain or, at least, maintain her weight. Supplements were suggested, and Lois took several varieties along to try at home. As a nurse, I realized she was entering a territory from which there was no recovery. Still, her oncologist felt there was a chance with the CMF protocol. With just two rounds of chemo, her markers already fell to 362 by May 20. The chemo was working, but Lois was deteriorating in front of me. Even Lois held out hope she could tolerate enough chemotherapy to get back on her feet and back to work before the end of the year.

Lois realized, without her management of the support group and the newsletter, the breast cancer support group she cofounded in 1993 was going to disappear. I think, somehow, she did not have the heart, or strength, to say good-bye to the group or the newsletter. Fortunately, the oncology nurse who worked with the support group all those years wrote the final two-page letter to the group's current and former members. The letter essentially told everyone the group was disbanding at the end of 2010 after being inexistence since 1993, a period of seventeen years, a phenomenon in itself. Though there were a few final events for the support group throughout the remainder of the year to celebrate the ending of the group, Lois would not get to any of them. It was an absence she regretted but could do nothing about.

When April and May passed, and Lois saw she was not recovering as quickly as she expected, she questioned me to what we would need to do if she did not get strong enough to return to work. I suggested a call to her workplace to see if there was anything she could do for them from home, as she did before. If she ever tried to call, I did not know. I do know her pain from the pleurodesis in late April

George S. J. Anderson

did not start to improve until the end of May. She remained exhausted most of the time and slept almost as many hours as she was awake. She maintained contacts with her advocacy associates by phone and over the Internet on days she was strong enough for activity. Nausea, vomiting, and constipation were her major adversaries. She struggled daily with one, or all of them. She managed to stay in good humor and made light of her symptoms most of the time. Instead of complaining, she went on the computer and investigated alternative treatments, often consulting experts she met at professional conferences over the years.

By the beginning of June 2010, Lois was doing much better and asked her oncologist when she could return to work. Though she felt she had more than enough downtime at home, she wasn't completely healed from the talc procedure. A test to evaluate the success of the procedure was scheduled for June 17, 2010. Her oncologist and the thoracic surgeon felt she might recover more quickly if she had home oxygen to help with breathing. An attempt to set a time to be evaluated was tried, but she refused, telling each of them her oxygen saturations were fine when she was tested. And in fact, she was correct. When tested, prior to the procedure with a compromised right lung, her oxygen saturations were between 97 and 100 percent, even with activity. Though she was improving, she still had serious problems with pain. At the time, Lois was on a list of over twenty medications (types, not times). Two medications were injections, the other eighteen or so were assorted long- and short-acting pain medications, stool softeners, laxatives, a gamma-aminobutyric acid analogue (for neuropathic pain), reflux medication, and assorted medications for nausea and vomiting. Keeping a stable medication regimen was more than a challenge; it was a miracle of discipline and astute record management. With such enormous tasks before her, she created a medication schedule with records to evaluate results and had me keep track of it.

Late June and the early part of July were the best times Lois had since April. Though she was still not cleared to drive a car, she made good use of her time helping to cook meals, clean the house, and keep in touch with her friends and coworkers. There was a minimum of tests, and there were no chemotherapy treatments.

Lois had a port placed several years in the past, but over time, the port would not give a blood return, something the physicians needed for lab results. Without a blood return from the port, the nurses giving chemo were extremely skeptical of administering chemotherapy. A decision to place a new port was requested by her oncologist, which Lois agreed to immediately. There were no veins to draw blood from anymore, and having a technician try unsuccessfully several times to get blood was tiring. Placing a new port was a surgical procedure, which her oncologist explained he needed in place not only for the chemotherapy but also for the blood work he would require to evaluate her progress. He said he was willing to start chemotherapy whenever the port was safely in place and functioning.

The port could not be scheduled until late July, giving Lois a short respite. This was one of those magical times where she was feeling better than she had in months. When I wasn't working, we would take short trips. Nausea and vomiting continued to be a problem, but the oral antiemetics, prescribed around the clock, managed to suppress it most of the time. However, any motion, like riding a car or walking too fast, could set the nausea cycle off at any time. Short trips were all she could manage, and her world shrank to a five-mile radius around our home. Going out for dinner was no longer palatable, but she did enjoy going to the malls and shopping centers just to walk around. She also enjoyed going to the grocery store when we needed to do the weekly shopping. Small things began to matter more, spending time with me, conversations with our son about how he was doing in college now that he moved back in with us, and looking forward to spending time with my mother on nights I was working and our son had a late night class. Overall, she appeared to be recovering from the nausea and dehydration that set her back over the course of late May and early June.

My mother loved keeping vigil over Lois when no one could stay with her. Lois loved having her stay and keeping her company until our son returned from his late classes at college. My mother and Lois became very close over this time. Even the nights I was home, she would call or visit her anyway. It was one of those situations that went against the prediction that mothers-in-law and daughters-in-law didn't get along. Nothing could have been further from the truth. Lois once told me, "She is the only mother I have anymore." It was a sad truth; Lois's mother was gone almost three years, and I knew she missed her.

Lois's confrontations with joint pain and nausea were getting better, but our preplanned trip to Las Vegas had to be cancelled when she considered the rugged environment of the airports and the four- to five-hour flight from the east coast to get there. She was afraid she would not tolerate the long flight and considered what might happen if she were to get sick on the flight. So as an alternative, Lois attempted to schedule a short car trip to Philadelphia. However, when the time came, even this was too much for her to handle. Again, she cancelled the reservations, and we stayed within the five-mile radius so as not to get the nausea started again. Since we tried to plan for vacation, and I saved time to go to Las Vegas, I took a week and a half off at the end of June and early July.

I took Lois to an elegant restaurant nearby where she could dress up and feel like she was normal again. It was the first time in a restaurant in a very long time for her. Though she could not eat everything, her appetite seemed to be returning. The oncologist had not approved her to drive, but after he heard this remarkable improvement, Lois asked his permission to drive again. The oncologist was delighted to hear of her progress and allowed her to drive once more.

For Lois, there was something magical about driving. On the side of the actual, or real reasons for her to drive, was the problem she always had with nausea whenever she was a passenger. Driving meant whatever problems existed in the car, as a passenger, seemed to be overwritten in the driver's seat. So when the Fourth of July came around, Lois invited my mother, my son, and me to drive and see the fireworks displays in the area.

She was more than overjoyed to drive the car again, having driven it once on the trip to Philadelphia in December 2009. Since then, she was only the passenger, not the driver, and this was going to be her treat to everyone. On the night of the fireworks, the grounds were so busy, she couldn't get close enough to the display area to park the car. But as was her style, she found a parking lot near the fireworks display where we could all watch from the car. When the display was just about over, she drove to another location where the sky lit with colorful flames of colored light. Somewhere in our travels that night, Lois scraped the front bumper of the car, leaving scratches underneath. I left the scratches as a reminder of that last glorious night when Lois had her last good time showing us the fireworks displays. It was the best night we had in a long time, and Lois showed promise she was doing much better. She even gained most of her weight back by that time.

On a night in mid-July, after a morning I returned from a full night of work, Lois slept the entire day with me. We both woke up about ten o'clock that evening. It was my intent to make a list to go to the grocery store and go shopping that evening, but when I saw the time, I wasn't so sure. Lois looked over at me, now fully awake, and said, "Well, we can still go if you want to. The store is open twenty-four hours. Besides, we can park near the door, and we will probably have the entire store to ourselves. Why not?"

I looked at her, her head propped on one arm smiling at me, and then said, "We both need a bath, and then we need to get ready. It could be midnight or later until we are ready."

She gave me one of her devilish grins and said, "Go get your bath, and then you can help me get ready. I'm really awake right now, and I know you are too, so let's do it."

"I'm up for it if you are," I replied as I rolled out of bed. I pulled some summer clothes from the chest of drawers to wear after the bath.

I quickly got my shower and dressed. Lois stayed in bed to conserve her strength, then had me choose clothes for her from the closet, pointing to things she wanted to put on. When I had everything ready, she slowly moved into an upright position on the edge of the bed, testing her balance and assessing any signs the nausea might kick in. "So how do you feel?" I asked, thinking she might not be up to this little midnight excursion.

"Pretty good . . . a little sore in my knees and back, but considering that is where the metastasis is . . . not bad."

"Nausea?" I asked.

"None . . . in fact, I feel pretty good overall. Just make sure I get in and out of the bathtub okay."

"You need help getting your clothes off?" I asked with a sly smile on my face.

"I think I can do quite nicely by myself, thank you." She giggled, then said, "Typical male."

"You wouldn't have it any other way," I told her with a big smile on my face.

"You're right. But get out of my way so I can undress, then help me into the shower."

The playfulness we directed toward each other was typical of the days when we were more carefree and Lois was feeling good. It was nice to see her playful nature surface once again after feeling so downtrodden and serious over these long months. It was almost like she was reminding me she was not about to let cancer rule her. She was going to live her life until she couldn't. She never burdened anyone with her ailments or her problems. She wanted people to see her, not her cancer.

While Lois showered, I checked the things we needed for the week and made a list. After her shower, I helped her get dressed. She walked to the kitchen and looked over my list. She organized everything, matching coupons with things on the list to use at the store, and then found ones we would use because they were expiring. So armed with a store list and a handful of coupons, we set off for the store. We were in the parking lot by half past midnight.

Inside, the store was almost empty except for a familiar cashier who always waited on us. She greeted us and asked how we were doing. We nodded we were okay and went about finding the things we came for. Even though it was July, Lois brought a sweater to wear in the long freezer aisles where the cold air could affect her neuropathy and give her chills. She had a difficult time staying warm even in the summer months.

Some aisles were congested with skids fully loaded with boxes and containers waiting to be placed on the shelves. We saw a man setting up a floor cleaner at the rear of the store, but he was not ready to begin. Aisle by aisle, we walked slowly, picking up one item after another and placing them into the growing grocery cart. The store lights were just a dim phosphorescence, enough to see by but lowered to conserve energy. We entered the freezer aisle, noting how the luminescence of the freezer lights cast a bright bluish tint from both sides. The aisle was clear of displays that once sat there, presumably the efforts of the man preparing to clean the floors, leaving a long open corridor from one end to the other. The PA system was tuned to a station playing rock-and-roll tunes from the '60s and '70s. As we walked, I told Lois the titles of the songs I recognized on the PA.

Lois had little to say after we arrived at the store. Her lack of conversation concerned me, and I felt she may have not felt as well as she had when we started. When I said something to her, she just came back with "Let's just do the shopping and let me get my mind off cancer for a while." For the time, she was very serious. I believe she was trying to be normal for a while but had so much on her mind to consider. I look back over this time and wonder if she already had doubts about the proposed CMF protocol. Would it work, or would she tolerate it? During this time, while we waited for the port placement, the tumor markers went up from 362 (a marker taken in May 2010) to 1,020 (a result taken in the first week of July 2010). We both knew waiting to take chemo much longer meant the cancer might not be arrested. The best Lois and her oncologist hoped for was stabilization, allowing her to return to work. She hoped to survive another year or two. However, after the CMF was done, she realized there were no other options . . . but it would give her time to finish many projects she hoped to pick up again and pursue.

As we walked halfway down the freezer aisle, a song started playing over the PA system we both knew. It was an old song called "*Daydream Believer*" by the *Monkees*, a group Lois loved as a teenager. As the song started, we looked at each other and smiled. I stepped back from the grocery cart and moved down the aisle away from it. Then I turned, faced my wife, opened my arms, and bowed. She laughed and then said with a twinkle in her eye, "Do you want to?"

I looked up and down the lighted freezer aisle and smiled. "Sure, why not, no one is around."

She curtsied and then sauntered slowly into my arms. As I lightly placed my arms around her waist, she slid her arms around my neck and then looked into my eyes. The song played softly behind us, and the aisle became our dance floor. She was dressed in blue jeans, a light summer shirt, and a sweater. I was in a pair of summer shorts and an old T-shirt. Though it was one o'clock in the morning, we danced a slow rhythmical dance to music I never had the chance to dance to with my beautiful wife. We didn't need a ballroom with ladies adorned in gold and lace dancing in their fashionable gowns or men displayed in fine suits and egregious ties. We were two people dancing in the night, defying the odds we could dance. We felt young again, dressed in fine clothes, dancing slowly down the aisle lighted by freezer displays. To us, the store became a beautiful ballroom where we laughed and kissed like we did when we first met. The song lasted just a few minutes, but we wanted to dance forever in a place where we finally escaped the realities surrounding us.

When we stopped, still holding each other at arm's length, we heard clapping from the front of the store. We looked and realized our favorite cashier caught us in the act. We both took a bow and then finished our shopping with lighter hearts than we had in quite a while. When we finished, we emptied the cart where the cashier told us we danced beautifully. We shared our laughter and then said our good-byes to one another. I didn't know it at the time, but it would be the last time I had to dance with Lois. I never forgot the immense joy it gave us. When I feel empty, I think back on the night we danced and remember the fullness of those few minutes, and I don't feel empty anymore. I have no doubt she loved me, and I knew I loved her.

Looking back on July 2010, Lois had a very full schedule planned. But she had to cancel most of it to have her port placed on July 21. The week after the port was placed, Lois was to teach a group of LPNs about breast cancer advocacy but had to cancel. It was the first time in fifteen years she missed teaching the class. She also cancelled appointments with the American Cancer Society and the NBCC before surgery. She had the first chemotherapy on July 30, 2010, since February 4, 2010. If all went well, Lois hoped to return to work by the end of August.

The CMF protocol was given on a Friday. I did not have to be back at work until Monday evening. With Lois in a constant state of nausea, I didn't want to leave her alone after this first round of chemotherapy. But with elevated markers, I was also concerned that the cancer would become insurmountable, making it impossible for Lois to do much of anything . . . except prepare for her death. How she reacted physically to this protocol was crucial. If she could not tolerate it . . . the handwriting was on the wall. There may have been other alternatives, but of the ones capable of turning the cancer back again, this was the least stressful. Lois and I waited and watched as the weekend passed . . . hoping for the best.

She did well Saturday and Sunday. There was the usual facial flushing from the use of a steroid to reduce the feelings of nausea, but otherwise, she appeared to have very little problem tolerating the chemo. Lois did so well, I felt comfortable going to work that Monday. For the entire week, she continued to do well, and we thought she had a therapy she could rely on for a time. But when Friday came, she started with excessive joint and spine pain. With the pain taking up residence, the inevitable nausea moved in as well. I called the oncologist on Friday, and with some adjustments to her pain medications and antiemetics, Lois made it through the remainder of the week.

By Monday, the debilitating pain and severe nausea returned. The symptoms were so bad, that as the week opened, I requested getting few days off to be with her. Since I wasn't due back at work until the following weekend, I spent the time making sure she ate and drank anything she could keep down. There were days she felt good enough to get out of bed and do some things around the house. Then there were days she simply had to stay in bed and sleep after taking narcotics to keep the pain away. No matter what we tried, the nausea pervaded her life, never stopping completely.

Even with the severe nausea and pain, Lois convinced me she needed to get to the Photo License Center located about three miles from our home. She wanted her picture taken for a new driver's license, which was due that month. She told me her driving days were probably over but might need the identification to vote in November. I know I must have looked skeptical to her as I thought, *How is she going to pull this off?* She saw the quizzical look on my face and told me, "Don't worry about me. I'll just take my antiemetic before we leave, and you can drive. I'll take a plastic basin to 'throw up' in."

I shook my head. "Well, that makes me feel really confident. Besides, how are you going to look going into the Photo Center if you are vomiting?" I asked, hoping to appeal to vanity.

"Don't worry about it. I will settle down once we stop," she answered stubbornly. "I need my identification to vote, and I *will* vote this year. There are some people running we definitely don't want in, and I'm going to do my best to stop them," she told me without hesitation.

"Okay . . . I'll do my best to get you there," I said, resigned she was going to do this even if it killed us both.

So on August 13, 2010, a Friday no less, I managed to get Lois to the Photo Center to have the photo for her driver's license taken. The trip went just as she told me. She took her meds, and after we drove the three miles to the center, she started vomiting. I parked near the closest entrance I could. Then in what had to be sheer force of strength and stubborn willpower, Lois controlled her nausea. Her pain was poorly managed, but she wasn't leaving after making the trip to the Photo Center. I had to help her move from the car seat, getting her feet on the ground, where she struggled to a standing position. When standing, I asked her, "Are you going to be able to do this?"

"If I walk slow, then sit right away, I think I will be fine," she told me, holding back tears of pain and disgust as I took her by the hand.

"We probably have about twenty steps to the door and then whatever else lies beyond it. Don't think it will be too far," I said, trying to comfort her.

"I am going to do this," she said with a conviction I rarely saw coming from her anymore.

Lois began her slow steady walk with me at her side. I opened the doors in front of her and managed to get her to a chair in the front row. I then went to the desk and pulled one of those paper numbers they have for calling your name. I came back and gave the slip of paper to her. As I looked around, I felt we were lucky. The place wasn't too busy, and the three people in front of her gave her just enough time to rest and regain her composure before they took her up to get her picture. Before long, she had her new driver's license in her hand, and I could tell she felt better. For her, it was more than just a picture. If she lost her driver's license, I feel she would have felt she lost another piece of her identity. She did not want to be erased from the world. She still wanted to be a vital part of it, and losing another piece of her identity was too much, so she fought for it, as she always did, and won.

As we made our way back to the car, she vomited again. The strain of being the passenger in the car, the motion of walking, and the insurmountable pain she endured to do what she just did were too much. She told me, "Please help me into the car and get me back home. I feel so sick right now."

I hurried and opened the car door and gently guided her into the front seat, handing the plastic basin to her again when she was seated. She was gagging on nothing. There was nothing left in her to come up anymore. I looked over at her when I got into the driver's seat and saw she was trying to stifle her pain. "Should I go back home or take you to the doctor's office?" I asked, concerned she was too sick for me to manage at home.

"Just take me back home," she said stiffly while hanging her head over the basin.

I was able to get back home in about five minutes, but the nausea would not relent as she went into severe gagging just before

I pulled into our garage. I got out and quickly opened the door for her, waiting for the gagging to subside. She was crying. The gagging started savage cramping in her right rib cage, pulling on the bottom three ribs like an unseen monster. When she could manage, she walked slowly into the house and lay on the bed. "Please put your hands on my chest," she pleaded, tears of pain trekked over her cheeks in abandon.

I pulled up her blouse and saw the effects of vomiting curled the bottom three ribs of the right chest wall. I put my hands over the site and put firm light pressure on them. The muscles in the right chest wall would, over time, tighten and spasm, causing a great deal of pain and limit her ability to move the right arm. However, the curling of the lower rib cage was in such a severe spasm, I wasn't certain I would be able to do anything about it. I think Lois had more faith in my abilities than I did as she looked at me, pleading for my help. I placed my hands over the ridge and felt the site tighten and distend from muscles pulling up on the ribs. She winced as I put my hands over it. As it always worked in the past, the spasm released, allowing the ribs to settle back in place after about twenty minutes. I looked into her face and saw the tears were gone, and she regained her composure.

"Is it starting to feel any better?" I asked, watching the tension leave her face.

"Yeah, it's better. That was pretty bad," she told me. "Are your hands tired, or can you just let them there a few more minutes?"

"No, I can leave them on for a while yet. Are you still spasming?" I asked, thinking she still felt something I couldn't feel with my hands.

"No, but I'm afraid to move. The spasms may start again . . . They were really bad this time. Probably the worst I ever had," she told me.

"Well, at least you have your photo ID," I said, smiling at her.

"Yeah, at least that much is done. That way I will get to vote in November," she told me, smiling as she closed her eyes and entered the realm of sleep even before I pulled my hands off the troublesome ribs.

I look back to this time, remembering the sheer will and determination she had to go for her license. It showed how much she believed in the freedoms and rights some of us take for granted. She believed one person did have the power to make a difference. Not only did she believe it, but she lived it as well. She might have been very ill, but it did not stand in the way of a true warrior and hero. I have never experienced such resolve from any person I ever knew, and I felt blessed and honored to know her and love her.

I needed to go to work that night, and I employed the attentions of my mother and my son to keep watch over her. Lois had terrible pain in her joints, and the nausea prevented her from eating or drinking much of anything. Most times when she asked for something to drink, it would only be some weak tea. I was expecting the nausea to subside a week or two after the chemo she had at the end of July, but instead, the nausea continued to increase as the time wore on. I managed to work my two shifts on Friday and Saturday nights, but when I arrived home on Sunday morning, Lois was unable to move off the bed. The pain was back with a vengeance. Nothing I had in the house could help reduce the pain, and she was barely able to contain herself. I called the oncologist office and was told to get an ambulance to get her into the emergency room. The nurse on call was calling the oncologist working the hospital to be ready for her. They would get her into a room as soon as we arrived.

Lois stopped me from making the call to the ambulance right away. Though she was in severe pain, she insisted on getting a shower before she went into the hospital. Our son and I did what we could to help her, but every step she made was agony. She made it into the shower but had no energy left to bathe herself, so she asked me to help her. Every touch I made elicited a wince of pain. When I tried to get her out of the shower, she could not do it. I dried her off and then used a towel to wrap around her hair. I called our son to help me carry her back to the bed and then called the ambulance. She told me she could not stand the pain, and she felt like she was going to pass out. I just managed to get her dressed in clean pajamas when the ambulance crew came into the house. My son got them through the door and then made their way back to the bedroom. Her pain was intense; she begged them not to move her. The team reassured her, but she was not convinced. I leaned over her, telling her how gentle they would be and how I was going to be with her every step of the way. I knew they had to get her into the hospital quickly, as they managed to lift her to the stretcher and onto the ambulance. I still felt her pain could be controlled, as well as the nausea, once the IV medications could be given. Somehow, we were still in the dance, and we were dancing.

I followed them to the emergency room, and as promised, Lois was seen immediately. IVs were started via her new port, and she was medicated with pain medications and antiemetics before being taken to her room. I stayed behind, filling out the obligatory paperwork needed for the insurance before following her to the oncology floor. Our son packed an overnight bag somehow, and I eventually took everything to her room. When I arrived at the room, Lois was awake and had a weak, sleepy smile on her face.

"How are you feeling?" I asked with some trepidation.

"Better now," she said weakly. "The pain is almost gone, and I don't feel nauseated anymore."

"You gave me a scare. I wasn't sure you were going to make it for a while," I said, stifling back a tear.

"Come and sit with me," she told me.

I put down the bag with her belongings and pulled a chair next to the bed. "Is this better?" I asked.

"Yeah. Just sit there with me until I fall asleep and hold my hand." She smiled as she closed her eyes.

"You know I will," I said, leaning over to kiss her on the forehead.

"So what's in the overnight bag?" she asked with her eyes closed.

"Don't know exactly. You know Jimmy packed it while I was getting you ready."

"I know he didn't get everything. When I wake up, I'll go through it and tell you what I need," she said, her sense of organization still alive and well.

I had to smile when she told me she still wanted to make some choices for herself, even if it was only the things she thought should have been packed for a trip to the hospital. I told her just before she fell asleep, "I'll be here when you wake up."

"I know ... love you," she told me from the edge of wakefulness and sleep. Unable to keep up any further conversation, she went into a deep sleep.

While she slept, I realized she wasn't going to be able to take another chemotherapy treatment, no matter what it was. For a while, I felt like I couldn't breathe. This was the end of everything. She wasn't going back to work. She wasn't going to change the world with her expertise and advice. She was quickly becoming one of those faceless statistics she, many times, attempted to personalize. It was all just numbers. No one really saw the pain, the loss, or the value of such a person as she had become. I never met such a courageous person. She had such grace, wisdom, and understanding of those she cared about. She never complained that she was one of the people affected by breast cancer. She never asked for the many accolades people bestowed upon her. She would have been happy doing the work she did for breast cancer survivors and patients without ever being noticed. But that was not the way her life played out.

I called our son Jim, giving him the room number at the hospital. I asked him to contact everyone who might want to see her. I asked him to bring some flowers to brighten up the stark hospital room and some toiletries his mother might need. I knew this would take him a little while to accomplish. It was good he was holding down the proverbial fort while I got Lois settled. I told him I was staying and would try to get a little sleep myself until he could get in. He told me he would take care of everything then come in. Jim could be counted on to do the right thing and get things accomplished. I felt secure letting him handle things while I got some sleep.

With everything being taken care of by our son, I just sat there beside her and held her hand. *What comes next?* I thought. Every answer I had in my soul screamed out in resistance as I watched her slowed breathing. Knowing she was out of pain and comfortable again made it easier for me to relax. I was awake over twenty-six hours when I fell asleep in the chair next to her, still holding her hand. I knew Lois would need to have a serious discussion with everyone very soon. As I fell asleep, I tried to clear my mind of it.

Lois spent the next week in the hospital, returning on Friday, August 20, 2010, at 2:00 p.m., to our home. While at the hospital, Lois was on IV fluids, many antiemetics, and a change in pain medications. Before she left, a twenty-four-hour period without IVs or IV medications of any kind was attempted. She was only able to tolerate fluids the whole day Thursday, and by Friday, she was only able to tolerate full liquids. Her appetite was dramatically suppressed, and advancing her diet was going to take a very long time. Tumor markers drawn in the hospital told her the chemo she had taken in July was moderately effective, bringing down the markers over two hundred points. The chemotherapy could be effective, but her tolerance of it was in question. Her oncologist decided to hold the next treatment and consider other alternatives to giving the next one. Lois considered everything and told him she needed time to think, but she also wanted him to take some time to come up with another plan, if possible. She did not want to end up in the hospital feeling like this after every treatment. She knew her options were slim, yet she still hoped something could be done.

During the week she spent recuperating at the hospital, Lois and I had some very frank and open conversations about what could happen if she could not tolerate any other treatments. I continued to remain optimistic, telling her, "I want you around until I reach sixty, longer if you can manage."

"But if I can't eat, what will happen to me?" she asked seriously.

"I guess you will get slim and trim . . ." trying to lighten her mood.

She laughed. "It's a hell of a diet program." Then she looked toward me and gave me another serious look. "If my oncologist can't come up with something, I'm afraid I won't be seeing the ripe old age of sixty with you." She stopped for a moment, letting this fatal reality sink in. "I have a lot of questions to ask him when we see him, and I don't know if you or I will like what he has to say."

"Well, let's leave that conversation for the time when we see him. Maybe we can get all our questions down on paper so when we do see him, we will have everything we need to decide what to do next." Our eyes looked on one another, but I could see Lois was not convinced there was anything left to do.

"If there is nothing left to try, my time is limited. You know that . . . right?" she said, as she placed her hand over mine.

"Maybe that's a question we need to ask. What kind of time would he give you if you were to stop treatments?" I stared at her; my heart was breaking, and I think hers was too. "He still may have a trick or two up his sleeve that neither of us thought about," I said, again trying to keep her spirits up.

"I'll have eighteen years of beating this come October 12, you know . . ." She looked deep in my eyes, keeping my attention. "I'd like to make it twenty years to see the age of sixty with you, but . . ." she stammered. For the first time since I knew her, it seemed she didn't know how to say something.

"You're not sure you can stay with me that long, are you?" I asked, knowing how hard it was for her to give up, if that was what she was trying to say.

"There is still so much to do," she said. "I was hoping to be around long enough to see our son graduate from college . . . I know he would want me to be there."

"Yes, he would . . . and if it is possible, you will be too," I said, trying to be encouraging.

"I'm getting weaker. I was really hoping to turn this around again and get back to work, at least for a little while, and keep pushing advocacy for breast cancer."

"It may still be possible," I said, but beneath the conversation, I understood she was considering the possibility there was nothing left to try. I took her hand in mine and said, "If it comes down to the choice where you have to stop everything . . . I will understand. I won't like it . . . I never said I would like it when a time like this came. But I think you need to hear what your oncologist has to say . . . then decide. Any decision you make before hearing what he has to say would be premature and foolish."

Again, she looked at me seriously and said, "I know. I just wanted to make sure you understood there may not be anything left to try . . . and if he does have a suggestion of what to do next, will I be able to tolerate it?"

My thoughts were, in part, a mixture of optimism and guarded logic. Lois's point of not being able to tolerate further treatments was very valid. Even if her oncologist could come up with a solution to the nausea and weight loss, could any treatment he offered still be effective against the cancer? If not, I think in hindsight, it was Lois's way of telling me she had enough and wanted to live out the remainder of her life the best she could. She may have been saying, "I give up," but knowing Lois, she still wanted to hear the arguments for continued treatments and against them. It was going to be her decision either way, even if she knew, at this point, she wanted to stop.

One of the key elements behind Lois's chronic nausea was dehydration. Keeping her hydrated with IV fluids was almost as good as the best antiemetic or increases in pain medications. It was evidence: almost every time she had severe pain and nausea, a bag of IV fluids would inevitably improve both symptoms, or erase them entirely. The extreme chronic nausea eliminated Lois's desire to eat or drink, and if she did consume anything, the vomiting that came afterward caused losses of essential fluids and nutrients. As a result of this cycle of events, Lois requested her physician to order a course of IV fluids throughout the following week before she left the hospital. The fluids could be given at the infusion center at the cancer center outpatient clinic not far from our home.

The music was still playing, and we were dancing. We returned home from the hospital on Friday, and I had the entire weekend off with her. On Monday, August 23, 2010, we were to go for her first IV infusion.

The weekend went very well. Although Lois tried to eat small amounts of food, she preferred to drink warm tea. She still had problems with the unabated nausea but felt well enough to go to the grocery store with me. She pushed the cart, more so for support than anything else. She had pain in her knees and back but felt she wanted to contribute to the household chores by shopping with me. She did very well negotiating the store aisles and traffic. When we returned, she was so tired she went to bed and slept almost three hours. I put the groceries away myself, thinking how courageous she had been to get out of the house for a while. She had spent most of the last three months or four months in either the hospital or at home in bed. Her short trips outside the house were getting less and less. At home, when she was feeling good, she booted up the computer and continued her advocacy concerns with other survivors and agencies like the American Cancer Society and the NBCC. She spoke on the phone with members of her hospice and explained some of the paperwork to the people who had stepped in over her absence. All in all, though she was very ill, she made every attempt to stay in touch with everyone.

Fluid replacement started at the infusion center the Monday after she left the hospital for dehydration and uncontrolled pain. Since it was a very long walk from the parking lot to the infusion room, I had my uncle who volunteers with the Lion's Club in our area bring a used wheelchair to the house for Lois to use. Lois could still walk short distances, but the pain was still such an issue that reducing her activity was a better decision than allowing her to walk so far. Lois took all of this in good humor and grace. She enjoyed having me push her around on the wheelchair and told people along the way that I was her chauffer. She always remained upbeat, though we were both still thinking, *What else can be done?* I could see that she was weakening physically, but she still had a strong resolve to continue, to survive.

The third fluid replacement was to be done on Friday. The two replacements done to date had little effect on her condition. We knew the outcome of this replacement therapy was tenuous at best. Looking over the long term, we both knew how severe the consequences of little or no chemotherapy would be. Questions of how long she would survive like this, or what undiscovered therapies might still be available, plagued us.

As I wheeled Lois to the infusion room, I was deep in thought. The nausea and vomiting were barely controlled in the three or four months since the pleurodesis in late April. Though she gained some weight afterward, she had not regained all of it. Tumor markers after the pleurodesis were 325-250 but sharply rose to 1,050 in two months' time. The cancer was thriving. Without chemotherapy to arrest it, the cancer cells would run rampant. Then came more dire news: a recent CT scan showed two new sites on her liver not present on previous studies. Again, it was evidence the cancer was spreading to organs never affected before. The one chemotherapy treatment of CMF put her in the hospital for a week. Another round might be something she could not survive, much less tolerate. So our question to each other was, what options does she have? What can be done to arrest the nausea and vomiting . . . and the subsequent weight loss? Just two weeks before her hospital admission, her weight was 115 pounds, about ten pounds lighter than her normal weight. Now her weight after a week in the hospital and a week of IV therapy was only 106 pounds. It was a nine-pound weight loss in only two weeks.

We agreed, the signs were ominous. When we arrived at the waiting room of the infusion center, I wheeled Lois to a space beside a chair. I went to the receptionist and informed her Lois was there for IV therapy. Before that Friday, Lois and I discussed what was in store if she couldn't complete another treatment. We had serious discussions with each other about hospice and "end of life" concerns. Yet our discussions bordered the academic, not a personal one. I believe we weighed the possibilities together and concurred this moment in time might be the end of the things (treatments) to be of any help. Still, we needed information from the physician to turn our concerns from the idealistic to the real. This was the path Lois wanted to follow until we walked into the waiting room that Friday.

I barely had Lois through the door and settled when one of the social workers we met many years ago, when Lois ran the breast cancer support group, engaged us in a conversation. I had no contact with this social worker in almost ten years. It seemed to me, this chance encounter was contrived before we ever entered the building. She spoke to Lois about considering her thoughts of stopping chemotherapy and allowing breast cancer to take its course. Of course, Lois and I had spoken of these things, so it was certainly a good prediction we discussed stopping everything . . . though we still stood on the edge of the knife. A push, one way or another, would have been enough to topple the decision. She spoke to Lois about setting up a disability claim for her, along with other concerns that would come up from going on disability. I looked on in disbelief, noting Lois's inability to comprehend all that was said to her, her resignation to the evidence she knew to be true, and the abandonment of the possibility there might still be hope offered at the hands of her oncologist.

As I said, it was ten years since I saw this particular social worker; and on this Friday, she magically appeared with the right things to say at "almost" the right time. It was too coincidental to deny. To add to the dismay, the infusion nurse who knew Lois since the beginning of her ordeal with breast cancer, armed with similar information, mulled an astutely similar conversation over with Lois. I knew the social worker and the nurse meant well. They had a job to do, and they did it well. It was well timed . . . Lois and I were teetering on a decision and needed input . . . but they took the decision away from Lois to say "no more."

Though I had nothing but admiration and respect for both the social worker and Lois's favorite nurse, I felt deflated. I could see in Lois's eyes, she felt the same way. When the social work said good-bye to Lois in the waiting room, it felt like she was saying good-bye forever. The same was true of her nurse at the infusion center. Even though events certainly spoke of stopping, the discussion to get to that point had not yet been verbalized or worked through. It felt like they wanted Lois under the gravestone . . . and we both felt it. A saying from one of our modern-day poets summarizes how damaging this day was for us. *"People will forget what you said. They will forget what you did. But they will never forget how you made them feel."* I remembered the dream Lois once had a very long time ago. It was about the ship where she had been checking off names of all the people who would help her on her journey. I now thought, they are standing on the shoreline with Lois on the ship alone, ready to make sail. It had to be lonely on an empty ship completely aware you were embarking to a place over the mysterious horizon . . . to a point unknown.

The next day, Lois was not sure what to do or say. She was caught in the kind of limbo between life as she knew it and the impending yawn of death. She was afraid. Being afraid was not new to her. Many times in her past, we never knew if the next treatment would work or not. So far, all of them had. But this time, there was nothing left to try; no magical drug would pull her back. Her tumor markers were rising. New areas in her body showed metastasis. Nothing she ate or drank stayed down. It was true . . . the outlook wasn't good. Still, she needed and wanted to speak with her oncologist to know if her fears were valid; and if they were, how much time did she have left?

I think Lois took account of everything that Friday. Her health was not good, but the surreal dimensions of it were not explored. The oncologist never had a chance to go over any options with her, and even if she could not do another cycle of chemotherapy, could the nausea be controlled? After all, there was still a position waiting for her. If nausea could be stabilized, there was an off chance she still might be able to work for a short time, however long that might be. Things were still not so dire but ominous.

I brought in the mail the next day, Saturday, August 28, 2010. There was a bunch of sales catalogs and about four pieces of real mail. Lois had been lying down in the bedroom watching television when I brought the mail into her. I told her, "It doesn't look like much. I'll leave you to look through it while I get some things done."

"Go ahead, but can you bring back my 'slitter'?" she smiled, knowing I knew what she wanted was a metal envelope opener we kept in a kitchen drawer with other accumulated paraphernalia, like pens, pencils, tape, and glue.

When I returned to the bedroom, she was crying inconsolably. "What's wrong?" I asked, seeing her hold an innocuous piece of paper that looked like something sent by a promotion for a magazine.

"I no longer have a job to go back to," she told me as she handed me the piece of paper.

I read the nonjudgmental form letter that stated the agency she worked for was allowing her to stay on full benefits until November 6, 2010, but that she had to turn in her cell phone, keys, and her badge. Any hope she would be able to return to work was dashed to pieces. From what I could surmise, they were done with her. She had the right to long-term disability, but it was Saturday . . . No one she could even call until Monday. So within two subsequent days, Lois gave up her right to live and pursue treatment and lost her place, her identity, in this world. It was a two-punch knockdown I didn't feel she would be able to recover from.

I was angry at both facilities. Why tell a patient dire news on a Friday, when after a patient has thought about the ramifications, there would be questions that needed to be asked? Certainly, we were there the previous Monday; why didn't this discussion come up then? Or Wednesday, for that matter? Second, why send out such a formidable letter that would only reach you on a Saturday when nothing could be sorted out until Monday, at best? Again, it could have been mailed so it would have come during a business day. Both situations put Lois in a place where she felt defenseless and alone. It was like both institutions were taking "sucker punches" at her, and even if she could have gotten up, she wasn't going to be able to deliver any of her own. Cowards do this. There is no conscionable reason I can come up with that services a patient or an employee with actions where they cannot respond immediately.

If the news, on both fronts, had waited until Monday, she could have, at least, defended herself. Or at best, she would have had time to think and ask questions of those who would have been available. As it was, no one was there, and she felt isolated and abandoned.

This was the person who fought so avidly for the rights of breast cancer patients, fought for legislation, advocated for change, met with state senators, and talked to state and national representatives in Washington DC to advocate for breast cancer patients and survivors across the nation being brought to her knees by those she fought for.

When Sunday came, she could barely talk. She was so subdued; she only whispered or spoke in a very soft voice, like her voice would betray she still existed. There was no command; there was no force, just resignation. The woman who was a reigning voice for breast cancer survivors and patients was finally silenced. Even the simplest action of getting out of bed was too much to ask of her. I felt so badly for her. We talked the entire day away about what may be ahead of us, but she made no attempt to act on anything we spoke of. This was very uncharacteristic of her. She didn't want anyone called. She just wanted to be alone with me, and for that time, this was good enough for me.

I looked at her body, thinning as it was, clothes barely able to stay up from loss of weight, and I felt angry. Angry, because there was nothing I could do for her. Nothing I could say, nothing I did would make any difference now. It was such a short time to live. It was something Lois and I spoke about, how much she still wanted to do but was not going to get the chance. Yet when I looked back over her short life, she did more than ten people in her lifetime. I told her again if she could draw life from her spirit instead of her body, she would have lived past one hundred. She laughed and then said, "That's not how it works."

On Monday, August 30, 2010, Lois was very weak and in a lot of pain when she woke up. She told me her knees were giving her a lot of trouble again and was afraid they would buckle if she put her slight weight on them. I gave her something for nausea and pain so she could make it to the infusion center for IV fluids. I knew her intake of oral fluids and food at home was not enough to keep her going anymore. I knew the IV fluids would help as they had in the past. After I helped her into her clothes, packed up the wheelchair, and made our way to the infusion room, she had her fluids. The IVs perked her up a little, but when I got her back home, she went to bed, exhausted from the short three-mile trip. She slept the rest of the day away. I wasn't sure if she felt this way from physical exhaustion or from emotions not played out in their final dance.

It was just a little thing anymore to see her get up and about, just to look out the windows, or walk about the house. It meant a lot to my son, and I just to know she was still able to do it. In these afternoons after IV therapy, I would find her exhausted and sleeping soundly. Before I would leave for work in the evenings, I would wake her to give her medications and an injection of a blood thinner in her abdomen to keep clots from forming in her legs. The sites I used to administer these were disappearing, as she had very little abdominal fat to rotate sites anymore. Still, there always seemed to be another way to get one more injection into her. Though she didn't like the injections, she was always gracious and thankful I could do them for her. So when it was time to kiss her good-bye for the evening, she would always have the injection ready for me to administer. However, on the nights I worked now, she rarely had them ready anymore, so I prepared them myself. She would always apologize, saying she would have gotten it for me. I never complained; she had enough on her plate for a dozen people.

Unless the nausea, keeping her from any nutritional intake, abates, we fear her time with us is limited. Yet we still have to speak in the hypothetical sense, since we have not spoken to the oncologist. We need to hear his outlook on the things that have happened, hear his words of consequences, and hear of his foretelling.

On Tuesday, August 31, 2010, the day starts early, since we need to see the oncologist at 9:45 a.m. Our alarm goes off at 8:00 a.m. We need to get ready. I go to the kitchen and gather all of her medications together. This morning, there are five of them to take before she can even consider moving from beneath the covers. I made hot tea, which is something palatable to her, then took the medications to the bedroom, where she is still sleeping. She wakes up in pain, so she also takes a strong narcotic from me to stave it off. About a half an hour later, she is comfortable enough to move off the bed. I have clothes waiting for her after she showers. When she is dressed, we make our way into the car and put her wheelchair in the trunk.

We make our way to the infusion center where I pull close to the curb nearest the entrance and stop. I pull the wheelchair from the trunk, while people drive around me or yell, "You going to be long? My mother has an appointment here, and she's sick." I pull Lois from the car, barely able to get to the wheelchair on her own, while the guy blows his horn, thinking this will hurry me. I stay oblivious to him as I wheel her inside the sliding glass doors to wait for me until I park the car. I park then find her inside the glass doors smiling at me as I push her to the infusion room.

I sense a little more urgency from her this morning. I know we are going to discuss stopping treatments for now. She already knows this conversation will occur. She has the social worker and me in tow for this. Almost like the first time, the term "breast cancer" was spoken to us almost eighteen years ago . . . the whole thing seems surreal. I'm watching a play where the actors are Lois, the social worker, and me. Then enters the oncologist, saying, without treatments, she will have four to six months left to her life. I think he is being conservative, realizing her weight has dropped to just one hundred pounds. In the past week, she lost five pounds already. For someone weighing a hundred pounds and losing three to four pounds a week, you just have to do the math and know it may not be as long as he predicts. The choice to stop everything leaves us all emotional and in tears. The oncologist is a human being. He stoops over and hugs my wife, wiping tears away as he does. He has never shown emotions before, but he does now, acknowledging Lois as one of his most challenging patients. He tells her he has learned much from her he would not have learned without knowing her. He feels she was a partner and a colleague with her care. It was the last time Lois ever had the chance to see or talk with him. I think it may have been too painful for him.

Before Lois left the office, she asked to be put on home care so any continuing IV therapy could be done at home. This way, she could stay home and not be carted from home to the infusion center three times a week. Her oncologist felt this was a good idea and told her he still held out hope she could turn around and try chemotherapy again. The oncologist explained, though she did not tolerate the treatment well, the chemo successfully backed the markers down over two hundred points. Yet he understood how devastating the treatment was on her overall health. Still he held out hope. He wanted to do another marker in late September, but Lois could not see the point and decided against it. Now we held our breath and waited.

With our son back at home attending college and working, I had a live-in sitter for the nights I worked. Over the successive months, word went out to family and friends that Lois stopped treatments and was living out the rest of her days at home. In spite of the grave prognosis, Lois continued to stay in touch with her colleagues both at work and her breast cancer advocacy groups by phone and the Internet, hoping to influence people to stand with her during the elections on November 2, 2010. She was still up and about, going to the store with me when she could, and even picked out a suit for me to wear to her funeral, she later told me. Though she was dying, she did not want any of us to be sad. She lightened the mood about her condition with every visitor, every encounter she had.

Lois had visitors come to the house from all over the country. One of her friends came all the way to Pennsylvania from Florida just to see her. People from all over our local area, Philadelphia, and Washington DC came to our home. Those who could not visit made calls from New York, Virginia, Arizona, all along the West Coast, and the Midwest. Her friends and colleagues who could make it to our home in Pennsylvania made the journey. Many of her friends came weekly or biweekly to visit. A group of women from Philadelphia made the two-and-a-half-hour trip three or four times over her remaining months. Lois wrote the following letter to her friends over the Internet in mid-September.

(Letter from Lois A. Anderson dated September 13, 2010)

Dear Friends,

It is with a heavy heart that I write this note. I am sorry I cannot deliver this message in person. I wish to make all of you aware that I was given a very grave prognosis last week when I saw my oncologist. It seems that I have reached the end of the line with treatments for my breast cancer. The last one we tried in August sent me spinning and I ended up in the hospital once again with uncontrolled nausea and vomiting after treatment. There were some more metastatic sites found on my CT-scan while I was in the hospital.

As of this writing I am at home taking it easy and letting this surreal information sink in. If you would care to visit, please give a call to make sure I am able to have visitors.

Take care,

Lois

When my eighty-something-year-old mother realized Lois was dying, she and Lois spoke of "end of life" situations. Lois and I had living wills, durable power of attorney, wills, and power of attorney papers drawn up many years before when she was first diagnosed. The two of them looked these papers over and found them to be in order. However, we never purchased a cemetery plot on which to be buried or considered a funeral home. My mother had possession of four lots. She wanted to give two lots to us, one for Lois, and one for myself. However, there was the problem of signing papers and looking the lots over. The whole idea of considering these things seemed morose and melancholy to me. Yet as Lois pointed out, there were things she and my mother discussed that needed to be done before she was too weak to do any of it. So before she was too weak to get out anymore, the three of us went to the cemetery and made the arrangements for her burial site.

Lois continued to work on advocacy concerns from home when she felt well enough to get to her computer. She used her time to work on disability forms and made calls during the day to prepare and tie up loose ends with the insurance companies. When she was tired, she lay down beside me and held my hand while I was sleeping. Many times when I woke up I found her hand clasping mine, and I knew she was trying to comfort me.

We missed our thirty-third wedding anniversary on September 18 the year before, and I made it my business to be off for our thirty-fourth. I wanted to take her someplace, but she was not up to it. So I found some movies and bought a dozen red roses to mark the occasion. She cried when she saw the roses. I stifled back a tear, knowing we would never see our next anniversary together. We could have been melancholy, but we found some old picture albums and saw the many places we had been over our lifetime, and somehow it made us happy to know we visited so many places together. We lay together on the bed and watched "chick flicks" until she fell asleep.

Home care nurses came three times a week and administered IV fluids. Our nurse evaluated how well the nausea was controlled, how her pain was doing, and evaluated her weight. Constipation was an enormous problem to consider because of the pain medications and the antiemetics. Many times, very strong laxatives were needed, and occasionally an oil retention enema to relieve this. While this is not something we talk about in polite conversations, the constipation contributed significantly to the nausea and her inability to eat anything. By the time her fifty-eighth birthday arrived on October 6, 2010, she weighed less than ninety pounds. On October 12, 2010, I brought her eighteen pink roses and one white one to signify she had survived eighteen years with breast cancer. The white one, as Lois knew, was for hope for the next year. It was a bittersweet moment for us both.

By the end of October, Lois was very weak and was not out of the house for several weeks. She managed to keep informed of the upcoming election and was determined to make it to the polls to vote. Her nausea was so bad, when I asked her to walk to the end of the driveway, a matter of a hundred feet, she started getting nauseated and had to go back. I could not see how she would ever make the three-mile trip to vote. She was on the Internet with her friends who advocated for breast cancer concerns, and she gave her opinion as to who she wanted in and who she wanted out. She was determined not to allow certain seats to be taken by people she did not feel would do a good job or had a history of ignoring the public's needs. She felt she had to vote and wanted to be sure everyone else did as well. So as a final tribute to her political advocacy, I took her to the polls on November 2, 2010.

The morning of the elections, Lois managed to get showered and dressed herself. She put on makeup to cover her pale complexion and wore clothes once too tight for her but still fit loosely over her emaciated body. By the time she exerted the energy to get ready, she was exhausted. The nausea was getting bad, and she took an antiemetic to stifle it. However, within minutes of taking it, she vomited even before I got her to the car. I asked her, "Are you sure you are going to be able to do this?"

The question seemed to make her angry. "Don't worry about me . . . If I throw up, then I throw up. But I'm going to vote." She was stubborn and brave, feeling she could, at least, try to make this last bit of difference with her vote.

I managed to get her into the car without further trouble and positioned a large plastic basin she had from the hospital in front of her. I shut the car door for her so she didn't have to move. She was trying to stay rigidly still, knowing motion would stir the nausea up again. I started the car and pulled it to the end of the driveway, stopping to look both ways for oncoming traffic. Even before I pulled out, Lois started retching clear fluid. Tears welled in her eyes from the exertion of vomiting so forcefully. Before I pulled out, I asked, "Are you going to be all right?"

"Just get the car moving and let's get there," she chided me with some emphasis.

"All right . . ." I said skeptically. "I hope I can get you there in one piece."

"Just do it," Lois seethed through clenched teeth, as if this would prevent her from getting nauseated again.

I pulled away from the driveway and drove the car as smoothly as I could the three miles to the voting site. Lois brought her hard-fought driver's license so they could see her photo ID, as did I. As Lois predicted, once I had the car moving at an even pace, she was all right. Still, she clenched her teeth and remained quiet for the short trip. When I parked the car, the pent-up nausea hit her hard. The hard spasmodic vomiting left her rib cage sore and cramped. I went to the passenger side door and opened it. She asked me to put my hands on her cramped ribs, which I did there in the parking lot. I'm sure anyone passing by certainly wondered what I was doing with my hands up her shirt.

"You're going to get me arrested doing this," I said with lighthearted sincerity.

"If you make me laugh, I'm going to throw up on you next," she said, as a smile reeked through the grimace.

"The ribs are easing up . . . How is the nausea doing?"

"I feel better, but let me catch my breath a little. The air is cold, and it's making it hard to breathe."

"Do you want me to start the car and let you warm up a little?" I asked, seeing some of her energy returning.

"Yes, I think that would help. Then we should go in."

I started the car, letting the heater warm the air inside. Her color was returning, and she said she was ready to try it after about five minutes. We walked to the door like any other couple going to the polls. We gave our names at the desk then cast our votes. When Lois was done, she was smiling ear to ear. She took a sticker that said "I voted" and stuck it on her pocketbook. We walked back to the car like nothing happened on the way, then made our way back home.

We made it to the garage door before the vomiting hit her hard again. The forcefulness of the vomiting was so hard, it doubled her over, making her gasp for breath between spasms. She could not get out of the car because the episode followed with terrible abdominal spasms. She was crying out from the pain. I went into the house, found the antiemetics, and gave one to her, thinking she probably lost her last dose with the emesis. I put my hands on her chest wall again and tried to warm her up to a point where the spasms would allow her to stand up. When she could finally stand, I put my arm around her waist and took her weight on my hip and led her back to the bedroom. I got her into bed, clothes and all, and then covered her with blankets. Almost immediately, she went into a deep sleep.

I watched as she drew air into her damaged lungs, breathing deeply like she had run a marathon. In fact, for a person with a compromised respiratory system, bone metastasis, and almost uncontrolled nausea, she probably had. It was perhaps one of the bravest things I ever saw her do. She believed in the right to vote, and nothing, not even her physical condition, was going to stop her. When I think of how easy it is for most of us to go out to vote and those who rescind the right to do so, I remember this day and marvel at the supreme effort she put into getting herself to the voting booth.

I was never able to get her out of the house again. I knew her days of venturing out into the cold air were over. But I was very proud of her.

November 6 was fast approaching, and the end of her full-time benefits was ending. She would soon be on disability benefits, and my insurance would be the only one to take care of her medical bills. Lois made many calls in October and early November to set up her own hospice. She kept notes on every phone call she made and whom she spoke with. By November 7, home care was over, and hospice stepped in. Without eating, she had weakened significantly. She was still able to get out of bed and get around the house with little difficulty. Lois continued to manage her own health care in both the physical sense and in the financial (or insurance) sense. She was a social worker for hospice for over five years and understood the "ins and outs" of insurers and policies regarding end-of-life decisions and planning. Though her body betrayed her, her mind did not. She was just as clear minded as she had ever been.

My mother turned eighty-two in 2010. She was confused about Medicare, Social Security, and private insurers, as many people her age were. During the times when my mother stayed with Lois, they spoke of these matters. Much later, I learned Lois assisted her to make decisions after explaining the details within the systems and how they could affect her. My mother said she felt Lois was one of the most intelligent people she ever met. The two of them worked together to get the best coverage for her age group and financial situation. Again, Lois continued to look out for people other than her. She was always the doer, never the taker. She remained alive and vibrant.

It was during this time, she worked by phone with her previous insurer, and now, the secondary insurer, to cover all of her expenses, both in the past and in the future, until she died. On good days, which became less existent as November wore away to nothing, Lois created a list of names and phone numbers I was to notify when she passed away. Her list was so detailed with policy numbers, alternate phone numbers, dates of purchase, and values of policies, it was easily followed. The whole idea of planning for her death, making certain everything was in place for our son and me to continue afterward, was surreal. It was like watching a normal, healthy person getting their business affairs in order so they could pass everything on to the next owner without complications. She performed all this from our bedroom or, when she could, from the living room sofa, using two landlines and her cell phone. When she was finished with calls, she would write a summary of what she accomplished and created files for me to use after she died.

As I've said, it seemed surreal at the time, but everything she did prior to her death helped me follow up on her affairs afterward. It was the kindest, most loving thing I ever saw anyone do.

She remained active until the end of November when she needed to stay on oxygen all the time. The idea of dying did not appeal to her, and she had no intention of letting go without a fight. Just after Thanksgiving, Lois decided to have Christmas dinner at our house. When she told me about her ambitious plan, I was incredulous. "How are we going to do this?" I asked her. She then informed me of how it was going to be done. Somehow, I should have known she had everything under control from the beginning. I just couldn't believe how thorough she had been. She thought everything through. She informed me she made calls to her sister, who was to make the turkey, calls to her two brothers, her aunts, my brother, my mother, and everyone else coming to the house on Christmas Day. They were all coming Christmas morning to make the house ready for dinner. She had a big smile on her face when she told me what she planned. I knew I should not have been surprised. She already enlisted my son and my mother, both of whom had stayed the nights with her, to conjure all this up. From her bed, on oxygen, nauseated, and in severe pain much of the time, she came up with a list of things I was to get at the store. She also made a list of everything our relatives were bringing for Christmas dinner. She was quite pleased with herself, knowing she still had something to plan for, something to contribute to life.

Christmas was fast approaching. Lois was always the shopper for the family, and this year was no exception. Using many store catalogs that drown our mailbox around Christmas, Lois managed to pick out several things for everyone that put a kind of personal touch on things. Packages started arriving daily, and we were not allowed to see what came inside. In spite of her failing health, she was putting together a Christmas event that would not be forgotten for a very long time. It was our last Christmas together, and she wanted it to be special, not just for our son and me but for everyone as well. She was feeling very pleased, enlisting my mother to do most of the Christmas wrapping and boxing up of the gifts for our son and myself.

Even though Lois tried to get all the insurance issues concluded in November, there were still some loose ends to deal with during the middle of December. Our insurance agent had to come to the house to explain options and sign papers. Lois listened intently to what he had to say and then had very intelligent questions to ask him afterward. Her body was failing, but her mind remained sharp and focused. Using what the agent told us and using Lois's good judgment, we concluded our business with all the insurances about December 17, 2010. From here, the dust would settle where it may.

As the year drew to a close, Lois's condition declined steadily. Her weight was just over seventy pounds. She could not eat anything. One favorite food I could get her to eat was apple slices and soft cheese. Though it wasn't much, just seeing her take something made me feel better. The nausea never stopped but was managed. The pain was constant; rarely was it completely controlled. She was sleeping almost twenty hours a day, waking up only for visitors or to see the news reports.

On December 20, 2010, an event occurred that was mystical, magical, and something Lois was able to see from a bedroom window with some help from our son. It was the night of the winter's solstice and an eclipse of the moon. I told Lois she managed to stay with us long enough to experience an event so rare it hadn't occurred since the year 1638, almost four centuries ago. Lois told me that night she probably wouldn't be around for another one, which made me laugh. I told her, "Well, neither will I." She smiled and then put her hand over mine as we watched the eclipse through the bedroom window. I knew, even before the shadow of the moon was complete, the music had faded . . . the dance was over.

The Last Road

Tell me about her last road . . .

Darkness addressed me in my world, but here in the dream within a dream, it was the gloaming. Just below the horizon, the darkness waited, striking at the light that became incessantly more beautiful as it faded in the sky beneath the Poet's Tree. I feel hollowed out by life, like a structure still standing with gutted ruins, lingering in the dying fires surrounding the fabled village of Stock. She is dying, and no amount of love, no amount of care, and no cadence of soft words will stop her journey down the Last Road. I wait. I watch. I feel the precious moments of life slipping away like drops bleeding from a broken glass.

I have come to know Timothy's pain, and his is mine. We have journeyed far together to come to this place. And I . . . still grope with my mind and my memories of what was, to find what will become. We will all walk the Last Road.

Alexis pulled a brush through her hair as she looked out the window of her room. The roaring fires once surrounding the village of Stock now smoldered, releasing a thin haze of smoke stubbornly clinging to the ground like a gray veil. Everywhere, the ring of metal hammers on iron spikes and the ripping sounds of saws tearing through newly felled timbers denied the silence she felt Catherine deserved in her final hours. The villagers were not wasting time rebuilding what they lost. In the aftermath, her father's farm became the refuge for many families burned out of their homes. Eric, Lamin, Andrew, and many of their newfound friends erected makeshift pole tents to create shelters on Jakob's farm. After such a terrible ordeal, her brothers did not have the heart to turn anyone away.

Alexis swept the brush through her hair once more, placing it on her late mother's dressing table positioned below the oval window. She turned back to face the room, swept up her hair with one hand, and with the other, bound it in a pink ribbon, tying it back over her shoulder. It was not just the efforts of her brothers that drew the villagers to their father's farmlands but also the arrival of Catherine and her parents to the two lower rooms of the farmhouse. After Catherine sealed the breach with her lifestone, she was brought here, where everyone believed Timothy would return . . . if he were still alive.

With the ribbon in place, Alexis went to a mirror positioned behind her bedroom door, doing a cursory inspection of her appearance before the expected assembly of visitors to her father's home. The activities inside the house fell to the resources of herself, Michael, and Leena. During the second day of the stone sickness, Catherine was still able to have visitors. But today, she did not know if Leena and Michael would allow anyone to visit.

She was hesitant to put her hand on the door handle. Alexis knew when the door opened, time would pursue her like a hungry wolf. If Timothy did not return with something to help Catherine, she would walk the Last Road without him. So many died already . . . Certainly death did not need another victim to complete its bitter score. With her brothers out of the house, keeping the homeless villagers from overrunning the boundaries of their home, it was up to Michael, Leena, and herself to maintain decorum and control the flow of visitors wanting to see Catherine.

Yesterday, the second day of the stone sickness, Leena suggested Catherine was almost out of time. Her daughter was in constant pain; unable to eat or drink anything, and many times she seemed unable to focus on anything happening around her. When she lost consciousness, the end was near. Alexis watched Leena hold her daughter's hand, rarely allowing it to fall from her grasp, then to Michael, taking control of the many visitors still arriving, just for a glimpse of his daughter. Alexis knew Catherine was increasingly listless in the last moments before she retired for the night. She thought Michael allowed too many visitors with benevolent intentions of staying a moment to offer their thanks and say farewell to his daughter.

Alexis absentmindedly looked at her hand resting on the door latch. It was something from a painting, not hers. She looked at her bare feet; she forgot her shoes. Her moment of inattentiveness delayed her departure, allowing just a breath of time to regain some courage while she pulled on her shoes and laced them up. She returned to the door, moved the latch, and then walked quietly to the balcony overlooking the lower rooms. The display of stillness she found there was foretelling. Today was different. The air was palpable with the presence of grief and silence. There were no muffled voices coming from the front door. It was unlike the hum of whispers and reverent speaking, which filled the rooms below her these past two days.

She took a moment to watch Michael and Leena sitting to either side of their daughter. Even before she reached the top of the staircase, where she would descend to reach them, she knew the moments left to them this day were more precious than any thanks, any monument her visitors secured to honor her memory. If Michael and Leena wanted to be selfish with their daughter, she could not fault them.

The back of the house was built with a stone-floored kitchen where Jakob and his family brought Alexis fruits and vegetables from the summer fields. There she would prepare the meals on an iron stove and place them on a long wooden table when they came in from their labors. Adjacent to the busy kitchen were the formal room where they kept a well-polished wooden table where they ate on special occasions and then the large entry room where they accepted visitors at the front of the house. Around three sides of the farmhouse was a covered porch, built by her father when her mother was still living, where her family spent many summer evenings watching sunsets fade away on the steps of the busy house.

The wooden table was pushed to the side of the formal room with chairs turned upside down on its top when Catherine arrived. Her brothers cleared a space wide enough to carry a small bed to the room where Catherine and her parents could stay. Leena and Michael sent word to her brother Stephan when they arrived to come as quickly as he could. He was coming from one of the most southern villages, the village of Rossland. He was making the long journey to Stock with his family with roads besotted with busy travelers, imbued with wagonloads of supplies, and ruined roads destroyed by the industry of the murdering orbs. He would have a difficult time getting here, and Leena was certain he would never get the chance to say good-bye to his sister. Even Alexis believed he would not arrive in time to see his sister alive.

Alexis remained in her thoughts haunted by one thing, the one thought that plagued her every time she tried to find the field of sleep, the one thought that lingered in her moments before waking . . . Was Timothy still alive? Was he killed when he tried to escape from the village of Glade with Victoria, Penny, Rand, and Leon? Did he die trying to save his beloved Catherine? Because if he survived, where was he when she needed him? *She did not know how to feel with her heart tormented by his absence—and for Catherine, who was steadily dying before her.*

In some way, Alexis felt Timothy was still alive, still trying to find a way to save Catherine. Yet hope slipped away like wine dripping from the bottom of a broken goblet. Before the end of this day, Catherine would die. It was the third day of her stone sickness, and no one survived beyond the third day. Catherine was so lethargic, yet when she woke, she cried out in pain. Alexis hoped, for her sake, she did not survive much longer. She felt guilty thinking her friend would be freed from her pain by death. The enigma of wanting to save her but needing to allow her to die defeated any sense of hope she still held in her heart of hearts. Catherine's sacrifice made all their lives possible again, but Catherine was rewarded with a death filled with unimaginable pain. If Timothy was alive, why didn't he send word of what he was doing or where he was?

The room where Catherine laid on the borrowed bed, greedily guarded by her parents, was strangely quiet. There were no visitors, and Alexis knew that if she asked, they would have told her they wanted Catherine's last moments to be with them alone. Alexis moved closer to where Leena held Catherine's hand in her own. Michael sat opposite her, head in his hands, not letting anyone see the tears that unsuccessfully waited there.

"I was expecting the room to be busy with visitors this morning," Alexis whispered, catching Leena off guard as her head jerked in attention toward Alexis.

Leena looked tired, with lines running from her eyes in some nondescript map. "She's too exhausted to see anyone today. I told Michael to keep everyone away. Your brothers are making sure everyone stays off the porches and away from the windows," Leena said, as she leaned down to hear Catherine whisper something to her.

Alexis tried to listen for Catherine's voice, but even in this quiet room, her whispers were too faint to hear. She watched Leena put her ear close to Catherine's lips, listening intently to the words that would burn in her memory for the remainder of her life. Catherine said many things to her mother over time, but these words would be indelible, visited over and over like a prayer to the Winds. Alexis understood. She lost her mother when an infection crept into body When sshe was dying, she made Alexis promise she would take care of her brothers and her father. She wanted them to know she loved them, then told her daughter Alexis, "I love you so much, my dear daughter." Those were the last words she ever heard her mother say. Those words could not be any clearer, either now or then, even if they had been clearly written on stone. She would never forget them.

Leena motioned for Alexis to come closer. "Catherine wants to say something to you before she is too weak to talk."

Alexis nodded and then walked to the head of the bed where the pale husk of the girl she knew as Catherine lay. She lay there with eyes open, yet she did not seem to see. Her lips were cracked and bleeding in places where the wounded edges no longer came together. Her face somehow sank in places, and there were dark hollows in the places where her blue unseeing eyes still showed a spark of life. Even in the ravages of the stone sickness, she was still beautiful. Catherine whispered something she could not hear as she looked to Leena to interpret what Catherine said.

"She wants you to lean in closer." Leena pulled away from her chair, offering it to Alexis. Alexis looked at Leena, not certain of what she wanted her to do. "It's okay. Please sit here. Catherine is too weak to do much more than whisper. Just get very close and listen."

Alexis walked to the chair and sat next to Catherine. Catherine seemed to struggle to find Alexis until she spoke up. "I'm here, Catherine . . . I'm here . . . It's Alexis." Alexis found Catherine's hand on the bedspread and held it. Catherine struggled again to say something, but she could not make it out. "I need to get closer, Catherine. Just wait, and then tell me what you want to say." Alexis put her ear just a finger's length from Catherine's lips. "Go on, Catherine. I'm here."

At first, the cracked lips seemed unable to produce anything but the fetid breath moving through them. Then she finally pronounced a word, "Sister . . ." she said.

"Sister?" Alexis said, deeply moved Catherine felt she was like a sister.

From beneath the dry lips, Catherine struggled. "I love you like a sister." She was tiring but struggled to continue. "Tell your brothers . . . thank you for helping me. They are brave, and I love them all." She struggled again to take a deep breath. She seemed to use all her energy trying to tell Alexis her final words.

"Rest now, Catherine. I will tell them," Alexis said with tears running down her face. She had made a slight move to leave the chair when Catherine's hand tightened on hers.

"Don't go," she whispered.

"I will stay for as long as you like." Alexis sobbed silently.

"Timothy?" she asked with a shuddered breath.

"We haven't heard anything from Timothy," Alexis said as calmly as she could, not wanting to upset her.

"He is on a great journey," she whispered with a faint smile. Then resigned to concluding, she said, "I am so tired."

Alexis knew Catherine could not continue talking much longer. She was exhausted. The stone sickness was well upon her, and every word had to be a small agony. She wanted to let her sleep and tried to pull her fingers from Catherine's grasp. But yet again, Catherine tightened her hold. She still had something she wanted to say.

"Come closer, my sister," she said to Alexis, panting horribly to catch her breath. "When you see my Timothy . . ." She stopped, panting until she could speak again. "Tell him . . . I love him more than anything."

Catherine expended a tremendous amount of her remaining energy just to tell her this. Her hand fell away weakly as Alexis pulled away from her. Her whisperings were so faint, even Leena, standing as close as she had been, did not hear what she said to her.

Leena watched as Alexis moved slowly from the offered chair with tears running down her face. The two women looked at one another, unable to speak. Catherine struggled to breathe, wheezing air over her dried lips. Alexis stood by the chair and nodded to Leena to return to her daughter. As they passed one another, Leena reached out to Alexis and hugged her. They wept in each other's embrace as Michael kept vigil from the other side of the bed in abject silence.

Michael's thoughts ran deep as he watched his daughter struggling to hold fast to her fragile life. He thought of all the people he buried along the Last Road on the way to the breach where his Catherine effectively ended her life by sacrificing her lifestone to save them all. He remembered Benjamin, Jakob, and all the others who fought and died trying to help Catherine make this sacrifice. And Timothy . . . what happened to him? Was he still on a quest to save Catherine? Had he died, or was he lying someplace injured, unable to go on? Was he just one more tragedy in a line of tragedies still waiting to be discovered? He listened as his daughter breathed heavily then started the incessant panting again. She would barely last until the dark time broke in a blaze of stars. It would be winter solstice tonight with a total eclipse of the moon. According to the heralds, who knew these things, an event like this had not occurred in almost four centuries. He hoped Catherine would still be here when it happened. Michael knew neither he nor his daughter would be here to see another one in this lifetime. They would both be with the Four Winds when the next one occurred. It wasn't much comfort to know, but this last shared experience with his daughter would be the last thing they would hold together.

Alexis walked into the kitchen and tried to keep busy. The day moved slowly as she walked to the back door and checked in with her brothers. People, when they saw her, came up and asked how Catherine was doing. She did not know what to tell them . . . she was dying; there was nothing left to say. The day passed, and the darkness walked slowly to her doorstep. She checked with Leena and Michael from time to time, but they were grieving and did not ask anything of her. Catherine had no more to say as all her remaining strength was exerted to breathe.

When the dark time came, Alexis made her rounds. Michael motioned for her to come to the bedside where he asked her to open the curtains over one of the windows. By the time he made the request, the moon was full and round, easily seen through the parlor window where he and Leena kept vigil over Catherine's bed.

"Sit with us, Alexis," Michael invited. "Tonight will be the full eclipse of the moon. Have you ever seen one?"

"Once, with my father," Alexis answered sadly, thinking of her father's absence.

Michael looked out the window in a dreamlike state, like the events happening around him didn't exist. He looked to Alexis, then to Leena, then Catherine. "This one will be magical, mystical, and hasn't happened for a very long time. I know Catherine will stay with us long enough to see it."

Alexis looked to Michael sadly. It wasn't much to cling to, but it was something. She brought a chair from the kitchen and pulled it next to Catherine's bed. They all watched as the dark edge slid over the white of the moon. Catherine's labored breathing went to shallow panting, still audible, while the darkness grew. By the time the moon was fully eclipsed, she stopped breathing. Catherine was gone. Wherever Timothy had gone, he was too late.

The Last Dream

Tell me about dreams . . .

It is time to tell you my deepest secret. I will hold you in my heart forever, like timeless pictures on the walls of my mind. She was dying. She had me call the entire family together on Christmas Eve just before midnight. She told me to get everyone together so she could say good-bye. I made the calls as quickly as I could then went back to sit with her.

"It's time for me to go," Lois told me calmly, as if nothing was wrong.

"Go where?" I asked, seeing her physical condition had not changed dramatically and saw no reason why she felt this way.

"I'm dying," she told me, looking directly into my eyes, with tears welling up in the corners.

"Are you feeling worse? Any pain, or did it get hard to breathe all of a sudden?" I asked, trying to find out if I could do something to make her feel any better.

"No . . . I don't feel any different," she told me, as I watched her analyze her symptoms as she had done so many times in the past.

I looked at her and tried to understand what she might have experienced to make her so afraid. I lay down beside her and took both of her hands into mine. Whatever calls I could not make, I assigned to our son. I gave him a nod when he came back to the room. He told us he contacted everyone, and they were on their way.

"I love you both so much," she told us when we were both in the room with her. Our adult son broke down in tears, as she pulled one hand from me and placed it on his face.

"What's wrong, Mom?" he asked, barely able to keep the tears away.

"I just woke up and knew my time was gone," she told him.

"But how do you feel?" I asked, still trying to find out if her body was as ready to go as her spirit must have been.

She turned to me, and her determination spooked me for a moment. "Nothing is different . . . I just know."

"Did you get hold of Lisa, Jim?" I asked, with obvious concern in my voice.

"Yes . . . I got her on my cell phone while you were on the other phone," he told me.

Lisa has been our hospice nurse for the last three months. She felt Lois was holding on just to get us through Christmas. Lisa was certain Lois did not want to die on an important holiday . . . She would not want us to remember her that way. However, at this moment, I wasn't so sure.

I've been a registered nurse for over thirty-five years, and it has been my experience that when someone tells me they are going to die . . . you better listen to them. Yet as I sat with my wife of thirty-four years, I was not as certain as I would have been with one of my patients. I looked across the bed to our son and said, "I think I am going to have to let this one for Lisa. I can't find anything wrong, but I believe what she tells me." I looked to my beautiful wife and told her, "Lois, if this is your time, don't be afraid. Jim and I are here, and we won't leave you. If you are to go tonight, Jim and I will be okay." My voice was breaking up. I just looked into her eyes. She was still here. She was still coherent and thinking. She was still breathing and said she didn't feel any different. I couldn't understand what happened.

The first of many doorbells rang. "Jim, should I get it, or are you okay?"

"I'm okay," he said, as he got up and left the room to answer the door.

Lois held on to me and told me, "I love you more than anything."

"I know you do, and I love you too," I told her, wiping my eyes before the first visitor made it back to our bedroom.

Somehow in those last few minutes before midnight, before the bells tolled the advent of Christmas, Lois assembled the whole family. Our hospice nurse, Lisa, was on her way. As the family arrived, everyone went back to see her. Lois seemed calmer and comfortable after she had the chance to see her family. When Lisa made it back to her, she did a thorough exam and could not find anything physically wrong with her other than the obvious signs of dehydration and marked weight loss. By this time, Lois lost almost half of her original weight, weighing perhaps seventy pounds of her normal 130-pound weight. The person before us was skeletal in comparison to the person she was only three months ago, but her mind and her spirit never changed. She told Lisa she had no pain, no breathing problems, no fever . . . Lisa could not find a thing. Yet at that moment, we all believed something changed profoundly. We all knew she was dying, but there was still something holding her to us. We never found out why she persevered, but I think she loved us all too much to leave.

Eventually, everyone went home, and Lois managed to get back to sleep. We all put it down to some kind of anxiety attack, but on Christmas Day, I found out what happened.

Lois planned our last Christmas by asking for help from everyone. The dinner, the presents, and the decorations were originated by her design or her designation of tasks to certain family members. By Christmas Day, she was too weak to hand out presents herself, so she had Jim and I give them out to everyone. Our traditional Christmas tree stood in our large recreation room as it always did, a place Lois could not even conceive of going in her condition. I didn't want her to miss her last Christmas without a tree, so I brought a small three-foot artificial tree, beautifully decorated with lights and ornaments, and placed it on the bed beside her. I had everyone place their presents around the small tree on the bed, and then I woke her up.

As many people as we could fit in our bedroom stood by the bedside as she opened her gifts. As she moved from one present to another, she would call the person who gave it to her to come to the bed as she opened it so she could thank them. Though the presents mainly consisted of clothing and movies, the delight of opening a Christmas present persisted in the inner child that knows they are loved. Her eyes shone like never before, as if this was the first Christmas she experienced instead of the last. She laughed and smiled, and in my eyes, it was perhaps the best Christmas present she could have given to all of us. She let us know she was content that we all loved her and made her a part of that last Christmas together. She didn't want to be a bystander with nothing to offer. Instead, she was the focus and the center of all the planning and commitments she drew from everyone. It was the most amazing culmination of planning I ever saw. Even in her most debilitated state, she pulled off a Christmas event that amazed everyone.

Unwrapping gifts left her tired but not exhausted. She issued orders for her sister and brothers to begin serving Christmas dinner to everyone once the presents were opened. Just before I left the room to help everyone with seating and dinnerware, she told me what had happened when she had called everyone on Christmas Eve. Her sister had not left the bedroom to go to the kitchen, and she too was curious as to what happened. Lois told us both, while the guests were milling about, that when she woke up on Christmas Eve, she saw a dark hole opening in the ceiling that was drawing her into it. This was why she called everyone to her bedside. Her sister and I realized what she saw was a foretelling of a kind, and we believed her. We also agreed if we saw something like that, we would have been terrified. We did not fault her for her actions.

The rest of the Christmas celebrations went well, and before the night was over, everyone helped put the house back in order again. Surprisingly, Lois remained awake and active until every one of her guests excused themselves and went home. Then she went into a deep sleep, waking up the next day feeling better than she had in a very long time.

I remained at home with her the rest of the week. My employer was aware of my situation at home and was very understanding of my need to be off with my wife. Lois and I enjoyed the time together, still utilizing pain medications, IV fluids, and dealing with the problems of pain, nausea, and suppressed appetite. Lois continued to have visitors from her friends and relatives who stopped in for short periods. She continued to be gracious and held very intelligent conversations with everyone who came, but her periods of wakefulness were shorter, requiring me to prevent some visits from happening.

By January 4, 2011, Lois requested that her IV fluids be stopped indefinitely. Both I and her hospice nurse knew she was asking everyone to let her go. It was a difficult measure to release when we all knew this predication would end her life over a matter of days. Still it was a conscious decision she made to let the cancer take her. We would not attempt any argument with her, as we all understood she did not want to exist like this, unable to participate in the lives and life around her. Even the times she was awake were numbered as an hour or two a day anymore. The pain medications coupled with the medications needed to stop the persistent nausea kept her in a steady state of lethargy. Many times we tried unsuccessfully to waken her. Lois had not used oxygen until January started, but now she wore it constantly, getting short of breath with any exertion. She could manage a short trip to the bathroom when she needed, but the energy she exerted to do so would leave her breathless, until she returned to bed.

By January 9, she was less responsive but woke up momentarily to tell me she was seeing things. She told me, with a smile, a horse came to visit her in her sleep, but it left. She said she knew it would come back after dark because it was a big animal and would not like being out in the dark by itself. I told her there was no horse to which she replied, "Yes, I know. I am seeing things that aren't there now, and I am confused." With that, she closed her eyes and went back to sleep. Sometime later, she called me and told me she saw George Washington floating across the bedroom ceiling. "I know it really isn't there, but I can see it," she told me.

It seemed Lois was slipping between two realities, one where she knew the vision wasn't real and a tenuous hold on the other. I had a book on dreams where I could look these symbols up, and the findings surprised me. The image of George Washington meant she was moving to a higher kind of existence, and the horse meant she was comfortable. Though she was dying and not always able to communicate what she was feeling, the analysis of the symbols seemed to be fairly accurate.

My birthday and my son's birthday both come in January. When my birthday passed at the early part of the month, I realized Lois had stopped her fluids to time her own death. My son's birthday comes at almost the end of the month, so when she passed on January 17, 2011, it was a date almost directly between our two birthdays. She knew she was going to die, but she was going to do it her way, and in her own time and terms, as she always did. Lois had remained in control of her faculties until January 13, when she went unresponsive. Yet even three hours before she died, she tried to open her eyes. We thought it was just a reflex, but when Jim and I opened her eyes so she could see us and told her we were going to be okay, she closed them. They remained closed until she died. I don't believe it was a reflex. She wanted to see us one more time before she left. If she thought she was dreaming, we were the last thing she saw before she went on her last journey . . . the last dream before her ship finally sailed over the horizon.

Sunset under the Poet's Tree

In the aftermath of Lois's death, I struggled to my place of dreams. On a night where exhaustion took its toll, I dreamed I was there. The dreams were unlike anything I experienced, no doubt the culmination of sadness, grief, and illness. The Poet's Tree loomed before me, burgeoning majestically above my head with multicolored blooms. A sky, an impossible silky blue, rippled with lines of incandescent gold. The air hinted textures of a soft breeze, as the rustling leaves betrayed it; the lingering sensation bathed the skin over my arms and face. The shadows failed to conceal the floor beneath the majestic limbs, profusely littered with white stones and strewn with pale rocks the size of loaves. The broad roughened trunk sustained its purpose and grew through them as its spiral ascension into the sky created a prodigious dome of leaves, fruits, and flowers.

As I walked across the unfamiliar stones, a peculiar sight emerged from the sun painted horizon. A presence, a human figure, approached from a distance. My journeys to this spiritual place never involved an invitation to anyone other than the souls of my own inventions. I sensed something wrong within the paradigm. Animal instincts told me to hasten away and hide, yet something held me. Told me to stay where I was . . .

I watched transfixed as a young man struggled over the rugged terrain beyond the perimeter of stones. I gauged him in my line of sight, considering his distance. He appeared distracted by the intense beauty and majesty of the natural structure that stood before him. He seemed unaware of my existence, never displaying the slightest acknowledgement of my presence beneath the vibrant woven branches. Yet my rational thoughts betrayed me, and I felt the Poet's Tree drawing him forward with calculated intention. Or perhaps, was it possible, this young man already knew the power of this place, somehow seeking it out as I did? I thought it best to observe first. Then if an intervention occurred, this vision, this mirage, or whatever it was could be real and not a dream. For now, I would wait.

In my dreams, there were dreams within dreams, where familiar people walked, interacted, spoke with me, and taught me lessons. I often spoke with my grandfather this way. This time was different. I had not yet passed into the place of dreaming. As I sat, watching the stranger close the distance between us, my mind filled with suppressed thoughts and questions. *Who was making their way to my sanctum under the Poet's Tree? Was he aware of my presence, or was this simply a metaphor of a reality I was about to learn?* I watched and waited while the figure struggled over the obstructions presented by phosphorescent foliage and sepulchral stones, making steady progress toward the mystical tree.

Ground mists covered the flatlands, swirling madly about his legs and feet like living tendrils and obscuring the secure footholds both from myself and this unwanted trespasser. Twice the intruder stumbled on loose rocks and caught in the twisted vines growing askew over the visible edges of the rocky perimeter. Still, he refused to abandon his steady advance to the base of the Poet's Tree. He broke through the last of the tangled foliage offered by the verdant flatlands and placed his feet onto the white stones. The temple stood before him; the white stone floor radiated like a pallid island around the massive tree. His footing secured on the whitened stones, he looked in awe at the mesmerizing branches above him. His attention was averted to the sights above him. His ambivalence blinded him to my presence for which I was grateful. I began elusive thoughts, believing he was just a passing phantom, a ghost, a lingering spirit. I almost convinced myself it was another trial of observation and discovery, until he fell.

The uneven stone surface eventually forced his attention to his footing then toward me. He looked shocked, startled by my presence, unbalanced by the uneven terrain; he fell to his haunches, legs twisting beneath him. Now, seeing each other at eye level, he said, *"I knew you would be here."*

"You can see me?" I asked, both shocked and perplexed by what this new interloper's presence might mean in this place . . . in this time out of time. Until this moment, I watched and listened to the strange interventions of souls past, teaching me about events I had forgotten or perhaps lessons I failed to learn earlier in my life . . . lessons that became focused as their stories revealed the truths underlying the insipid shell that contained them. This was a new situation where the ghost was as real as I was . . . a ghost that wanted to communicate, share ideas, and delve into mysteries that, up to this moment, remained silent.

"Yes, I can see you . . . and hear you," he said with an expression as stunned as my own.

"Why?" I asked, dumbfounded by my ability to interact with him. "What?" I asked, still confounded by the unlikely possibility this was happening. "Are you really here?"

"Yes, I'm really here. As to 'what' and 'why' . . . well, I guess that is for us to discover," he said, brushing off dead foliage and dust clinging loosely to his coat from his travels to this haven beneath the Poet's Tree. *"It is really beautiful."* His eyes wandered over the lush boughs and variegated colors, while I sought an answer as to what this stranger was doing here.

"How did you know about this place?" I asked, concerned others might be searching for this haven in my world of dreams.

"I am asleep under Timmerloo's hand," the young man told me with sadness in his eyes. *"Timmerloo told me, 'Sometimes you get the chance to change things.' I assured him I would try. Then I asked, 'How do I get to the poet?' 'In a place where your dreams become real . . .' Timmerloo said to me. I was confused by his response, so I said, 'I can only dream in my sleep.' He placed his hand on my head as I lay on a stone slab atop a high pinnacle where he placed me. He looked into my eyes and said, 'It is within sleep that we drop our inhibitions, shed our ties to the world that pulls us toward it, and unveils the person within the cloak.' . . . then I woke up walking through those flatlands,"* he said, pointing to the lush green surrounding the pale isle of stones around us.

The mention of Timmerloo's name sent waves of shock through me. Even in this dream, my appearance to this interloper must have changed when he saw "suffering" clothe me in graying raiments. *"Are you okay? You don't look too good."*

"Timmerloo, you say." My eyes widened with alarm and suspicion. "Timmerloo is just an invention I created to escape the realities of my world as my wife lay dying in the bed next to me. How can you know of this?"

"Am I a part of your inventions too?" the impetuous young man asked.

"Are you Timothy?" I stammered.

"Yes, and I have traveled more parcels and have been through more-strange adventures than I care to imagine trying to get here. My great love, Catherine, is going to die if I don't find a way to save her."

"By making her immortal?" I responded incredulously.

He looked at me, a searing wave of alarm, or possibly astonishment, branded his face. *"You are the poet . . ."*

"Poet?" I asked under my breath, lowering my head to my chest.

"Yes, Timmerloo said I was to find a poet beneath the great tree who would help me make Catherine immortal."

"No one can be immortal, Timothy. Not I, or you, my wife Lois, or even your Catherine. We are human, and we are given a short time to be alive, and then we are gone." He was looking at me as I raised my head to face him.

"She gave her life to save others. Certainly there is something you can tell me to do that will save her."

"Catherine is already gone. She has gone just like Lois has gone. She passed away by the dark eclipse of the moon."

Timothy looked at me, sickened with shock and grief of what he feared most. *"How can you know this? How can you say such things? You never met her, have never seen her."*

"I have known about her since the beginning, before you left the morning for Glade. I know about Benjamin, your father, Jakob, Catherine's mother, Leena, Rand, Leon, Penny, and Victoria. I know Timothy . . . I know."

"But how?" His words echoed in my ears, and I did not know how to answer them. *"Are you the poet?"* he asked me, sounding more like a plea than a question.

Timothy's tearful eyes twisted in horror. Then when his transient hold on the world disappeared, his bewildered eyes struggled with the puzzle within a puzzle, the paradox in a paradigm, the insolvable undecipherable enigma. Timothy would not understand my creation of the world he came from without resolute condemnation of my intentions. I needed to offer explanations that predicated truths yet did not erase the fragile world of my imagination. It wasn't Timothy I was afraid of . . . it was myself. In the quandary of offered explanations, I ventured from the sublime to the poetic. "Where I come from, Timothy, a very wise man once said, 'When I learned something, I had to let something go.'"

"What did he mean by that?" he asked with tearful resentment . . . not convinced his beloved Catherine was really gone from his world.

"I think it means when you are born, a higher power creates within each person a soul that is perfect. It is a spirit without imperfections, without marks, or colors, or lines worn or scratched into it." Timothy remained lost in thought, unconcerned about what I was trying to say, as I continued. "In this place beneath the Poet's Tree, a lifetime spans a single day. This day began for me at the birth of midnight, in darkness. Then when I matured and saw the first tendrils of light infuse my sight, I could see the world around me. In the beginning, it was an invisible world, wearing a dark cloak, finally discarded, able to be seen and explored. As the day progressed, I feared the world around me less and less. As the light revealed, I was given the chance to learn and do what I could until the sunset. When this sun shatters into beautiful striated colors, I can rest and look at the work I have done and how it has affected the world. I suspect when the sun sets in this world, I will be in the darkness once again to wait and reflect."

I could not tell if anything I said to Timothy had any effect on him. He still writhed in the turmoil of his lost Catherine. Finally, he looked up from his tears, and with bitter words, he said, *"Timmerloo lied when he told me I could make her immortal. You have no knowledge to make her immortal, and he knew it,"* he screamed violently. *"You are just a man like I am. No special powers . . . no incantations . . . no elixirs or magic that can bring her back. What, by the Winds, was I sent here for? Why have I struggled against impossible tasks, risking my own life and thinking I was saving the great love of my life by coming here?"*

"Immortality . . ."

"But Catherine is dead, you say . . . Immortality is not possible for the dead," Timothy screamed into the air.

"Being immortal has more to do with our memories than whether or not blood is pumping through our arms," I told him, equally distressed and equally loud, fueled in anger at his reaction.

We could not face each other for a time and sat on opposite sides of the great tree fixed in thought. It was Timothy who eventually spoke first, *"You have lost your wife, Lois, you told me."*

I looked into the boughs of flowers growing above me, hesitant to respond. Without moving, I spoke the words softly, "Yes, she is gone."

"And my Catherine?"

"Catherine has gone too."

"Then what is left?"

"We are."

Timothy got up from the other side of the tree and stood before me. *"And we are left to remain in pain until the day we die. Is that the wisdom you have to offer?"*

I looked up at the young man and saw where his tears dried and anger stabbed at it with bitter knives. "Both Lois and Catherine are heroes. They did something with their lives that was extraordinary."

"Dead heroes . . . That makes me feel so much better," he seethed, his tortured words indignant with sarcasm.

"Listen to me," I screamed at him, "we don't have the right or the power to say who dies and who doesn't. Maybe someday we will be put in that situation . . . maybe not. For your sake and mine, I hope neither one of us has to face that ordeal."

"But they did . . . didn't they? Lois and Catherine?"

It was a fair question. One I hadn't considered in my journey through the gray clouds of grieving. I laid my head in my arms so I didn't have to look into his eyes. For a character of my own imagination, he was discovering me as much as I was discovering him. "Both women had a choice," I said finally. "Lois and Catherine could have stayed to themselves, played it safe, or suffered in silence and did nothing. But they didn't. They saw the greater good in helping others even though it was a supreme sacrifice on both their parts. They saw a chance to change things, and that is what they did. Catherine saved the villages by giving her life. Lois's life work with breast cancer advocacy saved countless women from having to 'walk in her shoes,' as she so often told me. Their legacy is written in their deeds."

"And they were taken away from us in spite of their deeds, in spite of their legacy. In my world, the villages are probably proclaiming Catherine's sacrifice in great tributes and grandiose celebrations. They will honor her and reap praises upon her and her family. But the truth is, when a few solens pass, it will be hard for some of them to even remember her name or what she did. In a generation, when I become an old man, the young will not remember anything of this. Yet the foundations of why these same young people even exist, why they are even alive, will be forgotten. Though I won't let her be forgotten for as long as I live, others will. And when all that exists here, myself, my brothers and sister, Catherine's parents and brother, and the ones who counted her dear to them, passes into the darkness of the past, what will this matter? It was a sacrifice given in vain . . . a lesson

forgotten . . . a name never spoken again. It will become a dusty broken memory of a sacrifice given to save them all . . . Some may even argue that such a thing ever happened."

It was painful to hear Timothy's words. It was painful to know the truth he so eloquently defined. We would all forget. We might even deny the memories of both women's sacrifices over time, finding them too impossible to be true. In my world, the very science Lois promoted in her lifetime would become antiquated. The laws would change over passing years; the footsteps she made would fade in the dynamic wind of technology and wash away in the insatiable ebb and flow of time. How could a life so beautiful, so unselfish, that it was given back to its Maker to save others, be the empty fodder of skepticism and denial? How could we forget such unimaginable sacrifices that it would not concern the foundations of what made us the people we are? I understood what Timothy spoke of. Yet while we existed, we had the power to change things. I learned that somewhere.

"We must do our best for them," I said.

"They are dead. There is nothing you or I can do for them," he stated with repugnance. *"The time to be with them, love them, and have a life with them is gone. There is nothing left. Their memory and their deeds are withering into dust. They will be like they never were . . . empty air . . . voiceless . . . faceless!"* It was something about this final word that brought Timothy to his knees. He looked into the flowering boughs of the Poet's Tree and wept. *"I remember it now!"* he said, his shocked eyes locked mine in an epiphany.

"What . . . what do you remember?" I asked, trying to draw him out, concerned by the sudden ashen color of his face.

"A dream . . . ," he said, turning his face away from me, *"a dream I had troubling my sleep on the journey here."* I sat silent, waiting for Timothy to speak. He turned back, his chilled voice shuddered with stumbling words. *"I dreamed of a faceless bride . . . It was Catherine, wasn't it?"* I faced him, not knowing what to say. *"Did she come to me in dreams to tell me she loved me, but it wouldn't be her I would marry?"* he stared into the space between us, eyes focused and trapped inside the space of air separating us. *"I lost my life with her. I will never get it back."*

I remembered writing those words into his story. I thought it best to allow him this message from Catherine as her way of telling him she loved him, knowing he would never get to hear her words himself. I couldn't bear looking into his haunted eyes. I was looking into an abyss, the likes of which I had never seen. There was such emptiness in them I could not express. I felt it with him. We were travelers on the same sad journey. We could not go back. We had to move on. It was my January, written like a gospel of white bones. I wrote the queen's song as she lay dying on the withered bed, then watched as the winter's rain washed it all away. We could not leave this place until it was finished . . . until we made them immortal.

"It is within the telling of their stories that we make them immortal, Timothy."

"But words don't keep. They are forgotten over time. The telling becomes different every time they are spoken. And if no one listens . . ."

"Then we write them down for our time and for times we can no longer tell their stories. Lois and Catherine will live again and again as long as their stories are remembered."

"I don't know how to write. Some of the villagers are able to, and a few can read, but I cannot do either one. I always relied on my memory to keep the old stories," he told me sadly. *"Besides, I don't know your wife's story as well as you know mine."*

"You tell me Timmerloo sent you here."

Timothy started up when he heard me mention Timmerloo. *"Yes, you know that?"*

"He sent you to meet the poet . . . I think I am he. I know both our stories."

Timothy remained silent, looking at me, perhaps, for the first time. He took note of the differences in our clothing, the differences in our ages, and eventually realized I was not at all like any of the villagers he ever encountered. Finally, after long stares and silent contemplation, he said, *"Timmerloo said this was a way to make Catherine immortal. Though I must admit this is not what I imagined it would be."*

"Nor I, Timothy."

"I miss Catherine but understand how important it is to keep her memory alive. If we write their stories, anyone can return to the times when they lived and became heroes over and over, if they like. People will understand what Catherine and Lois sacrificed to help everyone. It is important to remember."

"First, I must tell you Lois's story so you can write it down with Catherine's. Then you must go to Timmerloo and learn the skills of reading and writing, for he is a great seeker."

"They should have been destroyed long ago for what they did to the villages," Timothy told me, alarmed I would suggest something that went against his principles.

"But they brought you to me. Certainly, there was no other way. Catherine was the only one who could seal the breach. Even if you stayed in Glade, you would have died. Events unfolding after your death, leading Catherine to the breach, would have failed. We were both doomed to lose our greatest loves. Still, we have a chance to show our worlds these women did not die in vain . . . to be forgotten."

"Seeking the help of Timmerloo and the others in the vaults of Winterland goes against everything I ever learned. I intend to pass through that wretched village and bring back help to destroy it completely when I return," Timothy said with steadfast conviction.

I could not break the years of hatred Timothy learned in the short time we had together. Then I remembered something. "Did you know your Catherine could read and write?"

"Her mother taught her. I knew."

"Then before you lead a war party into Winterland, learn something from Timmerloo. They are peaceful beings who saved your life and want to help you." Timothy looked at me, and his thoughts were murderous.

"They should have left me to die. I owe them nothing but my contempt for the centuries of murder, rape, and slander they placed upon the innocent people of the villages."

"Do you know of a book you gave Catherine before you left that day to Glade? It was made of tooled leather. Very beautiful . . . it was to be a ledger for her wedding, but she used it like a diary."

Timothy asked, *"How do you know this?"* shocked by details I knew about his life.

"Under the Poet's Tree, I have come to know a great many things. I also know Catherine wrote something in her diary for you to read. She hid it under her bed the day she went shopping with Leena and the orbs attacked. It lies there still. If you want to read it, you need to learn how."

"And write?"

"If her memory is to go on after everything goes back to normal in the villages . . . yes."

"Leena could teach me," Timothy piped up, thinking he found a way around Timmerloo's hand.

"Yes, she could. But your story of Catherine will be ordinary . . . in ordinary terms, which Leena could do. But to be extraordinary, to be remembered, it has to be Timmerloo."

"I will think about it," he told me. I returned a stern look, which he brushed aside. I didn't hold much hope for Timmerloo and his sentient pink orbs in Timothy's world after his return. Then Timothy asked, *"Do you know what Catherine wrote in her diary?"*

"Yes, but you must read it for yourself. I can't tell you."

"You said you would tell me Lois's story," Timothy stated formally.

"Yes, you must know her story before you leave." I turned my back to him and looked into the colorful boughs above my head. Without looking down, I asked, "Are you ready, Timothy?"

"Yes, begin . . ." Timothy said, as I leaned against the massive spiraling tree trunk, mesmerized by the beauty above me.

"Once upon a time, I met a girl. Her name was Lois, and she was the most beautiful girl I ever saw . . ." I paused, wondering if Timothy was paying attention. When I turned, he was gone. I saw him walking a great distance away. I watched him walk toward the far horizon. I wanted to call him back, but he disappeared, melting into the mists gathering in the flatlands. He returned to his world, called back, and awakened by the hand of Timmerloo. He would not return. I listened to a gentle breeze soughing through the leaves above me. I listened, hoping to hear a voice from the *Poet's Tree.*

"Tell me about the world" . . . the voice said.

"You have been with me from the beginning, haven't you?" I asked.

"You have told the story, and I am at peace."

"But I only have a little time to tell it."

"It will be enough. It may be like a fire that catches in someone's heart from time to time."

"The story?"

"Hope . . ."

"A fire that catches in someone's heart?"

"Like a moment of fire . . . unending . . . immortal . . ." Then silence spoke its unending cadence of emptiness before a voice whispered . . . "Tell me about the world . . ."

"I will . . ."

The world became a better place while she was here. She fought for better breast cancer treatments, and it happened. She fought for a stamp that celebrated Breast Cancer Awareness, and it happened. She fought for legislation through advocacy, and it happened. She battled a deadly disease valiantly and without compromise for almost two decades before it finally took her away. The only injustice would be forgetting she ever existed. The only affront would be not celebrating her unending belief in "hope." The world talks more openly now about breast cancer. Some still stumble over the word "breast" in a sentence, but it is far better than it was in 1992, when she was diagnosed. She became a force to be reckoned with on many levels. The work she did is felt now and will be for many years to come. She showed the worth of her being here, and I am grateful I had the chance to be with her, comfort her, and live my life with her. The world is a better place.

I want to believe Timothy went back to his world to forgive and learn what he could from Timmerloo. I want to believe he writes the story of Catherine and the sacrifice of her lifestone. I want to believe the villagers will read the pages he writes and let his inspiration write the unwritten pages Timmerloo once spoke of when Timothy sat by the hearth. I want to believe he rejoins his abandoned family in a joyous reunion celebration. I want to believe one day he finds a tooled leather-bound diary hidden beneath Catherine's bed. The one he once gave her. I want to believe he found the knowledge to read what she has written there . . . "I want you to know I love you more than anything." I want to believe in "hope" . . . for us all.

The last moments are the sweetest. Existing in long last rays of sunlight, distorted by air and objects in between, they are the last of the memories. And with these memories to support us, we have created legends and treasured stories, found worlds within and without boundaries, believed in a consciousness beneath our skin and beyond it that somehow gives us moments of peaceful recollection . . . a place to remember. It may be of little consequence to us, but it may be all of what truly exists . . . our memories. Like any sunset, we will remember its beauty, the intense coloration of the sky, the impending night's coolness, and how it touches us . . . each in our own unique way. And when night finally comes, when the last vestiges of light vanish, save the garden of stars in the darkening sky, we will remember the day that passed. How it was . . . the tender moments, the hard times, the peaceful, the common, the unusual, the heroic, the sad, and the joyful . . . When it is over, it will stand within the boundaries of the memories we shared with the one lost . . . the one who was chosen to fall off the edge of the world to become the last sunset . . . the last sunset under the Poet's Tree.

Epilogue

When I see and hear the ubiquitous hype and media coverage for celebrities receiving acclaim after facing their ordeals with breast cancer, I hear words like "bravery," "stamina," and "devastating disease," how well they are handling the diagnosis, and how heroically they are getting on with their lives." Most of these same celebrities are alive and well after their diagnosis because of the work done by women like my late wife, Lois A. Anderson. Yet most people have never heard of her. If you want to read a book about real bravery, real stamina, and the power to make real changes that matter to the breast cancer story, you need to take the time to read this book.

Lois came from a poor family, coming from conditions most of us would never ascend from, and made her mark upon the world. "I do not want to be forgotten," she told me after being diagnosed with stage III breast cancer at the age of thirty-nine. She lived eighteen years after that diagnosis and, in many ways, changed the world with her knowledge, support, and political advocacy. Many throw money at research in an effort to move breast cancer out of the ranks of an incurable cancer into one where most will survive it. Lois didn't have money. She didn't have the media to tell of her many battles. What she did have was a spirit of hope, which she used to battle breast cancer on all fronts.

This is the story of a remarkable woman who, in spite of the odds, not only survived but also turned an ordeal that would have devastated most of us into a shining example of what one person can do, even when they are facing death. "Sometimes you get the chance to change things," she often told me. In her short lifetime, even with cancer raging through her body, she took the chance and did that very thing. She not only fought her own personal battle with breast cancer but also fought the war against it.

My son and I prepared a video before she died that provided a cursory but thorough overview of Lois's accomplishments achieved over her lifetime. We were fortunate to have had the time to share the final versions with her. We had a chance to tell her we wanted to use it to celebrate her life in some way after she was gone. She told us she was very pleased and deeply moved by our efforts. Though she was always very modest about her achievements, many times keeping the real outcomes of her work quiet, even from us, she was very supportive of the video we made for her.

A few days after she died, our local newspaper ran a beautiful article about some of her accomplishments. When Jim and I told the newspaper about the video, they asked us if they could have a copy to attach to their webpage. My son and I agreed wholeheartedly and created a copy for them. It was a great tool to show people the enormous amount of good Lois generated for breast cancer survivors, current patients, and patients that would still continue to need care after her passing.

The enormous agenda of around-the-clock care, coupled with the emotional fallout of losing Lois, pummeled me into a position where I became ill. The winter was unforgiving, and we were beset within the worst assembly of snowstorms seen over past years. In order to open the grave site, about a foot of snow had to be removed on all sides just to get to the tent housing the site. On the day of the funeral, the temperatures were in single digits; I could barely speak because of laryngitis. Regardless of how I felt, many people wanted to speak with me; I eventually lost my voice completely by the end of the second day. Overall, between the viewing and the funeral, over 350 people came from everywhere to pay their respects, bearing the ice, snow, and freezing temperatures. Had the weather been more temperate, I suspect the numbers would have doubled.

When Lois died on January 17, 2011, it seemed to me some part of her continued to live on. After her death, there were many financial obligations and institutions I needed to work with to finalize unfinished business. One such institution worked with Lois's long-term disability benefits, which had only been in place for two months prior to her death. The insurance coordinator contacted me once before, when Lois was not doing well, asking me to call her back sometime after Lois had passed. Several days went by after the funeral before I remembered to make this call.

Using my broken, raspy voice, I explained to the insurance coordinator, I was making the follow-up call she requested. As things went, she needed Social Security numbers, addresses, and some other information then followed it with the obligatory "I'm sorry for your loss." I told her I missed my wife terribly, but I was certainly grateful her suffering was over. It was then the young woman realized Lois's birth date on some of the papers she had before her, indicating Lois was younger than she suspected. I told her Lois was only fifty-eight years old when she died. She asked what happened for her to die so young. I explained, Lois was a breast cancer survivor since 1992 when she was diagnosed at the age of thirty-nine, almost forty within the week of finding it. I told her our local newspaper set up a website with Lois's story, if she was interested. My sore throat decimated my voice to an almost inaudible whisper, allowing just a few moments to stay on the phone to give her the website to look up Lois's story herself. She thanked me after we made arrangements to speak again in two weeks for an update with information I didn't have available.

In two weeks, I called and answered some additional questions for her. I had to fax some papers, which then concluded our business with each other. I was about to end the call when she told me she went to the website and was very impressed with the life Lois lived. She went on to tell me, on the day we last spoke, she went home to find two of her friends committed suicide together. The news of that horrific event made her feel very saddened and depressed. For some reason, she told me, she remembered I had spoken very highly of Lois and, as a consequence of my conversation with her, decided to go to the website I suggested. She told me after she read the story and viewed the video, she felt so inspired by Lois's story, she told herself, "I want to be like Lois . . . I want to be that kind of person . . . not like my friends." It made me feel good to realize a stranger, not even affected by breast cancer, could be so inspired by her. Knowing this young woman would carry on, even with such a dark event looming over her, made me feel Lois's story would be worth telling. Somehow, I knew Lois was still somewhere making a difference.

Another event happened the week after Lois passed away. Lois always believed early detection was the best way to get ahead of breast cancer, making it treatable. So to back herself up, she asked many of the area high schools to give permission to come into the schools and teach the young girls self-breast exam and the importance of regular checkup with their physicians in their health classes. Needless to say, the idea was not well taken, and many schools turned down her offer. However, the first year she offered, she did get a chance to go to a few high schools and do a presentation. In one such class, one of my son's friends had the chance to hear Lois talk. She was perhaps seventeen or eighteen at the time. The schools never asked Lois to come back. Other than that one chance to make a difference, the doors were closed.

Two days after Lois died, this same young woman, now about thirty-two years old, remembered Lois's class and did a self-breast exam. She found a lump that turned out to be a stage III breast cancer. She called my son to let him know it was Lois's warning that day in her health class to do self-exam leading her to this discovery. She remembered how insistent Lois had been to drive the point home. Lois's death from breast cancer brought it all back to her. Two nights after she died, this young woman found the lump. By the end of the week, she knew she had breast cancer. The only reason she did the exam was woven in the memory of Lois's class when she was a teenager. The impact of Lois's death, somehow, made the memory real again.

Was it coincidence? Sure, after all, how much faith would you have to have to believe Lois had such sweeping influence over so many people? Still, my son's friend is alive and being treated because of this finding. Where would she have been if Lois never taught her class? Where would she have been in a year if her memory of Lois was never instilled? It was because she knew my son and met Lois that she was emotionally moved when she passed. Again, Lois's work was never completed . . . She is still out there.

I no longer hold my wife in my arms. I hold her in a much better place . . . my heart. It was perhaps the place where I held her all the times when I knew her, even during her short life and now after. Perhaps writing this book is my moment of fire. Yet when I think about it, it was her moment of fire that inspired me to write it. Memories fade in time. People who made those memories and keep them alive for a while will fade as well. Nothing in this place is truly "immortal." But perhaps these moments of fire will catch somewhere in another's heart and allow them to burn a while longer, leading a path of light to shine where it never did before. It is perhaps all we can ask of ourselves to keep that memory alive. We are finite. We all owe a death, but while we live, we need to discover those moments of fire that make us better people . . . make better lives for those around us now and for those who will walk these shores long after we have faded from them. It will be our moments of fire by which we will be remembered.

She has become the dream . . .
And I . . . still stand here breathing . . .
We will be known by our moments of fire . . .
Perhaps . . . this is one of mine.
George S. J. Anderson 2013

Acknowledgements

The preparation of this book would not have been possible without the help of many people. First and foremost, I wish to thank my good friend and colleague, Cherie Christopherson, who believed in my vision many times when I thought I was losing my perspective. She helped me stay on course and "keep at it" many times when I thought I would never finish. I thank you, Cherie, for your strength and perseverance. I could not have done it without you.

I wish to thank Donna Duncan from the Linda Creed Foundation for her help in researching some of the work my wife did over the years. And on that note, I wish to thank everyone at the Linda Creed Foundation in Philadelphia, Pennsylvania, for their loyal support and appreciation of the work Lois did during her lifetime.

My son, James T. Anderson, has been a staunch supporter and constant critic, evaluating my book from the very beginning, keeping me on track, and evaluating the context written between these covers. He has been my invaluable technical support for videos, advertising, and generally getting information out to the public. Thank you, Jim, from the bottom of my heart. I know your mother watches over you.

Finally, I want to thank my late wife, Lois Ann Anderson, for keeping such incredible records. Without her words to guide me, I would never have been able to piece all of this together. Wherever you are, I hope this book becomes your legacy of a life well lived and inspires others to have the kind of "hope" you so often envisioned. You are missed.

In Her Lifetime

Her Achievements

Lobbied for the first Breast Cancer Awareness postage stamp with Diane Sackett Nannery from New York. The stamp became a reality in early 1996, leading the way for other potential causes, like heart disease and domestic violence toward women, to become realities afterward.

She cofounded the breast cancer support group known as Surviving Breast Cancer in 1993. At its height, this group had a membership of over 350 women. Its legacy lasted from 1993 until 2010, when she was no longer able to continue it.

In 1994, she founded the first support group for men supporting their wives and significant others in a group called Men Supporting Women with Breast Cancer. This was the first support group of its kind anywhere in the country at the time.

She wrote a quarterly newsletter for her support group between the years 1993 and 2010. The newsletter was so well received that physicians and medical personnel requested copies just to keep informed of the advancements happening on the breast cancer front.

She was a member of the National Breast Cancer Coalition, where she was designated as a team leader and field coordinator. In this role, she functioned to enable advocacy for such things as getting mammograms paid yearly under Medicare rather than biyearly, as they were originally stated.

In 1997, she went up against the recommendations of the National Cancer Institute to raise the age a woman was to start getting mammograms from age forty to age fifty. The NCI gave her a little over two weeks to accomplish retrieving anecdotal evidence where women under the age of fifty were helped by a mammogram. She was able to collect 226 verifiable accounts in this time. While this is still a controversial subject, her outrage was echoed across the country by women everywhere. She was invited to a Senate subcommittee hearing, under then senator Arlen Specter, where she gave testimony in behalf of women under the age of fifty needing to be screened. The decision to keep the age of forty as the recommendation was retained.

She was nominated to be a consumer advocate reviewer to the Department of Defense Scientific Peer Review Panels for the Breast Cancer Research Program in 1995, 1996, 1997, 1998, and 2000. The object of these panels was to apply grants to scientific proposals that would impact breast cancer research and treatments nationwide and perhaps internationally. Her work as a reviewer on these panels helped many scientists bring new treatments to the forefront of the breast cancer battle.

In addition to these panels, she was also invited to be a consumer reviewer of their outcomes in 1996, 1997, 1998, and 2000.

She was a member of the Consumer Advisory Panel to the Oncology Nursing Society from 2000 until 2003.

She worked tirelessly with the American Cancer Society and was involved in the Reach to Recovery Program as a volunteer trainer and as an advisory board member. In addition to these duties, she was a member of the Volunteer Leadership Council and served as ACT LEAD for the Nineteenth District. These were activities that had nationwide impacts.

She reviewed grants, not only for the Department of Defense Breast Cancer Research Program, but also for the American Cancer Society and the Pennsylvania Health Department. These were activities that helped scientists on both the national level and the state level bring new treatments for breast cancer to the forefront.

Her work with other advocates from the NBCC and the Linda Creed Foundation in Philadelphia helped to found the Breast and Cervical Cancer Treatment Act. The effects of this legislation led Pennsylvania to adopt the Healthy Woman Program in Pennsylvania.

She worked with leaders of the Pennsylvania Breast Cancer Coalition to get legislation signed where a taxpayer could designate a portion of their tax dollars to go to a fund for breast and cervical cancer on the last line of the Pennsylvania tax form. The line still exists today as a result of her work and the efforts of breast cancer advocates across the state.

On the local level, she taught classes of LPN students the importance of breast health and advocacy from 1995 until 2010. She did this twice a year until she was too ill to continue.

She served as an ad hoc consumer reviewer on the Integration Panel of the Breast Cancer Research Program of the Department of Defense in 2004 and 2005.

She was the guest on many television, radio, and cable network programs who wanted her to share her experiences in our area. She was a member of the Speakers Bureau for our area and was invited to speak at many local events.

She did all this while holding a full-time job located an hour away from our home, pursuing her master's degree in social work, running a household, and first fighting stage III breast cancer in 1992 and 1993 and eventually stage IV by 2001 and almost every year afterward. It wasn't supposed to be her first priority . . . but it was.

Her Awards and Acknowledgements

1991-1992 **Who's Who in the East**

1996 **U.S. Postal Service Honorary Plaque Recipient for the first Breast Cancer Awareness Stamp**

1997 **The Jefferson Award**

1997 **The Golden Eagle Award**

1997 Special Resolution for Lois A. Anderson from the York County Commissioners for Breast Cancer Advocacy

1997-1998 Who's Who in Health Care and Medicine

1998 The JCPenney Golden Rule Award

1999 Outstanding Woman of the Year presented by the Pennsylvania Women of Today

2000-2003 Consumer Advocacy Panel Award for the Oncology Nurses Society

2002 McAuley Silver Award

2002 Suzanne M. Kaye Advocacy Award *Up to this time, only one person received this award besides Lois . . . Fran Visco, head of the National Breast Cancer Coalition in Washington DC.*

2003 Recognized by the Alpha Delta Mu National Honor Society at Temple University

2003 McAuley Silver Award (second time)

2003-2005 Recognized by the American Cancer Society with the Primary Care Physician's Award—Peer Review Committee

2004 Health Care Heroes Award

2008 Certificate of Excellence—ACT Lead for Congressional District #19

2008-2009 York College of Pennsylvania Distinguished Alumni Achievement Award

2009-2010 Elaine M. Ominsky PhD Humanitarian Award

Lois accepting an honorary award from the United States
Postal Service for her part in getting the first postage stamp
for breast cancer awareness in 1996.

Lois as she delivered testimony at the Senate Subcommittee
Hearing for then Senator Arlen Specter in 1997.

Lois displaying the "quilt" from the *Skin Deep Project* for the
American Cancer Society in 1998.

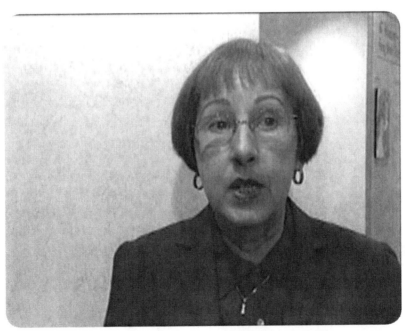
Lois giving a TV interview for 67 Counties, 67 Women for the
Pennsylvania Breast Cancer Coalition in 2001.

Lois with Senator Platts of Pennsylvania delivering an award in 2007.

Lois speaking to the Linda Creed Foundation on December 5, 2009
for the 2009 Elaine M. Ominsky PHD award.

Lois speaking at a luncheon for York College of Pennsylvania in early 2009.

CPSIA information can be obtained at www.ICGtesting.com
Printed in the USA
LVOW11s1302030614

388231LV00003B/9/P